The Symbolism
of the Psalms

A SPIRITUAL COMMENTARY

VOLUME I

by
Theodore D. Webber

The Apocryphile Press
1700 Shattuck Ave. #81
Berkeley, CA 94709
www.apocryphile.org

The Symbolism of the Psalms: A Spiritual Commentary, Vol. 1

Copyright © 2017 Theodore D. Webber
ISBN 978-1-944769-73-4
Printed in the United States of America

Please join our mailing list at
www.apocryphilepress.com/free
and we'll keep you up-to-date on all our new releases
—and we'll also send you a FREE BOOK.
Visit us today!

Table of Contents

Preface

The Symbolism of the Psalms is a comprehensive spiritual commentary on the Psalms which reveals the hidden spiritual meaning behind the literal sense of scripture, to open up the Word for study. Most who read the Bible take it on faith, or on the basis of church authority and tradition, that it is Divinely inspired. But what about a systematic proof, using internal evidence from the text itself, to demonstrate that it is indeed Divinely inspired? This work seeks to open up the literal sense of scripture, to show the spiritual and symbolic meaning behind each passage, in most cases covering each Psalm word by word with numerous cross references. The spiritual meaning of scripture is shown to be consistent throughout several passages, using a system of symbolic correspondences that pervades the entire scripture of the Bible. Each interpretation is systematically supported with evidence from scripture. Once one's mind becomes abstracted from the literal sense, it is lifted up towards higher level concepts of love and truth, and the most obscure passages become relevant to one's everyday life. The Old Testament no longer has to be a closed book, but is now open to the everyday student of the Bible who wishes to examine the truth of this matter for the sake of Truth. When reading the Psalms, in most cases readers of the Bible will simply skip over what they think are poetic and needless phrases, and pass them off as "figures of speech." But there is no needless word or phrase, or unnecessary repetition: for every aspect of scripture is describing something Divine, down to every "jot and tittle" (Matt. 5:18).

That there is a higher spiritual meaning to scripture hidden behind its literal sense is shown in the gospels, where Jesus gave many teachings in the form of parables to the masses, but gave the secret teaching only to his inner circle of disciples (Matt. 13:3, 10). In the parable of the sower and the seed, it is revealed that the "seed" is the Word of God that is implanted in the mind to those willing to receive it. And those who receive it properly, the idea or seed will grow to transform one's life into a life of love and service to others, which are symbolically portrayed as "bearing fruit" (Matt. 3:8). This hidden inner spiritual meaning is not restricted to just the parables of Jesus, but can be applied across all of scripture. This work is focused on the largest book of scripture, the Psalms, but the spiritual concepts mentioned here can be applied to all areas of scripture. This work will thus be useful to any study that wishes to explore to the meaning of many difficult passages that are hard to understand to most readers.

Theodore D. Webber
Mar. 16, 2017

The Spiritual Meaning of the Psalms

This work provides new translation and commentary on the spiritual symbolism of the Psalms, which reveals the inner spiritual meaning of each Psalm. This work thus provides a means to make the Psalms and scripture more applicable to everyone's spiritual life, for without understanding the spiritual sense of scripture there are many passages in the Psalms that will be passed over as meaningless or superfluous poetry. The symbolic spiritual interpretation of each Psalm has been collated from over 30 volumes among the theological works of Emanuel Swedenborg, who had experienced a series of waking visions over a period of 27 years in order to reveal the spiritual sense of scripture and the true nature of heaven and hell in the afterlife. Some of these visions of the afterlife have been partially confirmed with recent testimonies of the Near Death Experience, which was first made known to the public at large with the book *Life After Life*, by Raymond Moody. Swedenborg wrote volumes concerning the spiritual meaning of scripture, and scattered throughout these works are expositions of the Psalms. Others have attempted to disclose the hidden spiritual meaning of scripture without success as they were without the benefit of direct revelation. This work brings together this information to create a comprehensive spiritual commentary for each Psalm, with extensive cross references to other passages of scripture. In this manner, scripture is used to systematically interpret scripture, and a massive amount of evidence is presented here

1

for the reader to judge the truth for themselves. This work will thus be useful for Bible studies as it provides answers for those who desire to have a deeper understanding of scripture beyond its literal sense, which is often obscure and confusing without knowledge of the higher spiritual sense.

For this work a new translation of the Psalms was necessary, as each distinct Hebrew word has a distinct spiritual meaning which is lost in many passages in modern translations of the Bible. The need for this is very apparent as Swedenborg was careful to follow the literal sense of the Hebrew, and made use of a Latin translation of the Bible by Schmidius that was made direct from the Hebrew Masoretic.

The majority of Biblical scholarship and studies have concentrated on the literal sense of scripture, ignoring the spiritual meaning of scripture that makes it more relevant to our daily lives. This work takes the Psalms to a deeper spiritual level. The Psalms like the rest of scripture contains stories, parables, figures of speech, poetic references, seemingly meaningless repetition and symbolic visions that are hard to explain as Divine when one merely looks at the literal sense of the words. For example, one popular verse of the Psalms which is read at most funerals is *Yes, though I walk through the valley of the shadow of death, I will fear no evil* (Ps. 23:4). "Death" here is taken to mean the physical death of the body. However in the spiritual sense, death is not physical death, but spiritual death or separation from heaven. Walking through a valley is taken as merely a figure of speech. However in the spiritual sense, walking is not literally walking, but how one live's one's life according to the truth. A valley is not a valley, but a lower state of obscurity and unawareness during a state of depression and temptation. All of these meaning are through a consistent system of correspondences, where natural physical forms correspond to higher level spiritual concepts. These higher levels of meaning is what makes scripture Divinely inspired, without these higher levels of meaning the Bible would be just like any other ordinary work.

Throughout the history of Biblical interpretation, very few attempts have been made to uncover the spiritual allegorical meaning. None of them are as comprehensive and consistent as the one provided to Swedenborg through waking visions. In his work *Heavenly Arcana*, Swedenborg mentions the prevailing ignorance of the spiritual sense of scripture among many, which continues to this day:

"The Jews and also some Christians believe indeed that in these, and also in the rest of the passages of the Word, there is some meaning stored up, which they call mystical — the reason of the belief being that an idea of holiness in regard to the Word has been impressed upon them from early childhood; but when it is inquired what that mystical meaning is, they do not know. If they are told that because the Word is Divine, this meaning must necessarily be such as is in heaven among the angels; and that no other mystical meaning can exist in the Word, or if so, that it would be either fabulous or magical or idolatrous; and furthermore that this mystical meaning which is in heaven among the angels, is nothing else than what is called the spiritual and celestial senses, and treats solely of the Lord, of His kingdom, and of the church, consequently of good and truth; and that if they knew what good and truth, or what faith and love, are, they would be able to know that meaning — when this is told them, scarce any one believes it; nay, in such ignorance at the present day are they who are of the church, that what is related concerning the celestial and spiritual is scarcely comprehensible to them. Be it so; nevertheless since it has been granted me by the Divine mercy of the Lord to be at the same time in heaven as a spirit and on earth as a man, and accordingly to speak with angels, and this now continually for several years, I cannot do otherwise than open those things of the Word which are called mystical, that is, its interiors, which are the spiritual and celestial things of the Lord's kingdom." (*Heavenly Arcana*, n. 4923.2)

Swedenborg confirms that each particular word of scripture is holy, and that communication is effected with heaven through

scripture through Divine influx into the mind of the person that
reads it:

"...all the particulars of the Word are holy; but the holiness
therein is not apparent to the understanding, except of one who
knows its internal sense. And yet by influx from heaven it comes
to the apperception of him who believes the Word to be holy. That
influx is effected through the internal sense in which the angels
are; and although this sense is not understood by the man, still
it affects him, because the affection of the angels who are in it, is
communicated. From this it is plain also that the Word has been
given to man that he may have communication with heaven, and
that the Divine truth, which is in heaven, may affect him by
influx." (*Heavenly Arcana*, n. 5247.7)

The Word is written using symbolism, where each word or
phrase in the literal sense corresponds to a higher spiritual
meaning that is more abstract. Swedenborg calls this system of
symbolism "correspondences:"

"...the Word was written by pure correspondences, and thus
it is such as to conjoin heaven with man. For heaven is in the
internal sense of the Word, and to the internal sense the external sense corresponds. Wherefore when the Word is read by man,
the angels who are with him perceive it in the spiritual sense,
which is the internal sense. Hence the holy from the angels flows
in, whereby there is conjunction. To this end was the Word given
such as it is." (*Heavenly Arcana*, n. 10687)

The Word of scripture is Divinely inspired down to the letter,
but in the literal sense this is not apparent to most readers:

"The Word of the Lord was also given for that end, since each
and all things therein, even to the smallest iota, have correspondence and signification. Therefore by means of the Word alone
there is a connection of heaven with man. ...That this is the
case no one at this day knows. And so the natural man, when
he reads the Word and searches where the Divine lies concealed
therein and does not find it in the letter, because of its ordinary
style, begins first to hold it in low estimation, and then to deny
that it was dictated by the Divine Itself and sent down through

heaven to man; for he does not know that the Word is Divine by virtue of its spiritual sense, which is not apparent in the letter, but still is in the letter, and that that sense is presented to view in heaven when man reads it reverently, and that that sense treats of the Lord and His kingdom. It is these Divine things from which the Word is Divine, and through which holiness flows through heaven from the Lord even into the literal sense and into the very letter itself. But so long as man does not know what the spiritual is, neither can he know what the spiritual sense is, and thus not what correspondence is. And so long as man loves the world more than heaven, and himself more than the Lord, he does not desire to know these things nor to apprehend them; when yet from this was all ancient. intelligence, and from it is the wisdom of angels. The mystic arcana which diviners have vainly labored to discover in the Word, therein only lie concealed." (*Heavenly Arcana*, n. 9280.2-3)

"...the literal sense is the basis and fulcrum on which the spiritual sense rests, and with which it coheres in closest conjunction, insomuch that there is not even a jot or a point or a tittle in the letter of the Word which does not contain within it the holy Divine — according to the words of the Lord in Matthew: *Verily I say unto you, Till heaven and earth pass away, one jot or one tittle shall in no wise pass away from the law, till all things be accomplished* (v. 18); and in Luke: *It is easier for heaven and earth to pass away than for one tittle of the law to fall* (xvi. 17). That the law means the Word, may be seen above (n. 6752, 7463).

"Therefore also it has been effected through the Divine providence of the Lord that the Word as to every jot and tittle, especially the Word of the Old Testament, has been preserved from the time when it was written. It has also been shown from heaven that in the Word not only every expression, but also every syllable, and, what seems incredible, every tittle of a syllable in the original tongue involves what is holy, which becomes perceptible to the angels of the inmost heaven. That this is the case I can assert positively, but I am aware that it transcends belief. From this it is plain that the external rituals of the church, which represented the Lord and the internals of heaven and the church that are from the Lord, and which are prescribed in the Word of the Old Testament, have indeed been for the most part abrogated, but that still the Word remains in its Divine sanctity, since, as already said, each and everything therein still involve holy Divine things, which are perceived in heaven while the Word is being read; for in each particular there is a holy internal which is its internal sense, that is, its heavenly and Divine sense. This sense is the soul of the Word, and it is truth Divine itself proceeding from the Lord; thus it is the Lord Himself." (*Heavenly Arcana*, n. 9349.1-2)

The Book of the Psalms

The Psalms is one of the largest books of the Bible, containing 150 psalms of prayers and hymns. The Psalms are used for a variety of liturgical purposes, and many were originally composed for singing during worship. Among the Jews the Bible was divided into three main divisions: the Law or the first 5 books of Moses (the *Torah*), followed by the Prophets which includes the historical and prophetic works (the *Nevi'im*), and the Writings (*Ketuvim*). The order of the books in the Writings was never finalized by the Jews, however in most modern editions the first book of the Writings is the Psalms. A form of this three fold division of scripture was mentioned by Jesus to His disciples following His resurrection:

> "*These are my words that I spoke to you while I was still with you, that everything written about me in the Law of Moses and the Prophets and the Psalms must be fulfilled.*" (Luke 24:44)

Many Bibles do not follow this division of scripture as they are based on the order of books as found in the later Greek translation of the Old Testament, known as the Septuagint or LXX.

The New Testament frequently quotes from the Psalms as it contains several prophecies that were fulfilled by Jesus. These prophecies are a strong indication that the Word of scripture is focused on the Lord and His kingdom of heaven. Here is a sample of the main prophecies found in the Psalms that were fulfilled by the coming of Jesus:

† He would be the Son of God, begotten by Jehovah, fulfilled when Jesus was born of a virgin by the Holy Spirit (Ps. 2:6-7, 110:3)

† Children would give praise to Him (Ps. 8:2; Matt. 21:15-16)

† He would rise from the dead in a glorified body (Ps. 16:9-10; Acts 2:25-32)

† He would cry out, "My God, my God, why have you forsaken me?" (Ps. 22:1; Matt. 27:46)

† He would be forsaken and rejected by His own people (Ps. 22:6-8; Matt. 27:41-43)

† He would be hung in the crucifixion (Ps. 22:15)

† He would thirst during the crucifixion (Ps. 22:14-15; John 22:28,30)

† His hands and feet would be pierced during the crucifixion (Ps. 22:16; Matt. 27:38)

† His garments would be divided during the crucifixion (Ps. 22:18; John 19:23-24)

† Yet, the ends of the earth and a new people would worship Him (Ps. 22:27,30-31)

† False witnesses would testify against Him (Ps. 27:12, 35:11; Matt; 26:59-61)

† He would cry out, "Into your hands do I commit my spirit" (Ps. 31:5; Luke 23:46)

† They would attempt to take His life (Ps. 31:13)

† No bone of His body would be broken (Ps. 34:20; John 19:32-33)

† He would be hated without cause (Ps. 35:19, 69:4; John 15:24-25)

✝ He would fulfill and replace the rituals of the animal sacrifices (Ps. 40:6-8; Heb. 10:10-13)

✝ He would perform the will of God (Ps. 40:7-8; John 5:30)

✝ He would be betrayed by one of His own disciples (Ps. 41:9, 55:12-14; Mark 14:17-18)

✝ His throne would be eternal (Ps. 45:6-7; Heb. 1:8-9)

✝ He would ascend into heaven (Ps. 68:18)

✝ He would be zealous for the temple (Ps. 69:9; John 2:13-17)

✝ He would be abandoned by His disciples before His death (Ps. 69:20; Mark 14:33-41)

✝ He would be offered gall mingled with vinegar (Ps. 69:21; Matt. 27:34)

✝ He would call God His Father (Ps. 89:26; Matt. 11:27)

✝ He would be God's only begotten Son (Ps. 89:27; Col. 1:18)

✝ He would be a descendant of King David, and reign upon His throne forever (Ps. 89:29,35-36, 132:11; Matt. 1:1; Mark 16:19)

✝ He would calm the stormy sea (Ps. 107:29; Matt. 8:24-26)

✝ He would pray for His enemies (Ps. 109:4; Luke 23:34)

✝ His betrayer Judas would live a short life, and his office taken by another (Ps. 109:8; John 17:12; Acts 1:16-26)

✝ He would be mocked by many (Ps. 109:25; Mark 15:29-30)

✝ Although a descendant of the line of David, He would be known as Lord by king David (Ps. 110:1; Matt. 22:41-46)

✝ He would be rejected by the Jews, and become the foundation of the Christian Church (Ps. 118:22; Matt. 21:42-43)

Intertwined with the above prophecies, there are other prophecies that depict a completely different Messiah than the one presented by Jesus: in these prophecies the Messiah is described as a conquerer, one who arises to fight against and subdue the nations of the world, to judge the good and evil, and punish the wicked by fire. This is where the subject matter of the Psalms starts to become open to a variety of interpretations based on the literal sense. Here is a sampling of some of these prophecies:

† He shall speak to nations and kings in anger (Ps. 2:1)
† He shall rule the nations, reigning over the entire earth (Ps. 2:5, 18:43, 22:28, 46:10, 47:2,7, 72:8)
† He would reign from Jerusalem (Ps. 2:6, 132:13-14,17)
† Many would perish unless they worshipped the Son, or the King (Ps. 2:12, 10:16, 21:10)
† Upon the wicked He will rain fire and brimstone, and consume them with fire (Ps. 11:6, 21:9, 37:20, 50:3, 68:2, 97:3)
† His people will return from captivity (Ps. 14:7, 53:6, 69:35-36)
† The earth will shake, mountains will be overturned (Ps. 18:7)
† He shall descend from heaven (Ps. 18:9)
† He will fight against the wicked with arrows and lightnings (Ps. 18:14, 45:5)
† He would fight against enemies in battle and subdue them (Ps. 18:40, 47:3, 89:10,23, 91:7, 110:5-6, 118:10-13)
† He would pulverize His enemies like the dust (Ps. 18:42)
† Foreigners will fear Him (Ps. 18:44-45)
† The righteous will possess the earth (Ps. 37:9,22,29,34)
† He will make wars to cease on the earth (Ps. 46:9)
† His people will walk in the blood of their enemies (Ps. 68:23)
† Kings shall bring presents to the temple in Jerusalem (Ps. 68:29, 72:10)

It is from these prophecies in the Psalms, as well as others throughout scripture, that the Jews expected the Messiah to conquer the world and rule the world from Jerusalem. This was the main reason why Jesus was rejected by the Jews, for they were expecting a literal earthly kingdom, not a spiritual kingdom. As they were not fulfilled or did not happen during His ministry, many now assume these will be fulfilled in the future when He returns in the Second Coming. But is this the proper way to interpret these prophecies, that God will come in anger to judge the world, destroy the wicked by fire, and rule over the kingdoms of the earth? It is perhaps from these prophecies that

the disciples had asked Jesus to destroy the wicked by fire from
heaven, for which Jesus severely rebuked them (Luke 9:52-56).

So what is the proper way to interpret these prophecies in
the Psalms? Jesus made it very clear – His kingdom was a spiritual kingdom, not an earthly kingdom of this world:

> *My kingdom is not of this world: if my kingdom were of
> this world, then would my servants fight, that I should not
> be delivered to the Jews: but now is my kingdom not from
> hence.* (John 18:36)

> *And when he was demanded of the Pharisees, when the
> kingdom of God should come, he answered them and said,
> The kingdom of God cometh not with observation: Neither
> shall they say, Lo here! or, lo there! for, behold, the kingdom
> of God is within you.* (Luke 17:20-21)

When Jesus spoke to the people he spoke in parables, but
revealed the hidden spiritual meaning of the parables to his disciples. This hidden spiritual meaning contained the "mysteries
of the kingdom of heaven:"

> *And the disciples came, and said unto him, Why speakest
> thou unto them in parables? He answered and said unto
> them, Because it is given unto you to know the mysteries of
> the kingdom of heaven, but to them it is not given.* (Matt.
> 13:10-11)

Unknown to most, this way of speaking in parables actually
pervades all of scripture. The parables of the Gospels is one
area of scripture where for the first time Jesus began to speak
openly of the internal spiritual symbolism of scripture. Before
He ascended to heaven, Jesus had promised that in the future
much more would be revealed through the Holy Spirit:

> *I have yet many things to say unto you, but ye cannot bear
> them now.*

> *Howbeit when he, the Spirit of truth, is come, he will guide
> you into all truth.* (John 16:12-13)

As foretold by Jesus, the internal spiritual sense of scripture has been revealed, and this work seeks to show this revelation for the book of the Psalms. If we take another look at the prophecies of the Psalms in light of the spiritual sense of scripture, we can derive the following interpretation: the "nations" and "kings" that fight against the Messiah are not political nations and kings, but rather the evils and falsities of hell which attacked the Lord in severe temptations while He was incarnate in His human form. The wars and battles that are described in the Psalms are not literal political wars or battles, but rather represents a spiritual conflict, and all spiritual conflicts are fought between truth and falsehood which takes place in a state of temptation. In the Lord, this spiritual battle was a battle between Jehovah and all of hell. "Jerusalem" is not the literal city of Jerusalem, but rather the church where there is the doctrine of truth (see John 4:20-23). For the Messiah to be anointed as King is for the Divine to become merged with the human in Jesus Christ. For many to perish if they would not worship the Son is for the evil to suffer spiritual death should they not fight against their sins through repentance in Jesus Christ. For them to be consumed and destroyed by fire is for one to be spiritually destroyed through self consumption in one's evil desires from the love of self. For the earth to shake and mountains to be overturned signifies the end and destruction of the old church that had become corrupted by falsehoods and evils. For the people to be gathered back into the land of Israel signifies the establishment of a new Church; to be delivered from captivity is to be brought out of falsehoods and into the truth; to dwell in the land is to live according to good, and ultimately have eternal life in heaven. This is the meaning of these prophecies, when the internal spiritual sense is understood and opened from the literal sense. The proof that this indeed is the proper interpretation of these prophecies is explained in detail throughout this work.

These prophecies thus describe the spiritual war that the Lord fought against all of hell in order to redeem humanity. This was done by Jehovah by becoming incarnate in human form. The

Psalms declare this, for in many passages it is Jehovah Himself who sits on the throne (see Ps. 9:4,7, 11:4, 45:6, 47:8, 89:14, 93:2, 97:2, 103:19), it is Jehovah Himself who is Saviour (see Ps. 17:7, 106:21), it is Jehovah Himself who is Redeemer (see Ps. 19:14, 78:35), it is Jehovah Himself who is King (see Ps. 5:2, 10:16, 24:7-10, 29:10, 44:4, 47:2,6-7, 74:12, 84:3, 95:3, 98:6, 145:1). All of these positions and titles are given to Jesus in the New Testament – both Jehovah and Jesus are also known as "Lord." By assuming a lower human nature, Jehovah could fight against hell by admitting temptations from hell in His human. This continued until the human was made Divine, when the Lord's body was glorified and raised from the dead. In this manner hell was conquered, as now the Holy Spirit could flow from Jesus to all humanity. Swedenborg confirms that many of the Psalms were fulfilled with the Lord's combats with the hells:

"...the Lord fought from His own power against all the hells, and utterly subdued and subjugated them; and, by His having at the same time glorified His Human, He keeps them subdued and subjugated forever. For, before the Lord's Coming, the hells had grown up to such a height that they began to infest the angels of heaven themselves; and, in like manner, every man coming into the world and going out of the world. The reason that the hells had grown up to such a height was that the church was utterly devastated; and men in the world, from idolatries, were in nothing but falsities and evils; and the hells are from men. Hence it was that no man could have been saved unless the Lord had come into the world. These combats of the Lord are much treated of in the Psalms of David and in the Prophets, though little in the Evangelists. These combats are what are meant by the temptations which the Lord endured, the last of which was the passion of the cross. It is from them that the Lord is called the Saviour and Redeemer. This is so far known in the church that they say that the Lord conquered death, or the devil, that is, hell; and that He rose again with victory; as also, that, without the Lord, there is no salvation. That He also glorified His Human, and that He thereby became the Saviour, Redeemer, Reformer, and Regenerator forever, will be seen in what follows. That the Lord became the Saviour by combats or temptations is manifest from the passages adduced in abundance above (n. 12-14), and from this in Isaiah: *The day of vengeance is in My heart, and* THE YEAR OF MY REDEEMED *is come. I have trodden them down in My anger; I have brought down their victory to the earth:* THEREFORE HE BECAME THEIR SAVIOUR (lxiii. 4, 6, 8); the Lord's combats are treated of in that chapter. And in David: *Lift up your heads, ye gates; and be ye lifted up, ye everlasting doors; that* THE KING OF GLORY *may come in. Who is this* KING OF GLORY? JEHOVAH STRONG AND MIGHTY, JEHOVAH MIGHTY IN BATTLE (Ps. xxiv. 7, 8); this also is concerning the Lord." (*Doctrine of the Lord*, n. 33)

The temptations that the Lord endured are especially described in the Psalms:

"That the Lord while He was in the world endured such temptations, is only briefly described in the Gospels, but more fully in the prophets, and especially in the Psalms of David. In the Gospels it is only said that He was led into the wilderness, and was afterward tempted by the devil, and that He was there forty days, and with the wild beasts (Mark i. 12, 13; Matt. iv. 1). But that from His first boyhood even to the end of His life in the world, He was in temptations, that is, in combats with the hells, He did not reveal, in accordance with these words in Isaiah: *He bore oppression, and was afflicted, yet He opened not His mouth: He is led as a lamb to the slaughter, and as a sheep before her shearers is dumb, He opened not His mouth* (liii. 7). His last temptation was in Gethsemane (Matt. xxvi.; Mark xiv.), and then the passion of the cross; that thereby He fully subdued the hells, He Himself teaches in John: *Father, save Me from this hour. But for this cause came I unto this hour. Father, glorify Thy name. Then came there a voice out of heaven,* saying, *I have both glorified it and will glorify it. ...Then said Jesus, Now is the judgment of this world: now shall the prince of this world be cast out* (xii. 27, 28, 31). The prince of the world is the devil, thus all hell; glorifying means making the Human Divine. The reason why mention is made only of the temptation after forty days in the wilderness, is, that forty days signify and involve temptations to the full, and thus temptations during many years (n. 8098, 9437); the wilderness signifies hell, and the wild beasts with which He fought there, the diabolical crew." (*Heavenly Arcana*, n. 9937.7)

Thus when warfare and battles are mentioned in the Psalms, they refer to not literal earthly warfare, but rather spiritual warfare against the hells:

"In the Word, where mention is made of war, is meant in the internal sense spiritual war, which is against falsities and evils, or what is the same thing, which is against the devil, that is, the hells (n. 1664, 2686). The wars or combats of the Lord against the hells are described in the internal sense both in the historical and in the prophetical books of the Word, in like manner the wars and combats of the Lord for man." (*Heavenly Arcana*, n. 8273.4)

It was through combatting temptations admitted into His human form that Jehovah fought against the hells. Thus many of the Psalms are prayers to be delivered from temptation, which Jesus uttered as prayers while in His lower human state (see Ps. 22:1, 31:5). These prayers were prayed to the Father as a distinct person, but this is an appearance in His human form as His very soul is the Father (see John 14:8-11). This lower state of humiliation continued until Jesus had made His very human body one with the Divine. Salvation continues to be effected when each person resists temptation, acknowledging the Lord to help deliver them which is done by an influx of the Holy Spirit through the Divine Human of Jesus Christ. Thus the Psalms asking for deliverance are applicable to each person resisting sin and temptation in repentance, but were ultimately fulfilled by the Lord during His incarnation when He resisted the temptations of all of hell to deliver all of humanity. We thus participate in the process of salvation that Jesus accomplished through repentance. As Paul stated, we are *buried with him in baptism, wherein also ye are risen with him through the faith of the operation of God, who hath raised him from the dead* (Col. 2:12).

To be buried with Jesus is to allow the old self to die through repentance, to be baptized is to be reformed and regenerated by the truth, to be raised from the dead is to live a new spiritual life.

Many of the Psalms are meant to be sung in worship as glorification of the Lord for deliverance from sin and the bondage of hell. Songs of worship glorifying the Lord were not only sung among the Jewish church, but a more ancient church of the Middle East that had preceded it which had been given prophecies concerning the Lord's coming. Swedenborg comments on the purpose of these songs and their purpose in the following passage:

"To sing a song means to glorify, and thus a song glorification, because songs in the Ancient Church and afterward in the Jewish Church were prophetic and treated of the Lord, especially that He was to come into the world, and to destroy the diabolical crew, then more raging than ever, and to liberate the faithful from their assaults. And because the prophecies of songs contained such things in the internal sense, therefore by songs is signified glorification of the Lord, that is, celebration of Him from gladness of heart; for gladness of heart is especially expressed by song, since in song gladness as it were of itself breaks forth into sound. Therefore it is that Jehovah, that is, the Lord, is called in songs Hero, a Man of war, the God of armies, Conqueror, Strength, Defence, a Shield, Salvation; and the diabolical crew which was destroyed, is called the enemy which was smitten, swallowed up, overwhelmed, cast into hell.

"They who knew nothing of the internal sense believed also formerly that such things as were in the world were meant, as worldly enemies, battles, victories, overthrows, overwhelmings, of which the songs treated in the outward sense; but they who knew that all the prophecies involved things heavenly and Divine, and that these were represented in them, knew that the subject of those prophecies was the damnation of the unbelieving and the salvation of the believing by the Lord, when He should come into the world. And then they who knew this to be the case and meditated upon it and were affected thereby, had internal gladness, but others only external. The angels also who were with men were then at the same time in glorification of the Lord. Therefore they who sang and they who heard the songs had heavenly gladness from the holy and blessed feeling which flowed in out of heaven, in which gladness they seemed to themselves to be as it were taken up into heaven. Such an effect had the songs of the church among the ancients. Such an effect also they should have at this day, for the spiritual angels are especially affected by songs which relate to the Lord, His kingdom, and the church. That the songs of the church had such an effect, was not only because gladness of heart was rendered active by them, and broke forth from within even to the outmost fibres of the body, and moved these fibres with a glad and at the same time holy tremor, but also because there is glorification of the Lord in the heavens by choirs, and thus by the concordant singing of many. For this reason also angelic speech is harmonious, falling into rhythmic measures... and of angelic speech, that it falls into rhythmic measures... From this origin glorifications of the Lord among the ancients who were of the church were performed by songs, psalms, and musical instruments of various kinds; for the ancients who were of the church derived a joy exceeding all other joys from calling to mind the Lord's promised coming and the salvation of the human race through Him." (*Heavenly Arcana*, n. 2861.2-3; see also *Heavenly Arcana*, 8261.2,5-6)

A Note on the Translation and Text

In order to provide an accurate interpretation of the spiritual sense of scripture, the entire translation of the Psalms of the King James Version has been compared to the original Hebrew and corrected where needed. In order to retain familiarity with modern readers the text was first updated into modern English. From this base text numerous corrections were made to ensure the consistent translation of each Hebrew word. Use was made of various Hebrew lexicons: Strong's Corcordance, Brown Driver Biggs, and the Hebrew and Aramaic Lexicon of the Old Testament. Occasionally the Chicago Assyrian Dictionary was consulted for cognates to uncertain Hebrew words. In addition to this, translation notes from Biblical scholars of other translations were also consulted. The majority of the corrections are minor and merely improves the consistency between the original Hebrew and English. However there are many corrections of mistranslations that were necessary in order to determine the spiritual sense of scripture. For Swedenborg's own commentary he made use of a literal translation of the scriptures from the Hebrew into Latin by Schmidius published in 1696, and this translation follows a similar philosophy in translation in trying to be as close to the original Hebrew as possible.

The translation of each Psalm is first presented in its original poetic structure showing the stanzas, which are useful in dividing the Psalm into thematic sections. Verses that are common to one stanza are indented and the verse numbers are shifted to the right as they do not always accurately portray the poetic verse. For each Psalm, there is a short summary followed by a detailed commentary drawn from the writings of Emanuel Swedenborg, revealing the symbolic spiritual sense of the scripture, with cross references to other Psalms that cover the symbolic meaning of the word in question.

All quotes of Swedenborg's works are from the e-book *The Divine Revelation of the New Jerusalem: Expanded Edition* (39 volumes), where all references and indexes are hyperlinked for ease of study. This work is an updated version of the Rotch edition, containing the following works which are also published separately:

- † *Heavenly Arcana* (volumes 1-20), also known as *Arcana Coelestia* (indicated by "A.C." in the quotes)
- † *Heaven and Hell* (volume 21)
- † *The Final Judgment*, also containing *The White Horse, Earths in the Universe, Summary Exposition* (volume 22)
- † *The Doctrines of the New Jerusalem* (volume 23), containing *The Four Doctrines* and *New Jerusalem and Its Heavenly Doctrines*.
- † *Angelic Wisdom concerning Divine Love and Wisdom* (volume 24)
- † *Angelic Wisdom concerning Divine Providence* (volume 25)
- † *Apocalypse Revealed* (volume 26-28)
- † *Angelic Wisdom concerning Marriage Love* (volume 29)
- † *True Christian Religion* (volumes 30-32)
- † *The Book of Jasher*
- † *Apocalypse Explained* (6 volumes, expanded edition only)

Psalm 1

Happy is the man who walks not in the counsel of the wicked, (1)
Nor stands in the way of sinners,
Nor sits in the seat of the scoffers.
For instead his delight is in the law of Jehovah, (2)
And in His law he meditates day and night.
And he shall be like a tree planted by streams of water, (3)
Which gives its fruit in its time.
And his leaf shall not fade away,
And all whatsoever he does shall prosper.
~
The wicked are not so, (4)
For instead they are like the chaff which the wind blows away.
Therefore the wicked shall not rise in the judgment, (5)
Nor sinners in the congregation of the righteous.
For Jehovah knows the way of the righteous, (6)
But the way of the wicked shall perish.

Psalm Commentary 1

Summary: Eternal life of the righteous (v. 1-3) is contrasted with the condemnation of the wicked (v. 4-6). Those who refuse and turn against evil shall have eternal happiness (v. 1). Their heart and mind are guided by the Word (v. 2) and live a life of good works (v. 3). The Lord will judge between the good and the evil, in which the evil will perish (v. 4-6).

Happy is the man who walks not in the counsel of the wicked...

True happiness is spiritual, and the ultimate origin of spiritual happiness is derived from the happiness of eternal life. True spiritual happiness can only increase insofar as one withdraws from evil and falsity, which is the subject of this Psalm. The Hebrew word for "happy" is the same word for the name of the tribe of Asher, and the spiritual meaning can be discerned from Swedenborg's commentary on the birth of Asher in Genesis 30:13 where the word "happy" is translated as "blessed." Swedenborg notes that this spiritual happiness is not perceived directly in the body except through an obscure external enjoyment:

"And Leah said, In my blessedness; for the daughters will call me blessed. That this signifies in the supreme sense eternity, in the internal sense the happiness of eternal life, and in the external sense the enjoyment of affections, is evident from the signification of blessedness, and from the signification of 'the daughters will call me blessed.' ...Furthermore, as regards the happiness of eternal life, the man who is in affection for good

and truth cannot perceive it when he is living in the world, but a certain enjoyment instead. The reason is, that in the body he is in worldly cares and in anxieties thence which prevent the happiness of eternal life, which is inwardly in him, from being manifested in any other way at that time.

"Asher in the original language signifies blessedness; but it involves all that is signified by the words of his mother Leah, 'in my blessedness; for the daughters will call me blessed,' namely, the enjoyment of affections, that corresponds to the happiness of eternal life. This... conjoins the external man with the internal; for when a man perceives this corresponding enjoyment in himself, his external man is then beginning to be conjoined to his internal." (*Heavenly Arcana*, n. 3938.1,7, 3939; see also *Heavenly Arcana*, n. 6408; *Apocalypse Explained*, n. 438)

The more one is closely conjoined to the Lord in love, the more happy one becomes, and this comes from doing His will: *If ye know these things, happy are ye if ye do them* (John 13:17). However it is necessary in one's spiritual development to pass through periods of temptation of sadness, in such a way one withdraws from evil in repentance and becomes more closely conjoined to the Lord. Even the angels, in order to be perfected, must pass through alternating states of happiness and sadness, for inasmuch as they are led by the Lord they are in love and truth, but inasmuch as they withdraw to their own self into the love of self, they enter a state of obscurity and lack of enjoyment. In such a way they are perfected to eternity (see *Heaven and Hell*, n. 157-158).

Happy is the man who walks not in the counsel of the wicked,
Nor stands in the way of sinners,
Nor sits in the seat of the scoffers. (Ps. 1:1)

To walk is to live by falsehood (see Ps. 56:13, 81:13); the counsel of the wicked is falsity derived from evil. Standing up pertains to one's intention from the will (see Ps. 139:2); a way signifies falsehood (see Ps. 18:42, 25:4,12, 37:23, 86:11) and sin is evil against the good of love (see Ps. 25:7, 32:1, 51:1-3). Sitting or seat pertains to one's will (see Ps. 9:7, 107:4,36, 139:2). From the will one sits, to think from the will is to stand, and to act from the thought of the will is to walk.

"Walking and journeying pertain to man's movements, and thence signify progression of life, or progression of the thought from an intention of the will; but standing and sitting pertain to man's rest, and thence signify the being (*esse*) of life, from which is its existence (*existere*); thus they signify making to live... What further is signified by 'to sit' in the spiritual sense, can be seen from the following passages. In David:—

> *Blessed is the man who walketh not in the counsel of the wicked, and standeth not in the ways of sinners, and sitteth not in the seat of scoffers (Ps. i. 1).*

Here the expressions 'to walk,' 'to stand,' and 'to sit,' are used as following one another, for 'to walk' pertains to the life of thought from intention, 'to stand' to the life of the intention from the will, and 'to sit' to the life of the will, thus it is life's being (*esse*). Moreover, 'counsel,' of which 'walking' is predicated, has respect to thought, 'way,' of which 'standing' is predicated, has respect to the intention, and 'to sit in a seat' has respect to the will, which is the being (*esse*) of man's life." (*Apocalypse Explained*, n. 687.5-6)

"To walk with God is to teach and live according to the doctrine of faith, but to walk with Jehovah is to live a life of love. To walk is a customary form of expression signifying to live — as to walk in the law, to walk in the statutes, to walk in the truth. To walk has reference properly to a way, which is of truth, and consequently of faith or of the doctrine of faith." (*Heavenly Arcana*, n. 519)

As walking signifies the progression of one's life, sitting pertains to one's permanent state within:

"... sitting signifies remaining in a state; for movements from place to place signify changes of state of the interiors... Therefore tarryings or sittings signify permanent abidings in the state of the interiors. Because sittings have such a signification, therefore to sit down was an accepted ceremony among the children of Israel when they represented a permanent state of the interiors..." (*Heavenly Arcana*, n. 9422.2)

To "sit with scoffers" is to be in a permanent state of the will that refuses to change. In other passages scoffers represent a permanent state where one refuses correction (see Prov. 9:7-8, 13:1; Isa. 28:22). It is only by admission of fault, and then accepting correction, can a permanent state of the will be changed.

For instead his delight is in the law of Jehovah,
And in His law he meditates day and night. (Ps. 1:2)

This verse is based on Joshua 1:8, which is the first book after the 5 books of the law of Moses. The book of Joshua concerns the entrance of the Israelites into the land of Canaan, which in the spiritual senses signifies entrance into the kingdom of heaven. The law can pertain to the Word in general, or specifically to the internal things of the Word (see Ps. 19:7). The law of Jehovah are laws in regards to love and charity as the name Jehovah signifies the Lord as to Divine love (see Ps. 18:31, 28:1, 68:26, 82:1, 147:7), and delight is joy of the will. Meditation is perception of good (see Ps. 19:14); day signifies a state of enlightenment (see Ps. 32:4, 74:16, 136:8) and night a state of obscurity (see Ps. 3:8, 16:7, 32:4, 74:16, 91:6, 104:20, 136:9). As stated above, one passes through states of enlightenment and obscurity in one's spiritual development to eternity.

And he shall be like a tree planted by streams of water,
Which gives its fruit in its time.
And his leaf shall not fade away,
And all whatsoever he does shall prosper. (Ps. 1:3)

A tree signifies a person as to their spiritual growth (see Ps. 104:16); to be planted by streams of water is to be grounded in the truths of faith, signified by water (see Ps. 18:15, 23:2, 29:3, 42:1, 46:3, 66:12, 77:19, 78:13,16, 104:3, 136:6). Fruits are good works which come about from the truths of faith (see Ps. 21:10, 72:16, 107:37, 127:3, 148:9). True good works are those that are done without thought of return, and these are to be distinguished from the "works" spoken of in the letters of Paul which for the most part concern the external rituals of the Mosaic law which were abrograted. Leaves represent the knowledges of truths with man, and that which is done according to truth is said to prosper.

"That a tree signifies man, is evident from the following passages in the Word: *All the trees of the field shall know that I, Jehovah, will humble the high tree, will exalt the low tree, and will dry up the green tree, and will make the dry tree to flourish* (Ezek. xvii. 24). *Blessed is the man whose delight is in the law; he shall be like a tree planted by the rivers of waters, that bringeth forth his fruit in his season* (Ps. i. 1-3; Jer. xvii. 8). *Praise Jehovah, ye fruitful trees* (Ps. cxlviii. 9). *The trees of Jehovah are full* (Ps. civ. 16). *The axe lieth at the root of the tree; every tree that beareth not good fruit shall be cut down* (Matt. iii. 10; vii. 16-21). *Either make the tree good and its fruit good, or make the tree corrupt and its fruit corrupt; for the tree is known by its fruit* (Matt. xii. 33; Luke vi. 43, 44). *I will kindle a fire, which shall devour every green tree and every dry tree* (Ezek. xx. 47). Because a tree signifies man, it was a law that the fruit of a tree serviceable for food in the land of Canaan should be counted as uncircumcised for three years (Lev. xix. 23)." (*True Christian Religion*, n. 468)

"...'trees' signify such things as are with man in his interiors, which are of his mind (*mens*) or disposition (*animus*); 'boughs' and 'leaves' signifying those things that are of the knowledges of truth and good, and 'fruits' the goods of life themselves. This signification of trees draws its origin from the spiritual world; for in that world trees of every kind are seen, and the trees that are seen correspond to the interiors of the angels and spirits which are of their mind; the most beautiful and fruitful trees to the interiors of those who are in the good of love and thence in wisdom; trees less beautiful and fruitful to those who are in the good of faith; but trees bearing leaves only, and without fruits, to those who are only in the knowledges of truth; and horrible trees, with noxious fruits, to those who are in knowledges and in evil of life. To those, however, who are not in knowledges, and who are in evil of life, no trees appear, but stones and sands instead. These appearances in the spiritual world really flow from correspondence, for the interiors of the minds of those there are by such effigies presented actually before their eyes...

"Because the 'fruits of the tree' signified the goods of life, it was also commanded:—

> *That in the feast of tabernacles they should take the fruits of the tree of honor, and the boughs, and be glad before Jehovah, and thus should keep the feast (Lev. xxiii. 40, 41).*

For by 'tabernacles' were signified the goods of heavenly love, and holy worship therefrom (see *A. C.*, n. 414, 1102, 2145, 2152, 3312, 4391, 10545); and by the 'feast of tabernacles' was signified the implantation of that good or love (n. 9296). Because 'fruits' signified the goods of love which are goods of life:—

> *It was amongst the blessings that the tree of the field should give its fruit, and among the curses that it should not bear fruit (Lev. xxvi. 4, 20).*

So also it was a command that when any city was besieged:—

> *They should not lay the axe to any tree of good fruit (Deut. xx. 19, 20).*

From all this it can be seen that 'fruits' signify the goods of love, or what is the same, the goods of life, which are also called 'works,' as likewise in these passages in the Evangelists:—

> *The axe lieth unto the root of the tree; every tree that bringeth not forth good fruit shall be hewn down and cast into the fire (Matt. iii. 10; vii. 16-21).*

> *Either make the tree good and the fruit good, or else make the tree corrupt and the fruit corrupt; for the tree is known by its fruit (Matt. xii. 33; Luke vi. 43, 44).*

> *Every branch that beareth not fruit shall be taken away; but every branch that beareth fruit shall be pruned, that it may bring forth more fruit (John xv. 2-8).*

A certain man had a fig-tree planted in his vineyard; and he came seeking fruit thereon, but found none. And he saith unto the vine dresser, Behold, for three years I come seeking fruit from the fig-tree, and find none; cut it down; why should it make the ground unfruitful? (Luke xiii. 6-9).

Jesus saw a fig-tree by the way; He came to it, and found nothing thereon but leaves only; and He said, Nevermore from thee shall there be fruit. And immediately the fig-tree withered away (Matt. xxi. 19; Mark xi. 13, 14, 20).

The 'fig-tree' signifies the natural man and its interiors, and 'fruits' signify his goods (A. C., n. 217, 4231, 5113); but 'leaves' signify knowledges (n. 885). From this it is clear what is signified by the fig-tree's withering away because the Lord found on it leaves only and no fruit." (*Apocalypse Explained*, n. 109.2,6)

The wicked are not so, for instead they are like the chaff,
Which the wind blows away from the face of the earth. (Ps. 1:4)

Chaff signifies an external life in which there is nothing of good, and represents how truth not adjoined to the will of one's life becomes dissipated. This is because wheat represents the good of love or charity (see Ps. 81:16), and chaff is the external husk without the kernel. Wind is the Divine influx of truth which explores and judges the wicked (see Ps. 11:6, 18:15, 48:7, 78:26, 83:15), and separated the good from the evil just as wind separates the wheat from the chaff.

"In Matthew: *Whose fan is in His hand, and He will thoroughly cleanse His threshing floor; and He will gather His wheat into the barn, but the chaff He will burn up with unquenchable fire* (iii. 12). John the Baptist thus speaks of the Lord; the wheat stands for the good of love and charity, the chaff for that in which there is nothing of good." (*Heavenly Arcana*, n. 3941.9).

"The truth which man only knows or apprehends, remains outside of his will, and so outside of his life; for man's will is his life. But when man wills the truth, it is then on the threshold of his life; and when from willing he does it, then the truth is in the whole man; and when he does it frequently, it not only recurs from habit, but also from affection, and so from freedom. Let any one who pleases, consider whether man can be imbued with anything but that which he does from will. That which he only thinks and does not do, and still more that which he thinks and is not willing to do, is merely outside of him, and is also dissipated like chaff by the slightest wind, as it is in fact dissipated in the other life; from which it may be known what faith is without works." (*Heavenly Arcana*, n. 4884.2).

Therefore the wicked shall not rise in the judgment,
Nor sinners in the congregation of the righteous.
For Jehovah knows the way of the righteous:
But the way of the wicked shall perish. (Ps. 1:5-6)

To not rise is to not be raised to eternal life in heaven due to a life not according to Divine truth, as all judgment is according to Divine truth (see Ps. 36:6, 37:6, 72:2, 89:14, 92:12). The wicked are those who are in the falsity of evil; sinners are those who are in evil (see Ps. 25:7, 32:1, 51:1-3) and the congregation of the righteous is the heaven of those who do good (see Ps. 36:6, 37:6, 72:2, 89:14, 92:12). The way of the righteous is to be in the truth from good and the way of the wicked is falsity of evil as way signifies truth or falsehood (see Ps. 18:42, 25:4,12, 37:23, 86:11); to perish is to spiritually die from falsehoods (see Ps. 88:11). When speaking of the church, the word "assembly" refers to the truths of good of the church (see Ps. 68:26, 107:32) and "congregation" to the good of the church which can be seen in the passage concerning the killing of the Passover lamb (Ex. 12:6):

"*And the whole assembly of the congregation of Israel shall kill it.* That this signifies preparation for enjoying by all in general who are of the spiritual church, is evident from the signification of killing, when said of the lamb or of the she goat to be used for the passover, as preparation for enjoying, namely, the good of innocence, which is signified by the lamb and the goat; and from the signification of the whole assembly of the congregation of Israel, as all in general who are of the spiritual church (see n. 7830);

by the assembly of the congregation are signified the truths of good which belong to those who are of that church, for assembly is predicated of truth (n. 6355), and congregation of good."

Psalm 2

Why do the nations make commotion, (1)
And the people meditate vanity?
The kings of the earth take a stand, (2)
And the rulers take counsel together,
Against Jehovah and against His anointed.
Let us break their bands asunder, (3)
And cast away their ropes from us.
   He who sits in the heavens shall laugh, (4)
   The Lord shall scorn them.
   Then shall He speak to them in His anger, (5)
   And trouble them in His ferocity:
   But I have anointed My king, (6)
   Upon Zion, my holy mountain.
   I will recount the statute, Jehovah has said to me, (7)
   You are my Son, this day I have begotten You.
   Ask of me, and I shall give the nations for Your inheritance, (8)
   And the ends of the earth for Your possession.
   You shall *shepherd* them with a rod of iron, (9)
   You shall dash them in pieces like a potter's vessel.
And now be prudent, ye kings, (10)
Be chastised, ye judges of the earth.
Serve Jehovah with fear, (11)
And be glad with trembling.
Kiss the Son lest He be angry, (12)
And ye perish *from* the way.
For His anger is kindled but a little,
Happy are all who seek refuge in Him.

Psalm Commentary

2

Summary: Those who should be in the truths and goods of the church are against the Lord, thus one should separate from them (v. 1-3). Their falsehoods shall be accounted as nothing (v. 4) and the Lord shall assume His human form (v. 5-7) by which He will disperse falsehoods from evil (v. 8-9). Let them acknowledge and worship the Divine Human of the Lord lest they perish (v. 10-12).

Why do the nations make commotion,
And the people meditate vanity? (Ps. 2:1)

In the spiritual sense "nations" represent those who are in good or evil (see Ps. 18:43, 102:15, 106:5 and 79:1, 80:8, 106:27), and "people" are those who are in truth or falsity (see Ps. 2:1, 3:8, 18:43, 74:18, 102:15). Agitation is evil of the the will, and vanity is falsity of doctrine (see Ps. 4:2, 144:8). Without understanding the spiritual sense, many will falsely conclude that passages that mention nations and peoples concern political earthly kingdoms, which is not the case:

"'The nations have become tumultuous and the peoples have meditated vanity,' signifies the state of the church and of the former heaven that was to pass away, 'nations' meaning those who are in evils, and 'peoples' those who are in falsities (see above, n. 175, 331b, 625); (*Apocalypse Explained*, n. 684.11)

"'Nations and peoples' are often mentioned in the Word, and those who know nothing of the spiritual or internal sense of the Word, believe that peoples and nations are to be understood. But 'peoples' mean those who are in truths, or in the contrary sense those who are in falsities, and 'nations' those who are in goods, or in the contrary sense, those who are in evils. And as such are meant by 'peoples' and by 'nations,' so abstractly from persons 'peoples' mean truths or falsities, and 'nations' goods and evils; for the true spiritual sense is abstracted from persons, spaces, times, and like things, that are proper to nature. With these the natural sense of the Word, which is the sense of its letter, is at one; and the sense that is at one with these serves as a basis to the sense that is apart from them. For all things that are in nature are ultimates of Divine order, and the Divine does not rest in the middle, but flows down even to its ultimates, and there subsists. From this it is that the Word in the letter is such as it is, and unless it were such it would not serve as a basis for the wisdom of angels who are spiritual. It can be seen from this how mistaken those are who despise the Word on account of its style. 'Nations' signify those who are in good, and in the abstract, goods, because men who lived in ancient times were divided into nations, families, and houses; and they then loved each other mutually; and the father of a nation loved the whole nation which was from him; thus the good of love reigned among them. For this reason 'nations' signified goods. But when men came into the opposite state, which took place in the following ages when empires were established, then 'nations' signified evils." (*Apocalypse Explained*, n. 175.1-2)

The kings of the earth take a stand,
And the rulers take counsel together,
Against Jehovah and against His anointed. (Ps. 2:2)

The "kings of the earth" represent those who are in falsehoods (see Ps. 2:10, 24:7-10, 72:11, 89:20,39, 95:3, 105:20,30, 110:5); the earth represents the church fallen into falsehood (see Ps. 9:8, 24:1, 60:2, 90:2, 96:13). Rulers represent those who are

in evils (see Ps. 105:20). Jehovah is the Lord as to Divine love
(see Ps. 18:31, 28:1, 68:26, 82:1, 147:7); the anointed (Hebrew
Messiah) represents the Divine good in the Divine Human of
the Lord (see Ps. 89:20, 132:17). Kings were anointed to represent the descent of Divine good into the human form, which was
fulfilled by the incarnation of the Lord in the Divine Human:

"By the Anointed of Jehovah is also meant the Lord in the
following passages — *The kings of the earth set themselves, and
the rulers take counsel together, against Jehovah, and against
His Anointed. ...I have anointed My king upon Zion, the mountain of My holiness* (Ps. ii. 2, 6). The kings of the earth here
are falsities, and the rulers evils which are from the hells, and
against which the Lord when He was in the world, fought, and
which He conquered and subdued; the Anointed of Jehovah is
the Lord as to the Divine Human, for from that He fought; Zion
the mountain of holiness, upon which He is said to be anointed
to be king, is the celestial kingdom, which is in the good of love;
and this kingdom is the inmost of heaven and the inmost of the
church." (*Heavenly Arcana*, n. 9954.14)

"Kings were anointed that they might represent the Lord in
relation to judgment from Divine truth; therefore in the Word
'kings' signify Divine truths (see above, n. 31). Kings were
called 'the anointed of Jehovah,' and it was therefore sacrilege
to do harm to them, because 'anointed of Jehovah' means the
Lord in respect to the Divine Human, although, in the sense of
the letter the term is applied to the king anointed with oil; for
the Lord, when He was in the world, in respect to His Human
was the Divine truth itself, and in respect to the very *esse* of
His life, which with man is called the soul from the father, was
the Divine good itself of the Divine love; for He was conceived
of Jehovah, Jehovah in the Word meaning the Divine good
of the Divine love, which is the *esse* of the life of all; consequently the Lord alone was the Anointed of Jehovah in very
essence and in very deed, since there was in Him the Divine
good of the Divine love, and the Divine truth proceeding from
that good itself in His Human while He was in the world (see

above, n. 63, 200, 228, 328; and in *The Doctrine of the New Jerusalem*, n. 293-295, 303-305). Moreover, earthly kings were not 'the anointed of Jehovah,' but were so called because they represented the Lord, who alone was 'the Anointed of Jehovah,' therefore because they were anointed it was sacrilege to harm the kings of the earth. But the anointing of the kings of the earth was an anointing with oil, while the anointing of the Lord in respect to the Divine Human was accomplished by the Divine good itself of the Divine love; and this is what the 'oil' signified and the 'anointing' represented. For this reason the Lord was called the Messiah and Christ, Messiah in the Hebrew signifying anointed, and Christ the like in Greek (*John* i. 41; iv. 25). From this it can be seen, that when 'the anointed of Jehovah' is mentioned in the Word, in a representative sense the Lord is meant... 'The anointed of Jehovah' means the Lord also in the following passages. In *David*:—

> *The kings of the earth set themselves and the rulers took counsel together against Jehovah and against His anointed. I have anointed My king upon Zion, the mountain of My holiness* (Ps. ii. 2, 6).

'The kings of the earth' are falsities, and the 'rulers' are evils from the hells, against which the Lord fought when He was in the world, and which He conquered and subdued; 'the anointed of Jehovah' is the Lord in respect to the Divine Human from which He fought; 'Zion, the mountain of holiness upon which he is said to have been anointed as a king,' is the celestial kingdom, which is in the good of love; this kingdom is the inmost of heaven and the inmost of the church." (*Apocalypse Explained*, n. 375.16-17, 19; see also *Apocalypse Explained*, n. 684.11; *Heavenly Arcana*, n. 9954.10)

"That in ancient times they anointed stones set up as statues, is manifest from Gen. xxviii. 18, 19, 22. That they also anointed warlike arms, shields and bucklers, 2 Sam. i. 21; Isa. xxi. 5. That it was commanded that they should prepare holy oil, with which they should anoint all the holy things of the church; that with it they anointed the altar and all its vessels, also the tabernacle and all things of it, Exod. xxx. 22-33; xl. 9-11; Lev. viii. 10-12; Num. vii. 1. That they anointed with it those who should discharge the duties of the priesthood, and their garments, Exod. xxix. 7, 29; xxx. 30; xl. 13-15; Lev. viii. 12; Ps. cxxxiii. 1-3. That with it they anointed the prophets, 1 Kings xix. 15,16. That they anointed the kings with it, and that the kings were on that account called the anointed of Jehovah, 1 Sam. x. 1; xv. 1; xvi. 6, 13; xxiv. 6, 10; xxvi. 9, 11, 16, 25; 2 Sam. i. 16; ii. 4, 7; v. 17; xix. 21; 1 Kings i. 34, 35; xix. 15, 16; 2 Kings ix. 3; xi. 12; xxiii. 30; Lam. iv. 20; Hab. iii. 13; Ps. ii. 2, 6; xx. 6; xxviii. 8; xlv. 7; lxxxiv. 9; lxxxix. 20, 38, 51; cxxxii. 17. Anointing with the oil of holiness was commanded, because oil signified the good of love, and represented the Lord, who as to His Human is the very and the only Anointed of Jehovah, anointed not with oil, but with the Divine good itself of the Divine love; therefore also He was called the Messiah in the Old Testament and the Christ in the New (John i. 41; iv. 25): and Messiah and Christ signify Anointed. Hence the priests, kings, and all things of the church were anointed, and when anointed were called holy; not that they were holy in themselves, but because they thereby represented the Lord as to His Divine Human. Hence it was sacrilege to harm a king, because he was the anointed of Jehovah (1 Sam. xxiv. 7, 11; xxvi. 9; 2 Sam. i. 16; xix. 21)." (*Apocalypse Revealed*, n. 779)

Let us break their bands asunder,
And cast away their ropes from us.
He who sits in the heavens shall laugh,
The Lord shall scorn them. (Ps. 2:3-4)

Bands are conjunctions with hell through evil, and ropes are conjunctions with hell through falsehood which keep one in bondage (see Ps. 18:4-5). The one who "sits in the heavens" is the Divine itself, as sitting refers to the will or one's interiors (see Ps. 1:1, 107:4,36, 139:2); the Lord (Hebrew *Adonai*) is Divine good in the Divine Human (see Ps. 68:17,26, 105:21,

110:1, 114:7). To laugh is to have a spiritual affection for truth; to scorn is to reject falsity from knowledges of truth. Laughter is the meaning of the name Isaac (see Gen. 17:17):

"*And laughed*. That this signifies affection for truth, may be evident from the origin and essence of laughter. Its origin is nothing but affection either for what is true, or for what is false, from which is the gladness and merriment that show forth in the face in laughter, and make it plain that such is its essence." (*Heavenly Arcana*, n. 2072).

There are four stages of liberation from evil and falsity. The first is one of bondage to evil and aversion to truth (v. 1-2). The second is doubts about the truth are dispelled by reason (v. 3-4). The third is one of affirmation (v. 5-6) which is the rejection of evil and falsity. These states of reformation are described in the following passage:

"For the first state is, that the mind is held in doubt; the second state is, that the doubt is dispelled by reason; the third is affirmation; and the last is acting. In this manner good with truths introduces itself from the intellectual part into the voluntary and is appropriated." (*Heavenly Arcana*, n. 4097)

Then shall He speak to them in His anger,
And trouble them in His ferocity: (Ps. 2:5)

In many passages of scripture God is described as angry, but this is an appearance to those who are in evil who suffer from the punishment of their own evil. God is love itself and incapable of anger. Anger is related to punishment of evil, and ferocity is related to punishment of falsehood:

"In the Word in many passages it is said of Jehovah that He burns with anger and is wroth, and also that He consumes and destroys. But it is so expressed because it so appears to the man who turns himself away from the Lord, as is the case when he does evil; and since then he is not heard and is even punished, he believes that the Lord is in anger against him, when yet the Lord is never angry and never consumes, for He is mercy itself and good itself." (*Heavenly Arcana*, n. 10431)

"In many places in the Word, anger and fury are mentioned together; and anger there is predicated of evil, and wrath or fury of falsity; because they who are in evil become angry, and they who are in falsity become furious: and in the Word, each is attributed to Jehovah, that is, to the Lord; but it is meant that it is the feeling of man against the Lord" (*Apocalypse Revealed,* n. 635; for anger and fury see also Deut. 29:27; Isa. 10:4-7, 13:9, 34:2, 53:6, 66:15; Jer. 7:20, 33:5; Eze. 5:13; for "fury of anger" see also Deut. 6:14-15; Isa. 13:13; Ps. 78:49-50)

But I have anointed My king,
Upon Zion, my holy mountain. (Ps. 2:6)

To anoint is a ritual that represents the descent of the Divine into the human, which was fulfilled by the incarnation (see Ps. 2:2, 89:20, 132:17). Zion represents the highest heaven where love to the Lord is primary (see Ps. 14:7, 20:2, 48:11, 51:18, 102:13, 128:5, 133:3, 147:12), and "holy mountain" signifies good from truth or spiritual good where love to the neighbor from truth is dominant (see Ps. 15:1). Holiness is predicated of truth, as it is truth which cleanses one from sin (see Ps. 5:7, 65:4). This describes the union of the Divine with the human in the Lord, after the Divine had descended through the highest heaven signified by "Zion" and the intermediate spiritual heaven signified by "holy mountain." The land of Canaan, Jerusalem and Mount Zion do not refer to the physical places, but rather to the spiritual kingdom of heaven and the church:

"It is known, that by the land of Canaan the church is signified, because the Word was there, and through it the Lord was known: also that in the midst of it was the city of Zion and below it the city of Jerusalem, both upon a mountain. Hence by Zion and Jerusalem the inmost things of the church are signified. And because the church in heaven makes one with the church on earth, therefore by Zion and Jerusalem is meant the church in both: but by Zion the church as to love, and by Jerusalem the church as to doctrine from love. It is called Mount Zion, because love is signified by a mountain (n. 336)." (*Apocalypse Revealed,* n. 612)

I will recount the statute, Jehovah has said to me,
You are my Son, this day I have begotten You. (Ps. 2:7)

To recount is to know the quality of a thing (see Ps. 147:4); statutes signify external rituals (see Ps. 19:8, 89:31, 119:8, 147:19) which were all fulfilled by the coming of the Lord in human form (see Ps. 50:16). The word saying concerns the perception of the will (see Ps. 33:9) and is thus mentioned with Jehovah, or the Lord as to Divine love. A revelation of the Divine will is here made concerning the symbolism of the external statutes of the Jewish rituals, which were all fulfilled in ultimate form in the incarnation of the Lord. This is a prophecy concerning the virgin birth of Jesus: the day in which he was begotten was the time in which Jehovah became incarnate in human form through the conception and birth of his human form from his human mother Mary (see Ps. 110:3; Luke 1:35). The human form is the Son of God born in time to the virgin Mary, and it was only later in the fourth century A.D. that the First Council of Nicaea invented the doctrine of a Son born from eternity:

"By Son, also, is meant the Lord as to the Human, in David: *I will declare the decree, Jehovah said, Thou art My Son; today I have begotten Thee. ...Kiss the Son, lest He be angry, and ye perish in the way* (Ps. ii. 7, 12). Here a Son from eternity is not meant, but the Son born in the world; for it is prophetical of the Lord, who was to come: therefore it is called the decree, which Jehovah declared to David; and in the same Psalm it is written, in the previous verse, *I have anointed my King upon Zion* (v. 6); and in the following, *I will give to Him the nations for an inheritance* (v. 8); therefore *today,* there, is not from eternity, but in time, for with Jehovah the future is present." (*True Christian Religion,* n. 101)

"...'the Anointed of Jehovah' means here the Lord in relation to the Divine Human, for it is said, "Jehovah said unto Me, Thou art My Son, this day have I begotten Thee; kiss the Son lest ye perish; blessed are all they who put their trust in Him." In the sense of the letter this indeed is said of David, but in the Word "David" means the Lord in relation to Divine truth, or as a King (see above, n. 205). It is evident also that the Lord's coming and finally the Last Judgment by Him, and afterwards His sovereignty over all things of the world, are here treated of…

"'I have anointed My king upon Zion, the mountain of My holiness,' signifies the Lord's Human in relation to Divine truth proceeding from the Divine good of His Divine love, and thus His sovereignty over all things of heaven and the church, 'Zion' and 'the mountain of holiness' meaning heaven and the church; and thus all things of heaven and the church; 'I will declare the statute' signifies an arcanum of the Divine providence and will; 'Jehovah said unto Me, Thou art My Son, this day have I begotten Thee,' signifies the Lord as the Anointed, Messiah, Christ, and King, thus in relation to His Human conceived and afterwards born of the Divine Itself, that is, Jehovah; 'this day' signifies what is decreed from eternity and looks therefrom to the conjunction and union accomplished in time." (*Apocalypse Explained*, n. 684.10,12)

"That 'Zion' signifies heaven and the church, in which the Lord reigns by His Divine truth, can be seen from the following passages. In David:—

> *I have anointed My king upon Zion, the mountain of My holiness. I will declare the decree, Jehovah hath said unto Me, Thou art My Son, this day have I begotten Thee. I will give the nations for Thine inheritance, and the ends of the earth for Thy possession. Kiss the Son, lest He be angry and ye perish in the way, for His anger will shortly burn forth. Happy are all they who trust in Him* (Ps. ii. 6-8, 12).

This evidently was not said of David, but of the Lord, for it is said, 'Thou art My Son, this day have I begotten Thee. I will give the nations for Thine inheritance, and the ends of the earth for Thy possession;' also 'Kiss the Son, lest He be angry and ye perish in the way; Happy are all they who trust in Him;' nothing of which can be said of David. Therefore 'to anoint a king upon Zion, the mountain of holiness,' signifies the Lord's rule in heaven and in the church by means of Divine truth. (What 'to be anointed' and 'one anointed' signify, in reference to the Lord, may be seen above, n. 375d, 375e (v., vi.)). 'King' signifies the Lord in respect to Divine truth, 'Zion' heaven and the church, and 'to declare the decree' His coming; 'Thou art, My Son, this day have I begotten Thee,' signifies the Divine Human, which also is the Son of God" (*Apocalypse Explained*, n. 850.3)

Ask of me, and I shall give the nations for Your inheritance,
And the ends of the earth for Your possession. (Ps. 2:8)

Nations signify internal goods (see Ps. 2:1, 18:43, 79:1, 80:8, 102:15, 106:5,27) which the Lord acquired by the power of Divine truth as signified by inheritance (Ps. 68:9, 69:35-36). The ends of the earth the ultimate external of the church which is remote from spiritual good and truth (see Ps. 46:9, 48:10, 65:5); to possess is to acquire from love (see Ps. 69:35-36). The Lord has united His human with Divine love, and thereby saved the human race which had become separated from heaven. In this manner the Lord in His human acquired all power over all things of the heaven and the church:

"'Ask of Me, and I will give the nations for thine inheritance, and the uttermost parts of the earth for Thy possession,' signifies His kingdom and dominion over all things of heaven and the church, which shall be His" (*Apocalypse Explained*, n. 684.13)

"...that He has all power in the heavens and on earth is meant by 'I will give the nations for Thine inheritance, and the ends of the earth for Thy possession'" (*Apocalypse Explained*, n. 850.3)

You shall shepherd them with a rod of iron,
You shall dash them in pieces like a potter's vessel. (Ps. 2:9)

To shepherd or feed is to instruct in good and truth (see Ps. 23:1, 80:1); a rod of iron is the power of spiritual truth (see

Ps. 23:4, 45:6, 105:16, 110:2, 125:3) in the external natural, signified by iron (see Ps. 105:18). Spiritual truths are taught by
external natural truths, which dissipates falsities in the external natural signified by potter's vessel.

"*And he shall rule them with a rod of iron*, signifies by truths
from the literal sense of the Word, and at the same time by rational principles from natural light. These things are signified by a
rod or staff of iron, because by a rod or staff in the Word power
is signified, and by iron is signified natural truth, consequently
the natural sense of the Word and at the same time the natural
light of man. In these two the power of truth consists. That the
Divine truth is in its power in the natural sense of the Word,
which is the sense of its letter, may be seen in the *Doctrine of
the New Jerusalem respecting the Sacred Scripture* (n. 37-49);
for the reason that the sense of the letter is the basis, container,
and support of its spiritual sense (n. 27-36). And that all power
is in ultimates, which are called things natural, may be seen in
the *Angelic Wisdom concerning the Divine Love and the Divine
Wisdom* (n. 205-221); consequently in the natural sense of the
letter of the Word, and in man's natural light. These, therefore,
are the iron rod with which he shall govern the nations, that is,
shall overcome the evils which are from hell. Similar things are
signified by a rod in these passages: *Thou shalt break in pieces
the nations with a rod of iron, as a potter's vessel thou shalt
disperse them* (Ps. ii. 9). *The woman brought forth a man-child,
that was to govern all nations with a rod of iron* (Apoc. xii. 5).
*Out of the mouth of Him who sat upon the white horse proceeded
a sharp sword, that with it He should smite the nations; but
He shall govern them with a rod of iron* (Apoc. xix. 15). *Jehovah shall smite the wicked with the rod of His mouth* (Isa. xi.
4)." (*Apocalypse Explained*, n. 148; see also *Heavenly Arcana*,
n. 4876.9)

"*And He shall rule them with an iron rod*, signifies that He
is about to chastise evils by means of truths that are in the natural man. This is evident from the signification of 'ruling,' as
being to chastise, for it is added that 'He would shiver them as

pottery vessels,' and the evils which are signified are chastised by means of truths. It is evident also from the signification of 'an iron rod,' as being truths that are in the natural man; a 'rod' or 'staff' signifies the power by which chastisement is effected; and 'iron' truths in the natural man which chastise. ..."Iron" signifies truths in the natural man, because metals, as well as the other things of the earth, by correspondence signify things spiritual and celestial all of which have reference to truths and goods. 'Gold' signifies the good of the internal man; 'silver' its truth; 'copper' or 'brass' the good of the external or natural man; 'iron' its truth. For this reason the ages were called by the ancients after the names of the metals, namely, Golden, Silver, Copper, and Iron; the Golden Age from the most ancient men, who lived in the good of love; the Silver Age from the ancients after them who lived in truths from that good; the Copper Age from their posterity who were in external or natural good; the Iron Age from the posterity of these who were in natural truth alone without good." (*Apocalypse Explained*, n. 176)

A potter's vessel signify the falsities of things derived from one's own intelligence; that these are falsities is that one's own self intelligence has the self and the world in mind, which are opposed to the good and truth of heaven.

"*As the vessels of a potter shall they be broken in pieces*, signifies as of little or no account. The vessels of a potter is said because by them are signified the things of one's own intelligence, all of which are falsities, and in themselves of no account. So in David: *Thou shalt break in pieces the nations with a rod of iron, thou shalt disperse them as a potter's vessel* (Ps. ii. 9)." (*Apocalypse Revealed*, n. 148-149)

"*As earthen vessels shall they be shivered*, signifies the total dispersion of falsities. This is evident from the signification of 'earthen vessels,' as being such things in the natural man as are from self-intelligence; and all things in the natural man that have respect to the things of heaven and the church and which are from self-intelligence are falsities (of which presently). It is evident also from the signification of being 'shivered,' as being to be dispersed; 'to disperse' is said of falsities, as 'to shiver' is said of earthen vessels. ... That 'earthen vessels' signify such things as are from self-intelligence, thus the falsities that are in the natural man, is evident from various passages in the Word, of which I will cite the following as confirmation. In *David:*—

> *Thou shalt bruise the nations with an iron scepter; as a potter's vessel Thou shalt dash them in pieces* (Ps. ii. 9).

In this passage also 'to bruise the nations with an iron scepter' is to chastise and subdue the evils that are in the natural man. 'Scepter' here has the same signification as 'staff' or 'rod.' It is added 'as a potter's vessel,' because that signifies falsity from self-intelligence. In the sense of the letter this is a comparison, for it is said 'as a potter's vessel,' and 'as earthen vessels;' but in the internal sense comparisons axe not perceived as comparisons, since comparisons are equally from things significative (see *A. C.,* n. 3579, 8989). 'A potter's vessel,' or 'earthen vessel,' signifies what is false, because a potter is one who forms, and a vessel is what is formed; and when man forms the vessel it is a falsity, but when the Lord forms it with man it is a truth; consequently in the Word 'a potter's vessel' signifies either what is false or what is true, and 'a potter' signifies one who forms." (*Apocalypse Explained,* n. 177.1,5)

And now be prudent, ye kings:
Be chastised, ye judges of the earth. (Ps. 2:10)

Kings are those who are in falsehood (see Ps. 2:2, 24:7-10, 72:11, 89:20,39, 95:3, 105:20,30, 110:5) and judges are those who are in evil. In the opposite sense judges represent those who are in good:

"In old times a judge rode upon a she-ass, and his sons upon young asses; for the reason that the judges represented the goods of the church, and their sons truths therefrom. But a king rode upon a she-mule, and his sons upon mules, by reason that kings and their sons represented the truths of the church" (*Heavenly Arcana*, n. 2781.6).

As kings and judges have this meaning, to be prudent means to be in the truths of faith, and to be chastised is to apply the truths of faith to one's life by correcting one's evils (see Ps. 94:10). That chastise has this meaning can be seen in Jeremiah: *Your own evil shall chastise you, and your backslidings shall reprove you* (Jer. 2:19)

Serve Jehovah with fear,
And be glad with trembling. (see Ps. 2:11)

To serve is to be in truth (see Ps. 31:16, 69:36, 78:70, 89:3,20, 105:26) from Divine love signified by Jehovah (see Ps. 18:31, 28:1, 68:26, 82:1, 147:7); with fear is to do according to the good of love (see Ps. 33:18, 128:1, 147:11). To be glad is to be in affection for truth (Ps. 14:7); trembling is a holy reverence of mind. The meaning of fear depends on the context; throughout scripture there are three levels or degrees of fear in the worship of God:

"What fearing God signifies in the Word, may be evident from a great many passages when understood as to the internal sense. The fear of God there signifies worship, and indeed worship either from fear, or from the good of faith, or from the good of love" (*Heavenly Arcana*, n. 2826; see also *Heavenly Arcana*, n. 5459)

"That to fear God signifies to love the things that are God's, by doing them, and not being willing to do the things that are contrary to Him, is manifest from these passages: *What doth Jehovah thy God require of thee, but to fear Jehovah thy God, to walk in all His ways, and to love Him* (Deut. x. 12). *Ye shall walk after Jehovah your God, and fear Him, and keep His commandments* (Deut. xiii 4). *Jehovah thy God shalt thou fear, Him shalt thou serve, and to Him shalt thou cleave* (Deut. x. 20; vi. 2, 13, 24; viii. 6; xvii. 19; xxviii. 58; xxxi. 12). *O that there were in them a heart to fear Me, and to keep My commandments* (Deut. v. 29). *Teach me, O Jehovah, Thy way; unite my heart to the fear of Thy name* (Ps. lxxxvi. 11). *Blessed is he who feareth Jehovah, who walketh in His ways* (Ps. cxxviii. 1; cxii. 1; Jer. xliv. 10). *If I am a father, where is my honor? if I am a lord, where is my fear?* (Mal. i. 6; ii. 5; Isa. xi. 2, 3). *I will give them one heart and one way to fear Me; and I will put My fear in their heart, that they may not depart from Me* (Jer. xxxii. 39, 40). *The fear of Jehovah is the beginning of wisdom* (Ps. cxi. 10. Beside other places, as Isa. viii. 13; xxv. 3; xxix. 13; 1. 10; Jer. xxxiii. 9; Ps. xxii. 23; xxxiii. 8, 18; xxxiv. 7, 9; lv. 19; cxv. 13; cxlvii. 11; Apoc. xiv. 7; Luke i. 50). *But the fear of God with the evil is not love, but a fear of hell."* (*Apocalypse Revealed*, n. 527)

Kiss the Son lest Jehovah be angry,
And ye perish from the way. (Ps. 2:12)

The Son is the Lord in the Divine Human as to Divine truth (see Ps. 2:7); to kiss signifies to be conjoined in love for the Lord is love itself; for Jehovah to be angry is to be in the punishment from one's own evil causing opposition from Divine love which appears as anger (see Ps. 2:5, 78:49). It is through the Lord that all humanity has conjunction with God. To perish is to spiritually die from falsehoods (see Ps. 88:11) and way signifies one's falsehood (see Ps. 1:1, 18:42, 25:4,12, 37:23, 86:11).

"...'kiss the Son' signifies conjunction with the Lord by love, 'to kiss' signifying conjunction by love; 'lest He be angry, and ye perish in the way,' signifies lest evils assault you and you be condemned, for 'to be angry' when predicated of the Lord, signifies the turning away of men from Him, thus their anger and not the Lord's; and evils are what turn away, and then are angry; 'for His anger will shortly burn forth' signifies the Last Judgment, and the casting down of the evil into hell; 'blessed are all they who trust in Him' signifies salvation by love to the Lord and faith in Him." (*Apocalypse Explained*, n. 684.13; see also *Apocalypse Explained*, n. 850.3; *Heavenly Arcana*, n. 3573-74)

"In David: *Now, O ye kings, be intelligent; be instructed, ye judges of the earth; serve Jehovah with fear, and exult with trembling. Kiss the Son, lest He be angry, and ye perish in the way* (Ps. ii. 10-12). Kings stand for those who are in truths; and from truths they are often called the 'king's sons.' 'The Son' here stands for the Lord, Who is here called 'the Son,' because He is the truth itself, and all truth is from Him." (*Heavenly Arcana,* n. 2015.6; see also *Heavenly Arcana,* n. 9309)

For His anger is kindled but a little,
Happy are all who seek refuge in Him. (Ps. 2:12)

Anger is the punishment of evil whose desires are experienced as a burning fire; happiness is the happiness of eternal life (see Ps. 1:1).

"*When a fire shall have broken out.* That this signifies anger from affection for evil, is evident from the signification of fire, as love, here the love of evil and affection for it — of which just above (n. 9141). It is said affection for evil, because by affection is meant the continuous of love. That fire is anger from affection for evil, is because anger is from that source, since when that which a man loves is assailed, a fiery spirit bursts forth and as it were burns. Therefore anger is described in the Word by fire, and it is said to burn — as in David: *There went up a smoke out of His nostrils, and fire out of His mouth: coals did burn from Him* (Ps. xviii. 8). Again: *Kiss the Son, lest He be angry ...for His wrath will soon be kindled* (Ps. ii. 12). In Isaiah: *Who among us shall dwell with the devouring fire? who among us shall dwell with the fires of eternity?* (xxxiii. 14). Again: *He poured upon him the fury of His anger ...it set him on fire round about, yet he knew not; it burned him, yet he laid it not to heart* (xlii. 25). Again: *Behold, Jehovah will come in fire, and His chariots like the whirlwind; to recompense in the fury of His anger, and His rebuke in flames of fire* (lxvi. 15). And in Moses: *I looked back, and came down from the mount, when the mount was burning with fire. ...I was afraid by reason of the anger and hot displeasure wherewith Jehovah was wroth against us* (Deut. ix. 15, 19). In these and many other passages anger is described by fire. The anger is

attributed to Jehovah, that is, to the Lord, but it is in man
(n. 5798, 6997, 8282, 8483). The Lord appeared in mount Sinai
to the Israelitish people according to their nature, thus in fire,
smoke, and thick darkness (n. 6832). But it is to be known that
anger is fire bursting forth from affection for evil, while zeal
is fire bursting forth from affection for good (n. 4164, 4444,
8598). Therefore zeal also is described by fire — as in Moses:
Jehovah thy God is a devouring fire, a zealous God (Deut. iv.
24). And in Zephaniah: *I will pour upon them ...all the fury
of Mine anger; for all the earth shall be devoured in the fire
of My zeal* (iii. 8). That the zeal of Jehovah is love and mercy
and that it is called anger because it appears as anger to the
wicked when they rush into the punishment of their evil, may
be seen above (n. 8875)." (*Heavenly Arcana*, n. 9143)

Psalm 3

A Psalm of David, when he fled before Absalom his son.

~

Jehovah, how are my adversaries multiplied, (1)
Many are they who rise up against me.
Many are they who say of my soul, (2)
There is no salvation for him in God. (Selah)
But You, Jehovah, are a shield for me, (3)
My glory and the lifter of my head.
I called unto Jehovah with my voice, (4)
And He answered me out of His holy mountain. (Selah)
 I lied down and slept, I awoke, (5)
 For Jehovah supported me.
 I will not fear ten thousands of people, (6)
 Who have set themselves against me round about.
 Arise, Jehovah, (7)
 Save me, my God:
 For You will smite all my enemies upon the cheek,
 You will break the teeth of the wicked.
 Salvation belongs to Jehovah, (8)
 Your blessing is upon Your people. (Selah)

Psalm Commentary   3

Summary: The temptations of the Lord by the hells (v. 1-2), who called upon the Father for help (v. 3-4). The Lord's subjugation of the hells (v. 5-8).

Jehovah, how are my adversaries multiplied,
Many are they who rise up against me.
Many are they who say of my soul,
There is no salvation for him in God. (Ps. 3:1-2)

Adversaries are the evils of hell which constantly rises to fight against the good of heaven (see Ps. 27:12). The soul is one's spiritual life of the understanding (see Ps. 22:10, 31:9, 71:23, 107:9); salvation is deliverance from evil (see Ps. 14:7, 96:2) and God is the Lord as to Divine truth (see Ps. 18:31, 29:1, 68:17,24, 82:1, 95:3, 147:7).

"In a multitude of passages in the Word, 'adversaries' and 'enemies' are mentioned, and by them evils and falsities are meant, evils by 'adversaries,' and falsities by 'enemies;' for the Word in its bosom is spiritual, therefore in that sense no other than spiritual adversaries and enemies can be meant by 'adversaries and enemies.' That this is so can be seen from the following passages. In *David:*—

> *Jehovah, how are my adversaries multiplied, many are they*
> *who rise up against me, that say of my soul, There is no sal-*
> *vation for him in God (Ps. iii. 1, 2)." (Apocalypse Explained,*
> n. 671.3)

"*For destruction by those who rose up against them.* That this signifies that they lacked all power of resisting the evils [and falsities] which are from hell, is evident from the signification of destruction, as that they lacked all power of resisting evils and falsities, for this in the spiritual world is to have no power; and from the signification of those who rise up against, or enemies, as evils and their falsities, for these are the enemies which rise up in a spiritual sense. Wherefore also these are signified in the Word by enemies and those who rise up against one — as in David: *O Jehovah, how are mine enemies increased! Many are they who rise up against me; many which say of my soul, There is no salvation for him in God* (Ps. iii. 1, 2). ...by enemies and those who rise up against one are signified evils and falsities which are from hell. They are called those who rise up against, because evils and falsities rise up against goods and truths, but not the reverse." (*Heavenly Arcana*, n. 10481.1)

But You, O Jehovah, are a shield for me,
My glory and the lifter of my head. (Ps. 3:3)

A shield signifies the Lord's protection against evils and falsities, and a person's trust in the Lord (see Ps. 144:2). Glory is the Divine truth which should be acknowledged as coming from the Lord alone (see Ps. 8:5, 19:1, 24:7-10, 29:1, 73:24, 96:3); to lift the head is to deliver from hell and be elevated towards heaven (see Ps. 110:7).

"To lift up the head was a customary form of judgment with the ancients, when the bound, or in prison, were judged either to life or to death; when to life, it was expressed by lifting up the head, as in the Second Book of Kings: *Evil-merodach king of Babylon, in the year that he began to reign, did lift up the head of Jehoiachin king of Judah out of prison; and he spake kindly to him, and set his throne above the thrones of the kings that were with him in Babylon* (xxv. 27, 28). And so in Jeremiah: *Evil-merodach king of Babylon, in the [first] year of his reign lifted up the head of Jehoiachin king of Judah, and brought him forth out of prison* (lii. 31). But when they were judged to death, it was expressed by lifting up the head from off him, as in what follows concerning the baker: *Within yet three days shall Pharaoh lift up thy head from off thee* (verse 19).

"This form of judgment had its origin with the ancients, who were in representatives, from the representation of those who were bound in prison or in a pit; and as by these were represented those who were in vastation under the lower earth (n. 4728, 4744, 5038), therefore by lifting up their head was signified their liberation, for they are then elevated or lifted up out of vastation to the heavenly societies (n. 2699, 2701, 2704). To be lifted up or to be elevated is to advance toward interiors; for what is elevated or high is predicated of the interiors (n. 2148, 4210); and because it is toward interiors, it is toward heaven, for heaven is in the interiors. This was signified by lifting up the head." (*Heavenly Arcana*, n. 5124)

I called unto Jehovah with my voice,
And He answered me out of His holy mountain. (Ps. 3:4)

To call is to be receptive of the Lord and to answer signifies Divine influx providing inspiration as to truth and aid from mercy (see Ps. 4:1); the holy mountain represents good from truth or spiritual good (see Ps. 15:1).

I lied down and slept, I awoke,
For Jehovah supported me.
I will not be fear ten thousands of people,
Who have set themselves against me round about. (Ps. 3:5-6)

Evil and falsity have no power to those in good and truth as they are protected by the Lord. To lie down and sleep represents a state of rest following the conflict of temptation (see Ps. 4:8); to awake is to come into a new spiritual life by living by the truth (see Ps. 13:3, 76:5). The number ten thousand or myriad is predicated of falsehoods which are many (see Ps. 68:17, 91:7) and people are the falsehoods of hell (see Ps. 2:1, 3:8, 18:43, 65:7, 74:18, 102:15). Those who set themselves round about are the evils of hell.

"*And lay down in that place.* That this signifies tranquillity of state is evident from the signification of lying down, as being in a state of tranquillity; for lying down and sleeping mean nothing else. That this is the signification of lying down, in the internal sense, may be evident also from other passages in the Word, as will be seen below. With those who are to be regenerated, who are here treated of in the internal representative sense, the case is, that first of all they are in a state of tranquillity, or in a state of external peace — for external peace, or peace in externals, is called tranquillity; it is also produced from a Divine state of peace, which is inmostly within it, and comes into existence in externals by the removal of lusts and falsities, for these are what cause all restlessness.

"...In David: *I will lay me down and sleep; and I will awake; for Jehovah sustaineth me. I will not be afraid of ten thousands of the people, that have set themselves against me round about* (Ps. iii. 5, 6) — where to lay me down and sleep signifies a state of tranquillity and security. Again: *In peace will I both lay me down and sleep; for Thou, Jehovah, alone makest me to dwell in safety* (Ps. iv. 8). And again: *He will make me to lie down in green pastures: He will lead me to the waters of rest; He will restore my soul* (Ps. xxiii. 2, 3). From which passages it is manifest that a state of peace and tranquillity is signified by lying down; and that by lying down in that place is signified tranquillity of state, for place in the internal sense signifies state (n. 3692)." (*Heavenly Arcana*, n. 3696.5)

Arise, Jehovah,
Save me, my God:
For You will smite all my enemies upon the cheek,
You will break the teeth of the wicked. (Ps. 3:7)

Jehovah is the Lord as to Divine love (see Ps. 18:31, 28:1, 68:26, 82:1, 147:7); God is the Lord as to Divine truth (see Ps. 18:31, 29:1, 68:17,24, 82:1,6, 95:3, 147:7). Enemies are the falsehoods of hell which attack the truth (see Ps. 3:1, 27:12). To smite their cheek is to destroy interior falsehood, and to break the teeth of the wicked is to destroy exterior falsehoods:

"Arise, O Jehovah; save me, O my God; for Thou smitest all mine enemies upon the cheek; Thou breakest the teeth of the wicked (Ps. iii. 7).

'To smite the enemies upon the cheek' signifies to destroy interior falsities with those who are opposed to the goods and truths of the church; such persons and their falsities of evil are meant in the Word by 'enemies;' 'to break the teeth of the wicked' signifies to destroy exterior falsities, which are such as are based on the fallacies of the senses and are confirmed by them." (*Apocalypse Explained*, n. 556.7)

"By cheek is signified affection for interior truth, by the right cheek affection for truth from good, by dealing a blow is signified the act of hurting this affection... That to inflict a blow or to smite the cheek means to destroy truths, is plain from passages in the Word where mention is made of smiting the cheek. And because in the genuine sense it signifies the destruction of truth, therefore in the opposite sense it signifies the destruction of falsity, in which sense it occurs in David: *Thou wilt smite all mine enemies on the cheek bone; Thou wilt break the teeth of the wicked* (Ps. iii. 7)." (*Heavenly Arcana*, n. 9049.6,8).

"That the teeth signify natural truth, which belongs to the exterior understanding, and in the opposite sense the falsity which destroys that truth, is manifest from the following passages in the Word — that they signify natural truth, in Moses: *His eyes shall be redder than wine, and his teeth whiter than milk* (Gen. xlix. 12). In this passage also both eyes and teeth are mentioned together. The subject is Judah, by whom is meant the Lord as to the Divine celestial (n. 6363); the eyes signify the Divine intellectual of the Lord (n. 6379), and the teeth His Divine natural (n. 6380), thus also the Divine truth in the natural.

"In Amos: *I have given you emptiness of teeth in all your cities, and want of bread in all your places* (iv. 6) — where emptiness of teeth stands for penury of truth, and want of bread for penury of good. From this it is plain what is meant by the gnashing of teeth among those who are in hell (Matt. viii. 12; xiii. 42, 50; xxii. 13; xxv. 30; Luke xiii. 28), namely, the collision of falsities with the truths of faith. For the teeth, as already said, in the opposite sense signify the falsity which destroys truth — as in David: *Arise, O Jehovah; save me, O my God: for thou wilt smite all mine enemies upon the cheek bone; thou wilt break the teeth of the wicked* (Ps. iii. 7) — where the teeth of the wicked to be broken stand for the falsities by which they destroy truths." (*Heavenly Arcana*, n. 9052.2-3; see also *Heavenly Arcana*, n. 9049.7)

Salvation belongs to Jehovah:
Your blessing is upon Your people. (Ps. 3:8)

Salvation is deliverance from evil by the Lord's mercy (see Ps. 14:7, 96:2), and thus it is said to belong to Jehovah is the Lord as to Divine love (see Ps. 18:31, 28:1, 68:17, 26, 82:1, 147:7). Blessing is the influx of good from the Divine (see Ps. 16:7, 21:6, 24:5, 28:6, 31:21, 96:2), and people are those who are in good from truth or spiritual good (see Ps. 2:1, 18:43, 65:7, 74:18, 102:15):

"*Salvation unto Jehovah, Thy blessing upon Thy people* (Ps. iii. 8).

'The blessing of Jehovah upon His people' signifies influx and the reception of good and truth; those are called 'the people of Jehovah' who are in spiritual good (see above, n. 331)." (*Apocalypse Explained*, n. 340.20)

Psalm 4

To the chief musician on Neginoth, a Psalm of David.

~

In my call answer me, God of my righteousness: (1)
In adversity You have enlarged me,
Be gracious to me and hear my prayer.
Ye sons of men, how long will my glory be in dishonour? (2)
Why do you love vanity, seeking after lies? (Selah)
But know, for Jehovah sets apart the merciful for Himself, (3)
Jehovah will hear when I call to Him.
Be agitated and sin not, (4)
Speak with your own heart upon your bed, and be silent. (Selah)
  Sacrifice sacrifices of righteousness, (5)
  And trust in Jehovah.
  Many say, Who will show us good? (6)
  Jehovah, lift up the light of Your face upon us.
  You have given joy to my heart, (7)
  More than the time when their grain and their new wine
  are multiplied.
  In peace I will both lie down and sleep: (8)
  For You alone, Jehovah, make me to dwell in safety.

Psalm Commentary 4

Summary: Respecting the Lord, when in great temptations (v. 1-2). The Lord should be feared as He has protection from the Father (v. 3-4). Exhortation to repent (v. 5-8).

In my call answer me, God of my righteousness:
In adversity You have enlarged me. (Ps. 4:1)

To call and answer signifies reciprocal conjunction between man and God, inasmuch as one approaches God, God will approach that person:

"...we may often read in the Word that the Lord answers those who call and cry; as Ps. iv. 1; xvii. 6; xx. 9; xxxiv. 4; xci. 15; cxx. 1. Also that He gives to those who ask (Matt. vii. 7, 8; xxi. 22; John iv. 13, 14; xv. 7; xvi. 23-27). But still the Lord gives them to ask, and what to ask; and therefore the Lord knows it before; but still the Lord wishes that man should ask first, to the end that it may be as of himself, and so be appropriated to him. Otherwise if the petition itself were not from the Lord, it would not have been said in those places, that they should receive whatever they asked." (*Apocalypse Revealed*, n. 376)

"...the expression 'to answer' frequently occurs in the Word, and it signifies, in reference to the Lord, influx, inspiration, perception, and information, likewise mercy and aid... 'to answer' means not to answer but to flow into the thought, to give perception, and to give help from compassion; from this it is that 'answers,' in reference to the Lord, signify perceptions from influx. It is to be noted that whatever comes from the Lord into the perception is called influx." (*Apocalypse Explained*, n. 471.2; see also Isa. 49:8, Ps. 13:3, 17:6, 20:9, 34:4, 91:15, 120:1)

The "God of my righteousness" is the Divine truth, as signified by God (see Ps. 18:31, 29:1, 68:17,24, 82:1, 95:3, 147:7), which proceeds from Divine good, signified by righteousness (see Ps. 36:6, 37:6, 72:2, 89:14, 92:12). To be enlarged is to be brought into truth after the distress of the temptation of falsehoods. The word "enlarge" also means width – and in the spiritual sense "width" (from north to south) has regard to truth (see Ps. 18:19, 31:8, 104:25), and "length" (west to east) has regards to what is good:

"The breadth of the earth signifies the truth of the church, because there are four quarters in the spiritual world, the east, west, south, and north; and the east and west make its length and the south and north its breadth: and because they who are in the good of love dwell in the east and west, therefore also good is signified by the east and west, and so by length; and because they who are in the truths of wisdom dwell in the south and north, therefore also truth is signified by the south and north, and so by breadth. But on this more may be seen in the work on *Heaven and Hell*, published at London, 1758 (n. 141-153). That truth is signified by breadth may be evident from these passages in the Word: *O Jehovah, Thou hast not shut me up into the hand of the enemy, Thou hast made my feet to stand in a broad place* (Ps. xxxi. 8). *I called upon Jah in straitness, He answered me in a broad place* (Ps. cxviii. 5). *Jehovah led me forth into a broad place, He delivered me* (Ps. xviii. 19). *I am He who raiseth up the Chaldeans, a nation bitter and swift, who walketh in the breadths of the earth* (Hab. i. 6). *Ashur shall pass through Judah, he shall overflow and go over, and the stretching out of his wings shall fill the breadth of the land* (Isa. viii. 8). *Jehovah shall feed them as a sheep in a broad place* (Hos. iv. 16; beside other places, as Ps. iv. 1; lxvi. 12; Deut. xxxiii. 20)." (*Apocalypse Revealed*, n. 861)

Be gracious to me and hear my prayer. (Ps. 4:1)

To receive grace is to receive spiritual truth and comfort and hope of mind, and is sought by those in humiliation of thought (see Ps. 103:8); prayer is according to the good of one's life (see Ps. 66:19, 72:15).

"*And I will be gracious to whom I will be gracious, and will shew mercy on whom I will shew mercy.* That this signifies that Divine truth and good shall be revealed to those who receive, is evident from the signification of being gracious, as giving spiritual truth and good, in this case revealing it, because the subject is the internal and the external of the church, of worship, and of the Word; and from the signification of showing mercy, as endowing with celestial truth and good, here revealing it. That it is with those who receive, is because the internal things of the Word, of the church, and of worship are revealed to no others than those who receive.

"That to be gracious is to endow with spiritual truth and good, and to show mercy to endow with celestial truth and good, is because grace is predicated of faith and mercy of love, and the good of faith is spiritual good and the good of love is celestial good." (*Heavenly Arcana*, n. 10577.1-2)

In the following passage grace is translated as favor:

"*And gave him favor in the eyes of the prince of the prison.* That this signifies relief thence in temptations, is evident from the signification of giving favor, as relief — for giving favor in temptations is comforting and relieving by hope; and from the signification of a prince, as a primary truth" (*Heavenly Arcana*, n. 5043)

Ye sons of men, how long will my glory be in dishonour?
Why do you love vanity, seeking after lies? (Ps. 4:2)

Sons in general signify truths (see Ps. 17:14, 45:16, 127:3, 128:3,6); sons of men (Heb. *'iysh*) refer to those who are in a false rationality from their self intelligence (see Ps. 49:2, 80:17); glory is the Divine truth (Ps. 8:5, 19:1, 24:7-10, 29:1, 73:24, 96:3) which is turned to dishonor when one attributes good or truth to one's self instead of God. Vanity is falsity of doctrine (see Ps. 144:8) and lies are falsity of life.

"By seeing or by vision, when said of the prophets, is signified in the internal sense revelation which regards doctrine, and by divining or by divination is signified revelation which regards life; and because vanity signifies falsity of doctrine, and a lie falsity of life, therefore it is said, they have seen vanity and divination of a lie. Again in Ezekiel: *In seeing there is to thee vanity, in divining there is to thee a lie* (xxi. 29). In Zechariah: *The teraphim speak iniquity, and the diviners see a lie, and they tell dreams of vanity* (x. 2). In Jeremiah: *The prophets have seen vanity* (Lam. ii. 14). That vanity is falsity of doctrine and of religion, is also plain in Hosea: *They are become vanity; in Gilgal they sacrifice bullocks* (xii. 11). In Jeremiah: *My people hath forgotten Me, they have burned incense to vanity* (xviii. 15); in like manner in other passages (see Isa. v. 18; xxx. 28; lix. 4; Ps. xii. 2; cxix. 37; cxliv. 7, 8)." (*Heavenly Arcana*, n. 9248.2)

But know, for Jehovah sets apart the merciful for Himself:
Jehovah will hear when I call to Him.
Be agitated and sin not:
Speak with your own heart upon your bed, and be silent. (Ps. 4:3-4)

To be "set apart" is to separate the good from the evil before the last judgment, as in the case where the same word is mentioned in Exodus (see Ex. 8:22, 9:4). The merciful are those who are in the good of love (see Ps. 25:10, 26:3, 36:5, 89:14, 103:8). Hearing, when said of the Lord, signifies Divine providence (see Ps. 17:6). To be agitated is to resist from one's thought and to not sin is to not do evil against the good of love (see Ps. 25:7, 32:1); to speak or say signifies perception of the will (see Ps. 33:9) and is thus mentioned with heart which signifies the will (see Ps. 7:9, 22:10, 24:4, 51:10, 64:6, 66:18, 71:23, 78:8, 86:11). The bed signifies doctrine regarding good; to be silent is to silence falsehoods from one's own self.

"A bed signifies doctrine from correspondence; for as the body reclines in its bed, so does the mind in its doctrine. But by a bed is signified doctrine which any one procures to himself either from the Word or from his own intelligence; for in it his mind rests, and as it were sleeps. The beds in which they lie in the spiritual world are from no other origin. Every one there has a bed according to the quality of his knowledge and intelligence; there are magnificent for the wise, mean for the unwise, and filthy for falsifiers. This is signified by a bed in Luke; *I say unto you, in that night there shall be two in one bed; the one shall be taken, and the other left* (xvii. 34). This is concerning the final judgment. Two in one bed are two in one doctrine, but not in similar life. In John: *Jesus said to the sick man, Arise, take up thy bed, and walk: and he took up his bed, and walked* (v. 8-12): and in Mark: *Jesus said to the palsied, Son, thy sins are forgiven thee: and He said to the scribes, Which is the easier, to say, Thy sins are forgiven thee, or to say, Take up thy bed, and walk? Then said He, Arise, take up thy bed, and walk: and he took up his bed, and went forth from them* (ii. 5, 9, 11, 12). That something is here signified by the bed is manifest; because Jesus said, *Which is the easier to say, Thy sins are forgiven thee, or to say, Take up thy bed, and walk?* By carrying the bed, and walking, is signified to meditate on doctrine; it is thus understood in heaven. Doctrine is also signified by a bed in Amos: *As the shepherd taketh out of the mouth of the lion, so shall the sons of Israel be taken out, that dwell in Samaria, in the corner of a bed, in the extremity of a couch* (iii. 12). In the corner of a bed and in the extremity of a couch means more remotely from the truths and goods of doctrine. By a bed and a couch and by a bedchamber, the like is signified elsewhere; as in Isaiah xxviii. 20; lvii. 2, 7, 8; Ezek. xxiii. 41; Am. vi. 4; Mic. ii. 1; Ps. iv. 4; xxxvi. 4; xli. 3; Job vii. 13; Lev. xv. 4, 5." (*Apocalypse Revealed*, n. 137)

Sacrifice sacrifices of righteousness,
And trust in Jehovah.
Many say, Who will show us good?
Jehovah, lift up the light of Your face upon us. (Ps. 4:5-6)

It is a spiritual law that one must first withdraw from evil (v. 4), and after that one can do good, but not before. Sacrifices are symbolic of the worship from the truths of faith (see Ps. 40:6, 50:8) which are derived from righteousness which is to do what is good (see Ps. 36:6, 37:6, 72:2, 89:14, 92:12). To trust is to have confidence of the will which is given to those who are in the good of charity (see Ps. 33:21) and is thus mentioned with Jehovah who is the Lord as to Divine love (see Ps. 18:31, 28:1, 68:26, 82:1, 147:7). Good comes from the Lord alone; to lift up the light of the Lord's face is to receive Divine truth as signified by light (see Ps. 11:4, 18:28, 36:9, 43:3, 104:2, 139:12) from Divine good as signified by face (Ps. 13:1, 22:24, 27:8-9, 31:16, 67:1):

"Among the ancients the face signified the internals, for the reason that the internals shine forth through the face; and in the most ancient times men were such that the face was in perfect accord with the internals, so that every one could see from a man's face of what disposition or mind he was. For they held it to be a monstrous thing to show one thing by the face and think another. Simulation and deceit were then abominable. Thus it was that the internals were signified by the face. When charity shone from the face the countenance was said to be lifted up; and when the opposite, the countenance was said to fall. And therefore it is predicated of the Lord that He lifts up His countenance upon man — as in the Blessing (Num. vi. 26, and Ps. iv. 6) — by which is signified that the Lord gives man charity. What the falling of His countenance signifies is evident in Jeremiah: *I will not cause My countenance to fall toward you, for I am merciful, saith Jehovah* (iii. 12). The countenance of Jehovah is mercy. When He lifts up His countenance upon any one, it means that out of mercy He gives him charity. When He causes His countenance to fall it is the reverse — that is, when man's countenance falls." (*Heavenly Arcana*, n. 358)

You have given joy to my heart,
More than the time their grain and their new wine are multiplied. (Ps. 4:7)

The joy of heart is the good of love; grain is lower natural good (see Ps. 65:9), wine is spiritual truth (see Ps. 23:5, 32:9, 104:15). As one advances from natural to spiritual, and from spiritual to celestial, one's joy increases in love.

> *"Who will show us good? Jehovah, lift Thou up the light of Thy faces upon us. Thou givest joy in my heart more than at the time when their corn and new wine are increased. In peace I at the same time lie down and sleep; for Thou alone, O Jehovah, dost make me to dwell securely (Ps. iv. 6-8);*

This describes the peace that those have who are in conjunction with the Lord through the reception of Divine good and Divine truth from Him, and that it is peace in which and from which is heavenly joy. Divine good is meant by 'Who will show us good?' and Divine truth by 'lift Thou up the light of Thy faces upon us,' 'the light of the Lord's faces' is the Divine light that proceeds from Him as a sun in the angelic heaven, which light is in its essence Divine truth (as may be seen in the work on *Heaven and Hell,* n. 126-140). Heavenly joy therefrom is meant by 'Thou givest joy in the heart;' multiplication of good and truth is meant by 'their corn and new wine are increased,' 'corn' signifying good, and 'new wine' truth. Because peace is in these and from these, it is said, 'In peace I at the same time lie down and sleep; for Thou alone, O Jehovah, dost make me to dwell securely,' 'peace' signifying the internal delight of heaven, 'security' the external delight, and 'to lie down and sleep' and 'to dwell' signifying to live." (*Apocalypse Explained,* n. 365.13)

In peace I will both lie down and sleep:
For You alone, Jehovah, make me to dwell in safety. (Ps. 4:8)

Peace is spiritual peace from the Lord (see Ps. 29:11) and the internal delight of heaven; to lie down and sleep is to arrive at a state of rest and tranquility after the conflict of temptation (see Ps. 3:5); to dwell in safety is to be in the external delight of heaven (see above passage on verse 7).

"By peace are signified all things in the complex which are from the Lord, and hence all things of heaven and the church, and the blessedness of life in them. These are of peace in the highest or inmost sense. It follows from this, that charity, spiritual security, and internal rest, are peace; for, when a man is in the Lord, he is in peace with his neighbor, which is charity; in protection against the hells, which is spiritual security; and when he is in peace with his neighbor, and in protection against the hells, he is in internal rest from evils and falsities." (*Apocalypse Revealed*, n. 306; see also Num. 6:24-26; Ps. 4:6-8, 29:11, 34:14, 37:11,37, 38:3, 55:18, 72:7, 85:9-10, 119:165, 120:6-7, 122:6-9, 128:5-6, 147:14; Isa. 9:6-7, 26:12, 32:17-18, 48:18,22, 52:7, 53:5, 54:10,13; Jer. 33:6,9; Lam. 3:15,17; Eze. 34:25,27, 37:25; Hag. 2:9; Zech. 8:16,19; Mal. 2:4-5; Matt. 10:12-14; Luke 1:79, 10:5-6; John 14:27, 16:33)

Psalm 5

To the chief Musician upon Nehiloth, A Psalm of David.

~

Give ear to my sayings, Jehovah, (1)
Consider my meditation.
Listen to the voice of my cry, my King, and my God: (2)
For unto You I will pray.
Jehovah, in the morning You shall hear my voice, (3)
In the morning I will set in order *my prayer* to You and watch.
    For You are not a God who delights in wickedness, (4)
    Evil shall not sojourn with You.
    The boastful shall not stay in front of Your eyes, (5)
    You hate all workers of iniquity.
    You shall make those who speak lies to perish, (6)
    Jehovah will abhor the bloody and deceitful man.
    But as for me, in the multitude of Your mercy I will come into Your house, (7)
    I will bow down toward Your holy temple in Your fear.
    Jehovah, lead me in Your righteousness, (8)
    Because of my opponents make Your way straight before me.
    For there is nothing steadfast in their mouth, (9)
    Their inward part is mischievous,
    Their throat is an open sepulchre,
    They flatter with their tongue.
    Hold them guilty, God, (10)
    Let them fall from their own counsels.
    Drive them out in the multitude of their transgressions,
    For they have rebelled against You.
But let all those who seek refuge in You rejoice, (11)

Let them forever shout for joy.
And You will shelter them,
And let them who love Your name exult in You.
For You will bless the righteous, Jehovah, (12)
You will compass him with good pleasure as scale armour.

Psalm Commentary 5

Summary: Prayer of the Lord to the Father for help (v. 1-3) against the evil, falsifiers and hypocrites (v. 4-10). The righteous will be preserved and have eternal happiness (v. 11-12).

Give ear to my sayings, Jehovah,
Consider my meditation.
Listen to the voice of my cry, my King, and my God,
For unto You I will pray.
Jehovah, in the morning You shall hear my voice,
In the morning I will set in order my prayer to You and watch.
(Ps. 5:1-3)

To give ear signifies Divine providence (see Ps. 17:6) from Divine mercy; to consider one's meditation is for Divine providence to be according to Divine truth. To cry is to be in sadness of mind from falsity against the truth and is thus mentioned with King and God, which signifies the Lord as to Divine truth. Prayer is from spiritual good (see Ps. 66:19, 72:15). The morning signifies the coming of the Lord, the good of love, and His kingdom (see Ps. 30:5, 46:5, 101:8, 110:3, 130:6, 143:7). To set in order one's prayer is to direct oneself to the Lord away from self, and to watch signifies to study one's life according to one's faith (see Ps. 13:3):

"*Watch, therefore, for ye know not the day nor the hour wherein the Son of Man cometh* signifies the study of life according to the precepts of faith, which is to watch. The time of acceptance, which is unknown to man, and the state of it, are signified by

67

their not knowing the day nor the hour in which the Son of Man
is to come. He who is in good, that is, he who does according to
the precepts, is called wise, and he who is in knowledges of truth
and does them not is called foolish, in another passage also in
Matthew: *Every one ...who heareth My words and doeth them, I
will liken him unto a wise man ...and every one who heareth My
words, and doeth them not, shall be likened unto a foolish man*
(vii. 24, 26)." (*Heavenly Arcana*, n. 4638.10)

For You are not a God who delights in wickedness,
Evil shall not sojourn with You. (Ps. 5:4)

The Lord is good and truth itself in whom there is no evil
or falsehood. To have no delight in wickedness signifies the evil
will have no happiness from love; for the evil to not sojourn with
the Lord signifies that the evil will refuse to be instructed in the
truth, as signified by sojourning:

"That to sojourn means to be instructed, is evident from the
signification of sojourning in the Word, which is to be instructed;
and this for the reason that sojourning and migration, or proceeding from place to place, is in heaven nothing but change of
state, as was shown above (n. 1376, 1379); therefore, whenever
travelling, sojourning, and passing from place to place, occur
in the Word, nothing else is suggested to the angels than such
change of state as they have. There are changes of state as well
of the thoughts as of the affections; changes of the state of the
thoughts are knowledges, and these are produced in the world
of spirits by instructions; which also was a reason why the men
of the Most Ancient Church, as they had communication with
the angelic heaven, from sojourning had a perception only of
instruction." (*Heavenly Arcana*, n. 1463)

The boastful shall not stay in front of Your eyes,
You hate all workers of iniquity.
You shall make them who speak lies to perish,
Jehovah will abhor the bloody and deceitful man. (Ps. 5:5-6)

The boastful are those who praise their own self and have no understanding of the truth, signified by eyes (see Ps. 11:4, 13:3, 31:9, 69:23); iniquity is evil done against the good of faith (see Ps. 51:1-3). Those who speak lies are those who are in a falsity of life (see Ps. 4:2, 144:8); to perish is to spiritually die from falsehoods (see Ps. 88:11). To abhor is to be in opposition due to inverted order (see Ps. 14:1); a bloody man is one who falsifies the truth and a deceitful man is one who intentionally deceives. The first 2 lines have regard to those who do evil against love; the second 2 line have regard to those who are against good from truth; and the third 2 lines have regard to those who are in falsehood against the truths of faith.

"That blood signifies the Divine truth may be clearly manifest from its opposite sense, in which it signifies the Divine truth of the Word falsified or profaned; as is manifest from these passages: *Who stoppeth his ears, lest he should hear of bloods, and shutteth his eyes, lest he should see evil* (Isa. xxxiii. 15). *Thou shalt destroy them who speak falsehood; the man of bloods and deceit Jehovah abhorreth* (Ps. v. 6). *Every one that is written among the living in Jerusalem, when the Lord shall have washed away the blood thereof out of the midst of it by the spirit of judgment and by the spirit of purifying* (Isa. iv. 3, 4). *In the day that thou wast born I saw thee trodden down in thy blood; and I said, In thy blood live; I washed and cleansed the blood from off thee* (Ezek. xvi. 5, 6, 9, 22, 36, 38). *They have wandered like blind men in the streets; they were polluted by blood, till they can do no more; they touch with their garments* (Lam. iv. 13, 14). *The garment is polluted with blood* (Isa. ix. 5). *Even in thy skirts is found the blood of the souls of the innocents* (Jer. ii. 34). *Your hands are full of blood; wash you, purify you, put away the evil of your doings* (Isa. i. 15, 16). *Your hands are defiled with blood, and your fingers with iniquity; your lips have spoken a lie; they hasten to shed innocent blood* (Isa. lix. 3, 7). *Jehovah goeth forth to visit the iniquity of the earth; then shall the earth reveal her blood* (Isa. xxvi. 21). *As many as received Him, to them gave He power to become children of God; who were born not of blood*

(John i. 12, 13). *In Babylon was found the blood of the prophets and of the saints* (Apoc. xviii. 24). *The sea became as the blood of a dead man, and the fountains of waters became blood* (Apoc. xvi. 3, 4; Isa. xv. 9; Ps. cv. 29). The same is signified by the streams, pools, and lakes of waters in Egypt being turned into blood (Exod. vii. 15-27). *The moon shall be turned into blood before the great day of Jehovah cometh* (Joel ii. 31). *The moon became blood* (Apoc. vi. 12). In these places, and many more, blood signifies the truth of the Word falsified, and also profaned; which can be still more manifestly seen from the passages read in the Word in their connection. Since therefore the truth of the Word falsified or profaned is signified by blood in the opposite sense, it is manifest that by blood in the genuine sense the truth of the Word not falsified is signified." (*Apocalypse Revealed*, n. 379)

Whereas lying is to speak falsehood, deceit and bearing false witness is to intentionally mislead (see Ps. 78:57):

"By a lie in the Word falsity and false-speaking are signified, and by deceit is signified each from design... The deceitful are signified in the Word by poisonous serpents, and by crocodiles and vipers; and deceit is signified by their poison." (*Apocalypse Revealed*, n. 624; see also Ex. 21:14; Ps. 5:6, 17:1, 24:4, 35:20-21, 46:3, 50:19, 52:2,4, 72:14, 109:2, 119:118, 120:2-3; Job 13:7, 27:4, Isa. 53:9; Jer. 5:26-27, 8:5, 9:5-6, 14:14, 23:26; 48:10; Hos. 7:16, 11:12; Zeph. 1:9; Mic. 6:12; John 1:47)

"In the spiritual sense by bearing false witness is meant persuading that falsity of faith is truth of faith, and that evil of life is good of life, and the converse; but to do these things from design and not from ignorance, thus to do them after one knows what is true and good, and not before; for the Lord says, *If ye were blind, ye would not have sin; but now ye say, We see; therefore your sin remaineth* (John ix. 41). This falsity is meant in the Word by a lie, and the design by deceit, in these passages: *We have made a covenant with death, and with hell have we made an agreement, we have made a lie our trust, and under falsehood have we hid ourselves* (Isa. xxviii. 15). *They are a rebellious people, lying sons, they will not hear the law of Jehovah* (xxx. 9).

From the prophet even to the priest, every one doeth a lie (Jer. viii. 10). *The inhabitants speak a lie, and their tongue is deceitful in their mouth* (Mic. vi. 12). *Thou wilt destroy them who speak a lie; Jehovah abhorreth a man of deceit* (Ps. v. 6). *They have taught their tongue to speak a lie; thine habitation is in the midst of deceit* (Jer. ix. 5, 6). Because a lie means falsity, the Lord says that *the devil speaketh a lie from his own* (John viii. 44). A lie signifies falsity and false speaking in other passages also (Jer. xxiii. 14, 32; Ezek. xiii. 6-9, 19; xxi. 29; Hos. vii. i; xii. 1; Nah. iii. 1; Ps. cxx. 2, 3)." (*True Christian Religion*, n. 322)

"...'to speak a lie' signifies to teach falsely from ignorance of truth; but 'deceit' signifies falsity that is not from ignorance of truth, but from deliberation, thus from the purpose of deceiving, as is the case with the wicked. ..."deceit" does not mean deceit in the natural sense, which consists of deceitful plotting and malicious falsehood against another, but deceit in the spiritual sense, in which 'deceit' means thought from the intention of the will, or intentionally and deliberately speaking falsities and per-suading to them, and thereby destroying the soul." (*Apocalypse Explained*, 866.3-4)

But as for me, in the multitude of Your mercy I will come into Your house,
I will bow down toward Your holy temple in Your fear. (Ps. 5:7)

The house of the Lord signifies heaven and the church in respect to good (see Ps. 23:6, 65:4, 92:13, 105:21) and is thus mentioned with mercy which signifies Divine love (see Ps. 25:10, 26:3, 36:5, 89:14, 103:8). The temple signifies heaven and the church in respect to truth (see Ps. 18:6, 48:9, 65:4) and in the highest sense refers to the Divine Human (see Ps. 68:29, 138:2). To fear the Lord is to follow His commandments by doing them (see Ps. 2:11, 33:18, 128:1, 147:11). Since a temple represents those who live by the truth, it is mentioned along with holiness, for it is living by the truth which makes one holy or sanctified (see Ps. 65:4):

"They are called saints who live according to the truths of
the Word; not that they are holy, but that the truths in them are
holy; and these are holy when they are from the Lord in them,
and the Lord is in them when the truths of His Word are in them
(John xv. 7). By virtue of truths from the Lord the angels are
called holy (Matt. xxv. 31; Luke ix. 26): and the prophets likewise (Luke i. 70; Apoc. xviii. 20; xxii. 6): and also the apostles
(Apoc. xviii. 20). Hence it is, that the temple is called *the temple
of holiness* (Ps. v. 7; lxv. 4): that Zion was called *the mountain of
holiness* (Isa. lxv. 11; Jer. xxxi. 23; Ezek. xx. 40; Ps. ii. 6; iii. 4;
xv. 1): that Jerusalem is called *the holy city* (Isa. xlviii. 2; lxiv.
10; Apoc. xxi. 2, 10; Matt. xxvii. 53): that the church is called
a people of saints (Isa. lxii. 12; lxiii. 18; Ps. cxlix. 1): and also *a
kingdom of saints* (Dan. vii. 18, 22, 27). They are called saints
because the angels, in the abstract sense, signify Divine truths
from the Lord; the prophets, truths of doctrine; the apostles, the
truths of the church; the temple, heaven and the church as to
Divine truth; and likewise Zion, Jerusalem, and the people and
kingdom of God. That no one is holy of himself, not even the
angels, may be seen Job xv. 14, 15; but from the Lord, because
the Lord alone is holy, Apoc. xv. 4, n. 173." (*Apocalypse Revealed*,
n. 586)

Jehovah, lead me in Your righteousness,
Because of my opponents make Your way straight before me.
(Ps. 5:8)

Jehovah is the Lord as to Divine love (see Ps. 18:31, 28:1,
68:26, 82:1, 147:7) and righteousness is to do good by that love
(see Ps. 36:6, 37:6, 72:2, 89:14, 92:12). Opponents are those who
are in falsehoods from evil; the way is truth (see Ps. 1:1, 18:42,
25:4,12, 37:23, 86:11); to make it straight is to correct the falsehood of ignorance into truth leading to good signified by straight,
as length pertains to good (see Ps. 4:1).
   "In Luke: *Every valley shall be filled, and every mountain and
hill shall be brought low; and the crooked shall become straight,
and the rough ways smooth* (iii. 5) — where valley stands for

what is lowly (n. 1723, 3417), mountain and hill for what is exalted (n. 1691), the crooked become straight for the evil of ignorance turned into good, since length and the things relating to length are predicated of good (n. 1613); the rough ways made smooth stand for the falsities of ignorance being turned into truths. That way is predicated of truth, see above (n. 627, 2333)." (*Heavenly Arcana*, n. 3527.3)

For there is nothing steadfast in their mouth,
Their inward part is mischievous.
Their throat is an open sepulchre,
They flatter with their tongue.
Hold them guilty, God,
Let them fall from their own counsels. (Ps. 5:9-10)

The mouth signifies the external understanding (see Ps. 37:30, 135:16); the inward part signified the internal understanding. The throat or neck signifies the conjunction of interiors with exteriors (see Ps. 18:40), a sepulchre is the hell of evil who are spiritually dead (see Ps. 88:5), and one's tongue is a false principle of persuasion (see Ps. 35:28, 57:4, 140:11). To be held guilty by God is to be judged according to Divine truth; to fall is to pervert the truth (see Ps. 7:15) and one's own counsels are one's own falsehoods.

> "There is nothing right in the mouth of any one, their midst is perditions; their throat is an open sepulchre, they flatter with their tongue (Ps. v. 9).

'In the mouth' signifies outwardly, the 'midst' inwardly; that there is hell within is signified by 'their throat is an open sepulchre;' and that outwardly there is hypocrisy and seeming sanity is signified by 'they flatter with their tongue.'" (*Apocalypse Explained*, 659.11)

"And put a necklace of gold about his neck. That this signifies a significative of the conjunction of interiors with exteriors, effected by good, is evident from the signification of the neck, as influx and also the communication of higher with lower things, or what is the same, of interiors with exteriors (see n. 3542); hence a necklace, because it encircles the neck, is a significative of their conjunction. A necklace of gold signifies conjunction through good, or effected by good, because gold signifies good (n. 113, 1551, 1552). A sign of the conjunction of interior with exterior truth is signified by a necklace upon the throat, in Ezekiel: *I decked thee with ornaments, and I put bracelets upon thy hands, and a necklace upon thy throat* (xvi. 11)." (*Heavenly Arcana*, n. 5320)

The word for "flatter" can also be translated as "smooth" and is predicated of truth or falsehood:

"...that smooth is predicated of truth, and in an opposite sense of falsity, is manifest also from these passages in the Word — in Isaiah: *Ye that inflame yourselves with gods, under every green tree ...among the smooth stones of the valley is thy portion* (lvii. 5, 6) — where inflaming is predicated of evil, and the smooth stones of the valley, of falsity. Again: *The workman encourages the melter, him who smootheth the hammer with the stroke of the anvil, saying of the soldering, It is good* (xli. 7) — where the workman encouraging the melter is predicated of evil, and smoothing the hammer, of falsity. In David: *They make thy mouth smooth as butter when his heart approacheth, his words are softer than oil* (Psalm lv. 21) — where a smooth or alluring mouth is predicated of falsity, and the heart and soft things therefrom, of evil. Again: *Their throat is an open sepulchre, they speak smooth things with their tongue* (Ps. v. 9). The throat an open sepulchre is predicated of evil, the tongue speaking smooth things, of falsity." (*Heavenly Arcana*, n. 3527.3)

Drive them out in the multitude of their transgressions,
For they have rebelled against You. (Ps. 5:10)

The word transgression (or trespass) signifies anything done contrary to the truth of faith from a perverted understanding (see Ps. 25:7, 32:1), rebellion signifies revolt against the truth of faith or to reject what is good in state of temptation (see Ps. 78:56).

"Inasmuch as trespasses are evils that are contrary to truths of faith, they are both transgressions and revolts, which indeed in the original tongue are signified by the same expression, as is manifest in David: *Thrust them out for the multitude of their transgressions, who rebel against Thee* (Ps. v. 10). The expression to rebel is used when there is both revolt and transgression." (*Heavenly Arcana*, n. 9156.3)

But let all those who seek refuge in You rejoice,
Let them forever shout for joy.
And You will shelter them,
And let them who love Your name exult in You.
For You will bless the righteous, Jehovah,
You will compass him with good pleasure as scale armour.
(Ps. 5:11-12)

To seek refuge is to have trust from faith in the Lord; to shout for joy is to have joy from love; forever is eternity in the celestial heaven (see Ps. 145:13). To be sheltered is to be protected by the holy of truth, as the word for shelter is related to pavilion (see Ps. 31:20). To exult is to have happiness from affection for truth and name is every truth of doctrine by which the Lord is known and worshipped (see Ps. 74:18, 96:2). The righteous are those who do good (see Ps. 36:6, 37:6, 72:2, 89:14, 92:12); to be blessed is to receive good and happiness from the Lord (see Ps. 3:8, 16:7, 21:6, 24:5, 28:6, 31:21, 96:2). To be compassed with good pleasure like scale armour signifies protection by Divine love against falsities which attack what is good (see Ps. 35:2).

"*Thou dost bless the righteous; Thou wilt compass him with Thy good pleasure as with a shield* (Ps. v. 12).

Here 'good pleasure' stands plainly for the Divine love, from which the Lord protects every one; protection by the Lord from love is signified by 'Thou wilt compass him as with a shield.'" (*Apocalypse Explained*, n. 295.8

Psalm 6

To the chief musician on Neginoth upon Sheminith, a Psalm of David.

~

Jehovah, reprove me not in Your anger, (1)
And chasten me not in Your fury.
Be gracious to me, Jehovah, for I am weak, (2)
Heal me, Jehovah, for my bones are troubled.
And my soul is greatly troubled, (3)
But You, Jehovah, how long?
   Return, Jehovah, rescue my soul, (4)
   Save me for Your mercies' sake.
   For in death there is no remembrance of You, (5)
   In hell who shall confess You?
   I am weary with my sighing, (6)
   In all the night I make my bed to swim,
   I water my couch with my tears.
   My eye wastes away from provocation, (7)
   It waxes old with all my adversaries.
Depart from me all ye workers of iniquity, (8)
For Jehovah has heard the voice of my weeping.
Jehovah has heard my supplication, (9)
Jehovah will receive my prayer.
Let all my enemies be ashamed and greatly troubled, (10)
Let them return and be ashamed suddenly.

Psalm Commentary 6

Summary: Prayer of the Lord to the Father in an extreme state of temptation (v. 1-3, 4-7), who overcame and subjugated the hells (v. 8-10).

Jehovah, reprove me not in Your anger,
And chasten me not in Your fury. (Ps. 6:1)

Reproof is correction for falsehood (see Ps. 94:10), and chastisement correction for evil (see Ps. 2:10, 94:10). Reproof is also used in the sense to judge between two in an argument (see Gen. 31:37, Job 9:33). Anger is punishment due to evil (see Ps. 2:5, 78:49) and fury punishment due to falsehood:

"Fury and anger are frequently mentioned in the Word, but in the internal sense they do not signify fury and anger, but repugnance, and this for the reason that whatever is repugnant to any affection produces fury or anger, so that in the internal sense they are only repugnances; but the repugnance of truth is called fury, and the repugnance of good is called anger; and in an opposite sense fury is the repugnance of falsity or its affection, that is, principles of falsity; and anger is the repugnance of evil or its lust, that is, self-love and the love of the world." (*Heavenly Arcana*, n. 3614.2)

Be gracious to me, Jehovah, for I am weak,
Heal me, Jehovah, for my bones are troubled.
And my soul is greatly troubled,
But You, Jehovah, how long? (Ps. 6:2-3)

78

To receive grace is to receive spiritual good and truth, and comfort and hope of mind in temptations (see Ps. 4:1) and is sought by those in humiliation of thought (see Ps. 103:8); to be weak is to have no power against falsehoods; to be healed is to be saved and preserved from evils (see Ps. 30:2); bones refer to one's external knowledge from the self (see Ps. 22:14,17, 34:20, 35:10) which becomes troubles during temptation. The soul is one's spiritual life from the understanding (see Ps. 22:10, 31:9, 71:23, 107:9); to ask how long is to have doubt about the end to the conflict of temptations.

Return Jehovah, rescue my soul,
Save me for Your mercies' sake.
For in death there is no remembrance of You,
In hell who shall confess You? (Ps. 6:4-5)

To rescue the soul is to be delivered from falsehoods; to be saved is to be delivered from evil by Divine mercy (see Ps. 14:7, 96:2). Death is spiritual death which is a life separate from heaven (see Ps. 9:13, 102:20, 106:28) and also refers to those who are spiritually dead due to evil; hell is the condemnation that follows afterwards and also refers to those who are in the falsity of evil (see Ps. 18:5). Remembrance signifies presence and conjunction in love (see Ps. 8:4); to confess is to have affection for the good of love (see Ps. 7:17, 35:18, 89:24) which is absent for those who are in hell as they have blinded themselves from their own falsehoods.

"...in the Word 'life' signifies the life of heaven with man, which is there also called 'life eternal;' while 'death' signifies the life of hell, which life in the Word is called 'death,' because it is the privation of the life of heaven. ... That 'to live,' or 'being alive,' signifies spiritual life in man, and 'being dead' deprivation of that life, and damnation, can be seen from many passages in the Word, of which I will cite the following...

In *David*:—

> *Behold the eye of Jehovah is upon them who fear Him, to deliver their soul from death, and to keep them alive in famine* (*Ps.* xxxiii. 18, 19).

In the same:—

> *Thou hast delivered my soul from death, and my feet from stumbling, that I may walk before God in the light of the living* (*Ps.* lvi. 13).

In *Jeremiah*:—

> *Behold, I set before you the way of life and the way of death* (xxi. 8).

In *John*:—

> *Jesus said, Verily, verily, I say unto you, he who heareth My Word hath eternal life, and shall not come into condemnation, but shall pass from death into life* (v. 24).

It is clear that in these passages 'death' means damnation, and 'life' salvation. Because 'death' is damnation it is also hell, for which reason hell is commonly called 'death' in the Word, as in these passages. In *Isaiah*:—

> *Hell will not confess Thee, nor will death praise Thee; they who go down into the pit will not hope on Thy truth. The living, the living, he shall confess Thee* (xxxviii. 18, 19).

In the same:—

> *We have made a covenant with death, and with hell we have made a vision* (xxviii. 15).

In *Hosea*:—

> *I will ransom them from the hand of hell; I will redeem them from death. O death, I will be thy plague! O hell, I will be thy perdition!* (xiii. 14).

In *David:*—

> *In death there is no remembrance of Thee; in hell who shall confess Thee?* (Ps. vi. 5).

In the same:—

> *The cords of death compassed me, and the cords of hell* (Ps. xviii. 4, 5).

In the same:—

> *Like sheep shall they be laid in hell; death shall feed them* (*Ps.* xlix. 14).

In the same:—

> *Jehovah, thou hast brought up my soul from hell; Thou hast made Me to live* (Ps. xxx. 3).

In the *Apocalypse:*—

> *A pale horse, and he who sat upon him whose name was death, and hell will follow him* (vi. 8).

And in another place:—

> *Death and hell were cast into the lake of fire* (xx. 14).

As 'death' signifies damnation and hell, its meaning in the following passages is evident. In *Isaiah:*—

> *He will swallow up death for ever; and the Lord Jehovih will wipe away tears from off all faces* (xxv. 8).

In the same:—

> *That he might give the wicked to their sepulchre, and the rich in their deaths* (liii. 9).

In *David:*—

> *Jehovah, Thou liftest me up from the gates of death* (Ps. ix. 13).

In the same:—

> *Thou shall not be afraid for the arrow that flieth by day, nor for the death that wasteth at noonday (Ps.* xci. 5, 6).

In *John:*—

> *If any one keep My word he shall never see death* (viii. 51).

In the *Apocalypse:*—

> *He who overcometh shall not be destroyed in the second death* (ii. 11).

In *Matthew:*—

> *One of His disciples said, Lord, suffer me first to go away and bury my father. Jesus said, Follow Me, and let the dead bury the dead* (viii. 21, 22)

On account of this signification of 'the dead':—

> *The sons of Aaron were forbidden to touch any dead body (Lev.* xxi. 2, 3, 11);

Likewise the priests, the Levites (*Ezek.* xliv. 25);
  Likewise the Nazirite (*Num.* vi. 6, 7);
  And whoever of the sons of Israel touched the dead must be cleansed by the water of separation (*Num.* xix. 11 to the end).

From these passages it can be seen what is meant by 'the dead,' namely, those who have not in themselves the life of heaven, and consequently are in evils and in falsities therefrom. These are meant also in the following passages. In *David:*—

> *They joined themselves also unto Baal-peor, and ate the sacrifices of the dead (Ps.* cvi. 28).

In the same:—

> *He hath made me to sit in darkness, like the dead of eternity (Ps.* cxliii. 3)...

As 'death' signifies damnation and hell, soon the other hand 'life' signifies salvation and heaven; as in the passages that follow. In *Matthew:*—

Narrow is the gate and straitened is the way which leadeth unto life (vii. 14).

In the same:—

It is good to enter into life with one eye, rather than having two eyes to be cast into the hell of fire (xviii. 9).

In the same:—

If thou wilt enter into life, keep the commandments (xix. 17).

In *John:*—

They shall come forth; they who have done good unto the resurrection of life (v. 29).

From this it is that salvation is called 'eternal life' (as in *Matt.* xix. 16, 29; xxv. 46; *Mark* x. 30, 31; *Luke* x. 25; xviii. 18, 30; *John* iii. 14-16, 36; xvii. 2, 3; and other places). For the same reason heaven is called 'the land of the living,' as in *David:*—

O Jehovah, Thou art my reliance, my part in the land of the living (*Ps.* cxlii. 5).

In the same:—

That thou mayest see the good of Jehovah in the land of the living (*Ps.* xxvii. 13)." (*Apocalypse Explained*, n. 186.1-2,4-8)

I am weary with my sighing,
In all the night I make my bed to swim,
I water my couch with my tears.
My eye wastes away from provocation,
It waxes old with all my adversaries. (Ps. 6:6-7)

To be weary is grief of the will due to temptations; night signifies a state of obscurity as to truth (see Ps. 3:8, 16:7, 32:4, 74:16, 91:6, 104:20, 136:9); bed signifies one's understanding of

doctrine in a lower natural state (see Ps. 4:4, 41:3); couch signifies the good of doctrine (Ps. 4:4) and to shed tears is sadness
of mind due to falsehoods against the truth. One's eye is one's
internal spiritual understanding (see Ps. 11:4, 13:3, 31:9, 69:23)
which wastes away due to provocation which is temptation of
the will (see Ps. 10:14, 78:58). To wax old is for good to decline
due to attacks from evils, signified by adversaries (see Ps. 3:1,
27:12).

"A 'tear from the eyes' signifies grief of mind on account of
falsities and from falsities, because the 'eye' signifies the understanding of truth; a 'tear' therefore signifies grief because there
is no understanding of truth, consequently because of falsities.
'Tear' has a similar signification in *Isaiah:*—

> *He will swallow up death for ever, and the Lord Jehovih will
> wipe away tears from off all faces* (xxv. 8).

This signifies that the Lord by His coming will remove evils and
falsities with those who live from Him, so that there will be no
grief of mind on account of them and from them; 'death' signifies
evil, because spiritual death is from it; and 'tear' is predicated of
falsity. It is to be noted, that both 'shedding tears' and 'weeping'
signify grief on account of falsities and from falsities, but 'shedding tears' grief of mind, and 'weeping' grief of heart on account
of falsities. Grief of mind is grief of the thought and understanding, which pertain to truth, and grief of heart is grief of the affection or will, which pertain to good; and as there is everywhere in
the Word a marriage of truth and good, both 'weeping' and 'tears'
are mentioned in the Word when grief is expressed on account of
falsities of doctrine or of religion. That 'weeping' means grief of
heart can be seen from the fact that 'weeping' bursts forth from
the heart and breaks out into lamentations through the mouth;
and that 'shedding tears' is grief of mind can be seen from this,
that it issues forth from the thought through the eyes. In both
weeping and in the shedding of tears water comes forth which
is bitter and astringent, and this occurs through an influx into
man's grief from the spiritual world, where bitter water corre-

sponds to the lack of truth because of falsities, and to consequent grief; therefore those who are in truths grieve on account
of falsities. From this it can be seen why it is that in the Word,
where 'tears' are mentioned 'weeping' also is mentioned, namely,
that it is on account of the marriage of good and truth in every
particular of the Word. I will only adduce the following passages
in evidence of this. In *Isaiah:*—

> *I will weep with weeping for Jazer, the vine of Sibmah; I will
> water thee with my tears, O Heshbon and Elealeh* (xvi. 9).

In *Jeremiah:*—

> *In secret places my soul shall weep, and mine eyes shall run
> down with tears* (xiii. 17).

In the same:—

> *Who will give mine eyes a fountain of tears, that I may weep
> day and night* (ix. i).

In *Lamentations:*—

> *In weeping she will weep in the night, and her tears are on
> her cheeks* (i. 2).

In *Malachi:*—

> *Covering the altar of Jehovah with tears, with weeping, and
> with sighing* (ii. 13).

In *David:*—

> *They who sow with tears and he who weeping beareth the
> casting of seed* (Ps. cxxvi. 5, 6).

In *Jeremiah:*—

> *Refrain thy voice from weeping, and thine eyes from tears*
> (xxxi. 16).

In the same:—

> *Let the mourning-women make haste and take up a lamenta-
> tion over us, that our eyes may flow down with tears* (ix. 18).

Here we have 'lamentation' in place of weeping, because it is the voice of weeping. In *David*:—

> *I am weary with my sighing, all the night do I bathe my bed;*
> *with my tears I make my couch to melt (Ps. vi. 6).*

Here 'to bathe the bed' means by weeping, which is of the mouth, because it is said of sighing; while 'to drench the couch,' which has a like meaning, has reference to tears. These passages have been cited that from them also it may be known that two like expressions in the Word, especially in the Prophets, are not vain repetitions, but that one has reference to good, and the other to truth." (*Apocalypse Explained*, n. 484.2-4)

Depart from me all ye workers of iniquity,
For Jehovah has heard the voice of my weeping. (Ps. 6:8)

Workers of iniquity are those who do evil against the good of faith (see Ps. 51:1-3); weeping is grief of the will due to evil (see Ps. 6:6) and for Jehovah to hear signifies Divine providence (see Ps. 17:6). In a higher sense this refers to the suppression of hells by the Lord after overcoming all temptations and becoming united with His Divine, thus the first line is quoted to refer to the judgment of the wicked (see Mat. 7:23, 25:41; Luke 13:27).

Jehovah has heard my supplication,
Jehovah will receive my prayer.
Let all my enemies be ashamed and greatly troubled,
Let them return and be ashamed suddenly. (Ps. 6:9-10)

The word supplication is from the word favour, which is to implore God from humiliation of thought (see Ps. 103:8). Prayer is according to the good of one's life (see Ps. 4:1, 66:19, 72:15). Enemies are the falsehoods of hell which attack the truth (see Ps. 3:1, 27:12); for them to return is for them to be punished by their own evil.

Psalm 7

Shiggaion of David, which he sang unto Jehovah, concerning the words of Cush the son of Benjamin.

~

Jehovah my God, in You I seek refuge, (1)
Save me from all those who pursue me, and deliver me:
Lest he tear apart my soul like a lion, (2)
Severing while there is none to deliver.
Jehovah my God, if I have done this, (3)
If there be injustice in my hands,
If I have rewarded evil to him who was at peace with me, (4)
And have delivered my adversary without cause:
Let the enemy pursue my soul and overtake it, (5)
And let him tread down my life upon the earth,
And make my glory reside in the dust. (Selah)
    Arise, Jehovah, in Your anger, (6)
    Lift up Yourself against the wrath of my adversaries,
    And wake up for me to the judgment that You have commanded.
    And the congregation of the nations shall compass You about, (7)
    And over them return on high.
    Jehovah shall adjudicate the people, (8)
    Judge me, Jehovah, according to my righteousness and integrity upon me.
    Oh let the evil of the wicked cease but establish the righteous, (9)
    And prove the hearts and kidneys, righteous God.
        My shield is upon God, (10)
        Who saves the upright in heart.
        God is a righteous judge, (11)
        And He is *not* indignant every day.

If he return not, He will whet His sword, (12)
He has bent His bow and prepared it,
And He has prepared for him the instruments of death, (13)
He makes His arrows burning.
Behold, he has birth pangs with iniquity, (14)
And has conceived toil and begotten falsehood.
He dug a well and searched it out, (15)
And he is fallen into the pit which he made.
His toil shall return upon his own head, (16)
And his violence shall come down upon the crown of his head.
I will confess Jehovah according to His righteousness, (17)
And I will make music to the name of Jehovah Most High.

Psalm Commentary 7

Summary: Prayer of the Lord to the Father for help against the hells (v. 1-2) and proclamation of innocence (v. 3-5). Let there be judgment between the good and evil (v. 6-9), for the evil will be punished and conquered (v. 14-17).

Jehovah my God, in You I seek refuge:
Save me from all those who pursue me, and deliver me:
Lest he tear apart my soul like a lion,
Severing while there is none to deliver. (Ps. 7:1-2)

To seek refuge in the Lord is to have trust in Him; to be saved is to be delivered from evil (see Ps. 14:7, 96:2). To tear apart the soul is to destroy the truth; lions signify the power of falsity from evil (see Ps. 10:9, 17:12, 57:4); to sever is to destroy good.

"Many times in the Word that which is torn is mentioned, and by it is meant in the proper sense that which has perished by falsities from evils; but that which has perished by evils is called a carcass. When only the torn is mentioned, both are signified, for the one involves the signification of the other; but it is otherwise when both are mentioned, for then a distinction is made. Because that which is torn signifies in the spiritual sense that which had perished by falsities from evils, therefore it was forbidden in the representative church to eat anything torn — which by no means would have been thus forbidden unless that spiritual evil had been understood in heaven. Otherwise, what harm would there have been in eating flesh torn by a wild beast?

89

"Of torn things, that they were not to be eaten, it is thus written in Moses: *The fat of a carcass and the fat of that which is torn may be used for any service, only eating ye shall not eat of it* (Lev. vii. 24). Again: *A carcass and that which is torn he shall not eat, to defile himself therewith: I am Jehovah* (Lev. xxii. 8). And again: *Men of holiness ye shall be unto Me; therefore ye shall not eat any flesh that is torn in the field; ye shall cast it to the dogs* (Exod. xxii. 31). In Ezekiel: The prophet said, *Ah Lord Jehovih! behold, my soul hath not been polluted; for from my youth up even till now have I not eaten a carcass or that which was torn, that there might not come abominable flesh into my mouth* (iv. 14). From these passages it is plain that it was an abomination to eat that which was torn, not because it was torn, but because it signified the tearing of good by falsities which are from evils, and a carcass signified the death of good by evils.

"The rending of good by falsities from evils is meant also in the following passages from David in the internal sense: The likeness of the wicked *is as a lion, he desireth to rend, and as a young lion he sitteth in secret places* (Ps. xvii. 12). Again: *They opened their mouth against me, a rending and a roaring lion* (Ps. xxii. 13). And yet again: *Lest they tear my soul like a lion, rending it while there is none to deliver* (Ps. vii. 2). A lion represents those who vastate the church. Where it is said of Joseph above, that he was sold by his brethren, and his tunic stained with blood was sent to his father, then his father also said, *It is my son's tunic. ... Joseph is surely torn in pieces* (Chap. xxxvii. 33). That to be torn in pieces is to be dissipated by falsities from evil, may be seen where this is explained (n. 4777)." (*Heavenly Arcana*, n. 5828.4-6)

Jehovah my God, if I have done this,
If there be injustice in my hands,
If I have rewarded evil to him who was at peace with me,
And have delivered my adversary without cause:
Let the enemy pursue my soul and overtake it,
And let him tread down my life upon the earth,
And make my glory reside in the dust. (Ps. 7:3-5)

To do is the intention of the will; injustice in the hands is to commit an external act according to falsehood (see Ps. 24:4, 73:13). To reward evil to one who was at peace is to do evil against spiritual truth, for peace signifies freedom from the conflict of temptation which is fought against by spiritual truth (see Ps. 4:8, 29:11). Adversaries are evils which attack what is good (see Ps. 3:1, 27:12); to "deliver" them here is in the sense of preserving evils against punishment. Enemies that pursue the soul are falsehoods of hell (see Ps. 3:1, 27:12) which destroy one's spiritual understanding of the truth signified by soul (see Ps. 22:10, 31:9, 71:23, 107:9); to tread down one's life upon the earth is to destroy all spiritual truths by means of the corporeal sensual (see Ps. 44:5, 68:30); glory is truth (see Ps. 8:5, 19:1, 24:7-10, 29:1, 73:24, 96:3) and dust is the condemnation of hell (see Ps. 22:29, 44:25, 72:9).

"'to trample down the life to the earth and make glory to dwell in the dust' signifies to destroy by means of the corporeal-sensual all truths of heaven and the church; for these constitute spiritual life, and are signified by 'glory;' 'dust,' too, is predicated of the corporeal-sensual, and this is also meant by 'walking upon the belly and eating dust,' as is here and there said of the serpent." (*Apocalypse Explained*, n. 632.9)

Arise, Jehovah, in Your anger,
Lift up Yourself against the wrath of my adversaries,
And wake up for me to the judgment that You have commanded.
And the congregation of the nations shall compass You about,
And over them return on high.
Jehovah shall adjudicate the people:
Judge me, Jehovah, according to my righteousness and integrity
upon me. (Ps. 7:6-8)

Anger is punishment due to evil against the good of love (see Ps. 2:5, 78:49); wrath is evil agains the good of faith (see Ps. 78:49) which is here derived from evils which attack good as signified by adversary (see Ps. 3:1, 27:12). God is the Lord as to Divine truth (see Ps. 18:31, 29:1, 68:17,24, 82:1, 95:3, 147:7) and judgment is the Divine truth which judges (see Ps. 36:6, 37:6, 72:2, 89:14, 92:12). The congregation is the good of the church (see Ps. 1:5) and nation are those who are in good (see Ps. 2:1, 18:43, 79:1, 80:8, 102:15, 106:5,27); to return on high is to be elevated to higher internal spiritual truths of love and in the highest sense refers to the glorification of the Lord and His ascension into heaven. To adjudicate is to judge those in the external natural; to judge is to judge those of the spiritual church. To be judged according to righteousness is to be judged according to one's deeds (see Ps. 36:6, 37:6, 72:2, 89:14, 92:12) and integrity is according to truth. The word for adjudicate is the origin of name of the tribe of Dan, which signifies those who are in external natural truths and not yet in affection for good:

"Dan shall judge his people, as one of the tribes of Israel. Dan shall be a serpent upon the way, an arrow-snake upon the path, biting the horse's heels, and his rider shall fall backward. I wait for Thy salvation, O Jehovah. 'Dan' signifies those who are in truth and not as yet in good; 'shall judge his people, as one of the tribes of Israel' signifies that he is one of the truths in general which the tribes of Israel represent. 'Dan shall be a serpent upon the way' signifies their reasoning about truth, because good does not as yet lead; 'an arrow-snake upon the path' signifies from truth concerning good; 'biting the horse's heels' signifies fallacies from lowest nature; 'and his rider shall fall backward' signifies that hence comes receding. 'I wait for Thy salvation, O Jehovah' signifies unless the Lord brings aid." (*Heavenly Arcana*, n. 6395)

Oh let the evil of the wicked cease but establish the righteous:
And prove the hearts and kidneys, righteous God. (Ps. 7:9)

To prove the heart is to purify the good of the will (see Ps. 22:10, 24:4, 51:10, 64:6, 66:18, 71:23, 78:8, 86:11); to prove the kidneys is to purify the thoughts (see Ps. 51:6, 73:21, 139:13):

"Establish Thou the righteous; for Thou who provest the hearts and the reins art a righteous God (Ps. vii. 9); 'the righteous' are those who love to do what is true and good, their goods and truths are purified by the Lord, which is meant by 'seeing' and

by 'proving the reins and the hearts.'" (*Apocalypse Explained*, n. 167.4)

As kidneys filter out that which needs to be expelled from the body, it signified exploration according to the truth (see Ps. 51:6, 139:13). Swedenborg saw that different societies of heaven correspond with different parts of the body, and that all of heaven formed one Man. Below he describes the character of those who belong to the kidneys:

"I have often observed that they who constitute the province of the kidneys and ureters are quick to explore or to search out the quality of others, what they think and what they will, and that it is their desire to find causes for convicting them of some fault, mostly for the purpose of punishing them; and I have talked with them about that desire and end. Many of this kind, when they lived in the world, were judges, who rejoiced at heart when they found cause which they believed just, to fine, chastise, and punish. The operation of such is felt in the region at the back where are the kidneys, ureters, and bladder. They who belong to the bladder extend toward hell [gehenna], where some of them sit as it were in judgment.

"The methods by which they explore or search out the dispositions of others are very numerous; but it is permitted to present only the following one. They induce other spirits to speak — a thing which is effected in the other life by an influx that cannot be intelligibly described, and if the induced speech flows easily, they judge from it that such is the quality of the spirits: they induce also a state of affection. But they who explore in this way are among the grosser of them, and others use other methods. There are some who as soon as they approach perceive another's thoughts, desires, and acts, and also what he has done that is a sorrow to him. This they seize upon, and also condemn, if they think that there is just cause. It is a wonderful thing in the other life, which scarcely any one in the world can believe, that as soon as any spirit comes to another, and more so when he comes to a man, he instantly knows his thoughts and affections, and what he has been doing, thus all his present state, just as if he had been a long time with him — so perfect is the communication. But there are differences in these perceptions, some spirits perceiving interior things, and others perceiving only exterior ones. These, if they are in the desire of knowing, explore the interiors of others by various means.

"The methods by which they punish who constitute the province of the kidneys, ureters, and bladder in the Greatest Man, are also various; for the most part they remove joyous and glad things, and induce such as are joyless and sad. By this desire those spirits communicate with the hells; but by the justness of the cause, which they enquire into before punishing, they communicate with heaven. For this reason they are kept in that province.

"From these things it may be evident what is signified when it is said in the Word, that Jehovah tries and searches the reins and the heart, and that the reins chasten — as in Jeremiah: *Jehovah trieth the reins and the heart* (xi. 20). In the same: *Jehovah who triest the just, and seest the reins and the heart* (xx. 12). In David: *The just God trieth the hearts and reins* (Ps. vii. 9). Again: *O Jehovah, explore my reins and my heart* (Ps. xxvi. 2). Again: *Jehovah, Thou hast possessed my reins* (Ps. cxxxix. 13). In the Apocalypse: *I am He who searcheth the reins and heart* (ii. 23). In these passages spiritual things are signified by the reins, and celestial things by the heart; that is, the things which are of truth are signified by the reins, and those which are of good by the heart. The reason of this is, that the reins purify the serum, and the heart purifies the blood itself; hence by trying, exploring, and searching the reins, is signified to try, explore, and search out the quantity and quality of truth, or the quantity and quality of faith in man. That this is the signification, is plain also in Jeremiah: *Jehovah, Thou art near in their mouth, but far from their reins* (xii. 2); and in David: *Jehovah, behold Thou desirest truth in the reins* (Ps. li. 6). That chastening is attributed to the reins, is clear also in David: *My reins chasten me in the night seasons* (Ps. xvi. 7)." (*Heavenly Arcana*, n. 5382-5385)

"*And the two kidneys, and the fat that is upon them.* That this signifies the interior truth of the external or natural man and its good, is evident from the signification of the kidneys, as interior truths — of which below; and from the signification of fat, as good — of which above (n. 10029); that it is the good of that truth is because it was the fat upon the kidneys. The good of that truth is said, because every good has its truth, and every truth its good. There are innumerable kinds of good, and every kind of good has truth which is of the same kind; for in the whole heaven there are goods and truths which constitute the life there, and they are everywhere various. The quality of the good which is signified by the fat upon the kidneys, is evident from the truths which are signified by the kidneys. By the kidneys are signified truths exploring, purifying, and chastening, taking this signification from their function. Hence what is signified by kidneys or reins in the following passages is manifest: *Jehovah ...who triest the reins and the heart* (Jer. xi. 20). And in David: *Thou who triest the hearts and the reins, O just God* (Ps. vii. 9). Again: *O Jehovah ...try my reins and my heart* (Ps. xxvi. 2). Again: *O Jehovah, Thou possessest my reins* (Ps. cxxxix. 13). And in the Apocalypse: *I am He who searcheth the reins and the heart* (ii. 23). To search and to try or prove the kidneys or reins is to explore the truths of faith; and to search and prove the heart is to explore the goods of love, for the heart is the good of love (n. 3883-3896, 7542, 9050). That the truths of faith are signified by the kidneys, appears clearly in David: O Jehovah, *Thou desirest truth in the reins* (Ps. li. 6). That by the kidneys is signified interior truth and its exploration, is because by the ureters and the bladder which go forth from the kidneys is signified exterior truth and its examining, as also chastening (n. 5381-5384)." (*Heavenly Arcana*, n. 10032)

My shield is upon God,
Who saves the upright in heart.
God is a righteous judge,
And He is not indignant every day.

If he return not, He will whet His sword,
He has bent His bow and prepared it,
And He has prepared for him the instruments of death,
He makes His arrows burning. (Ps. 7:10-13)

A shield is protection against evil and falsity (see Ps. 3:3) from Divine truth, and is thus mentioned with God who is the Lord as to Divine truth (see Ps. 18:31, 29:1, 68:17,24, 82:1, 95:3, 147:7); the upright in heart are those who live by the truth (see Ps. 11:3). God as a righteous judge is to judge by truth from good as righteous signifies those who do good (see Ps. 14:5, 36:6, 37:6,17, 72:2, 89:14, 92:12). A sword represents truth which fights against falsehood (see Ps. 22:16, 37:14, 45:3, 57:4, 59:7, 64:3, 78:62,64, 149:5); a bow signifies doctrine of truth (see Ps. 11:2, 18:34, 37:15, 46:9, 77:17-18, 78:9,57); death is spiritual death (see Ps. 6:5, 9:13, 33:19, 102:20, 106:28); arrows are truths that fight against falsehoods (see Ps. 11:2, 46:9, 77:17-18, 78:9,57, 91:5), here from the love of evil signified by burning. However God does not do these things to punish man, but rather one punishes one's self through one's own evil and falsehood:

"It is here attributed to God that He is indignant with the wicked, that He whets His sword, that He bends and makes ready His bow, prepares instruments of death, and makes His arrows burning; but in the spiritual sense it is meant that man does this in respect to himself. These things are attributed to God in the sense of the letter, because that sense is natural, and is for the natural man who believes that for these reasons God is to be feared; and with him fear works as love works afterwards, when he becomes spiritual. This makes clear what these words signify, namely, that it is the evil man who is indignant with God, that he whets the sword against himself, and bends the bow and makes it ready, he prepares the instruments of death, and makes his arrows burning. 'He whetteth the sword' signifies that he acquires for himself falsity, by which he combats against truths; 'He bendeth the bow and maketh it ready,' signifies that from falsities he frames for himself doctrine opposed to truths; and 'He prepares the instruments of death, and maketh His arrows burning,' signifies that from infernal love he frames for himself principles of falsity by which he destroys good and its truth." (*Apocalypse Explained*, n. 357.23)

Behold, he has birth pangs with iniquity,
And has conceived toil and begotten falsehood. (Ps. 7:14)

The "birth pangs with iniquity" is punishment from evil done against the good of faith (see Ps. 51:1-3); "to conceive toil" means to initiate the conflict of temptation from one's falsehood:

"*For God hath made me forget all my toil.* That this signifies removal after temptations, is evident from the signification of forgetting, as removal (see n. 5170, 5278); and from the signification of toil, as conflicts, and thus temptations. Hence it follows that by the words, God hath made me forget all my toil, is signified removal after temptations, that is, the removal of evils which have caused pain. That this is signified, is plain also from what is related of Joseph in the land of Canaan among his brethren, and afterward in Egypt — in the land of Canaan that he was cast into a pit and sold, in Egypt that he served and was kept in prison for some years. That temptations are signified by these events, has already been shown, and that they are what are meant by the toil is plain." (*Heavenly Arcana*, n. 5352)

He dug a well and searched it out,
And he is fallen into the pit which he made. (Ps. 7:15)

To dig a well is to devise falsehood, a pit signifies falsehood (see Ps. 28:1, 69:15, 88:4,6) and to fall into a pit is to pervert the truth:

"And since a pit is falsity, therefore also the Lord when He spake concerning the falsities of the church said, *If the blind lead the blind, both shall fall into a pit* (Matt. xv. 14) — where the blind man is one who is in erroneous ideas, and falling into a pit is perverting truth." (*Heavenly Arcana*, n. 9086.2)

His toil shall return upon his own head,

And his violence shall come down upon the crown of his head.
(Ps. 7:16)

One's head is insanity opposed to wisdom (see Ps. 68:21); toil is the conflict of temptation from falsehood (see Ps. 7:14) and violence is the destruction of the good of charity (see Ps. 27:12); the crown of one's head represents wisdom from love or in the opposite sense the insanity of evil (see Ps. 132:18). That violence represents the destruction of charity is shown from the commentary on Gen. 6:11:

"In Ezekiel: *The land is full of judgment of bloods, and the city is full of violence* (vii. 23) — where judgment of bloods stands for the destruction of faith, and violence for the destruction of charity. Again: *If he beget a son that is violent, a shedder of blood, that doeth any one of these things ...if he hath eaten upon the mountains, and defiled his neighbor's wife, hath wronged the poor and needy, hath taken plunder, hath not restored the pledge, and hath lifted up his eyes to idols, hath committed abomination, hath given forth upon usury, and hath taken increase; shall he live? he shall not live ...dying he shall die* (xviii. 10-13). Here a son that is violent and a shedder of blood is described, and all the works of charity which it destroys are told; thus a son that is violent and a shedder of blood is a destroyer of charity and faith." (*Heavenly Arcana*, n. 6353.6-7)

I will confess Jehovah according to His righteousness:
And I will make music to the name of Jehovah Most High.
(Ps. 7:17)

Confession is to worship from the good of love (see Ps. 7:17, 35:18, 89:24) and righteousness is to do what is good (see Ps. 14:5, 36:6, 37:6,17, 72:2, 89:14, 92:12); to make music is to worship from truth spiritual truth (see Ps. 57:7); the name of the Lord is every truth of doctrine (see Ps. 74:18, 96:2).

"But what confessing and confession mean, may be evident from the passages in the Word in which these expressions occur — as in Isaiah: *In that day thou shalt say, I will confess to Thee, O Jehovah; though Thou wast angry with me, Thine anger is*

*turned away, and Thou hast comforted me. ...And in that day ye
shall say, Confess to Jehovah, call upon His name, make known
His doings among the people, make mention that His name is
exalted* (xii. 1, 4). In David: *We confess to Thee, O God, we confess;
that Thy name is near, Thy wondrous works declare* (Ps. lxxv. 1).
Again: *A psalm for confession: Make a joyful noise to Jehovah, all
the earth. ...He hath made us, and not we ourselves, His people
and the flock of His pasture. Enter into His gates with confession, into His courts with praise: confess ye to Him, and bless His
name. For Jehovah is good, His mercy is forever, and His truth
even to generation and generation* (Ps. c. 1-5). Here it is manifest
what confessing and confession mean, namely, acknowledging
Jehovah or the Lord, and the things which are His. That this
acknowledgment is doctrine and the Word, is manifest.

"Again in Isaiah: *Jehovah will comfort Zion, He will comfort
all her waste places. ...Joy and gladness shall be found therein,
confession and the voice of melody* (li. 3). And in Jeremiah: *Thus
saith Jehovah, Behold, I will turn again the captivity of Jacob's
tents, and have compassion on his dwelling-places, and the city
shall be built upon her own heap, and the palace shall be inhab-
ited after the manner thereof; and out of them shall proceed confession, and the voice of them who make merry* (xxx. 18, 19). In
David: *I will confess to Jehovah according to His justice, and I
will sing praise to the name of Jehovah Most High* (Ps. vii. 17).
Again: *When I shall go ...to the house of God, with the voice of joy
and of confession, with a multitude who keep a festival* (Ps. xlii.
4). Again: *I will confess unto Thee O Lord among the nations, I
will sing praises unto Thee among the peoples, for Thy mercy is
great, even to heaven* (lvii. 9, 10).

"From these passages it is manifest that confession has reference to the celestial of love, and is distinguished from what
relates to the spiritual of love; for it is said confession and the
voice of joy, confession and the voice of them who make merry, I
will confess unto Thee among the nations, and I will sing praises
unto Thee among the peoples — confession and confessing being
what is celestial, and the voice of joy, the voice of them who make

merry and sing praises, being what is spiritual. It is also said, confess among the nations, and sing praises among the peoples, because nations signify those who are in good, and peoples those who are in truth... — that is, those who are in celestial love, and those who are in spiritual love. In the Word, with the Prophets, two expressions for the most part occur, one having reference to the celestial or good, and the other to the spiritual or truth, in order that there may be a Divine marriage in every part of the Word, thus a marriage of good and truth... From this it is also manifest that confession involves the celestial of love, and that genuine confession, or that which is from the heart, can only be from good, the confession which is from truth being called the voice of joy, the voice of them who make merry, and that sing praises." (*Heavenly Arcana*, n. 3880.2-4)

The title Most High signifies the inmost Divine, or Divine love:

"...by high is signified what is Divine. High means what is Divine because by it is meant heaven where the Divine is. Therefore in the Word it is said of Jehovah or the Lord that He dwells on high, and He Himself is called the Highest — as in Isaiah: *Jehovah is exalted; for He dwelleth on high* (xxxiii. 5). Again: *Thus saith the high and lofty One that inhabiteth eternity, Whose name is Holy: I dwell in the high and holy place* (lvii. 15). And in David: Jehovah *sent from on high, He took me* (Ps. xviii. 16). Therefore Jehovah is called the Highest (Deut. xxxii. 8; Dan. iv. 17, 32, 34; vii. 18, 22, 25; Ps. vii. 17; ix. 2; xviii. 13; xlvi. 4; l. 14; lvii. 2; lxxxii. 6). Because high signified heaven and the Divine therein, therefore Divine worship was instituted on mountains and on high places by those who were of the representative church; and for that reason also it was performed in lofty places which they built for themselves, as frequently mentioned in the historical and prophetical portions of the Word — as in Ezekiel: *Thou hast built unto thee an eminent place, and hast made thee a lofty place in every street. Thou hast built thy lofty place at every head of the way* (xvi. 24, 25, 31). That the Divine was signified by what is high, was because by the starry heaven was signified the angelic heaven, and it was also believed that it was there, though the wiser among them knew that heaven was not on high, but where the good of love is, and this within man, wheresoever he may be. That high things mean the interiors, or the goods which are there, may be seen above (n. 450, 1735, 2148, 4210, 4599)." (*Heavenly Arcana*, n. 8153)

"*Blessed be God Most High.* That this signifies the Lord's internal man, is evident from the things which were said just above concerning the internal man. Jehovah was called God Most High in the Ancient Church, for the reason that height represented and therefore signified the internal, and thus the Most High signified the inmost. Hence the worship of the Ancient Church was upon high places, mountains, and hills. The inmost also has the same relation to the exterior and the outermost as the highest bears to the lower and the lowest. The Most High or the Inmost is the Celestial of Love, or Love itself. Jehovah, or the Lord's internal, was the very Celestial of Love, that is, Love itself, to which no other attributes are fitting than those of pure Love, thus of pure Mercy toward the whole human race; which is such that it wishes to save all and make them happy for ever, and to bestow on them all that it has; thus out of pure mercy to draw all who are willing to follow, to heaven, that is, to itself, by the strong force of love." (*Heavenly Arcana*, n. 1735)

Psalm 8

To the chief musician upon Gittith, a Psalm of David.

~

Jehovah, our Lord, (1)
How magnificent is Your name in all the earth!
Who have set Your splendour above the heavens.
Out of the mouth of babes and sucklings You have *perfected praise,* (2)
Because of Your adversaries, to put away the enemy and the avenger.
When I see Your heavens, the work of Your fingers, (3)
The moon and the stars, which You have established:
What is man, that You remember him? (4)
And the son of Man, that You visit him?
   But You have made him a little lower than God, (5)
   And have crowned him with glory and grandeur.
   You made him to rule over the works of Your hands, (6)
   You have put all things under his feet:
   All flocks and kine, all of them, (7)
   And also the beasts of the field,
   The birds of the air, (8)
   And the fish of the sea passing through the paths of the seas.
   Jehovah, our Lord, (9)
   How magnificent is Your name in all the earth!

Psalm
Commentary

8

Summary: A song in praise of the Father by the Lord to regard His innocence, and give help against the hells (v. 1-3). The state of the humiliation of the Lord (v. 4, 5) and His glorification (v. 5-9).

Jehovah, our Lord,
How magnificent is Your name in all the earth!
Who have set Your splendour above the heavens. (Ps. 8:1)

Jehovah is the Lord as to Divine love (see Ps. 18:31, 28:1, 68:26, 82:1, 147:7); Lord (Hebrew *Adonai*) is Divine good in the Divine Human (see Ps. 68:17,26, 105:21, 110:1, 114:7); and magnificence is good in external acts of power (see also Ex. 15:6,11). The name of the Lord signifies Divine truth (see Ps. 74:18, 96:2) or the Divine Human. The earth is the church as to truth (see Ps. 9:8, 24:1, 60:2, 90:2, 96:13). Splendour is the Divine truth from which is heaven (see Ps. 45:3, 96:6, 104:1, 111:3).

The name of God signifies everything of love and faith by which God is worshipped, however in later and modern times many became focused on the literal name of God itself:

"They who were of the Ancient Church did not by a name understand the name, but all the quality (see n. 144, 145, 440, 768, 1754, 1896, 2009); and thus by the name of God all that in one aggregate by which God was worshipped, consequently every thing of love and faith; but when the internal of worship perished, and only the external remained, they then began to

104

understand by the name of God nothing else than the name, so much so that they worshipped the name itself, feeling no care about the love and the faith from which they worshipped. On this account the nations began to distinguish themselves by the names of their gods; and the Jews and Israelites set themselves up above the rest, because they worshipped Jehovah, placing the essential of worship in uttering the name and invoking it, when in truth the worship of a name only is no worship, and may also be found among the worst of men, who thereby profane the more." (*Heavenly Arcana*, n. 2724)

In the most internal sense, the name of God is His Divine Human:

"*This is My name for ever*. That this signifies that the Divine Human is the quality of the Divine Itself, is evident from the signification of the name God, as all in one complex whereby God is worshipped, thus His quality (see n. 2724, 3006, 6674); and since the Divine Itself cannot be worshipped, because it cannot be approached either by faith or by love, being above every idea — according to the Lord's words in John: *No man hath seen God at any time; the only begotten Son, Who is in the bosom of the Father, He hath declared Him* (i. 18) and again, *Ye have neither heard His voice at any time, nor seen His shape* (v. 37) — therefore it is the Divine Human, because the quality of the Divine Itself, which can be approached and worshipped.

"That the Divine Human is the name of Jehovah, is plain in John: *Jesus said, Father, glorify Thy Name; then came there a voice from heaven, I have both glorified, and will glorify again* (xii. 28). Here the Lord as to the Divine Human calls Himself the name of the Father. And in Isaiah: *I Jehovah have called Thee in justice, and will hold Thy hand, because I will keep Thee, and give Thee for a covenant of the people, for a light of the Gentiles; to open the blind eyes, to bring out the bound from the prison, and them who sit in darkness out of the prison house. I am Jehovah; that is My Name: and My glory will I not give to another* (xlii. 6-8). Here and in the preceding verses of the chapter, the Lord is plainly treated of: that He it is Who is meant by the name of

Jehovah, is plain from this, that it is said, My glory will I not give to another; which words when spoken of the Lord, mean giving glory to Himself, because they are one.

"And in Moses: *Behold, I send an Angel before thee, to keep thee in the way, and to bring thee into the place which I have prepared. Take heed of His face, and hear His voice, for He will not bear your transgression; for My name is in the midst of Him.* (Exod. xxiii. 20, 21). That by the angel of Jehovah is here meant the Lord as to the Divine Human, may be seen above (n. 6831); and as the Divine Human is the quality of the Divine Itself, therefore it is said that the name of Jehovah is in the midst of Him. In the Lord's Prayer, also, by *Our Father ...in the heavens; hallowed be Thy Name,* is meant the Lord as to the Divine Human; and also all in one complex whereby He is to be worshipped." (*Heavenly Arcana*, n. 6887.1-3)

Out of the mouth of babes and sucklings You have perfected praise,
Because of Your adversaries, to put away the enemy and the avenger. (Ps. 8:2)

Babes signify celestial love, and sucklings innocence, and praise is affection for truth (see Ps. 7:17, 35:18). Truth is perfected out of love and innocence. Adversaries are evils of hell against the good of love, enemies are the falsehoods against the good of faith (see Ps. 3:1, 27:12), and an avenger is one who does harm against external knowledges of truths and good. That an avenger refers to those who do harm against the externals of faith, can be seen where the same word is used to not avenge Cain which in the spiritual sense signifies faith separate from charity (see Gen. 4:15, 24 and *Heavenly Arcana*, n. 395, 432), and in the laws protecting servants (see Ex. 21:20-21 and *Heavenly Arcana*, n. 9036) who represent those who are in external truths (see Ps. 89:50).

"That in the Word a sucking child signifies innocence, is also plain from other passages, as in David: *Out of the mouth of infants and sucklings hast thou established strength* (Ps. viii. 2;

Matt. xxi. 16); where infants denote celestial love, and sucklings innocence. In Jeremiah: *Wherefore commit ye great evil against your souls, to cut off from you man and woman, infant and suckling out of the midst of Judah, that I should leave you none remaining?* (xliv. 7); where infant and suckling in like manner denote celestial love and the innocence thereof; and when these become none, then there are no longer any remains, that is, any good and truth remaining stored up by the Lord in the internal man; that these are remains, may be seen above (n. 1906, 2284); for all goods and truths perish with innocence, inasmuch as innocence is immediately from the Divine itself, and thus is the very essential in them." (*Heavenly Arcana*, n. 3183.3)

"In Matthew: The children cried in the temple, *Hosanna to the son of David.* The priests were indignant; but *Jesus saith unto them ...Did ye never read, Out of the mouth of babes and sucklings Thou hast perfected praise?* (xxi. 15, 16; Ps. viii. 2.) The children's crying, Hosanna to the son of David, was to represent that only innocence acknowledges and receives the Lord — that is, they who have innocence. By, Out of the mouth of babes and sucklings Thou hast perfected praise, is signified that praise can come to the Lord by no other way than through innocence; for by this alone is effected all communication and all influx, and consequently access. It is for this reason that the Lord says, *Unless ye be converted, and become as children, ye shall not enter into the kingdom of the heavens* (Matt. xviii. 3)." (*Heavenly Arcana*, n. 5236.4)

"In the following passages also innocence is signified by infants or little children — in Matthew: *Out of the mouth of babes and sucklings Thou hast perfected praise* (xxi. 16; Ps. viii. 2). Again: *Thou hast hid these things from the wise and understanding, and hast revealed them unto babes* (xi. 25; Luke x. 21); for innocence, which is signified by babes, is wisdom itself, since genuine innocence dwells in wisdom (n. 2305, 2306, 4797). For this reason it is said, 'Out of the mouth of babes and sucklings Thou hast perfected praise,' and also that such things have been revealed unto babes." (*Heavenly Arcana*, n. 5608.6)

When I see Your heavens, the work of Your fingers,
The moon and the stars, which You have established (Ps. 8:3)

God's work is the regeneration of each person spiritually, from which are the heavens (see Ps. 107:24, 111:2,7). The fingers of God signify power from Divine good by the truth (see Ps. 144:1):

"*This is the finger of God.* That this signifies that the power was from the Divine, is evident from the signification of the finger of God, as power from the Divine; the finger is power because fingers are of the hands, and by hands is signified power (see n. 878, 4931-4937, 6344, 6424, 6948). That finger is power, is evident also from the following passages: *When I consider Thy heavens, the work of Thy fingers, the moon and the stars which Thou hast ordained* (Ps. viii. 3). And in Luke: *Jesus said, If I by the finger of God cast out devils, surely the kingdom of God is come unto you* (xi. 20). That Jesus took the deaf man who had an impediment in his speech apart from the people, *and put His finger into his ears, and spat, and touched his tongue* (Mark vii. 32, 33), was also a representative of Divine power.

"That the thumb and finger are the power of good by truth, is plain here from the internal sense. Power is also signified by finger in David: *Blessed be Jehovah who teacheth my hands combat, and my fingers war* (Ps. cxliv. 1), and in Isaiah: *He shall not look to the altars, the work of his hands, and ...that which his fingers have made* (xvii. 8). Altars stand for worship in general (n. 4541); the work of the hands, and what the fingers have made, for such things as are from the proprium, thus which are from man's own power." (*Heavenly Arcana*, n. 7430.1,3)

The heavens are not the visible sky, but the spiritual heavens. In heaven the Divine love is seen as a sun in the highest heaven (see Ps. 50:1, 72:5,7, 74:16, 89:36, 104:19, 136:8, 148:3) and the Divine truth is seen as a moon in the lower spiritual heaven (see Ps. 72:5,7, 74:16, 89:37, 104:19, 136:9, 148:3):

"The angels taken together are called heaven, because they constitute heaven; but yet it is the Divine proceeding from the Lord, which flows in with angels and is received by them, that

makes heaven in general and in particular. The Divine proceeding from the Lord is the good of love and the truth of faith. In
the degree, therefore, in which they receive good and truth from
the Lord, they are angels and are heaven. …The Divine proceeding from the Lord is called in heaven Divine truth, for a reason
that will presently appear. This Divine truth flows into heaven
from the Lord from His Divine love. Divine love and Divine truth
therefrom are by comparison as the fire of the sun and the light
therefrom in the world, love as the fire of the sun, and truth
therefrom as the light from the sun." (*Heaven and Hell*, n. 7, 13)

"The Sun of heaven is the Lord, the light there is Divine
truth, and the heat is Divine good, which proceed from the Lord
as a Sun. From this origin are all things that exist and are seen
in the heavens." (*Heaven and Hell*, n. 117)

"Since the Lord is seen in heaven as the Sun, from the Divine
Love which is in Him and from Him, all in the heavens turn
constantly to Him, those in the celestial heaven as to the Sun,
and those in the spiritual heaven as to the Moon." (*Heaven and
Hell*, n. 123)

The sun, moon and the stars are representations of the three
main degrees or levels of heaven – the first level of those who
are primarily in love, the second level those who are primarily
in spiritual truth, and the third are those who are in knowledges
of good and truth which is represented by stars (see Ps. 136:9,
147:4, 148:3).

"Love and faith are first called great lights, and then love is
called the greater light and faith the lesser light; and it is said of
love that it shall rule the day, and of faith that it shall rule the
night. As these are things unknown, and are especially hidden
in this end of days, it is permitted of the Lord's Divine mercy
to disclose how the matter is. The reason why they are hidden
especially in this end of days is, that now is the consummation
of the age and there is almost no love, and consequently almost
no faith — as the Lord Himself predicted in the Evangelists,
in these words: *The sun shall be darkened, and the moon shall
not give her light, and the stars shall fall from heaven, and the*

powers of the heavens shall be shaken (Matt. xxiv. 29). By the sun
is here meant love, which is obscured; by the moon faith, which
does not give her light; by the stars knowledges of faith, which
fall from heaven, and which are the virtues and powers of the
heavens." (*Heavenly Arcana*, n. 32)

What is man, that You remember him?
And the son of Man, that You visit him? (Ps. 8:4)

Man (Hebrew *enosh*) are those who are in good from external
truths (see also Ps. 49:2, 80:17); the son of Man (Hebrew *adam*)
are those who are in spiritual truths (see Ps. 49:2, 57:4, 80:17,
89:47). The "Son of Man" is a Messianic title which refers to the
Lord in His Divine Human, while He was incarnated in a lower
natural state. To remember signifies to have compassion or conjunction through love; to visit is to explore one's state by means
of Divine truth. With men there is only conjunction with the
Lord through good and truth; but in the Lord there was a complete union between the Divine and the human. In the highest
sense this verse describes the Lord's state of humiliation before
He had yet united His human to the Divine.

"That remembering, when said of the Lord, means having
compassion, and therefore out of mercy preserving or delivering,
is evident from the following passages — in David: *Jehovah hath
made known His salvation: His justice hath He openly showed
before the eyes of the nations. He hath remembered His mercy
and His truth toward the house of Israel* (Ps. xcviii. 2, 3). Again:
Jehovah *hath remembered us in our low estate: for His mercy
is for ever* (Ps. cxxxvi. 23). Again: *Remember not the sins of my
youth, nor my transgressions; according to Thy mercy remember
Thou me, for Thy goodness' sake, O Jehovah* (Ps. xxv. 7). Again:
*He remembered for them His covenant, and repented according
to the multitude of His mercies* (Ps. cvi. 45). Again: *He hath made
His wonderful works to be remembered: Jehovah is gracious and
full of compassion. He hath given meat unto them who fear Him:
He hath remembered for ever His covenant* (Ps. cxi. 4, 5). Again:

Remember not against us former iniquities: let Thy mercies pre-vent us (Ps. lxxix. 8).

"In Luke: *God hath accepted His servant Israel, that He might remember His mercy. ...To shew mercy toward our fathers, and to remember His holy covenant* (i. 54, 72). Again in David: *What is man that Thou art mindful of him?* (Ps. viii. 4). And again: *Remember me, O Jehovah, with the favor of Thy people* (Ps. cvi. 4). Again: *Jehovah hath been mindful of us: He blesseth* (Ps. cxv. 12). In the First Book of Samuel: *If Thou wilt indeed look upon the affliction of Thine handmaid, and remember me, and not forget Thine handmaid* (i. 11) — the prayer of Hannah the mother of Samuel; and when she bare him, it is said, *Jehovah remembered her* (verse 19), that is, looked upon her affliction and showed mercy — in like manner in many other passages (Lev. xxvi. 41, 42, 45; Num. x. 9; Isa. xliii. 25; xlix. 1; lxiv. 9; Jer. xxxi. 34)." (*Heavenly Arcana*, n. 9849.2-3)

Remember also signifies conjunction through love:

"That remembering is conjunction, is because the remember-ing of any one in the other life conjoins; for as soon as any spirit calls another to mind, he appears present, and so present that they talk together. It is for this reason that angels and spirits can meet all persons whom they have known or have heard of, can see them present and speak with them, when the Lord per-mits them to call them to mind (see n. 1114)." (*Heavenly Arcana*, n. 5229)

Visitation is related to judgment:

"This last time in the Word is called visitation, and is pred-icated both of the church in general, and also of those who are within the church in particular; of the new church which is born, and of the old church which expires; in particular of the man of the church who is saved, and of him who is condemned.

"That these things are signified in the Word by visitation, and the day of visitation, may be evident from the following pas-sages — in Luke: *Blessed be the Lord, the God of Israel; for He hath visited, and wrought redemption for His people. ...Through*

the bowels of mercy of our God, whereby the day-spring from on
high hath visited us, to give light to them who sit in darkness
and the shadow of death (i. 68, 78, 79). This is the prophecy of
Zacharias concerning the Lord Who was born; to be visited here
stands for the raising up of a new church, and the enlightenment
then of those who were in ignorance of the truth and good of
faith, thus their deliverance; wherefore it is said, He hath visited and redeemed His people, He hath visited to give light to
them who sit in darkness and the shadow of death." (*Heavenly
Arcana*, n. 6588)

But You have made him a little lower than God,
And have crowned him with glory and grandeur. (Ps. 8:5)

The word for "God" is mistranslated as "angels" in most
translations to make this Psalm refer to mankind in general.
However, this is a prophecy concerning the coming of the Lord,
who lowered Himself to become incarnate in human form and is
thus described being a "little lower than God." The elevation of
His human form to Divinity is then described as bring crowned,
which also signifies a state of wisdom from love (see Ps. 132:18).
Glory is Divine truth (see Ps. 19:1, 24:7-10, 29:1, 73:24, 96:3) and
excellence is Divine good (see Ps. 104:1, 111:3). To give glory and
grandeur means to ascribe all truth and good to the Lord:

"By giving to the Lord glory and honor nothing else is meant
in the Word but to acknowledge and confess that all truth and
all good are from Him, and thus that He is the only God; for He
has glory from the Divine truth and honor from the Divine good.
These things are signified by glory and honor in the following
passages: *Jehovah made the heavens; glory and honor are before
Him* (Ps. xcvi. 5, 6). *O Jehovah God, Thou art very great; Thou
art clothed with glory and honor* (Ps. civ. 1). *The works of Jehovah are great; glory and honor are His work* (Ps. cxi. 2, 3). *Glory
and honor Thou layest upon Him, blessings for ever* (Ps. xxi. 5,
6). These things are said of the Lord. *Gird Thy sword upon Thy
thigh, O mighty in glory and honor; in Thine honor mount up,
ride upon the Word of truth* (Ps. xlv. 3, 4). *Thou hast made him*

little less than the angels; Thou hast crowned him with glory and honor (Ps. viii. 5). *The glory of Lebanon hast Thou given unto it, the honor of Carmel and Sharon: they shall see the glory of Jehovah, and the honor of our God* (Isa. xxxv. 1, 2). These and the foregoing are concerning the Lord; besides other places, as Ps. cxlv. 4, 5, 12; Apoc. xxi. 24, 26. Besides, where the Divine truth is treated of in the Word, the word glory is used (n. 629); and where the Divine good is treated of, honor." (*Apocalypse Revealed*, n. 249)

You made him to rule over the works of Your hands,
You have put all things under his feet. (Ps. 8:6)

This concerns the power given to the Lord over all heaven and earth (see Matt. 28:18). To rule is to have all power from Divine good (see Ps. 105:20); the work of His hands is the Divine work of spiritual regeneration (see Ps. 107:24, 111:2,7). For all things to be under the feet means the Lord made His very human Divine as the feet signifies the external natural (see Ps. 8:6, 41:9, 49:5, 99:5, 105:18). It was through the work of sanctification of the human of the Lord, by making it one with the Divine, that the Lord spiritually regenerates each person through repentance.

"*Thou madest Him to have dominion over the works of Thy hands; Thou hast put all things under His feet* (*Ps.* viii. 6). This is said of the Lord; His dominion over all things of heaven and the church is meant by 'all things are put under His feet.' And in *Isaiah:*—

I will make the place of My feet honorable (lx. 13).

'The place of the Lord's feet' in a general sense means all things of heaven and the church, since the Lord as a sun is above the heavens; but in a particular sense 'the place of His feet' signifies the church, for the Lord's church is with men in the natural world, and the natural is the lowest, into which the Divine closes, and upon which it as it were subsists. This is why the church on the earth is also called 'the footstool of the Lord,' as in the same:—

The earth is My footstool (lxvi. 1; *Matt.* v. 35).

Also in *Lamentations:*—

> *He hath cast down from the heavens unto the earth the splendor of Israel, and doth not remember His footstool* (ii. 1).

And in *David:*—

> *We will come into His tabernacles, we will bow down at His footstool* (*Ps.* cxxxii. 7).

This is said of the Lord, and 'His footstool' signifies the church on the earth." (*Apocalypse Explained*, n. 606)

All flocks and kine, all of them, and also the beasts of the field, The birds of the air and the fish of the sea passing through the paths of the seas. (Ps. 8:7-8)

Animals in general signify the affections and feelings of a person, each of which corresponds to a particular animal which Swedenborg clearly saw in the spiritual world (see *Heavenly Arcana*, n. 6048). A flock is internal good (see Ps. 114:6, 144:13) and kine is external good (see Ps. 68:30, 106:19-20, 144:13); the "beasts of the field" signify the affections of the voluntary; the "birds of the air" signify the intellectual; the "fish of the sea" represents the sensual affections for knowledges in the natural man, or those of the lowest heaven; paths of the sea are knowledges of what is good (see Ps. 25:4).

> *"Thou madest him to have dominion over the works of Thy hands. Thou hast put all things under His feet, the flock and herds, yea, the beasts of the fields, the bird of heaven, and the fishes of the sea* (*Ps.* viii. 6-8).

This whole psalm treats of the Lord and His dominion over all things of heaven and the church; the things of heaven and the church are meant here and elsewhere in the Word by 'the works of the hands of Jehovah;' and as it is over these things that the Lord has dominion, and as spiritual things in the Word are expressed by natural things, for the Word in its bosom is spiritual, so by 'flock,' 'herds,' 'the beasts of the field,' 'the birds of heaven,' and 'the fishes of the sea,' these are not meant, but the spiritual things of heaven and the church. 'Flock and herds' signify spiritual things and natural things that are from a spiritual origin, a 'flock,' that is, lambs, kids, she-goats, sheep, and rams, signifying spiritual things, and 'herds,' which are bullocks, oxen, cows, and camels, natural things from spiritual things; 'beasts of the field' signify the affections of the natural man, 'birds of the heavens' thoughts therefrom, and 'fishes of the sea,' the knowledges (*scientifica*) of the sensual-natural man. Except for this meaning, why should the Lord's dominion over these be described?" (*Apocalypse Explained*, n. 650.6; see also *Apocalypse Explained*, n. 342.6, 513.9; *Apocalypse Revealed*, n. 567; *Heavenly Arcana*, n. 10609.3; for birds see *Heavenly Arcana*, n. 776.1-2)

As dominion first proceeds over animals, or things of the will, this particular passage treats of the celestial man who is primarily in the good of love:

"So long as a man is spiritual his dominion proceeds from the external man to the internal, as is here said: *Let them have dominion over the fish of the sea, and over the fowl of the heavens, and over the beast, and over all the earth, and over every creeping thing that creepeth upon the earth*. But when he becomes celestial and does good from love, his dominion proceeds from the internal man to the external; just as the Lord, in David, says of Himself, and thus at the same time of the celestial man who is His likeness — *Thou hast made him to have dominion over the works of Thy hands; Thou hast put all things under his feet; the flock and all cattle, and also the beasts of the fields, the fowl of the heavens, and the fish of the sea, and whatsoever passeth through the paths of the seas* (Ps. viii. 6-8). Here therefore the beasts are first mentioned, then the fowl, and then the fishes of the sea; because the celestial man goes forth from love, which is of the will. It is otherwise with the spiritual man, with whom the fishes and the birds precede — which are things of the understanding, that relates to faith — and the beasts follow." (*Heavenly Arcana*, n. 52)

Beasts of the field concern affections related to the church: since a field represents something that is cultivated that can grow produce it signifies the doctrine of truth, and the good of life conjoined with doctrine, (see Ps. 96:12):

"'...beasts of the fields' [are] affections of good in the natural man that pertain to the church (for 'field' signifies the church), 'birds of heaven' signify the thoughts of the rational man, and 'fishes of the sea' knowledges." (*Apocalypse Explained*, n. 1100.4)

More specifically flocks and kine signify internal and external goods:

"*Thy flocks, and thy herds.* That this signifies goods internal and external, is evident from the signification of flocks, as internal goods, and from the signification of herds, as external goods (see n. 2566, 5913). That by flocks are signified internal goods, is because to flocks belong lambs, sheep, kids, she-goats, rams, and he-goats, by which are signified such things as are of innocence, of celestial and spiritual love in the internal man; and by herds are signified external goods, because to herds belong oxen, bullocks, calves, by which are signified such things as are of good and truth in the external man; what is signified by oxen has been already shown (n. 2180, 2566, 2781), also what by bullocks and by calves (n. 1824, 2830), what by lambs (n. 3519, 3994, 7840), what by sheep (n. 4169), what by kids and by she-goats (n. 3519, 4005, 4006, 4871), what by rams (n. 2830, 4170), and what by he-goats (n. 4169, 4769)." (*Heavenly Arcana*, n. 8937; see also *Heavenly Arcana*, n. 6048)

"That a bullock signifies the good of innocence and of charity in the external or natural man, is because those animals which were from the herd signified affections for good and truth in the external or natural man, and those which were from the flock affections for good and truth in the internal or spiritual man (n. 2566, 5913, 6048, 8937, 9135). The animals which were from the flock were lambs, she-goats, sheep, rams, he-goats; and those which were from the herd were oxen, bullocks, and calves. Lambs and sheep signified the good of innocence and of charity in the internal or spiritual man; therefore calves and bullocks, because they were of a tenderer age than oxen, signified the like in the external or natural man." (*Heavenly Arcana*, n. 9391.1)

Birds signify things of the understanding:

"*Say to the bird of every wing, and to every beast of the field, Come to the great sacrifice upon the mountains of Israel: so will I set My glory among the nations* (Ezek. xxxix. 17, 21; Apoc. xix. 17: besides other places, as Isa. xviii. 1, 6; Ezek. xxxviii. 20; Hos. ix. 11; xi. 9, 11: Zeph. i. 3; Ps. viii. 6, 8; l. 11; civ. 10, 12). That birds signify the things of the understanding and hence of thought and design is clearly manifest from the birds in the spiritual world, where there appear also birds of every genus and species; in heaven such as are most beautiful, birds of paradise, turtle-doves, and pigeons, and in hell dragons, screech-owls, horned owls, and other similar ones; all of which are representations to the life, of thoughts from good affections in heaven, and of thoughts from evil affections in hell." (*Apocalypse Revealed*, n. 757)

At the lowest level, fish signify affections for external knowledges:

"*And to all the fishes of the sea.* That this signifies outward knowledges is evident from the signification of a fish. Fishes in the Word signify knowledges which spring from things of sense. For knowledges are of three kinds, intellectual, rational, and sensual. All these are planted in the memory, or rather memories, and are called forth thence in the regenerate man, through his internal man. These knowledges which are from things of sense come to man's sensation or perception when he lives in the body, for he thinks from them. The other knowledges, which are interior, do not so come before man puts off the body and comes into the other life. That fishes or the creeping things which the waters produce signify outward knowledges, may be seen above (n. 40); and that a whale or sea monster signifies the generals of outward knowledges (n. 42). It may be evident moreover from the following passages in the Word — in Zephaniah: *I will consume man and beast; I will consume the fowls of the heavens, and the fishes of the sea* (i. 3) — where the fowls of the heavens stand for things of reason, and the fishes of the sea for lower things of reason, or for man's thought from sensuous knowledges.

"In Habakkuk: *And makest man as the fishes of the sea, as the creeping things that have no ruler over them* (i. 14) — where making man as the fishes of the sea means that he is altogether sensual. In Hosea: *Therefore shall the land mourn, and every one that dwelleth therein shall languish, with the wild animal of the field and the fowl of heaven; yea, the fishes of the sea also shall be taken away* (iv. 3) — where fishes of the sea stand for knowledges from things of sense. In David: *Thou hast put all things under His feet: all sheep and oxen, yea, and the beasts of the field, the fowl of the air, and the fish of the sea, whatsoever passeth through the paths of the seas* (Ps. viii. 6-8) — describing the dominion of the Lord in man, the fish of the sea standing for outward knowledges. That seas signify the gathering together of knowledges, outward or inward, may be seen above (n. 28). In Isaiah: *The fishers also shall lament, and all they who cast angle into the Nile shall mourn, and they who spread nets upon the faces of the waters shall languish* (xix. 8) — fishers standing for those who trust only in things of sense, and out of these hatch falsities, the subject being Egypt, or the realm of outward knowledge." (*Heavenly Arcana*, n. 991.1-2)

"These are meant in the Word by the fishes of the sea, which are sensual affections, the lowest affections of the natural man; for such affections appear in the spiritual world at a distance like fishes, and as if in the sea; because the atmosphere in which they are appears watery, and hence in the eyes of those who are in the heavens and upon the earth there, as a sea (see above, n. 238; and concerning fishes, n. 405)." (*Apocalypse Revealed*, n. 290)

> *Jehovah, our Lord, how magnificent is Your name in all the earth!* (Ps. 8:9)

Jehovah is the Divine itself, the Lord (Hebrew *Adonai*) is the Divine Human, and His name in all the earth is the Divine proceeding (see also v. 1).

Psalm 9

To the chief musician upon Muthlabben, a Psalm of David.

~

I will confess, Jehovah, with all my heart, (1) [*aleph*]
I will recount all Your wondrous works.
I will rejoice and exult in You, (2)
I will make music to Your name, Most High.
    When my enemies are turned back, (3) [*beth*]
    They shall stumble and perish from Your presence.
    For You have executed my judgment and my adjudication, (4)
    You sat in the throne judging in righteousness.
    You have rebuked the nations, (5) [*gimel*]
    You have made the wicked to perish,
    You have blotted out their name forever and ever.
    The enemy came to an end in perpetual waste places, (6) [*he*]
    And You have uprooted cities,
    Their memorial is perished with them.
    And Jehovah shall sit forever, (7) [*vav*]
    He has established His throne for judgment.
    And He shall judge the world in righteousness, (8) [*vav*]
    He shall adjudicate the people in uprightness.
    And Jehovah will be a high fort for the contrite, (9) [*vav*]
    A high fort in times of adversity.
    And they who know Your name will trust in You: (10) [*vav*]
    For You have not forsaken those who enquire after You, Jehovah.
Make music unto Jehovah who dwells in Zion, (11) [*zayin*]
Proclaim among the people His doings.
For He who enquires after blood remembers them, (12)
He forgets not the cry of the afflicted.

119

Be gracious to me Jehovah, (13) [*cheth*]
See my affliction from those who hate me,
You who lift me up from the gates of death:
That I may recount all Your praise in the gates of the daughter of
Zion, (14)
I will be glad in Your salvation.
The nations are sunk down in the pit that they made, (15) [*teth*]
In the net which they hid is their own foot caught.
Jehovah is known by the judgment which He executes, (16)
The wicked is snared in the work of his own hands. Meditation.
(Selah)
The wicked shall turn away to hell, (17) [*yod*]
All the nations that forget God.
For the needy shall not always be forgotten, (18) [*kaph*]
The hope of the afflicted shall *not* perish for ever.
Arise, Jehovah, let not man prevail, (19)
Let the nations be judged upon Your presence.
Put them in fear, Jehovah, (20)
That the nations may know themselves to be but men. (Selah)

Psalm Commentary 9

Summary: Thanksgiving and joy of the Lord (v. 1-2) that the evil have been judged and destroyed (v. 2-10). Praise of God for deliverance of the righteous (v. 11-12) for the evil have been conquered and condemned to hell (v. 13-20).

I will confess Jehovah with all my heart,
I will recount all Your wondrous works.
I will rejoice and exult in You,
I will make music to Your name, Most High. (Ps. 9:1-2)

Confession is worship from affection for the good of love (see Ps. 7:17, 35:18, 50:14, 89:24), thus here it is mentioned with the name Jehovah which is the Lord as to Divine love (see Ps. 18:31, 28:1, 68:26, 82:1, 147:7) as well as the heart which signifies the will (see Ps. 7:9, 22:10, 24:4, 51:10, 64:6, 66:18, 71:23, 78:8, 86:11). To recount is to know the quality of a thing (see Ps. 147:4); wondrous works are acts of Divine power which confirm belief (see Ps. 71:7, 78:43, 105:5). To "rejoice and exult" is joy from the will (see Ps. 14:7); to make music is to worship from truth spiritual truth (see Ps. 57:7) and is thus mentioned with name which signifies the truths of doctrine (see Ps. 74:18, 96:2).

When my enemies are turned back,
They shall stumble and perish from Your presence.
For You have executed my judgment and my adjudication,
You sat in the throne judging in righteousness.
You have rebuked the nations,

You have made the wicked to perish,
You have blotted out their name forever and ever.
The enemy came to an end in perpetual waste places,
And You have uprooted cities,
Their memorial is perished with them. (Ps. 9:3-6)

Enemies are the falsehoods of hell which attack the truth (see Ps. 3:1, 27:12); to turn back is to turn towards self love and to stumble is to fall into falsity (see Ps. 64:8). To perish is to spiritually die from falsehoods (see Ps. 88:11); the Lord's presence or face is Divine love (see Ps. 4:6, 13:1, 22:24, 27:8-9, 31:16, 67:1). Judgment is internal truth and adjudication is external truth (see Ps. 7:8); the throne is the heaven as to Divine truth from which there is judgment (see Ps. 9:4, 93:1, 103:19, 122:5) which is according to good signified by righteousness (see Ps. 36:6, 37:6, 72:2, 89:14, 92:12). Nations are those who are in evils (see Ps. 2:1, 18:43, 79:1, 80:8, 102:15, 106:5,27); the wicked are those who are in falsehoods and to perish is to spiritually die from them (see Ps. 88:11). For their name to be blotted out is to be removed from heaven due to the quality of their state of life (see Ps. 69:28). The perpetual waste places are the evils of hell (see Ps. 33:11, 46:8); cities are false doctrines (see Ps. 31:21, 46:4, 48:8, 107:36, 122:3) and their memorial is false worship derived therefrom (see Ps. 135:13).

And Jehovah shall sit forever:
He has established His throne for judgment. (Ps. 9:7)

For Jehovah to sit forever is to be the center of all being (see Ps. 1:1, 107:4,36, 139:2); forever is eternity in the celestial heaven of love (see Ps. 145:13); His throne is the Divine truth by which all are judged (see Ps. 9:4, 93:1, 103:19, 122:5). All are judged according to how they lived after death.

"As Jehovah, that is, the Lord, is the very being (*esse*) of every one's life, therefore He is said 'to sit.' In *David:*—

Jehovah shall sit to eternity (Ps. ix. 7).

In the same:—

> *Jehovah sitteth at the flood, and sitteth a King to eternity* (*Ps.* xxix. 10).

In the same:—

> *God reigneth over the nations; God sitteth upon the throne of His holiness* (*Ps.* xlvii. 8).

In *Matthew:*—

> *When the Son of man shall come in His glory; and all His holy angels with Him, then shall He sit upon the throne of His glory* (xxv. 31).

'To sit upon the throne of His glory' signifies to be in His Divine truth, from which is judgment. So again in the same:—

> *When the Son of man shall sit on the throne of His glory ye also shall sit upon twelve thrones, judging the twelve tribes of Israel* (xix. 28; *Luke* xxii. 30).

Since 'angels,' as well as 'the twelve apostles' and 'the twelve tribes of Israel,' signify all the truths of the church, and in the highest sense, Divine truth, therefore 'to sit upon thrones' means not that they themselves will sit, but the Lord as to Divine truth, from which is judgment; and 'to judge the twelve tribes of Israel' signifies to judge all according to the truths of their church. From this it is clear that 'to sit upon a throne,' in reference to the Lord, signifies one who judges, thus to judge. It is called 'a throne of glory,' because 'glory' signifies Divine truth" (*Apocalypse Explained*, n. 687.7; see also *Apocalypse Explained*, n. 253, *Apocalypse Revealed*, n. 229).

"In very many other places, too, a throne is attributed to Jehovah or the Lord, and this because in thrones is a representative of a kingdom. When Divine truth and judgment are talked about in a higher heaven, then a throne appears in the lowest heaven. This is why, as already said, a throne is representative, and is so often spoken of in the prophetic Word, and why from most ancient times thrones became the insignia of kings, and as such signify royalty — as is seen also in the following passages. In Moses: *Moses built an altar, and called the name of it Jehovah-nissi; and he said, Because a hand is against the throne of Jah, Jehovah will have war with Amalek from generation to generation* (Exod. xvii. 15, 16). What is meant by a hand being against the throne of Jah, and by Jehovah's having war with Amalek from generation to generation, no one can know except from the internal sense, and unless he knows what is meant by a throne, and what by Amalek. By Amalek in the Word are signified the falsities which assail truths (n. 1679), and by a throne the Divine truth itself which is assailed.

"In David: *Jehovah, Thou hast maintained my judgment and my cause; Thou safest on the throne, the judge of justice. ...Jehovah shall endure forever: He hath prepared His throne for judgment* (Ps. ix. 4, 7)" (*Heavenly Arcana*, n. 5313.10-11)

And He shall judge the world in righteousness,
He shall adjudicate the people in uprightness. (Ps. 9:8)

To judge is to judge those who are in internal good, for world signified those of the church who are in good (see Ps. 24:1, 60:2, 90:2, 93:1, 96:13) and the righteous are those who do good (see Ps. 36:6, 37:6, 72:2, 89:14, 92:12). To adjudicate is to judge those in the external natural (see Ps. 7:8). People are those of the church as to truth (see Ps. 2:1, 3:8, 18:43, 65:7, 74:18, 102:15); uprightness is truth from good (see Ps. 11:3, 25:21, 96:10, 143:10).

"By the world is not signified the world of lands, but the church in it, in the following passages: *The earth shall mourn and be confounded, the world shall languish and be confounded* (Isa. xxiv. 4). *The lands shall learn Thy judgments, and the inhabitants of the world Thy justice* (Isa. xxxvi. 9). *Who maketh the earth by Thy power, who prepareth the world by Thy wisdom* (Jer. x. 12; li. 15). *The foundations of the world were revealed by the blast of Thy breath* (Ps. xviii. 15). *The earth is Jehovah's and the fullness thereof, the world and they who dwell therein: He hath founded it upon the seas, and established it, upon the floods*

(Ps. xxiv. 1, 2). *The heavens are Thine, the earth also is Thine; the world and the fullness thereof Thou hast founded* (Ps. lxxxix. 11). *He will make them to inherit the throne of glory; for the pillars of the earth are Jehovah's, and He hath set the world upon them* (1 Sam. ii. 8). *O Babylon, thou hast made the world a wilderness; thou hast destroyed thy land, and slain thy people* (Isa. xiv. 17, 20). Besides other places, as Isa. xviii. 3; xxvi. 18; xxvii. 6; xxxiv. 1; Nah. i. 5; Ps. ix. 8; Ps. lxxvii. 18; Ps. xcviii. 9; Lam. iv. 12; Job xviii. 18; Matt. xxiv. 14; Luke xxi. 26; Apoc. xvi. 14. But it is to be known, that when the world and the earth are named together, the church as to good is signified by the world, and the church as to truth by the earth." (*Apocalypse Revealed*, n. 551)

> "*Jehovah shall judge the world in righteousness, He shall judge the peoples in uprightness* (Ps. ix. 8).

Because the 'world' means the church in respect to good, and 'righteousness' is predicated of good, it is said 'Jehovah shall judge the world in righteousness;' and as those are called 'peoples' who are in truths, and 'uprightness' means truths, as above, it is said, 'He shall judge the peoples in uprightness.' In *Jeremiah:*—

> *Jehovah maketh the earth by His power, and prepareth the world by His wisdom, and by His intelligence He stretcheth out the heavens* (x. 12; li. 15).

'Jehovah maketh the earth by His power' signifies that the Lord establishes the church by the power of Divine truth; 'He prepareth the world by His wisdom' signifies that He forms the church that is in good from Divine good by means of Divine truth; 'by His intelligence He stretcheth out the heavens' signifies that thus He enlarges the heavens." (*Apocalypse Explained*, n. 741.14)

And Jehovah will be a high fort for the contrite,
A high fort in times of adversity.
And they who know Your name will trust in You:
For You have not forsaken those who enquire after You, Jehovah.
(Ps. 9:9-10)

The contrite are those who have a humble will from a state of temptation (see Ps. 44:19); times of adversity are states of temptations of evil attacking what is good (see Ps. 3:1, 27:12). Those who know God's name are those who know the truth of doctrine concerning the Lord (see Ps. 74:18, 96:2); to trust is to have confidence of the will which is given to those who are in the good of charity (see Ps. 33:21); those who enquire after the Lord are those in ignorance who seek the truth; to be forsaken is to be lacking in truth (see Ps. 27:9).

Make music unto Jehovah who dwells in Zion,
Proclaim among the people His doings.
For He who enquires after blood remembers them,
He forgets not the cry of the afflicted. (Ps. 9:11-12)

To make music is to worship from truth spiritual truth (see Ps. 57:7); Jehovah is the Lord as to Divine love (see Ps. 18:31, 28:1, 68:17, 26, 82:1, 147:7) and Zion is the church that is in celestial love (see Ps. 2:6, 14:7, 20:2, 48:11, 51:18, 102:13, 128:5, 133:3, 147:12). People are those in the church who are in truth (see Ps. 2:1, 18:43, 102:15); to proclaim His deeds is to teach how the Lord reforms each person through repentance. To "enquire after blood" is to explore one's conscience as to violence done against love or charity:

"*Therefore also, behold, his blood is required.* That this signifies the stings of conscience thence, is evident from the signification of blood, as violence offered to good or to charity (see n. 374, 1005). When this violence or this blood is required [or searched out], it causes internal anxiety, which is called stings of conscience; but this is so only with those who have been in anxiety when they sinned (n. 5470)." (*Heavenly Arcana*, n. 5476)

The afflicted are those who are lacking in knowledges of truth (see Ps. 35:10, 37:14, 40:17). To cry is grief on account of falsehood:

"That a cry is falsity, and that sin is evil, may be evident from the signification of a cry in the Word. That a cry signifies falsity can be evident to no one unless he knows the internal sense of the Word. The word sometimes occurs in the Prophets, and when wasting and desolation are there treated of, it is said that they howl and cry. This signifies that good and truth are vastated, and cry is there the word by which falsity is described in the internal sense; as in Jeremiah: *A voice of the cry of the shepherds, and the howling of the masters of the flock, for Jehovah layeth waste their pasture* (xxv. 36); where the cry of the shepherds means that they are in falsity, from which there is wasting." (*Heavenly Arcana*, n. 2240)

Be gracious to me, Jehovah,
See my affliction from those who hate me,
You who lift me up from the gates of death (Ps. 9:13)

To receive grace is to receive spiritual good and truth, and comfort and hope of mind in temptations (see Ps. 4:1) and is sought by those in humiliation of thought (see Ps. 103:8); affliction is to be in a state of lacking knowledges of truth (Ps. 35:10, 37:14, 40:17); those who hate are the evils of hell. The gates of death are the gates of hell (see Ps. 69:12, 127:5), and to be lifted up from them is to be delivered from them (see Ps. 3:3). When "death" is mentioned in scripture it is not talking about physical death, but spiritual death in hell:

"That by death is signified spiritual death, or damnation, is evident from very many passages in the Word, of which it will suffice to adduce the following. In Isaiah: *With justice shall He judge the poor, and reprove with equity for the meek of the earth. But He shall smite the earth with the rod of His mouth, and with the breath of His lips shall He cause the wicked to die* (xi. 4) — speaking of the Lord. The rod of His mouth and the breath of His lips stand for the Divine truth from which is judgment; to die means to be damned. Again: *He will swallow up death for ever; and the Lord Jehovih will wipe away the tear from off all faces* (xxv. 8). Again: *The dead shall not live; the Rephaim shall not rise; because Thou hast visited and destroyed them* (xxvi. 14). Again: *Thy dead shall live; My dead bodies shall arise* (xxvi. 19). Again: *Ye have said, We have made a covenant with death, and with hell have we made an agreement ... Your covenant with*

*death shall be disannulled, and your agreement with hell shall
not stand* (xxviii. 15, 18).

"In Jeremiah: *Ye look for light, but He turns it into the shadow
of death, He makes it gross darkness* (xiii. 16). In Ezekiel: *Ye have
profaned Me among My people for handfuls of barley and for pieces
of bread, to slay the souls that should not die, and to make souls to
live that should not live* (xiii. 19). In Hosea: *I will ransom them from
the hand of hell; I will free them from death: O death, I will be thy
plagues; O hell, I will be thy destruction* (xiii. 14). In David: *Thou
liftest me up from the gates of death* (Ps. ix. 13). Again: *Enlighten
mine eyes, lest I sleep the sleep of death* (Ps. xiii. 3). Again: *The
cords of death compassed me, and ...the cords of hell*(Ps. xviii. 4, 5).
Again: *They are appointed as a flock for hell; death shall pasture
them* (Ps. xlix. 14). In the Apocalypse: *I have the keys of hell and
of death* (i. 18). Again: *He who overcometh shall not be hurt of the
second death* (ii. 11)." (*Heavenly Arcana*, n. 6119.2-3)

*That I may recount all Your praise in the gates of the daughter
of Zion:
I will be glad in Your salvation.* (Ps. 9:14)

To recount is to know the quality of a thing (see Ps. 147:4); to
praise is to worship from affection for truth (see Ps. 7:17, 35:18).
As knowledge and truth are external to the celestial heaven this
is done at the gates, which signify knowledges which introduce
to the goods and truths of the church (see Ps. 24:7-10). Zion is the
heaven and the church of celestial love (see Ps. 2:6, 14:7, 20:2,
48:11, 51:18, 102:13, 128:5, 133:3, 147:12); as daughters signify
affections (see Ps. 45:9-10) the daughter of Zion is the affection
for good. To be glad is to be happy from affection for truth (see
Ps. 14:7); salvation is deliverance from evil (see Ps. 14:7, 96:2).

"That the celestial church, or the Lord's celestial kingdom, is
called the daughter of Zion from affection for good, or from love
to the Lord Himself, may be seen further in Isaiah (x. 32; xvi. 1;
lii. 2; lxii. 11; Jer. iv. 31; vi. 2, 23; Lam. i. 6; ii. 1, 4, 8, 10; Mic. iv.
10, 13; Zech. ii. 14; Ps. ix. 14). And that the spiritual church, or
the Lord's spiritual kingdom, is called the daughter of Jerusalem

from affection for truth, and so from charity toward the neighbor, in Jeremiah (Lam. ii. 15)." (*Heavenly Arcana*, n. 2362.3; see also *Apocalypse Revealed*, n. 612)

Gates signify knowledges which introduce one into the church and heaven:

"*Having twelve gates*, signifies all the knowledges of truth and good there, by which a man is introduced into the church. By the gates are signified knowledges of truth and good from the Word, because by them a man is introduced into the church; for the wall, in which the gates were, signifies the Word; as explained just above (n. 898): and it is said in what follows, that *the twelve gates were twelve pearls, each one of the gates was one pearl* (vers. 21); and by pearls the knowledges of truth and good are signified (n. 727). That a man is introduced into the church by them, as into a city through the gates, is manifest. That twelve signifies all, may be seen above (n. 348). Knowledges of truth and good are signified by gates in these places also: *I will lay thy foundations with sapphires, and I will make thy stones of ruby, and thy gates of carbuncles* (Isa. liv. 11, 12). *Jehovah loveth the gates of Zion more than all the dwellings of Jacob, glorious things are to be declared of thee, O city of God* (Ps. lxxxvii. 2, 3). *Enter into His gates with thanksgiving, be thankful unto Him, bless His name* (Ps. c. 4). *Our feet have stood within thy gates, O Jerusalem, Jerusalem is built as a city that is compact together* (Ps. cxxii. 2, 3). *Praise Jehovah, O Jerusalem, for He strengthened the bars of thy gates, He blesseth thy children within thee* (Ps. cxlvii. 12, 13). *That I may show forth all Thy praises in the gates of the daughter of Zion* (Ps. ix. 14)." (*Apocalypse Revealed*, n. 899)

The nations are sunk down in the pit that they made:
In the net which they hid is their own foot caught.
Jehovah is known by the judgment which He executes:
The wicked is snared in the work of his own hands. Meditation.
The wicked shall turn away to hell,
All the nations that forget God. (Ps. 9:15-17)

Nations are those who are in evils (see Ps. 2:1, 18:43, 79:1, 80:8, 102:15, 106:5,27) who become imprisoned by their own falsehoods in hell signified by the pit (see Ps. 28:1, 69:15, 88:4,6). One's foot is one's lower external natural (see Ps. 8:6, 41:9, 49:5, 99:5, 105:18) and a net represents external material desires (see Ps. 10:9) which draw one down towards hell. Judgment is according to Divine truth (see Ps. 36:6, 37:6, 72:2, 89:14, 92:12); to be snared is to fall into the allurement of evil (see Ps. 18:5, 38:12) and the work of one's hands is one's evil deeds. Meditation signifies the perception of good (see Ps. 19:14). To wicked who turn away towards hell are those who are in falsity from evil as signified by hell (see Ps. 18:5); nations are those who are in evils (see Ps. 2:1, 18:43, 79:1, 80:8, 102:15, 106:5,27); to forget God is to be in a state of non-conjunction due to falsity from evil (see Ps. 13:1 and 8:4).

For the needy shall not perpetually be forgotten,
The hope of the afflicted shall not perish for ever. (Ps. 9:18)

The needy are those who are lacking in good and yet desire it (see Ps. 35:10, 37:14, 40:17, 109:16, 113:7) and to be forgotten is to be in state that is non receptive of Divine compassion as signified by remembrance (see Ps. 8:4); to be afflicted is to be lacking in knowledges of the truth (see Ps. 35:10, 37:14, 40:17) and to perish is to spiritually die from falsehoods (see Ps. 88:11). In the following passage the word afflicted is translated as miserable, and needy as poor:

Arise, Jehovah, let not man prevail,
Let the nations be judged upon Your presence.
Put them in fear, Jehovah,
That the nations may know themselves to be but men. (Ps. 9:19-20)

For Jehovah to arise, not letting man (Hebrew *enosh*) prevail, is for Divine love to overcome one's lower natural; nations are evils (see Ps. 2:1, 18:43, 79:1, 80:8, 102:15, 106:5,27) which will be judged according to one's interiors, signified by presence or face (see Ps. 4:6, 13:1, 22:24, 27:8-9, 31:16, 67:1). For nations to acknowledge that they are but men is to know that all evil is from their lower selfish nature.

Psalm 10

Why do you stand afar off, Jehovah? (1) [*lamed*]
You hide in times of adversity.
    With pride the wicked hotly pursues the afflicted, (2)
    Let them be taken in the schemes that they have devised.
    For the wicked praises according to his soul's longing, (3)
    And the greedy curses, he spurns Jehovah.
    The wicked in the haughtiness of his nose will not enquire after Him, (4)
    God is not in any of his schemes.
    His ways are perverted at all times, (5)
    Your judgments are far above from in front of him,
    He testifies at all his adversaries.
    He has said in his heart, I shall not be moved, (6)
    In generation and generation which will not be with evil.
    His mouth is full of cursing and deceit and fraud, (7)
    Under his tongue is toil and iniquity.
    He sits in ambush in the villages, (8)
    In the secret places he kills the innocent,
    His eyes are hidden against the hapless.
    He lies in ambush secretly as a lion in his covert, (9)
    He lies in ambush to catch the afflicted,
    He catches the poor when he draws him into his net.
    He crouches, he stoops down, (10)
    And the hapless fall by his numerous ones.
    He has said in his heart, God has forgotten, (11)
    He hides His face, He will not see it perpetually.
Arise Jehovah, God lift up Your hand, (12) [*qoph*]
Forget not the afflicted.

Why does the wicked spurn God? (13)
He has said in his heart, You will not enquire after it.
You have seen, for you behold toil and provocation, (14) [*resh*]
To give with Your hand.
The hapless forsakes himself upon You,
You are the helper of the orphan.
Break the arm of the wicked and the evil, (15) [*shin*]
Enquire after his wickedness till You find none.
Jehovah is King forever and ever, (16)
The nations are perished out of His land.
Jehovah, You have heard the longing of the meek, (17) [*tav*]
You will prepare their heart, You will cause Your ear to listen:
To judge the orphan and the contrite, (18)
That the man of the earth may no more frighten.

Psalm Commentary 10

Summary: God appears distant in states of temptation (v. 1). The evil do evil to the good and deny God, and are hypocrites and deceitful (v. 1-11). Prayer to the Father, for their requital, and for judgment upon them (v. 12-18).

Why do you stand afar off, Jehovah?
You hide in times of adversity. (Ps. 10:1)

For Jehovah to stand afar off is for Divine mercy and love to appear absent in a state of temptation; times of adversity is to be in a state where evil attacks good (see Ps. 3:1, 27:12).

With pride the wicked hotly pursues the afflicted,
Let them be taken in the schemes that they have devised.
For the wicked praises according to his soul's longing,
And the greedy curses, he spurns Jehovah.
The wicked in the haughtiness of his nose will not enquire after
Him,
God is not in any of his schemes. (Ps. 10:2-4)

To be afflicted is to be lacking in knowledges of truth (see Ps. 35:10, 37:14, 40:17); those who devise falsehood will be punished by their own falsehood. To praise the longing of the soul is to be in affection for falsehood based on one's selfish love, as signified by praise (see Ps. 7:17, 35:18). To curse is to be in falsity against good (see Ps. 10:7); to spurn Jehovah is to reject Divine love from one's evil of the will. The haughtiness of the nose is to be in selfish pride; to not enquire after God is to be in falsehood.

God is the Lord as to Divine truth (see Ps. 18:31, 29:1, 68:17,24, 82:1, 95:3, 147:7); ways are falsehoods (see Ps. 1:1, 18:42, 25:4).

His ways are profane at all times,
Your judgments are far above from in front of him,
He testifies at all his adversaries.
He has said in his heart, I shall not be moved,
In generation and generation which will not be with evil.
His mouth is full of cursing and deceit and fraud,
Under his tongue is toil and iniquity. (Ps. 10:5-7)

To be profane is to falsify what is holy from one's own self-ish loves (see Ps. 74:7). Judgments are from Divine truth (see Ps. 36:6, 37:6, 72:2, 89:14, 92:12) which are above thoughts of falsehood; to testify against adversaries is to attack good (see Ps. 3:1, 27:12). To say signifies perception of the will (see Ps. 33:9) and to not be moved is to be established in one's falsehood; for happiness to not be in evil from generation and generation is to believe there will be no punishment of one's enjoyment of evil in each state of falsehood signified by generation (see Ps. 14:5, 22:30, 33:11, 145:13). The mouth is the external understanding (see Ps. 5:9, 37:30, 135:16); cursing is falsehood against good, deceit is falsehood against the truth with the intent to deceive (see Ps. 5:6), and fraud is to deceive in one's external actions. The tongue is a false opinion or persuasion hidden beneath the external understanding (see Ps. 35:28, 57:4, 140:11); toil is the conflict of temptation through falsehood (see Ps. 7:14) and iniq-uity is evil done against the good of faith (see Ps. 5:9-10).

He sits in ambush in the villages,
In the secret places he kills the innocent,
His eyes are hidden against the hapless. (Ps. 10:8)

To "sit in ambush in the villages" means the evil destroy the external things of the church; to "kill the innocent" in secret places means the evil destroy the interior things of the church. The Hebrew word for hapless comes from a root meaning to be dark or unhappy and refer to those who are in obscurity as to external truth. The word for village can also be translated as court which signifies the external things of heaven and the church (see Ps. 65:4, 84:2,10, 92:13):

"*In their villages.* That this signifies the external things of the church, is evident from the signification of villages, as those things which are the externals of faith, thus of the church; the external things of the church are rituals, the internal things are doctrinal teachings, when these are not merely of knowledge but of life. External things were represented by villages, because they were outside of the cities, but internal things by the cities themselves..." (*Heavenly Arcana*, n. 3270)

The innocent are those who are in interior good who are in love and charity:

"*And the innocent and the just slay thou not.* That this signifies a turning away from destroying interior and exterior good, is evident from the signification of the innocent, as he who is in interior good, and thus in the abstract sense as interior good..." (*Heavenly Arcana*, n. 9262)

"Charity without innocence is not charity, and still less is it love to the Lord. For this reason innocence is the very essential of love and charity, and accordingly of good. The proprium of innocence is, to know, acknowledge, and believe, not with the mouth but with the heart, that nothing but evil is from one's self, and that all good is from the Lord; and therefore that one's proprium is nothing but blackness, that is to say, not only his voluntary proprium which is evil, but also his intellectual proprium which is falsity. When man is in this confession and belief from the heart, the Lord flows in with good and truth, and insinuates into him a heavenly proprium, which is white and lustrous. No one can ever be in true humiliation, unless he is in this acknowledgment and belief from the heart; for he is then in annihilation of himself, and even loathing of himself, and thus in absence from himself; and in this manner he is then in a state for receiving the Divine of the Lord. It is by this means that the Lord flows in with good into a humble and contrite heart." (*Heavenly Arcana*, n. 3994)

"Within the church, they who have not some measure of innocence and of charity toward the neighbor, howsoever they are acquainted with truth and profess it with the lips, still in no wise acknowledge it in heart. Outside of the church, among the Gentiles who are called to the truth of faith, or are instructed concerning it in the other life, no others receive it than those who are in innocence, and live in mutual charity together; for innocence and charity make the ground in which the seeds of faith may take root and grow up." (*Heavenly Arcana*, n. 3111.2)

He lies in ambush secretly as a lion in his covert,
He lies in ambush to catch the afflicted,
He catches the afflicted when he draws him into his net. (Ps. 10:9)

To lie in ambush secretly as a lion in the covert is to be against interior truth. A lion signifies the power of falsity destroying (see Ps. 17:12, 57:4). The afflicted are those who are lacking in knowledges of truth (see Ps. 35:10, 37:14, 40:17); to be caught in a net is to be trapped by lower material desires.

"...the voice of roaring of the lion is falsity; to spread the net over him is to allure by the enjoyments of earthly loves and by reasonings from them..." (*Heavenly Arcana*, n. 9348.4).

He crouches, he stoops down,
And the hapless may fall by his numerous ones.
He has said in his heart, God has forgotten,
He hides His face, He will not see it perpetually. (Ps. 10:10-11)

The word crouch can also be translated as crush, which signifies a state of temptation where there is a lack of influx of truth from heaven (see Ps. 44:19); to stoop down is for there to be a lack of influx of good; the hapless are those in obscurity as to knowledges of the truth (see Ps. 10:9); to fall is to pervert the truth (see Ps. 7:15). To say signifies perception of the will (see Ps. 33:9) and so is mentioned with the heart which signifies the will (see Ps. 7:9, 22:10, 24:4, 51:10, 64:6, 66:18, 71:23, 78:8, 86:11); that God has forgotten is to deny God's compassion for the good (see Ps. 8:4); for the Lord to hide His face is to be in a state separate from Divine mercy in one's own evil loves (see Ps. 13:1, 22:24); to state that God will not see is to be in false-hood against Divine truth.

Arise Jehovah, God lift up Your hand:
Forget not the afflicted.
Why does the wicked spurn God?
He has said in his heart, You will not enquire after it.
You have seen, for you behold toil and provocation,
To give with Your hand.
The hapless forsakes himself upon You,
You are the helper of the orphan. (Ps. 10:12-14)

Jehovah is the Lord as to Divine love (see Ps. 18:31, 28:1, 68:26, 82:1, 147:7), God is the Lord as to Divine truth (see Ps. 18:31, 29:1, 68:17,24, 82:1, 95:3, 147:7), and hand is the power of truth (see Ps. 20:6, 44:3, 45:4, 80:15,17, 89:13,21, 110:1, 121:5). To not forget the afflicted is to bring knowledge of truth to those who are infested with falsities (see Ps. 35:10, 37:14, 40:17). To spurn God is to reject the Divine truth from one's falsehood signified by wicked; to say signifies perception of the will (see Ps. 33:9) and so is mentioned with the heart which signifies the will (see Ps. 7:9, 22:10, 24:4, 51:10, 64:6, 66:18, 71:23, 78:8, 86:11); that God will not enquire signifies a believe that evil will be hidden. Toil is the conflict of temptation from falsehood (see Ps. 7:14) and provocation is temptation of the will (see Ps. 78:58). The hapless are those in obscurity as to knowledges of the truth (see Ps. 10:9) and to be forsaken is be destitute of truth (see Ps. 27:9); an orphan represents those who are in truth but not yet in good (see Ps. 68:5, 94:6, 146:9). God as a helper signifies aid from Divine mercy:

"For [he said], The God of my father was my help. That this signifies the Lord's mercy and presence in the church, is evi-dent from the signification of father, as the church as to good (see n. 5581), and as the Ancient Church (n. 6050, 6075, 6846); from the signification of the God of my father, as the Divine of the Ancient Church, which was the Lord (n. 6846, 6876, 6884);

and from the signification of help, when predicated of the Lord, as mercy; for help from Him is of mercy, and also of presence, since where the reception of mercy is, there is presence; and this is especially in the church, because there is the Word, and by means of the Word the Lord's presence." (*Heavenly Arcana*, n. 8652)

Break the arm of the wicked and the evil,
Enquire after his wickedness till You find none. (Ps. 10:15)

To "break the arm" is to break the power of falsity from evil (see Ps. 77:15, 89:21, 136:12) where the wicked are those who are in evil against the good from truth and the evil are against the good of love; to "enquire after wickedness" is to explore one as to evil and falsehood from Divine truth before judgment.

"That the hands, arms, and shoulders correspond to power in the Greatest Man, is because the strength and powers of the whole body and of all its viscera have reference to them; for the body exerts its strength and powers by the arms and hands. It is for this reason also that power is signified in the Word by the hands, arms, and shoulders. That this is signified by the hands, may be seen above (in n. 878, 3387); and that it is signified by the arms also, is plain from many passages — as from the following: *Be Thou their arm every morning* (Isa. xxxiii. 2). *The Lord Jehovih shall come as a mighty one, and His arm shall rule for Him* (xl. 10). *He worketh it with the arm of His strength* (xliv. 12). *Mine arms shall judge the peoples* (li. 5). *Put on strength, O arm of Jehovah* (li. 9). *I looked, and there was no one helping ...therefore Mine own arm brought salvation unto Me* (lxiii. 5). *Cursed is the man that trusteth in man, and maketh flesh his arm* (Jer. xvii. 5). *I have made the earth, the man and the beast ...by My great power and by My outstretched arm* (xxvii. 5; xxxii. 17). *The horn of Moab is cut off, and his arm is broken* (xlviii. 25). *I will break the arms* of the king of Egypt *...but I will strengthen the arms of the king of Babylon* (Ezek. xxx. 22, 24, 25). O Jehovah, *break Thou the arm of the wicked* (Ps. x. 15). *According to the greatness of Thine arm preserve Thou the children of death* (lxxix. 11). *Brought us forth out of Egypt with a mighty hand and with an outstretched arm* (Deut. xxvi. 8; xi. 2, 3; vii. 19; Jer. xxxii. 21; Ps. cxxxvi. 12). From these passages it may also be evident that by right hand in the Word, is signified superior power, and by sitting at the right hand of Jehovah omnipotence (Matt. xxvi. 63, 64; Luke xxii. 69; Mark xiv. 61, 62; xvi. 19)." (*Heavenly Arcana,* n. 4933)

Jehovah is King forever and ever,
The nations are perished out of His land.
Jehovah, You have heard the longing of the meek,
You will prepare their heart, You will cause Your ear to listen:
To judge the orphan and the contrite,
That the man of the earth may no more frighten. (Ps. 10:15-18)

Jehovah is Lord as to Divine love (see Ps. 18:31, 28:1, 68:26, 82:1, 147:7) and King as to the Divine truth (see Ps. 2:2, 72:11, 89:20,39, 95:3, 105:20,30). Heaven is derived from the good and truth of the Lord: forever is eternity in the celestial heaven of love (see Ps. 145:13) and ever is eternity in the spiritual heaven of truth. Nations are those who are in evil (see Ps. 2:1, 18:43, 79:1, 80:8, 102:15, 106:5,27) who perish which is to spiritually die from falsehoods (see Ps. 88:11), and are thus removed from the land or earth which signifies the church as to truth (see Ps. 9:8, 24:1, 60:2, 90:2, 96:13). For Jehovah to hear signifies Divine providence (see Ps. 17:6); the longing of the meek is the desire of those who are humble in heart; to prepare their heart is to establish their love in truth; to listen is to attend to something in regard to love (see Ps. 5:2); to judge the orphan is to deliver those who are in truth but not good (see Ps. 68:5, 94:6, 146:9); the crushed are those have a humble will from temptation (see Ps. 44:19); the "man of the earth" are those who are in falsehoods who attack the truth.

Psalm 11

To the chief musician, a Psalm of David.

~

In Jehovah I seek refuge, (1)
How say ye to my soul, Flutter, bird, to your mountain?
For behold, the wicked bend the bow, (2)
They prepare their arrow upon the string,
To shoot under dusk at the upright in heart.
For the foundations are broken down, (3)
What can the righteous do?
    Jehovah is in His holy temple, (4)
    Jehovah's throne is in heaven.
    His eyes behold,
    His eyelids prove the sons of Man.
    Jehovah proves the righteous, (5)
    But His soul hates the wicked and he who loves violence.
    Upon the wicked He shall rain *coals*, fire and brimstone, (6)
    And a raging spirit shall be the portion of their cup.
    For Jehovah is righteous, He loves righteousness, (7)
    His face beholds the upright.

Psalm Commentary 11

Summary: The Lord arouses Himself to fight for the good against the evil (v. 1-2) for the church is destroyed (v. 3). Exploration by Divine truth (v. 4-5) after which the evil are punished and the righteous are protected (v. 6-7).

In Jehovah I seek refuge:
How say ye to my soul, Flutter, bird, to your mountain?
For behold, the wicked bend the bow,
They prepare their arrow upon the string,
To shoot under dusk at the upright in heart. (Ps. 11:1-2)

To seek refuge in Jehovah is to trust in the Lord as to Divine love (see Ps. 18:31, 28:1, 68:26, 82:1, 147:7). The soul is one's spiritual life of the understanding (see Ps. 22:10, 31:9, 71:23, 107:9) and birds signify rational and intellectual thought (see Ps. 8:8, 50:11); to flutter or wander is to not know what is true and good (see Ps. 56:8). A mountain here signifies the love of self (see Ps. 46:2, 144:5). A bow signifies the doctrine of falsity (see Ps. 7:12-13, 11:2, 18:34, 37:15, 46:9, 77:17-18, 78:9,57); arrows are the falsities derived from doctrine (see Ps. 7:12-13, 11:2, 46:9, 77:17-18, 78:9,57, 91:5). To shoot under dusk is to be under the falsity of appearances; the upright in heart are those who are in truth from good (see Ps. 9:8, 11:3, 25:21, 96:10, 143:10).

"As the bow signifies the doctrine of truth, so in the opposite sense it also signifies the doctrine of falsity. The same things in the Word have usually an opposite sense, as has been said

142

and shown in several places — thus in Jeremiah: *Behold, a people cometh from the north country, and a great nation shall be stirred up from the sides of the earth; they lay hold on bow and spear; they are cruel, and shall not have compassion; their voice shall roar like the sea, they shall ride upon horses set in array as a man for battle, against thee, O daughter of Zion* (vi. 22, 23); where bow stands for the doctrine of falsity. In the same: *Behold, a people cometh from the north, and a great nation, and many kings shall be stirred up from the sides of the earth, they lay hold on bow and spear, they are cruel, and have no compassion* (l. 41, 42); where the meaning is similar. In the same: *They bend their tongue; their bow is a lie, and not for truth, they are grown strong in the land; for they have gone forth from evil to evil, and have not known Me* (ix. 3).

"That the bow is the doctrine of falsity is plainly manifest, for it is said, 'They bend their tongue; their bow is a lie, and not for truth.' In the same: *Jehovah Zebaoth said, Behold, I will break the bow of Elam, the chief of his might* (xlix. 35). In David: *Come, behold the works of Jehovah, Who hath made desolations in the earth; He maketh wars to cease unto the end of the earth, He breaketh the bow, He cutteth the spear in sunder, He burneth the chariots in the fire* (Ps. xlvi. 9). In the same: *In Judah is God known, His name is great in Israel; in Salem also shall be His tabernacle, and His dwelling-place in Zion; there brake He the fiery shafts of the bow, the shield and the sword, and the war* (Ps. lxxvi. 1-3). In the same: *Lo, the wicked bend the bow, they make ready their arrows upon the string, to shoot in darkness at the upright in heart* (Ps. xi. 2). Here the bow and arrows plainly stand for doctrinals of falsity." (*Heavenly Arcana*, n. 2686.7-8)

"As most of the things in the Word have also an opposite sense, so likewise have javelins, darts, arrows, bows, and a shooter; and they signify falsities, the doctrine of falsity, and those who are in falsity. So in Moses: *Joseph is the son of a fruitful one, the son of a fruitful one by a fountain of daughters, he goeth upon the wall; they grieved him, and shot at him, and the archers hated him* (Gen. xlix. 22, 23). In Jeremiah: *They bend*

*their tongue, their bow is a lie, ...and not for truth; ...their tongue
is a lengthened arrow, it speaketh deceit* (ix. 3, 8). In David: *They
have sharpened their tongue like a sword, they have aimed their
arrow, a bitter word, to shoot in secret places at the perfect; suddenly will they shoot at him, and will not fear. They will make
strong for themselves an evil word, they will tell of the hiding of
snares* (Ps. lxiv. 4-6). In the same: *Lo, the wicked bend the bow,
they make ready their arrow upon the string, to shoot in the darkness at the upright in heart* (Ps. xi. 2). In the same: *His truth is
a shield and buckler. Thou shalt not be afraid for the terror by
night, for the arrow that flieth by day* (Ps. xci. 4, 5)." (*Heavenly
Arcana*, n. 2709.4)

"To fight against evils and falsities is also to fight against the
hells, because evils and falsities are thence; hence this also is
signified. That a bow in the Word signifies doctrine combating in
both senses, may be evident from these passages: *The arrows of
Jehovah are sharp, and all His bows bent; the hoofs of His horses
are counted as flint* (Isa. v. 28). *The Lord hath bent His bow as
an enemy* (Lam. ii. 4). *Jehovah, Thou ridest upon Thy horses;
Thy bow shall be made naked* (Hab. iii. 8, 9). *He gave the nations
before him, and made him to rule over kings; He gave them as
dust to His sword, as stubble to His bow* (Isa. xli. 2). In these passages a bow, because belonging to Jehovah or the Lord, signifies
the Word, from which the Lord fights in man against evils and
falsities. *I will cut off the chariot from Ephraim, and the horse
from Jerusalem; and the bow of war shall be cut off, and He shall
speak peace to the nations* (Zech. ix. 10). *They bend their tongue,
their bow is a lie, and not the truth* (Jer. ix. 3). *Behold, the wicked
bend their bow, they make ready their arrows upon the string, to
shoot in the darkness the upright in heart* (Ps. xi. 2)." (*Apocalypse
Revealed*, n. 299)

"...a 'bow' signifies the doctrine of truth combating against
falsities and evils and dispersing them. That this is the signification of 'bow' can be seen further from its contrary sense, in which
'bow' signifies the doctrine of falsity fighting against truths and
goods and destroying them; and 'darts' and 'arrows' its falsities

themselves. In this sense 'bow' is mentioned in the following passages. In *David:*—

> *Lo, the wicked bend the bow, they make ready their arrow upon the string, that they may shoot in darkness at the upright in heart (Ps. xi. 2).*

'The wicked bend the bow' signifies that they frame doctrine; 'they make ready the arrow upon the string' signifies that they apply into it falsities that appear as truths; 'to shoot in darkness at the upright in heart' signifies to deceive those who are in truths from good; 'bow' here meaning the doctrine of falsity, 'arrow' the falsity itself; 'to shoot' meaning to deceive, and 'darkness' appearances; for such as these reason from appearances in the world and from fallacies, also by the application of the sense of the letter of the Word." (*Apocalypse Explained*, n. 357.12)

For the foundations are broken down,
What can the righteous do? (Ps. 11:3)

The foundations are the truths of faith upon which the church is based (see Ps. 11:3, 18:7,15, 24:2, 75:3, 82:5, 104:5) which if destroyed by falsity then affects those who are in the good of charity, signified by righteous (see Ps. 14:5, 36:6, 37:6,17, 72:2, 89:14, 92:12).

"In the Word the foundations of the earth are mentioned several times; and by them are not meant the foundations of the earth, but the foundations of the church: for the earth signifies the church (n. 285); and the foundations of the church are none other than those which are from the Word, and are called doctrines: for the Word itself founds the church. Doctrines from the Word are also signified by foundations in these passages: *Do ye not understand the foundations of the earth?* (Isa. xl. 21.) *I will put My words into thy mouth, to plant the heavens and to found the earth* (Isa. li. 16). *They do not acknowledge, they do not understand, they walk in darkness, all the foundations of the earth totter* (Ps. lxxxii. 5). *The Word of Jehovah, who stretcheth forth the heavens and the foundations of the earth, and who formeth the spirit of man within him* (Zech. xii. 1). *Jehovah hath kindled a fire in Zion, and it hath devoured the foundations thereof* (Lam. iv. 11). *The wicked shoot in darkness at the upright in heart, because the foundations are undermined* (Ps. xi. 2, 3). *Hear ye, O mountains, the controversy of Jehovah, the strength, the foundations of the earth, for Jehovah hath a controversy with His people* (Mic. vi. 2). *The cataracts on high were opened, and the foundations of the earth were shaken, the earth is broken in pieces, the earth is rent, the earth is moved exceedingly* (Isa. xxiv. 18-20; beside other places, as Isa. xiv. 32; xlviii. 13; li. 13; Ps. xxiv. 2; cii. 25; civ. 4, 5; 2 Sam. xxii. 8, 16). He who does not think that the earth signifies the church, can think no otherwise here than merely naturally, yea, materially, when he reads of the foundations of the earth: the same as it would be, if he did not think that the city Jerusalem here signifies the church, while he reads of its wall, gates, foundations, streets, measures, and other particulars which are described in this chapter as relating to a city; when yet they relate to the church, and thus are not to be understood materially, but spiritually." (*Apocalypse Revealed*, n. 902)

Jehovah is in His holy temple,
Jehovah's throne is in heaven.
His eyes behold,
His eyelids prove the sons of Man.
Jehovah proves the righteous,
But His soul hates the wicked and he who loves violence.
(Ps. 11:4-5)

The holy temple represents the heaven as to Divine truth (see Ps. 18:6, 65:5 and 5:7) and the Lord's throne signifies the judgment by the Divine truth (see Ps. 9:4,7 93:1, 103:19, 122:5). Eyes signifies the understanding of truth (see Ps. 13:3, 31:9, 69:23) and in reference to the Lord signify Divine foresight (see Ps. 17:6). It also signifies the presence of the Lord in the truths and goods of faith and love. To behold is to have Divine foresight to those who are good; for the eyelids to prove is for those who are in truth to undergo temptation and be reformed by it. The sons

of Man (Hebrew *adam*) are those who are in spiritual truths (see
Ps. 49:2, 57:4, 80:17, 89:47). To prove is to explore by means of
Divine truth, the righteous are those who do good (see Ps. 36:6,
37:6, 72:2, 89:14, 92:12). The wicked are those in the falsehood
of evil; those who love violence are those who by hatred destroy
the good of charity (see Ps. 7:16, 27:12).

"It is said in the eyes of Jehovah, and thereby is signified the
Divine presence of the Lord in the truths and the goods of faith
and of love with men on earth and with angels in the heavens.
The reason why the presence of the Lord is in the truths and the
goods of faith and of love, is, that these are from the Lord Himself, and when the Lord is present with men and with angels
in these, He is then present in His own with them, and not in
their proprium, for this is evil. So also it is that by eyes in the
Word, where referring to men who receive the Divine things of
the Lord, is signified faith and also intellect that receives; for the
intellect is the internal eye, and faith is truth which is seen and
perceived...

"It shall also be told whence such faculty of seeing comes. It is
real light which illumines the understanding, a light altogether
distinct from the light which illumines the sight of the body. The
light which illumines the understanding is from heaven, but that
which illumines the sight of the body is in the world. The light
of heaven is from the Lord as the Sun there, and is in its essence
Divine truth proceeding from the Divine good of the Lord. Thus
it is plain whence it is that by the eyes, when with reference to
Jehovah, is signified the Divine presence of the Lord, and that
by the eyes, when with reference to men who receive the Divine
truth of the Lord, or His light, is signified faith and an enlightened understanding.

"That it is real light which illumines minds and constitutes
understanding with men, is not known in the world, though
sight and light are attributed by men to the understanding, and
the Lord in the Word is many times called the Light, and thereby
is understood that He is seen by faith and the light thereof...

"From these considerations it may be evident what is signified in the Word by the eyes of Jehovah — as in Isaiah: *Incline
Thine ear, O Jehovah, and hear; open Thine eyes, O Jehovah,
and see* (xxxvii. 17). In Jeremiah: *I will set Mine eye upon them
for good, and I will bring them again to their own land, and I
will build them* ...(xxiv. 6). And in David: *Behold, the eye of Jehovah is upon them who fear Him* (Ps. xxxiii. 18). Again: *Jehovah is
in the temple of His holiness, the throne of Jehovah is in heaven;
His eyes behold, His eyelids try, the sons of man* (Ps. xi. 4); and
elsewhere." (*Heavenly Arcana*, n. 10569.2-5)

"By eye in these places is not meant the eye, but the understanding of truth. Since the understanding of truth is signified
by the eye, it was therefore among the statutes for the sons of
Israel, that one blind or disordered in the eye, of the seed of
Aaron, should not come near to offer sacrifice, nor enter within
the veil (Lev. xxi. 18, 20): also that what was blind should not be
offered in sacrifice (Lev. xxii. 22; Mal. i. 8). From these things
what is meant by the eye when speaking of man is manifest.
Hence it follows that by the eye, when speaking of the Lord, is
meant His Divine wisdom, also His omniscience and providence;
as in these passages: *Open thine eyes, O Jehovah, and see* (Isa.
xxxvii. 17). *I will set Mine eye upon them for good, and will build
them up* (Jer. xxiv. 6). *Behold, the eye of Jehovah is upon them
who fear Him* (Ps. xxxiii. 18). *Jehovah is in the temple of holiness; His eyes behold, His eyelids try, the sons of man* (Ps. xi. 4)."
(*Apocalypse Revealed*, n. 48)

*Upon the wicked He shall rain coals, fire and brimstone,
And a raging spirit shall be the portion of their cup.* (Ps. 11:6)

Coals of fire and brimstone signify the love of self with its
lusts (see Ps. 78:48). A "raging spirit" is drunkenness, which is
punishment for those who falsify and profane the truth as signified by wine (see Ps. 75:8), or for those who reason against
faith (see Ps. 107:27). A cup signifies truth in its most outward
or external form as Divine truth flows downward from heaven,
which is punishment to the wicked.

*"Upon the wicked Jehovah shall rain snares, fire and brim-
stone* (Ps. xi. 6) — where fire and brimstone are the evils of the
love of self and the world. That fire has this signification, may be
seen above (n. 1297, 1861, 5071, 5215, 6314, 6832, 7324, 7575,
9144), and also sulphur (n. 2446)." (*Heavenly Arcana*, n. 9348.9)
"That brimstone is the hell of the evils of the love of self, and
fire the hell of the falsities therefrom, is evident from the signification of brimstone and its fire, in the Word, as the love of self
with its lusts and falsities, thus as hell; for hell consists of such
things. That brimstone and fire have this signification is evident
in David: *Jehovah shall rain upon the wicked snares, fire and
brimstone* (Ps. xi. 6)." (*Heavenly Arcana*, n. 2446)
"By the fire is signified love of self and of the world, which
love is the selfhood of man's will (n. 450, 465, 494): by the smoke
the pride of one's own intelligence is signified, which is the self-
hood of his understanding, going forth from the love of self and
of the world, as smoke from a fire (n. 422): and by the brimstone
is signified the lust of evil and falsity, which is the general self-
life flowing forth from those two. But these things do not appear
from their discourses before men in the world, but manifestly
before the angels in heaven; therefore it is said that viewed interiorly they are such. Fire signifies infernal love, and brimstone
the lusts flowing forth from that love through the pride of one's
own intelligence, in the following passages: *I will make it rain
fire and brimstone upon him* (Ezek. xxxviii. 22). *Jehovah will
rain upon the wicked fire and brimstone* (Ps. xi. 6)." (*Apocalypse
Revealed*, n. 452; see also *Apocalypse Explained*, n. 578.7)
"...Jehovah in no wise caused it to rain brimstone and fire,
that is, in no wise condemned to hell; but that they who were in
evil and thence in falsity did this, because they separated themselves from good, and so cast themselves upon the laws of order
from truth alone... That in the Word evil, punishing, cursing,
damnation, and other things are attributed to Jehovah, or the
Lord, as here that He made it rain brimstone and fire, may be
seen in Ezekiel: *I will contend against him with pestilence and
with blood, ...fire and brimstone will I make it rain upon him*

(xxxviii. 22). In Isaiah: *The breath of Jehovah is like a stream of brimstone, kindling* (xxx. 33). In David: *Jehovah shall rain upon the wicked snares, fire and brimstone* (Ps. xi. 6)." (*Heavenly Arcana*, n. 2447.4-5)

> *"Jehovah shall rain upon the wicked snares, fire, and brimstone, and a wind of tempests shall be the portion of their cup* (Ps. xi. 6).

In the same:—

> *There is a cup in the hand of Jehovah, and He hath mixed it with wine, He hath filled it with mixture, and hath poured it out thence; but the dregs of it all the wicked of the earth shall suck out and drink* (Ps. lxxv. 8).

'Snares, fire, and brimstone,' signify falsities and evils leading astray, and 'a wind of tempests' signifies vigorous assault upon truth. These are called 'the portion of a cup,' because a 'cup,' as a containant signifies these. 'To mix' and 'to fill with mixture' signify to falsify truth and to profane it." (*Apocalypse Explained*, n. 960.6)

"...by containers in the Word the same is signified as by things contained; as by a cup the same as by wine, and by a platter the same as by food. That by cups, goblets, vials, and plates, similar things are signified as by their contents, will be seen in what now follows. ...the Lord always operates from inmosts through ultimates, or in fullness. This is the reason that vials were given to the angels: by which are signified containing goods and truths, such as those of the literal sense of the Word, by which falsities and evils are detected. That the literal sense of the Word is a container, may be seen in the *Doctrine of the New Jerusalem concerning the Sacred Scriptures* (n. 27-36, and 37-49). That by vials, plates, cups, and goblets, and by bottles, those things are signified which are contained in them, may be evident from the following passages: Jehovah said, *Take the cup of anger from My hand, and make all the nations to drink: and if they refuse to take the cups, thou shalt say, ye shall certainly drink* (Jer. xxv. 15, 16, 28). *Babylon hath been a golden cup in the hand of Jehovah, that made the whole earth drunken* (Jer. li. 7). *I will give the cup of thy sister into thine hand; thou shalt be filled with drunkenness and sorrow, with the cup of desolation, with the cup of thy sister Samaria* (Ezek. xxiii. 31-34). *The cup of Jehovah shall go around to thee, that there may be vomit upon thy glory* (Hab. ii. 16). *Even unto thee, O daughter of Edom, shall the cup pass over; thou shalt be made drunken and shalt make thyself naked* (Lam. iv. 21). *Jehovah shall rain upon the wicked terrible winds; this shall be the portion of their cup* (Ps. xi. 6)." (*Apocalypse Revealed*, n. 672)

For Jehovah is righteous, He loves righteousness;
His face beholds the upright. (Ps. 11:6-7)

Jehovah is the Lord as to Divine love (see Ps. 18:31, 28:1, 68:26, 82:1, 147:7) and the righteous are those who do good (see Ps. 14:5, 36:6, 37:6,17, 72:2, 89:14, 92:12); the Lord loves those who are in love as all love is from Him. The upright are those in truth from good (see Ps. 9:8, 11:3, 25:21, 96:10, 143:10) which the Lord beholds from His Divine truth.

Psalm 12

To the chief musician upon Sheminith, a Psalm of David.

~

Save, Jehovah, for the merciful cease, (1)
For the faithful disappear from the sons of Man.
They speak vanity, a man with his neighbour, (2)
They speak with flattering lips with a double heart.
Jehovah shall cut off all flattering lips, (3)
The tongue that speaks great things:
Who have said, With our tongue will we prevail, (4)
Our lips are with us: who is lord to us?

~

For the devastation of the afflicted, (5)
For the groaning of the needy,
Now I will arise, says Jehovah,
I will set him in safety, he will testify.
The speech of Jehovah is pure speech: (6)
As silver refined in a furnace of earth,
Purified seven times.
You, Jehovah, shall keep them, (7)
You shall preserve them from this generation forever.
The wicked walk round about, (8)
Vileness is exalted among the sons of Man.

Psalm
Commentary

12

Summary: There is no longer any good, but hypocrites (v. 1-4). The Lord will to eternity deliver the good as against the evil (v. 5-8).

Save, Jehovah, for the merciful cease,
For the faithful disappear from the sons of Man.
They speak vanity, a man with his neighbour,
They speak with flattering lips with a double heart. (Ps. 12:1-2)

The merciful are those who are in love towards the Lord and others (see Ps. 25:10, 26:3, 36:5, 89:14, 103:8); the faithful are those who live by the truth; the sons of Man (Hebrew *adam*) are those who are in spiritual truths (see Ps. 49:2, 57:4, 80:17, 89:47). To speak vanity is to teach the falsity of doctrine (see Ps. 4:2, 144:8) and neighbours are those who are in similar falsehoods (see Ps. 122:8). Flattering lips is the hypocrisy of one's doctrine signified by lips (see Ps. 12:4, 81:5), and a double heart is the hypocrisy of the will.

Jehovah shall cut off all flattering lips,
The tongue that speaks great things:
Who have said, With our tongue will we prevail;
Our lips are with us: who is lord to us? (Ps. 12:3-4)

Tongue and lips correspond to one's intellectual. To say signified perception of the will (see Ps. 33:9) and tongue signifies a false persuasion (see Ps. 35:28, 57:4, 140:11); flattering lips

154

signify the false doctrine of hypocrites (see Ps. 5:9 and 81:5). To ask who is lord is to have no regard for what is good, as signified by lord (see Ps. 68:17,26, 105:21, 110:1, 114:7).

"That a lip signifies doctrine is seen from the following places in the Word — in Isaiah: The seraphim cried and said, *Holy, holy, holy, Jehovah of Hosts. ...And the prophet said, Woe is me! for I am cut off, because I am a man of unclean lips, and I dwell in the midst of a people of unclean lips; for mine eyes have seen the King, Jehovah of Hosts. Then flew one of the seraphim unto me ... and he touched my mouth with it, and said, Lo, this hath touched thy lips; and thine iniquity is taken away, and thy sin is purged* (vi. 3, 5-7). Lips here stand for interior things of man, and so for internal worship, from which is adoration, as is represented here with the prophet. That his lips were touched, and that thus his iniquity was taken away and his sin purged, any one may see was a representative of interior things that are signified by the lips, which are things of charity and its doctrine... In Zephaniah: *Then will I turn to the peoples with a clean lip, that they may all call upon the name of Jehovah, to serve Him with one shoulder* (iii. 9). A clean lip manifestly stands for doctrine. In Malachi: *The law of truth was in his mouth, and perversity was not found in his lips. ...For the priest's lips should keep knowledge, and they should seek the law at his mouth; for he is the messenger of Jehovah of Hosts* (ii. 6, 7). This is said of Levi, by whom the Lord is represented; lips stand for doctrine from charity. In David: *Who have said, With our tongue will we prevail; our lips are with us* (Ps. xii. 4). Here lips stand for falsities. Again: *My soul shall be satisfied as with marrow and fatness; and my mouth shall praise Thee with lips of songs* (lxiii. 5). In Isaiah: *In that day there shall be five cities in the land of Egypt speaking with the lip of Canaan, and swearing to Jehovah of Hosts* (xix. 18). Lip stands for doctrine." (*Heavenly Arcana*, n. 1286.1,4)

From the devastation of the afflicted,
From the groaning of the needy,
Now I will arise, says Jehovah,

I will set him in safety, he will testify. (Ps. 12:5)

Devastation is deprivation of the truth (see Ps. 40:2, 46:8); the afflicted are those who are infested with falsities (see Ps. 35:10, 37:14, 40:17); groanings grief of heart due to evil against good; the needy are those who are lacking in the knowledge of good (see Ps. 35:10, 37:14, 40:17, 109:16, 113:7). To arise is for truth to judge; to say signified perception of the will (see Ps. 33:9) from the Divine love signified by Jehovah; to be set in safety is to deliver from evil and to testify is to be in truth against falsehood.

The speech of Jehovah is pure speech:
As silver refined in a furnace of earth,
Purified seven times. (Ps. 12:6)

The speech of Jehovah refined as silver and purified seven times is the holiness of the Divine truth of the Word, as silver signifies truth (see Ps. 2:9, 5:7, 68:13,30, 105:37, 115:4). The number seven is holy, as there are six stages of development in temptations and combats against evil and falsity, until one reaches a state of peace, signified by the seventh day or Sabbath.

"*The sayings of Jehovah are pure sayings, as silver refined in a crucible purified seven times* (*Ps.* xii. 6).

'Silver' signifies truth from the Divine; 'purified seven times' means wholly and fully pure." (*Apocalypse Explained,* n. 257.5; see also *Heavenly Arcana,* n. 1551.4)

"...as the six days of labor are related to the seventh day of rest, or the holy day, so the number two is related to three; and therefore the third day in the Word is taken for the seventh, and involves almost the same, on account of the Lord's resurrection on the third day. And hence the Lord's coming into the world, and in glory, and every coming of the Lord, is described equally by the seventh and by the third day. For this reason the two days that precede are not holy, but relatively profane. Thus in Hosea: *Come and let us return unto Jehovah, for He hath wounded, and He will heal us; He hath smitten and He will bind us up. After two days will He revive us; on the third day He will raise us up, and we shall live before Him* (vi. 1, 2). And in Zechariah: *It shall come to pass in all the land, saith Jehovah, that two parts therein shall be cut off and die, and the third shall be left therein; and I will bring the third part through the fire, and will refine them as silver is refined* (xiii. 8, 9). And silver was most pure when purified seven times (Ps. xii. 6). From all which it is plain that as seven does not signify seven, but things that are holy, so by pairs are signified not pairs, but things relatively profane." (*Heavenly Arcana*, n. 720)

You, Jehovah, shall keep them,
You shall preserve them from this generation forever.
The wicked walk round about,
Vileness is exalted for the sons of Man. (Ps. 12:7-8)

For Jehovah to keep them signifies to be kept from evil; to be preserved from this generation is to be preserved from falsehoods, signified by generation (see Ps. 14:5, 22:30, 33:11, 145:13). The wicked are those who are in evil who are outside of heaven; vileness is profanation of spiritual truths as signified by the sons of Man (see Ps. 49:2, 57:4, 80:17, 89:47).

Psalm 13

To the chief musician, a Psalm of David.

~

How long, Jehovah? Will You forget me perpetually? (1)
How long will You hide Your face from me?
How long shall I take counsel in my soul, (2)
Having sorrow in my heart daily?
How long shall my enemy be exalted over me?
Look! Answer me, Jehovah my God, (3)
Enlighten my eyes lest I sleep *in* death;
Lest my enemy say, I have prevailed against him, (4)
And my adversaries be glad when I am moved.
   But I have trusted in Your mercy, (5)
   My heart shall be glad in Your salvation,
   I will sing unto Jehovah, (6)
   For He has dealt bountifully with me.

Psalm
Commentary
13

Summary: The state of the Lord's temptations, and the grievous insurrection of the infernals against Him (v. 1-4). He has confidence respecting the victory (v. 5-6).

How long, Jehovah? Will You forget me perpetually?
How long will You hide Your face from me? (Ps. 13:1)

This describes the state of temptation, where the Lord appears absent. To forget is to be in a state of non conjunction with the truth; for the Lord to hide his face is to be in a state of self love separate from Divine mercy (see Ps. 22:24). To forget also signifies a state of non-conjunction:

"*But forgot him.* That this signifies removal, is evident from the signification of forgetting, when not remembering is non-conjunction, as removal: for it is according to non-conjunction that removal takes place." (*Heavenly Arcana*, n. 5170)

To hide the face is to be in a state of no mercy:

"*Saying, Ye shall not see my face.* That this signifies that there will be no compassion, is evident from the signification of the face when predicated of man, as his interiors, that is, his affections and thoughts therefrom (see n. 358, 1999, 2434, 3527, 3573, 4066, 4796, 4797, 5102); but when predicated of the Lord, it is mercy or compassion. Therefore not to see his face means that there will be no mercy, or no compassion; for the Lord is represented here by Joseph in the supreme sense. Not that the Lord has no compassion, for He is mercy itself; but when there

160

is no medium that conjoins, it seems to man as if there were no compassion in the Lord. The reason is, that if there is not a conjoining medium, there is no reception of good; and when there is no reception of good, evil is in its place. If man then cries out to the Lord, and, because he cries from evil and thus for himself against all others, is not heard, it appears to him as if there were no compassion. That the face of Jehovah or the Lord is mercy, may be evident from the Word; for the face of Jehovah or the Lord is in the proper sense the Divine love itself; and because it is the Divine love, it is of mercy, for this from love is turned toward the human race subjected to so much misery...

"On the other hand the opposite is to conceal or hide and also to turn away the face, which signifies not to be merciful — as in Isaiah: *In the overflowing of My wrath I hid My face from thee for a moment; but with everlasting kindness will I have mercy on thee* (liv. 8) — where the overflowing of wrath stands for temptation, and because the Lord appears not to be merciful therein it is said, 'I hid My face from thee for a moment.' In Ezekiel: *I will turn away My face from them* (vii. 22). In David: *How long wilt Thou forget me, O Jehovah? for ever? How long wilt Thou hide Thy face from me?* (Ps. xiii. 1.) In the same: *Hide not Thy face from me; put not Thy servant away in anger* (Ps. xxvii. 9). Again: *Jehovah, why easiest Thou off my soul? why hidest Thou Thy face from me?* (Ps. lxxxviii. 14.) And again: *Make haste to answer me, O Jehovah; my spirit is consumed. Hide not Thy face from me, lest I become like them who go down into the pit. Cause me to hear Thy mercy in the morning* (Ps. cxliii. 7, 8)." (*Heavenly Arcana*, n. 5585.1,5)

How long shall I take counsel in my soul, having sorrow in my heart daily?
How long shall my enemy be exalted over me? (Ps. 13:2)

Counsel of the soul is thought of the spiritual understanding (see Ps. 22:10, 31:9, 71:23, 107:9); to have sorrow in the heart is grief due to evil attacking what is good as the heart signifies the love of the will (see Ps. 7:9, 22:10, 24:4, 51:10, 64:6, 66:18, 71:23,

78:8, 86:11). For the enemy to be exalted is to be in a state where falsity prevails over truth (see Ps. 3:1, 27:12).

Look! Answer me, Jehovah my God,
Enlighten my eyes lest I sleep in death (Ps. 13:3)

To look and answer means to receive Divine influx of truth and good (see Ps. 4:1). To enlighten the eyes is to enlighten the spiritual understanding (see Ps. 11:4, 31:9, 69:23); sleep is a state of spiritual unawareness or a natural life without the spiritual (see Ps. 76:5, 78:65) and death is spiritual death, which is separation from heaven (see Ps. 6:5, 102:20, 106:28).

"That a dictate from within is signified by their eyes being opened, is evident from similar expressions in the Word — as from what Balaam says of himself, who because he had visions called himself *the man whose eyes are opened* (Num. xxiv. 3, 4). And of Jonathan — when he tasted of the honey-comb, and it was dictated to him from within that it was evil — it is said his eyes saw, that is, were enlightened, so that he knew what he had not known (1 Sam. xiv. 27-29). Moreover, in many places in the Word the eyes are taken for the understanding, and so for an inward dictate therefrom — as in David: *Enlighten mine eyes lest I sleep the sleep of death* (Ps. xiii. 3) — eyes meaning the understanding. In Ezekiel: *Which have eyes to see and see not* (xii. 2) — meaning, which are not willing to understand. In Isaiah: *Cover their eyes, lest they see with their eyes* (vi. 10); signifying that they should be made blind lest they understand. Moses said to the people, *Jehovah hath not given you a heart to know, and eyes to see, and ears to hear* (Deut. xxix. 4) — heart standing for will, eyes for understanding. In Isaiah it is said of the Lord, that He would *open the blind eyes* (xlii. 7); and in the same prophet: *The eyes of the blind shall see out of obscurity and out of darkness* (xxix. 18). (*Heavenly Arcana*, n. 212; see also *Apocalypse Revealed*, n. 48; *Apocalypse Explained*, n. 152.10)

Those who are not living by the truth are said to be in a sleep:

"*Be watchful*, signifies that they should be in truths, and in life according to them. Nothing else is signified by watching in the Word. For he who learns truths, and lives according to them, is like him who is awakened out of sleep and becomes watchful. But he who is not in truths, but only in worship, is like him who is sleeping and dreaming. Natural life, viewed in itself, or without spiritual life, is nothing but sleep; but natural life in which there is spiritual life is watchfulness: and this is not procured in any other way than through truths; which are in their light and in their day, when the man is in life according to them. This is signified by watching in these places: *Watch ye, because ye know not what hour the Lord will come* (Matt. xxiv. 42). *Blessed are the servants, whom the Lord, when He cometh, shall find watching: be ye ready, because at an hour when ye think not, the Son of Man shall come* (Luke xii. 37, 40). *Watch ye, because ye know not when the Lord of the house shall come; lest, coming suddenly, He find you sleeping: what I say unto you, I say unto all, Watch* (Mark xiii. 35-37). *The virgins, while the bridegroom tarried, slumbered and slept: and the five foolish ones came and said, Lord, open unto us: but the Lord shall answer, I know you not: Watch therefore, because ye know neither the day nor the hour in which the Son of Man will come* (Matt. xxv. 1-13). Because the Lord's coming is called the morning (n. 151), and truths are then opened, and it becomes light, therefore that time is called the beginning of the watches (Lam ii. 19); and the Lord is called the watcher (Dan. iv. 13): and it is said in Isaiah, *Thy dead shall live; awake, ye inhabitants of the dust* (xxvi. 19). But that the state of the man who is not in truths is called slumber and sleep, may be seen (Jer. li. 39, 57; Ps. xiii. 3; Ps. lxxvi. 6; Matt. xiii. 25; and elsewhere)." (*Apocalypse Revealed*, n. 158)

"Because 'to be awake' signifies to receive spiritual life, therefore 'sleeping' signifies natural life apart from spiritual life, since natural life compared with spiritual life is as sleep compared with wakefulness, as has been said above. This is what 'sleeping' signifies in *Matthew:*—

*The kingdom of the heavens is like unto a man that sowed
good seed in his field; but while men slept the enemy came
and sowed tares among the wheat* (xiii. 24, 25).

In *Jeremiah:*—

*When they have grown warm, I will set their feasts, and I
will make them drunken, that they may sleep the sleep of an
age, and not awake* (li. 39, 67).

In *David:*—

*Look! answer me, Jehovah my God! lighten Thine eyes lest
I sleep death (Ps.* xiii. 3)." (*Apocalypse Explained*, n. 187.8)

"*Happy is he who is awake,* signifies the happy state of those
who look to the Lord. This is evident from the signification of
'happy,' as being to be in a happy state; also from the signification of 'being awake,' as being to acquire for oneself spiritual life
(see n. 187); and this is acquired by man's looking to the Lord,
because the Lord is Life itself, and from Him alone is life eternal.
When a man is in life from the Lord he is in wakefulness; but
when he is in life from himself he is asleep; or what is the same,
when a man is in spiritual life he is in wakefulness, but when he
is in natural life separated from the spiritual he is asleep; and
what a man then sees is like what he sees in a dream. To live this
life is meant also by 'sleeping and slumbering' in the Word (as in
Matt. xiii. 25; xxv. 5, 6; *Mark* iv. 26, 27; xiii. 36; *Isa.* v. 27; *Jer.* li.
39, 57; *Ps.* xiii. 4; lxxvi. 7; and elsewhere). This makes clear what
is signified by 'being awake.'" (*Apocalypse Explained*, n. 1006.1)

*Lest my enemy say, I have prevailed against him,
And my adversaries be glad when I am moved.* (Ps. 13:4)
　　An enemy signifies a falsehood that attacks the truth, and an
adversary signifies an evil which hates what is good (see Ps. 3:1,
27:12).

*But I have trusted in Your mercy,
My heart shall be glad in Your salvation.
I will sing unto Jehovah,*

For He has dealt bountifully with me. (Ps. 13:5-6)

To trust is to have confidence of the will which is given to those who are in the good of charity (see Ps. 33:21) and is thus mentioned with mercy which is Divine love (see Ps. 25:10, 26:3, 36:5, 89:14, 103:8); to be glad is to have joy from affection for the truth (see Ps. 14:7); salvation is deliverance from evil (see Ps. 14:7, 96:2). To sing is to worship from spiritual good (see Ps. 33:3, 57:7); Jehovah is the Lord as to Divine love (see Ps. 18:31, 28:1, 68:26, 82:1, 147:7) and to deal bountifully is to give as to good.

Psalm 14

To the chief musician, a Psalm of David.

~

The fool has said in his heart, (1)
There is no God.
They are corrupt, they have done abominable deeds,
There is none who does good.
Jehovah looked down from heaven upon the sons of Man, (2)
To see if there were any who were prudent to enquire after God.
They have all turned aside, they are altogether become filthy: (3)
There is none who does good, no, not one.
   Have all the workers of iniquity no knowledge? (4)
   Who eat up my people as they eat bread,
   They call not upon Jehovah.
   There were they dreading a dread, (5)
   For God is in the generation of the righteous.
   Ye have shamed the counsel of the afflicted, (6)
   For Jehovah is his refuge.
   Who shall give the salvation of Israel out of Zion? (7)
   When Jehovah returns the captivity of His people,
   Jacob shall be glad, and Israel shall rejoice.

Psalm Commentary 14

Summary: There is no longer any understanding of truth or will of good whatever (v. 1-3). They do not acknowledge God (v. 4). They are against good and truth (v. 5-6). There will be a new church from the Lord (v. 7).

The fool has said in his heart there is no God,
They are corrupt, they have done abominable deeds,
There is none who does good, no, not one. (Ps. 14:1)

To be foolish is to be in denial of God, or to know the Word and not do it (Matt. 7:24-26). To say signifies perception of the will (see Ps. 33:9) and so is mentioned with the heart which signifies the will (see Ps. 7:9, 22:10, 24:4, 51:10, 64:6, 66:18, 71:23, 78:8, 86:11); to be corrupt is to be in a false persuasion of thought. To do abominable deeds is to do works of evil to become averse to good. As the Lord is the source of all good, those who deny good are incapable of doing good as their intent will be focused on serving their self.

"That to corrupt is predicated of persuasions, is evident in Isaiah: *They shall not hurt, nor corrupt, in all the mountain of My holiness; for the earth shall be full of the knowledge of Jehovah* (xi. 9); and so in chapter lxv. 25th verse, where to hurt has relation to the will, or to lusts, and to corrupt relates to the understanding, or to persuasions of falsity. Again: *Woe to the sinful nation, a people laden with iniquity, a seed of evil-doers, children that are corrupters* (i. 4). Here as in other places, 'nation' and the 'seed of evil-doers' stand for evils which are of the will, or lusts; 'people' and 'children that are corrupters,' for falsities which are of the understanding, or of persuasions. In Ezekiel: *Thou wast more corrupt than they in all thy ways* (xvi. 47). Here 'corrupt' is predicated of things of the understanding, or reason, or thought; for 'way' is a word that signifies truth. In David: *They have done what is corrupt, and have done abominable work* (Ps. xiv. 1). Here 'what is corrupt' is put for dreadful persuasions, and 'abominable' for the filthy lusts which are in the work, or from which the work is done. In Daniel: *After sixty and two weeks shall the Messiah be cut off, and there shall be none belonging to Him; and the people of the prince that shall come shall corrupt the city and the sanctuary, and the end thereof shall be with a flood* (ix. 26). Here likewise to corrupt stands for persuasions of what is false, of which a flood is predicated." (*Heavenly Arcana*, n. 622)

"*For that is an abomination unto the Egyptians.* That this signifies that they are in opposition, is evident from the representation of the Egyptians, as those who are in inverted order (see n. 5700); and from the representation of the Hebrews, to eat with whom was an abomination to the Egyptians, as those who are in genuine order (n. 5701): thus they were in opposition to each other, whence comes aversion, and at length abomination. In regard to this abomination it should be known that those who are in inverted order, that is, in evil and falsity therefrom, become at last so averse to the good and truth of the church that when they hear them, and especially when they hear the interior things of them, they abominate them to such an extent that they feel in themselves a sort of nausea and retching." (*Heavenly Arcana*, n. 5702)

Jehovah looked down from heaven upon the sons of Man,
To see if there were any who had prudence to enquire after God.
They have all turned aside, they are altogether become filthy:
There is none who does good, no, not one. (Ps. 14:2-3)

The sons of Man (Hebrew *adam*) are those who falsified spiritual truths (see Ps. 49:2, 57:4, 80:17, 89:47); to have prudence to

enquire after God is to have wisdom. To turn aside and become
filthy is to turn away from truth to falsehood; to not do good is to
turn towards selfish love.

Have all the workers of iniquity no knowledge?
Who eat up my people as they eat bread,
They call not upon Jehovah.
There were they dreading a dread,
For God is in the generation of the righteous.
Ye have shamed the counsel of the afflicted,
For Jehovah is his refuge. (Ps. 14:4-6)

Iniquity is evil done against the good of faith (see Ps. 5:9-10).
To eat people is to destroy truths from falsehood (see Ps. 2:1, 3:8,
18:43, 65:7, 74:18, 102:15); to eat bread is to appropriate evil (see
Ps. 78:24, 128:2). Dread is a fear of punishment by those who
are in evil in the presence of the Divine. God is Divine truth (see
Ps. 18:31, 29:1, 68:17,24, 82:1, 95:3, 147:7), the generation of the
righteous are those who have eternal life from truths from good
(see Ps. 22:30, 33:11 and 36:6, 37:6,17, 72:2, 89:14, 92:12). Counsel is falsehood from a lack of truth signified by afflicted (see
Ps. 35:10, 37:14, 40:17). Generation in scripture always refer to
spiritual generations (see Ps. 22:30, 33:11, 145:13):

"...those things which are begotten from the internal afterward, are more interior; for those things which have been begotten before, serve successively for producing those which are
begotten afterward more interiorly, since the internal by degrees
elevates the natural to itself. This is plain from the generation
of all things of the intellectual in man; for man is first sensual,
afterward he becomes more and more interior, until he becomes
intellectual. It is the same with the new generation, which comes
by faith and charity; and thus man is perfected by degrees — see
what was said above of successive elevation toward interiors,
when man is being regenerated (n. 6183).

"That generation in the Word signifies what is of faith and
charity, is because no other generation than spiritual can be
understood in the internal sense. This generation is also meant

in David — *They shall fear a fear; for God is in the generation of the just* (Ps. xiv. 5). The generation of the just stands for truths from good, for justice is predicated of good." (*Heavenly Arcana,* n. 6239.1-2)

Who shall give the salvation of Israel out of Zion? (Ps. 14:7)

Zion signifies the heaven and the church of celestial love (see Ps. 2:6, 14:7, 20:2, 48:11, 51:18, 102:13, 128:5, 133:3, 147:12) from which there is salvation for the spiritual church signified by Israel (see Ps. 14:7, 22:23, 78:5, 105:23, 106:26-27, 114:2, 136:11). Salvation is deliverance from evil by Divine mercy (see Ps. 96:2) and belongs to the Lord alone:

"'Salvation unto Him,' signifies that salvation is from Him, since He is salvation; for everything of salvation and of eternal life is from the Lord and is with man and angel; for all the good of love and all the truth of faith with man are the Lord's with him, and not the man's; for it is the Divine proceeding, which is the Lord in heaven with the angels and in the church with men, and from the good of love and the truth of faith come salvation and eternal life; so when it is said that salvation is the Lord's, and that the Lord Himself is salvation, it is clear how this is to be understood, as in the following passages. In *Isaiah:*—

Lo, this is our God; we have waited for Him that He may save us; this is Jehovah; we have waited for Him; let us exult and be glad in His salvation (xxv. 9).

In the same:—

My salvation shall not delay; and I will give salvation in Zion, My splendor in Israel (xlvi. 13).

In the same:—

I have given Thee for a light to the nations, that Thou mayest be My salvation unto the end of the earth (xlix. 6).

In the same:—

Say ye to the daughter of Zion, Behold thy salvation cometh
(lxii. 11).

In *David:*—

Jehovah shall give out of Zion the salvation of Israel, when
He shall bring back the captivity of His people (Ps. xiv. 7;
liii. 6).

This is said of the Lord, who is here called salvation, from the
act of saving, and for the reason that He is salvation with man,
for so far as the Lord is with man so far man has salvation. So
in *Luke:*—

Simeon said, Mine eyes have seen Thy salvation, which
Thou hast prepared before the face of all peoples (ii. 30, 31).

Again, this is why the Lord was called 'Jesus,' for *Jesus* means
salvation." *(Apocalypse Explained*, n. 460.2)

When Jehovah returns the captivity of His people,
Jacob shall be glad, and Israel shall rejoice. (Ps. 14:7)

To go into captivity signifies to be misled and captivated by
falsity (see Ps. 68:18, 78:61); for the people to return is to establish a new church in truth (see Ps. 2:1, 3:8, 18:43, 65:7, 74:18,
102:15). Jacob signifies the external church of those who are in
knowledge of the truth but not yet in good (see Ps. 77:15, 78:5,
132:5); Israel signifies the internal spiritual church of those who
are in good from truth (see Ps. 22:23, 78:5, 105:23, 106:26-27,
114:2, 136:11). To be glad is to have affection for truth, to rejoice
is from joy from affections of love.

"*Who will give out of Zion the salvation of Israel? When Jeho-*
vah shall bring back the captivity of His people Jacob shall exult,
Israel shall be glad (Ps. xiv. 7; liii. 6). Here also 'Zion' means
those who are in the good of love from the Lord; deliverance from
evils by the Lord and salvation are meant by 'Who will give out
of Zion the salvation of Israel?' 'To bring back the captivity of His
people' means deliverance from falsities and evils; "Jacob shall
exult, Israel shall be glad," means the joy with those who are in

the external church and of those who are in the internal church because of their deliverance, 'Jacob' meaning those who are of the external church, and 'Israel' those who are of the internal church; and both mean the Gentiles." (*Apocalypse Explained*, n. 811.22)

"By going into captivity is signified to be led away by their own falsities and evils into hell. By captivity spiritual captivity is here meant, which is to be seduced, and so led away from truths and goods, and to be led on into falsities and evils. That this spiritual captivity is meant by captivity in the Word, may be evident from the following passages: *Hear, all people, and behold my sorrows; my virgins and my young men have gone into captivity* (Lam. i. 18). *God forsook His habitation and tent, where He dwelt among men, and hath delivered His strength into captivity* (Ps. lxxviii. 60, 61). *The wind shall lead away all thy shepherds, and thy lovers shall go away into captivity; then shalt thou be ashamed for all thy wickedness* (Jer. xxii. 22). *I will make Mine arrows drunk with the blood of the pierced, and of the captivity* (Deut. xxxii. 42). *They are bent and bowed down, and their soul shall go into captivity* (Isa. xlvi. 1, 2). *Jehovah hath sent Me to bind up the broken-hearted, to proclaim liberty to the captives, and to the bound* (Isa. lxi. 1; Luke iv. 18, 19). *I will raise him up in justice; he shall let go My captivity, not for price nor reward* (Isa. xlv. 13). *Thou hast gone up on high, Thou hast led captivity captive* (Ps. lxviii. 18). *Shall the captivity of the just be delivered? even the captivity of the mighty shall be taken away, and the prey shall be delivered from the violent* (Isa. xlix. 24, 25). *Shake thyself from the dust, sit down, O Jerusalem; loose thyself from the bands of thy neck, O captive daughter of Zion* (Isa. lii. 1, 2. Beside other places, as Jer. xlviii. 46, 47; l. 33, 34; Ezek. vi. 1-10; xii. 1-12; Ob. i. 11; Ps. xiv. 7; liii. 6; Jer. l. 33, 34). By the captivities of the children of Israel by their enemies, spoken of in the book of Judges, and 2 Kings xxv., and in the prophets, spiritual captivities were represented and hence signified, which are treated of elsewhere." (*Apocalypse Revealed*, n. 591)

"It is said 'rejoice and be glad' because of the marriage of good and truth; for 'joy' is predicated of good because it relates to love, for it belongs especially to the heart and will, and 'gladness' is predicated of truth, because it relates to the love of truth, for it belongs especially to the mind and its thought; therefore we speak of 'joy of heart' and 'gladness of mind.' Everywhere in the Word there are two expressions, one of which has reference to good and the other to truth, and this because it is the conjunction of good and truth that makes both heaven and the church; therefore both heaven and the church are compared to a marriage, for the reason that the Lord is called 'Bridegroom' and 'Husband,' and heaven and the church are called 'bride' and 'wife.' Every one, therefore, who is not in that marriage is not an angel of heaven nor a man of the church; and the reason is that there is no good with any one unless it is formed by truths, nor is there truth with any one unless it is made living by good; for every truth is a form of good, and all good is the being (*esse*) of truth, and as one is not possible without the other it follows that there must needs be a marriage of good and truth with the man of the church as well as with an angel of heaven. Moreover, all intelligence and wisdom are from that marriage, for from it truths and goods are continually born, by which the understanding and will are formed. ...In place of joy exultation is also mentioned, because exultation, like joy, is predicated of good, because it relates to love, to the heart, and to the will..." (*Apocalypse Explained*, n. 660.2, 4; see also Ps. 5:11, 14:7, 31:7, 32:11, 48:11, 53:6, 118:24; Isa. 16:10, 25:9, 65:18; Jer. 48:33; Joel 2:21,23; Hab. 3:18; Zeph. 3:14; Luke 1:14).

Psalm 15

A Psalm of David.

~

Jehovah, who shall sojourn in Your tent? (1)
Who shall reside in Your holy mountain?
    He who walks perfectly and who works righteousness, (2)
    And speaks the truth in his heart.
    He backbites not with his tongue, (3)
    He does no evil against his neighbour,
    And he does not bear reproach against his kin.
    In his eyes that which should be rejected is despised, (4)
    And he honours those who fear Jehovah.
    He swears to a *neighbour* and changes not,
    He gives not his silver with usury, (5)
    And takes not a bribe against the innocent.
    He who does these things,
    Shall never be moved.

Psalm Commentary 15

Summary: Who shall go to heaven (v. 1)? Those who reject evil (v. 2-4) and who do what is good (v. 4-5).

Jehovah, who shall sojourn in Your tent?
Who shall reside in Your holy mountain? (Ps. 15:1)

A tent signifies the holiness of love or the celestial heaven (see Ps. 52:5, 61:4, 132:3) and to sojourn is to be instructed (see Ps. 5:4). Mountains in general signify the good of love in the celestial heaven (see Ps. 18:7, 36:6, 46:2, 65:6, 68:15-16, 72:3, 97:8, 104:10, 114:4,6, 121:1, 133:3, 147:8, 148:9), but here mountain is predicated of what is holy. Holy signifies the Divine truth which sanctifies (see Ps. 5:7, 65:4), thus "holy mountain" refers to good from truth, or spiritual good, which is a lower degree of good than the good of love of the celestial heaven.

"That dwelling in tents denotes the holy of love is evident from the signification of tents in the Word — as in David: *O Jehovah, who shall abide in Thy tent, who shall dwell in the mountain of Thy holiness? He who walketh uprightly and worketh justice, and speaketh truth in his heart* (Ps. xv. 1, 2). What it is to dwell in a tent or in the mountain of holiness is here described by holy acts of love — which are walking uprightly, and working justice. Again: *Their line is gone out through all the earth, and their speech to the end of the world. In them hath He set a tent for the sun* (xix. 4); where the sun stands for love. And again: *I will abide in Thy tent forever, I will trust in the covert of Thy wings* (lxi. 4); where the tent stands for what is celestial; the covert of the wings for the spiritual therefrom. In Isaiah: *A throne is established in mercy, and one sat thereon in truth, in the tent of David, judging and seeking judgment and hastening justice* (xvi. 5). Here also the tent stands for the holy of love, as is indicated by the judging judgment and hastening justice. Again: *Look upon Zion, the city of our set feasts. Thine eyes shall see Jerusalem a quiet habitation, a tent that shall not be removed* (xxxiii. 20); where the heavenly Jerusalem is spoken of.

"In Jeremiah: *Thus saith Jehovah, Behold I bring back the captivity of Jacob's tents, and will have compassion on his dwelling-places; and the city shall be built upon her own heap* (xxx. 18). The captivity of tents stands for the vastation of things celestial, or holy things of love. In Amos: *In that day I will raise up the tabernacle of David that is fallen, and close up the breaches thereof; and I will raise up his ruins, and I will build it as in the days of old* (ix. 11); where likewise the tabernacle stands for what is celestial and the holy things thereof. In Jeremiah:*The whole land is spoiled, suddenly are My tents spoiled, My curtains in a moment* (iv. 20). And in another place: *My tent is spoiled and all My cords are broken; My sons are gone forth of Me, and they are not; there is none to stretch forth My tent any more and to set up My curtains* (x. 20); where the tent stands for what is celestial, and curtains and cords for spiritual things therefrom. Again: *Their tents and their flocks shall they take, they shall carry away for themselves their curtains and all their vessels and their camels* (xlix. 29). This is said of Arabia and the sons of the East, by whom are represented those who possess things celestial or holy. And again: *In the tent of the daughter of Zion the Lord hath poured out His fury like fire* (Lam. ii. 4) — denoting the vastation of celestial or holy things of faith.

"The reason why a tent is taken in the Word to represent the celestial and holy things of love is, that in ancient times they performed holy worship in their tents; and when they began to profane their tents by profane kinds of worship, the tabernacle was built, and afterward the temple. Tents therefore signified the same as the tabernacle, and afterward the temple. For the same reason a holy man is called a tent, a tabernacle, and also a temple of the Lord. That a tent, the tabernacle, and the temple, have the same signification, is evident in David: *One thing have I asked of Jehovah, that will I seek after; that I may dwell in the house of Jehovah all the days of my life, to behold Jehovah in pleasantness, and to inquire early in His temple. For in the day of trouble He shall keep me secretly in His tabernacle, in the covert of His tent shall He hide me; He shall lift me up upon a rock. And now shall my head be lifted up against mine enemies round about me and I will offer in His tent sacrifices of shouting* (Ps. xxvii. 4-6).

"In the highest sense the Lord as to His Human Essence is the tent, the tabernacle, and the temple. Hence every celestial man is so called; and every thing celestial and holy. Now, because the Most Ancient Church was more beloved by the Lord than the churches that followed it, and also because they dwelt among themselves alone, or in their own families, and so celebrated holy worship in their tents, therefore tents were accounted holier than the temple, which was profaned. In remembrance therefore the feast of tabernacles was instituted, when they gathered in the increase of the land — during which like the most ancient people, they dwelt in tents (Lev. xxiii. 39-44; Deut. xvi. 13; Hos. xii. 9)." (*Heavenly Arcana*, n. 414.1-4; see also *Heavenly Arcana*, n. 10545.6, *Apocalypse Explained*, n. 799.7, *Apocalypse Revealed*, n. 585)

The phrase "holy mountain" and the word "hill" signify spiritual good:

"Since 'a mountain' signified the good of love, and in the highest sense, the Divine good, and from the Divine good Divine truth proceeds, so Mount Zion was built up above Jerusalem, and in the Word 'Mount Zion' signifies the church that is in the good of love to the Lord, and 'Jerusalem' the church that is in truths from that good, or the church in respect to doctrine. For the same reason Jerusalem is called 'the mountain of holiness,' also 'the hill;' for 'the mountain of holiness,' likewise 'hill' signify spiritual good, which in its essence is truth from good, as can be seen from the following passages. In *Isaiah:*—

> *It shall come to pass in the latter end of days that the moun-tain of Jehovah shall be on the head of the mountains, and shall be lifted up above the hills; whence all nations shall flow unto it; and many peoples shall go and say, Come ye, let us go up to the mountain of Jehovah, to the house of the God of Jacob* (ii. 2, 3).

In the same:—

> *In that day a great trumpet shall be blown, and the perish-ing in the land of Assyria shall come, and the outcasts in the land of Egypt, and they shall bow down to Jehovah in the mountain of holiness at Jerusalem* (xxvii. 13).

In *Joel:*—

> *Blow ye the trumpet in Zion, and cry aloud in the mountain of holiness* (ii. 1).

In *Daniel:*—

> *Let thine anger and Thy wrath be turned back from Thy city Jerusalem, the mountain of Thy Holiness* (ix. 16).

In *Isaiah:*—

> *They shall bring all your brethren out of all nations unto Jehovah, unto the mountain of My holiness, Jerusalem* (lxvi. 20).

In the same:—

> *He who putteth His trust in Me shall have the land for a heritage, and shall possess as an inheritance the mountain of My holiness* (lvii. 13).

In *Ezekiel:*—

*In the mountain of My holiness, in the mountain of the height
of Israel, there shall all the house of Israel, all of them in the
land, serve Me* (xx. 40).

In *Micah:*—

*In the latter end of days it shall be that the mountain of
the house of Jehovah shall be established on the top of the
mountains, and shall be lifted up above the hills; and the
peoples shall flow unto it* (iv. 1).

Besides many passages elsewhere in which 'the mountain
of holiness,' 'Mount Zion,' and 'the mountain of Jehovah' are
mentioned:—

The mountain of holiness (*Isa.* xi. 9; lvi. 7; lxv. 11, 25; *Jer.*
xxxi. 23; *Ezek.* xxviii. 14; *Dan.* ix. 20; xi. 45; *Joel* ii. 1; iii. 17;
Obad. verse 16; *Zeph.* iii. 11; *Zech.* viii. 3; *Ps.* xv. 1; xliii. 3).

And Mount Zion (*Isa.* iv. 5; viii. 18; x. 12; xviii. 7; xxiv. 23; xxix.
8; xxxi. 4; xxxvii. 32; *Joel* iii. 5; *Obad.* verses 17, 21; *Micah* iv. 7;
Lam. v. 18; *Ps.* xlviii. 11; lxxiv. 2; lxxviii. 68; cxxv. 1).

Because 'Mount Zion' signified Divine good and the church in
respect to Divine good, it is said in *Isaiah:*—

*Send ye [the lamb of] the ruler of the land from the cliff
towards the wilderness unto the mountain of the daughter
of Zion* (xvi. 1).

And in the *Apocalypse:*—

*A lamb standing upon the Mount Zion, and with him a
hundred forty and four thousand* (xiv. 1)." (*Apocalypse
Explained*, n. 405.26)

*He who walks perfectly and who works righteousness,
And speaks the truth in his heart.* (Ps. 15:2)
    To walk is to live according to the truth (see Ps. 1:1, 56:13,
81:13); perfectly is to be in the good from truth; to work
righteousness is to be in the good of charity (see Ps. 14:5, 36:6,

37:6,17, 72:2, 89:14, 92:12); to "speak the truth in the heart" is to be in truths from love as the heart signifies the good of the will (see Ps. 7:9, 22:10, 24:4, 51:10, 64:6, 66:18, 71:23, 78:8, 86:11).

"*And be perfect.* That this signifies the good of charity is evident from the signification of being perfect, which is to do good from truth; that is, to do good from a conscience of truth, and thus from charity, for this makes conscience (concerning which signification, see n. 612). But as the Lord is treated of in the internal sense, by perfect is signified the good of charity; for good proceeds from charity, so that the truth which is therefrom itself is good." (*Heavenly Arcana*, n. 1994; perfect is mistranslated as upright in *Heavenly Arcana*, n. 612.1-3)

"Frequent mention is made by the Lord of the Father Who is in the heavens, and then is meant the Divine in heaven, thus Good from which heaven is. The Divine regarded in Himself is above the heavens, but the Divine in the heavens is good which is in truth that proceeds from the Divine. This is meant by the Father in the heavens — as in Matthew: *That ye may be sons of your Father which is in the heavens. That ye may be perfect, as your Father which is in the heavens is perfect* (v. 45, 48; vi. 1)" (*Heavenly Arcana*, n. 8328)

"'He who walketh in integrity' signifies one who is in good in respect to life and in truths in respect to doctrine; therefore it is added, 'who doeth justice and speaketh the truth;' 'doing justice' signifying to be in good in respect to life, and 'speaking the truth' to be in truths in respect to doctrine." (*Apocalypse Explained*, n. 799.7)

He backbites not with his tongue,
He does no evil against his neighbour,
And he does not bear reproach against his kin.
In his eyes that which should be rejected is despised,
But he honours those who fear Jehovah. (Ps. 15:3-4)

A spiritual life is one that rejects falsehoods and evils. To not backbite with the tongue is to not entertain a false opinion or persuasion (see Ps. 35:28, 57:4, 140:11); to not do evil to one's neighbour is to not do harm against one in a similar truth of faith (see Ps. 122:8); to not bear reproach against one who is near is to not bear falsehood against a similar truth of faith. Eyes signify spiritual understanding (see Ps. 11:4, 13:3, 31:9, 69:23) which rejects falsehood and evil; to honour is to acknowledge good (see Ps. 8:5) which comes from fear of the Lord, which is to live by His commandments (see Ps. 2:11, 33:18, 128:1, 147:11).

He swears to a neighbour and changes not,
He gives not his silver with usury,
And takes not a bribe against the innocent.
He who does these things,
Shall never be moved. (Ps. 15:4-5)

To swear to one's neighbour is to confirm a similar truth and not change towards falsehood (see Ps. 63:11, 89:3,35, 105:9, 110:4, 132:1) and a neighbour is one in a similar truth of faith (see Ps. 122:8); to not give silver with usury is to not teach the truth for the sake of self profit as silver signifies truth (see Ps. 2:9, 5:7, 12:6, 68:13,30, 105:37, 115:4); to take a bribe against the innocent is to do good for the sake of self reward, which is against the good of love as all acts are regarded from one's intent. To shun evil as sin is to live forever in heaven.

"...it is evident that it was permitted them to swear by the name of Jehovah, or by Jehovah; but it is evident that it was nothing else than a representative of the confirmation of the internal man. But it is known that internal men, that is, those who have conscience, have no need to confirm anything by an oath; and that they do not thus confirm. To them oaths are a cause of shame. They can indeed say with some manner of asseveration that a thing is so, and can also confirm the truth by reasons; but to swear that it is so, they cannot. They have an internal bond by which they are bound, namely, that of conscience. To superadd to this an external bond, which is an oath, is like imputing to them that they are not upright in heart. The internal man is also of such a character that he loves to speak and act from freedom, but not from compulsion; for with them the internal compels the

external, but not the reverse. On which account they who have
conscience do not swear; still less do they who have perception of
good and truth, that is, celestial men. These do not even confirm
themselves or one another by reasons, but only say that a thing
is so, or is not so (n. 202, 337, 2718); wherefore they are still far-
ther removed from taking an oath.

"For these reasons, and because oaths were among the representatives which were to be abrogated, the Lord taught that
one should not swear at all, in these words in Matthew: *Ye have
heard that it was said, Thou shalt not forswear thyself; but shalt
perform unto the Lord thine oaths. But I say unto you, Swear
not at all; neither by the heaven, for it is God's throne; nor by the
earth, for it is the footstool of His feet; nor by Jerusalem, for it is
the city of the great king; neither shalt thou swear by thy head,
for thou canst not make one hair white or black. But let your
speech be, Yea, yea; nay, nay; and whatsoever is more than these,
is of evil* (v. 33-37). By these words is meant that one should not
swear at all by Jehovah, nor by anything which is of Jehovah or
the Lord." (*Heavenly Arcana*, n. 2842.9-10)

"*Thou shalt not be to him as a usurer.* That this signifies that
it shall be done from charity, is evident from the signification of
a usurer, as one who does good for the sake of gain; for a usurer
lends money to another for the sake of usury, and brings aid to
another for the sake of recompense. And because genuine charity regards not gain or recompense as an end, but the good of
the neighbor, therefore by, Thou shalt not be as a usurer, is signified that it shall be done from charity. He who does not know
what Christian charity is, may suppose that it consists not only
in giving to the needy and the poor, but also in doing good to a
fellow citizen, to one's country, and to the church, for any cause
whatever, or for any end whatever. But it is to be known that the
end is what determines the character of all the deeds of a man.
If his end or intention is to do good for the sake of reputation,
or to procure honors or gain, then the good which he does is not
good, because it is done for the sake of himself, and thus also
from himself. But if his end is to do good for the sake of a fellow

citizen, or of his country, or of the church, thus for the sake of the neighbor, then the good which a man does is good, for it is done for the sake of good itself, which in a general sense is the real neighbor (n. 5025, 6706, 6711, 6712, 8123); and thus also it is done for the sake of the Lord, for such good is not from man, but from the Lord, and what is from the Lord is the Lord's. It is this good which is meant by the Lord's words in Matthew: *Inasmuch as ye did it unto one of the least of these My brethren, ye did unto Me* (xxv. 40).

"As it is with good, so also it is with truth. They who do truth for the sake of truth, do it also for the sake of the Lord, because they do it from the Lord. To do truth for the sake of truth is to do good; for truth becomes good when from the intellectual it enters into the will, and from the will goes forth into act. To do good in this manner is Christian charity. They who do good from Christian charity sometimes have regard to reputation there-from, thus for honor or for gain, but altogether otherwise than they who regard these things as an end; for they regard what is good and just as the essential and only real thing, and thus in the highest place, and then they regard gain and honor, and consequent reputation, as relatively not essential, and thus in the lowest place. They who are of such a character, when they have in view what is just and good, are like those who fight in battle for their country and at the time have no concern for their life, nor for their rank and possessions in the world, which are then relatively of no account. But they who regard themselves and the world in the first place are such that they do not even see what is just and good, because they have in view only them-selves and their gain.

"From these things it is plain what it is to do good for the sake of self or the world, and what it is to do good for the sake of the Lord or the neighbor, and what the difference is between them — a difference as great as between two opposites, thus as great as between Heaven and Hell. Moreover they who do good for the sake of the neighbor or the Lord are in heaven; but they who do good for the sake of self and the world are in hell. For

they who do good for the sake of the neighbor and the Lord love
the Lord above all things and the neighbor as themselves, which
are the chief of all the commandments (Mark xii. 28-31). But
they who do all things for the sake of themselves and the world
love themselves above all things, thus more than they love God,
and not only do they despise their neighbor, but even hold him
in hatred if he does not make one with themselves and become
theirs. This is meant by what the Lord teaches in Matthew: *No
man can serve two masters: for either he will hate the one, and
love the other; or else he will hold to one and despise the other.
Ye cannot serve God and mammon* (vi. 24). There are those who
serve both; but they are those who are called lukewarm, and
neither cold nor hot, who are spewed out (Apoc. iii. 15, 16). From
these things it is now plain what was represented by usurers
who took usury, namely, they who do good for the sake of gain.

"Hence it is clear why it is said that one should not be as
a usurer and should not lay usury upon a brother — as also
in other passages in Moses: *Thou shalt not put usury on thy
brother; usury of silver, usury of victuals, usury of any thing that
is lent upon usury. Upon a stranger thou mayest put usury; but
upon thy brother thou shalt not put usury: that Jehovah thy God
may bless thee in all that thou puttest thine hand unto, in the
land whither thou goest in to possess it* (Deut. xxiii. 19, 20; Lev.
xxv. 36-38). To put upon a brother the usury of silver is to lend
truths or to instruct for the sake of gain; to put the usury of victuals is to lend the goods of truth for the sake of gain; for silver
is truth (n. 1551, 2954, 5658, 6914, 6917), and victuals or food is
the good of truth (n. 5147, 5295, 5340, 5342, 5410, 5426, 5487,
5576, 5582, 5588, 5655, 5915, 8562). That Jehovah will bless
those who do not do so, in all that they put their hand unto in
the land, is because they are in affection for good and truth, and
thus in the happiness of angels in heaven, for in this affection,
or in the good of this love, man's heaven consists (n. 6478, 9174).
The reason why it was allowed to put usury upon strangers was,
that by strangers are signified those who do not acknowledge
and receive anything of good and truth (n. 7996), and thus who

do good only for the sake of gain. These are to serve man, because they are servants respectively (n. 1097).

"So in David: *He who walketh uprightly, and worketh justice, and speaketh truth in his heart. ...He who putteth not out his silver to usury, and taketh not a reward against the innocent. He who doeth this shall never be moved* (Ps. xv. 2, 5) — where to put out his silver to usury is to teach for the sake of gain alone, and thus to do good for the sake of recompense. In like manner in Ezekiel: *If a man be just, and do judgment and justice ...give not forth upon usury, neither take any increase* (xviii. 5, 8). Again: *He who holdeth off his hand from the needy, that receiveth not usury nor increase, that executeth My judgments, who walketh in My statutes ...he shall surely live* (xviii. 17). Again: *In thee have they taken ...to shed blood; thou hast taken usury and increase, and thou hast taken gain of thy companions by violence* (xxii. 12). This is said of the city of bloods, by which is signified the falsity that destroys truth and good (n. 9127); taking usury and increase is doing good for the sake of gain and recompense, and thus not from charity. That genuine charity is free from all claim of merit, may be seen above (n. 2371, 2373, 2400, 4007, 4174, 4943, 6388-6390, 6392, 6478)." (*Heavenly Arcana*, n. 9210.1-5)

Psalm 16

Michtam of David.

~

Keep me, God, (1)
For I seek refuge in You.
You have said unto Jehovah, You are my Lord, (2)
My goodness is not beyond You.
To the holy ones who are in the earth, (3)
And the magnificent in whom is all my delight:
Their suffering shall be multiplied who hasten after another, (4)
I will not pour out their drink offerings of blood,
And I will not bear their names on my lips.
   Jehovah is the portion of my part and my cup, (5)
   You uphold my lot.
   The lines have fallen to me in pleasant places, (6)
   Moreover a goodly inheritance is upon me.
   I will bless Jehovah who has counseled me, (7)
   Moreover my kidneys chastise me in the nights.
   I have set Jehovah in front of me continually, (8)
   For He is at my right hand, I shall not be moved.
Therefore my heart rejoices, (9)
And my glory is glad,
Moreover my flesh shall reside in safety.
For You will not forsake my soul in hell, (10)
You will not suffer your Holy One to see corruption.
You will let me know the path of life, (11)
In Your presence is fullness of joy,
In Your right hand there are pleasures for evermore.

Psalm Commentary 16

Summary: The Lord's trust in Himself (v. 1-2) for delivering the good whom the evil infest (v. 3-4). His is the Divine (v. 5-6) and the Divine power (v. 7-8). His Human glorified will rise again (v. 9-11).

Keep me, God,
For I seek refuge in You.
You have said unto Jehovah, You are my Lord,
My goodness is not beyond You.
To the holy ones who are in the earth,
And the magnificent in whom is all my delight:
Their suffering shall be multiplied who hasten after another,
I will not pour out their drink offerings of blood,
And I will not bear their names on my lips (Ps. 16:1-4)

God is the Lord as to Divine truth (see Ps. 18:31, 29:1, 68:17,24, 82:1, 95:3, 147:7) which preserves those who trust in Him from falsity and evil. To say signifies perception of the will (see Ps. 33:9) and Jehovah is the Lord as to Divine love (see Ps. 18:31, 28:1, 68:26, 82:1, 147:7); the Lord (Hebrew *Adonai*) is Divine good in the Divine Human (see Ps. 68:17,26, 105:21, 110:1, 114:7). One's good is derived and originates from God alone. The holy ones are those in spiritual truths (see Ps. 5:7, 65:4) and the earth is the church as to truth (see Ps. 9:8, 24:1, 60:2, 90:2, 96:13). The magnificent are those who are in good (see Ps. 8:1) and are thus associated with delight or joy from the good of love. Suffering or wounds signify the harm from doing evil (see Ps. 38:4-5); a "drink offering of blood" signifies those who have profaned and falsified the Divine truth signified by blood (see Ps. 5:6, 16:4, 105:29), for in the positive sense to drink is to be instructed in the truth (see Ps. 78:15). To not bear the name on the lip is to not follow after their false doctrine (see Ps. 12:4, 81:5).

"In Moses: It shall be said, *Where are their gods, the rock in which they trusted; which did eat the fat of their sacrifices, and drank the wine of their drink offering? Let them rise up and help* them (Deut. xxxii. 37, 38). Gods stand for falsities as above, that did eat the fat of their sacrifices for their destroying the good of worship, that drank the wine of their drink offerings for their destroying the truth of worship. Drink offerings are also predicated of blood, in David: *Their sorrows shall be multiplied; they have hastened to another; their drink offerings of blood will I not offer, and I will not take up their names upon my lips* (Ps. xvi. 4); and by them are signified the profanations of truth; for blood in that sense is violence offered to charity (n. 374, 1005), and profanation (n. 1003)." (*Heavenly Arcana*, n. 4581.11)

Jehovah is the portion of my part and my cup,
You uphold my lot,
The lines have fallen to me in pleasant places;
Moreover a goodly inheritance is upon me. (Ps. 16:4-6)

Jehovah is the Lord as to Divine love (see Ps. 18:31, 28:1, 68:26, 82:1, 147:7); one's portion is one's eternal inheritance from good. The word "lot" can also be translated as "pebble," and refers to casting lots by drawing pebbles from a cup. Rocks signify truth (see Ps. 18:46, 19:14, 28:1, 78:15) and a cup signifies external truth (see Ps. 11:6); one's lot is one's eternal inheritance from truth. The lines falling in pleasant places refer to the borders of a plot of land received by lot, and spiritually refer to one's eternal portion from knowledges of truth and good, for to measure is to know one's quality of state (see Ps. 31:8, 39:4, 40:5). The pleasant places refer to spiritual happiness of doing good from truth; a goodly inheritance is one's spiritual inheritance from the faith of charity (see Ps. 68:9, 69:35-36). In the highest sense this refers to the deliverance of those infested by falsehoods by Lord, who is Jehovah in human form, described as having Jehovah (the Divine itself) as the portion of His cup (the external human form.)

"*And the land that it is pleasant.* That this signifies that in that, namely happiness, are they who are in the Lord's kingdom, is evident from the signification of land, as the church... and from the signification of being pleasant, as signifying the happiness in works of good without recompense. It is said that he shall see rest that it is good, and the land that it is pleasant, and by both is signified the happiness which is in the Lord's kingdom, because to see rest that it is good, refers to what is celestial or to good, and to see the land that it is pleasant, refers to what is spiritual or to truth, and this on account of the marriage of good and truth (n. 6343)." (*Heavenly Arcana*, n. 6392)

I will bless Jehovah who has counseled me,
Moreover my kidneys chasten me in the nights.
I have set Jehovah in front of me continually,
For He is at my right hand, I shall not be moved. (Ps. 16:7-8)

To bless Jehovah is to acknowledge that all that is good comes from the Lord (see Ps. 3:8, 16:7, 21:6, 24:5, 28:6, 31:21, 96:2); counsel is to guided from Divine good. Kidneys correspond to truth which explores and judges a person to purify from falsities (see Ps. 7:9); to chasten is to correct evils (see Ps. 2:10, 94:10). Night is the state when falsity is dominant (see Ps. 3:8, 16:7, 32:4, 74:16, 91:6, 104:20, 136:9). To set Jehovah in front is to have Divine love as the focus of one's life, as Jehovah signifies the Lord as to Divine love (see Ps. 18:31, 28:1, 68:26, 82:1, 147:7). The right hand signifies power from Divine truth (see Ps. 20:6, 44:3, 45:4, 80:15,17, 89:13,21, 110:1, 121:5); to not be moved is to not fall into falsity (see Ps. 104:5).

"*I will bless Jehovah, who hath given me counsel; also my reins chastise me in the night (Ps. xvi. 7).*

'Night' signifies the state of man when falsities rise up; the consequent combat of truths with falsities is signified by 'my reins chastise me.'" (*Apocalypse Explained*, n. 167.5)

"By blessing is meant all the good which man has from the Lord, as power and opulence, and the things which accompany them; but especially all spiritual good, as love and wisdom, charity and faith, and hence the joy and happiness which are of life eternal: and because all these are from the Lord, it follows that they are in Him; for unless they were in Him, they could not be in others from Him. Hence it is, that the Lord is called Blessed in the Word, and also Blessing, that is blessing itself. That Jehovah, that is, the Lord, is called Blessed, is manifest from these places: *The High priest asked Jesus, Art thou the Christ the Son of the Blessed?* (Mark xiv. 61). *Jesus said, Ye shall not see Me hereafter, until ye say, Blessed is He who cometh in the name of the Lord* (Matt. xxiii. 39; Luke xiii. 35). *Melchizedek blessed Abram, and said, Blessed be God Most High, who hath given thine enemies into thy hand* (Gen. xiv. 18-20). *Blessed be Jehovah the God of Shem* (Gen. ix. 26). *Blessed be Jehovah, who hath heard my voice* (Ps. xxviii. 6). *Blessed be Jehovah, because He hath made marvelous His kindness* (Ps. xxxi. 21). *Blessed be Jehovah from everlasting even to everlasting* (Ps. xli. 13. So, too, Ps. lxvi. 20; Ps. lxviii. 19, 35; Ps. lxxii. 18, 19; Ps. lxxxix. 52; Ps. cxix. 12; Ps. cxxiv. 6; Ps. cxxxv. 21; Ps. cxliv. 1; Luke i. 68). Hence it is that it is here said Blessing, as also vers. 12; and chap. vii. 12: and in David, *Glory and honor hast Thou laid upon Him, since Thou makest Him a blessing for ever* (Ps. xxi. 5, 6): this is concerning the Lord. It may be seen from these things what is meant in the Word by blessing God; that it is to ascribe to Him all blessing; also by praying that He would bless, and by giving thanks because He has blessed; as may be evident from these passages following: The mouth of Zacharias was opened, and he spake, blessing God (Luke i. 64, 68). Simeon took up the infant Jesus in his arms, and blessed God (Luke ii. 28). *Bless ye Jehovah, who hath counselled for me* (Ps. xvi. 7). *Bless ye the name of Jehovah, preach the good tidings of His salvation from day to day* (Ps. xcvi. 1-3). *Blessed be the Lord from day to day: bless ye God in the congregations, the Lord from the fountain of Israel* (Ps. lxviii. 19, 26)." (*Apocalypse Revealed*, n. 289).

Therefore my heart rejoices,
And my glory is glad,
Moreover my flesh shall reside in safety. (Ps. 16:9)

To rejoice is to have joy from love of the will and is thus mentioned with heart (see Ps. 7:9, 22:10, 24:4, 51:10, 64:6, 66:18, 71:23, 78:8, 86:11); glory is the Divine truth (see Ps. 8:5, 19:1, 24:7-10, 29:1, 73:24, 96:3) and to be glad is to be happy from the mind or thought (see Ps. 14:7). Flesh signifies one's will or the voluntary (see Ps. 63:1, 78:39) and here refers to one's will to do good; safety is the external delight of heaven (see Ps. 4:8); to not be forsaken is to be preserved from falsehood (see Ps. 27:9); the soul is one's life of the spiritual understanding (see Ps. 22:10, 31:9, 71:23, 107:9); hell is one's state of final condemnation and also represents those in the falsity of evil (see Ps. 18:5).

"Flesh also signifies good in many other passages in the Word, as in these: *I will take away the heart of stone from their flesh, and will give them a heart of flesh* (Ezek. xi. 19; xxxvi. 26). *My flesh longeth for thee in a land of drought* (Ps. lxiii. 1). *My heart and my flesh cry out for the living God* (Ps. lxxxiv. 2). *My flesh shall dwell in trust* (Ps. xvi. 9). *When thou seest the naked that thou cover him, and that thou hide not thyself from thy flesh* (Isa. lviii. 7)." (*Apocalypse Revealed*, n. 832)

For You will not forsake my soul in hell,
You will not suffer your Holy One to see corruption.
You will let me know the path of life,
In Your presence is fullness of joy,
In Your right hand there are pleasures for evermore. (Ps. 16:10-11)

This verse is a prophecy concerning the Lord's resurrection following His descent into the lower regions of hell while His body lay in the tomb (see Acts 2:23-28, 13:35-37). While flesh and blood suffer corruption, the body of the Lord did not suffer this fate as it was glorified and made Divine. The Holy One is the one who is Divine truth itself (see Ps. 71:22). Corruption can also be translated as pit which concerns those caught in the lower earth (see Ps. 28:1, 69:15, 88:4,6). These were delivered and ascended into heaven upon the death and resurrection of Jesus Christ (see Matt. 27:52-53, 1 Pet. 3:19). The "path of life" is the truth of good (see Ps. 25:4) that leads to the eternal life of heaven, and in the highest sense life is the Lord Himself (see Ps. 27:13, 36:9). The presence or face of the Lord signifies His Divine love (see Ps. 4:6, 13:1, 22:24, 27:8-9, 31:16, 67:1); fullness or to be filled with food is to receive good from the joy of love (see Ps. 14:7). His right hand is the power from His Divine truth (see Ps. 20:6, 44:3, 45:4, 80:15,17, 89:13,21, 110:1, 121:5) and pleasures for evermore refer to happiness in spiritual truths (see Ps. 16:6). When Jesus was glorified His human became united with the Divine love, and had all Divine omnipotence (Matt. 28:18). Thus when scripture states that Jesus rose from the dead to sit at the right hand of God it means His human had Divine omnipotence, as the Lord had become united with the Father.

Psalm 17

A Prayer of David.

~

Hear, Jehovah, what is right, (1)
Listen to my cry.
Give ear to my prayer,
Which is not with deceitful lips.
Let my judgment come forth from Your presence, (2)
Let Your eyes behold uprightness.
You have proven my heart, (3)
You have visited by night.
You have refined me, You shall find nothing,
I intend that my mouth shall not disobey.
As for the works of Man *they are* by the word of Your lips, (4)
As for me, I have kept from the paths of robbers.
Hold up my steps, (5)
That my footsteps slip not.
I have called upon You, for You will answer me, God, (6)
Incline Your ear to me, my speech.
    Set apart Your mercy, Saviour of those who seek refuge, (7)
    From those who rise up by Your right hand.
    Keep me as the apple, the daughter of the eye, (8)
    Hide me under the shadow of Your wings,
    From the face of the wicked who devastate me, (9)
    My enemies against the soul encircle upon me.
    They are enclosed in their own fat, (10)
    With their mouth they speak in pride.
    They have now compassed us in our steps, (11)
    They have set their eyes to stretch out in the earth:

His likeness is as a lion that longs to tear apart, (12)
And as a young lion dwelling in secret places.
    Arise, Jehovah, confront his face, have him bow, (13)
    Rescue my soul from the wicked by Your sword,
    From *murderers* by Your hand, Jehovah, (14)
    From *murderers* of this age who have their portion in this life.
    And with Your hidden treasure fill their belly,
    The sons are satisfied and leave the rest to their babes.
    As for me, I will behold Your face in righteousness, (15)
    I shall be satisfied when I awake to Your figure.

Psalm Commentary   17

Summary: The Lord concerning the integrity of His life (v. 1-5) from the Divine in Himself (v. 6) from which He is sustained against the evil who rise up against Him and wish to slay Him (v. 7-12). Nevertheless He cannot be hurt (v. 13) and yet they possess the Word (v. 14). He will be glorified (v. 15).

Hear, Jehovah, what is right, listen to my cry,
Give ear to my prayer which is not with deceitful lips.
Let my judgment come forth from Your presence,
Let Your eyes behold uprightness.
You have proven my heart,
You have visited by night. (Ps. 17:1-3)

Jehovah is the Lord as to Divine love (see Ps. 18:31, 28:1, 68:26, 82:1, 147:7) and is the origin of righteousness which is the good of charity (see Ps. 14:5, 36:6, 37:6,17, 72:2, 89:14, 92:12). Listen and cry are predicated of what is good (see Ps. 5:2 and Ps. 30:5, 61:1, 88:2). Prayer is according to the good of one's life (see Ps. 4:1, 66:19, 72:15); deceitful lips signifies false doctrine (see Ps. 12:4, 81:5) with intent to deceive others. Prayers are heard only as far as they are in accordance with good and truth. Judgment is Divine truth which judges (see Ps. 36:6, 37:6, 72:2, 89:14, 92:12) which comes from God's presence or face which signifies His Divine good (see Ps. 4:6, 13:1, 22:24, 27:8-9, 31:16, 67:1). His eyes signify Divine foresight (see Ps. 17:6) and upright is truth from good (see Ps. 9:8, 11:3, 25:21, 96:10, 143:10). To prove the

heart means to explore the will, to visit in the night is to explore
the thoughts in a state of obscurity as to the truth (see Ps. 3:8,
16:7, 32:4, 74:16, 91:6, 104:20, 136:9).

You have refined me, You shall find nothing,
I intend that my mouth shall not disobey.
As for the works of Man they are by the word of Your lips,
As for me, I have kept from the paths of robbers.
Hold up my steps,
That my footsteps slip not.
I have called upon You, for You will answer me, God:
Incline Your ear to me, hear my speech. (Ps. 17:3-6)

To refine is to become purified through temptation (see
Ps. 66:10). The mouth is the external understanding (see Ps. 5:9,
37:30, 135:16) and the wages of Man (Hebrew *adam*) is one's
reward of heaven or hell according to one's good or evil (see
Ps. 109:20). The word of the lips are the truths of doctrine (see
Ps. 12:4, 81:5); paths are falsehoods concerning evil (see Ps. 25:4);
robbers are those who take away that which is good through
falsehood. Steps concern how one lives one's life; feet refer to
the external natural (see Ps. 8:6, 41:9, 49:5, 99:5, 105:18). To
answer signifies Divine influx of good and truth to those willing
to receive it (see Ps. 4:1). Hearing in reference to the Lord signifies Divine providence:

"That hearing in the supreme sense signifies providence,
may be evident from what was said above (n. 3863) concerning
seeing, as in the supreme sense foresight; for the Lord's fore-
seeing is the seeing from eternity to eternity that so a thing is;
but the Lord's providing is the ruling that a thing be so, and the
bending of man's freedom to good, so far as He foresees that man
suffers himself to be bended in freedom (see n. 3854)...

"That hearing in the supreme sense signifies providence, and
seeing foresight, is evident from the passages in the Word where
eyes and ears are predicated of Jehovah, or the Lord — as in
Isaiah: *Incline Thine ear, O Jehovah, and hear; open Thine eyes,*
O Jehovah, and see (xxxvii. 17). In Daniel: *O my God, incline*

*Thine ear, and hear; open, O Jehovah, Thine eyes, and see our
desolations* (ix. 18). In David: *O God, incline Thine ear unto me,
and hear my speech* (Ps. xvii. 6). Again: *Incline Thine ear unto
me, and save me* (Ps. lxxi. 2). Again: *Give ear to my supplications,
in Thy truth answer me, and in Thy justice* (Ps. cxliii. 1). In Jeremiah: *O Jehovah ...Thou heardest my voice; hide not thine ear at
my breathing, at my cry* (Lam. iii. 55, 56). In David: *O Jehovah
...hide not Thy face from me, in the day of my distress; incline
Thine ear to me; in the day when I call, answer me* (Ps. cii. 1, 2).
It is known that Jehovah has not ears nor eyes, like a man, but
that it is an attribute predicable of the Divine, which is signified by ear and by eye, namely, infinite will and infinite understanding. Infinite will is providence, and infinite understanding
is foresight; these are what are understood by ear and eye in the
supreme sense, when they are attributed to Jehovah." (*Heavenly
Arcana*, n. 3869.3,13)

*Set apart Your mercy, Saviour of those who seek refuge,
From those who rise up by Your right hand.
Keep me as the apple, the daughter of the eye,
Hide me under the shadow of Your wings* (Ps. 17:7-8)

God's mercy is His Divine love (see Ps. 25:10, 26:3, 36:5,
89:14, 103:8) by which there is salvation (see Ps. 14:7, 96:2), and
His right hand is power from Divine truth (see Ps. 20:6, 44:3,
45:4, 80:15,17, 89:13,21, 110:1, 121:5). Those who rise up refer
to the evils of hell which rise up to attack the good of heaven, for
hell always rises up to attack, but heaven defends (see Ps. 3:1).
Fruit represents the good works of life (see Ps. 1:3, 21:10, 72:16,
107:37, 127:3, 148:9) and here apple signifies the good of wisdom;
daughters signify affections (see Ps. 45:9-10), in this case affection of spiritual understanding signified by eye (see Ps. 11:4,
13:3, 31:9, 69:23). Wings represent the power of spiritual truth,
which protect against falsehoods:

"That wings are spiritual truths, is because birds in general signify intellectual things and thoughts (n. 40, 745, 776,
3219, 5149, 7441); and for this reason wings are spiritual truths,

inasmuch as all the intellectual is from these truths. The intellectual derived from falsities, however discerning and acute it appears, is not the intellectual; for the real intellectual sees from the light of heaven, and the light of heaven is spiritual truth, that is, the truth of faith. Wherefore where there is not the truth of faith, there is not light, but thick darkness, and an intellectual in thick darkness is no intellectual. Wings also are the powers which belong to spiritual truth from its good; for the wings with birds are as the hands or arms with man, and by the arms and hands are signified powers ...That wings are truth Divine is also evident from the following passages: *They that wait upon Jehovah shall renew their strength, they shall mount up with wings as eagles* (Isa. xl. 31). In David: God *rode upon a cherub, and did fly: yea, He flew swiftly upon the wings of the wind* (Ps. xviii. 10; civ. 3) — describing the Divine truth and its power. Again: *Jehovah shall cover thee under His wing, and under His wings shalt thou take refuge: His truth is a shield and a buckler* (Ps. xci. 4). To be covered with the wing of Jehovah and to take refuge under His wings stands for protection and confidence which is of faith. The like is meant by being hid under the shadow of God's wings (Ps. xvii. 8), and taking refuge under the shadow of His wings (Ps. xxxvi. 7; lvii. 1; lxi. 4), and rejoicing in the shadow of His wings (Ps. lxiii. 7)." (*Heavenly Arcana*, n. 8764.2,8; see also *Apocalypse Revealed*, n. 245)

From the face of the wicked who devastate me,
My enemies against the soul encircle upon me.
They are enclosed in their own fat,
With their mouth they speak in pride. (Ps. 17:9-10)

The face of the wicked is the evil of falsity which destroys that which is good; enemies are the falsehoods of hell which attack the truth (see Ps. 3:1, 27:12) and the soul is the spiritual life from the understanding (see Ps. 22:10, 31:9, 71:23, 107:9). "Against the soul" can be literally translated as "in the soul" indicating internal spiritual temptations. Fat signifies celestial good (see Ps. 23:5, 36:8, 63:5, 65:11, 81:16, 92:14, 147:14), but

here refers to those who are in the love of self; their mouth is the
external understanding of falsehood (see Ps. 5:9, 37:30, 135:16)
derived from the love of self signified by speaking proudly. The
symbolism of fat is described in the following passage:

"As the Jewish and Israelitish nation was only in external
worship, and not also in internal worship, and in consequence
was in no good of love and in no good of charity and faith:—

> It was forbidden them to eat the fat and blood, and it was
> declared that they would be cut off if they should eat them
> (*Lev.* iii. 17; vii. 23, 26).

But to those who are in internal worship and from that in external worship, such as those must be who will be of the Lord's New
Church, it is said:—

> That they shall eat fat till they be full, and drink blood till
> they be drunken (*Ezek.* xxxix. 19);

'fat' here signifying all the good of heaven and of the church, and
'blood' all their truth. In the contrary sense those who are 'fat'
signify those who are nauseated at good, or who at least despise
and reject it (*Deut.* xxxii. 15; *Jer.* v. 28; l. 11; *Ps.* xvii. 10; xx.
4; lxviii. 31; cxix. 70; and elsewhere)." (*Apocalypse Explained*,
n. 1159.4)

Casting me out they have now compassed me,
They have set their eyes to stretch out in the earth:
His likeness is as a lion that longs to tear apart,
And as a young lion dwelling in secret places. (Ps. 17:11-12)

This may prophetically refer to Jesus being crucified outside
of the city, with His arms stretched out on the cross (see note
on translation). To be cast out is for good to be rejected by evil;
eyes are internal falsehoods of the understanding which are
opposed to truths of the church signified by earth (see Ps. 9:8,
24:1, 60:2, 90:2, 96:13). A lion represents the power of falsity
from evil destroying (see Ps. 10:9, 57:4). A lion that tears apart
is falsity that destroys external good (see Ps. 7:2); a young lion

dwelling in secret places is interior falsity that destroys internal good (see Ps. 91:13).

"Because 'the kings of Judah and Israel' represented the Lord in respect to Divine truth, and because a 'throne' represented the judgment, which is effected according to Divine truth, and because 'lions' represented power, guard, and protection against falsities and evils, therefore near the two stays of the throne built by Solomon there were two lions, and twelve lions on the six steps on the one side and on the other (1 *Kings* x. 18-20). From this it can be seen what 'lions' in the Word signify when the Lord, heaven, and the church are treated of. 'Lions' in the Word signify also the power of falsity from evil by which the church is destroyed and devastated. As in *Jeremiah:*—

> *The young lions roar against her, they give forth their voice, they reduce the land to wasteness* (ii. 15).

In *Isaiah:*—

> *A nation whose arrows are sharp, and all his bows bent, the hoofs of his horses are accounted as rock, his roaring like that of a lion, he roareth like a young lion, and he growleth and seizeth the prey* (v. 28, 29).

Besides many other places (as in *Isa.* xi. 6; xxxv. 9; *Jer.* iv. 7; v. 6; xii. 8; l. 17; li. 38; *Ezek.* xix. 3, 5, 6; *Hos.* xiii. 7, 8; *Joel* i. 6. 7; *Ps.* xvii. 12; xxii. 13; lvii. 4; lviii. 6; xci. 13)." (*Apocalypse Explained*, n. 278.11)

Arise, Jehovah, confront his face, have him bow,
Rescue my soul from the wicked by Your sword,
From murderers by Your hand, Jehovah,
From murderers of this age who have their portion in this life
(Ps. 17:13-14)

For Jehovah to confront the face and have him bow down is to subdue evil; to rescue the soul from the wicked is to deliver from falsehoods (see Ps. 91:14) by truth fighting against falsity, signified by sword (see Ps. 7:12, 22:16, 37:14, 45:3, 57:4, 78:62,64,

149:5). The first instance of murderers are those who extinguish falsehoods and are thus mentioned with hand, which signifies the power of Divine truth (see Ps. 20:6, 44:3, 45:4, 80:15,17, 89:13,21, 110:1, 121:5); the second instance of murderers are evils which destroy good, or one's spiritual life, as they only have regard to the life of the body.

And with Your hidden treasure fill their belly,
The sons are satisfied and leave the rest to their babes. (Ps. 17:14)

The belly signifies internal reception of the Word (see Ps. 31:9, 40:8, 127:3); the hidden treasure is the spiritual sense hidden behind its literal sense, signified by treasure (see Ps. 33:7, 135:4,7). Sons signify those in truth (see Ps. 45:16, 127:3, 128:3,6) who are satisfied from the Word; babes are those who are in the innocence of love (see Ps. 8:2). The spiritual meaning of belly is explained from the Apocalypse:

"*And when I had eaten it my belly was made bitter,* signifies that it was perceived and ascertained that the Word was inwardly undelightful because of the adulterated truth of the sense of its letter. This is evident from the explanations above (n. 617, 618), where there are like words. The 'belly' here signifies the interiors of the Word, which are called spiritual, because exploration was represented by 'devouring or eating up the little book,' which means the Word, and by its taste, which means perception; therefore the first perception is signified by the taste in the mouth, where the little book was 'sweet as honey.' The first perception of the Word is such as is the perception of the sense of its letter, that is, as the Word is outwardly. The other perception however is signified by its taste when it has come into the belly, which is said to be made bitter by it. This other perception of the Word is such as the perception of its spiritual sense is, that is, as the Word is inwardly. Consequently, as the 'mouth' signifies what is exterior, so here the 'belly' signifies what is interior, because inwardly received and ascertained. The 'belly' signifies interior things because the belly stores up the food inwardly, and 'food' signifies everything that nourishes the soul; also because the belly, like the bowels, is within or in the midst of the body; for this reason the 'belly,' and also the 'bowels,' signify in the Word interior things. That the 'belly,' and the 'bowels' signify interior things can be seen from the following passages. In *Ezekiel:*—

> *Son of man, feed thy belly and fill thy bowels with this roll* (iii. 1, 3).

This has a similar signification as what is now being explained in the *Apocalypse,* that 'he took and ate up the little book,' for the 'roll' has a similar signification as 'the little book,' namely, the Word, and 'to feed the belly and fill the bowels with the roll' signifies to explore how the Word is understood in the church, which is done by the reading and perception of it. In *David:*—

> *Fill their belly with Thy treasure; the sons are fed to the full, and what remains to them they leave to their babes* (Ps. xvii. 14).

'Treasure' signifies the truth of the Word, 'belly' the interior understanding, so 'to fill their belly with treasure' signifies to instruct their interior understanding in the truths of the Word; that thence those who are affected by truths are fully instructed is signified by 'the sons are fed to the full,' 'sons' signifying those who are in the affection of truth; and the sons' 'babes,' truths in their birth; of such it is said that 'what remains to them they leave to their babes.' It is here said the interior understanding, for man has an exterior understanding and an interior understanding; the exterior understanding is of the natural mind, and the interior understanding is of the spiritual mind; the interior understanding is signified by the 'belly.'...

The 'bowels' have a similar signification as the 'belly,' as can be seen from the following passages. In *Isaiah:*—

> *My bowels are moved like a harp for Moab, and My inward part for Kir-heres* (xvi. 11).

In *David:*—

Bless Jehovah, O my soul, and all my bowels the name of His holiness (Ps. ciii. 1).

In the same:—

I have desired to do Thy will, O my God, and Thy law is in my bowels (Ps. xl. 8)." (Apocalypse Explained, n. 622.1-3, 10)

As for me, I will behold Your face in righteousness:
I shall be satisfied when I awake to Your figure. (Ps. 17:15)

The face of God is His Divine good (see Ps. 4:6, 13:1, 22:24, 27:8-9, 31:16, 67:1) which flows in as righteousness which is to do what is good (see Ps. 36:6, 37:6, 72:2, 89:14, 92:12). To be satisfied or filled is to appropriate what is good; to awake is to come out of a merely natural life and be enlightened and receive spiritual life by living by the truth (see Ps. 13:3, 76:5, 78:65). The Hebrew word for "figure" is also used concerning the appearance of an angel or spirit (see Job 4:16), and in the highest sense refers to the Divine Human of the Lord. This thus also describes how one will awake after death to the spiritual life, to see God's face in the light of heaven. In the highest sense this refers to the union of the Divine with the human in the Lord.

Psalm 18

To the chief musician, of the servant of Jehovah, of David, who spake
unto Jehovah the words of this song in the day that Jehovah delivered him from the hand of all his enemies, and from the hand of Saul.
And he said, I will love You, Jehovah, my perseverance. (1)

~

Jehovah is my cliff, and my fortress, and my deliverer, (2)
My God, my rock, in whom I seek refuge,
My shield, and the horn of my salvation, my high fort.
I will call upon Jehovah with praise, (3)
And I shall be saved from my enemies.
 The cords of death surrounded me, (4)
 And the torrents of Belial terrified me.
 The cords of hell compassed me about, (5)
 The snares of death confronted me.
 In my distress I called upon Jehovah, (6)
 And cried to my God.
 He heard my voice out of His temple,
 And my cry came before Him in His ears.
  And the earth shook and quaked, (7)
  And the foundations of the mountains were agitated,
  And they were shaken for He was upset.
  There went up a smoke in His nostrils, (8)
  And fire out of His mouth devoured: coals were kindled by it.
  And He stretched out the heavens, and came down, (9)
  And thick fog was under His feet.
  And He rode upon a cherub, and flew, (10)
  And He soared upon the wings of the wind.
  He made darkness His secret place, (11)

His pavilion round about Him were darkness of waters, clouds of
the skies.
From the brightness in front of Him His clouds passed, (12)
Hail and coals of fire.
And Jehovah thundered in the heavens, (13)
And the Most High gave His voice,
Hail and coals of fire.
And He sent out His arrows and scattered them, (14)
And He shot out lightnings and routed them.
And the channels of waters were seen, (15)
And the foundations of the world were uncovered,
From Your rebuke, Jehovah,
From the breath of the spirit of Your nostrils.
He sent from above, He took me, (16)
He drew me out of many waters.
He delivered me from my strong enemy, (17)
And from those who hated me for they persisted after me.
They confronted me in the day of my calamity, (18)
But Jehovah was my support.
And He brought me forth to a broad place, (19)
He rescued me for He was delighted in me.
Jehovah rewarded me according to my righteousness, (20)
According to the cleanness of my hands He has returned to me.
For I have kept the ways of Jehovah, (21)
And have not done wickedly against my God.
For all His judgments were in front of me, (22)
And I did not put away His statutes from me.
And I was perfect with Him, (23)
And I kept myself from my iniquity.
And Jehovah returned to me according to my righteousness, (24)
According to the cleanness of my hands in front of His eyes.
With the merciful You will be merciful, (25)
With a perfect mighty one You will be perfect,
With the pure You will be pure, (26)
And with the perverse You will struggle.
For You will save the afflicted people, (27)
And will bring down exalted eyes.
For You will light my lamp, (28)
Jehovah my God will enlighten my darkness.

For with You I have run through a troop, (29)
And by my God I have leaped over a wall.
As for God, His way is perfect, (30)
The saying of Jehovah is refined,
He is a shield to all who seek refuge in Him.
For who is God beside Jehovah? (31)
And who is a rock except our God?
It is the God who girds me with valour, (32)
And makes my way perfect.
He makes my feet like that of a hind, (33)
And makes me to stand upon my high places.
He teaches my hands for war, (34)
And a bow of brass is bent in my arms.
And You have given me the shield of Your salvation, (35)
And Your right hand has sustained me,
And Your meekness has increased me.
You have enlarged my steps under me, (36)
And my ankles falter not.
I have pursued my enemies and overtaken them, (37)
And I did not return till they were consumed.
I have stricken them and they were not able to rise, (38)
They are fallen under my feet.
And You have girded me with valour for the battle, (39)
You have made those who rose up against me to bow under me.
And You have given to me the necks of my enemies, (40)
And I have put an end to them who hate me.
They cried but there was none to save, (41)
Unto Jehovah but He answered them not.
And I pulverized them as dust upon the face of the wind, (42)
I emptied them out as the mire in the streets.
You have rescued me from the arguing of the people, (43)
And You have made me the head of the nations,
A people whom I have not known shall serve me.
At the hearing of the ear they shall hearken to me, (44)
Sons of foreigners shall submit themselves to me.
Sons of foreigners shall fade away, (45)
And tremble out of their enclosures.
Jehovah lives, and blessed be my rock, (46)
And let the God of my salvation be exalted.

It is God who gives me vengeance, (47)
And He subdues people under me.
He rescues me from my enemies, (48)
Yes, You lift me up above those who rise up against me,
You have delivered me from the violent man.
Therefore I will confess You among the nations, Jehovah, (49)
And make music to Your name.
He magnifies salvation to His king, (50)
And does mercy to His anointed,
To David and to his seed for evermore.

Psalm Commentary 18

Summary: Confidence of the Lord from the Divine against the hells (v. 1-3) and combats of the Lord against the hells (v. 4-6), by which He descended and subjugated them (v. 7-11, 12-15), after which the righteous were delivered by the Divine truth (v. 16-19) and were rewarded according to their deeds (v. 20-24). From this they have Divine influx (v. 25-29). Acknowledgment of Jehovah (v. 30-32) and influx from the Divine (v. 33-36) by which the Lord fought against temptations from hell and defeated them (v. 37-41) and created a new church that worshipped Him (v. 42-45). Praise of the new church for deliverance from evil (v. 46-50).

Jehovah is my cliff, and my fortress, and my deliverer,
My God, my rock, in whom I seek refuge,
My shield, and the horn of my salvation, my high fort.
I will call upon Jehovah with praise,
And I shall be saved from my enemies. (Ps. 18:2-3)

A cliff represents external truth, a fortress represents spiritual truth which defend against falsehoods, and a deliverer represents the Lord who is truth itself who delivers one out of falsehoods (see Ps. 91:14). A rock signifies the Lord as to Divine truth (see Ps. 18:46, 19:14, 28:1, 78:15) and to seek refuge is to have faith. A shield here is external truth which protects against evil and falsity (see Ps. 144:2). A horn signifies the power of truth (see Ps. 22:21, 44:5, 89:17, 112:9, 132:17, 148:14) through which there is salvation or deliverance from evil (see Ps. 14:7, 96:2), thus "horn of salvation" represents spiritual truth. A high fort

211

represents internal celestial truth. Praise is worship from affection for truth (see Ps. 7:17, 35:18); enemies are falsehoods which
attack the truth (see Ps. 3:1, 27:12).

*"I will love Thee, O Jehovah, my strength; Jehovah is my
rock, and my fortress, and my deliverer, my God, my strong rock
in whom I trust, my shield, and the horn of my salvation* (Ps.
xviii. 1, 2; 2 Sam. xxii. 2, 3). The horn of salvation stands for
truth as to power. Here strength, rock, fortress, God, strong rock,
and shield, are all significative of the power of truth." (*Heavenly
Arcana*, n. 2832.2)

A cliff is distinct from rock - a cliff signifies external truth, as
opposed to internal spiritual truth:

*"He made him to ride on the high places of the earth, and fed
him with the produce of the fields, he made him to suck honey
out of the cliff; and oil out of the flint of the rock* (Deut. xxxii.
13).This is in the song of Moses, which treats of the church in
its beginning, and afterward in its progress, and finally in its
end. Those that constituted the Ancient Church are described by
these words, not those however who constituted the Israelitish
Church, for these were evil from the beginning even to the end,
as can be seen from their fathers in Egypt, and afterwards in
the wilderness; but the Ancient Church, the men of which are
meant by 'their fathers,' was that which the Lord 'made to ride
on the high places of the earth, and fed with the produce of the
fields.' That to these the good of natural love and the good of
spiritual love with their delights were given by means of truths,
from which they had their intelligence and according to which
they lived, is signified by 'he made him to suck honey out of the
cliff, and oil out of the flint of the rock,' 'honey' signifying the
delight of natural love, 'oil,' the delight of spiritual love, and 'the
cliff' and 'the flint of the rock,' truth from the Lord. (That 'oil'
signifies the good of love and charity, may be seen above, n. 375;
and that 'cliffs' and 'rocks' signify truth from the Lord, n. 411,
443a)." (*Apocalypse Explained*, n. 619.10)

*The cords of death surrounded me,
And the torrents of Belial terrified me.*

The cords of hell compassed me about,
The snares of death confronted me. (Ps. 18:4-5)

This describes the Lord's combats with the hells. The cords of death are temptations from the hell of evils which holds the will in bondage; the torrents of Belial represent a flood of false temptations; the cords of hell are temptations from the hell of falsehoods which holds the mind in bondage; snares signify the allurement and deception of evil.

"The *cords* and *snares of death* that compassed and prevented, signify temptations; which, because they are from hell, are also called the cords of hell. These, and all the other things in this Psalm, treat of the combats and of the victories of the Lord. Wherefore it is also said, *Thou wilt make Me the Head of the nations: a people which I have not known shall serve Me* (verse 43)." (*Doctrine of the Lord*, n. 14)

"*For it will be a snare unto thee.* That this signifies by the allurement and deception of evils, is evident from the signification of a snare, when applied to evils, as allurement and deception." (*Heavenly Arcana*, n. 9348)

In Hebrew the word "cord" can also be translated to refer to a band or a a group of people, as cords represent what binds a group together. Swedenborg describes the appearance of these cords in the spiritual world:

"...in the other life there appear ropes or cords of various twist and thickness, and by them are represented various modes of conjunction. For this reason it is that by ropes or cords in the Word also are signified the things which conjoin, as in the following passages — in Isaiah: *Woe unto them who draw iniquity with cords of vanity, and sin as it were with cart ropes* (v. 18) — where cords of vanity are conjunctions of falsities, by which there is iniquity or evil of life." (*Heavenly Arcana*, n. 9854.2)

"The very cause of the wicked man's leading himself deeper into evil, is that he introduces himself more and more interiorly, and also more and more deeply, into infernal societies, as he wills and does evil; hence also the enjoyment of evil grows; and this so occupies his thoughts, that at length he feels nothing sweeter. And he who has introduced himself more interiorly and deeply into infernal societies, becomes as if he were bound around with cords; but as long as he lives in the world, he does not feel the cords; they are as of soft wool, or of smooth threads of silk, which he loves because they titillate: but after death, these cords from being soft become hard, and instead of titillating they become galling." (*Angelic Wisdom concerning Divine Providence*, n. 296)

Floods represent spiritual temptations from hell:

"As all spiritual temptations come through falsities that break into the thoughts and infest the interior mind, thus through reasonings from falsities, so temptations are signified by the inundations of waters and by the irruptions of rivers and torrents. As in *Jonah:*—

> *Thou hadst cast me into the depths, even into the heart of the seas; and the river was round about me; all Thy waves and Thy billows passed over me* (ii. 3).

In *David:*—

> *The cords of death compassed me, and the brooks of Belial terrified me* (*Ps.* xviii. 4).

In *Matthew:*—

> *And the rain descended, and the rivers came, and the winds blew and beat upon that house; yet it fell not, for it was founded upon a rock* (vii. 25, 27).

In *Luke:*—

> *When a flood arose, the stream dashed against that house and could not shake it; for it had been founded upon a rock* (vi. 48, 49)." (*Apocalypse Explained*, n. 518.38)

Death is spiritual death (see Ps. 6:5, 9:13, 102:20, 106:28) and hell is the condemnation that follows it which can be seen in Rev. 6:8:

"*And the name of him who sat upon him was Death, and hell followed with him*, signifies the extinction of spiritual life, and hence condemnation. By death is here signified spiritual death, which is the extinction of spiritual life; and by hell condemnation is signified, which follows that death. Every man has spiritual life, indeed, from creation, and thence from birth; but that life is extinguished, when God, the holiness of the Word, and eternal life, are denied. It is extinguished in the will, but remains in the understanding, or rather in the faculty of understanding. By the latter, man is distinguished from the beasts. Since death signifies the extinction of spiritual life, and hell condemnation thence, therefore death and hell are named together in some passages, as in these: *I will redeem them out of the hand of hell; I will deliver them from death: O death, I will be thy plague; O hell, I will be thy destruction* (Hos. xiii. 14). *The cords of death encompassed me, the cords of hell encompassed me, the snares of death prevented me* (Ps. xviii. 4, 5; Ps. cxvi. 3). *Like sheep they are laid in hell; death feedeth upon them; hell is their habitation; but God will redeem my soul from the hand of hell* (Ps. xlix. 14, 15). *I have the keys of hell and of death* (Apoc. i. 18)." (*Apocalypse Revealed*, n. 321)

In another sense, death is spiritual death for those who are in evil, otherwise called devils, and those of hell are those in the falsehoods of evil, otherwise called satans (see Ps. 38:20, 71:13, 109:6). Death an hell are mentioned together in the same way evil and its accompanying falsehood are mentioned together, which can also be seen in Rev. 20:13:

"*And death and hell gave up the dead which were in them*, signifies the men of the church, impious at heart, who were in themselves devils and satans, called together to judgment. No others are meant by death and hell, but they who were interiorly in themselves devils and satans; by death they who were interiorly in themselves devils, and by hell they who were interiorly in themselves satans; consequently all the impious in heart: and yet in externals they appeared like men of the church; for no others were called to this universal judgment: for they who

in externals are like men of the church, whether they be of the
laity or of the clergy, and in internals are devils and satans, are
judged, because with them the externals are to be separated
from the internals; and they also can be judged, because they
have known and professed the things which are of the church.
That by death are meant the impious in heart who in themselves
were devils, and by hell they who in themselves were satans, is
manifest from its being said that death and hell were cast into
the lake of fire (vers. 14 following): and neither death nor hell
can be cast into hell; but they who are death and hell as to their
interiors, that is, who are in themselves devils and satans. Who
are meant by the devil and satan may be seen above (n. 97, 841,
856); and that they are death who in themselves are devils, just
above (n. 866). Death and hell are also spoken of elsewhere, as,
the Son of Man said, I have the keys of death and of hell (Apoc.
i. 18). *The name of him who sat upon the pale horse was Death,
and hell followed him* (Apoc. vi. 8). So also Hos. xiii. 14; Ps. xviii.
4, 5; xlix. 14, 15; cxvi. 3." (*Apocalypse Revealed*, n. 870)

In my distress I called upon Jehovah,
And cried to my God.
He heard my voice out of His temple,
And my cry came before Him in His ears. (Ps. 18:6)

Jehovah is the Lord as to Divine love (see Ps. 18:31, 28:1,
68:26, 82:1, 147:7) and to call upon Him is to ask for deliverance
from evil; to cry to God is to ask for deliverance from falsehood.
The temple is the heaven as to Divine truth (see Ps. 48:9, 65:4).
His face ("before Him") is His Divine good (see Ps. 4:6, 13:1,
22:24, 27:8-9, 31:16, 67:1); ears or hearing in reference to the
Lord signifies Divine providence (see Ps. 17:6).

"In the highest sense, 'temple' signifies the Lord's Divine
Human, and in the relative sense, heaven; and as it signifies
heaven, it also signifies the church, for the church is the Lord's
heaven on earth; and as 'temple' signifies heaven and the church
it also signifies Divine truth proceeding from the Lord, for the
reason that this makes heaven and the church; for those who

receive Divine truth in soul and heart, that is, in faith and love, are they who constitute heaven and the church. As such is the signification of 'temple,' it is said, 'the temple of My God;' 'My God,' when said by the Lord, meaning heaven and Divine truth there, which also is the Lord in heaven... That 'temple' in the Word signifies the Lord's Divine Human, and in the relative sense, heaven and the church, consequently also Divine truth, can be seen from the following passages. In *John:*—

> *The Jews asking, What sign showest Thou unto us, that Thou doest these things? Jesus answered and said unto them, Destroy this temple, and in three days I will raise it up. Then said the Jews, In forty and six years was this temple built, and wilt Thou raise it up in three days? But He was speaking of the Temple of His body* (ii. 18-23).

That 'temple' signifies the Lord's Divine Human is here openly declared; for 'destroying the temple and raising it up after three days' means the Lord's death, burial, and resurrection. In *Malachi:*—

> *Behold, I send My messenger, and he shall prepare the way before Me; and the Lord shall suddenly come to His temple, and the Angel of the covenant whom ye seek* (iii. 1).

Here also 'temple' means the Lord's Divine Human; for the Lord's coming is here treated of, therefore 'coming to His temple' signifies to His Human.

...That it may be known that 'temple' means heaven and the church, as also Divine truth proceeding from the Lord, I will cite these passages here, lest the mind should cling to the idea that a mere temple is meant, and not something more holy; for the temple in Jerusalem was holy because it represented and thus signified what is holy. That 'temple' signified heaven is evident from these passages. In *David:*—

> *I called upon Jehovah, and cried unto my God: He heard my voice from His temple* (Ps. xviii. 6).

In the same:—

> *A day in Thy courts is better than thousands. I have chosen to stand at the door in the house of my God, rather than to dwell in the tents of wickedness* (Ps. lxxxiv. 10).

In the same:—

> *The righteous shall flourish like the palm-tree; he shall grow like a cedar in Lebanon. They who are planted in the house of Jehovah shall flourish in the courts of our God* (Ps. xcii. 12, 13).

In the same:—

> *One thing have I asked of Jehovah; that I may dwell in the house of Jehovah, and to early visit His temple* (Ps. xxvii. 4)." (*Apocalypse Explained*, n. 220.1, 2-3, 7)

And the earth shook and quaked,
And the foundations of the mountains were agitated,
And they were shaken for he was upset. (Ps. 18:7)

The earth signifies the church on earth as to truth (see Ps. 9:8, 24:1, 60:2, 90:2, 96:13); the foundations are the truths of faith on which the church is based (see Ps. 11:3, 24:2, 75:3, 82:5, 104:5); the mountains are the goods of love (see Ps. 36:6, 46:2, 65:6, 68:15-16, 72:3, 97:8, 104:10, 114:4,6, 121:1, 133:3, 147:8, 148:9). These become agitated and shake when they become falsified. An earthquake signifies the time when the state of the church changes and comes to an end:

"*I called upon Jehovah, and cried unto my God. Then the earth tottered and quaked, and the foundations of the mountains trembled and tottered when He was wroth* (Ps. xviii. 6, 7). Here the 'earth' stands for the church, which is said to 'totter and quake' when it is perverted by the falsification of truths; and then 'the foundations of the mountains' are said 'to tremble and totter' for the goods of love, which are founded upon the truths of faith, vanish; 'mountains' meaning the goods of love (as above),

and their 'foundations' the truths of faith; which also shows that
the 'earth' is the church." (*Apocalypse Explained*, n. 304.15; see
also *Heavenly Arcana*, n. 9643.3)

"*The earth tottered and quaked; the foundations of the mountains trembled, because He was wroth* (Ps. xviii. 7). This does
not mean that it was the earth and its foundations that tottered
and quaked, but the church and the truths upon which it was
founded; for 'earth' signifies the church, and the 'foundations of
the mountains' signify the truths on which the church is founded,
which are truths from good; 'because He was wroth' has the like
signification as 'the wrath of Jehovah,' in the Word. Its being
said that 'the earth tottered and quaked, and the foundations
of the mountains trembled,' is from appearances in the spiritual
world, where such things occur when the state of the church is
changed with those who dwell there. Moreover, those who are in
truths there dwell at the foot of mountains, for all the dwelling
places of the angels are so arranged that those who are in the
good of love to the Lord dwell upon mountains, and those who
are in truths from that good dwell lower down. When the state of
these in respect to truths is changed, their habitations, and thus
the foundations of the mountains, tremble. That there are such
things in the spiritual world, and that they exist from changes
of the state of the church there, no one except he to whom it is
revealed can know." (*Apocalypse Explained*, n. 400.6)

"Earthquakes signify changes of state in the church, because
the earth signifies the church (n. 285): and because, in the spiritual world, when the state of the church is anywhere perverted,
and a change is made, there is an earthquake; and because this
foreshadows their destruction, they are in terror. For the earths
or lands in the spiritual world are similar as to their appearance
to the lands in the natural world (n. 260); but because the lands
there, like all other things in that world, are from a spiritual
origin, they are therefore changed according to the state of the
church with them who dwell upon them: and when the state of
the church is perverted, they quake and tremble, yea, sink down
and are moved out of their place. That it was so done when the

final judgment was impending and taking place, may be seen in the small work on the *Final Judgment*. It may be evident from these things, what is signified by quakings, concussions, and commotions of the earth, in the following passages: *There shall be pestilences, famines, and earthquakes in divers places* (Matt. xxiv. 7; Mark xiii. 8; Luke xxi. 11). The words here are said concerning the final judgment. *In the fire of indignation I have spoken, Surely in that day there shall be a great earthquake, that every man upon the face of the earth should shake, and the mountains should be overturned* (Ezek. xxxviii. 18-20). *There was a great earthquake, such as was not since men were made upon the earth* (Apoc. xvi. 18). *I will shake the heavens, and the earth shall be shaken out of its place, in the indignation of Jehovah Zebaoth* (Isa. xiii. 12, 13). *The foundations of the earth have been shaken; the earth hath been shaken exceedingly, because its transgression is heavy upon it* (Isa. xxiv. 18-20). *The earth is smitten and shaken, and the foundations of the mountains, because He was wroth* (Ps. xviii. 7). *The mountains tremble before Jehovah. and the rocks are overturned* (Nah. i. 5, 6). In like manner elsewhere, as Jer. x. 10; xlix. 21; Joel ii. 10; Hag. ii. 6, 7; Apoc. xi. 19; and elsewhere. But these things are to be understood as being done in the spiritual world, and not in the natural world: there they signify such things as are said above." (*Apocalypse Revealed*, n. 331)

There went up a smoke in His nostrils,
And fire out of His mouth devoured: coals were kindled by it. (Ps. 18:8)

Smoke is falsity from evil (see Ps. 11:6, 68:2, 144:5); fire is punishment due to the evil (see Ps. 2:12, 11:6, 21:9, 68:2, 97:3); coals are the desires of evil (see Ps. 78:48) from which there is punishment.

"'Smoke' signifies the falsity of evil, because it proceeds from fire, and 'fire' signifies the loves of self and the world and thence all evils; consequently the hells that are in falsities from the evils of those loves, and still more the hells where those are who have falsified the Word by adapting it to favor those loves, appear in a fire like that of a great furnace, from which a dense smoke mingled with fire goes up. I have also seen those hells, and it was evident that it was the loves with those who were in them that presented the appearance of such a fire, and the falsities flowing forth from those loves that presented the appearance of the fiery smoke. …'Smoke and fire' have a like signification in *David:*—

Because He was wroth there went up a smoke out of His nostrils, and fire out of His mouth devoured, coals burned from Him; He bowed heaven also and came down; and gross darkness was under His feet (Ps. xviii. 7-9; 2 Sam. xxii. 8, 9).

This does not mean that smoke and a devouring fire went up from Jehovah, for there is no anger in Him; but it is so said because the Lord so appears to those who are in falsities and evils, for they regard Him from their falsities and evils. The like is signified by the following in the same:—

He looketh on the earth and it trembleth; He toucheth the mountains and they smoke (Ps. civ. 32).

In the same:—

Bow Thy heavens, O Jehovah, and come down; touch the mountains, that they may smoke (Ps.cxliv. 5)." (Apocalypse Explained, n. 539.1,5-6)

"In like manner in Joel: *The day of Jehovah . . . A fire devoureth before Him, and behind Him a flame burneth (ii. 1, 3).* In David: *There went up a smoke out of His nostrils, and fire out of His mouth devoured, coals did burn from Him . . . and thick darkness was under His feet (Ps. xviii. 8, 9).* In Moses: *A fire is kindled in Mine anger, and it shall burn unto the lowest hell, and shall devour the earth and her increase, and set on fire the foundations of the mountains (Deut. xxxii. 22);* where fire stands for the hatreds and smoke for the falsities which are in men; which are attributed to Jehovah or the Lord for the reasons that have been given. In the hells also the appearance is that Jeho-

vah or the Lord does this, but it is just the reverse; they do this
to themselves, because they are in the fires of hatred. Hence it is
manifest how easily a man can fall into fantasies if the internal
sense of the Word be not known." (*Heavenly Arcana*, n. 1861.14)

"*When a fire shall have broken out.* That this signifies anger
from affection for evil, is evident from the signification of fire,
as love, here the love of evil and affection for it — of which just
above (n. 9141). It is said affection for evil, because by affection
is meant the continuous of love. That fire is anger from affection
for evil, is because anger is from that source, since when that
which a man loves is assailed, a fiery spirit bursts forth and as it
were burns. Therefore anger is described in the Word by fire, and
it is said to burn — as in David: *There went up a smoke out of His
nostrils, and fire out of His mouth: coals did burn from Him* (Ps.
xviii. 8). Again: *Kiss the Son, lest He be angry . . . for His wrath
will soon be kindled* (Ps. ii. 12). In Isaiah: *Who among us shall
dwell with the devouring fire? who among us shall dwell with the
fires of eternity?* (xxxiii. 14). Again: *He poured upon him the fury
of His anger . . . it set him on fire round about, yet he knew not;
it burned him, yet he laid it not to heart* (xlii. 25). Again: *Behold,
Jehovah will come in fire, and His chariots like the whirlwind;
to recompense in the fury of His anger, and His rebuke in flames
of fire* (lxvi. 15). And in Moses: *I looked back, and came down
from the mount, when the mount was burning with fire. . . . I
was afraid by reason of the anger and hot displeasure wherewith
Jehovah was wroth against us* (Deut. ix. 15, 19). In these and
many other passages anger is described by fire. The anger is
attributed to Jehovah, that is, to the Lord, but it is in man (n.
5798, 6997, 8282, 8483)." (*Heavenly Arcana*, n. 9143)

"The state of an evil man when he is angry, is similar indeed
to that of smoke, which when fire is applied kindles into flame;
for falsity of evil in the intellectual is like smoke, and anger is
like the flame of enkindled smoke. There is also a correspondence between them, and therefore in the Word smoke stands
for what is false, and its flame for anger — as in David: *There
went up a smoke out of His nostrils, and fire out of His mouth:*

coals did burn from Him (Ps. xviii. 8). And in Isaiah: *Wickedness burneth as the fire; it devoureth the briers and thorns; and
kindleth in the thickets of the forest, and they mount up as the
rising of smoke, in the wrath of Jehovah Zebaoth* (ix. 18, 19) —
where smoke is falsity, from the kindling of which is anger. That
smoke stands for falsity may be seen above (n. 1861)." (*Heavenly
Arcana*, n. 9144.3)

"It is because of this effect of the Divine love flowing down
out of heaven, that in the Word anger and wrath are so often
attributed to Jehovah, that is, to the Lord, anger from fire, and
wrath from the heat of fire; there is also the expression 'the fire
of His anger,' and that 'He is a consuming fire,' with many other
like expressions, which do not mean that the fire proceeding
from the Lord is such, for in its origin it is Divine love, but that
it becomes such with the evil, who by reason of its flowing into
them become angry and wrathful. ...This is why Jehovah, that
is the Lord, is called in the Word 'a consuming fire,' as in the
following passages:—

Jehovah God is a consuming fire (Deut. iv. 24).

In *Isaiah:*—

*Behold, Jehovah will come in fire and His chariots like a
storm, in flames of fire. For in fire Jehovah will plead, and
in His sword with all flesh; and the slain of Jehovah shall
be multiplied* (lxvi. 15, 16).

In the same:—

Thou shalt be visited with a flame of devouring fire (xxix. 6).

In the same:—

*In the indignation of the anger of Jehovah, and in a flame
of a devouring fire, in scattering, and inundation, and hailstones* (xxx. 30).

In *David:*—

There went up a smoke out of His nostrils, and fire out of His mouth devoured; coals were kindled by it. At the brightness that was before Him the clouds passed, hail and coals of fire. Jehovah thundered out of the heavens, and the Most High gave forth His voice, hail and coals of fire (Ps. xviii. 8, 12, 13).

In the same:—

Our God shall come, and shall not keep silence; a fire shall devour before Him (Ps. l. 3).

In the same:—

Jehovah shall rain upon the wicked snares, fire, and brimstone (Ps. xi. 6).

In *Ezekiel:*—

I will set My faces against them, that although they go out from the fire yet the fire shall devour them. And I will make the land a waste, because they have committed trespasses (xv. 4, 6-8).

In *Moses:*—

A fire has been kindled in Mine anger, and shall burn even unto the lowest hell, and it shall devour the earth and its produce, and shall set on fire the foundations of the mountains (Deut. xxxii. 22).

Such things appear in the spiritual world when Divine good and truth come down out of heaven towards the lower parts where the evil are who are to be separated from the good and dispersed; and these things are said because of these appearances there. And as the fire that comes down out of heaven, which in its origin is Divine love, becomes, when it is received by the evil there, a consuming fire, in the Word such fire is predicated of Jehovah. Infernal fire has no other source than the change of the Divine love into evil loves, and into direful cupidities of doing evil and inflicting injury." (*Apocalypse Explained*, n. 504.19, 20)

And He stretched out the heavens, and came down,
And thick fog was under His feet. (Ps. 18:9)

This describes the descent of the Lord as to Divine truth into the literal sense of the Word, which covers the spiritual sense of the Word as a cloud or thick fog with its literal sense (see Ps. 18:11, 68:4, 77:16, 89:37, 97:2, 99:7, 104:3, 105:39, 147:8). To stretch the heavens is to enlarge heaven by the inflow of truth Divine (see Ps. 104:2). Feet signifies the lower external natural (see Ps. 8:6, 41:9, 49:5, 99:5, 105:18), which is the literal sense.

"Jehovah *bowed the heaven . . . and thick darkness was under His feet. . . . He made darkness His hiding place . . . darkness of waters, thick clouds of the heavens. At the brightness before Him His thick clouds passed* (Ps. xviii. 9, 11, 12). Here the subject is the coming and presence of the Lord in the Word; the thick darkness under His feet is the sense of the letter of the Word; likewise the darkness of waters and the thick clouds of the heavens. That nevertheless the Divine truth, such as it is in the heavens, is in that sense, is signified by making darkness His hiding place; and that at the presence of the Lord the internal sense appears, such as it is in heaven, in its glory, is signified by His thick clouds passing at the brightness before Him. In Nahum: *Jehovah hath His way in the whirlwind and in the storm, and the clouds are the dust of His feet* (i. 3) — where also the clouds are the Word in the sense of the letter, which sense likewise is the whirlwind and the storm, wherein Jehovah hath His way." (*Heavenly Arcana*, n. 9406.5)

And He rode upon a cherub, and flew,
And He soared upon the wings of the wind. (Ps. 18:10)

This describes the descent of the Divine truth into the literal sense of the Word. Cherub are angelic guards lest the celestial heaven of love should be profaned (see Ps. 80:1, 99:1); wings are spiritual truths which guard and protect against falsehoods (see Ps. 17:8, 68:13, 91:4), and wind is Divine influx from the higher heavens into the lower regions (see Ps. 18:15, 48:7, 78:26, 83:15).

"Jehovah bowed the heavens, He came down, and thick dark-
ness was under His feet; and He rode upon a cherub, He did fly,
and was borne upon the wings of the wind (Ps. xviii. 9, 10). Jehovah 'bowed the heavens, He came down,' signifies visitation,
which precedes the Last Judgment; 'thick darkness under His
feet' signifies the falsities of evil in lower things; 'He rode upon
a cherub, He did fly, and was borne upon the wings of the wind,'
signifies omnipresence with the Divine, "the wings of the wind"
meaning Divine truth in ultimates" (*Apocalypse Explained,* n.
419.12)

"But that by the clouds of heaven the Word in the sense of
the letter is meant, and by the glory and power in which also He
is then to come (Matt. xxiv. 30) the spiritual sense of the Word is
meant, has been heretofore concealed, because hitherto no one
has even by conjecture reached the conclusion that there is a
spiritual sense in the Word such as this sense is in itself. Now
because the Lord has opened to me the spiritual sense of the
Word, and it has been granted me to be together with angels and
spirits in their world as one of them, it has been disclosed that
by the clouds of heaven is meant the Word in the natural sense,
and by glory the Word in the spiritual sense, and by power the
Lord's power through the Word. That this is the signification of
the clouds of heaven, may be seen from the following passages
in the Word: *There is none like unto the God of Jeshurun who*
rideth in the heaven, and in magnificence upon the clouds (Deut.
xxxiii. 26). *Sing unto God, sing praises to His name, extol Him*
who rideth upon the clouds (Ps. lxviii. 4). *Jehovah riding upon*
a swift cloud (Isa. xix. 1). To ride signifies to instruct in Divine
truths from the Word, for a horse signifies the understanding of
the Word (see *Apocalypse Revealed,* n. 298). Who does not see
that God does not ride upon the clouds? Again: *God rode upon*
the cherubs and put for His tent the clouds of the heavens (Ps.
xviii. 10, 11). Cherubs also signify the Word, as may be seen in
the *Apocalypse Revealed* (n. 239, 672). *Jehovah bindeth up the*
waters in His clouds, and He spreadeth out His cloud over the
throne (Job xxvi. 8, 9). *Ascribe ye strength unto God; His strength*

is in the clouds (Ps. lxviii. 34). *Jehovah created over every dwelling-place of Zion a cloud by day, for upon all the glory shall be a covering* (Isa. iv. 5). The Word in the sense of the letter was also represented by the cloud in which Jehovah descended upon Mount Sinai, when He promulgated the law: the things of the law then promulgated were the first fruits of the Word. In confirmation the following may also be added: There are clouds in the spiritual world as well as in the natural, but from a different origin. In the spiritual world there are sometimes bright clouds over the angelic heavens, but dusky clouds over the hells. Bright clouds over the angelic heavens signify obscurity there, from the literal sense of the Word; but when those clouds are dispersed, this signifies that they are in its clear light from the spiritual sense: but dusky clouds over the hells signify the falsification and profanation of the Word. The origin of this signification of the clouds in the spiritual world is that the light which proceeds from the Lord as the sun there, signifies Divine truth; therefore He is called the Light (John i. 9; xii. 35). It is owing to this that the Word itself, which is kept in the shrines of the temples, appears encompassed with clear white light; and its obscurity is induced by clouds." (*True Christian Religion*, n. 776)

"Jehovah *bowed the heavens, and came down, and thick darkness was under His feet; and He rode upon a cherub* (Ps. xviii. 9, 10). Thick darkness here stands for clouds; to ride upon a cherub represents the Lord's providence lest man should of himself enter into the mysteries of faith which are in the Word (n. 308)." (*Heavenly Arcana*, n. 2761.4)

"*Jehovah bowed the heavens, and came down, and rode upon the cherubs* (Ps. xviii. 10, 11). To ride upon the cherubs, to sit, and to be seated upon them is upon the ultimate sense of the Word." (*Apocalypse Revealed*, n. 239)

"Inasmuch as this cherub was like an eagle, and the eagle appeared as flying, it shall be told also what 'flying' signifies in the Word. 'Flying' signifies circumspection and presence, because a bird when it flies looks all about from on high, and thus by its sight is present everywhere and round about But when 'flying' in the Word is attributed to Jehovah, it signifies omnipresence, because omnipresence is infinite circumspection and infinite presence. This then is why this cherub appeared 'like an eagle flying;' for 'cherubim' signify in general the Lord's Providence that the higher heavens be not approached except from the good of love and of charity; and this cherub signifies Divine intelligence (as was shown just above). That 'flying' in the Word, in reference to the Lord signifies omnipresence, and in reference to men circumspection and presence, can be seen from the following passages. In *David:*—

> *God rode upon a cherub, He did fly, and was borne upon the*
> *wings of the wind (Ps. xviii. 10; 2 Sam. xxii. 11).*

'He rode upon a cherub' signifies the Divine Providence; 'He did fly' signifies omnipresence in the spiritual world; 'and was borne upon the wings of the wind' signifies omnipresence in the natural world. These words from *David* no one can understand except from the spiritual sense." (*Apocalypse Explained*, n. 282.1-2; see also *Apocalypse Explained*, n. 283.5)

"'To fly' signifies, in reference to the Lord, to enlighten, because 'to fly' is said of the understanding, and of the extension of its vision round about, therefore in reference to the Lord, 'to fly' signifies the enlightenment of the understanding. That in reference to the Lord, 'to fly' signifies omnipresence, may be seen above (n. 282); consequently it signifies also enlightenment, for where the Lord is present there is enlightenment. 'To fly' has the same signification in *David:*—

> *God rode upon a cherub, He did fly, and was borne upon the*
> *wings of the wind (Ps. xviii. 10; 2 Sam. xxii. 11).*

A 'cherub' signifies the inmost heaven, 'to ride' signifies to give understanding and to enlighten; 'to fly' and 'to be borne upon the wings of the wind' have a like meaning; but 'to ride' here signifies to give understanding to and to enlighten here the inmost heaven, which is signified by a 'cherub;' 'to fly' also signifies to give understanding to and to enlighten the middle heaven; while

'to be borne upon the wings of the wind' signifies to give understanding to and to enlighten the ultimate heaven. (That 'to ride'
signifies to give understanding, see above, n. 355c, 364b; and that
a 'cherub,' signifies the inmost heaven, n. 313a, 322, 362, 462).
'To fly' signifies to enlighten the middle heaven, because that
heaven is the spiritual heaven, and spiritual things in the Word
are signified by various birds, and by their wings and flights. 'To
be borne upon the wings of the wind' signifies to enlighten the
ultimate heaven, because 'wings' are for flight, and here signify
enlightenment, and 'wind' signifies the spiritual of that heaven;
thus all this describes the omnipresence of the Lord in the heavens, thence also the enlightenment of the understanding; for as
was said above, where the Lord is present there is enlightenment." (*Apocalypse Explained*, n. 529.2)

"That by flying is signified to perceive and to instruct, and in
the highest sense to look out for and to provide, is also evident
from these passages: *God rode upon a cherub, He did fly, and
was borne upon the wings of the wind* (Ps. xviii. 11; 2 Sam. xxii.
11). *I saw an angel flying through the midst of heaven, having
the everlasting gospel* (Apoc. xiv. 6)." (*Apocalypse Revealed*, n.
245)

> "*God rode upon a cherub and did fly, and was borne upon
> the wings of the wind. He made darkness His hiding place;
> His tent round about Him the darkness of waters, the clouds
> of the heavens. At the brightness before Him the clouds
> passed* (Ps. xviii. 10-12).

This, too, describes the enlightenment of the Word, and thus of
the church; enlightenment by the influx of Divine truth from
the heavens is signified by 'God rode upon a cherub and did fly;'
Divine truth in ultimates which is enlightened is signified by
'the wings of the wind,' 'the darkness of waters,' and 'the clouds
of the heavens,' these signifying the various degrees of the understanding receiving enlightenment; that the obscurities of the
ultimate sense are thereby dissipated is meant by 'at the bright-

ness before Him the clouds passed.'" (*Apocalypse Explained*, n. 594.6)

He made darkness His secret place,
His pavilion round about Him were dark waters, clouds of the
skies. (Ps. 18:11)

A pavilion is the holy of truth (see Ps. 31:20). This interior holy truth is hidden by external truths, signified by dark waters and clouds of the skies (see Ps. 18:9, 68:4, 77:16, 89:37, 97:2, 99:7, 104:3, 105:39, 147:8).

"Jehovah God *rode upon a cherub and did fly, and flew swiftly upon the wings of the wind. He made darkness His hiding-place, and His surroundings His tent* [succoth], *darkness of waters, thick clouds of the skies* (Ps. xviii. 11, 12). And again: *He bowed the heavens, and came down, and thick darkness was under His feet. And He rode upon a cherub and did fly, and flew swiftly upon the wings of the wind. And He put darkness round about Him for tents* [succoth], *gathering of waters, thick clouds of the skies* (2 Sam. xxii. 10-12) — where the subject is the Divine revelation or Word. To bow the heavens and come down, means to hide the interiors of the Word; the thick darkness under His feet means that the things which appear to man are darkness in comparison — such is the literal sense of the Word; to ride upon a cherub means that it was so provided; to put darkness round about Him for tents, or His surroundings for His tent, denotes the holy of truth in its hiding-place, namely, within in the literal sense; the gathering of waters, thick clouds of the skies, are the Word in the letter." (*Heavenly Arcana*, n. 4391.1-2)

From the brightness in front of Him His clouds passed,
Hail and coals of fire.
And Jehovah thundered in the heavens,
And the Most High gave His voice,
Hail and coals of fire.
And He sent out His arrows and scattered them,
And He shot out lightnings and routed them. (Ps. 18:12-14)

Brightness is enlightenment from Divine truth and the clouds are the literal sense of the Word in which is hidden the spiritual sense. Hail are the falsities of evil which destroy truths (see Ps. 78:47-48, 105:32); and coals of fire are the lusts of self love (see Ps. 78:48). Thunder from Jehovah is revelation of the Divine truth from the higher heaven (see Ps. 29:3) which effects judgment upon the evil; arrows are Divine truths and lightnings are truths which enlighten the understanding (see Ps. 77:18, 97:4, 135:7, 144:6) which scatter those of the hells who are in falsehoods and evils.

"*And there followed hail and fire mingled with blood*, signifies falsity from infernal love destroying good and truth and falsifying the Word. Falsity destroying good and truth is signified by the hail; by the fire is signified infernal love, and by the blood the falsification of truth. That hail signifies falsity destroying good and truth, will be seen below: that fire is love in both senses, the heavenly and the infernal, may be seen (n. 468): that blood is the Lord's Divine truth, which is also the Word, and in the opposite sense the Word falsified (n. 379). From these gathered into one sense, it is manifest that by *there followed hail and fire mingled with blood*, is signified falsity from infernal love destroying good and truth, and falsifying the Word. These things are signified because in the spiritual world such things appear, when the sphere of the Lord's Divine love and Divine wisdom descends into societies below, where are falsities from infernal love, and the Word is falsified by them. Similar things are signified by hail together with fire in the following passages; *At the brightness before Him the clouds passed away, hailstones and coals of fire: the Most High gave His voice, hailstones and coals of fire; and He sent His arrows, and scattered them* (Ps. xviii. 12, 13)." (*Apocalypse Revealed*, n. 399; see also *Heavenly Arcana*, n. 7553.5)

"*At the brightness before Him His clouds passed, with hail and coals of fire. Jehovah thundered in the heavens, and the Most High uttered His voice, hail and coals of fire. And He sent forth His arrows and scattered them, and many lightnings and discomfited them (Ps.* xviii. 12-14). Here 'hail and fire' have a similar signification as the 'hail and fire' in this passage in the *Apocalypse,* namely, falsities and evils destroying the truths and goods of the church. It is said that such things are from Jehovah, because Divine truth coming down out of heaven is changed with the evil into infernal falsities, as has been said above; and from this change there spring forth many appearances such as the fall of hail and fire; and yet these things are not out of heaven from the Lord, but from those who are in the falsities of evil, who turn the influx of Divine truth and good into the falsity of evil. It has been granted me to perceive these changes, when Divine truth flowed down out of heaven into some hell. ...From this it can be seen what the origin is of the appearances of hail and fire in the spiritual world, and why it is said that 'Jehovah causes them to rain,' when yet there is nothing from Jehovah but what is good; and when Jehovah, that is, the Lord, renders the influx powerful, it is not that He may destroy the evil but that He may rescue and protect the good, for He thus conjoins the good to Himself more closely and interiorly, and thus they are separated from the evil, and the evil perish; for if the evil were not separated the good would perish and the angelic heaven would fall to ruin." (*Apocalypse Explained*, n. 503.7; see also *Heavenly Arcana*, n. 7573.4)

"*Jehovah thundered from heaven, and the Most High gave forth His voice and sent forth His arrows and scattered them, lightning, and discomfited them* ([2 Sam.] xxii. 14, 15). Thunders are here described by 'thundering from heaven' and by 'giving forth a voice,' flying thunderbolts by 'arrows,' and all these signify Divine truths, and "lightning" their light; and as these vivify and illustrate the good, so they terrify and blind the evil, which is meant by 'He sent forth arrows and scattered them, lightning, and discomfited them;' for the evil cannot bear Divine truths, nor any light at all from heaven, therefore they flee away at their presence." (*Apocalypse Explained*, n. 273.5; see also Ex. 19:16; Ps. 71:7; Rev. 6:1, 8:6, 10:3-4, 11:19, 14:2, 19:6)

And the channels of waters were seen,
And the foundations of the world were uncovered, (Ps. 18:15)

The "channels of waters" are the knowledges of truths of the church (see Ps. 42:2) and the "foundations of the world" are the truths of faith upon which the good of the church is based (see Ps. 11:3, 18:7,15, 24:2, 75:3, 82:5, 104:5) which get overturned in the last judgment due to falsifications and perversions of doctrine in the church.

"The channels of waters appeared and the foundations of the world were revealed at Thy rebuke, O Jehovah, at the breath of the spirit of Thy nostrils (Ps. xviii. 15; 2 Sam. xxii. 16). That all things of the church in respect to its truths and goods were overturned from the foundation is signified by 'the channels of waters appeared and the foundations of the world were revealed;' 'the channels of waters' meaning the truths, and 'the foundations of the world' its goods, and 'to appear' and 'to be revealed' meaning to be overturned from the foundation. That this destruction is from the hatred and fury of the evil against Divine things is signified by 'at Thy rebuke, O Jehovah, at the breath of the spirit of Thy nostrils;' the 'rebuke' and 'the spirit of Jehovah's nostrils' have a similar signification as 'His anger and wrath' mentioned elsewhere in the Word. But since the Lord has no anger or wrath against the evil, while the evil have against the Lord, and as anger and wrath appear to the evil when they perish to be from the Lord, therefore this is so said according to that appearance. 'The breath of the spirit of Jehovah's nostrils' means also the east wind, which destroys by drought, and overturns by its penetrating power." (*Apocalypse Explained*, n. 741.22)

"Since a foundation is the truth of faith, and a city the doctrine thereof, therefore in the Word the foundation of the city is named when truth of doctrine is meant — as in David: *The channels of waters appeared, and the foundations of the city were discovered, at the rebuke of Jehovah (Ps. xviii. 15)."* (*Heavenly Arcana*, n. 9643.3)

From Your rebuke, Jehovah,

From the breath of the spirit of Your nostrils. (Ps. 18:15)

The rebuke of Jehovah is the punishment of evil; wind or breath of the Lord signifies Divine influx of the truth into the lower regions which punishes the falsehood of evil (see Ps. 11:6, 18:15, 48:7, 78:26, 83:15); spirit signifies Divine truth (see Ps. 33:6, 51:11, 104:4, 143:10).

"It is to be known, that a final judgment takes place, when the evil are multiplied to such a degree under the heavens in the world of spirits, that the angels in the heavens cannot stand in the state of their love and their wisdom; for they then have no support and foundation. And because this takes place from the multiplication of the evil below, the Lord, therefore, that He may preserve their state, flows in more and more strongly with His Divine; and this is done until they cannot be preserved by any influx, unless the evil below are separated from the good: and this is effected by a lowering and drawing near of the heavens, and hence a stronger influx, until the evil cannot endure it; and the evil then flee away, and cast themselves into hell. ... That wind signifies influx, properly the influx of truth into the under-standing, may be evident from the following passages: *The Lord Jehovah said, Come from the four winds, O breath, and breathe into these slain, that they may live* (Ezek. xxxvii. 9, 10). *Four chariots were seen, to which there were four horses; these are the four winds of the heavens* (Zech. vi. 1, 5). *Ye must be born again: the wind bloweth where it listeth, and thou knowest not whence it cometh and whither it goeth* (John iii. 7, 8). *The Maker of the earth hath established the world by His wisdom; He bringeth forth the wind out of His treasuries* (Jer. x. 12, 13; li. 15, 16; Ps. cxxxv. 7). *Jehovah maketh His wind to blow, and the waters flow; He declareth His Word, His statutes and His judgments* (Ps. cxlvii. 17-19). *Let the stormy wind praise Jehovah, that doeth His word* (Ps. cxlviii. 8). *Jehovah maketh the winds His angels* (Ps. civ. 3, 4). *Jehovah did fly upon the wings of the wind* (Ps. xviii. 9, 10; civ. 3). The wings of the wind are the Divine truths which flow in. On this account the Lord is called the breath of the nostrils (Lam. iv. 20); and it is said that He breathed into the nostrils of Adam *the breath of life* (Gen. ii. 7): also, that He breathed upon the disciples, and said, *Receive ye the Holy Spirit* (John xx. 21, 22). The Holy Spirit is the Divine truth proceeding from the Lord, the influx of which into the disciples was represented and hence is signified by His breathing upon them. That wind and breathing signify the influx of the Divine truth into the understanding, is from the correspondence of the lungs with the understanding, on which see the *Angelic Wisdom concerning the Divine Love and the Divine Wisdom* (n. 371-429). " (*Apocalypse Revealed*, n. 343)

"Because now by the wind of the nostrils of Jehovah is signified the life which is from the Lord, and thus in the universal sense heaven, and because by the presence of the Lord, or by the presence of heaven where the Lord is, evils and falsities are cast into hell (n. 8265), therefore also this effect is signified by the wind of the nostrils of Jehovah — as in David: *The channels of the sea appeared, the foundations of the world were laid bare, at the rebuke of Jehovah, at the blast of the breath of His nostrils* (Ps. xviii. 15; 2 Sam. xxii. 16). And in Isaiah: *The breath of Jehovah, like a stream of brimstone, doth kindle it* (xxx. 33). Again: *Yea, they are not planted; yea, they are not sown; yea, their stock taketh not root in the earth: moreover He bloweth upon them, and they wither, and the whirlwind taketh them away as stubble* (xl. 24). And in David: *He sendeth out His word, and melteth them: He causeth His wind to blow, the waters flow* (Ps. cxlvii. 18). Hence also it is, that by the nostrils, when predicated of Jehovah or the Lord, is also signified wrath, thus the punishment, vastation, and damnation of those who are in evils and falsities (as in Num. xxv. 4; Deut. vii. 4; Judges ii. 14; Isa. ix. 21; Jer. iv. 8; Hosea xiv. 4; Ps. vi. 1; lxxxvi. 15; ciii. 8; cxlv. 8: and in many other passages); and by blowing with the nostrils, or breathing, is signified to be angry (Deut. iv. 21; Isa. xii. 1; Ps. ii. 12; vi. 1; lx. 3; lxxix. 5; lxxxv. 5; Job iv. 9)." (*Heavenly Arcana*, n. 8286.4)

"That Holy proceeding from the Lord, and flowing in through angels and spirits with man, whether manifestly or not, is the

Holy Spirit with him; for it is Divine truth proceeding from the Lord that is called in the Word the holy (see n. 9680).

"For this reason it is that the Holy Spirit is called the Spirit of Truth, that it is said that *He will guide into all truth; for He shall not speak of Himself, but what things soever He shall have heard* from the Lord; and that *what He shall receive from Me* [the Lord] He shall declare (John xvi. 13, 14); and also that when the Lord departed from the disciples, *He breathed on them, and saith unto them, Receive ye the Holy Spirit* (John xx. 21, 22). Breathing signifies the life of faith (n. 9229, 9281); and hence breathing upon by the Lord signifies the faculty imparted of perceiving Divine truths, and thus of receiving that life. Wherefore also the name, spirit, is derived from blowing and from wind, because from breathing, and therefore spirit is sometimes called wind. That breathing, which is of the lungs, corresponds to the life of faith, and that the pulse, which is of the heart, corresponds to the life of love, may be seen above (n. 3883-3896, 9300, 9495).

"The same is signified by breathing into in the Book of Genesis: *And Jehovah breathed into man's nostrils the breath of lives* (ii. 7). Therefore the Lord is called, *The breath of our nostrils* (Lam. iv. 20). And because Divine truth consumes and vastates the evil, therefore it is said in David: *The foundations of the world were laid bare . . . at the blast of the breath of Thy nostrils* [*nose*] (Ps. xviii. 15). And in Job: *By the breath of God they perish, and by the breath of His nostrils are they consumed* (iv. 9). And in David: *By the word of Jehovah were the heavens made; and all the host of them by the breath of His mouth* (Ps. xxxiii. 6). The Word of Jehovah is Divine truth, in like manner the breath or spirit of His mouth. That it means the Lord, is evident in John: *In the beginning was the Word, and the Word was with God, and God was the Word. . . . All things were made by Him. . . . And the Word became flesh, and dwelt among us* (i. 1, 3, 14)." (*Heavenly Arcana*, n. 9818.14-16; for passages that show the "Spirit of God" is the Divine truth, see also *Apocalypse Explained*, n. 183.12)

"In *Jeremiah*:—

The wild asses pant for breath like whales; their eyes were consumed because there was no herb (xiv. 6).

'To pant for breath like whales' signifies that there is no truth to be imbibed; 'because there was no herb' means because there is no truth in the church. As the evil are cast down by a more powerful influx of Divine truth and good proceeding from the Lord as a sun, as has been said above, so the casting down of those who are in the falsities of evil is described also by 'the breath of the nostrils of Jehovah.' As in *Isaiah*:—

Topheth is prepared of old; the pile thereof is fire and much wood made ready; the breath of Jehovah like a brook of brimstone doth kindle them (xxx. 33).

In *David*:—

The channels of waters appeared, and the foundations of the world were disclosed, at the rebuke of Jehovah, at the blast of the breath of Thy nostrils (Ps. xviii. 15).

In *Moses*:—

By the breath of Thy nostrils the waters were heaped up; Thou didst blow with Thy wind, the sea covered them (*Exod.* xv. 8, 10).

And in *Job*:—

Plotters of iniquity, by the blast of God they perish, by the breath of His nostrils are they consumed (iv. 8, 9).

In all these passages 'the blast,' 'the breath,' and 'the breathing of the nostrils of Jehovah' means the Divine proceeding, which disperses and casts down the evil when it flows in intensely and strongly; but respecting this influx more will be said in what follows, where 'tempests,' 'storms,' and 'the east wind' are treated of." (*Apocalypse Explained*, n. 419.10)

He sent from above, He took me,
He drew me out of many waters.

He delivered me from my strong enemy,
And from those who hated me for they persisted after me.
They confronted me in the day of my calamity,
But Jehovah was my support.
And He brought me forth to a broad place,
He rescued me for He was delighted in me. (Ps. 18:16-19)

Following the exploration of the Divine, the good are separated from the evil and the good are elevated towards heaven. To
be drawn out of the waters is to become elevated by the truth out
of the falsehoods of hell (see Ps. 144:7). Enemies are falsehoods
which attack the truth (see Ps. 3:1, 27:12); those who hate are
the evils which attack what is good. To persist after is for evil to
oppose good; the day of calamity is to be in a weak state as to
truth. Support or staff signifies the power of good (see Ps. 18:18,
23:4, 105:16); a broad place has reference to truth based on the
spiritual meaning of breadth or width (see Ps. 4:1, 31:8, 104:25);
to be delighted is to be in conjunction from love.

"They came upon me in the day of my calamity: but Jehovah
was my staff. He brought me forth into a large place (Ps. xviii.
18, 19) — where the day of calamity stands for a weak state in
respect to the faith of truth; Jehovah being a staff stands for
power then; bringing forth into a large or broad place means into
the truths which are of faith — that this is meant by bringing
forth into a broad place may be seen shown above (n. 4482). So
also in Isaiah: *The Lord Jehovah of hosts doth take away from*
Jerusalem and from Judah staff and stay, the whole staff of
bread and the whole staff of water (iii. 1) — where to take away
staff and stay means the power and strength of life derived from
truth and good, the staff of bread meaning power from good and
the staff of water power from truth. Staff or stay in the original
tongue is a term implying to lean upon and be supported, which
in the spiritual world is effected by truth and good." (*Heavenly*
Arcana, n. 9028)

Jehovah rewarded me according to my righteousness,
According to the cleanness of my hands He has returned to me.

For I have kept the ways of Jehovah,
And have not done wickedly against my God.
For all His judgments were in front of me,
And I did not put away His statutes from me.
And I was perfect before Him,
And I kept myself from my iniquity.
And Jehovah returned to me according to my righteousness,
According to the cleanness of my hands in front of His eyes. (Ps. 18:20-24)

One's reward is eternal life in heaven according to how one lived their life (see Ps. 109:20). Righteousness is the interior good of charity (see Ps. 14:5, 36:6, 37:6,17, 72:2, 89:14, 92:12) and cleanness of the hands is exterior good or the removal of external evils (see Ps. 24:4, 73:13). To "keep the ways of Jehovah" means to live by the truth signified by way (see Ps. 1:1, 18:42, 25:4,12, 37:23, 86:11); to not wickedly depart from God is to avoid following falsehood. Judgments are internal spiritual truths (see Ps. 36:6, 37:6, 72:2, 89:14, 92:12); statutes are the external rituals and truths of the church (see Ps. 19:8, 89:31, 119:8, 147:19). To be perfect means to be in good from truth (see Ps. 15:2); to keep from iniquity is to refrain from evil against the good of faith (see Ps. 5:9). Righteousness is internal good; the cleanness of hands is exterior good.

With the merciful You will be merciful,
With a perfect mighty one You will be perfect,
With the pure You will be pure,
And with the perverse You will struggle.
For You will save the afflicted people,
And will bring down exalted eyes.
For You will light my lamp,
Jehovah my God will enlighten my darkness.
For with You I have run through a troop,
And by my God have I leaped over a wall. (Ps. 18:25-29)

The Lord is perceived in the manner in which one receives Him. The merciful are those who are in the good of love (see Ps.

25:10, 26:3, 36:5, 89:14, 103:8); the perfect are those who are
in good from truth (see Ps. 15:2); the pure are those who purify
themselves from evils and falsehoods by the truth. The perverse
are those who distort the truth; the afflicted are those who are
lacking in knowledges of truth (see Ps. 35:10, 37:14, 40:17);
"exalted eyes" are those in the pride of their own intelligence.
Light is Divine truth (see Ps. 4:6, 11:4, 36:9, 43:3, 104:2, 139:12)
and a lamp is related to the holy things of love; to enlighten the
darkness is to dispel falsehoods of ignorance (see Ps. 104:20).
A troop signifies those who are in evil works, and as legs correspond to one's power to do good (see Ps. 147:10) to run through
them is to oppose through good. A wall is a falsehood that defends
against truth (see Ps. 55:10).

*"Thou makest my lamp to shine; Jehovah God maketh bright
my darkness (Ps.* xviii. 28). 'To make a lamp to shine' signifies
to enlighten the understanding by Divine truth; and 'to make
bright the darkness' signifies to disperse the falsities of ignorance by the light of truth." (*Apocalypse Explained,* n. 274.2)

"When I sit in darkness Jehovah shall be a Light unto me
([Mic.] vii. 8). ...'darkness' signifies the falsities of ignorance,
such as existed, and as exist at this day among the upright Gentiles. These falsities are altogether distinct from the falsities of
evil, which have evil stored up in them because they are from
evil, while the former have good stored up in them because they
have good as an end. Those, therefore, who are in these falsities can be instructed in truths, and they also when instructed
receive truths in the heart, for the reason that good, which is in
their falsities, loves truth, and also conjoins itself to truth when
it is heard. It is otherwise with the falsities of evil; these are
averse to all truth and cast it off because it is truth, and thus
is not in agreement with evil. Again, 'darkness' signifies in the
Word mere ignorance from lack of truth (as in *David, Ps.* xviii.
29; cxxxix. 11, 12)." (*Apocalypse Explained,* n. 526.15-16)

As for God, His way is perfect,
The saying of Jehovah is refined,

He is a shield to all who seek refuge in Him.
For who is God beside Jehovah?
And who is a rock except our God? (Ps. 18:30-31)

The way of God is truth (see Ps. 1:1, 18:42, 25:4,12, 37:23, 86:11); to be perfect is to be in good from truth (see Ps. 15:2). The term "saying" is used for the perception of the will (see Ps. 33:9) and is thus mentioned with Jehovah which signifies the Lord as to Divine love (see Ps. 28:1, 68:26, 82:1, 147:7); to be refined is to become purified from evils and falsities (see Ps. 66:10) and a shield is truth which protects from evil and falsity (see Ps. 144:2). In the spiritual sense, to ask who is God beside Jehovah is to acknowledge that there is only one God (see Ps. 77:13, 88:6) and that Divine truth comes from Divine love signified by Jehovah (see Ps. 28:1, 68:26, 82:1, 147:7); a rock signifies truth (see Ps. 18:46, 19:14, 28:1, 78:15) and God is the Lord as to Divine truth (see Ps. 18:31, 29:1, 68:17,24, 82:1, 95:3, 147:7).

"It is said 'Who is God save Jehovah, and who is a Rock besides my God?' because where Divine good is treated of the Lord is called 'Jehovah,' and where Divine truth is treated of He is called 'God,' and also 'Rock,'" (*Apocalypse Explained*, n. 411.9)

It is the God who girds me with valour,
And makes my way perfect. (Ps. 18:32)

To gird or put on clothing is to know and perceive truths from the light of good (see *Heavenly Arcana*, n. 10087); valour is to be more excellent in doctrine; way is the truth (see Ps. 1:1, 18:42, 25:4,12, 37:23, 81:13, 86:11) and to be perfect is to be in good from truth (see Ps. 15:2). The word for valour is translated as "activity" in the following commentary on Gen. 47:6:

"*And if thou knowest, and there be among them, men of activity.* That this signifies the more excellent things in doctrine, is evident from the signification of men of activity, as things more excellent in doctrine, for man signifies one who is intelligent, and also truth (see n. 158, 265, 749, 1007, 3134, 4823), consequently doctrine, and active signifies excellent; for activity in the original tongue is expressed by a word that also signifies

strength and valor, which in the internal sense are things which
have power, and thus surpass in excellence." (*Heavenly Arcana*,
n. 6413.1-2, 4-6)

He makes my feet like that of a hind,
And makes me to stand upon my high places. (Ps. 18:33)

To have feet like a hind means freedom in natural affections
(see Ps. 42:1); to stand is to live a new spiritual life (see Ps. 31:8,
40:2); upon high places is to become elevated from the natural
into the spiritual (see Ps. 27:5).

"*Is a hind let loose.* That this signifies the freedom of natural
affections, is evident from the signification of a hind, as natural
affection — of which below; and from the signification of being
let loose, as freedom, for a hind let loose has freedom. Deliverance from a state of temptations is compared to a hind let loose,
because the hind is an animal of the forest, loving freedom more
than other animals, in which the natural also resembles it; for
this loves to be in the enjoyment of its affections, consequently
in freedom, for freedom is of the affections. That by a hind is signified natural affection, is because it is among the beasts which
signify affections, as all those are which are for food and use,
as lambs, sheep, goats, and kids, also oxen and cows. But these
beasts also signify spiritual affections, because burnt-offerings
and sacrifices were made of them, whereas hinds, because they
were not so used, signified only natural affections...

"Natural affections are also signified by hinds in David:
Jehovah *maketh my feet like hinds', and setteth me upon my high*
places (Ps. xviii. 33). And in Habakkuk: *Jehovih, the Lord, is my*
strength, Who maketh my feet like hinds', and maketh me to walk
upon my high places (iii. 19.) To make the feet like hinds' means
the natural in liberty of affections... That to make the feet as
hinds' has this signification, may be evident from this, that to
make the feet nimble and active to run like hinds' feet, is nothing
spiritual; but that something spiritual is involved, is plain from
what immediately follows, that Jehovah will set him and cause
him to walk upon his high places, whereby is signified spiritual

affection, which is above the natural. So with this passage in Isaiah: *The lame shall leap as a hart* (xxxv. 6), for by the lame is signified one who is in good, but not yet genuine (n. 4302).

"And in Jeremiah: *From the daughter of Zion all her honor is departed; her princes are become like harts, they have found no pasture* (Lam. i. 6) — where the daughter of Zion stands for affection for good, which affection is of the celestial church (n. 2362); princes for the primary truths of that church... which are compared to harts, whereby are signified affections for natural truth; and by the harts not finding pasture, are signified natural affections without truths and their goods...

"So by hinds in Jeremiah: *The earth is crumbled, for that no rain hath been in the land, the plowmen were ashamed, they covered their heads. Yea, the hind also in the field calved, but forsook it, because there was no grass* (xiv. 4, 5). Hind is here affection for natural good; calving in the field is joining natural affections with spiritual which are of the church; but because those affections were without truths and goods, it is said that she forsook, because there was no grass. Every one may see that there is an internal sense in what is here said concerning the hind; for without an internal sense what could be here meant by the hind calving in the field, but forsaking, because there was no grass?

"In like manner in David: *The voice of Jehovah hath made the hinds to calve, and strippeth the forests bare; but in His temple every one saith, Glory* (Ps. xxix. 9). That there is an internal sense which is spiritual, in "the voice of Jehovah hath made the hinds to calve," is manifestly evident from this, that immediately afterward it is said, "but in His temple every one saith, Glory," which words do not combine with those which precede concerning hinds and forests, without a spiritual sense." (*Heavenly Arcana*, n. 6413.1-2, 4-6)

He teaches my hands for war,
And a bow of brass is bent in my arms. (Ps. 18:34)

Hands signify the power of truth (see Ps. 20:6, 44:3, 45:4, 80:15,17, 89:13,21, 110:1, 121:5) and war is spiritual warfare between truth and falsity (see Ps. 24:8, 27:3, 46:9, 76:3); a bow signifies doctrine (see Ps. 7:12-13, 11:2, 37:15, 46:9, 77:17-18, 78:9,57) which here concerns charity, as brass is natural good (see Ps. 2:9); arms are the power of good though truth (see Ps. 10:15, 77:15, 89:21, 136:12).

"*God teacheth my hands war and placeth a bow of brass in mine arms* (*Ps.* xviii. 34). 'War' here signifies war in a spiritual sense, which is war against evils and falsities; this is the war that God teaches; and 'the bow of brass' signifies the doctrine of charity; God places this in the arms, that is, makes it to prevail." (*Apocalypse Explained*, n. 357.4)

"*Jehovah who teacheth my hands war, that a bow of brass may be let down upon his arms* (*Ps.* xviii. 34). 'To teach the hands war' does not mean war against enemies in this world, but against enemies in hell, which is carried on by the combats of truth against falsities and against evils. The appearance is that such a war is there meant as David waged against his enemies, and thus that Jehovah taught him such war, and how to let down a bow of brass upon the arms; nevertheless spiritual war is meant, also a spiritual bow, which is the doctrine of truth, and 'the bow of brass' means the doctrine of the good of life, and this because the Word regarded in its essence is spiritual." (*Apocalypse Explained*, n. 734.6)

And You have given me the shield of Your salvation,
And Your right hand has sustained me,
And Your meekness has increased me.
You have enlarged my steps under me,
And my ankles falter not. (Ps. 18:35-36)

A shield signifies protection from evil and falsity by the Lord (see Ps. 144:2) and salvation is deliverance from evil (see Ps. 14:7, 96:2); the right hand signifies the power by Divine truth (see Ps. 20:6, 44:3, 45:4, 80:15,17, 89:13,21, 110:1, 121:5). To be meek is to be in the good of charity (see Ps. 37:11); to enlarge or widen one's steps is to increase one's instruction in the truth (see

Ps. 4:1, 18:19, 31:8, 104:25). Ankles or feet represent one's lower natural desires (see Ps. 8:6, 41:9, 49:5, 99:5, 105:18).

I have pursued my enemies and overtaken them,
And I did not return till they were consumed.
I have stricken them and they were not able to rise,
They are fallen under my feet.
And You have girded me with valour for the battle,
You have made those who rose up against me to bow under me.
And You have given to me the necks of my enemies,
And I have put an end to them who hate me.
They cried but there was none to save,
Unto Jehovah but He answered them not. (Ps. 18:37-41)

This concerns the Lord's combats with the hells through temptations in His human, and conquering temptations through the Lord. Enemies are the falsehoods of hell (see Ps. 3:1, 27:12); to pursue is to search them out from the truth; for them to be consumed is to be destroyed from one's own evil. To strike them so that they do not rise is to be deprived of good; to fall is to pervert the truth (see Ps. 7:15) and to be under the feet is to subdue the falsehoods of one's lower natural as signified by feet (see Ps. 8:6, 41:9, 49:5, 99:5, 105:18). To gird or put on clothing is to know and perceive truths from the light of good (see Ps. 18:32); valour is excellence in doctrine (see Ps. 18:32); battle is warfare between truth and falsity (see Ps. 18:34, 24:8, 27:3, 46:9, 76:3); to make them kneel down is to subdue them into order. The neck signifies conjunction for it connects the head to the body, to have the necks of the enemies is to separate from falsehoods so that they can no longer disjoin or block communication of good and truth from heaven:

"That the neck signifies what conjoins, is because the higher things in man, which are of the head, communicate with the lower things which are of his body, by the intermediate neck; hence both influx and communication, consequently conjunction, is signified by that intermedium — as may be still more evident from the correspondences of the Greatest Man with the things which are of the human body, which are treated of at the conclusion of the chapters. The like is hence signified by neck in the Word — as in Isaiah: *His breath as an overflowing stream, will divide even unto the neck* (xxx. 28) — where an overflowing stream stands for falsity thus overflowing; dividing even unto the neck, stands for falsity closing up and thus intercepting communication, and thus the conjunction of what is superior with what is inferior, which conjunction is precluded and intercepted when spiritual good and truth are not received." (*Heavenly Arcana*, n. 3542.2)

And I pulverized them as dust upon the face of the wind,
I emptied them out as the mire in the streets. (Ps. 18:42)

This describes the conquest of the hells by the Lord after they were separated from the good. Dust signifies condemnation towards hell as it concerns the lowest things of the sensual (see Ps. 22:29, 44:25, 72:9); the face of the wind is the evil of their own falsehood; wind is also Divine influx of truth which punishes the wicked (see Ps. 11:6, 18:15, 48:7, 78:26, 83:15). The "mire in the streets" signifies the falsity of their love for what is evil which led to their condemnation, for ways and paths signifies truths or falsities (see Ps. 1:1, 25:4,12, 37:23, 86:11).

"'Street' signifies the truth of doctrine, and in the contrary sense the falsity of doctrine, because in the spiritual sense a 'way' signifies truth leading to good, and in the contrary sense falsity leading to evil (see above, n. 97); and streets are ways in a city, and as a 'city' signifies doctrine, so a 'street' signifies the truth and the falsity of doctrine. Moreover, in the spiritual world there are cities, and streets in them, as in the cities of the world; and what each one is in respect to the affection of truth and intelligence therefrom is known there merely from the place where he dwells and from the streets in which he walks. Those who are in a clear perception of truth dwell in the southern quarter of the city and also walk there; those who are in a clear affection of the good of love dwell in the eastern quarter and also walk there;

those who are in an obscure affection of the good of love dwell in the western quarter and also walk there; and those who are in an obscure perception of truth dwell in the northern quarter and also walk there. But in the cities where those live who are in the persuasion of falsity from evil the reverse is true. This makes clear why it is that a 'street' signifies truth or falsity leading." (*Apocalypse Explained*, n. 652.2)

"As 'street' signifies the truth of doctrine leading, and in the contrary sense falsity, 'the clay of the streets,' 'the mire,' and 'dung' signify the falsity of the love of evil, in the following passages. In *Isaiah*:—

Their carcass has become as the dung of the streets (v. 25).

In the same:—

He shall make him to be trodden down like the clay of the street (x. 6).

In *Micah*:—

She shall be trodden down like the mire of the streets (vii. 10).

In *David*:—

I will beat them small as the dust before the faces of the wind, I will spread them out as the mire of the streets (*Ps.* xviii. 42).

All this, too, is from the appearances in the spiritual world; in the cities there in which falsities from evil reign the streets appear full of dung, mire and clay." (*Apocalypse Explained*, n. 652.29)

You have rescued me from the arguing of the people,
And You have made me the head of the nations,
A people whom I have not known shall serve me. (Ps. 18:43)

The "arguing of the people" are disputes against the truth by falsehoods (see Ps. 35:1); to be rescued is to be delivered from falsehoods (see Ps. 91:14); to be head of the nations is for the Lord to become united with the Father or Divine good, for nations signify all goods (see Ps. 2:1, 18:43, 102:15, 106:5). Upon the glorification of the Lord the church was established among the Gentiles who were in obscurity as to the truth; to hear with the ear signifies obedience (see Ps. 40:6).

"In the Most Ancient and in the Ancient Church, the many families which acknowledged one father constituted one nation. But as to nations signifying in the internal sense worships of the church, and this as to things good or evil in the worship, the case is this: as families and nations are viewed by angels, they have no conception of a nation, but only of the worship in it; for they regard all men according to their actual quality, or according to what they are. The quality or character of a man according to which he is regarded in heaven is his charity and faith. This any one may clearly apprehend if he considers that when he looks at any man, or any family, or nation, he thinks for the most part of what quality they are — every one from that which is dominant in himself at the time. The idea of their quality comes instantly to mind, and in himself he estimates them from that. Still more does the Lord; and from Him angels cannot but regard a man, a family, or a nation, according to their quality as to charity and faith. And hence it is that in the internal sense nothing else than the worship of the church is signified by nations, and this in respect to its quality, which is the good of charity, and the truth of faith therefrom. When the term nation occurs in the Word, angels do not dwell at all in the idea of a nation, according to the historical sense of the letter, but in the idea of the good and truth in the nation that is named.

"Further, as regards nations signifying things good and evil in worship, the case is this: in the most ancient times, as has been stated before, men lived distinguished into nations, families, and houses, in order that the church on earth might represent the kingdom of the Lord, wherein all are distinguished into societies, and societies into greater, and these again into still greater societies, and this according to differences of love and of faith, in general and in particular (see n. 684, 685). Thus they are likewise distinguished as into houses, families, and nations. And hence in the Word houses, families, and nations, signify goods of love and thence of faith; and a distinction is there made, with exactness, between nations and people. A nation signifies good or evil, and a people truth or falsity, and this so constantly that it is never otherwise…

"In David: *Thou wilt deliver Me from the strivings of the people, thou wilt place Me at the head of the nations. A people whom I have not known shall serve Me* (Ps. xviii. 43). Here likewise the people stand for those who are in truths, and the nations for those who are in good. They are both mentioned because they constitute the man of the church." (*Heavenly Arcana*, n. 1258, 1259.1,5; see also *Apocalypse Revealed*, n. 483, *Apocalypse Explained*, n. 331.7)

At the hearing of the ear they shall hearken to me,
Sons of foreigners shall submit themselves to me.
Sons of foreigners shall fade away,
And tremble from their enclosures. (Ps. 18:44-45)

This describes the last state of the existing church which becomes estranged from the Lord in their worship. The foreign sons are those who are in the falsehoods of external worship only (see Ps. 144:5). To fade away is to decline from truth into falsehood; to tremble from enclosures is to be in fear against the truth from a state of falsehood, similar to the meaning for a pit (see Ps. 28:1, 69:15, 88:4,6). In the following passage "sons of the foreigner" is translated as "sons of the stranger" –

"…those who placed worship solely in externals were represented by the Gentiles, whom they called strangers, who were their servants and performed menial services in the church — as in Isaiah: *And strangers shall stand and feed your flocks, and the sons of the stranger shall be your ploughmen and your vine-dressers. But ye shall be named the priests of Jehovah: men shall call you the ministers of our God: ye shall eat the wealth of the gentiles, and in their glory shall ye boast yourselves* (lxi. 5, 6). Here celestial men are called priests of Jehovah, spiritual men the ministers of our God; those who place worship solely in externals are called the sons of the stranger, who should serve in their fields and vineyards." (*Heavenly Arcana*, n. 1097)

Jehovah lives, and blessed be my rock,
And let the God of my salvation be exalted. (Ps. 18:46)

"Jehovah lives" signifies the Lord is life itself (see Ps. 27:13, 36:9) and to bless Him is to acknowledge He is the source of all that is good (see Ps. 3:8, 16:7, 21:6, 24:5, 28:6, 31:21, 96:2); rock is the Divine truth (see Ps. 19:14, 28:1, 78:15). God is the Lord as to Divine truth; salvation is deliverance from evil (see Ps. 14:7, 96:2).

"'Jehovah liveth, and blessed be my Rock;' 'the God of my salvation shall be exalted' signifies that He must be worshiped by means of truths from good, from which is salvation; 'to be exalted,' in reference to God, is predicated of worship from good by means of truths." (*Apocalypse Explained*, n. 411.9)

It is God who gives me vengeance,
And He subdues people under me.
He rescues me from my enemies,
Yes, You lift me up above those who rise up against me,
You have delivered me from the violent man.
Therefore I will confess You among the nations, Jehovah,
And make music to Your name.
He magnifies salvation to His king,
And does mercy to His anointed,
To David and to his seed for evermore. (Ps. 18:47-50)

To bring down people is to overcome falsehoods (see Ps. 2:1, 3:8, 18:43, 65:7, 74:18, 102:15); to rescue is to lead away from falsities (see Ps. 91:14) and enemies are falsehoods which attack the truth (see Ps. 3:1, 27:12); to be lifted above those who rise up is to be saved from evil; to be delivered from violent men is to be delivered from those who pervert the truths of the Word (see Ps. 140:1). To confess is to worship from affection for the good of love (Ps. 7:17, 35:18, 50:14, 89:24); Jehovah is the Lord as to Divine love (see Ps. 18:31, 28:1, 68:26, 82:1, 147:7); nations are those who are in good (see Ps. 2:1, 18:43, 79:1, 80:8, 102:15, 106:5,27). To make music is to worship from truth spiritual truth (see Ps. 57:7) and name signifies every truth of doctrine (see Ps. 74:18, 96:2). Salvation is from Divine good (see Ps. 14:7, 96:2) which proceed through Divine truth, signified by king (see Ps. 2:2,10 24:7-10, 72:11, 89:20,39, 95:3, 105:20,30, 110:5). The anointed one signifies Divine good from Divine love in the Divine Human (see Ps. 2:2, 89:20); the Divine Human is represented by David (see Ps. 78:70, 89:3,20, 132:1,10); and his seed are those who are in faith from charity (see Ps. 21:10, 22:23, 30, 89:4, 106:27).

Psalm 19

To the chief musician, a Psalm of David.

~

The heavens recount the glory of God, (1)
And the firmament proclaims the work of His hands.
Day unto day utters speech, (2)
And night unto night shows knowledge.
Without speech and without words lacking, (3)
We will hear their voice.
Their line is gone out through all the earth, (4)
And their statements to the end of the world.
In them has He set a tent for the sun,
And He is as a bridegroom coming out of His chamber. (5)
He rejoices as a mighty one running the path,
His going forth is from the end of the heavens, (6)
And His circuit is upon the ends of them,
And nothing is hidden from His heat.
  The law of Jehovah is perfect, (7)
  Restoring the soul,
  The testimony of Jehovah is faithful,
  Making wise the simple.
  The precepts of Jehovah are right, (8)
  Rejoicing the heart.
  The commandment of Jehovah is pure,
  Enlightening the eyes.
  The fear of Jehovah is clean, (9)
  Standing for ever,
  The judgments of Jehovah are truth,
  They are righteous altogether.

More to be desired are they than gold, (10)
And than much pure gold,
And sweeter than honey,
And the dropping of honeycombs.

Also by them is Your servant warned, (11)
In keeping them there is much consequence.
Who can understand errors? (12)
Hold me guiltless from *my* secrets.
Also withhold Your servant from arrogant things, (13)
Let them not rule over me, then I shall be perfect,
And I shall be held guiltless from much transgression.
Let the sayings of my mouth and the meditation of my
heart, (14)
Be well pleasing in Your presence,
Jehovah, my rock and my redeemer.

Psalm
Commentary

19

Summary: Emanation of the Divine truth from the Lord (v. 1-4), from the first things to the last things of heaven and the church (v. 5-6). This Divine truth perfects man, because it is wisdom. (v. 7-10). There will be no pride (v. 11-13). Thus there will be what is pure and acceptable to the Lord (v. 14).

The heavens recount the glory of God,
And the firmament proclaims the work of His hands. (Ps. 19:1)

The heavens are the spiritual heavens of the truths of faith (see Ps. 135:6); the "glory of God" is the Divine truth (see Ps. 8:5, 24:7-10, 29:1, 73:24, 96:3); to recount is to describe the quality of a thing (see Ps. 147:4). The firmament represents the heaven of the good of charity (see Ps. 150:1); the work of His hands are all things of good that regenerate man (see Ps. 107:24, 111:2,7).

"That heaven in the internal sense means the angelic heaven, is from correspondence and also from the appearance. Wherefore when mention is made in the Word of the heavens, also of the heavens of heavens, in the internal sense are meant the angelic heavens. For the ancients had no other idea of the visible heaven than that the heavenly inhabitants dwelt there, and that the stars were their habitations. Similar also at this day is the idea of the simple, and especially of little children. So also it is usual to look upward to heaven when God is worshipped. This is also from correspondence; for in the other life a heaven with stars is seen, yet not the heaven which is seen by men in the world; but it is a heaven which is apparent according to the state of intelligence and wisdom of the spirits and angels. The stars there are [representative of] knowledges of good and truth, and the clouds which are sometimes seen under the heaven are of various signification according to their colors, their translucence, and their movements; the blueness of heaven is from truth transparent from good. From these things it may be evident that by the heavens are signified the angelic heavens; but by the angelic heavens are signified truths Divine, since angels are receptions of truth Divine proceeding from the Lord.

"Similar things are signified by the heavens in David: *Praise Jehovah, ye heavens of heavens, and ye waters that are above the heavens* (Ps. cxlviii. 4). Again: *Sing praises unto the Lord, that rideth upon the heaven of heaven of old* (Ps. lxviii. 32, 33). Again: *By the word of Jehovah were the heavens made, even all the host of them* (Ps. xxxiii. 6). Again: *The heavens declare the glory of God; and the firmament sheweth His handywork* (Ps. xix. 1)." (*Heavenly Arcana*, n. 9408.2-3)

The glory of God is the Divine truth:

"*And the glory of Jehovah abode upon mount Sinai.* That this signifies the interiors of the Word of the Lord in heaven, is evident from the signification of the glory of Jehovah, when spoken of the Word, as its internal sense, thus the interiors of the Word (see preface to Gen. xviii.; and n. 5922); and from the signification of mount Sinai, as the Divine truth proceeding from the Lord, and therefore heaven... That the interiors of the Word are called glory is because the Divine truth proceeding from the Lord as a sun is the light in heaven, which gives sight to the angels there and at the same time intelligence and wisdom... From that Divine light is all the glory in heaven, which is such as to exceed all human apprehension. From this it is plain why the internal sense of the Word is meant by glory; for the internal sense of the Word is Divine truth proceeding from the Lord in heaven, and therefore it is the light from which all glory there exists.

"This is meant by glory in many passages in the Word — as that they should see the Son of Man in a cloud with glory (Matt.

xxiv. 30; Luke xxi. 27), and that the Lord, after He had suffered, was to enter into His glory (Luke xxiv. 26); that when He should come in His glory, He was to sit upon the throne of His glory (Matt. xxv. 31) — where to sit upon the throne of glory is to judge from the Divine truth which is from Himself; also that Moses and Elijah were seen in glory (Luke ix. 30, 31), Moses and Elijah here standing for the Word (see preface to Gen. xviii.; and n. 2762, 5247, 9372). It is also meant by the glorification of the Lord, in John: *Now is the Son of Man glorified, and God is glorified in Him. ...God shall also glorify Him in Himself, and straightway shall He glorify Him* (xiii. 31, 32). To be glorified in God is to become Divine good, from which is Divine truth.

"And again: *Thy light shall break forth as the morning ...thy justice shall go before thee; the glory of Jehovah shall be thy rearward* (lviii. 8). Again: *It shall come, that I will gather all nations and tongues; and they shall come, and shall see My glory* (lxvi. 18). Again: *Jehovah of hosts shall reign in mount Zion, and in Jerusalem, and before the elders shall be His glory* (xxiv. 23). In Moses: *Jehovah said ...I live, and all the earth shall be filled with the glory of Jehovah* (Num. xiv. 20, 21). These passages relate to the Lord, and the glory is the Divine truth which is from Him. In Isaiah: *I saw the Lord sitting upon a throne, high and lifted up. ...Above Him stood the seraphim. ...And one cried unto another, Holy, holy, holy, Jehovah of hosts; the fullness of all the earth is His glory* (vi. 1-3). And in David: *The heavens declare the glory of God* (Ps. xix. 1). And again: *That the nations may fear the name of Jehovah, and the kings of the earth Thy glory: For Jehovah hath built up Zion, and He hath appeared in His glory* (Ps. cii. 15, 16)." (*Heavenly Arcana*, n. 9429.1-2, 6)

"...the angels of heaven perceive nothing else by glory but the Divine truth; and because all Divine truth is from the Lord, by giving glory to Him they understand acknowledgment and confession that all truth is from Him. For all the glory in the heavens is from no other source; and as far as a society of heaven is in Divine truth, so far all things shine in it, and so far the angels are in the splendor of glory. That the Divine truth is meant by glory, may be evident from these passages: *The voice of one crying in the wilderness, Prepare the way of Jehovah; the glory of Jehovah shall be revealed, and all flesh shall see it* (Isa. xl. 3, 5). *Arise, shine, for thy light is come, and the glory of Jehovah is risen upon thee; Jehovah shall arise upon thee, and His glory shall be seen upon thee* (Isa. xl. 1 to the end). *I will give thee for a covenant to the people, for a light of the nations, and My glory will I not give to another* (Isa. xlii. 6, 8). *For Mine own sake, for Mine own sake will I do it, and I will not give My glory to another* (Isa. xlviii. 11). *They shall fear His glory from the rising of the sun; the Redeemer shall come to Zion* (Isa. lix. 19, 20). *Thy light shall break forth as the morning, the glory of Jehovah shall gather thee* (Isa. lviii. 8). *He shall come to gather together all nations and tongues, that they may see My glory* (Isa. lxvi. 18). *Jehovah said, I live, and the whole earth shall be filled with the glory of Jehovah* (Num. xiv. 21). *The fullness of all the earth is His glory* (Isa. vi. 3). *In the beginning was the Word, and the Word was God; in Him was life, and the life was the light of men. That was the true light. And the Word was made flesh, and we saw His glory, the glory as of the only-begotten of the Father* (John i. 1, 4, 9). *These things said Esaias, when he saw His glory* (John xii. 41). *And they shall see the Son of Man coming in the clouds of heaven with glory* (Matt. xxiv. 30). *The heavens declare the glory of God* (Ps. xix. 1). *And all nations shall fear the name of Jehovah, and the kings of the earth Thy glory; for He hath built up Zion, and hath appeared in His glory* (Ps. cii. 15, 16). *The glory of God shall enlighten the Holy Jerusalem, and her lamp is the Lamb, and the nations which are saved shall walk in the light of it* (Apoc. xxi. 23-25). *The Son of Man shall come in His glory, and sit upon the throne of His glory* (Matt. xxv. 31; Mark viii. 38)." (*Apocalypse Revealed*, n. 629)

"For the sake of the end that the Lord might be constantly present, He has disclosed to me the spiritual sense of His Word, in which Divine truth is in its light, and in this light He is continually present. For His presence in the Word comes only by the spiritual sense; through the light of this, He passes into the shade in which is the sense of the letter; comparatively, as it is with the light of the sun in the day time, passing through a cloud that is interposed. That the sense of the letter of the Word is as a cloud, while the spiritual sense is the glory, and the Lord Himself is the sun from which the light comes, and that so the Lord is the Word, was shown above. That the glory in which He is to come (Matt. xxiv. 30) signifies Divine truth in its light, in which the spiritual sense of the Word is, is clearly evident from these passages: *The voice of him who crieth in the wilderness, Prepare ye the way of Jehovah: the glory of Jehovah shall be revealed, and all flesh shall see it together* (Isa. xl. 3, 5). *Arise, shine, for thy light is come, and the glory of Jehovah is risen upon thee* (ix. 1 to the end). *I will give Thee for a covenant of the people, for a light of the Gentiles, and My glory will I not give to another* (xlii. 6, 8; see also xlviii. 11). *Thy light shall break forth as the morning, the glory of Jehovah shall gather thee* (lviii. 8). *All the earth shall be filled with the glory of Jehovah* (Num. xiv. 21; Isa. vi. 1-3; lxvi. 18). *In the beginning was the Word; in Him was life, and the life was the light of men. That was the true light. And the Word was made flesh, and we beheld His glory, the glory as of the only-begotten of the Father* (John i. 1, 4, 9, 14). *The heavens will declare the glory of God* (Ps. xix. 1). *The glory of God will enlighten the holy Jerusalem, and the Lamb is the light thereof; and the nations that are saved shall walk in the light of it* (Apoc. xxi. 23, 24). So in many other places. Glory signifies Divine truth in its fullness, because all that is magnificent in heaven is from the light proceeding from the Lord, and the light proceeding from Him as the sun there is in its essence Divine truth." (*True Christian Religion*, n. 780)

Day unto day utters speech,
And night unto night shows knowledge.
Without speech and without words lacking,
We will hear their voice.
Their line is gone out through all the earth,
And their statements to the end of the world. (Ps. 19:3-4)

A day signifies a state of enlightenment in the truth (see Ps. 32:4, 74:16, 136:8), and night a state of obscurity or false-hood (see Ps. 3:8, 16:7, 32:4, 74:16, 91:6, 104:20, 136:9). Speech and words in the internal sense signifies thoughts of truth; to hear signifies obedience of the will (see Ps. 40:6). The earth represents those of the church in truth and the world those in the church as to good (see Ps. 9:8, 24:1, 60:2, 90:2, 96:13). The ends of the earth are the limits of the church where there is little spirituality (see Ps. 46:9, 48:10, 65:5).

In them has He set a tent for the sun,
And He is as a bridegroom coming out of His chamber. (Ps. 19:4-5)

Tents represent the celestial heaven or worship in the holy of love (see Ps. 15:1, 52:5, 61:4, 132:3), and the sun represents the Lord as to Divine love (see Ps. 8:3, 50:1, 72:5,7, 74:16, 89:36, 104:19, 136:8, 148:3). To rejoice is to have joy from love (see Ps. 14:7) which descends as the power of truth signified by a mighty one (see Ps. 21:13, 80:2).

"*In the heavens He hath set a tabernacle for the sun* (*Ps.* xix. 4). 'The sun' means here the Lord in relation to Divine love; and because He dwells in the good of His own love in the heavens it is said, 'In the heavens He hath set a tabernacle for the sun,' 'tabernacle' here meaning the Lord's heaven from the good of love." (*Apocalypse Explained*, n. 799.17)

The male is a form of truth and the female is a form of love, and the union of the two in marriage represents the conjunction of truth and good. A bridegroom thus signifies the affection for what is good and a bride the affection for truth:

"*And she took her veil and covered herself.* That this signifies appearances of truth, is evident from the signification of a veil with which brides covered the face when they first saw the bridegroom, as appearances of truth; for brides with the ancients represented affections for truth, and bridegrooms affections for good; or what is the same, the church, which was called a bride from affection for truth; affection for good which is from the Lord was the bridegroom, and hence the Lord Himself is called the bridegroom throughout the Word. Brides veiled their faces on their first coming to the bridegroom, that they might represent appearances of truth. Appearances of truth are not truths in themselves, but they appear as truths — concerning which see below. Affection for truth cannot come near to affection for good except by appearances of truth; nor is it stripped of appearances before it is conjoined; for then it becomes the truth of good, and becomes genuine so far as the good is genuine.

"Good itself is holy because it is the Divine proceeding from the Lord, and flows in by the superior way or gate in man; but truth so far as its origin is concerned, is not holy, because it flows in by a lower way or gate, and at first is of the natural man; but when it is elevated thence toward the rational man, it is by degrees purified; and at the first sight of affection for good, it is separated from knowledge, and puts on appearances of truth, and thus comes near to good; an indication that such is its origin, and that it could not support the first sight of Divine good, before it has entered into the bridegroom's chamber, that is, into the sanctuary of good, and conjunction has been effected; for then truth no longer looks at good from appearances, or through appearances, but it is looked at from good apart from them." (*Heavenly Arcana*, n. 3207; see also *Heavenly Arcana*, n. 9182.4-5)

He rejoices as a mighty one running the path,
His going forth is from the end of heavens,
And His circuit upon the ends of them,
And nothing is hidden from His heat. (Ps. 19:5-6)

A path is truth that concerns good (see Ps. 25:4) and running along it signifies instruction similar to sojourning (see Ps. 5:4). The "end of heaven" and the "circuit to the ends of it" signify the Divine influx of truth and good into the ultimate external heaven (see Ps. 12:8, 105:33). Heat is Divine influx influencing affections for good in the will (see Ps. 32:4, 74:17). Divine influx is from the interior heavens of love towards the exterior heavens, which are less perfect in form:

"How it is with these things cannot be known unless it is known how it is with interior and exterior things in the spiritual world. Those things which are best and purest, which therefore are more perfect than the rest, are in the inmost part; those which proceed thence toward exteriors, are less perfect according to the degree of removal from inmosts; and lastly those things which are in outmosts are the least perfect of all (n. 9648). Things are said to be less perfect, which can be more easily wrested from their form and beauty, and thus from their order. It is the same as with fruits, which contain in their inmost part seeds, on the outside of which is the pulp. The seeds are in a more perfect state than the pulp which is outside; as may be evident from this, that when the pulp decays, the seeds notwithstanding remain entire. The case is the same with the seeds; inmostly in them is the prolific part, and this is in a more perfect state than those parts of the seed which are outside; for the prolific part remains in its integrity and produces a new tree or plant, when the exterior parts are dissolved. The case is the same in heaven, where inmosts, since they are nearer to the Lord, are in a more perfect state than the exteriors. In consequence the inmost heaven excels the heavens which are beneath in wisdom and intelligence, and therefore in happiness. The case is still the same in every heaven, the inmost therein being more perfect than are the parts which are round about. It is the same with a man who is in the good of love and the truths of faith. His internal is in a more perfect state than his external, for the internal man is in the heat and light of heaven, but the external is in the heat and light of the world. It is the same in every perfect form; its inmost is the best. It is the inmost which is understood by the middle.

"...from end to end signifies the first end and the last, and thus from beginning to end, for the first end is the beginning. It is for this reason that by the ends are signified all things and everywhere — as in Jeremiah: *The sword of Jehovah devoureth from the end of the land unto the end thereof* (xii. 12). A sword stands for truth fighting against falsity and destroying it, and in the opposite sense for falsity fighting against truth and destroying it (n. 2799, 4499, 6353, 7102, 8294); devouring from the end of the land unto the end thereof stands for all things of the church, since the land or earth means the church (n. 9334). In David: *His going forth is from the end of the heavens, and His circuit unto the ends thereof* (Ps. xix. 6) — where also from the end of the heavens unto the ends thereof means all things and everywhere.

"In Mark: *He shall send forth His angels, and shall gather together His elect from the four winds, from the uttermost part of the earth even unto the uttermost part of heaven* (xiii. 27) — where the uttermost part or end of the earth and the uttermost part or end of heaven stand for all things external and internal of the church; that the earth is the external of the church, and heaven its internal, may be seen above (n. 1733, 1850, 2117, 2118, 3355, 4535) — where is set forth what is meant by the new earth and the new heaven. So with ends, in the plural number — as in Isaiah: *Look unto Me, and be ye saved, all the ends of the earth* (xlv. 22). And in David: *O God of our salvation, the confidence of all the ends of the earth, and of them who are afar off upon the sea* (Ps. lxv. 5). And also in the singular number, when it is said, even unto the end — as in Isaiah: *That My salvation may be even unto the end of the earth* (xlix. 6). Again: *Jehovah shall make it to be heard even unto the end of the earth, Say ye to the daughter of Zion, Behold, thy salvation cometh* (lxii. 11). And in Jeremiah: *A tumult shall come even unto the end of the earth* (xxv. 31). In these passages by even unto the end is involved from end to end." (*Heavenly Arcana*, n. 9666.2-4)

The law of Jehovah is perfect,
Restoring the soul:
The testimony of Jehovah is faithful,
Making wise the simple.
The precepts of Jehovah are right,
Rejoicing the heart:
The commandment of Jehovah is pure,

Enlightening the eyes.
The fear of Jehovah is clean,
Standing for ever:
The judgments of Jehovah are truth,
They are righteous altogether.
More to be desired are they than gold,
And than much pure gold,
And sweeter than honey,
And the dropping of honeycombs. (Ps. 19:7-10)

This describes the descent of the Divine truth in the natural. The "law of Jehovah" is Divine truth from Divine love flowing into the inmost soul giving spiritual life, which is described as perfect which is to be in good from truth (see Ps. 15:2). The law can also signify all things of the Word, which is based on love. The "testimony of Jehovah" is the Divine truth that testifies concerning the Lord; and is thus called faithful which is predicated of truth, which makes wise the simple. The "precepts of Jehovah" are external truths concerning good; to rejoice the heart is joy from love (see Ps. 14:7). The "commandments of Jehovah" are internal things of the Word which enlighten the eyes which signifies the spiritual understanding (see Ps. 11:4, 13:3, 31:9, 69:23). The "fear of Jehovah" signifies external obedience to God, and "judgments of Jehovah" are external truths of civil laws. Gold here is external knowledges of love (see Ps. 2:9, 19:10, 45:9, 72:15); honey is natural good and the dropping of the honeycomb is natural truth; sweetness is delight therefrom (see Ps. 55:14). The distinction between the law, judgments and statutes are described in the following passages:

"Now these are the judgments which thou shalt set before them signifies exterior truths, such as ought to be in the civil state where there is a representative. church, and which flow from the internal truths which are of order in the heavens; that these things are signified by the judgments which were to be set before the sons of Israel is evident from the signification of judgments, as truths (see n. 2235, 6397, 7206, 8685, 8695). The

reason why judgments are truths is that all judgment is effected by truths. Therefore by doing judgment in the Word is signified doing truth, that is, judging according to truths. But by judgments, in the plural, are signified civil laws, thus exterior truths such as are in the civil state. It is said where there is a representative church, for the reason that interiorly they contain and involve in them those truths which are of order in the heavens, as may be evident from their internal sense.

"The laws which were enacted and commanded the sons of Israel by the Lord were distinguished into commandments, judgments, and statutes. Those were called commandments which related to the life, those judgments which related to the civil state, and those statutes which related to worship." (*Heavenly Arcana*, n. 8972)

"*And kept My charge, My commandments, My statutes, and My laws.* That this signifies by continuous revelations from Himself — that is to say, as by temptations, so also by these revelations He united the Divine essence to the human — may be evident from this, that keeping His charge, commandments, statutes, and laws, involves all things of the Word — namely, charge all things of the Word in general, commandments the internal things, statutes the external things, and laws all things in particular. Inasmuch as this is predicated of the Lord, Who from eternity was the Word, and from Whom all those things are, in the internal sense it cannot be signified that He observed those things, but that He revealed them to Himself, when He was in a state of unition of the human with the Divine.

"...they who are in heaven are in the idea that all things of the Word in the internal sense treat of the Lord, and also that all things of the Word are from the Lord; likewise, that when He was in the world, He thought from the Divine and thus from Himself, and acquired to Himself all intelligence and wisdom by continuous revelations from the Divine; therefore they from the above words perceive nothing else. For keeping the charge, commandments, statutes, and laws, is not predicable of the Lord, since He Himself was the Word, consequently Himself was

the charge, Himself was the commandment, Himself the statute, and Himself the law; for all these things have respect to
Him, as the First from whom they are derived and as the Last to
whom they tend. Therefore by the above words, in the supreme
sense, nothing else can be signified than the unition of the Lord's
Divine with the human, by continuous revelations from Himself.

"That keeping the charge means all things of the Word in
general, and that commandments are the internal things of the
Word, statutes the external things, and laws all things of the
Word in particular, in a genuine sense, may be evident from
many passages viewed in the internal sense, some of which may
be adduced... *The law of Jehovah is perfect, restoring the soul; the
testimony of Jehovah is sure, making wise the simple. The precepts of Jehovah are right, rejoicing the heart; the commandment
of Jehovah is pure, enlightening the eyes. The fear of Jehovah is
clean, standing forever; the judgments of Jehovah are truth* (Ps.
xix. 7-9)." (*Heavenly Arcana*, n. 3382.1-4)

The testimony is the Divine truth that testifies concerning
the Lord, and also living a life according to the truth:

"As to the signification of the Testimony, a distinction is
made in the Word between laws, statutes, judgments, precepts,
testimonies, words, commands, truths, and covenants, as may
be evident from very many passages — especially from David, in
Psalm cxix., where these are all named, as testimonies in these
verses (2, 14, 31, 46, 59, 88, 95, 111, 119, 129, 138, 144, 168); in
like manner in other places, in David: *The law of Jehovah is perfect, restoring the soul; the testimony of Jehovah is sure, making
wise the simple. The statutes of Jehovah are right, rejoicing the
heart: the commandment of Jehovah is pure, enlightening the
eyes. ...The judgments of Jehovah are truth, justified together*
(Ps. xix. 7-9); and also in Moses (Deut. iv. 45; vi. 17, 20); and in
Jeremiah (xliv. 23); and in many other passages. From the above
it may be evident that the Testimony is Divine truth which testifies concerning the Lord, and thus is the Word, for the Word
in the supreme sense treats of the Lord alone, and therefore
in the internal sense testifies concerning Him, that is, teaches

Him and the truths of faith and the goods of love, which are from Him. In this sense the testimony is spoken of also in the Apocalypse: *That had been slain for the word of God, and for the testimony which they held* (vi. 9); and in another passage: *They overcame* the dragon *by the blood of the Lamb, and by the word of their testimony* (xii. 11). The blood of the Lamb is Divine truth proceeding from the Lord (n. 7846, 7877, 9127, 9393), and the word of testimony is Divine truth received by man; in like manner elsewhere (xii. 17 and xix. 10).

"That Divine truth proceeding from the Lord is called the testimony, is because it testifies concerning the Lord, as is evident from the words of the Lord Himself in John: *He who cometh from heaven is above all. ...What He hath seen and heard, that He testifieth. ...He who receiveth His testimony hath set his seal to this, that God is true* (iii. 31-33). Again: *I am he who testifieth of Myself, and the Father who sent Me testifieth of Me* (viii. 18). Again: *Search the Scriptures ...and these are they which testify of Me* (v. 39). And again: *The Comforter ...the Spirit of truth ...he shall testify of Me* (xv. 26). From these passages it is evident that Divine truth is called the testimony for the reason that it testifies concerning the Lord. This Divine truth is the Word, for the Word in the supreme sense, as was said above, treats of the Lord alone; therefore the Word is Divine, and from this is its holy. The Ten Words also, that is, the Law which was promulgated from mount Sinai and inscribed upon the two tables and deposited in the ark, is what is here called the Testimony — that this Law signifies the Word, that is, Divine truth proceeding from the Lord, in its whole complex, may be seen above (n. 9416)." (*Heavenly Arcana*, n. 9503.2-3)

"Since a covenant, or conjunction, is effected by the laws or precepts of love, it was also established by the laws of society given from the Lord in the Jewish church, called testimonies; and also by the rites of the church enjoined by the Lord, called statutes." (*Heavenly Arcana*, n. 1038.5)

The fear of Jehovah has regard to love, and judgment to the truths of faith:

"In David: *The precepts of Jehovah are right, rejoicing the heart; the commandment of Jehovah is pure, enlightening the eyes; the fear of Jehovah is clean, standing forever; the judgments of Jehovah are truth, justified together* (Ps. xix. 8, 9); where 'the fear of Jehovah is clean' means love, and 'the judgments of Jehovah are truth' means faith. That justice is predicated of the good of love, and judgment of the truth of faith, may be seen above (n. 2235); these are said to be justified together, when truth becomes good, or when faith becomes charity." (*Heavenly Arcana*, n. 2826.9)

> *"The judgments of Jehovah are truth, they are righteous altogether; more desirable than gold and than much fine gold; and sweeter than honey and the dropping of honeycombs (Ps. xix. 9, 10).*

In the same:—

> *I have not departed from Thy judgment; for Thou hast instructed me. How sweet are Thy words to my palate, more than honey to my mouth (Ps. cxix. 102, 103).*

'Judgments' signify the truths and goods of worship, therefore it is said 'the judgments of Jehovah are truth, they are righteous altogether;' 'righteous' signifies the good of life and worship therefrom; and as good is also signified by 'gold' and 'fine gold,' it is said that 'they are more desirable than gold and than much fine gold,' 'gold' meaning celestial good, 'fine gold' spiritual good, and 'desirable' means what belongs to affection and love. Since the goods by which a man is affected are delightful it is said that they are 'sweeter than honey and the dropping of honeycombs,' and that 'the words of Jehovah are sweet to the palate, more than honey to the mouth,' 'sweet' signifying what is delightful, 'honey' natural good, and 'the dropping of honeycombs' natural truth. And because 'honey' means natural good, and the 'mouth' signifies what is external, it is said 'more than honey to my mouth,' as in the *Apocalypse,* that 'the little book was sweet as honey in the mouth.'" (*Apocalypse Explained,* n. 619.14)

"In David: *The judgments of Jehovah are truth, just are they together; more to be desired are they than gold, than much fine gold, sweeter also than honey and the dropping of the honeycombs* (Ps. xix. 9, 10). The judgments of Jehovah stand for truth Divine; sweeter than honey and the dropping of the honeycombs, for enjoyments from good and pleasures from truth." (*Heavenly Arcana,* n. 5620.10)

Also by them is Your servant warned:
In keeping them there is much consequence.
Who can understand errors?
Hold me guiltless from my secrets.
Also withhold Your servant from arrogant things,
Let them not rule over me, then I shall be perfect,
And I shall be held guiltless from much transgression.
(Ps. 19:11-13)

The Lord withholds those who follow His commandments from evil. Servants are those who live by the truths of faith (see Ps. 31:16, 69:36, 78:70, 89:3,20); those who keep them are those who do them; the great outcome is eternal life in heaven according to how one lived their life (see Ps. 109:20). Errors are transgressions of ignorance (Lev. 4:13, Num. 15:22-24, Deut. 27:18, 1 Sam. 26:21, Job 6:24); secrets are iniquities done against the good of faith; arrogant things are evils against the good of love from self love. For sins to rule is for evil to dominate good (see Ps. 105:20); to be perfect is to be in good from truth (see Ps. 15:2). To be acquitted from transgression is to repent and turn away from evil done against the truth of faith (see Ps. 5:10, 25:7, 32:1, 51:1-3).

Let the sayings of my mouth and the meditation of my heart,
Be well pleasing in Your presence,
Jehovah, my rock and my redeemer. (Ps. 19:14)

The sayings of the mouth are the knowledges of good (see Ps. 33:9) of the external understanding (see Ps. 5:9, 37:30, 135:16); the meditation of the heart is the internal perception of good. To be well pleasing is to be in a state of conjunction (see Ps. 5:12, 40:8, 51:18, 69:13) with Divine love signified by presence or face (see Ps. 4:6, 13:1, 22:24, 27:8-9, 31:16, 67:1). Jehovah is the Lord as to Divine love (see Ps. 18:31, 28:1, 68:26, 82:1, 147:7); rock is the Lord as to the Divine truth (see Ps. 18:46, 78:15), and redeemer signifies liberation from evil (see Ps. 69:18, 107:2).

> *"Let the sayings of my mouth and the meditation of my heart be well pleasing before Thee, O Jehovah, my Rock and my Redeemer (Ps. xix. 14).*

'Jehovah the Rock' has a like signification as 'Jehovah God,' namely, the Lord in respect to Divine good and Divine truth; and He is called 'Redeemer' from regeneration, which is effected by Divine truth; 'sayings of the mouth' signify the understanding of truth, and 'the meditation of the heart' the perception of good." (*Apocalypse Explained*, n. 411.10)

Both Jehovah and Jesus are known as the Redeemer as they are one and the same:

"Because the Lord's Human was equally Divine with His Divine Itself that took on the Human, Jehovah is called 'the Redeemer' in the following passages. In *Isaiah:*—

> *Thus said Jehovah thy Redeemer, the Holy One of Israel, I am Jehovah thy God (xlviii. 17).*

In the same:—

> *Jehovah of Hosts is His name; and thy Redeemer, the Holy One of Israel; the God of the whole earth shall He be called (liv. 5).*

In *David:*—

> *O Jehovah, my Rock and my Redeemer (Ps. xix. 14).*

In *Jeremiah:*—

> *Their Redeemer is strong; Jehovah of Hosts is His name* (l. 34).

In *Isaiah:*—

> *Thou, O Jehovah, art our Father, our Redeemer; from everlasting is Thy name* (lxiii. 16).

From this it can now be seen how this saying of the Lord is to be understood:—

> *The Son of man came to give His soul a redemption for many* (*Matt.* xx. 28; *Mark* x. 46);

namely, that they might be delivered and freed from hell; for the passion of the cross was the last combat and complete victory by which He subjugated the hells, and by which He glorified His Human (see *The Doctrine of the New Jerusalem,* n. 293-297, 300-306)." (*Apocalypse Explained,* n. 328.22)

"That the God of Israel and the Holy One of Israel is the Lord as to the Divine Human, is also evident from this, that He is called the Redeemer, the Saviour, the Maker — the Redeemer, in Isaiah: *Our Redeemer, Jehovah of Hosts is His name, the Holy one of Israel* (xlvii. 4; also xli. 14; xliii. 14; xlviii. 17; liv. 5); also the Saviour (xliii. 3); and the Maker (xlv. 11). From this also it is plain that by Jehovah in the Word of the Old Testament, no other is meant than the Lord, for He is called Jehovah God and the Holy One of Israel, the Redeemer, the Saviour, the Maker — Jehovah the Redeemer and Saviour in Isaiah: *That all flesh may know, that I Jehovah am thy Saviour, and thy Redeemer, the Mighty One of Jacob* (xlix. 26). Again: *That thou mayest know that I Jehovah am thy Saviour and thy Redeemer, the Mighty One of Jacob* (lx. 16; as also xliii. 14; xliv. 6, 24; liv. 8; lxiii. 16; 5 Ps. xix. 14)." (*Heavenly Arcana,* n. 7091.4)

Psalm   20

To the chief musician, a Psalm of David.

~

Jehovah answer you in the day of adversity, (1)
The name of the God of Jacob elevate you,
May He send you help from the sanctuary, (2)
And sustain you out of Zion,
  May He remember all your offerings, (3)
  And make fat your burnt offerings. (Selah)
  May He give to you according to your own heart, (4)
  And fulfil all your counsel.
  We will shout for joy in your salvation, (5)
  And raise a banner in the name of our God,
  May Jehovah fulfil all your requests.
  Now I know that Jehovah saves His anointed, (6)
  He will answer him from His holy heaven,
  With the saving might of His right hand.
Some *swear* in the chariot and some *swear* in horses, (7)
But we will remember the name of Jehovah our God.
They bow and fall, (8)
But we are risen and testify.
Jehovah, save the king, (9)
May he answer us in the day we call.

Psalm Commentary 20

Summary: Praise of the Lord who sustains the church (v. 1-3) and from whom is salvation (v. 4-6). Those who trust in the Lord are saved, and those who trust in themselves shall perish (v. 7-9).

Jehovah answer you in the day of adversity,
The name of the God of Jacob elevate you,
May He send you help from the sanctuary,
And sustain you out of Zion (Ps. 20:1-2)

For Jehovah to answer signifies internal Divine influx giving help (see Ps. 4:1), in this case against evil signified by day of adversity (see Ps. 3:1, 27:12). Jacob is the external natural (see Ps. 14:7, 77:15, 78:5, 132:5) and the "God of Jacob" is good in external act (see Ps. 114:7); name is the quality of one's good in the external which elevates one to a more spiritual nature; to be elevated is to be delivered from falsehoods into interior truths derived from good (see Ps. 91:14). The sanctuary is the heaven of the truths of faith (see Ps. 19:1, 150:1) and Zion is the heaven of love (see Ps. 2:6, 14:7, 20:2, 48:11, 51:18, 102:13, 128:5, 133:3, 147:12):

"*The sanctuary, O Lord, which Thy hands have established.* That this signifies heaven where they are who are in the truth of faith from the Lord, is evident from the signification of the sanctuary, as heaven where the truth of faith is — of which presently; and from the signification of Thy hands have established, as that it is what is from the Lord. It is said of the sanctuary that Thy hands have established it, because the hands are predicated of truth and signify power. That the hands are predicated of truth, may be seen above (n. 3091, 8281), and also that they are power (n. 878, 3387, 4931-4937, 5327, 5328, 6292, 6947, 7011, 7188, 7189, 7518, 7673, 8050, 8069, 8153, 8281); likewise that the sanctuary is predicated of truth (n. 8302). But the expressions which precede, *The place for Thee to dwell in* and *which Thou hast made, O Jehovah,* are predicated of good, because they have reference to the mountain of inheritance, by which is signified heaven wherein is the good of charity (n. 8327). That there are expressions in the Word which are predicated of good and expressions which are predicated of truth, may be seen above (n. 8314).

"What is meant by the heaven in which is the good of charity, which is signified by the mountain of inheritance, and what by the heaven in which is the truth of faith, which is the sanctuary, shall be briefly told. The heaven in which is the good of charity is that in which the interior angels are, who are of the Lord's spiritual kingdom, and the heaven in which is the truth of faith is that in which the exterior are, who are of that kingdom. They who are interior are in charity itself and in faith therefrom; but they who are exterior are such as are in faith, but not yet in charity. These latter do good from obedience, but the former from affection. From this it is plain what is meant by the heaven in which is the good of charity and what by the heaven in which is the truth of faith.

"With regard to the sanctuary, it is in the supreme sense the truth of faith which is from the Lord, and hence in the representative sense it is the Lord's spiritual kingdom, also the spiritual church, and thus the regenerated man who is a church, and so also in a sense abstracted from these, it is the truth of faith, thus faith itself. What the holy is may be seen above (n. 8302). Therefore now it is, that heaven is called the sanctuary from the truth of faith which is from the Lord — as in David: *Jehovah answer thee in the day of trouble. ...Send thee help from the sanctuary, and support thee out of Zion* (Ps. xx. 1, 2) — where the sanctuary stands for the heaven in which is the truth of faith, and Zion for the heaven in which is the good of love." (*Heavenly Arcana*, n. 8330.1-3)

May He remember all your offerings,
And make fat your burnt offerings. (Ps. 20:3)

Offerings signifies worship from the truths of faith; to make fat is the reception of good as fat signifies celestial good (see Ps. 17:10, 23:5, 36:8, 63:5, 65:11, 81:16, 92:14, 147:14); burnt offerings signify worship from the good of love (see Ps. 40:6, 50:8, 66:15).

"*Jehovah shall remember all thy offerings and shall make fat thy burnt offering (Ps. xx. 3).* 'Offerings and burnt offering' signify worship, and 'to make fat' signifies worship from the good of love." (*Apocalypse Explained*, n. 1159.3)

"That by an offering [or gift] is meant worship may be evident from the representatives of the Jewish Church, in which sacrifices of every kind, as well as the first-fruits of the earth and of all its products, and the oblation of the first born, were called offerings, in which their worship consisted. And since they all represented heavenly things, and all had reference to the Lord, true worship was signified by these offerings, as may be known to every one. For what is a representative without the thing it represents, or what is an external without the internal, but a kind of idol, and devoid of life? The external has life from internals, or through internals from the Lord. Hence it is evident that the offerings of a representative church all signify worship of the Lord" (*Heavenly Arcana*, n. 349)

"Burnt offerings and sacrifices constituted the principal part of Divine worship with that people (n. 923, 2180), and therefore by burnt offerings and sacrifices in general is signified worship, and by the things which were offered in sacrifice, also by the whole process of the sacrifice, is signified the quality of worship, and by the fat and the burning thereof is signified the very celestial Divine itself, which is the good of love from the

Lord... In David: *Jehovah remember all thy offerings, and make fat thy burnt sacrifice* (Ps. xx. 3) — where to make fat the burnt sacrifice means to render the worship good." (*Heavenly Arcana*, n. 5943.5, 7)

"That burnt offerings in one complex signify representative worship, is evident also in the prophets — as in David: *Jehovah ...will send thee help from the sanctuary, and strengthen thee out of Zion; remember all thy offerings, and accept as fat thy burnt sacrifice* (Ps. xx. 2, 3). In Isaiah: *Every one who keepeth the sabbath from profaning it, and holdeth fast by My covenant; even them will I bring to My holy mountain, and make them joyful in My house of prayer; their burnt offerings and their sacrifices shall be accepted upon Mine altar* (lvi. 6, 7) — where burnt offerings and sacrifices stand for all worship — burnt offerings for worship from love, sacrifices for worship from faith from love. Internal things are here described, as usual in the prophets, by external." (*Heavenly Arcana*, n. 923)

May He give to you according to your own heart,
And fulfil all your counsel. (Ps. 20:4)

The heart is the desire of the will according to love (see Ps. 7:9, 22:10, 24:4, 51:10, 64:6, 66:18, 71:23, 78:8, 86:11); to fulfil all counsel is to fulfill the affection of one's understanding of Divine truth. Prayers are answered according to good and truth, or according to the Lord's kingdom and salvation:

"...he who is in faith from the Lord asks for nothing but what contributes to the Lord's kingdom and to himself for salvation; other things he does not wish, saying in his heart, Why should I ask for what does not contribute to this use? Therefore if he were to ask for any thing except what it is granted him from the Lord to ask he would have no faith of God, that is, no faith from the Lord. It is impossible for angels of heaven to wish and so to ask for any thing else, and if they were to do so they could have no faith that they would receive it." (*Apocalypse Explained*, n. 815.10)

We will shout for joy in your salvation,
And raise a banner in the name of our God,
Jehovah fulfil all your requests.
Now I know that Jehovah saves His anointed,
He will answer him from His holy heaven,
With the saving might of His right hand. (Ps. 20:5-6)

To shout for joy is to have joy from love (see Ps. 14:7) and salvation is deliverance from evil from Divine good (see Ps. 14:7, 96:2); to raise a banner or ensign is to gather together for spiritual combat (see Ps. 60:4). Jehovah is the Divine love itself, and the anointed is the Divine good from Divine love in the Divine Human (see Ps. 2:2, 89:20). The anointed is the Divine good from Divine love in the Divine Human (see Ps. 2:2, 89:20); for Jehovah to save His anointed means that the Lord glorified His human form in order to save all of humanity. To answer is to give help from Divine influx (see Ps. 4:1); the holy heaven is the heaven of Divine truth (see Ps. 5:7, 65:4); saving might is the power of truth to save (see Ps. 21:13, 80:2); the right hand is the power of Divine truth (see Ps. 18:35, 80:15,17, 89:13,21, 110:1, 121:5).

"Jehovah will send help for thee out of the sanctuary, and will sustain thee out of Zion. We will sing of thy salvation, and in the name of our God we will set up our banners. I know that Jehovah saveth His anointed; He answereth him from the heaven of His holiness with the might of the salvation of His right hand (Ps. xx. 2, 5, 6). This, too, was said of the Lord and of His victory over the hells, and the consequent salvation of men. Combats and victories are meant by 'answering His anointed from the heaven of His holiness with the might of the salvation of His right hand,' and the salvation of the faithful thereby is meant by 'His sustaining us out of Zion,' and by 'singing of His salvation.'" (*Apocalypse Explained*, n. 850.11)

"Thy right hand, O Jehovah, is become glorious in power. That this signifies that the omnipotence of the Lord was shown, is evident from the signification of the right hand of Jehovah,

as omnipotence, of which in what follows; and from the signification of, is become glorious in power, as, that it was shown, for
Divine power is shown by the strength by which it becomes glorious. That the right hand of Jehovah is omnipotence, is because
by hand in the Word is signified power, and thus by right hand,
eminent power. Therefore when the hand or right hand is said of
Jehovah, it means Divine power, or omnipotence...

"That the right hand of Jehovah means Divine power, or
omnipotence, is also evident from the following passages in
the Word: *Jesus said ...Henceforth ye shall see the Son of man
sitting at the right hand of power, and coming on the clouds
of heaven* (Matt. xxvi. 64; Mark xiv. 62). And in Luke: *From
henceforth shall the Son of man be sitting at the right hand
of the power of God*(xxii. 69). And also in David: *The saying of
Jehovah unto my Lord, Sit thou at my right hand, until I make
thine enemies a footstool for thy feet. ...Thou art a priest for ever
after the manner of Melchizedek. The Lord at thy right hand
hath stricken through kings in the day of His wrath* (Ps. cx. 1,
4, 5; Matt. xxii. 44). He who does not know that the right hand,
when said of Jehovah, signifies omnipotence, cannot have any
other idea from these words of the Lord, than that the Lord
will sit at the right hand of His Father, and have dominion like
one who sits at the right hand of a king on earth. But the internal sense instructs what is meant in those passages by sitting
at the right hand, namely, Divine omnipotence; thus also it is
said, sit at the right hand of power, and at the right hand of the
power of God...

"Divine power or omnipotence is also signified by the right
hand in the following passages in David: *Now know I that Jehovah saveth His Anointed; He will answer Him from heaven by
the strength of salvation of His right hand* (Ps. xx. 6). Again: *O
Jehovah, look down from the heavens, and behold, and visit this
vine; and the stock which Thy right hand hath planted. ...Let
Thy hand be upon ...the Son of man whom Thou madest strong
for Thyself* (Ps. lxxx. 14, 15, 17). Again: *Thou hast an arm with
might: strong is Thy hand, high is Thy right hand* (Ps. lxxxix.

13). Again: *Jah is my strength and song; He is become my salvation. The voice of rejoicing and salvation is in the tents of the righteous: the right hand of Jehovah hath done valiantly. The right hand of Jehovah is exalted: the right hand of Jehovah hath done valiantly* (Ps. cxviii. 14-16).

"In these passages the right hand of Jehovah stands for omnipotence, and in the supreme sense for the Lord as to Divine truth. This is more plainly seen elsewhere in David: *Let Thy hand, O Jehovah, be for the man of Thy right hand, for the Son of man whom Thou madest strong for Thyself* (Ps. lxxx. 17) — where the man of the right hand of Jehovah and the Son of man stand for the Lord as to Divine truth. Again: *Thou didst drive out the nations with Thy hand. ...They got not the land in possession by their own sword, neither did their own arm save them: but Thy right hand, and Thine arm, and the light of Thy countenance* (Ps. xliv. 2, 3) — where the light of the countenance of Jehovah is Divine truth from Divine good, so also the right hand and arm." (*Heavenly Arcana*, n. 8281.1-2,4-5)

Some swear in the chariot and some swear in horses:
But we will remember the name of Jehovah our God.
They bow and fall:
But we are risen and testify.
Jehovah, save the king:
May he answer us in the day we call. (Ps. 20:7-9)

Those who swear or take an oath in the chariot are those who are confirmed in the falsehood of their self-derived doctrine (see Ps. 18:10, 32:9, 45:4, 46:9, 68:8,17, 104:3, 136:6); those who swear or taken an oath in horses signify those who are confirmed in falsehood from their own understanding (see Ps. 147:10); the name of Jehovah is every truth of doctrine (see Ps. 74:18, 96:2) or the Divine Human through whom Jehovah is known (see Ps. 8:1). To bow is to be deprived of good (see Ps. 31:9, 38:6) and to fall is to pervert truth (see Ps. 7:15); to rise is to live a new spiritual life; to testify is to be in affirmation of the truth. Jehovah is the Divine itself and the king is the Lord as to Divine truth in human form (see Ps. 2:2, 72:11, 89:20,39, 95:3, 105:20,30). For Jehovah to save the king signifies the union of the Divine with the human in the Lord, which was done in order to save the human race. From this there is conjunction between the Divine and mankind through the Lord, signified by answering when one calls (see Ps. 4:1).

Psalm   21

To the chief musician, a Psalm of David.
~

Jehovah, the king shall rejoice in Your strength, (1)
And in Your salvation how exceedingly shall he be glad!
You have given him his heart's longing, (2)
And have not withheld the request of his lips. (Selah)
For You met him with the blessings of goodness, (3)
You set a crown of pure gold on his head.
He asked life from You, (4)
You gave to him length of days forever and ever.
His glory is great in Your salvation, (5)
Splendour and grandeur You have laid upon him.
For You have made him to be a blessing for ever, (6)
You have made him to rejoice with joy with Your face.

   For the king trusts in Jehovah, (7)
   And in the mercy of the Most High He shall not be moved.
   Your hand shall find all Your enemies, (8)
   Your right hand shall find those who hate You.
   You shall make them as a fiery oven in the time of Your presence, (9)
   Jehovah shall swallow them up in His anger,
   And fire shall devour them.
   You shall make their fruit to perish from the earth, (10)
   And their seed from the sons of Man.
   For they stretched out evil against You, (11)
   They devised a scheme, they were unable.
   For You shall appoint them a shoulder, (12)
   You shall prepare with Your bow string against their faces.
   Be exalted, Jehovah, in Your strength, (13)
   We will sing and make music of Your might.

Psalm Commentary 21

Summary: From the Divine the Lord shall be given everything, thus the Lord has all good and truth from which He has glory and honour (v. 1-6). From the Divine truth the Lord has all power from which He conquers all the enemies of hell for which He is praised (v. 9-13).

Jehovah, the king shall rejoice in Your strength,
And in Your salvation how greatly shall he be glad!
You have given him his heart's longing,
And have not withheld the request of his lips. (Ps. 21:1-2)

Jehovah is the Divine itself, the king is the Lord as to the Divine truth in human form (see Ps. 2:2, 72:11, 89:20,39, 95:3, 105:20,30), and strength is the power of Divine good (see Ps. 21:13, 29:1, 95:4, 96:6) which the Lord had from the Divine within Him. Salvation is deliverance from evil by Divine good (see Ps. 14:7, 96:2). Rejoice is joy of the heart or will, and gladness is happiness of the mind or thought (see Ps. 14:7). The Lord's love for the human race is the heart's longing; the corresponding prayer is signified by the request of his lips which was according to the doctrine of Divine truth (see Ps. 12:4, 81:5).

For You met him with the blessings of goodness,
You set a crown of pure gold on his head.
He asked life from You,
You gave to him length of days forever and ever. (Ps. 21:3-4)

This concerns the union of the Divine with the human in the Lord. Blessings of goodness is Divine good and to bless is to acknowledge all good is from the Lord alone (see Ps. 3:8, 16:7, 21:6, 24:5, 28:6, 31:21, 96:2); a crown is wisdom (see Ps. 132:18) which is from love, signified by gold (see Ps. 2:9, 19:10, 45:9, 72:15). The Lord was given eternal life as the Divine within Him is life itself – *For as the Father has life in himself, so he has granted the Son also to have life in himself* (John 5:26). Length is one's state as to good (see Ps. 4:1) and days is one' state as to truth (see Ps. 32:4, 74:16, 136:8); forever is eternity of the celestial kingdom (see Ps. 145:13) and ever is eternity in the spiritual kingdom.

His glory is great in Your salvation:
Splendour and grandeur You have laid upon him.
For You have set him to be blessings for ever:
You have made him to rejoice with joy with Your face. (Ps. 21:5-6)

All truth and good was given to the Lord. Glory is the Divine truth (see Ps. 8:5, 19:1, 24:7-10, 29:1, 73:24, 96:3) which became great in the salvation of the human race which originates from Divine good (see Ps. 14:7, 96:2). Splendour is also the Divine truth (see Ps. 45:3, 96:6, 104:1, 111:3) and grandeur is the Divine good (see Ps. 104:1, 111:3), which were united together in the Divine Human. From the Lord in His Divine Human all humanity receives good signified by blessings (see Ps. 3:8, 16:7, 21:6, 24:5, 28:6, 31:21, 96:2) for ever; rejoice and joy is to be happy from love (see Ps. 14:7) which is from Divine love signified by face (see Ps. 4:6, 13:1, 22:24, 27:8-9, 31:16, 67:1).

"*O Jehovah, Thou hast prevented the King with the blessings of goodness. Thou hast set a crown of fine gold on his head. Glory and honor dost Thou lay upon him. For Thou settest him blessings for ever* (Ps. xxi. 3, 5, 6). 'The King' here does not mean David, but the Lord, who is called 'King' from the spiritual Divine that proceeds from His Divine Human; and because 'blessing' signifies the acknowledgment, glorification, and thanksgiving because every good and truth, and thence heaven and eternal

happiness, are from Him, it is evident what is signified by 'Thou
hast prevented the King with the blessings of goodness,' and by
'Thou settest him blessings for ever.'" (*Apocalypse Explained*,
n. 340.7)

"*And thou shalt be a blessing.* That this signifies that each
and everything is from the Lord, may be evident from the signification of a blessing. Blessing is predicated of all good things; in
the external sense, of corporeal, worldly, and natural good things;
in the internal sense, of spiritual and celestial good things. To be
a blessing is to be the source of all good things, and the giver of
all those good things; this can by no means be said of Abram,
and hence it is plain that by Abram is represented the Lord,
Who alone is a blessing. So too in what is said of Abraham hereafter, as: *Abraham shall surely become a great and numerous
nation, and all the nations of the earth shall be blessed in him*
(Gen. xviii. 18); of Isaac, *In thy seed shall all the nations of the
earth be blessed* (Gen. xxvi. 4); and of Jacob, *In thee and in thy
seed shall the families of the earth be blessed* (Gen. xxviii. 14).
That nations cannot be blessed and are not blessed in Abraham,
Isaac, and Jacob, and in their seed, but in the Lord, may be evident to every one. This is clearly said in David: *His name shall
endure for ever; before the sun shall the name of His Son endure;
and all nations shall be blessed in Him* (Ps. lxxii. 17); where the
Lord is spoken of. Again: *Thou shalt set Him for blessings for
ever* (Ps. xxi. 6); which also is concerning the Lord. In Jeremiah:
The nations shall be blessed in Him, and in Him shall they glory
(iv. 2). From these passages it is now evident that a blessing signifies the Lord, and that when He is called a blessing, it signifies
that from Him are all celestial and spiritual things, which alone
are good; and because they alone are good, they alone are true;
therefore as far as there are celestial and spiritual good things
in natural, worldly, and corporeal things, so far these are good,
and so far are blessed." (*Heavenly Arcana*, n. 1420)

For the king trusts in Jehovah,
And in the mercy of the Most High he shall not be moved.

Your hand shall find all your enemies:
Your right hand shall find those who hate you. (Ps. 21:7-8)

The king is the Lord as to Divine truth in human form (see Ps. 2:2, 72:11, 89:20,39, 95:3, 105:20,30); to trust is to have confidence of the will which is given to those who are in the good of charity (see Ps. 33:21) and is thus mentioned with Jehovah, which signifies the Divine itself or Divine love. Mercy is the Divine love (see Ps. 25:10, 26:3, 36:5, 89:14, 103:8) and the Most High is the interior Divine (see Ps. 7:17); to not be moved is to not be affected by falsehood. Hand is the power of truth (see Ps. 20:6, 44:3, 45:4, 80:15,17, 89:13,21); enemies are the falsehoods of hell (Ps. 3:1, 27:12) and those who hate are the evils of hell.

You shall make them as a fiery oven in the time of Your presence:
Jehovah shall swallow them up in His anger,
And fire shall devour them. (Ps. 21:9)

Fire is the punishment of those who are in evil (see Ps. 2:12, 11:6, 18:8, 68:2, 97:3); the presence or face of God is Divine good (see Ps. 4:6, 13:1, 22:24, 27:8-9, 31:16, 67:1) which causes their torment due to their opposing evil.

"When 'fire' is predicated in the Word of the evil and of the hells, it signifies the love of self and of the world, and thence every evil affection and cupidity that torments the wicked after death in the hells. 'Fire' has this contrary signification for the reason that Divine love, when it comes down out of heaven and falls into the societies where the evil are, is changed into a love contrary to the Divine love, and thus into various heats of cupidity and of lusts, and so into evils of every kind, and also into torments, because evils carry with them the punishments of evil. From this change of the Divine love into infernal love with the evil, the hells where the love of self and the world and hatreds and revenge prevail, appear to be as if on fire, both within and round about, although the infernal crew that is in them perceive nothing fiery. Indeed, from these loves the crew that is in such hells appear with faces inflamed and reddened as from fire...

"Thou shalt make them as an oven of fire in the time of Thine anger, and fire shall devour them (Ps. xxi. 9).

In the same:—

Burning coals shall overwhelm the wicked; fire shall cast them into pits, they shall not rise again (cxl. 10).

In *Matthew:*—

Every tree that bringeth not forth good fruit shall be hewn down and cast into the fire. He will cleanse His floor, and gather His wheat into the garners, but the chaff He will burn with unquenchable fire (iii. 10, 12; Luke iii. 9, 17).

In the same:—

As the tares are burned with fire, so shall it be in the consummation of the age (xiii. 40).

In the same:—

The Son of man shall send forth His angels, and they shall gather out of His kingdom all things that cause stumbling, and them who do iniquity, and shall cast them into a furnace of fire (xiii. 41, 42, 50).

In the same:—

He said to them on the left hand, Depart from Me, ye cursed, into eternal fire, prepared for the devil and his angels (xxv. 41).

In the same:—

Whosoever shall say to his brother, Thou fool, shall be subject to the hell of fire (v. 22; xviii. 8, 9; Mark ix. 45, 47).

In *Luke:*—

The rich man in hell said, Father Abraham, send Lazarus that he may dip the tip of his finger in water and cool my tongue, for I am tormented in this flame (xvi. 24).

In the same:—

When Lot went out of Sodom it rained fire and brimstone from heaven and destroyed them; after the same manner shall it be in the day that the Son of man is revealed (xvii. 29, 80).

In the *Apocalypse:*—

If any one worship the beast he shall drink of the wine of the wrath of God, and he shall be tormented with fire and brimstone (xiv. 9, 10).

Again:—

The beast and the false prophet were cast alive into the lake of fire burning with brimstone (xix. 20).

Again:—

The devil was cast into the lake of fire and brimstone (xx. 10).

Again:—

Death and hell were cast into the lake of fire; and if any one was not found written in the book of life he was cast into the lake of fire (xx. 14, 15).

And again:—

The unfaithful, and murderers, and whoremongers, and sorcerers, and idolaters, and all liars, shall have their part in the lake which burneth with fire and brimstone (xxi. 8).

In these passages, 'fire' signifies all cupidity belonging to the love of evil, and its punishment, which is torment." (*Apocalypse Explained*, n. 504.15, 17)

You shall make their fruit to perish from the earth,
And their seed from the sons of Man. (Ps. 21:10)

Fruit are evil works (see Ps. 1:3, 72:16, 107:37, 127:3, 148:9); to perish is to spiritually die from falsehoods (see Ps. 88:11); the earth is the church as to truth (see Ps. 9:8, 24:1, 60:2, 90:2,

96:13). Seed is the falsehood of their evil which is opposite to the faith of charity (see Ps. 18:50, 22:23, 30, 89:4, 106:27); sons of Man (Hebrew *adam*) are those who are in spiritual truths (see Ps. 49:2, 57:4, 80:17, 89:47).

"...works of faith without charity are works of no faith, in themselves dead, since they are only of the external man. It is thus written of them in Jeremiah: *Wherefore doth the way of the wicked prosper? ...Thou hast planted them, yea, they have taken root; they have grown, yea, they bring forth fruit; Thou art near in their mouth, and far from their reins, ...How long shall the land mourn, and the herb of every field wither?* (xii. 1, 2, 4). They are 'near in the mouth but far from the reins' who are of faith separated from charity; of whom it is said that 'the land mourneth.' And in the same prophet such works are called 'the fruit of his doings': *The heart is deceitful above all things, and it is desperate, who knoweth it? I Jehovah search the heart, I try the reins, even to give every man according to his ways, according to the fruit of his doings* (xvii. 9, 10). And in Micah: *The land shall be in desolation, because of them who dwell therein, because of the fruit of their doings* (vii. 13). But it is declared in Amos that such fruit is no fruit, or that such work is dead, and that it perishes, fruit and root: *I destroyed the Amorite before them, whose height was like the height of the cedars; and he was strong as an oak; yet I destroyed his fruit from above and his roots from beneath* (ii. 9). And in David: *Their fruit shalt Thou destroy from the earth, and their seed from among the sons of men* (Ps. xxi. 10). On the other hand, the works of charity are living, and it is said of them that they 'take root downward and bear fruit upward' — as in Isaiah: *The escaped of the house of Judah that remain shall again take root downward and bear fruit upward* (xxxvii. 31). To 'bear fruit upward' is from charity. Such fruit is called 'the fruit of excellence' in the same prophet: *In that day shall the branch of Jehovah be for beauty and for glory, and the fruit of the earth for excellence and adornment to the rescued of Israel* (iv. 2); and it is 'the fruit of salvation,' as it is called in the same prophet: *Drop down ye heavens from above, and let the skies pour down justice;*

let the earth open, and let them bring forth the fruit of salvation,
and let justice spring up together. I Jehovah will create this (xlv.
8)." (*Apocalypse Revealed*, n. 348)

"Seed" is in reference to falsehoods, which bring forth evil
works:

"Their fruit will I destroy from the earth, and their seed from
the sons of man (Ps. xxi. 10).

In *Hosea:*—

I will sow Israel unto Me in the earth (ii. 23).

In *Zechariah:*—

I will sow Judah and Joseph among the peoples, and they
shall remember Me in remote places (x. 9).

In *Ezekiel:*—

I will look again to you, that ye may be tilled and sown; then
will I multiply man upon you, all the house of Israel, the
whole of it (xxxvi. 9).

In *Jeremiah:*—

Behold the days shall come in which I will sow the house of
Israel and the house of Judah with the seed of man and with
the seed of beast (xxxi. 27).

In *Matthew:*—

The seed sown are the sons of the kingdom (xiii. 38).

But it is not necessary to show here that the seed of the field has
a similar meaning as the seed of man, for here only what is signified by 'the seed of the woman' is what is to be explained and
confirmed from the Word.

Since 'seed' signifies the truth of doctrine from the Word,
and in the highest sense Divine truth, so in the contrary sense
'seed' signifies the falsity of doctrine and infernal falsity. As in
Isaiah:—

*Draw near hither, ye sons of the sorceress, ye seed of the
adulterer, and thou who hast committed whoredom. Against
whom do ye sport yourselves, against whom do ye make wide
the mouth and lengthen the tongue? Are ye not children of
transgression, the seed of a lie?* (lvii. 3, 4).

'The sons of the sorceress and the seed of an adulterer' signify falsities from the Word when it has been falsified and adulterated,
'the sons of the sorceress' meaning the falsities from the Word
falsified, and 'the seed of an adulterer,' falsities from the Word
adulterated. The Word is said to be falsified when its truths are
perverted, and to be adulterated when its goods are perverted,
as also when truths are applied to the loves of self. 'Children
of transgression and seed of a lie' signify falsities flowing from
such prior falsities. 'To sport themselves' signifies to take delight
in things falsified; 'to make wide the mouth' signifies delight in
the thought therefrom; and 'to lengthen the tongue' delight in
teaching and propagating such falsities. In *Isaiah:*—

*Woe to the sinful nation, a people heavy with iniquity, a seed
of evil doers, sons that are corrupters; they have forsaken
Jehovah, they have provoked the Holy One of Israel, they
have estranged themselves backwards* (i. 4).

'The sinful nation' signifies those who are in evils, and 'a people
heavy with iniquity' those who are in the falsities therefrom, for
'nation' is predicated in the Word of evils, and 'people' of falsities (see above, n. 175, 331, 626). The falsity of those who are
in evils is signified by 'a seed of evil doers,' and the falsities of
those who are in the falsities from that evil are signified by 'sons
that are corrupters.' (That 'sons' signify those who are in truths,
and in the contrary sense those who are in falsities, and in an
abstract sense truths and falsities, may be seen above, n. 724).
'They have forsaken Jehovah and have provoked the Holy One of
Israel' signifies that they have rejected Divine good and Divine
truth; 'Jehovah' meaning the Lord in relation to Divine good,
and 'the Holy One of Israel, 'the Lord in relation to Divine truth;
'their estranging themselves backwards' signifies that they

wholly departed from good and truth, and went away to infernal evil and falsity, for those in the spiritual world who are in evils and falsities turn themselves backward from the Lord (see in the work on *Heaven and Hell,* n. 123). In the same:—

> *Thou shalt not be joined with them in the sepulchre, for thou hast corrupted thy land, thou hast slain thy people; the seed of the evil shall not be named for ever* (xiv. 20).

This is said of Lucifer, by whom Babylon is meant; and 'the seed of the evil which shall not be named for ever' signifies the direful falsity of evil which is from hell. (The rest may be seen explained above, n. 589, 659e, 697). In *Moses:*—

> *He who hath given of his seed to Molech dying shall die, the people of the land shall stone him with stones. I will set My faces against that man, and I will cut him off from the midst of his people, because he hath given of his seed to Molech, to defile My sanctuary and to profane the name of My holiness* (*Lev.* xx. 3; xviii. 21).

'To give of his seed to Molech' signifies to destroy the truth of the Word and of the doctrine of the church therefrom, by application to the filthy loves of the body, as murders, hatreds, revenges, adulteries, and the like, which leads to the acceptance of infernal falsities instead of things Divine; such falsities are signified by 'the seed given to Molech.' Molech was the god of the sons of Ammon (1 *Kings* xi. 7); and was set up in the valley of Hinnom, which was called Topheth, where they burned up their sons and daughters (2 *Kings* xxiii. 10); the above mentioned loves are signified by that fire; and as 'seed given to Molech' signifies such infernal falsity, and stoning was the punishment of death for the injury and destruction of the truth of the Word and of doctrine therefrom, it is said that the man that 'hath given of his seed to Molech dying shall die, and the people of the land shall stone him with stones.' (That stoning was the punishment for injuring or destroying truth may be seen above, n. 655). That such falsity is destructive of every good of the Word and of the church is signified by 'I will set My faces against that man, and I will cut him off from the midst of his people, because he hath defiled My sanctuary and profaned the name of My holiness,' 'sanctuary' signifying the truth of heaven and the church, and 'the name of holiness' all that it is. From the passages quoted it can now be seen that 'seed' means in the highest sense Divine truth which is from the Lord, and thence the truth of the Word and of the doctrine of the church which is from the Word; while in the evil sense it means infernal falsity which is the opposite of that truth." (*Apocalypse Explained*, n. 768.22-25)

For they stretched out evil against You,
They devised a scheme, they were unable.
For You shall appoint them a shoulder,
You shall prepare with Your bow string against their faces.
(Ps. 21:11-12)

Evil is evil against the good a love; a scheme is an intentional falsehood against the truth. Shoulder signifies all Divine power resisting the hells; a bow signifies the doctrine of truth which fights against evil (see Ps. 7:12-13, 11:2, 18:34, 37:15, 46:9, 77:17-18, 78:9,57).

"That shoulders signify all force and power in resisting, in breaking, and in acting, is evident in Ezekiel: *Ye push with side and with shoulder, and thrust all the feeble sheep with your horns, till ye have scattered them abroad* (xxxiv. 21). Again in the same prophet: *Egypt is a staff of reed to the house of Israel. When they took hold of thee by the hand, thou didst break, and didst rend for them every shoulder* (xxix. 6, 7) — where rending every shoulder stands for depriving of all power of comprehending truths; Egypt is the perverted knowledge which deprives.

"In Zechariah: *They refused to hearken, and turned a stubborn shoulder* (vii. 11) — where turning a stubborn shoulder means resisting. In, David: *They imagined a wicked deed, they have not prevailed, for thou shalt offer to them the shoulder* (Ps. xxi. 11, 12) — where offering to them the shoulder also stands for resisting, and thus for power. That the shoulder means power, is plain from representatives in the other life, where they who resist seem to offer or oppose the shoulder." (*Heavenly Arcana*, n. 9836.4-5; see also *Heavenly Arcana*, n. 1085)

Be exalted, Jehovah, in Your strength,
We will sing and make music of Your might. (Ps. 21:13)

To exalt Jehovah is to worship by means of good from love (see also Ps. 18:46); strength is the power of good (see Ps. 29:1, 95:4, 96:6). To sing and make music is to worship from spiritual good and truth (see Ps. 33:3, 57:7); might is the power of truth (see Ps. 80:2) and refer's to the Lord's victory in combat against temptations. That strength is the power of good can be seen in the following comment on Gen. 49:3 where a similar Hebrew word is translated as "force" –

"*Excellent in dignity, and excellent in force.* That this signifies that glory and power are thence, is evident from the signification of excelling in dignity, as glory, for he who is in dignity is in glory; and from the signification of excelling in force, as power, for he who is in force is in power. Glory in this passage has reference to the truth of faith (see n. 5922), and power to the good of charity..." (*Heavenly Arcana*, n. 6345).

Might is power from truth, and is predicated of truth as the same word refers to men. It was thus used for those who were powerful in persuading according to religious faith. The same word is used for the false religion of Nimrod in ancient Babylon:

"*He was mighty in hunting before Jehovah.* That this signifies that he persuaded many, is evident from its being so with faith separate from charity; and also from the signification of hunting in the Word. Faith separate from charity is of such a nature that men are easily persuaded." (*Heavenly Arcana*, n. 1178)

"They called themselves men and mighty, from faith; for there is a term in the original language which expresses the idea of might and at the same time of man, which term in the Word is predicated of faith, and that in both senses." (*Heavenly Arcana*, n. 1179)

Psalm 22

To the chief musician upon Aijeleth Shahar, a Psalm of David.

~

My God, my God, why have You forsaken me? (1)
The words of my roaring are far from my salvation.
My God, I call by day, but You answer not, (2)
And in the night, and there is no silence for me.
But You are holy, (3)
Dwelling in the praises of Israel.
Our fathers trusted in You, (4)
They trusted and You rescued them.
They cried to You and they escaped: (5)
They trusted in You and were not ashamed.
   But I am a worm, and not a man, (6)
   A reproach of Man, and despised by the people.
   All who see me scorn me, (7)
   They open the lips, they wag the head:
   "He commits himself to Jehovah, let Him rescue him, (8)
   Let Him deliver him since He was delighted in him."
   For You are He who caused me to burst forth out of the belly: (9)
   You made me trust *when I was* upon my mother's breasts.
   I was cast upon You from the womb, (10)
   You are my God from my mother's belly.
   Be not far from me for adversity is near, (11)
   For there is none to help.
   Many bullocks have compassed me, (12)
   Strong ones of Bashan have surrounded me.
   They open their mouths against me, (13)
   As a lion, tearing apart and roaring.

I am poured out like water, (14)
And all my bones are separated,
My heart is like wax melted in the midst of my bowels.
My *palate* is dried up like a potsherd, (15)
And my tongue cleaves to my jaws,
And You have hung me in the dust of death.
For dogs have compassed me, (16)
The congregation of evildoers have encircled me.
They *pierced* my hands and my feet,
I may number all my bones, (17)
They look, they stare upon me.
They part my garments among them, (18)
And cast lots upon my clothing.
But You, Jehovah, be not far, (19)
My power, hurry to my help.
Deliver my soul from the sword, (20)
My only begotten from the hand of the dog.
Save me from the lion's mouth, (21)
And from the horns of the wild bulls answer me.
   I will recount Your name to my brethren, (22)
   In the midst of the assembly I will praise You.
   You who fear Jehovah, praise Him, (23)
   All the seed of Jacob, honour Him,
   And sojourn after Him, all ye the seed of Israel.
   For He has not despised, (24)
   And He has not detested the affliction of the afflicted,
   And He has not hid His face from him,
   And when he cried to Him, He heard.
   From You is my praise in the great assembly, (25)
   I will pay my vows in front of those who fear Him.
   The meek shall eat and be satisfied, (26)
   They shall praise Jehovah who enquire after Him,
   Your heart shall live for ever.
      All the ends of the earth shall remember and return unto
      Jehovah, (27)
      And all the families of the nations shall bow down before You.
      For the kingdom is Jehovah's, (28)
      And He is the ruler among the nations.
      All the fat ones upon earth shall eat and bow down, (29)

All who go down to the dust shall bow before Him,
And those who could not keep his own soul alive.
A seed shall serve Him, (30)
A generation to come shall be accounted to the Lord,
And they shall proclaim His righteousness, (31)
To a people that shall be born that He has done this.

Psalm Commentary

22

Summary: Prayer by the Lord to the Father that He be not forsaken (v. 1-5) seeing that He was more despised than all others (v. 6-8), that He was the Father's from conception (v. 9-10), that He was attacked by evils and falsehoods (v. 11-13) and was crucified (v. 14-18). Supplication that He be not forsaken (v. 19-21). A church will arise that will worship Him (v. 22-23, 25-26) for He was not forsaken (v. 24), and the church will be gathered from all parts to worship Him (v. 27-31).

My God, my God, why have You forsaken me?
The words of my roaring are far from my salvation. (Ps. 22:1)

The first line was uttered by Jesus on the cross (Matt. 27:46, Mark 15:34), and represents the despair He was in while in a state of humiliation, in which state He prays to the Father for deliverance. To be forsaken by God is to rejected due to falsehood, for God is the Lord in respect to Divine truth (see Ps. 18:31, 29:1, 68:17,24, 82:1, 95:3, 147:7). Roaring is grief of heart (see Ps. 32:3) and salvation is deliverance from evil by Divine mercy (see Ps. 14:7, 96:2).

If Jesus is Jehovah in human form, why does He pray to the Father? Jesus had two states of being; one of humiliation in his human nature (also known as "exinanition") in which He prayed to the Father, and another of being one with the Divine (also known as "glorification"):

"The reason that the Lord had those two states of exinanition and glorification, was, that there is no other possible way of progressing to union, since it is according to the Divine order, which is unchangeable. The Divine order is, that man should dispose himself for the reception of God, and prepare himself as a receptacle and habitation into which God may enter and dwell as in His temple. Man must do this from himself, but still acknowledge that it is from God; he must acknowledge this, because he does not feel the presence and operation of God, though God being intimately present operates in man all the good of love and all the truth of faith. According to this order every man proceeds and must proceed, that from being natural he may become spiritual. In like manner the Lord, that He might make His natural human Divine: it is from this cause that He prayed to the Father, that He did His will, that all He did and said He attributed to Him, and that upon the cross He said, *My God, My God, why forsakest Thou Me?* For in this state God appears absent; but after this state comes another which is a state of conjunction with God. In this man acts in like manner as before, but now from God; nor has he now need in like manner as before to ascribe to God all the good which he wills and does, and all the truth which he thinks and speaks, because this is inscribed upon his heart, and thereby is inwardly in all his actions and speech. In like manner the Lord united Himself to His Father, and the Father united Himself to Him; in a word, the Lord glorified His Human, that is, made it Divine, in the same manner in which He regenerates man, that is, makes him spiritual." (*True Christian Religion*, n. 105)

My God, I call by day, but You answer not,
And in the night, and there is no silence for me.
But You are holy, dwelling in the praises of Israel,
Our fathers trusted in You: they trusted and You rescued them.
They cried to You and they escaped:

They trusted in You and were not ashamed. (Ps. 22:2-5)

The day is a state of enlightenment (see Ps. 32:4, 74:16, 136:8) and night a state of obscurity (see Ps. 3:8, 16:7, 32:4, 74:16, 91:6, 104:20, 136:9). To not answer is for the Lord to appear absent (see Ps. 4:1). Holiness is predicated of Divine truth (see Ps. 5:7, 65:4) which is from the Lord alone; praise is worship from affection for truth (see Ps. 7:17, 35:18) and Israel is the spiritual heaven that is in good from truth (see Ps. 14:7, 22:23, 78:5, 105:23, 106:26-27, 114:2, 136:11). The Lord is present where there is love and affection for truth, and thus He is said to dwell in the praises of Israel, which is to be in good from truth. The rescue of the fathers refers to the deliverance of the Israelites from Egypt during the Passover; in a spiritual sense the fathers represent those who are in good (see Ps. 27:10, 45:16); to trust is to have confidence of the will which is given to those who are in the good of charity (see Ps. 33:21); to be rescued is to be led away from falsity (see Ps. 91:14). The ritual of the Passover foreshadowed the Lord's passion, and signifies the deliverance of the righteous from the dominion of hell at the time of the Lord's coming. To cry is to have distress from falsehood and to escape is to withdraw from it; to trust is to have confidence of the will from the good of charity (see Ps. 33:21) and to not be ashamed is to have no shame from committing evil.

But I am a worm, and not a man;
A reproach of Man, and despised by the people. (Ps. 22:6)

To be a worm and not a man means the Lord was in such a state where he had not yet made his human Divine, as His external human form had inherited evil tendencies from the human mother. A worm signifies the falsity of evil, a man signifies truth from good. A reproach of Man (Hebrew *adam*) is to be rejected by those who are in the evil of self love (see Ps. 36:6); to be despised by the people is rejection by those in falsehoods (see Ps. 2:1, 3:8, 18:43, 65:7, 74:18, 102:15).

"*And it bred worms.* That this signifies that thereby it became filthy, is evident from the signification of breeding worms, as producing what is filthy; for worms are produced from what is filthy and putrid. The falsity of evil, which is in good derived from the proprium, is compared to a worm, because they act in a similar manner; for falsity also consumes and thus torments. There are two things which make hell, as there are two which make heaven. The two which make heaven are good and truth, and the two which make hell are evil and falsity. Consequently there are those two in heaven which make happiness there, and there are two in hell which make torment there. The torment in hell caused by falsity is compared to a worm, and the torment from evil there is compared to fire — thus in Isaiah: *As the new heavens and the new earth, which I will make, shall remain before Me, saith Jehovah, so shall your seed and your name remain. And it shall come to pass from month to month, and from sabbath to his sabbath, that they shall stand before Me. ...And they shall go forth, and look upon the carcases of the men that have transgressed against Me: for their worm shall not die, neither shall their fire be quenched; and they shall be an abhorring unto all flesh* (lxvi. 22-24). In like manner it is said by the Lord in Mark, *Where their worm dieth not, and the fire is not quenched* (ix. 44, 46, 48) — speaking of Gehenna or hell. The filthiness of falsity is compared to a worm also in Moses: *Thou shalt plant vineyards, and dress them, but thou shalt neither drink of the wine, nor gather* [the grapes], *for the worm shall eat them* (Deut. xxviii. 39) — where wine stands for truth from good, and in the opposite sense falsity from evil (n. 6377)." (*Heavenly Arcana*, n. 8481)

All who see me scorn me,
They open the lips, they wag the head:
"He commits himself to Jehovah, let Him rescue him,
Let Him deliver him since He was delighted in him." (Ps. 22:7-8)

This portrays the derision the Lord experienced from the Jews while on the cross. Scorn is false knowledges, lips are the falsities of doctrine (see Ps. 12:4, 81:5), and head signifies insanity opposed to wisdom (see Ps. 68:21, 110:6) which all lead to opposition to Divine truth and salvation from it.

For You are He who caused me to burst forth out of the belly:
You made me trust when I was upon my mother's breasts.
I was cast upon You from the womb,
You are my God from my mother's belly. (Ps. 22:9-10)

In the spiritual sense, the fruit of the belly is one who is spiritually reborn or regenerated (see Ps. 132:11); the one from the belly is to be regenerated by spiritual truths as the belly signified the interior understanding of the Word (see Ps. 17:14, 31:9, 40:8, 127:3). To trust is to have confidence of the will which is given to those who are in the good of charity (see Ps. 33:21); the mother's breasts is good derived from the truth of the church as signified by mother (see Ps. 27:10,13). To be born from the womb signified to be regenerated as to the will regenerated in the will as to charity (see Ps. 44:25, 58:3, 71:6, 139:13). In the highest sense, this refers to the conception of the Son of God by the Holy Spirit.

"As rebirth, and hence the church, are signified by going forth from the womb, therefore the Lord is called in the Word, He who formeth from the womb, He who bringeth forth from the womb; and they who are regenerated and made a church are said to be carried from the womb — as in Isaiah: *Thus saith Jehovah who made thee, and formed thee from the womb, Who will help thee* (xliv. 2). Again: *Thus saith Jehovah, thy redeemer, and He who formed thee from the womb* (xliv. 24). Again: *Said Jehovah who formed me from the womb to be His servant, to bring Jacob again to Him, and that Israel be gathered unto Him* (xlix. 5). In David: *Thou art He who brought me forth from the womb* (Ps. xxii. 9). Again in Isaiah: *Hearken unto Me, O house of Jacob, and all the remnant of the house of Israel, which have been borne* [by Me] *from the belly, which have been carried from the womb* (xlvi. 3). In David: *The wicked are estranged from the womb; they go astray from the belly, with words of falsehood* (Ps. lviii. 3) — where being estranged from the womb means from the good which is of the church, and going astray from the belly means going astray from truth. In Hosea: *The sorrows of a travailing woman shall come upon him: he is an unwise son; for at the time, he standeth not in the womb of children* (xiii. 13) — where not standing in the womb of children means not being in the good of truth which is of the church." (*Heavenly Arcana*, n. 4918.2)

"Belly" also signifies the interior understanding of a person: "In *David:*—

> *I was cast upon Thee; from my mother's belly Thou art my God* (Ps. xxii. 10).

In the same:—

> *Thou dost possess my reins; Thou hast covered me in my mother's belly* (Ps. cxxxix. 13).

In the same:—

> *The wicked are estranged from the womb; they err from the belly, speaking falsehood* (Ps. lviii. 8).

So elsewhere. The 'belly' or 'bowels' signify the interiors of the thought or of the understanding, because there are two lives with man, the life of the understanding and the life of the will; to these two fountains of life all things of the body correspond; consequently under their direction all things of the body are acted upon and act, even to the extent that any part of the body that does not suffer itself to be put in action by the understanding and the will has no life. For this reason the universal body is subject to the control of these two lives, for all things in the body that are moved, and so far as they are moved by the respiration of the lungs, are subject to the control of the life of the understanding; and all things in the body that are brought into action, and so far as they are brought into action by the pulsation of the heart, are subject to the control of the life of the will. This is why 'soul' and 'heart' are often mentioned in the Word, and why the 'soul' signifies the life of the understanding, also the life of faith, for the soul is predicated of respiration; and why the 'heart' signifies the life of the will, also the life of the love. For the same reason 'the belly and bowels' are predicated of thought, which is of the understanding, and the 'heart' is predicated of affection, which is of the will." (*Apocalypse Explained*, n. 622.12-13)

"That natural births mentioned in the Word involve spiritual births, is clearly manifest from the following passages: *We have conceived, we have been in travail, we have as it were brought forth, we have not wrought any deliverance* (Isa. xxvi. 18). *At the presence of the Lord the earth travaileth* (Ps. cxiv. 7). *Hath the earth borne in one day? Shall I make the breach, and not cause to bring forth? shall I cause to bring forth, and shut the womb?* (Isa. lxvi. 8, 9). *Sin shall travail, and No shall be at the breaking forth* (Ezek. xxx. 16). *The sorrows of a travailing woman shall come upon Ephraim, he is an unwise son, for he doth not stay the time in the womb of sons* (Hos. xiii. 13); so also in many other places. Since in the Word natural generations signify spiritual generations, and these are from the Lord, He is called the Former and He who taketh from the womb; as is evident from the following: *Jehovah that made thee and formed thee from the womb* (Isa. xliv. 2). *He who took me out of the womb* (Ps. xxii. 10). *I have been laid upon Thee from the womb; Thou art He who took me out of my mother's bowels* (Ps. lxxi. 6). *Hearken unto Me, ye who are borne from the womb, carried from the belly* (Isa. xlvi. 3); besides other passages. The Lord is therefore called Father (as in Isa. ix. 6; lxiii. 16; John x. 30; xiv. 8, 9); and they who are in goods and truths from Him, are called sons of God and born of God, and brethren to one another (Matt. xxiii. 8); and also the church is called Mother (Hos. ii. 2, 5; Ezek. xvi. 45)." (*True Christian Religion*, n. 583)

Be not far from me for adversity is near,
For there is none to help.
Many bullocks have compassed me,
Strong ones of Bashan have surrounded me.
They open their mouths against me,
As a lion, tearing apart and roaring. (Ps. 22:11-13)

Adversity is evil which attacks what is good (see Ps. 3:1, 27:12); help is aid from Divine mercy (see Ps. 10:14). A bullock here signifies affection for evil from lusts in the external natural (see Ps. 8:7, 68:30, 106:19-20, 144:13), since bulls as wild and unrestrained animals represent the lower desires of the natural. The "strong ones of Bashan" signify the falsities of evil in the natural: Bashan was a region east of Jordan outside of Canaan, and as Canaan signifies heaven and the church Bashan signifies the evil of the natural (see Ps. 68:15) of those outside the church. Mouths are falsehoods of the external understanding (see Ps. 5:9, 37:30, 135:16); a lion is the power of falsity from evil which destroys (see Ps. 10:9, 17:12, 57:4); to tear apart is to destroy through falsity (see Ps. 7:2).

I am poured out like water,
And all my bones are separated,
My heart is like wax melted in the midst of my bowels. (Ps. 22:14)

This refers to Jesus's suffering on the cross, how he thirsted for water and was pierced in the side. But each thing suffered has a spiritual significance concerning the desolation of truth and corruption of good within the church. To be poured out like water is for truth (see Ps. 18:15, 23:2, 29:3, 42:1, 46:3, 66:12, 77:19, 78:13,16, 104:3, 136:6) to be rejected and profaned by by falsity; bones signify one's knowledge of the truth in the natural which do not cohere when falsified (see Ps. 34:20, 35:10). The heart is the love of the will (see Ps. 7:9, 22:10, 24:4, 51:10, 64:6, 66:18, 78:8); to be melted like wax is for one's internal love to be overcome by external evils; bowels here signify the Lord's love for the human race. As honey signifies natural good (see Ps. 19:10), wax would signify a life in which there was no good similar to chaff (see Ps. 1:4).

"...by bone and flesh is signified man's proprium, by bone his intellectual proprium, and by flesh his voluntary proprium; thus by bone the proprium as to truth, for this is of the intellect; and by flesh the proprium as to good, for this is of the will (n. 148, 149)." (*Heavenly Arcana*, n. 3812)

My palate is dried up like a potsherd,
And my tongue cleaves to my jaws,
And You have hung me in the dust of death. (Ps. 22:15)

For the palate to become dry as a potsherd is for the perception of truth to be overcome by the falsity derived from self intelligence signified by a potter's vessel (see Ps. 2:9). The tongue is one's confession of doctrine (see Ps. 35:28, 57:4, 140:11) which is said to cleave to the jaws which signifies external fallacies or thoughts of the corporeal-sensual (see *Apocalypse Explained*, n. 923.5); to be hung in the dust of death is to be condemned from falsehoods of the lower sensual (see Ps. 22:29, 44:25, 72:9) and was literally fulfilled by Jesus hanging on the cross. It was through the external natural of the body that the hells could tempt the Lord with evils and falsehoods.

"*But he who shall go forth out of thy bowels.* That this signifies those who are in love to the Lord and in love toward the neighbor, is evident from the signification of bowels, and of going forth out of the bowels, which is to be born; and here it means those who are born of the Lord. They who are born of the Lord, that is, who are regenerated, receive the Lord's life. The Lord's life, as was said, is the Divine love, that is, love toward the whole human race; or His will to save for ever, if possible, the whole of it, or all men. They who have not the Lord's love, that is, who do not love their neighbor as themselves, do not have the Lord's life, and so are not born of Him, or have not come forth out of His bowels; and therefore they cannot be heirs of His kingdom.

"From which it is evident that by coming forth out of the bowels, in the internal sense, are here signified those who are in love to Him and in love toward the neighbor. So in Isaiah: *Thus said Jehovah thy Redeemer, the Holy One of Israel; I am Jehovah thy God, Who teacheth thee to profit, Who leadeth thee in the way that thou shouldest walk. Oh that thou hadst hearkened to my commandments, and thy peace had been as a river, and thy justice as the billows of the sea, and thy seed had been as the sand, and the offspring of thy bowels as the gravel, of it* (xlviii. 17-19).

The seed as the sand, stands for good; and the offspring of the bowels as the gravel, for truth; thus for those who are in love, for they alone are in the love of good and truth.

"Moreover, in the Word bowels also signify love or mercy, for the reason that the bowels of generation, especially the mother's womb, represent and thus signify chaste marriage love, and the love for children that is from it. As in Isaiah: *The yearnings of Thy bowels and of Thy compassions toward me have restrained themselves* (lxiii. 15). In Jeremiah: *Is not Ephraim a dear son unto Me? Is he not a child of delights? ...Therefore My bowels are troubled for him; in mercy, I will have mercy upon him* (xxxi. 20).

"It is evident from this that the Lord's love itself, or mercy itself, and compassion toward the human race, are what are signified in the internal sense by bowels, and by coming forth out of the bowels; consequently by them that come forth out of the bowels are signified those who are in love." (*Heavenly Arcana*, n. 1803.1-4)

For dogs have compassed me,
The congregation of evildoers have encircled me. (Ps. 22:16)

Dogs are those who are in low morals and external pleasures who render the good of faith unclean by falsifications, thus the Lord said, *Give not that which is holy unto the dogs* (Matt. 7:6). The congregation of evildoers are those who are in evil (see Ps. 1:5).

"*Ye shall cast it to a dog.* That this signifies that it is unclean, is evident from the signification of dogs, as those who render the good of faith unclean by falsifications. For all animals in the Word signify affections and inclinations such as are in man, the gentle and useful animals signifying good affections and inclinations, but fierce and useless animals signifying evil affections and inclinations. That such things are signified by animals, is because the external or the natural man enjoys affections and inclinations, and also appetites and senses, similar to those of beasts. ...The reason why dogs signify those who render the good of faith unclean by falsifications, is, that dogs eat unclean things, and also bark at men and bite them. Therefore also it was that the nations outside the church, which were in falsities from evil, were called dogs by the Jews, and were accounted most vile." (*Heavenly Arcana*, n. 9231.1,2)

"*Dogs have compassed me: the assemblies of evildoers have inclosed me, piercing my hands and my feet. ...Deliver my soul from the sword: my only one from the power (hand) of the dog* (Ps. xxii. 16, 20). Dogs here stand for those who destroy the goods of faith, and who are therefore called assemblies of evil-doers; delivering the soul from the sword is delivering from the falsity that lays waste the truth of faith — that a sword means falsity laying waste the truth of faith may be seen above (n. 2799, 4499, 6353, 7102, 8294), and the soul the life of faith (n. 9050). Thus also it is plain that delivering the only one from the power of the dog means delivering from the falsity that lays waste the good of faith. That some were to be dragged and to be eaten by dogs (1 Kings xiv. 11; xvi. 4; xxi. 23, 24; 2 Kings ix. 10, 36; Jer. xv. 3) signified that they would perish by unclean things. That some compared themselves to dead dogs (1 Sam. xxiv. 14; 2 Sam. iii. 8; ix. 8; xvi. 9) signified that they were to be accounted as most vile and were to be cast out." (*Heavenly Arcana*, n. 9231.5)

They pierced my hands and my feet,
I may number all my bones,
They look, they stare upon me. (Ps. 22:17)

In the literal sense this is prophetic of the crucifixion of Jesus, but everything that happened in the crucifixion is symbolic of how the good and truth of the Lord was rejected by the Jewish church. To be pierced signifies to extinguish good and truth (see Ps. 88:5); pierced hands are destroyed external truths and pierced feet are destroyed external goods. Hands signify the external power of the truth (see Ps. 20:6, 44:3, 45:4, 80:15,17, 89:13,21, 110:1, 121:5); feet the lower natural (see Ps. 8:6, 41:9, 49:5, 99:5, 105:18); to number is to know the quality of a thing (see Ps. 147:4); bones are one's external knowledges of the truth (see Ps. 22:14, 34:20, 35:10). The Lord was denied and crucified by the Jews due to their distortions of external knowledges from the Word.

"*All my bones are out of joint; my heart is become like wax. …I can number all my bones. …They have parted my garments among them, and upon my vesture have they cast lots* (Ps. xxii. 14, 17, 18) — where the subject is the Lord's temptations as to Divine truths, which were the Lord's proprium, and hence are called my bones, and as to Divine good, which was the Lord's proprium, and hence is called my heart. That heart signifies good may be seen above (n. 3313, 3635); and because bones signify these truths, the numbering of which is desiring to dissipate them by reasonings and falsities, therefore also it immediately follows that they parted my garments, and cast lots upon my vesture, for garments also signify truths, but exterior (n. 297, 1073, 2576); dividing them and casting lots upon the vesture, involves the like — as also in Matthew (xxvii. 35). Again: *My soul exulteth in Jehovah; it shall be glad in His salvation. All my bones shall say …Who is like unto Thee* (Ps. xxxv. 9, 10) — where it is manifest that bones in the spiritual sense are the intellectual proprium. Again: *Thou shalt cause me to hear joy and gladness; the bones which Thou hast bruised shall exult* (Ps. li. 8) — where the exulting of the bones which were bruised, signifies recreation by truths after temptations.

"As bone signified the intellectual proprium, or proprium as to truth, and in the supreme sense the Divine truth which was the Lord's proprium, it was for this reason ordained as a statute of the passover, that they should not break a bone of the paschal lamb — as is thus expressed in Moses: *In one house shall it be eaten; thou shalt not carry forth of the flesh abroad out of the house; neither shall ye break a bone thereof* (Exod. xii. 46). And in another place: *They shall not leave of it until the morning, nor break a bone thereof* (Num. ix. 12). Not to break a bone, in the supreme sense, signifies not to violate truth Divine, and in the representative sense, not to violate the truth of any good whatever; for the quality of good and the form of good are from truths, and truth is the support of good, as bones are of flesh." (*Heavenly Arcana*, n. 3812.7-8)

They part my garments among them,
And cast lots upon my clothing. (Ps. 22:18)

At the crucifixion the Roman soldiers had parted the garments of Jesus, and spiritually signifies how the truths were dispersed by the Jews. Garments represent external truths which are dissipated by falsities (see Ps. 22:18, 102:26) and clothing represents internal truth. To cast lots or cause lots to fall is to pervert internal truth (see Ps. 7:15) signified by clothing.

"We read in David: *They parted (divided) My garments among them, and upon My vesture did they cast lots* (Ps. xxii. 18). In Matthew: *They parted (divided) His garments, casting lots: that it might be fulfilled which was spoken by the prophet* (xxvii. 35). Also in John: *The soldiers ...took His garments, and made four parts ...and the tunic; now the tunic was without seam, woven from the top throughout. They said therefore, Let us not rend (divide) it, but cast lots for it, whose it shall be: that the Scripture might be fulfilled* (xix. 23, 24). He who reads these words and knows nothing of the internal sense of the Word, is not aware that any arcanum lies concealed therein, when yet in each word there is a Divine arcanum. The arcanum was that Divine truths were dissipated by the Jews, for the Lord was the Divine truth; and hence He is called the Word (John i.). The Word is Divine truth; His garments represented truths in the external form, and His tunic truths in the internal form; the division of the garments represented the dissipation of the truths of faith by the Jews. That garments are truths in the external form may be seen above (n. 2576, 5248, 5954, 6918), also that a tunic is truth in the internal form (n. 4677). Truths in the external form are such as are the truths of the Word in the literal sense, but truths in the internal form are such as are the truths of the Word in the spiritual sense. The division of the garments into four parts signified total dissipation, in like manner as the division in Zechariah (xiv. 4), and in other passages; likewise the division into two parts, as we read of the veil of the temple (Matt. xxvii. 51; Mark xv. 38). The rending of the rocks also at that time (Matt. xxvii. 51) represented the dissipation of all things of faith, for a rock is the Lord as to faith and thus it is faith from the Lord." (*Heavenly Arcana*, n. 9093.5)

"When it is known from these examples what is signified by a tunic, it is manifest what is signified by the tunic of the Lord, of which it is thus written in John: *They took the garments, and made four parts, to every soldier a part ...and the tunic was without seam, woven from the top throughout. They said ...Let us not rend it, but cast lots for it, whose it shall be: that the Scripture might be fulfilled which saith, They parted My garments among them, and upon My vesture did they cast lots. These things the soldiers did* (xix. 23, 24; also Ps. xxii. 18). Who cannot see, if he thinks from reason at all enlightened, that these proceedings signified Divine things, and that otherwise they would not have been foretold by David? But what they signify cannot be known without the internal sense, and thus without knowledge therefrom what is signified by garments, by casting lots upon them and parting them, by a tunic, and by its being without seam, that is, woven throughout, and by soldiers. From the internal sense it is plain that by garments are signified truths, and by the garments of the Lord Divine truths; by casting lots and parting them is meant pulling these truths asunder and dispersing them (n. 9093); by the tunic Divine spiritual truth from the Divine celestial, the same as by Aaron's coat, since Aaron represented the Lord; so also by its being without seam and woven from the top throughout, the same is signified as by the chequered or woven work in Aaron's tunic. That the tunic was not rent signified that Divine spiritual truth proceeding immediately from Divine celestial truth could not be dispersed, because this truth is the internal truth of the Word, such as is with angels in heaven." (*Heavenly Arcana*, n. 9942.13)

"That violence was done to the Word in the sense of the letter, but not to the Word in the spiritual sense, is signified also by the soldiers dividing the Lord's garments, but not His tunic, of which it is said in *John:*—

> *The soldiers took His garments, and made four parts, to every soldier a part, also the tunic. Now the tunic was without seam, woven from the top throughout. They said therefore one to another, Let us not divide it, but let us cast lots for it, whose it shall be. These things therefore the soldiers did* (xix. 23, 24).

And in *David:*—

> *They parted My garments, and cast the lot upon My vesture* (*Ps.* xxii. 18).

'The garments of the Lord which they parted' signify the Word in the letter; His 'tunic' the Word in the spiritual sense; 'soldiers' signify those of the church who should fight in behalf of Divine truth; therefore it is said, 'These things therefore the soldiers did.' (That 'tunic' signifies Divine truth, or the Word in the spiritual sense, see *A. C.,* n. 9826, 9942; that 'soldiers' signify those who are of the church, and who should fight in behalf of Divine truth, see above, n. 64, at the end, where these things are more fully explained). It should be known that each particular related in the Evangelists respecting the Lord's passion, involves and signifies how the church at that time, which was among the Jews, had treated Divine truth, thus the Word, for this was Divine truth with them; the Lord also was the Word, because He was Divine truth (*John* i. 1, 2, 14). But what each particular involves and signifies cannot be known except from the internal sense. Here it will be told only what 'the Lord's garments' signified, because the meaning of 'garments' is here treated of, namely, that they signify truths, and in reference to the Lord, Divine truths." (*Apocalypse Explained,* n. 195.21)

But come, O Jehovah, be not far,
My power, hurry to my help.
Deliver my soul from the sword,
My only begotten from the hand of the dog.

Save me from the lion's mouth:
And from the horns of the wild bulls, answer me. (Ps. 22:19-21)

Jehovah is the Lord as to Divine love (see Ps. 18:31, 28:1, 68:26, 82:1, 147:7); to not be far is to be in conjunction through love (see Ps. 34:18, 65:4, 69:18). Power is the power of Divine truth; help is aid from Divine mercy (see Ps. 10:14). The soul is one's life from the spiritual understanding (see Ps. 22:10, 31:9, 71:23, 107:9); the sword is falsity fighting against spiritual truths (see Ps. 7:12, 22:16, 37:14, 45:3, 57:4, 78:62,64, 149:5). The only begotten is the only begotten Son of God (see Ps. 2:7, 110:3; John 1:18, 3:16,18) or Jehovah incarnate; in a lower sense it refers to one who has been spiritually regenerated or reborn. The "hand of the dog" is the power of external falsehoods that falsify and profane the things of the church (see Ps. 22:16, 59:6). The mouth is the external understanding (see Ps. 5:9, 37:30, 135:16), and the lion is the power of external falsity destroying the truth (see Ps. 10:9, 17:12, 57:4); horns signify the power of external truths defending (see Ps. 44:5, 89:17, 112:9, 132:17, 148:14) from natural good signified by wild bulls (see Ps. 8:7, 22:12, 68:30, 106:19-20, 144:13).

"*Save me from the lion's mouth; and from the horns of the unicorn hear me* (*Ps.* xxii. 21); 'lion' signifying falsity vehemently destroying truth; and 'horns of unicorns' truths that prevail against falsities." (*Heavenly Arcana*, n. 316.24)

"In Moses: *The firstling of his ox, honor is his, and his horns are the horns of the unicorn; with them shall he push the peoples all of them, to the ends of the earth* (Deut. xxxiii. 17). This is the prophecy of Israel concerning Joseph, where the horns of the unicorn stand for the great power of truth, as is manifest also from its being said that he shall push the peoples with them to the ends of the earth. So too in David: *My horn shalt Thou exalt like the unicorn's* (Ps. xcii. 10). And in the same: O Jehovah, *save me from the mouth of the lion, and answer me from the horns of the unicorn* (Ps. xxii. 21). Divine truths, from their height, are called the horns of unicorns; hence the horn is so often said to be exalted, for exaltation signifies power from the interior." (*Heavenly Arcana*, n. 2832.4)

"As by a horn is signified truth in its power, and in the opposite sense falsity destroying truth, therefore speech is attributed to a horn (Apoc. ix. 13; Dan. vii. 8; Ps. xxii. 21)." (*Heavenly Arcana*, n. 10182.10)

I will recount Your name to my brethren:
In the midst of the assembly I will praise You. (Ps. 22:22)

The name of the Lord is the Divine Human (see Ps. 8:1); brothers are those who have done the good works of charity (see Ps. 122:8, 133:1); the assembly represents the truths of the church (see Ps. 1:5, 68:26, 107:32) and to praise is to worship from affection for truth (see Ps. 7:17, 35:18).

"In *Matthew:*—

> *The King answering said unto them, I say unto you, Inasmuch as ye did it unto one of the least of these My brethren ye did it unto Me* (xxv. 40).

It is evident from what there precedes that those whom the Lord here calls 'brethren' are such as have done the good works of charity; but let it be known that although the Lord is their Father He still calls them 'brethren;' He is their Father from the Divine love, but brother from the Divine that proceeds from Him. This is because all in the heavens are recipients of the Divine that proceeds from Him; and the Divine that proceeds from the Lord, of which they are recipients, is the Lord in heaven and also in the church; and this is not of angel or man, but is of the Lord with them; consequently the good of charity itself with them, which is the Lord's, He calls brother, in like manner also angels and men, because they are the recipient subjects of that good. In a word, the Divine proceeding, which is the Divine of the Lord in the heavens, is the Divine born of the Lord in heaven; from that Divine, therefore, angels who are recipients of it are called 'sons of God,' and as these are brethren because of that Divine received in themselves, it is the Lord in them who says 'brother,' for when angels speak from the good of charity they speak not from themselves but from the Lord. This, then, is why the Lord says, 'Inasmuch as ye did it unto one of the least of these My brethren ye did it unto Me.' So in the spiritual sense the brethren of the Lord are the goods of charity that are enumerated in the verses preceding, and these are called by the Lord 'brethren' for the reason just given. Moreover, 'the King,' who so calls them, signifies the Divine proceeding, which in one word is called Divine truth or the Divine spiritual, which in its essence is the good of charity. It is therefore to be kept in mind that the Lord did not call them 'brethren' because He was a man like them, according to an opinion that is received in the Christian world; and for this reason it is not allowable for any man to call the Lord 'brother,' for He is God even in respect to the Human, and God is not a brother, but the Father. In the churches on the earth the Lord is called brother, because the idea of His Human which they have formed is the same as their idea of any other man's human, when yet the Lord's Human is Divine. As 'kings' formerly represented the Lord in relation to Divine truth, and as Divine truth received by angels in the Lord's spiritual kingdom is the same as Divine spiritual good, and as spiritual good is the good of charity, therefore the kings appointed over the sons of Israel called their subjects 'brethren,' although on the other hand the subjects were not permitted to call their king 'brother,' still less should the Lord be so called, who is the King of kings and Lord of lords. So in *David:*—

> *I will declare Thy name to my brethren; in the midst of the congregation will I praise Thee (Ps. xxii. 22).*

In the same:—

> *I am become a stranger to my brethren, and an alien to my mother's sons (Ps. lxix. 8).*

In the same:—

> *For the sake of my brethren and companions I will speak, Peace be in thee (Ps. cxxii. 8).*

This was said by David as if respecting himself, and yet in the representative spiritual sense David here means the Lord. In *Moses:*—

> *Out of the midst of thy brethren shalt thou set a king over them; thou mayest not put a man that is an alien over them, who is not thy brother; but let him not exalt his heart above his brethren (Deut.* xvii. 15, 20).

The 'brethren' from whom a king might be set over them signify all who are of the church, for it is said, 'Thou mayest not put over them a man that is an alien;' 'a man that is an alien' and a 'stranger' signifying one who is not of the church." (*Apocalypse Explained*, n. 746.10-12)

You who fear Jehovah, praise Him;
All the seed of Jacob, honour Him;
And sojourn after Him, all ye the seed of Israel. (Ps. 22:23)

Those who fear Jehovah are those who do His will (see Ps. 2:11, 33:18, 128:1, 147:11) and to praise is to worship from affection for truth (see Ps. 7:17, 35:18); the seed of Jacob is the external church (see Ps. 14:7, 77:15, 78:5, 132:5); to honour the Lord is to acknowledge all good is from Him; the seed of Israel is the spiritual church (see Ps. 14:7, 78:5, 105:23, 106:26-27, 114:2, 136:11); to sojourn is to be instructed (see Ps. 5:4). Seed are those who in faith from charity or in truth of doctrine from the Word (see Ps. 18:50, 21:10, 22: 30, 89:4, 106:27).

"*And with your seed after you.* That this signifies those who are created anew, is evident from the signification of seed, as also from what follows. From the signification of seed inasmuch as seed signifies in the literal sense posterity, but in the internal sense faith; and since, as has been often said, there is no faith except where there is charity, so it is charity itself which is meant in the internal sense by seed. From what follows it is evident that not only the man who is within the church is meant, but also the man who is without the church, thus the whole human race. Wherever there is charity, even among nations most remote from the church, there is seed, for heavenly seed is charity. No one of men can do anything of good from himself, but all good is from the Lord. The good which the gentiles do is also from the Lord — of whom, by the Divine mercy of the Lord, we shall speak hereafter. That the seed of God is faith has been shown before (n. 255). By faith there, and elsewhere, is meant charity from which is faith; for there is no other faith that is faith, than the faith of charity... In David: *Ye who fear Jehovah, praise Him; all ye the seed of Jacob, glorify Him; and stand in awe of Him, all ye the seed of Israel* (Ps. xxii. 23) — where by the seed of Israel no other seed is meant than the spiritual church." (*Heavenly Arcana*, n. 1025.1,11; see also *Heavenly Arcana*, n. 2826.6)

For He has not despised,
And He has not detested the affliction of the afflicted,
And He has not hid His face from him,
And when he cried to Him, He heard. (Ps. 22:24)

The afflicted are those who are lacking in knowledges of the truth (see Ps. 35:10, 37:14, 40:17). For Jehovah to hide His face is for one to be left in one's own evils separate from Divine mercy (see Ps. 13:1, 89:14); those who turn to the Lord will be delivered from their evils and falsities.

"...'the face' of Jehovah or the Lord signifies, namely, the Divine love, and all good in heaven and in the church therefrom; and from this it can be known what is signified by 'hiding' or 'concealing the faces,' in reference to Jehovah or the Lord, namely, that it is to leave man in what is his own (*proprium*) and thus in the evils and falsities that spring forth from what is his own (*proprium*); for man viewed in himself is nothing but evil and falsity therefrom, and that he may be in good he is withheld from these by the Lord, which is effected by being elevated out of what is his own (*proprium*). From this it can be seen that 'hiding and concealing the faces,' in reference to the Lord, signifies to leave in evils and falsities..." (*Apocalypse Explained*, n. 412.18; see also Deut. 31:17-18, 32:20; Isa. 8:17, 59:2; Jer. 33:6; Eze.

7:22, 39:23,28-29; Lam. 4:16; Mic. 3:4; Ps. 13:1, 22:24, 27:9, 30:7, 44:24, 69:17, 88:14, 102:2, 104:29, 143:7)

From You is my praise in the great assembly,
I will pay my vows in front of them who fear Him.
The meek shall eat and be satisfied,
They shall praise Jehovah who enquire after Him,
Your heart shall live for ever. (Ps. 22:25-26)

To praise is to worship from affection for the truth (see Ps. 7:17, 35:18) and the assembly is the truths of the church (see Ps. 1:5, 68:26, 107:32); to pay vows signifies to be in a state of Divine providence (see Ps. 50:14) and to fear the Lord is to do His commandments. The meek are those who are in the good of charity (see Ps. 37:11) and to eat is to appropriate good in one's life. The heart is one's will (see Ps. 7:9, 22:10, 24:4, 51:10, 64:6, 66:18, 78:8), and those who have a will of good will have eternal life.

"*And Jacob vowed a vow.* That this signifies a state of providence, is evident from the signification of vowing a vow, as in the internal sense willing that the Lord may provide; hence, in the supreme sense, in which the Lord is treated of, a state of providence. That vowing a vow in the internal sense signifies willing that the Lord may provide, is from this, that in vows there is desire and affection that what is willed may come to pass, thus that the Lord may provide. Somewhat also of stipulation is implied, and at the same time somewhat of debt on the part of man, which he takes upon himself if he comes to possess the object of his wish — as here on the part of Jacob, that Jehovah should be to him for a God, and the stone which he set up for a pillar should be the house of God, and that he would tithe all that was given him, if Jehovah would keep him in the way, and would give him bread to eat and raiment to put on, and if he should return in peace to his father's house. From this it is manifest that vows at that time were special compacts, particularly to acknowledge God for their God, if He would provide for them what they desired, and also to repay Him by some gift, if He would so provide." (*Heavenly Arcana*, n. 3732)

All the ends of the earth shall remember and return unto Jehovah,
And all the families of the nations shall bow down before You.
For the kingdom is Jehovah's,
And He is the ruler among the nations.
All the fat ones upon earth shall eat and bow down,
All who go down to the dust shall bow before Him,
And those who could not keep his own soul alive. (Ps. 22:27-29)

The ends of the earth are the external limits of the church (see Ps. 46:9, 48:10, 65:5); to remember is to receive in faith and to return to Jehovah is to turn away from evil towards good. The families of the nations are those who are in good (see Ps. 2:1, 18:43, 102:15, 106:5); to bow down is to worship from a humble heart (see Ps. 45:11). The kingdom is the spiritual heaven of Divine truth; the Lord is called ruler from Divine good (see Ps. 2:2, 105:20). The fat ones who eat are those who appropriate good (see Ps. 78:24, 128:2); those who "go down to the dust" are those of the hells of evil (see Ps. 44:25, 72:9) and those who could not keep alive their soul are those of the hells of falsity as soul signifies the spiritual life of the understanding (see Ps. 22:10, 31:9, 71:23, 107:9).

"That by returning unto the ground out of which he was taken, is signified that the church would return to the external man, such as it was before regeneration, is evident from the ground's signifying the external man, as was said before. And that 'dust' signifies that this was condemned and infernal, is evident likewise from what has been said respecting the serpent — that he should eat dust, because he was accursed. To what was there shown concerning the signification of dust, may be added also what is said in David: *All they who go down to the dust shall bow themselves before Jehovah, and he whose soul He hath not made alive* (Ps. xxii. 29). And in another place: *Thou hidest Thy face, they are troubled; Thou takest away their breath, they die, and return to their dust* (civ. 29); which means that when they turn themselves away from the face of the Lord they expire, or die, and so return to the dust, that is, become damned and infernal." (*Heavenly Arcana*, n. 278)

A seed shall serve Him;
A generation to come shall be accounted to the Lord,
And they shall proclaim His righteousness,
To a people that shall be born that He has done this. (Ps. 22:30-31)

A seed are those who are in the faith of charity (see Ps. 18:50, 21:10, 22:23, 30, 89:4, 106:27); those who serve are those who live by the truth (Ps. 31:16, 69:36, 78:70, 89:3,20, 105:26); a generation to come is the new spiritual church that would follow the Lord (see Ps. 14:5, 33:11, 145:13); the Lord (Hebrew *Adonai*) is Divine good in the Divine Human (see Ps. 68:17,26, 105:21, 110:1, 114:7). To proclaim the Lord's righteousness is to acknowledge He is the source of all good (see Ps. 36:6, 37:6, 72:2, 89:14, 92:12) as He had united His human with the Divine, from which He regenerates every person. A people are those in the truth of a new church of the Lord (see Ps. 2:1, 3:8, 18:43, 65:7, 74:18, 102:15); to be born is to become spiritually regenerated.

"*A seed that shall serve Him shall be counted to the Lord for a generation (Ps.* xxii. 30). This also is said of the Lord; and "the seed that shall serve Him" means those who are in the truths of doctrine from the Word; and 'it shall be counted to the Lord for a generation' signifies that they shall be His to eternity; 'to be counted' signifying to be arranged and disposed in order, here to be numbered with or added to, thus to be His." (*Apocalypse Explained*, n. 768.12; see also *Apocalypse Revealed*, n. 565, *Heavenly Arcana*, n. 10249.6))

Psalm 23

A Psalm of David.

~

Jehovah is my shepherd, (1)
I shall not want.
He makes me to couch in spring meadows, (2)
He guides me beside waters of rest.
He restores my soul, (3)
He leads me in the roads of righteousness for His name's sake.
Yes, though I walk through the valley of the shadow of death, (4)
I will fear no evil.
For You are with me,
Your rod and Your staff comfort me.
You arrange a table before me in front of my adversaries: (5)
You anoint my head with oil,
My cup is completely full.
Surely goodness and mercy shall pursue me all the days of
my life, (6)
And I will dwell in the house of Jehovah for length of days.

Psalm Commentary 23

Summary: The Lord teaches all concerning the goods and truths of heaven and the church hence there will be no fear of the hells for the Lord protects against them (v. 1-4). He imparts goods and truths in abundance for eternity (v. 5-6).

Jehovah is my shepherd,
I shall not want. (Ps. 23:1)

Jesus declared Himself to be the shepherd of the flock (Matt. 26:31, John 10:11-16) showing that Jesus is Jehovah in human form. In the spiritual sense to be a shepherd is to lead by way of the truth towards what is good (see Ps. 80:1).

"[*Jehovah is*] *my shepherd; I shall not want. He will make me to lie down in pastures of the tender herb; He will lead me to the waters of rest. Thou wilt arrange a table before me in the presence of mine enemies; my head wilt Thou make fat with oil; my cup will overflow* (Ps. xxiii. 1, 2, 5). This means, in the internal sense, that he who trusts in the Lord is led into all the goods and truths of heaven, and overflows with the enjoyments thereof; 'my shepherd' means the Lord; 'the pastures of the tender herb' signify the knowledges of truth and good; 'the waters of rest' signify the truths of heaven therefrom" (*Apocalypse Explained*, n. 375.34)

To feed or to pasture is to instruct (see Ps. 78:71):

"That feeding is being instructed, is plain from those places in the Word where we read of it — as in Isaiah: *Then shall He give the rain of thy seed, wherewith thou sowest the ground; and*

bread of the increase of the ground, and it shall be fat and rich;
in that day shall thy cattle feed in a broad meadow (xxx. 23) —
where cattle stand for those who are in good and truth, feeding
in a broad meadow, for being abundantly instructed.

"In the same: *I have given Thee for a covenant of the people,*
to restore the land, to make them inherit the desolate heritages;
saying to them who are bound, Go forth; to them who are in dark-
ness, Show yourselves. They shall feed in the ways, and on all
hillsides shall be their pasture (xlix. 8, 9). This is said of the
coming of the Lord, feeding in the ways meaning being instructed
in truths... and pasture standing for the instruction itself. In
Jeremiah: *Woe unto the shepherds that destroy and scatter the*
flock of My pasture! ...Therefore thus saith Jehovah, the God of
Israel, against the shepherds that feed My people (xxiii. 1, 2).
Shepherds stand for those who instruct, and flock for those who
are instructed... thus feeding stands for instructing.

"As it has become customary to call teachers shepherds, and
learners a flock, it has also become common to speak of feeding, when talking of preaching, or of instruction from doctrine
from the Word; but this is done by way of comparison, and not
from the signification, as in the Word. The reason why feeding
is spoken of in the Word from its signification, is, that when
instruction or doctrine from the Word is spoken of in heaven,
then in the world of spirits, where spiritual things appear naturally, are represented to the sight, meadows green with grass,
herbage, and flowers, with flocks therein; and this with every
variety, according to what is being said in heaven about instruction and doctrine.

"In the same: *I will bring Israel again to his habitation, that*
he may feed on Carmel and Bashan; and his soul shall be satis-
fied upon the mountain of Ephraim and in Gilead (l. 19) — feeding on Carmel and Bashan meaning to be instructed in the goods
of faith and of charity. Again: *From the daughter of Zion all her*
honor is departed; her princes are become like harts that find no
pasture (Lam. i. 6). In Ezekiel: *I will feed them in a good pasture,*
and upon the mountains of the height of Israel shall their fold be;

there shall they lie down in a good fold, and on fat pasture shall they feed upon the mountains of Israel (xxxiv. 14).

"In Hosea: *Now will Jehovah feed them as a sheep in a broad place* (iv. 16) — feeding in a broad place meaning to instruct in truths. That breadth is truth, may be seen above... In Micah: *Thou, Bethlehem Ephrathah ...out of thee shall He come forth unto Me who shall be ruler in Israel. He shall stand and shall feed in the strength of Jehovah* (v. 2, 4). Again: *Feed Thy people with Thy rod, the flock of Thy heritage, which dwell solitarily ... let them feed in Bashan and Gilead, as in the days of old* (vii. 14). In Zephaniah: *The remnant of Israel ...shall feed and lie down, and none shall make them afraid* (iii. 13).

"In David: *Jehovah is my shepherd. ...He will make me to lie down in green pastures; He will lead me to the waters of rest* (Ps. xxiii. 1, 2). Again: *It is He who hath made us, and not we; we are His people, and the flock of His pasture;* or, according to another reading, *therefore we are His; we are His people, and flock of His pasture* (Psalm c. 3). In the Apocalypse: *The Lamb which is in the midst of the throne shall feed them, and shall guide them unto living fountains of waters* (vii. 17). In John: *I am the door: by Me if any man enter in, he shall be saved, and shall go in and go out, and shall find pasture* (x. 9). Again: Jesus said to Peter, *Feed My lambs;* and a second time, *Feed My sheep;* and a third time, *Feed My sheep* (xxi. 15-17)." (*Heavenly Arcana*, n. 5201.2-7)

He makes me to couch in spring meadows (Ps. 23:1)

To couch or lie down is to be in a state of tranquility and safety after temptation (see Ps. 3:5, 4:8, 104:22). The sprouting vegetation of spring represents knowledges of truth and good (see Ps. 37:2, 103:15, 104:14, 147:8). Meadow is distinct from pasture (see Ps. 100:3) which represents a state of peace from good, mentioned below as "folds of peace":

"In regard to peace, it signifies in the supreme sense the Lord Himself, and hence in the internal sense His kingdom, and is the Lord's Divine inmostly affecting the good in which are those who are there... *The folds of peace art laid waste, because of the burning of the anger of Jehovah* (xxv. 37). ...peace in the supreme sense signifies the Lord; and in a representative sense it signifies His kingdom, and good from the Lord therein, thus the Divine which flows into good, or into affections for good, which also causes joy and happiness from the inmost. " (*Heavenly Arcana*, n. 3780.2,4)

He guides me beside waters of rest,
He restores my soul,
He leads me in the roads of righteousness for His name's sake.
(Ps. 23:2-3)

Waters signify the truths of faith (see Ps. 18:15, 23:2, 29:3, 42:1, 46:3, 66:12, 77:19, 78:13,16, 104:3, 136:6) which leads to a state of peace free from the conflict of temptation (see Ps. 95:11). To restore the soul is to bring one's spiritual understanding into the truth; to be led is to be led towards good (see Ps. 5:8, 23:3, 27:11); the roads of righteousness are the truths of good (see Ps. 36:6, 37:6, 72:2, 89:14, 92:12). In scripture water always has reference to the truth:

"As it is not yet known that 'waters' in the Word signify the truths of faith and the knowledges of truth, I would like, since this signification may possibly appear remote, to show here briefly that this is what is meant in the Word by 'waters.' This, moreover, is necessary, because without a knowledge of what 'waters' signify, it cannot be known what baptism signifies, nor the 'washings' in the Israelitish church so frequently referred to. 'Waters' signify the truths of faith, as 'bread' signifies the good of love. 'Waters' and 'bread' have this signification because things that pertain to spiritual nourishment are expressed in the sense of the letter by such things as belong to natural nourishment; for bread and water, which include in general all food and drink, nourish the body, while the truths of faith and the good of love nourish the soul. This also is from correspondence, for when 'bread' and 'water' are read of in the Word, angels, because they are spiritual, understand the things by which they are nourished, which are the goods of love and the truths of faith." (*Apoc-*

alypse Explained, n. 71.1; see also Isa. 11:9, 12:3, 33:15-16, 34:10, 41:17,18,20, 44:3, 48:21, 51:14, 58:10-11; Jer. 2:13, 14:3, 17:13, 31:9; Eze. 4:16-17, 12:18-19; Am. 8:11-13; Zech. 14:8; Ps. 23:1-2, 63:1, 147:18, 148:4; John 4:7-15, 7:37-38; Apoc. 21:6, 22:1,17)

Yes, though I walk through the valley of the shadow of death,
I will fear no evil:
For You are with me,
Your rod and Your staff comfort me. (Ps. 23:4)

To walk in a valley is to be in an obscure understanding of the truth in a lower natural state (see Ps. 65:13, 104:8); the "shadow of death" is the falsity of evil of those who have destroyed good (see Ps. 44:19); death is spiritual death in hell (see Ps. 6:5, 9:13, 102:20, 106:28). Rods or scepters signify the power of truth (see Ps. 2:9, 45:6, 105:16, 110:2, 125:3) and staffs signify the power of good (see Ps. 18:18, 105:16), by which one is protected from falsity and evil.

"In David: *Yea, though I walk through the valley of the shadow of death, I will fear no evil* (Ps. xxiii. 4) — where the valley of the shadow of death stands for lower things, which are relatively in shade.

"As valleys were between mountains and hills, and below them, therefore by valleys are signified the lower or exterior things of the church, because by hills and mountains are signified its higher or interior things, by hills things which are of charity, and by mountains those which are of love to the Lord..." (*Heavenly Arcana*, n. 4715.5-6)

"In Hosea: *My people ask counsel of their wood, and their staff will answer them; for the spirit of whoredom hath caused them to err* (iv. 12). Asking counsel of wood means consulting evils; the staffs answering means that falsity is thence, which has power from the evil which they confirm; the spirit of whoredom stands for a life of falsity from evil. In David: *Yea, though I walk through the valley of the shadow of death, I will fear no evil; for Thou art with me; Thy rod and Thy staff, they comfort me* (Ps. xxiii. 4). Thy rod and Thy staff stand for the Divine truth and good, which have power. Again: *The staff of wickedness shall not rest upon the lot of the just* (Ps. cxxv. 3)." (*Heavenly Arcana*, n. 4876.8)

"...by a staff is signified great power, which is from the Lord, here that of knowing the state of the church, because the temple and the altar were measured by the staff; and by measuring is signified to know, and by the temple and the altar the church is signified, spoken of in what follows. Power is signified by a staff, because wood, of which staves were made among the ancients in the church, signifies good; and because it is in place of the right hand, and supports it; and by the right hand power is signified. Hence it is that a sceptre is a short staff, and by a sceptre is signified the power of a king. Sceptre and staff are also the same word in the Hebrew language. That a staff signifies power is manifest from these passages: *Say ye, How is the strong staff broken, the beautiful staff; descend from glory, and sit in thirst* (Jer. xlviii. 17, 18). *Jehovah will send the staff of thy strength out of Zion* (Ps. cx. 2). *Thou didst strike through with staves the head of the unbelieving* (Hab. iii. 14). *Israel the staff of Jehovah's inheritance* (Jer. x. 16; li. 19). *Thy rod and Thy staff shall comfort me* (Ps. xxiii. 4). *Jehovah hath broken the staff of the ungodly* (Isa. ix. 4; xiv. 5; Ps. cxxv. 3). *My people inquire of a stock; and their staff answers them* (Hos. iv. 12). *Jehovah that removeth from Jerusalem the whole staff of bread and the whole staff of water* (Isa. iii. 1; Ezek. iv. 16; v. 16; xiv. 13; Ps. cv. 16; Lev. xxvi. 26). By the staff of bread and of water the power of good and truth is signified, and by Jerusalem the church." (*Apocalypse Revealed*, n. 485)

"Divine truth in respect to power is signified elsewhere in the Word by 'rods' and 'staffs,' as can be seen from the following passages. In *David:*—

Yea, when I shall walk in the shady valley I will fear no evil to me; Thy rod and Thy staff will comfort me; Thou wilt make ready before me a table in the presence of mine ene-

mies; and Thou wilt make fat my head with oil and my cup
will abound (Ps. xxiii. 4, 5).

'To walk in a shady valley' signifies in the spiritual sense an
obscure understanding that does not see truths from light; 'Thy
rod and Thy staff will comfort me' signifies that spiritual Divine
truth together with natural Divine truth will protect, for these
have power; 'rod' meaning spiritual Divine truth [or, the power
of truth], 'staff' natural Divine truth [or, the power of good], the
two together meaning these in respect to their power to protect,
for 'to comfort' means to protect. As 'rod and staff' signify Divine
truth in respect to power, it is next said, 'Thou wilt make ready
before me a table, Thou wilt make fat my head with oil, my cup
will abound,' which signifies spiritual nourishment through
Divine truth; for 'to make ready a table' signifies to be nourished
spiritually; 'to make fat the head with oil' signifies with the good
of love, and 'cup' signifies with the truth of doctrine from the
Word, 'cup' standing here for 'wine.'" (*Apocalypse Explained*,
n. 727.2)

You arrange a table before me in front of my adversaries (Ps. 23:5)

A table is arrangement to receive heavenly influx in regards
to love and to have instruction thence (see Ps. 128:3); adversaries are evils which attack what is good (see Ps. 3:1, 27:12).

"'table' signifies spiritual nourishment; 'to make fat the head
with oil' signifies wisdom which is from good; 'my cup will overflow,' signifies intelligence which is from truths, 'cup' signifying
the like as 'wine.'" (*Apocalypse Explained*, n. 375.34)

"*And thou shalt make a table.* That this signifies a receptacle
of celestial things, is evident from the signification of the table,
as heaven as to the reception of such things as are from the Lord
there, which are good of love and good of faith, and blessedness
and happiness therefrom. These things are signified by a table,
because by foods are signified the celestial things which are of
the good of love and of faith, and thus wisdom and intelligence,
which even in common speech are called heavenly foods, and are
likewise meant by foods in the Word... Moreover these things

are occasionally exhibited representatively in heaven by a table, upon which are foods of every kind. From this it is plain that by the table is signified a receptacle of celestial things, thus heaven as to the reception of such things as are from the Lord. These things are likewise signified by a table in Luke *Jesus said …I appoint unto you even as My Father appointed unto Me My kingdom; that ye may eat and drink at My table in My kingdom* (xxii. 29, 30). And in Matthew: *Many shall come from the east even to the west, and shall sit down with Abraham, and Isaac, and Jacob, in the kingdom of the heavens* (viii. 11). Also in David: *I will fear no evil. …Thou wilt prepare a table before me in the presence of mine enemies: Thou wilt anoint my head with oil; my cup shall run over. Goodness and mercy shall follow me* (Ps. xxiii. 4-6)." (*Heavenly Arcana*, n. 9527)

You anoint my head with oil (Ps. 23:5)

To anoint with oil is to receive celestial good (Ps. 17:10, 23:5, 36:8, 63:5, 65:11, 81:16, 92:14, 147:14) and to testify of gladness of mind and heart; the head signifies wisdom or interior spiritual things (see Ps. 133:2) and oil is celestial good (see Ps. 36:8, 52:8, 89:20, 104:15, 133:2).

"Because oil signified the good of charity, therefore also the sick were anointed with oil and were healed, as we read of the Lord's disciples, who went forth and cast out demons, and anointed with oil them who were sick and healed them (Mark. vi. 13). And in David: *Thou wilt anoint my head with oil; my cup shall run over* (Ps. xxiii. 5) — where anointing the head with oil signifies presenting with heavenly good." (*Heavenly Arcana*, n. 9780.8)

"…it had become customary to anoint themselves and others in order to testify gladness of mind and goodwill, is evident from the following passages — in Daniel: *I Daniel was mourning three weeks. I ate no pleasant bread, neither came flesh nor wine into my mouth, neither with anointing was I anointed, till three weeks of days were fulfilled* (x. 2, 3). In Matthew: *Thou, when thou fastest, anoint thy head, and wash thy face; that thou be not seen of men to fast, but of thy Father in secret* (vi. 17, 18). To fast means to be in mourning. In Amos: *They who drink out of bowls of wine, and anoint themselves from the firstfruits of the oils; but they are not grieved for the breach of Joseph* (vi. 6). In Ezekiel: *I washed thee with waters; yea, I washed away thy bloods, and I anointed thee with oil* (xvi. 9) — speaking of Jerusalem, by which is signified the church. In Micah: *Thou shalt tread the olive, but shalt not anoint thee with oil* (vi. 15). In Moses: *Thou shalt have olive trees throughout all thy borders, but thou shalt not anoint thyself with the oil; for thine olive shall be shaken off* (Deut. xxviii. 40).

"In Isaiah: *To give unto them a mitre for ashes, the oil of joy for mourning* (lxi. 3). In David: *Thy God hath anointed thee with the oil of gladness above thy fellows* (Ps. xlv. 7). Again: *Thou preparest a table before me in the presence of mine enemies; Thou anointest my head with oil* (Ps. xxiii. 5). Again: *My horn shalt Thou exalt like the horn of the unicorn: I shall grow old with fresh oil* (Ps. xcii. 10). Again: *Wine maketh glad the heart of man, to make his face to shine with oil* (Ps. civ. 15). In Mark: The disciples going out *anointed with oil many that were sick, and healed them* (vi. 12, 13). And in Luke: Jesus said unto Simon, *I entered into thine house. ...My head with oil thou didst not anoint: but this woman hath anointed My feet with ointment* (vii. 44, 46). From these examples it is plain that it was customary to anoint themselves and others with oil; not with the oil of holiness with which the priests, the kings, the altar, and the tabernacle were anointed, but with common oil, for the reason that this oil signified the gladness and satisfaction which are of the love of good; but the oil of holiness signified the Divine good, of which it is said: *Upon the flesh of man shall it not be poured, neither shall ye make any like it, according to the quality thereof ...it shall be holy unto you. Whosoever shall prepare any like it, or whosoever shall put any of it upon a stranger, he shall be cut off from his people* (Exod. xxx. 32, 33, 38)." (*Heavenly Arcana*, n. 9954.19-20)

My cup is completely full. (Ps. 23:5)

A cup represents external reception of the truth in the lower natural (see Ps. 11:6, 16:5, 23:5). Each person has the potential to become a recipient of Divine love and truth, which is represented as a table and a cup. This is the origin of the ritual of communion or the Eucharist.

"...a cup is often mentioned in the Word, and by it in the genuine sense is signified spiritual truth, that is, the truth of faith which is from the good of charity — the same as by wine; and in the opposite sense is signified falsity by which comes evil, and also falsity from evil. That a cup signifies the same as wine, is because a cup is what contains, and wine is what is contained, and hence they constitute one thing, and so the one is understood by the other.

"That such is the signification of cup in the Word, is plain from the following passages: Jehovah, *Thou preparest a table before me in the presence of mine enemies; Thou anointest my head with oil; my cup runneth over* (Ps. xxiii. 5). Preparing a table and anointing the head with oil, stands for being gifted with the good of charity and love; my cup runneth over means that the natural is thence filled with spiritual truth and good." (*Heavenly Arcana*, n. 5120.2-3)

Surely goodness and mercy shall pursue me all the days of my life, And I will dwell in the house of Jehovah for length of days. (Ps. 23:6)

Mercy is Divine love (see Ps. 25:10, 26:3, 36:5, 89:14, 103:8) from which is all good; the house of Jehovah is the heaven as to love (see Ps. 65:4, 92:13, 105:21). The days of the life is spiritual life to eternity as to truth; "length of days" in a general sense signifies eternal life (*Heavenly Arcana*, n. 650), but in a more spiritual sense it describes one's eternal progression towards the good of love of the Lord as signified by length (see Ps. 4:1).

"That dwelling is being and living, thus a state, is evident from many passages in the Word — as in David: *I will dwell in the house of Jehovah for length of days* (Ps. xxiii. 6). *One thing have I asked of Jehovah, that will I seek after; that I may dwell in the house of Jehovah all the days of my life* (Ps. xxvii. 4). *He who worketh deceit shall not dwell in the midst of My house* (Ps. ci. 7) — where dwelling in the house of Jehovah means being and living in the good of love, for this is the house of Jehovah." (*Heavenly Arcana*, n. 3384.2)

Psalm 24

A Psalm of David.

~

The earth is Jehovah's, and her fullness, (1)
The world and they who dwell therein.
For He has founded her upon the seas, (2)
And established her upon the rivers.
 Who shall ascend the mountain of Jehovah? (3)
 And who shall rise in His holy place?
 He who is innocent of hands and pure of heart, (4)
 Who has not lifted up *his* soul to vanity, nor sworn deceitfully.
 He shall receive the blessing from Jehovah, (5)
 And righteousness from God of his salvation.
 This is the generation of those who enquire after Him, (6)
 Who seek Your face, Jacob. (Selah)
  Lift up your heads, ye gates, (7)
  And lift up the everlasting doors, and the King of glory shall
  come in.
  Who is this King of glory? (8)
  Jehovah strong and mighty, Jehovah mighty in battle.
  Lift up your heads, ye gates, (9)
  And lift up the everlasting doors, and the King of glory shall
  come in.
  Who is this King of glory? (10)
  Jehovah of hosts, He is the King of glory. (Selah)

Psalm Commentary

24

Summary: The church is the Lord's through the Word (v. 1-2). Those who are not in falsity and evil shall belong to the church (v. 3-4) who will receive the Lord (v. 5-6) who conquered the hells and glorified His human (v. 7-8).

The earth is Jehovah's, and her fulness,
The world and they who dwell therein. (Ps. 24:1)

The earth is the church as to truth and the world is the church as to good (see Ps. 9:8, 60:2, 90:2, 96:13); its fullness is all truth and good of the church (see Ps. 50:12, 89:11):

> *"Let all the earth fear Jehovah, let all the inhabitants of the world stand in awe of Him (Ps. xxxiii. 8).*

Here, too, the 'earth' signifies those who are in the truths of the church, and 'the inhabitants of the world' those who are in the goods of the church. In the same:—

> *The earth is Jehovah's and the fullness thereof, the world and they who dwell therein; He hath founded it upon the seas, and established it upon the rivers (Ps. xxiv. 1, 2).*

Here, also, the 'earth' signifies the church in respect to truth, and 'the fullness thereof' signifies all truths in the complex; and the 'world' signifies the church in respect to good, and 'they who dwell' signify goods in the complex." (*Apocalypse Explained*, n. 741.8)

336

"By the world is not signified the world of lands, but the church in it, in the following passages: *The earth shall mourn and be confounded, the world shall languish and be confounded* (Isa. xxiv. 4). *The lands shall learn Thy judgments, and the inhabitants of the world Thy justice* (Isa. xxxvi. 9). *Who maketh the earth by Thy power, who prepareth the world by Thy wisdom* (Jer. x. 12; li. 15). *The foundations of the world were revealed by the blast of Thy breath* (Ps. xviii. 15). *The earth is Jehovah's and the fullness thereof, the world and they who dwell therein: He hath founded it upon the seas, and established it, upon the floods* (Ps. xxiv. 1, 2). *The heavens are Thine, the earth also is Thine; the world and the fullness thereof Thou hast founded* (Ps. lxxxix. 11). *He will make them to inherit the throne of glory; for the pillars of the earth are Jehovah's, and He hath set the world upon them* (1 Sam. ii. 8). *O Babylon, thou hast made the world a wilderness; thou hast destroyed thy land, and slain thy people* (Isa. xiv. 17, 20). Besides other places, as Isa. xviii. 3; xxvi. 18; xxvii. 6; xxxiv. 1; Nah. i. 5; Ps. ix. 8; Ps. lxxvii. 18; Ps. xcviii. 9; Lam. iv. 12; Job xviii. 18; Matt. xxiv. 14; Luke xxi. 26; Apoc. xvi. 14. But it is to be known, that when the world and the earth are named together, the church as to good is signified by the world, and the church as to truth by the earth." (*Apocalypse Revealed*, n. 551)

For He has founded her upon the seas,
And established her upon the rivers. (Ps. 24:2)

The foundations of the earth are the truths on which the church is based (see Ps. 11:3, 18:7,15, 75:3, 82:5, 104:5); seas are knowledges of truth in general (see Ps. 33:7, 69:34, 77:19, 89:25, 104:5-6,25) and rivers are the truths of faith (see Ps. 89:25, 46:3-5, 78:15-20, 97:8, 107:33).

"*The earth is Jehovah's and the fullness thereof, the world and they who dwell therein; and He hath founded it upon the seas, He hath established it upon the rivers* (Ps. xxiv. 1, 2). The 'earth' and the 'world' stand for the church, and 'fullness' for all things thereof; the 'seas upon which He hath founded it,' mean the knowledges of truth in general; the 'rivers' doctrinals; because the church is founded on both of these, it is said that 'He hath founded it upon the seas, and established it upon the rivers.' That this cannot be said of the earth and the world is clear to any one." (*Apocalypse Explained*, n. 304.16)

"*The heavens are Thine, the earth also is Thine; the world and the fullness thereof, Thou hast founded them* (Ps. lxxxix. 11). And again: *The earth is Jehovah's, and the fullness thereof; the world, and they who dwell therein. For He hath founded it upon the seas, and established it upon the floods* (Ps. xxiv. 1, 2) — where also the fullness stands for truth and good; the earth for the church in a specific, and the world for the church in a universal sense. That Jehovah founded the world upon the seas, is upon what is of knowledge (n. 28); and that He established it upon the floods, is upon what is of intelligence (n. 3051). Who cannot see that it is not meant that Jehovah founded the world upon the seas, and established it upon the floods, for the world is not founded and established thereon. He therefore who considers may see that by seas and by floods something else is signified, and that this something else is the spiritual or the internal of the Word." (*Heavenly Arcana*, n. 6297.3)

"*Jehovah hath founded the world upon the seas, and established it upon the rivers* (*Ps.* xxiv. 2). The 'world' signifies heaven and the church in the whole complex, the 'seas' signify cognitions and knowledges which are the ultimates of the church, and in particular, the cognitions of truth and good, such as are in the sense of the letter of the Word; 'rivers' signify introduction through knowledges into heavenly intelligence. This makes clear the meaning of these words in the spiritual sense, namely, that the interior things of heaven and the church, which are called celestial and spiritual, are founded upon the cognitions of truth and good which are in the sense of the letter of the Word rationally understood. It is said, 'He hath founded the world upon the seas and established it upon the rivers,' because there are seas and rivers in the boundaries of heaven, represented by the Sea Suph, the sea of the Philistines, the river Euphrates, and the river Jordan, which were the boundaries of the land of Canaan;

and because what is ultimate means in the Word what is lowest, it is said that Jehovah 'founded' and 'established' upon these. Evidently the earth is not founded upon seas and rivers." (*Apocalypse Explained*, n. 518.23)

"That the sea is a collection of knowledges, is from this, that waters, springs, and rivers signify truths, and therefore collections of these are signified by the seas. That this is so, is also evident from passages in the Word where mention is made of the sea or of seas — as in David: *The earth is Jehovah's, and the fullness thereof; the world, and they who dwell therein. He hath founded it upon the seas, and established it upon the rivers* (Ps. xxiv. 1, 2) — where the earth and world stand for the church; the seas upon which He hath founded the world, for truths of knowledge; the rivers upon which He hath established it, for the truths of faith. That the earth, the world, seas, and rivers are not meant here, is plain, for the world is not founded upon the seas, nor is it established upon rivers." (*Heavenly Arcana*, n. 9755.3)

> "The earth and the world Jehovah hath founded upon the seas, and established upon the rivers. Who shall ascend into the mountain of Jehovah, and who shall stand in the place of His holiness? (Ps. xxiv. 2, 3).

The establishment of the church is described by 'founding the earth and the world upon the seas, and establishing them upon the rivers,' as can be seen above (n. 304c, 518d, 741b). That the establishment of the church is signified is evident from what here follows, namely, 'Who shall ascend into the mountain of Jehovah, and who shall stand in the place of His holiness?' 'The mountain of Jehovah' means Zion, which signifies where the Lord reigns by means of the Divine truth, and 'the place of His holiness' means Jerusalem, where the temple was, which signifies the church as to doctrine. All this makes clear that 'the founding of the world' signifies the establishment of the church. For the 'world' has a similar meaning as 'heaven and earth;' and the expression 'to found the earth' is used because the 'earth' signifies the church on earth, and upon this heaven as to its holy things is founded. This also makes clear the signification of 'the foundations of the earth' in the following passages. In *Isaiah:*—

> *Do ye not know, do ye not hear, hath it not been declared to you from the beginning, do ye not understand the foundations of the earth?* (xl. 21).

In the same:—

> *The foundations of the earth are corrupted* (xxiv. 18; likewise *Isa.* lxiii. 12; *Jer.* xxxi. 37; *Micah* vi. 2; *Ps.* xviii. 7, 15; lxxxii. 5; and elsewhere)." (*Apocalypse Explained*, n. 1057.5)

"By rivers are signified truths in abundance, because truths are signified by waters (n. 50); and by fountains of waters the Word is signified (n. 384)... That rivers signify truths in abundance may be evident from the following passages: *Behold, I do a new thing: I will give waters in the desert and rivers in the wilderness, to give drink to My people, My chosen* (Isa. xliii. 19, 20). *I will pour water upon him who is thirsty, and rivers upon the dry ground; I will pour My spirit upon thy seed, and My blessing upon thine offspring* (Isa. xliv. 3).*Then the tongue of the dumb shall sing; for in the wilderness shall waters break out, and rivers in the plain of the desert* (Isa. xxxv. 6). *I will open rivers upon the slopes, and I will put fountains in the midst of the valleys, I will make the wilderness a pool of waters, and the dry land springs of water* (Isa. xli. 18). *Jehovah hath founded the world upon the seas, He hath established it upon the rivers* (Ps. xxiv. 2). *I will put His hand in the sea, and His right hand in the rivers* (Ps. lxxxix. 25). *Was Jehovah incensed at the rivers? was Thy anger against the rivers? was Thy wrath against the sea, that Thou dost ride upon Thy horses?* (Hab. iii. 8). *A river whose streams shall gladden the city of God* (Ps. xlvi. 3, 4, 5). *He showed me a pure river of water of life, going forth from the throne of God and of the Lamb* (Apoc. xxii. 1). *He clave the rocks in the desert, and gave them drink from the great deeps; He smote the rock and the rivers gushed out* (Ps. lxxviii. 15, 16, 20; cv. 41). *Then the waters shall fail in the sea, and the rivers shall be dried up* (Isa. xix. 5-7; xlii. 15; 1. 2; Nah. i. 4; Ps. cvii. 33; Job xiv. 10, 11). *Jesus said, If any one come unto Me, as the Scripture hath said, Out of his belly shall flow rivers of living water* (John vii. 37, 38. Beside other places, as Isa. xxxiii. 21; Jer. xvii. 7, 8; Ezek. xxxi. 3, 4; xlvii. 1-12; Joel iii. 18; Zech. ix. 10; Ps. lxxx. 11; xciii. 3-5; xcviii. 7, 8; cx. 7; Num. xxiv. 6, 7; Deut. viii. 7)." (*Apocalypse Revealed*, n. 409)

Who shall ascend the mountain of Jehovah?
And who shall rise in His holy place?
He who is innocent of hands and pure of heart,
Who has not lifted up his soul to vanity, nor sworn deceitfully.
He shall receive the blessing from Jehovah,
And righteousness from God of his salvation.
This is the generation of those who enquire after Him,
Who seek Your face, Jacob. (Ps. 24:3-6)

The mountain of Jehovah is the heaven of love (see Ps. 18:7, 36:6, 68:15-16, 72:3, 104:10, 114:4,6, 121:1, 133:3, 147:8, 148:9); the holy place or sanctuary is the heaven of truth (see Ps. 19:1, 20:2, 68:24, 150:1). Innocence of hands refers to exterior good, and to be pure of heart refers to interior good (see Ps. 73:13). To lift the soul to vanity is to follow the falsity of doctrine (see Ps. 4:2, 144:8); to swear deceitfully is to confirm falsehood (see Ps. 15:4, 63:11, 89:3,35, 105:9, 110:4, 132:1) to intentionally mislead others (see Ps. 5:6). To be blessed is to receive happiness and good from the Lord (see Ps. 3:8, 16:7, 21:6, 24:5, 28:6, 31:21, 96:2); righteousness is good (see Ps. 14:5, 36:6, 37:6,17, 72:2, 89:14, 92:12) from truth signified by God (see Ps. 18:31, 29:1, 68:17,24, 82:1, 95:3, 147:7); salvation is deliverance from evil (see Ps. 14:7, 96:2). A generation signifies those who in the truths of faith (see Ps. 14:5, 22:30, 33:11, 145:13); to seek God's face is to seek His Divine love (see Ps. 4:6, 13:1, 22:24, 27:8-9, 31:16, 67:1); Jacob is the external church that is in external knowledges of good and truth (see Ps. 14:7, 77:15, 78:5, 132:5).

"Those therefore who receive Divine good and Divine truth from the Lord, are called:—

Blessed (Ps. xxxvii. 22; cxv. 15; *Matt.* xxv. 34).

That 'blessing' has no other meaning, when said of man, than the reception of Divine truth and Divine good, because in them are heaven and eternal happiness, can be seen from the following passages. In *David:*—

> *The clean in hands and the pure in heart shall receive a blessing from before Jehovah, and righteousness from the God of our salvation (Ps.* xxiv. 4, 5).

'The clean in hands' signify those who are in truths from faith, and 'the pure in heart' those who are in good from love; of such it is said that they 'shall receive a blessing from before Jehovah, and righteousness from the God of salvation,' and 'receiving a blessing' signifies the reception of Divine truth, and 'receiving righteousness' the reception of Divine good." (*Apocalypse Explained*, n. 340.9-10)

Lift up your heads, ye gates,
And lift up the everlasting doors, and the King of glory shall come in.
Who is this King of glory?
Jehovah strong and mighty, Jehovah mighty in battle.
Lift up your heads, ye gates,
And lift up the everlasting doors, and the King of glory shall come in.
Who is this King of glory?
Jehovah of hosts, He is this King of glory. (Ps. 24:7-10)

Gates are the knowledges of good and truth which introduce into the church (see Ps. 9:14), and also signify the communication of good and truth from heaven (see Ps. 78:23, 84:10). The king is the Lord as to Divine truth in His human form (see Ps. 2:2, 72:11, 89:20,39, 95:3, 105:20,30); glory is the Divine truth of heaven (see Ps. 18:31, 29:1, 68:17,24, 82:1, 95:3, 147:7). To be strong is to have power from good (see Ps. 21:13, 29:1, 95:4, 96:6); to be mighty is to have power from truth (see Ps. 21:13, 80:2). Wars signify spiritual combat against the hells (see Ps. 18:34, 27:3,

46:9, 76:3), which is done by the Lord in saving man in repentance and spiritual regeneration. Jehovah of hosts is the Divine power of good (see Ps. 46:7); hosts in themselves are the goods and truths of heaven (see Ps. 33:6, 103:21). As Jehovah is King in the Old Testamant so Jesus is King in the New Testament, demonstrating that Jesus is Jehovah in human form. Gates are the entrances to the spiritual kingdom; everlasting doors is the entrance into the celestial heaven of love, as signified by everlasting (see Ps. 145:13). Gates and doors represent communication with heaven, thus the Lord says, *Behold, I stand at the door, and knock: if any man hear my voice, and open the door, I will come in to him, and will sup with him, and he with me* (Rev. 3:20). From the spiritual gates of heaven there is influx of good and truth into each person:

"As regards the signification of a gate, there are in general two gates with every man; the one extends toward hell, which is opened to evils and falsities therefrom; in that gate are infernal genii and spirits; the other gate extends toward heaven, which is opened to good and the truths therefrom; in this gate are angels. There is thus a gate which leads to hell, and a gate which leads to heaven. The gate of hell is opened to those who are in evil and falsity, and only through chinks round about above does anything of the light from heaven enter, by means of which they are able to think and reason, but the gate of heaven is opened to those who are in good and truth therefrom.

"For there are two ways which lead into man's rational mind — a higher or internal one, through which good and truth from the Lord enter, and a lower or external one, through which evil and falsity come up from hell. The rational mind itself is in the middle, and to it these ways tend...

"In David: *Lift up your heads, O ye gates; and be ye lifted up, ye everlasting doors; and the King of glory shall come in. Who is this King of glory? Jehovah strong and mighty, Jehovah mighty in battle. Lift up your heads, O ye gates; lift them up, ye everlasting doors* (Ps. xxiv. 7-10). In the same: *Praise Jehovah, O Jerusalem; praise thy God, O Zion: for He hath strengthened the bars of thy gates, He hath blessed thy children within thee* (Ps. cxlvii. 12, 13).

"From these passages it is manifest that the gate of heaven is where angels are with man, that is, where there is influx of good and truth from the Lord; and thus that there are two gates, as was said. Concerning these two gates the Lord speaks thus in Matthew: *Enter ye in by the narrow gate; for wide is the gate and broad the way that leadeth to destruction, and many are they who enter in thereby; for narrow is the gate and straitened the way that leadeth unto life, and few are they who find it* (vii. 12-14; Luke xiii. 23, 24)." (*Heavenly Arcana*, n. 2851.2-3, 14-15)

"...gates in a good sense stand for opening into heaven — as in David: *Lift up your heads, O ye gates; and be ye lifted up, ye everlasting doors; and the King of glory shall come in* (Ps. xxiv. 7-10). Moreover by gates in the Word is signified entrance into heaven and into the church by truth and good, and also the influx of truth and of good with man." (*Heavenly Arcana*, n. 10483.5)

"*Lift up your heads, O ye gates; be ye lift up, ye doors of the world: and the King of glory shall come in* (Ps. xxiv. 7, 9) — where the doors of the world being lift up stands for the opening and elevation of hearts to the Lord, Who is the King of glory, and thereby giving communication, that is, that He may flow in with good of charity and with truth of faith. The Lord is called the King of glory from truth which is from good." (*Heavenly Arcana*, n. 8989.5)

"Since, as was said above, 'doors' and 'gates' signify admission, and in particular, introductory truths, which are truths from good from the Lord, it is clear what 'doors' and 'gates' signify in the following passage. In *David:*—

> *Lift up your heads, O ye gates; and be ye lifted up, ye everlasting portals, that the King of glory may come in* (Ps. xxiv. 7, 9)." (*Apocalypse Explained*, n. 208.12)

"For all the things that are beheld in the heavens are correspondences; hence also the ways and the gates: for ways correspond to and hence signify truths; and gates correspond to and signify entrance. Since the Lord alone leads man to heaven, and opens the door, He therefore calls Himself the way, and also the door: the way in John: *I am the way, the truth, and the life* (xiv. 6): and the door in the same: *I am the door of the sheep; by Me if any one enter in, he shall be saved* (x. 7, 9). Since there are both ways and doors in the spiritual world, and angelic spirits actually go in the ways, and enter through the doors, when they enter into heaven, therefore doors, gates, and portals are often mentioned in the Word, and by them entrance is signified; as in these places: *Lift up your heads, O ye gates; lift up, ye doors of the world; that the King of glory may come in* (Ps. xxiv. 7, 9). *Open ye the gates, that the just nation that doeth truth may come in* (Isa. xxvi. 2)." (*Apocalypse Revealed*, n. 176)

As Jehovah descended as to the Divine truth or Word to become incarnate, in a higher sense the "King of glory" represents the Lord who fought against the power of hell through His Human:

"That glorification, where the Lord is treated of, is the uniting of His Human with the Divine Itself which was in Him, thus with Jehovah His Father, by which union He made His Human also Divine good, is manifest from the passages in the Word where mention is made of glory and glorification, when spoken of Jehovah or the Lord — as in Isaiah: *The glory of Jehovah shall be revealed, and all flesh shall see it together, for the mouth of the Lord hath spoken it* (xl. 5). Again: *I Jehovah have called thee in righteousness ...to open the blind eyes, to bring forth from the prison him who was bound; I am Jehovah; that is My name: and My glory will I not give to another* (xlii. 6-8). And again: *Jehovah shall arise upon thee, and His glory shall be seen upon thee; the nations shall walk to thy light* (lx. 2, 3). These passages refer to the Lord, and by the glory of Jehovah is meant the Lord as to Divine truth, for Divine truth proceeding from the Lord is the glory of Jehovah (n. 9429). That Divine truth is from no other source the Lord teaches in John: *Ye have neither heard His voice* [the Father's] *at any time, nor seen His form* (verse 37). And since it is the Lord, it is Jehovah Himself, for He says, *I am Jehovah; that is My name: and My glory will I not give to another.*

"Hence also it is that the Lord is called the King of glory — as in David: *Lift up your heads, O ye gates, and be ye lifted up ye everlasting doors; and the King of glory shall come in. Who is this King of glory? Jehovah strong and mighty, Jehovah mighty in battle* (Ps. xxiv. 7-10). The Lord is here called the King of glory from Divine truth from which He fought, conquered, and subdued the hells; that this was done from His Human when He was in the world may be seen above (n. 9715, 9809, 10019); hence it is that He is called Jehovah strong and mighty, and also Hero in Isaiah: *Unto us a child is born, unto us a son is given ... and His name shall be called God, Mighty, the Father of Eternity* (ix. 6)." (*Heavenly Arcana*, n. 10053.2-3)

"With regard to combats and victories over the hells the case is this. He who once overcomes them overcomes them for ever; for by victory he procures to himself power over them, since he so far confirms in himself and so far appropriates to himself the good which is of love and the truth which is of faith, against which afterward the hells dare nothing. The Lord, when He was in the world, admitted the combats of temptations into Himself from all the hells, and by these combats made the Human in Himself Divine, and at the same time brought back the hells under obedience forever... Therefore it is that the Lord alone has power over the hells to eternity, and from Divine power fights for man. For this reason now it is that the Lord is called a man of war, and also a mighty man — as in Isaiah: *Jehovah shall go forth as a mighty man; He shall stir up zeal like a man of war. ... He shall prevail over His enemies* (xlii. 13). And in David: *Who is this, the King of glory? Jehovah strong and mighty, Jehovah mighty in war. Who is this King of glory? Jehovah of hosts* (Ps. xxiv. 8, 10)." (*Heavenly Arcana*, n. 8273.3)

"Inasmuch as Divine truth is represented by royalty in the Word, the Lord as to the Divine truth being represented by kings (see the passages cited just above), therefore to the Divine truth as to a king is attributed glory — as in David: *Lift up your heads,*

O ye gates; and be ye lift up, ye doors of the world: and the King of glory shall come in. Who is this, the King of glory? Jehovah strong and mighty, Jehovah mighty in battle. Lift up your heads, O ye gates; yea, lift them up, ye doors of the world: and the King of glory shall come in. Who is He, this King of glory? Jehovah of hosts, He is the King of glory (Ps. xxiv. 7-10). In Isaiah: *Jehovah of hosts shall reign in mount Zion, and in Jerusalem, and before His elders shall be glory* (xxiv. 23) — glory standing for Divine truth. Jehovah is called Jehovah of hosts or Jehovah of armies, where the Divine truth is treated of, for by armies are signified truths (see n. 3448)." (*Heavenly Arcana*, n. 5922.15)

Psalm 25

Of David.

~

Unto You, Jehovah, I lift up my soul, (1) [*aleph*]
My God, I trust in You. (2)
Let me not be ashamed, [*aleph*]
Let not my enemies exult over me.
Also let all who wait on You not be ashamed, (3) [*gimel*]
Let them be ashamed who deal treacherously without cause.
 Let me know Your ways, Jehovah, (4) [*daleth*]
 Teach me Your paths.
 Let me tread in Your truth and teach me, (5) [*he*]
 For You are God of my salvation,
 On You I wait every day.
 Remember Your compassion, Jehovah, and Your mercies, (6) [*zayin*]
 For they have been from everlasting.
 Remember not the sins of my youth and my transgressions: (7)
 [*cheth*]
 According to Your mercy remember me for Your goodness' sake,
 Jehovah.
  Good and upright is Jehovah, (8) [*teth*]
  Therefore He will instruct sinners in the way.
  He will cause the meek to tread in judgment, (9) [*yod*]
  And He will teach the meek His way.
  All the paths of Jehovah are mercy and truth, (10) [*kaph*]
  To those who observe His covenant and His testimonies.
  For Your name's sake, Jehovah, (11) [*lamed*]
  Forgive my iniquity, for it is great.
 Who is this, the man who fears Jehovah? (12) [*mem*]

He shall instruct him in the way that he shall choose.
His soul shall tarry for the night in goodness, (13) [*nun*]
And his seed shall possess the earth.
The secret counsel of Jehovah is with those who fear Him, (14)
[*samech*]
And He will let them know His covenant.
My eyes are continually toward Jehovah, (15) [*ayin*]
For He shall bring forth my feet out of the net.
Face towards me, and be gracious to me, (16) [*pe*]
For I am an only child and afflicted.
The adversities of my heart are enlarged: (17) [*tsade*]
Bring me out of my distresses.
See my affliction and my toil, (18) [*resh*]
And forgive all my sins.
See my enemies for they are many, (19) [*resh*]
And they hate me with violent hatred.
Keep my soul, and deliver me: (20) [*shin*]
Let me not be ashamed; for I seek refuge in You.
Let integrity and uprightness preserve me, for I wait on You, (21)
[*tav*]
Ransom Israel, God, out of all his adversities. (22)

Psalm Commentary 25

Summary: Prayers of the church to the Lord, that they may be protected from the hells (v. 1-3), that they may be taught truths (v. 4-7), that their sins may be forgiven from mercy (v. 8-11). Thus they will have good, and conjunction (v. 12-15). Prayer of the church to the Lord, and in the highest sense, of the Lord to the Father, that, because He alone fights, He may assist against the hells and provide redemption (v. 15-22).

Unto You, Jehovah, I lift up my soul,
My God, I trust in You.
Let me not be ashamed,
Let not my enemies exult over me.
Also let all who wait on You not be ashamed,
Let them be ashamed who deal treacherously without cause.
(Ps. 25:1-3)

Jehovah is the Lord as to Divine love (see Ps. 18:31, 28:1, 68:26, 82:1, 147:7) and the soul is one's spiritual life as to the understanding (see Ps. 22:10, 31:9, 71:23, 107:9); to be lifted up is to be elevated away from the love of self towards the love of God and others. God is the Lord as to Divine truth (see Ps. 18:31, 29:1, 68:17,24, 82:1, 95:3, 147:7) and to trust is to have confidence of the will which is given to those who are in the good of charity (see Ps. 33:21). To not be ashamed is to have no shame from committing evil; enemies are falsehoods which attack the truth (see Ps. 3:1, 27:12) which exult when truth is overcome; to

351

deal treacherously is to act against the laws of Divine order (see
Ps. 78:57).

Let me know Your ways, Jehovah,
Teach me Your paths.
Let me tread in Your truth and teach me,
For You are God of my salvation,
On You I wait every day. (Ps. 25:4-5)

Ways signify truth (see Ps. 1:1, 18:42, 37:23, 86:11), and
paths are truths that concern what is good. To tread in the truth
is to live by it; to be taught is to be taught what is good. The "God
of my salvation" is the Divine truth that concerns deliverance
from evil by Divine good (see Ps. 14:7, 96:2).

"That way means truth is from the appearance in the spiritual world, where also are ways and paths, and in the cities,
streets with rows of dwellings, and spirits go in no other direction than to those with whom they are consociated by love. It is
for this reason that the quality of the spirits there in regard to
truth is known from the way which they go, for all truth leads to
its love, inasmuch as that is called truth which confirms what is
loved. Therefore it is that way in common human speech is used
also for truth, for the speech of man has derived this, like many
other things, from the spiritual world.

"From this now it is that in the Word by way or highway,
path, by-path, going, and street with rows of houses, are signified truths and in the opposite sense falsities — as is plain
from the following passages. In Jeremiah: *Stand ye in the ways*
and see, and ask for the old paths, where is the best way (vi.
16). Again: *Amend your ways, and your doings. …Trust ye not in*
lying words (vii. 3-5). Again: *Learn not the way of the nations* (x.
2). Again: *I give to every man according to his ways, according to*
the fruit of his doings (xvii. 10). Again: *They have caused them*
to stumble in their ways, in the ancient paths, that they might
walk in by-paths, in a way not cast up (xviii. 15). Again: *I will*
give them one heart and one way (xxxii. 39). In David: *Shew me*
Thy ways, O Jehovah; teach me Thy paths. Lead me in Thy truth

(Ps. xxv. 4, 5). In the Book of Judges: *In the days of Jael, the highways ceased, and they who walked in byways went through crooked paths* (v. 6). In Isaiah: *Get you out of the way, turn aside out of the path. ...Thine ears shall hear a word behind thee, This is the way, walk ye in it* (xxx. 11, 21). Again: *The ways are desolated, the wayfaring man hath ceased* (xxxiii. 8). Again: *A highway shall be there, and a way, and it shall be called The way of holiness; the unclean shall not pass over it; but it shall be for those: the wayfaring men, yea fools, shall not err therein* (xxxv. 8)." (*Heavenly Arcana*, n. 10422.2-3; see also *Heavenly Arcana*, n. 627.3, 2333.4)

When way and path are mentioned together, the word "way" concerns truth itself, and "path" is truth that concerns what is good. This can be seen in Swedenborg's commentary on Isa. 2:3:

> "*Many peoples shall go and say, Come ye, and let us go up to the mountain of Jehovah, to the house of the God of Jacob, and He will teach us of His ways that we may go in His paths...*

This treats of the Lord's coming, and that those who will be of His New Church are to be instructed in truths, by which they will be led to heaven. 'The mountain of Jehovah' and 'the house of Jacob' signify the church in which is love to the Lord and worship from that love; a summoning to that church, and thus to the Lord, is signified by 'Many peoples shall go and say, Come ye, and let us go up to that mountain;' that they will be instructed in truths by which they will be led is signified by 'He will teach us of His ways that we may go in His paths,' 'ways' meaning truths and 'paths' the precepts of life..." (*Apocalypse Explained*, n. 734.2; see also *Heavenly Arcana*, n. 6395)

Remember Your compassion, Jehovah, and Your mercies,
For they have been from everlasting.
Remember not the sins of my youth and my transgressions:
According to Your mercy remember me for Your goodness' sake,
Jehovah. (Ps. 25:6-7)

Compassion is the conjunction of good and truth in innocence (see Ps. 40:11); mercy is Divine love (see Ps. 25:10, 26:3, 36:5, 89:14, 103:8); everlasting is eternity in the celestial heaven of love (see Ps. 145:13). Sins are evils agains the good of love from a depraved will, and transgressions is evil against the truth of faith from a perverted understanding (see Ps. 5:10, 25:7, 32:1, 51:1-3). The "sins of my youth" are those done in a state of ignorance or innocence (see Ps. 103:5, 127:4). To remember is to have compassion (see Ps. 8:4).

"*Remember, O Jehovah, Thy tender mercies, and Thy loving kindnesses. ...Remember not the sins of my youth, nor my transgressions* (Ps. xxv. 6, 7) — where sins stand for evils from a depraved will, and transgressions for evils from a perverted understanding." (*Heavenly Arcana*, n. 9156.2)

Good and upright is Jehovah,
Therefore He will instruct sinners in the way.
He will cause the meek to tread in judgment,
And He will teach the meek His way. (Ps. 25:8-9)

Good is Divine good and upright is truth from good (see Ps. 9:8, 11:3, 25:21, 96:10, 143:10); Jehovah is the Lord as to Divine love (see Ps. 18:31, 28:1, 68:26, 82:1, 147:7) from which all good is derived. As the Lord is good itself, so He instructs all through the Divine truth to lead away from sin which is evil against good (see Ps. 25:7, 32:1, 51:1-3). The meek are those who are in the good of charity (see Ps. 37:11); to tread in judgment is to live by the truth (see Ps. 36:6, 37:6, 72:2, 89:14, 92:12). Judgments here are truths that regard life; way here is external knowledge of the truth (see Ps. 1:1, 18:42, 25:4,12, 37:23, 86:11).

All the paths of Jehovah are mercy and truth,
To those who observe His covenant and His testimonies.
For Your name's sake, Jehovah,
Forgive my iniquity, for it is great. (Ps. 25:10-11)

Paths are truths which primarily consider what is good (see Ps. 25:4); mercy and truth are Divine love and Divine truth (see

Ps. 26:3, 36:5, 89:14, 103:8). In the literal sense the covenant is the Word of the Old and New Testaments, but in a spiritual sense the covenant is the conjunction between God and man in love (see Ps. 89:3,28, 105:8, 111:9). The testimony is truth that testifies of the Lord or that which is good (see Ps. 19:7, 78:5). Iniquity concerns evil done against the good of faith (see Ps. 51:1-3).

"Because the good of love and the truth of faith are in the closest conjunction, and the one is not given without the other, therefore this form of speaking was usual among the ancients, because it was known to them that the good of love was inseparable from the truth of faith, and for this reason also these two are often spoken of conjointly in the Word — as in Exodus: *Jehovah ...great in mercy and truth* (xxxiv. 6). In the Second Book of Samuel: David said unto the men of Jabesh, *Jehovah do mercy and truth with you* (ii. 5, 6). In the same: David said unto Ittai the Gittite, *Return thou, and take back thy brethren; mercy and truth be with thee* (xv. 20). In Hosea: *Jehovah hath a controversy with the inhabitants of the land, because there is no truth, and no mercy, and no knowledge of God in the land* (iv. 1). In David: *All the paths of Jehovah are mercy and truth unto such as keep His covenant* (Ps. xxv. 10). Again: *Withhold not Thou Thy mercies from me, O Jehovah: let Thy mercy and Thy truth continually preserve me* (Ps. xl. 11). Again: *I will sing of the mercies of Jehovah for ever: with my mouth will I make known Thy truth to generation and generation. For I have said, Mercy shall be built up for ever; Thy truth shalt Thou establish in the very heavens. ...Justice and judgment are the support of Thy throne: mercy and truth stand before Thy face* (Ps. lxxxix. 1, 2, 14); and in other passages in David, Ps. xxvi. 3; xxxvi. 5; lvii. 3, 10; lxi. 7; lxxxv. 10; lxxxvi. 15; lxxxix. 24, 33; xcii. 2)." (*Heavenly Arcana*, n. 6180.2)

"That the compact of a covenant on the part of the Lord is mercy and election, is evident in David: *All the paths of Jehovah are mercy and truth unto such as keep His covenant and His testimonies* (Ps. xxv. 10). In Isaiah: *The mountains shall depart, and the hills be removed; but My mercy shall not depart ...neither shall the covenant of My peace be removed, saith Jehovah who hath mercy on thee* (liv. 10). In Moses: *Jehovah thy God, He is God; the faithful God, keeping covenant and mercy with them who love Him, and keep His commandments, to the thousandth generation* (Deut. vii. 9, 12). Again: *If ye will keep My covenant, ye shall be unto Me for a peculiar treasure from among all peoples* (Exod. xix. 5). Again: *I will have respect unto you, and make you fruitful, and multiply you, and will establish My covenant with you* (Lev. xxvi. 9). To have respect unto them is of mercy, to make them fruitful and multiply them is to endow them with charity and faith; they who are endowed with those gifts are called the elect; so these things are of election, also that they shall be for a peculiar treasure." (*Heavenly Arcana*, n. 6804.10)

Who is this, the man who fears Jehovah?
He shall instruct him in the way that he shall choose.
His soul shall tarry for the night in goodness,
And his seed shall possess the earth. (Ps. 25:12-13)

To fear Jehovah is to live by His commandments (see Ps. 2:11, 33:18, 128:1, 147:11) and to worship Him; to be instructed in the way is to learn the truth signified by way (see Ps. 1:1, 18:42, 25:4,12, 37:23, 81:13, 86:11). To tarry for the night in goodness is to be protected from the falsity of evil; seed is the faith of charity (see Ps. 18:50, 21:10, 22:23,30, 89:4, 106:27) and the earth are those who are in the truths of the church (see Ps. 9:8, 24:1, 60:2, 90:2, 96:13).

"*What man is he who feareth Jehovah? him shall He teach the way that He shall choose* (Ps. xxv. 12); where the man who feareth Jehovah stands for him who worships Him; and that this is said of the spiritual man is manifest from its being said, Him shall He teach the way." That a way is truth, may be seen above (n. 627, 2333). And again with similar meaning: *Blessed is every one who feareth Jehovah, who walketh in His ways* (Ps. cxxviii. 1)." (*Heavenly Arcana*, n. 2826.6)

The secret counsel of Jehovah is with those who fear Him,
And He will let them know His covenant.
My eyes are continually toward Jehovah,

For He shall bring forth my feet out of the net. (Ps. 25:14-15)

The "secret counsel of Jehovah" are good intentions of the will that flow in from Jehovah or the Lord as to Divine love (see Ps. 18:31, 28:1, 68:26, 82:1, 147:7); to fear the Lord is to live by His commandments (see Ps. 2:11, 33:18, 128:1, 147:11) from which there is conjunction with the Lord by love signified by covenant (see Ps. 25:10, 89:3,28, 105:8, 111:9). Eyes are spiritual understanding (see Ps. 11:4, 13:3, 31:9, 69:23); to bring one's feet out of the net is to withdraw from external material desires (see Ps. 10:9 and 8:6, 41:9, 49:5, 99:5, 105:18). That "secret counsel" concerns the intentions of the will is shown where Israel speaks of his sons Simeon and Levi, where Simeon represents the falsity of the will and Levi its evil where the same word is used (translated below as "secret"):

"*Into their secret let not my soul come.* That this signifies that spiritual good is not willing to know the evils which are of their will, is evident from the representation of Israel, who says this of himself, as spiritual good (see n. 6340); and from the signification of not coming into a secret, as not being willing to know, namely, the evils of the will, signified by Simeon and Levi (n. 6352): it is said, my soul, because by soul is there signified the life of good belonging to spiritual good..." (*Heavenly Arcana*, n. 6354)

Face towards me, and be gracious to me,
For I am an only child and afflicted.
The adversities of my heart are enlarged:
Bring me out of my distresses. (Ps. 25:16-17)

God's face is His Divine mercy (see Ps. 4:6, 13:1, 22:24, 27:8-9, 31:16, 67:1); to receive grace is to receive spiritual good and truth, and comfort and hope of mind in temptations (see Ps. 4:1) and is sought by those in humiliation of thought (see Ps. 103:8). To be an only child is to be left to one's own self without internal good from the Lord; to be afflicted is to be lacking in knowledge of the truth (see Ps. 35:10, 37:14, 40:17). Adversities of heart are evils of the will (see Ps. 3:1, 27:12); to be enlarged is for evils to

become increased with falsehoods (see Ps. 4:1); distress is a state
of temptation.

See my affliction and my toil,
And forgive all my sins.
See my enemies for they are many,
And they hate me with violent hatred. (Ps. 25:18-19)

To be in affliction is to be lacking in knowledge of the truth
(see Ps. 35:10, 37:14, 40:17) and toil is the conflict of temptation
(see Ps. 7:14). Sins are evil against the good of love (see Ps. 25:7,
32:1, 51:1-3). Enemies are falsities which attack the truth (see
Ps. 3:1, 27:12); those in violent hatred are those who destroy the
good of charity (see Ps. 7:16, 27:12).

Keep my soul, and deliver me:
Let me not be ashamed; for I seek refuge in You.
Let integrity and uprightness preserve me, for I wait on You,
Ransom Israel, God, out of all his adversities. (Ps. 25:20-22)

The soul is one's spiritual life of the understanding (see
Ps. 22:10, 31:9, 71:23, 107:9) and to be delivered is to be led away
from falsity; to not be ashamed is to not fall into evil. Integrity
is to live by the truth, and similarly uprightness is to be in truth
from good (see Ps. 9:8, 11:3, 96:10, 143:10). To ransom signifies
to deliver from falsity (see Ps. 25:22, 26:11, 31:5, 69:18, 71:23,
119:134); adversities are evils which attack what is good (see
Ps. 3:1, 27:12).

"That an upright man is one who is true, from good, or who
speaks and does truth, from charity, is evident from the words
walk and way being often applied to the upright or to uprightness; also righteous or righteousness — which words pertain to
truth — as in David: *I will teach the upright in the way. When will
he come unto me? I will walk within my house in the uprightness
of my heart* (Ps. ci. 2); and in the sixth verse: *He who walketh in
the way of the upright, he shall minister unto me.* Again: *Blessed
are the upright in the way, who walk in the law of Jehovah* (Ps.
cxix. 1). And again: *Uprightness and integrity shall preserve*

me (xxv. 21). And in another place: *Mark the upright man, and behold the righteous, for the end of that man is peace* (xxxvii. 37). It is evident from these passages that he is called just who does good, and he is called upright who does truth therefrom — which also is to do justice and judgment. Holiness and justice are the celestial of faith; uprightness and judgment are the spiritual therefrom." (*Heavenly Arcana*, n. 612.3)

The word integrity (Hebrew *thum*) is also the origin for the Hebrew word for "Thummim," which along with "Urim" was used by the high priest to divine answers to questions:

"...Urim means a glowing fire, and Thummim the shining forth therefrom; the glowing fire is Divine truth from the Divine good of the Divine love of the Lord, and the shining forth is that same truth in ultimates and thus in the effect. It is also to be known that Thummim in the Hebrew language means integrity, but in angelic language a shining forth. It is said in angelic language, because the angels converse with one another from the very essence of the subject perceived inwardly in themselves, and thus according to its quality. From this the speech flows forth into a suitable sonorous form, audible only to angels; the shining forth of Divine truth thus produces the sonorous *Thummim;* whence comes its name. The like is perceived by angels, when *thum* is read in the Hebrew tongue, by which is signified what is complete or entire, or integrity. It is for this reason that by integrity or uprightness in the internal sense of the Word is signified Divine truth in its effect, which is a life according to the Divine commandments — as may be evident from many passages in the Word (as Josh. xxiv. 14; Judges ix. 16, 19; Ps. xxv. 21; xxxvii. 37; lxxxiv. 11; ci. 2; cxix. 1)." (*Heavenly Arcana*, n. 9905.3)

Psalm 26

Of David.

~

Judge me, Jehovah, for I have walked in my integrity, (1)
And I have trusted in Jehovah, I shall not falter.
Prove me, Jehovah, and try me, (2)
Refine my kidneys and my heart.
  For Your mercy is in front of my eyes, (3)
  And I have walked in Your truth.
  I have not sat with vain men, (4)
  And I will not go in with secretive ones.
  I have hated the assembly of evil doers, (5)
  And I will not sit with the wicked.
  I will wash my hands in innocence, (6)
  And I will compass Your altar, Jehovah:
  To make the voice of confession heard, (7)
  And to recount all Your wondrous works.
  Jehovah, I have loved the habitation of Your house, (8)
  And the place of the tabernacle of Your glory.
Gather not my soul together with sinners, (9)
Nor my life with bloody men:
In whose hands is depravity, (10)
And their right hand is full of bribes.
But as for me, I will walk in my integrity, (11)
Ransom me, and be gracious to me.
My foot stands in uprightness, (12)
In the assemblies I will bless Jehovah.

Psalm Commentary 26

Summary: Prayer of the Lord to the Father that His Human be sanctified (v. 1-2). To the Lord belongs perfection, purity and innocence (v. 3-6). He has the Divine love of saving (v. 7-8). He is in combats with the malicious (v. 9-10) and there is redemption when He conquers (v. 11-12).

Judge me, Jehovah; for I have walked in my integrity:
And I have trusted in Jehovah; I shall not falter.
Prove me, Jehovah, and try me,
Refine my kidneys and my heart.
For Your mercy is in front of my eyes,
And I have walked in Your truth. (Ps. 26:1-3)

To walk in integrity is to live by the truth (see Ps. 25:21, 96:10, 143:10); to trust is to have confidence of the will from the good of charity (see Ps. 33:21); to falter is to fall into temptation. To prove is to purify the will through temptation (see Ps. 7:9); to try is to purify the thoughts from falsehood. Kidneys concern the exploration and judgement of thoughts by the truth (see Ps. 7:9); the heart is the love of one's will (see Ps. 7:9, 22:10, 24:4, 51:10, 64:6, 66:18, 78:8). Mercy is the Divine love (see Ps. 25:10, 36:5, 89:14, 103:8) which is always conjoined to Divine truth. Eyes are the spiritual understanding (see Ps. 11:4, 13:3, 31:9, 69:23); to walk in the truth is to live by it (see Ps. 1:1, 56:13).

"Since there are two things to which all things of the church have reference, namely, love and faith, and since mercy is of love, and grace as well as truth is of faith, therefore in the Word it is said mercy and grace when the Lord is implored, and it is said mercy and truth when the Lord is described — as in the following passages: *Thy mercy is before mine eyes: and I walk in Thy truth* (Ps. xxvi. 3). Again: *Thy mercy, O Jehovah, is in the heavens; and Thy truth reacheth unto the skies* (Ps. xxxvi. 5). Again: *God shall send from the heavens His mercy and His truth. Thy mercy is great unto the heavens, and Thy truth unto the skies* (Ps. lvii. 3, 10). Again: *Mercy and truth are met together; justice and peace have kissed each other* (Ps. lxxxv. 10). And Again: *I will sing of the mercy of Jehovah for ever; with my mouth Thy truth to generation and generation. For I have said, Mercy shall be built up for ever; Thy truth shalt Thou establish in the very heavens. ...Justice and judgment are the foundation of Thy throne: mercy and truth shall stand before Thy face* (Ps. lxxxix. 1, 2, 14)." (*Heavenly Arcana*, n. 10577.3)

I have not sat with vain men,
And I will not go in with secretive ones.
I have hated the assembly of evil doers,
And I will not sit with the wicked. (Ps. 26:4-5)

Sitting concerns the interiors of one's will (see Ps. 1:1, 9:7, 107:4,36, 139:2); vain men are the falsities of doctrine (see Ps. 4:2, 144:8); to not go with secretive ones is to not consent to evil. The assembly of evil doers are those in the falsehoods of evil (see Ps. 1:5, 68:26, 107:32); to sit with the wicked is to be interior evil of the will as signified by sitting (see Ps. 1:1, 9:7, 69:35, 107:4,36, 139:2)

I will wash my hands in innocence,
And I will compass Your altar, Jehovah:
To make the voice of confession heard,
And to recount all Your wondrous works. (Ps. 26:6-7)

Inasmuch as evils are removed, one approaches God. To wash one's hands in innocence is to remove exterior evils (see Ps. 24:4, 73:13); to compass the altar is to remove interior evils, as the altar

represents Divine good (see Ps. 43:4, 84:3). The "voice of confession" is spiritual truth; confession itself is worship from affection
for the good of love (see Ps. 7:17, 35:18). To recount is to know
the quality of a thing (see Ps. 147:4); wondrous works are acts of
Divine power which cause belief (see Ps. 71:7, 78:43, 105:5). The
symbolism of the altar is explained in the following passage:

"There were two things by which the Lord as to the Divine
Human was represented, the temple and the altar. That He was
represented by the temple, He Himself teaches in John: *Jesus
said, Destroy this temple, and in three days I will raise it up. ...
He spake of the temple of His body* (ii. 19, 21). That He was represented by the altar, may also be evident from His own words when
He speaks of the temple and at the same time of the altar, in Matthew: *Ye fools and blind, because ye say, Whosoever shall swear
by the temple, it is nothing; but whosoever shall swear by the gold
of the temple, he is a debtor. ...Whether is greater, the gold, or the
temple that sanctifieth the gold? Likewise, Whosoever shall swear
by the altar, it is nothing; but whosoever shall swear by the gift that
is upon it, he is a debtor. Ye fools and blind; for whether is greater,
the gift, or the altar that sanctifieth the gift? He who sweareth by
the altar, sweareth by it, and by all things thereon. And he who
sweareth by the temple, sweareth by it, and by Him that dwelleth
therein. And he who sweareth by heaven, sweareth by the throne of
God, and by Him who sitteth thereon* (xxiii. 16-22). From this it is
plain that, as the temple, so also the altar was a representative of
the Divine Human of the Lord; for the same is said of the altar as
of the temple, namely, that it is that which sanctifieth the gift that
is upon it; thus that the altar was the subject from which came
sanctification; consequently that it was also the representative of
the Divine Human of the Lord, from which all the holy proceeds.
But the altar was a representative of the Lord as to His Divine
good, whereas the temple was a representative of Him as to His
Divine truth, and thus as to heaven; for the Divine truth proceeding from the Lord makes heaven...

"Because by the altar was represented the Lord as to Divine
good, therefore it was the very holy of holies, and sanctified

everything which touched it — as may be evident from what follows in this same book, where it is said, *Seven days thou shalt make atonement for the altar, and sanctify it; that the altar may be holy of holies: and whatsoever toucheth it shall be made holy* (Exod. xxix. 37); and therefore the fire upon the altar was perpetually burning, and was never put out (Lev. vi. 13); and from that fire was taken fire for the incense, and from no other source (Lev. x. 1-6); for by the fire of the altar was signified the Divine good of the Divine love of the Lord...

"That the altar was a representative of the Lord, is plain from the following passages in David: *Let Thy light and Thy truth ... bring me unto the mountain of Thy holiness, and to Thy tabernacles, that I may go in unto the altar of God, unto God* (Ps. xliii. 3, 4). And again: *I wash mine hands in innocence; and I compass Thine altar, O Jehovah* (Ps. xxvi. 6)." (*Heavenly Arcana*, n. 9714.3-4)

Jehovah, I have loved the habitation of Your house,
And the place of the tabernacle of Your glory. (Ps. 26:8)

Habitation signifies the heaven as to good, and house also signifies the heaven and the church in respect to good (see Ps. 23:6, 65:5, 105:21; the tabernacle of glory is the spiritual heaven of those who are in heavenly truths as signified by glory (see Ps. 8:5, 19:1, 24:7-10, 29:1, 73:24, 96:3). Love, habitation and house signify the three degrees of love in heaven; likewise place, tabernacle and glory signify the three degrees of truth in heaven.

"That the habitation of Jehovah or the Lord is heaven, and also good, because in good heaven consists, is evident from the following passages: *Look down from the habitation of Thy holiness, from heaven, and bless Thy people Israel* (Deut. xxvi. 15)." (*Heavenly Arcana*, n. 8309.2)

"Because the dwelling signifies heaven where the Lord is, it also signifies the good of love and of faith, for these make heaven; and because all good is from the Lord, and heaven is called heaven from love and faith in the Lord, therefore also the dwelling in the supreme sense signifies the Lord — as is plain in many passages of the Word (Isa. lxiii. 15; Jer. xxv. 30; Ezek. xxxvii. 26, 27; Ps. xxvi. 8; xliii. 3; xc. 1; xci. 9; Exod. xv. 13; Deut. xii. 5: and in other places). From this it is evident that the tabernacle was called the sanctuary and the dwelling of Jehovah because of this representation." (*Heavenly Arcana*, n. 9481.3)

Gather not my soul together with sinners,
Nor my life with bloody men:
In whose hands is a crime,
And their right hand is full of a bribe.
But as for me, I will walk in my integrity:
Ransom me, and be gracious to me.
My foot stands in uprightness:
In the assemblies I will bless Jehovah. (Ps. 26:9-12)

The soul is one's spiritual life from the understanding (see Ps. 22:10, 31:9, 71:23, 107:9); the life is one's spiritual life of the will. Sinners are those with a depraved will who do evil against the good of love (see Ps. 25:7, 32:1, 51:1-3); bloody men signify falsehoods that do violence against the truth (see Ps. 5:6, 16:4, 105:29). Hands concern external acts (see Ps. 24:4, 73:13) a crime is an external act of evil, and a bribe is an external act of falsehood distorting the truth. Thus bribe is mentioned with the right hand, which signifies the power of truth (see Ps. 20:6, 44:3, 45:4, 80:15,17, 89:13,21, 110:1, 121:5) and those who are in the light of truth (see Ps. 73:22, 89:12, 137:5). To walk in integrity is to live by the truth (see Ps. 25:21 and also Ps. 1:1, 56:13); to ransom is to become spiritually liberated from falsehood by means of truth (see Ps. 25:22, 26:11, 31:5, 49:15, 69:18, 71:23, 119:134, 130:7); to receive grace is to receive spiritual good and truth, and comfort and hope of mind in temptations (see Ps. 4:1) and is sought by those in humiliation of thought (see Ps. 103:8). The foot is the lower natural (see Ps. 8:6, 41:9, 49:5, 99:5, 105:18) and to be upright is to be in truth from good (see Ps. 9:8, 11:3, 25:21, 96:10, 143:10). To bless Jehovah is to acknowledge all good and happiness comes from the Lord (see Ps. 3:8, 16:7, 21:6, 24:5, 28:6, 31:21, 96:2).

Psalm 27

Of David.

~

Jehovah is my light and my salvation, whom shall I fear? (1)
Jehovah is the stronghold of my life, whom shall I dread?
When the evil came near against me to eat my flesh, (2)
My adversaries and enemies stumbled and fell.
Though a camp should encamp against me, my heart shall not fear, (3)
Though war should rise against me, in this I will trust.

One thing I have asked from Jehovah that I will seek: (4)
That I may dwell in the house of Jehovah all the days of my life,
To behold the pleasantness of Jehovah,
And to seek in His temple.
For He shall hide me in His pavilion in the day of evil, (5)
He shall hide me in the secret of His tent.
He shall lift me up upon a rock,
And now shall my head be lifted up above my enemies round about me. (6)
And I will sacrifice in His tent sacrifices of a trumpet blast,
I will sing and make music unto Jehovah.

~

Hear, Jehovah, when I call with my voice: (7)
And be gracious to me, and answer me.
To you, my heart, He has said, Seek My face! (8)
Your face, Jehovah, I will seek.
Hide not Your face from me, (9)
Turn not Your servant aside in anger.
You have been my help, leave me not,

And forsake me not, God of my salvation.
When my father and my mother forsake me, (10)
Then Jehovah will gather me in.
Instruct me, Jehovah, *in* Your way, (11)
And lead me in an upright path, because of my opponents.
Give me not to the will of my adversaries, (12)
For false witnesses are risen up against me and a testifier of violence.
I believe to see the goodness of Jehovah in the land of the living: (13)
Wait on Jehovah, persevere, (14)
And He shall encourage Your heart and to wait on Jehovah.

Psalm
Commentary

27

Summary: The Lord has no fears of the hells that fight against Him (v. 1-3). The union of the Divine with the Human (v. 4-6) and the union of the Human with the Divine (v. 7-10). The Lord's subjugation of the hells (v. 11-14).

Jehovah is my light and my salvation,
Whom shall I fear?
Jehovah is the stronghold of my life,
Whom shall I dread?
When the evil came near against me to eat my flesh,
My adversaries and enemies stumbled and fell.
Though a camp should encamp against me,
My heart shall not fear:
Though war should rise against me,
In this I will trust. (Ps. 27:1-3)

Jehovah is the Lord as to Divine love (see Ps. 18:31, 28:1, 68:26, 82:1, 147:7); light is the Divine truth (see Ps. 4:6, 11:4, 18:28, 36:9, 43:3, 104:2, 139:12) and salvation is deliverance from evil by Divine mercy (see Ps. 14:7, 96:2). To have no fear nor dread is to have no fear from the evil and falsity of hell. Stronghold or strength is the power to do good (see Ps. 21:13, 29:1, 95:4, 96:6); one's life is one's spiritual life of the will. The evil that came near to eat the flesh signifies the hatred of the hells against the will to do good, as flesh signifies the voluntary proprium (see Ps. 16:9, 63:1, 78:39, 84:2). Adversaries are evils which attack good and enemies are falsehoods which attack the truth (see Ps. 3:1, 27:12); to stumble is to be deprived of good and to fall is to pervert the truth (see Ps. 7:15). A camp is the evils and falsities of hell arranged in order against the Lord; war is spiritual combat between the Lord and the hells (see Ps. 18:34, 24:8, 46:9, 76:3); to trust is to have confidence of the will which is given to those who are in the good of charity (see Ps. 33:21).

"And Jacob said when he saw them, This is the camp of God. That this signifies heaven is because the camp of God signifies heaven, for the reason that an army signifies truths and goods (n. 3448), and truths and goods are arranged by the Lord according to heavenly order; hence the laying out of a camp is arrangement according to armies, and heavenly order itself, which is heaven, is a camp. This camp or this order is such that it can in no way be broken through by hell, though hell is in the continual effort to break through it. Hence also that order, or heaven, is called a camp, and the truths and goods, that is, the angels, who are arranged according to that order, are called armies. From this it is now manifest whence the camp of God signifies heaven. It is that order itself, and thus heaven itself, which was represented by the encampments of the sons of Israel in the wilderness; and their dwelling together therein according to tribes was called a camp. The tabernacle which was in the midst, and around which they encamped, represented the Lord Himself...

"As most things in the Word have also an opposite sense, so likewise has a camp, which then signifies evils and falsities, and accordingly hell — as in David: Though the evil *should encamp against me, my heart shall not fear* (Ps. xxvii. 3). In the same: *God hath scattered the bones of him who encampeth against thee; thou hast put them to shame, because God hath rejected them* (Ps. liii. 5). By the camp of Assyria, in which the angel of Jehovah smote a hundred and eighty-five thousand (Isa. xxxvii. 36), nothing else is meant; and the same by the camp of the Egyptians (Exod. xiv. 20)." (*Heavenly Arcana,* n. 4236.1,4)

"That by wars in the Word spiritual wars are signified, which are fightings against the truth, and are carried on by reasonings from falsities, is evident from these passages: *Spirits of demons go forth to gather them together to the battle in the great day of God Almighty* (Apoc. xvi. 14). *The dragon was wroth with the woman, and went away to make war with the remnant of her seed, who keep the commandments of God, and have the testimony of Jesus Christ* (Apoc. xii. 17). *It was given to the beast of the dragon to make war with the saints* (Apoc. xiii. 7). *Consecrate the battle against the daughter of Zion, and let us go up at noon* (Jer. vi. 4). *Ye have not gone up into the breaches to stand in the battle in the day of Jehovah* (Ezek. xiii. 5). *In Salem is the tabernacle of God, and His dwelling-place in Zion; where He brake the fiery darts, the bow, and the battle* (Ps. lxxvi. 2, 3). *Jehovah shall go forth as a mighty man, He shall stir up zeal as a man of war* (Isa. xiii. 13; Ps. xxiv. 8). *In that day Jehovah shall be for a spirit of judgment to him who sitteth in judgment, and for strength to them who turn the battle from the gate* (Isa. xxviii. 6). *Deliver me from the evil man, and from the man of violence preserve me; the whole day they gather together for war, they sharpen their tongues as serpents* (Ps. cxl. 2-4). *Many shall come in My name, saying, I am Christ, and shall deceive many; and ye shall hear of wars and rumors of wars; see that ye be not troubled* (Matt. xxiv. 5, 6; Mark xiii. 6, 7; Luke xxi. 8, 9). The wars of the kings of the north and of the south, and the other wars, in Daniel, chap. x., xi., xii., signify no other than spiritual wars: besides the wars in other places, as Isa. ii. 3-5; xiii. 4; xxi. 14, 15; xxxi. 4; Jer. xlix. 25, 26; Hos. ii. 18; Zech. x. 5; xiv. 3; Ps. xxvii. 3; xliv. 9, 10." (*Apocalypse Revealed*, n. 500)

One thing I have asked from Jehovah that I will seek,
That I may dwell in the house of Jehovah all the days of my life,
To behold the pleasantness of Jehovah,
And to seek in His temple.
For He shall hide me in His pavilion in the day of evil,
He shall hide me in the secret of His tent.
He shall lift me up upon a rock,

*And now shall my head be lifted up above my enemies round
about me.* (Ps. 27:4-5)

To seek is to seek after truth; to dwell is to dwell in love (see
Ps. 1:1, 9:7, 107:4,36, 139:2); the house of Jehovah is the celestial
heaven of love (see Ps. 23:6, 65:5, 105:21); the days of one's life
are all states of one's eternal life in heaven. The pleasantness
of Jehovah is the happiness of doing good from Divine love; the
temple is the spiritual heaven of truth (see Ps. 18:6, 48:9, 65:4).
The pavilion is the holy of truth (see Ps. 31:20); the tent is the
holy of love (see Ps. 15:1, 52:5, 61:4, 132:3) and the day of evil is
the falsity of evil; the secret of His tent is the heaven of celestial
love which guards against evil (see Ps. 15:1, 61:4, 132:3). To be
lifted upon a rock signifies to be instructed in interior truths
as rock signifies the Divine truth (see Ps. 18:46, 19:14, 28:1,
78:15); to lift up the head is to be delivered from hell and raised
to heaven (see Ps. 3:3).

*"One thing have I asked of Jehovah, that will I seek, that
I may dwell in the house of Jehovah all the days of my life, to
behold the pleasantness of Jehovah, and to visit in the morning
His temple; for He shall hide me in His tent in the evil day, He
shall conceal me in the secret place of His tabernacle, He shall
exalt me upon a rock (Ps. xxvii. 4, 6).* Here 'the house of Jehovah,'
'the temple,' 'the tent,' and 'the tabernacle,' are mentioned; and
'house of Jehovah' signifies the church that is in the good of love
to the Lord, 'temple' the church that is in truths from that good,
'the tent of Jehovah' Divine truth, and 'the tabernacle' Divine
good; thence it is clear that 'to dwell in the house of Jehovah all
the days of one's life' does not mean to dwell in the house of Jehovah, but in the good of love to the Lord; and that 'to visit in the
morning the temple of Jehovah' does not mean to visit the temple
every morning, but to seek and learn the truths of that good; so
'to hide in the tent' signifies to continue in Divine truth, and to
be defended from falsities; and 'to conceal in the secret place of
the tabernacle' signifies to continue in Divine good and to be

defended from evils; 'to exalt upon a rock' signifies to instruct in interior truths." (*Apocalypse Explained*, n. 799.6)

Pleasantness is the delight of doing good, as indicated in the commentary of Gen. 49:15 where a similar Hebrew word is used:

"*And the land that it is pleasant.* That this signifies that in that, namely happiness, are they who are in the Lord's kingdom, is evident from the signification of land, as the church, and thus also the Lord's kingdom (n. 662, 1066, 1067, 1413, 1607, 1733, 1850, 2117, 2118, 4447) — that land has this signification is because the land of Canaan, which is meant by land in the Word, represented the Lord's kingdom, and this because the church had been there from the most ancient time (n. 3038, 3481, 3686, 3705, 4447, 4454, 4516, 4517, 5136); and from the signification of being pleasant, as signifying the happiness in works of good without recompense." (*Heavenly Arcana*, n. 6392)

And I will sacrifice in His tent sacrifices of a trumpet blast,
I will sing and make music unto Jehovah. (Ps. 27:6)

The tent represents the celestial heaven (see Ps. 15:1, 52:5, 61:4, 132:3) and a trumpet blast signifies worship from celestial good (see Ps. 33:3, 47:5); to sing is to worship from spiritual good and to make music is to worship from spiritual truth (see Ps. 33:3, 57:7).

Hear, Jehovah, when I call with my voice:
And be gracious to me, and answer me.
To you, my heart, He has said, Seek My face!
Your face, Jehovah, I will seek.
Hide not Your face from me,
Turn not Your servant aside in anger.
You have been my help, leave me not,
And forsake me not, God of my salvation. (Ps. 27:7-9)

Hearing by the Lord signifies Divine providence (see Ps. 17:6); To receive grace is to receive spiritual good and truth, and comfort and hope of mind in temptations (see Ps. 4:1) and is sought by those in humiliation of thought (see Ps. 103:8); to answer is to

receive Divine influx of perception and help (see Ps. 4:1). To see
God's face is to know and acknowledge Him in love and truth (see
Ps. 42:2). The heart is one's will (see Ps. 7:9, 22:10, 24:4, 51:10,
64:6, 66:18, 78:8) and to say signifies perception of the will (see
Ps. 33:9); the Lord's face is Divine good (see Ps. 4:6, 13:1, 22:24,
31:16, 67:1). For God to hide the face signifies for one to be left to
their own evils from their self (see Ps. 13:1, 22:24); for the servant
to be turned aside is to stop following the truth, signified by serving (see Ps. 31:16, 69:36, 78:70, 89:3,20). Help is aid from Divine
mercy against evil (see Ps. 10:14). The word "leave" here is the
departure of good, and "forsake" is the departure of truth and is
thus mentioned with God who is the Lord as to Divine truth (see
Ps. 18:31, 29:1, 68:17,24, 82:1, 95:3, 147:7). Thus in Psalm 22:1 it
is said, *My God, my God, why have You forsaken me?*

Face signifies the Divine good of the Lord:

"Because 'the faces of Jehovah,' or of the Lord, signify the
Divine good united to Divine truth going out and proceeding from
His Divine love, therefore also 'the faces of Jehovah' signify the
interiors of the church, of the Word, and of worship, for Divine
good is in the interior of these; the exteriors of the church, of the
Word, and of worship are only the effects and works therefrom.
The interiors of the church, of the Word, and of worship are sig-
nified by 'seeing,' 'seeking,' and 'entreating the faces of Jehovah.'
In *Isaiah:*—

> *What is the multitude of your sacrifices unto Me? when ye
> shall come to see the faces of Jehovah* (i. 11, 12).

In *Zechariah:*—

> *The inhabitants of one city shall go to another, saying, In
> going let us go to entreat the faces of Jehovah, and to seek
> Jehovah of Hosts; thus many peoples and numerous nations
> shall come to seek Jehovah of Hosts in Jerusalem, and to
> entreat the faces of Jehovah* (viii. 21, 22).

In *David:*—

My heart said unto thee, Seek ye my faces; Thy faces, O Jehovah, I do seek (Ps. xxvii. 8).

In the same:—

We will make a joyful noise unto the Rock of our salvation; we will come before His faces with confession (Ps.xcv. 1, 2).

In *Malachi:*—

Entreat the faces of God that He may be gracious unto us (i. 9).

In *David:*—

My soul thirsteth for God, for the living God; when shall I come to appear before the faces of God? Hope thou in God, for I shall yet confess to Him; His faces are salvations (xlii. 2, 5).

In these passages, 'faces of Jehovah,' 'of God,' or 'of the Lord,' mean the interiors of the church, of the Word, and of worship, because Divine good and Divine truth, thus the Lord Himself, are in these interiors, and from them in externals; but are not in externals, namely, of the church, of the Word, and of worship apart from these." (*Apocalypse Explained*, n. 412.11)

When my father and my mother forsake me,
Then Jehovah will gather me in. (Ps. 27:10)

Father signifies good (see Ps. 45:16, 78:57) and mother truth, and these are said to be forsaken when one recognizes that no good and truth come from one's self, but rather evil and falsehood. When the self is subdued in humiliation, then there is conjunction with the Lord in Divine love, signified by Jehovah (see Ps. 18:31, 28:1, 68:26, 82:1, 147:7).

"*My father and my mother have forsaken me, but Jehovah taketh me up* (Ps. xxvii. 10) — where father and mother stand for good and truth, which are said to have forsaken, when man observes that of himself he is not able to do anything good, or to know anything true; that it is not to be understood as if David was forsaken by his father and mother, is manifest." (*Heavenly Arcana*, n. 3703.11)

Instruct me, Jehovah, in Your way,
And lead me in an upright path, because of my opponents.
Give me not to the will of my adversaries:
For false witnesses are risen up against me, and a testifier of
violence. (Ps. 27:11-12)

To be instructed in the way is to be instructed in truth signified by way (see Ps. 1:1, 18:42, 25:4,12, 37:23, 86:11); to be led to be led towards what is good (see Ps. 5:8, 23:3, 27:11); and upright path is to be in truth from good (see Ps. 9:8, 11:3, 25:21, 96:10, 143:10); paths concerns truths which consider what is good (see Ps. 25:4); opponents are those who are in evils. The "will" can be literally translated as soul, and refers to the desire of one's understanding (see Ps. 22:10, 31:9, 71:23, 107:9). The will of adversaries thus refers to the false intents of evils that attack what is good (see Ps. 3:1, 27:12); false witnesses are those in affirmation against the truth; a testifier of violence is to be in affirmation against the good of charity (see Ps. 7:16).

"*To be a witness of violence.* That this signifies no affirmation of such things as are contrary to the good of charity, is evident from the signification of a witness, as confirmation (see n. 4197, 8908); and from the signification of violence, as the destruction of the good of charity (n. 6353); and thus a witness of violence is affirmation contrary to the good of charity." (*Heavenly Arcana*, n. 3703.11)

I believe to see the goodness of Jehovah in the land of the living:
Wait on Jehovah, persevere,
And He shall encourage Your heart and to wait on Jehovah.
(Ps. 27:13-14)

Jehovah is the Lord as to Divine love (see Ps. 18:31, 28:1, 68:26, 82:1, 147:7) from whom comes all that is good; the land of the living is the heavenly kingdom. To persevere is to have power from truth; to be encouraged in the heart is to become strengthened in the will to do good as the heart signifies the will (see Ps. 7:9, 22:10, 24:4, 51:10, 64:6, 66:18, 71:23, 78:8, 86:11). Jehovah is life itself from whom there is spiritual life on earth and eternal life in heaven:

"There can be only one Life, from which is the life of all; and there can be no life — which is life — except through faith in the Lord, Who is Life; nor can there be faith in which is life except from Him, thus in which He is. Therefore it is said in the Word that the Lord alone liveth; and He is called *Jehovah who liveth* (Jer. v. 2; xii. 16; xvi. 14, 15; xxiii. 7; Ezek. v. 11): *He who liveth for ever* (Dan. iv. 34; Apoc. iv. 10; v. 14; x. 6): In David, *The Fountain of life* (Ps. xxxvi. 9): In Jeremiah, *The Fountain of living waters* (xvii. 13). Heaven, because it lives from Him, is called, *The land of the living* (Isa. xxxviii. 11; liii. 8; Ezek. xxvi. 20; xxxii. 23-27, 32; Ps. xxvii. 13; lii. 5; cxlii. 5). And they who are in faith in the Lord are called *the living* — as in David: *Who putteth our soul among the living* (Ps. lxvi. 9). And they who are in faith are said to be *in the book of lives* (Ps. lxix. 28); and in *the book of life* (Apoc. xiii. 8; xvii. 8; xx. 15). And therefore they who receive faith in Him are said to be *made alive* (Hosea vi. 2; Ps. lxxxv. 6). It follows from this that those on the other hand who are not in faith are called dead — as also in Isaiah: *The dead shall not live, the Rephaim shall not rise; because Thou hast visited and destroyed them* (xxvi. 14); that is, those who are puffed up with the love of self; to rise again signifies to enter into life. They are also said to be *pierced* (Ezek. xxxii. 23-26, 28-31). And hell is called *death* (Isa. xxv. 8; xxviii. 15). They are also called by the Lord dead (Matt, iv. 16; John v. 25; viii. 21, 24, 51, 52)." (*Heavenly Arcana*, n. 290)

"That by quickening and giving life is signified spiritual life, or new life through regeneration, may be evident from this alone, that the spiritual of the Word cannot be anything else. There is natural life and there is spiritual life. Natural life is understood in the literal sense of the Word, but spiritual life in the internal sense; and indeed in many passages by saving alive and by life is understood in the literal sense spiritual life itself — as in Eze-kiel: *When I say unto the wicked, Thou shalt surely die; and thou givest him not warning, nor speakest to warn the wicked from his wicked way, to give him life* (iii. 18). Again: *Ye have profaned Me among My people for handfuls of barley and for pieces of bread, to slay the souls that should not die and to make the souls to live that should not live. ...Ye strengthen the hands of the wicked, that he should not return from his evil way, by giving him life* (xiii. 19, 22). In Hosea: *After two days will* Jehovah *make us live:* and *in the third day He will raise us up, that we may live before Him* (vi. 2). In David: *Unless I had believed to see good in the land of life* (Ps. xxvii. 13)." (*Heavenly Arcana*, n. 5890)

Psalm 28

Of David.

~

Unto You, Jehovah, I will call, (1)
My rock, be not still with me:
Lest You hold Your peace with me,
And I become like those who go down into the pit.
Hear the voice of my supplication, when I cry to You, (2)
When I lift up my hands toward the oracle of Your sanctuary.
Draw me not away with the wicked and with the workers of
iniquity, (3)
Who speak peace to their neighbours but evil is in their heart.
Give to them according to their deeds, (4)
And according to the wickedness of their doings:
    Give to them according to the work of their hands,
    Render to them their reward.
    For they understand not the works of Jehovah nor the work of His
    hands, (5)
    He shall break them down and not build them up.
    Blessed be Jehovah, (6)
    For He has heard the voice of my supplications.
Jehovah is my strength and my shield, (7)
My heart trusted in Him and I am helped.
And my heart exults,
And with my song I will confess Him.
Jehovah is strength to *His people*, (8)
And He is the saving stronghold of His anointed.
Save Your people and bless Your inheritance, (9)
And shepherd them and lift them up forever.

Psalm Commentary 28

Summary: Prayer of the Lord to the Father for deliverance from the evils and falsehoods of hell (v. 1-3), and that they would be judged according to their works (v. 4-6). Praise to the Father for the deliverance of the Lord and through Him those who are in good and truth (v. 7-9).

Unto You, Jehovah, I will call,
My rock, be not still with me:
Lest You hold Your peace with me,
And I become like those who go down into the pit. (Ps. 28:1)

Jehovah is the Lord as to Divine love (see Ps. 18:31, 28:1, 68:26, 82:1, 147:7); rock signifies the Lord as to Divine truth (see Ps. 18:46, 19:14, 28:1, 78:15). To not be still is to guard against evil; to not hold peace is to guard against falsehood. A pit signifies a state of falsity and the falsehood of the lower earth close to hell (see Ps. 28:1, 69:15, 88:4,6).

"*Unto Thee do I call, O Jehovah my Rock; be not silent from me; lest Thou be silent from me (Ps. xxviii. 1).* Here, too, 'Jehovah' and 'Rock' are mentioned, because 'Jehovah' means the Lord in respect to Divine good, and 'Rock' the Lord in respect to Divine truth, and as both are meant it is twice said, 'be not silent from me,' 'lest Thou be silent from me;' one having reference to Divine good, the other to Divine truth, for in the Word there is a heavenly marriage in every particular, which is the marriage of good and truth." (*Apocalypse Explained*, n. 411.10)

"That pits are falsities, is because men who have been in principles of falsity, are after death kept awhile under the lower earth, until falsities have been removed from them, and as it were rejected to the sides. These places are called pits, and those who go into them are such as must be in vastation (n. 1106-1113, 2699, 2701, 2704). It is for this reason that by pits, in the abstract sense, are signified falsities. The lower earth is next under the feet, and the region round about for a short distance. Here are most persons after death, before they are taken up into heaven. This earth is also frequently mentioned in the Word. Beneath it are the places of vastation, which are called pits, and below them and round about for a considerable extent, are the hells." (*Heavenly Arcana*, n. 4728.1)

Hear the voice of my supplication, when I cry to You,
When I lift up my hands toward the oracle of Your sanctuary.
Draw me not away with the wicked and with the workers of iniquity,
Who speak peace to their neighbours but evil is in their heart.
(Ps. 28:2-3)

Hearing signifies Divine providence (see Ps. 17:6); the voice of supplications is prayer from internal spiritual truth (see Ps. 86:6); hand is the power of truth (see Ps. 20:6, 44:3, 45:4, 80:15,17, 89:13,21, 110:1, 121:5) and thus the lifting up of the hands is faith looking upward to the Lord. The oracle (from a word meaning "to speak") signifies the Divine truth of the Lord in the celestial heaven, as the oracle was the name for the innermost sanctuary of the Jewish temple (see below). The wicked are those who do evil against good; the workers of iniquity are those who commit evil against the good of faith (see Ps. 51:1-3). Neighbours are those in a similar truth of faith (see Ps. 122:8); to speak peace is to have an external appearance of no conflict; evil of the heart is hidden internal evil of the will (see Ps. 7:9, 22:10, 24:4, 51:10, 64:6, 66:18, 71:23, 78:8, 86:11).

"*And it came to pass, when Moses held up his hand.* That this signifies when faith with those who were of the spiritual church looked toward the Lord, is evident from the representation of Moses, as truth Divine — of which frequently above; and from the signification of holding up the hand, as directing spiritual power upward, thus to the Lord. That the hand is spiritual power, maybe seen above (n. 6947, 7011); and because spiritual power it is faith; for all power in the spiritual world, that is, against falsities from evil, is of truth from good, or of faith from charity (n. 3563, 4932).

"What it is to look toward the Lord, and what it is to look toward the world and self, thus what it is to look above self and what to look below self, has been already shown (n. 7814-7821), namely, that to look above self is to look to the neighbor, to our country, to the church, to heaven, thus to the Lord (n. 7814, 7815, 7817); that to look below self is to look to the world and to self (n. 7817); and to look above self and below self is to regard as an end and to love above all things (n. 7818); and that man is distinguished from brutes by this, that he can look above self and below self, and that when he looks above self, he is a man, but when below self, he is a beast (see n. 7821); and that to look above self is to be elevated by the Lord (n. 7816)" (*Heavenly Arcana*, n. 8604.1-2)

The oracle represents the third celestial heaven, as the plan of the Jewish temple was divided into three sections to represent the three heavens:

"...the Tent of meeting represented the three heavens, its court the lowest or first heaven; the tent itself as far as the veil, wherein were the tables for the loaves, the altar of incense, and the lampstand, represented the middle or second heaven; and the ark, which was within the veil, upon which was the mercy-seat with the cherubim, represented the inmost or third heaven; and the law itself which was in the ark, represented the Lord in relation to Divine truth or the Word..." (*Apocalypse Explained*, n. 700.1)

Give to them according to their deeds,
And according to the wickedness of their doings:

Give to them according to the work of their hands,
Render to them their reward.
For they understand not the works of Jehovah nor the work of
His hands,
He shall break them down and not build them up.
Blessed be Jehovah,
For He has heard the voice of my supplications. (Ps. 28:4-6)

One's eternal reward will be according to what one has done
in their life. Deeds are what are done according to the will, the
wickedness of one's doings is the evil thought of the deed, and
the work of one's hands is the external act (see Ps. 24:4, 73:13).
One's reward is eternal life in heaven or condemnation towards
hell. The works of Jehovah is the Divine operation to regenerate the will and the work of His hands is the Divine operation
to regenerate the understanding (see Ps. 107:24, 111:2,7). To be
broken down is to be destroyed by falsities; to not be built up is
to not be spiritually regenerated from collecting knowledges of
good and truth (see Ps. 112:3). To bless Jehovah is to acknowledge all good is from the Lord (see Ps. 3:8, 16:7, 21:6, 24:5, 28:6,
31:21, 96:2); to hear signifies Divine providence (see Ps. 17:6);
supplication is a request from spiritual truth (see Ps. 86:6).

Jehovah is my strength and my shield,
My heart trusted in Him and I am helped.
And my heart exults,
And with my song I will confess Him.
Jehovah is the stronghold of His people,
And He is the saving strength of His anointed.
Save Your people and bless Your inheritance,
And shepherd them and lift them up forever. (Ps. 28:7-9)

Strength is the power of good (see Ps. 21:13, 29:1, 95:4, 96:6);
a shield is truth which defends against evil and falsity (see
Ps. 144:2). The heart is one's desire of the will (see Ps. 7:9, 22:10,
24:4, 51:10, 64:6, 66:18, 71:23, 78:8, 86:11); to trust is to have
confidence of the will from the good of charity (see Ps. 33:21);
help is aid from Divine mercy (see Ps. 10:14); to exult is to have

joy from love (see Ps. 14:7) and to confess is to worship from
affection for the good of love (see Ps. 7:17, 35:18, 89:24). Stronghold or strength is the power to do good (see Ps. 21:13, 29:1, 95:4,
96:6) and people are those of the church in truth (see Ps. 2:1, 3:8,
18:43, 65:7, 74:18, 102:15). The anointed is the Messiah, and signifies Divine good united in the Divine Human from which there
is salvation (see Ps. 2:2, 89:20, 132:17). Salvation is deliverance
from evil by Divine love (see Ps. 14:7, 96:2); to bless is to give
good and happiness (see Ps. 3:8, 16:7, 21:6, 24:5, 28:6, 31:21,
96:2). People are those of the spiritual church and their inheritance is the spiritual heaven (see Ps. 69:35-36); to shepherd is to
lead into the good and truth of heaven (see Ps. 23:1, 80:1); to lift
them up forever is to lead them towards interior truths; forever
is eternity in the celestial heaven (see Ps. 145:13).

"Blessing involves every good, celestial, spiritual, and also
natural. These are signified by blessing in the internal sense;
and in the external sense by blessing is signified every worldly,
corporeal, and earthly good; but these, if they be a blessing, will
be of necessity from internal blessing; for this alone is blessing,
because it is eternal and joined with every felicity, and is the
very being of blessings. For what really is, unless it be eternal?
Every other being ceases to be. It was a customary saying with
the ancients — Blessed be Jehovah, by which they meant that
from Him is every blessing, that is, every good. And it was also
a form of thanksgiving, that the Lord blesses, and that He has
blessed — as in David (Psalm xxviii. 6; xxxi. 21; xli. 13; lxvi. 20;
lxviii. 19, 35; lxxii. 18, 19; lxxxix. 52; cxix. 12; cxxiv. 6; cxxxv. 21;
cxliv. 1; and many other places)." (*Heavenly Arcana*, n. 1096.1)

Psalm 29

A Psalm of David.

~

Give unto Jehovah, ye sons of gods, (1)
Give unto Jehovah glory and strength,
Give unto Jehovah the glory of His name, (2)
Bow down to Jehovah in holy attire.
  The voice of Jehovah is upon the waters, (3)
  The God of glory thunders, Jehovah is upon many waters.
  The voice of Jehovah is with power, (4)
  The voice of Jehovah is with grandeur.
  The voice of Jehovah breaks the cedars, (5)
  And Jehovah breaks the cedars of Lebanon.
  And He makes them to skip like a calf, (6)
  Lebanon and Sirion like the son of a wild bull.
  The voice of Jehovah hews the flames of fire, (7)
  The voice of Jehovah makes the wilderness to travail, (8)
  Jehovah makes the wilderness of Kadesh to travail.
  The voice of Jehovah makes the hinds to calve, (9)
  And He makes the forests bare,
    And in His temple every one says, the glory of Jehovah.
He sits upon the flood, (10)
And Jehovah sits a King forever.
Jehovah will give strength to His people, (11)
Jehovah will bless His people with peace.

Psalm Commentary   29

Summary: Those who are in the truths of the Word will adore the Lord who is the Word (v. 1-2). The power of the Divine truth from the Word dissipates falsities and reforms the natural (v. 3-9) which is from the Lord alone (v. 10-11).

Give unto Jehovah, ye sons of gods, (Ps. 29:1)

The "sons of gods" are those who are in the truths of the Word (see Ps. 89:6); gods are recipients of Divine truth (see Ps. 29:1, 82:1, 95:3).

"And because the Divine truth in the heavens is what in the Word of the Old Testament is meant by God, in the original language God is called *Elohim* in the plural; and also the angels who are in the heavens, because they are recipient of the Divine truth, are called gods — as in David: *Who in heaven can be compared unto Jehovah? or be likened unto Jehovah among the sons of the gods?* (Ps. lxxxix. 6). Again: *Give unto Jehovah, O ye sons of the gods, give unto Jehovah glory and strength* (Ps. xxix. 1). Again: *I said, ye are gods, and all of you sons of the Most High* (Ps. lxxxii. 6). And in John: *Jesus said, Is it not written in your law, I said, Ye are gods? If He called them gods, unto whom the Word ...came* (x. 34, 35); and also in the passages where the Lord is called *God of gods,* and *Lord of lords* (as Gen. xlvi. 2, 3; Deut. x. 17; Num. xvi. 22; Dan. xi. 36; Ps. cxxxvi. 2, 3)." *(Heavenly Arcana,* n. 7268.2; see also *Heavenly Arcana,* n. 4402.8)

Give unto Jehovah glory and strength,
Give unto Jehovah the glory due to His name,
Bow down to Jehovah in holy attire. (Ps. 29:1-2)

To give glory is to acknowledge all truth is from the Lord
(see Ps. 8:5, 19:1, 24:7-10, 73:24, 96:3) and to give strength is to
acknowledge that all power to do good comes from the Lord (see
Ps. 21:13, 95:4, 96:6). Jehovah is the Divine itself; His name is
the Divine Human (see Ps. 8:1) or the truths of doctrine through
which He is known (see Ps. 74:18, 96:2). To bow down is to worship from a humble heart (see Ps. 45:11); holy attire represents
worship from Divine truth.

"*To Him be glory and strength for ever and ever*, signifies who
alone has Divine majesty and Divine omnipotence to eternity. By
glory in the Word, where the Lord is spoken of, the Divine majesty is meant, and it is predicated of his Divine wisdom: and by
strength is meant the Divine omnipotence, and it is predicated
of His Divine love; and by for ever and ever is meant eternity."
(*Apocalypse Revealed*, n. 22)

The voice of Jehovah is upon the waters,
The God of glory thunders, Jehovah is upon many waters.
(Ps. 29:3)

This describes the Divine truth proceeding from the Lord
described as the voice of Jehovah and its effect on evils and falsities. Waters are the truths of faith (see Ps. 18:15, 23:2, 29:3,
77:19, 78:16). The voice of Jehovah upon the waters is Divine
truth concerning good as Jehovah is the Lord as to Divine love
(see Ps. 18:31, 28:1, 68:26, 82:1, 147:7); the God of glory is Divine
truth as God is the Lord as to Divine truth (see Ps. 18:31, 29:1,
68:17,24, 82:1, 95:3, 147:7) and glory is the Divine truth in
heaven (see Ps. 8:5, 19:1, 24:7-10, 73:24, 96:3). Thunder is perception of instruction of truth (see Ps. 18:13, 77:18, 81:7), but in
a higher sense represents Divine truth from the higher heavens
descending into the lower heavens.

"That a voice in the Word signifies Divine truth which is heard
and perceived in the heavens and on earth, is evident from the

following passages — in David: *The voice of Jehovah is upon the waters. …The voice of Jehovah is in power; the voice of Jehovah is with glory. The voice of Jehovah breaketh the cedars. …The voice of Jehovah cleaveth as a flame of fire. The voice of Jehovah shaketh the wilderness. …The voice of Jehovah maketh the hinds to calve …but in His temple every one saith, Glory* (Ps. xxix. 3-9). In this psalm Divine truth is described as destroying falsities and evils; this Divine truth is the voice of Jehovah; but the glory which is spoken of is Divine truth in heaven and in the church. That glory means the Divine truth may be seen above (n. 9429); also that the temple is heaven and the church (n. 3720)." (*Heavenly Arcana*, n. 9926.2; see also *Apocalypse Explained*, n. 261.1)

The voice of the Lord from heaven is described as many waters and thunder in Rev. 14:2:

"*And I heard a voice from heaven as the voice of many waters*, signifies the Lord speaking through the New Heaven from Divine truths. By a voice from heaven is signified voice or speech from the Lord through heaven: for where a voice is heard from heaven, it is from the Lord; here, through the New Heaven from Christians, which is meant by the Mount Zion upon which the Lamb was seen to stand, and with Him a hundred forty-four thousand (n. 612, 613). By many waters Divine truths are signified (n. 50). The Lord speaking through heaven from Divine truths is similarly spoken of in these passages following: *The voice of the Son of Man was heard as the voice of many waters* (Apoc. i. 15). *And a voice out of the throne, as the voice of many waters* (Apoc. xix. 6). *And the voice of the God of Israel like the voice of many waters* (Ezek. xliii. 2). *The voice of Jehovah is upon the waters, Jehovah is upon many waters* (Ps. xxix. 3). *The sound of the wings of the cherubs was as the sound of great waters* (Ezek. i. 24). By the cherubs the Word is signified (n. 239), and thus the Divine truth, from which the Lord speaks.

"*And as the voice of a great thunder*, signifies the Lord speaking through the New Heaven from the Divine love. That lightnings, thunders, and voices signify enlightenment, perception, and instruction, may be seen above (n. 236); and that the seven thunders speaking signify the Lord speaking through the universal heaven (n. 472). When the Lord speaks through heaven, He speaks from the third heaven through the second heaven, and thus from love through the Divine wisdom; for the third heaven is in His Divine love, and the second heaven in His Divine wisdom. The Lord never speaks in any other way, when He speaks from the higher heavens; and this is what is meant by a voice as of many waters and by a voice of great thunder. Many waters are the Divine truths of the Divine wisdom, and a great thunder is the Divine good of the Divine love." (*Apocalypse Revealed*, n. 614-615)

That waters represent the truths of faith is explained further in the following passage:

"Except a man be born of water and of the spirit he cannot enter into the kingdom of God (iii. 5).

'Waters' here are the truths of faith, and 'spirit' a life according to them (see *The Doctrine of the New Jerusalem*, n. 202-209, *seq.*). Because it had not been known that 'waters' signified the truths of faith, and that all things that were instituted among the sons of Israel were representative of spiritual things, it was believed that by the washings that were prescribed for them their sins were wiped away; yet this was not at all the case; those washings only represented purification from evils and falsities by means of the truths of faith and a life according to them… From this it is now clear that by 'the voice,' which was 'as the voice of many waters,' is meant Divine truth; as likewise in *Ezekiel:*—

Behold the glory of the God of Israel came from the way of the east, and His voice was like the voice of many waters; and the earth was enlightened by His glory (xliii. 2).

And in *David:*—

The voice of Jehovah is upon the waters, Jehovah upon many waters (Ps. xxix. 3).

And in the following words in the *Apocalypse:*—

> *I heard a voice from heaven, as the voice of many waters* (xiv. 2).

I know that some will wonder why 'waters' are mentioned in the Word, and not *the truths of faith,* since the Word is to teach man about his spiritual life; and since, if the expression *the truths of faith* had been used, instead of 'waters,' man would have known that the waters of baptism and of washings contribute nothing to the purifying of man from evils and falsities. But it is to be known, that the Word in order to be Divine, and at the same time useful to heaven and the church, must be wholly natural in the letter, for if it were not natural in the letter there could be no conjunction of heaven with the church by means of it; for it would be like a house without a foundation, and like a soul without a body, for ultimates enclose all interiors, and are a foundation for them (see above, n. 41). Man also is in ultimates, and upon the church in him heaven has its foundations. For this reason the style of the Word is such as it is; and as a consequence, when man from the natural things that are in the sense of the letter of the Word thinks spiritually, he is conjoined with heaven, and in no other way could he be conjoined with it." (*Apocalypse Explained*, n. 71.3-4; see also *Apocalypse Revealed*, n. 50)

The voice of Jehovah is with power,
The voice of Jehovah is with grandeur.
The voice of Jehovah breaks the cedars,
And Jehovah breaks the cedars of Lebanon.
And He makes them to skip like a calf,
Lebanon and Sirion like the son of a wild bull.
The voice of Jehovah hews the flames of fire,
The voice of Jehovah makes the wilderness to travail,
Jehovah makes the wilderness of Kadesh to travail.
The voice of Jehovah makes the hinds to calve,
And makes the forests bare,
And in His temple every one says, the glory of Jehovah. (Ps. 29:4-9)

Power is the power of Divine truth (see Ps. 65:6); and grandeur is Divine good (see Ps. 104:1, 111:3). For the voice of Jehovah to break the cedars is to dissipate falsities of the understanding (see Ps. 80:10, 92:12, 104:16, 148:9); for Jehovah to break the cedars of Lebanon is to dissipate falsities of the rational. To make them skip like a calf is to give joy to the natural affection for the truth. Lebanon is rational truth, Sirion is the good of the rational, and the son of a wild bull signify sensual affections as bulls signify natural affections (see Ps. 8:7, 68:30, 106:19-20, 144:13). To hew the flames of fire is to dissipate the love of the world (see Ps. 105:32); to make the wilderness travail is to dispel ignorance of the truth (see Ps. 55:7, 65:12, 107:4,35) while being regenerated (see Ps. 114:7); to shake the wilderness of Kadesh is to dispel contentions regarding the truth. Hinds represent those outside the church that are in natural good (see Ps. 18:33, 42:1); for them to calve is to become spiritually regenerated. To make the forests bare is to destroy knowledges of falsity (see Ps. 96:12, 132:6); the temple is the church as to Divine truth (see Ps. 18:6, 48:9, 65:4) which is also signified by glory (see Ps. 8:5, 19:1, 24:7-10, 29:1, 73:24, 96:3). The glory that is declared in the temple is the Divine truth in heaven and the church which is from the Lord himself.

"The voice of Jehovah is upon the waters, the God of glory maketh it to thunder, Jehovah is upon the great waters; the voice of Jehovah breaketh the cedars, yea, Jehovah breaketh in pieces the cedars of Lebanon; He maketh them also to skip like a calf, Lebanon and Sirion like the son of unicorns: the voice of Jehovah cutteth like a flame of fire; the voice of Jehovah maketh the wilderness to tremble, it maketh the wilderness of Kadesh to tremble. The voice of Jehovah maketh the hinds to be in travail, and maketh bare the forests; but in His temple doth every one speak of glory (Ps. xxix. 3-9). He who does not know that the particular things here said are in every expression Divinely holy, may say within himself if he is merely natural, 'What is this, — that Jehovah sitteth upon the waters; that by His voice He breaketh the cedars, maketh them to skip like a calf, and Lebanon like the son

of unicorns; maketh the hinds to be in travail? and so on:' for he does not know that the power of Divine Truth, or of the Word, is described by these things in the spiritual sense. But in that sense, by the *voice of Jehovah* which is the *thunder* there, is meant the Divine Truth, or the Word, in its power: by the *great waters* upon which Jehovah sitteth, are meant its truths; by the *cedars* and by *Lebanon,* which He *breaketh* and *breaketh to pieces,* are meant the falsities of the natural man; and by the *calf,* and the *son of unicorns,* the falsities of the natural and of the sensual man; by the *flame of fire,* the affection for falsity; by the *wilderness,* and the *wilderness of Kadesh,*the church where there is no truth and no good; by the *hinds,* which the *voice of Jehovah maketh to be in travail,* are meant the Gentiles who are in natural good; and by the *forests* which He *maketh bare,* are meant the knowledges and cognitions which the Word opens to them: and therefore it follows that *In His temple doth every one speak of glory;* by which is meant that in everything in the Word there are Divine Truths; for the *temple* signifies the Lord, and hence the Word, also heaven and the church; and *glory* signifies the Divine Truth." (*Doctrine of the New Jerusalem respecting the Sacred Scripture,* n. 18.4)

Lebanon signifies the rational, as do the cedars of Lebanon:

"The intellectual things of the celestial man are compared to a garden of trees of every kind; his rational things, to a forest of cedars and similar trees, such as were in Lebanon; but his knowledges are compared to oak-groves, and this from their intertwined branches, such as are those of the oak. By trees themselves are signified perceptions; as by the trees of the garden of Eden eastward, inmost perceptions, or those of intellectual things, as shown above (n. 99, 100, 103); by the trees of the forest of Lebanon, interior perceptions, or those of rational things; but by the trees of an oak-grove, exterior perceptions, or those of knowledge, which belong to the external man." (*Heavenly Arcana,* n. 1443; see also *Heavenly Arcana,* n. 119, 2588.15)

A calf signifies affection for the Divine truth:

"*And the second animal was like a calf,* signifies the Divine truth of the Word as to affection. By the beasts of the earth the various natural affections are signified: they also are those affections; and by a calf is signified the affection for knowing. This affection is represented by a calf in the spiritual world; hence it is also signified by a calf in the Word; as in Hosea: *We will repay to Jehovah the calves of our lips* (xiv. 2). The calves of the lips are confessions from affection for truth. In Malachi: *Unto you who fear my name shall the sun of righteousness arise, with healing in His wings, that ye may grow up as fattened calves* (iv. 2). A comparison is made with fattened calves, because those are signified by them who are filled with the knowledges of truth and good from the affection for knowing them. In David: *The voice of Jehovah maketh the cedars of Lebanon to skip as a calf* (Ps. xxix. 6). By the cedars of Lebanon the knowledges of truth are signified: hence it is said that the voice of Jehovah maketh them to skip as a calf. The voice of Jehovah is the Divine truth, here affecting." (*Apocalypse Revealed*, n. 242)

A hind signifies natural affections (see Ps. 18:33, 42:1). An alternative vocalization of the Hebrew yields "strong tree" or "oak" instead of "hind," which in the spiritual sense signifies the exterior knowledges of the natural man (see translation note). For the hinds to calve or give birth means to become regenerated:

"*And they brought forth.* That this signifies fruitfulness, is evident from the signification of bringing forth and of birth. In the internal sense of the Word, none but spiritual and celestial things are signified; on which account, where mention is made of conception or conceiving, bearing or bringing forth, birth or being born, of generation or generating, and also of those who beget, as father and mother, and those who are begotten, as sons and daughters, all these things are meant only in a spiritual sense, for the Word in itself is spiritual and celestial; and it is so here with bringing forth, by which is signified fruitfulness as to the things of doctrine.

"That by bearing in the Word no other bearing is meant, may be evident from the passages that follow. In Samuel: *The full have hired out themselves for bread, and the hungry have ceased, until the barren hath borne seven, and she who hath many children hath languished. Jehovah killeth and maketh alive, He causeth to go down into hell, and bringeth up* (1 Sam. ii. 5, 6). In Jeremiah: *She who hath borne seven languisheth, she breatheth out her soul; her sun is gone down while it is yet day* (xv. 9). In Isaiah: *Sing, O barren, that did not bear; break forth into singing and cry aloud, that did not travail with child; for more are the children of the desolate than the children of the married wife, said Jehovah* (liv. 1). In David: *The voice of Jehovah maketh the hinds to calve, and strippeth the forests bare; and in His temple every one speaketh His glory* (Ps. xxix. 9)." (*Heavenly Arcana,* n. 2584.1-2)

Kadesh signifies a state of contention about the truth:

"That Kadesh signifies truths concerning which there is contention, is evident in Ezekiel, where the boundaries of the Holy Land are described: *The corner of the south southward from Tamar as far as the waters of Meriboth-* (contentions) *Kadesh, an inheritance to the great sea, and the corner of the south southward* (xlvii. 19; xlviii. 28); where the south stands for the light of truth; its boundary, by which is signified contention about truths, is called Kadesh.

"Kadesh also was where Moses smote the Rock, out of which waters came forth; which waters were called Meribah, from contention (Num. xx. 1, 2, 11, 13). By the Rock, as is known, the Lord is signified; by waters, in the internal sense of the Word, are signified spiritual things, which are truths; they were called 'the waters of Meribah,' because there was contention about them. That they were also called 'the waters of the contention of Kadesh,' is evident in Moses: *Ye rebelled against My mouth in the wilderness of Zin, in the contention of the assembly, to sanctify Me by the waters in their eyes. These are the waters of contention of Kadesh in the wilderness of Zin* (Num. xxvii. 14; Deut. xxxii. 51). So, too, it was to Kadesh that the explorers returned from the land of Canaan, and where they murmured and contended, not being willing to enter into the land (Num. xiii. 26)." (*Heavenly Arcana,* n. 1678.2-3)

He sits upon the flood,
And Jehovah sits a King forever.
Jehovah will give strength to His people,
Jehovah will bless His people with peace. (Ps. 29:10-11)

A flood signifies the judgment of the Divine truth upon the evil, whose false thoughts inundate them like a flood as they turn away from heaven (see Ps. 18:4, 32:6, 42:7, 69:1, 124:4). Jehovah to sit as a King is the Lord as to Divine truth in human form (see Ps. 2:2, 24:7-10, 72:11, 89:20,39, 95:3, 105:20,30); for the Lord to sit is to be the center of being and life (see Ps. 1:1, 9:7, 107:4,36, 139:2); forever is eternity in the celestial heaven (see Ps. 145:13). To give strength is to give the power of doing good (see Ps. 21:13, 29:1, 95:4, 96:6) to those who are in the truths signified by people (see Ps. 2:1, 3:8, 18:43, 65:7, 74:18, 102:15), to "bless His people with peace" is to allow those who are in truths to overcome the conflict of temptation and arrive at a state of peace (see Ps. 4:8):

"Jehovah bless thee and keep thee; Jehovah make His faces to shine upon thee, and be gracious unto thee; and Jehovah lift up His faces upon thee, and give thee peace (Num. vi. 24-26). Divine truth, from which is all intelligence and wisdom, with which the Lord flows in, is meant by 'Jehovah makes His faces to shine upon thee;' and protection thereby from falsities is meant by 'be gracious unto thee;' and the Divine good, from which is all love and charity, with which the Lord flows in, is meant by 'Jehovah lift up His faces upon thee;' and protection thereby from evils, and thence heaven and eternal happiness, are meant by 'give thee peace;' for when evils and falsities are removed and no longer infest, the Lord flows in with peace, in which and from which is heaven and the delight that fills with bliss the interiors of the mind, thus heavenly joy. (This benediction may also be seen explained above, n. 340b). 'Peace' has a like signification in *David:*—

Jehovah will bless His people with peace (Ps. xxix. 11)."
(*Apocalypse Explained*, n. 365.12)

Psalm 30

A Psalm, a Song at the dedication of the house of David.

~

I will exalt You, Jehovah, for You have drawn me up, (1)
And have not made my enemies to rejoice over me.
Jehovah my God, I cried to You, (2)
And You have healed me.
Jehovah, You have brought up my soul from hell, (3)
You have kept me alive from them who go down to the pit.
Make music unto Jehovah, ye His merciful ones, (4)
And confess for the remembrance of His holiness.
    For His anger is sudden, (5)
    In His good pleasure is life.
    In the evening weeping may tarry for the night,
    But loud joy is in the morning.
    And as for me, I said in my tranquility, (6)
    I shall never be moved.
    Jehovah, in Your good pleasure You have made my mountain to
    stand strong, (7)
    You hid Your face, I was troubled.
    To You, Jehovah, I called, (8)
    And toward Jehovah I sought grace.
What profit is there in my blood when I go down to the pit? (9)
Shall the dust confess You? Shall it proclaim Your truth?
Hear, Jehovah, and be gracious to me, (10)
Jehovah, be a helper for me.

You have turned my wailing into dancing for me, (11)
You have put off my sackcloth and girded me with joy,
So that my glory may make music to You, and not be silent, (12)
Jehovah my God, I will confess You forever.

Psalm Commentary 30

Summary: Praise for the glorification of the Human of the Lord, after He ascended from hell (v. 1-4) and having suffered temptations even to the cross (v. 5-8). Praise of the Father for deliverance (v. 9-12).

I will exalt You, Jehovah, for You have drawn me up,
And have not made my enemies to rejoice over me.
Jehovah my God, I cried to You,
And You have healed me.
Jehovah, You have brought up my soul from hell,
You have kept me alive from them who go down to the pit.
(Ps. 30:1-3)

To exalt Jehovah is to worship by means of good from love (see also Ps. 18:46); enemies are falsehoods which attack the truth (see Ps. 3:1, 27:12). To heal is to preserve the good against evil and in the highest sense refers to the union of the Lord's body with the Divine good. The souls is one's spiritual life of the understanding (see Ps. 22:10, 31:9, 71:23, 107:9) and hell is a state of condemnation in the afterlife for those in the falsity of evil (see Ps. 18:5). Pits represent a state of falsity from ignorance, and those who are in falsehoods are imprisoned in pits in the other life until the falsehoods are removed (see Ps. 28:1, 69:15, 88:4,6). In the highest sense this refers to the Lord's descent into hell and His subsequent ascension.

"For I am Jehovah who healeth thee. That this signifies that
the Lord alone preserves from evils, is evident from the signification of healing, as relieving and also preserving from evils, for,
when diseases signify evils, healing signifies relief and preserva-
tion from them — as indeed in many passages of the Word, thus
in Moses: *I kill, and I make alive; I wound, and I heal* (Deut.
xxxii. 39). And in Jeremiah: *Heal me, O Jehovah, that I may be
healed; save me, that I may be saved* (xvii. 14). Again: *I will make
healing to go up unto thee, and I will heal thee of thy wounds*
(xxx. 17). And in David: *Thou turnest all his bed in his sickness.
I said, O Jehovah, have mercy upon me: heal my soul; for I have
sinned against Thee* (Ps. xli. 3, 4). Moreover in many other passages, as in the following: (Isa. vi. 10; liii. 5; lvii. 18, 19; Jer. iii.
22; xvii. 14; Hosea vi. 1; vii. 1; xi. 3; xiv. 4; Zech. xi. 16; Ps. xxx. 2:
and elsewhere). And because healing has this signification, the
Lord also calls Himself a physician: *They that are strong need
not a physician, but they who are sick. ...I came not to call the
just, but sinners to repentance* (Matt. ix. 12, 13; Mark ii. 17; Luke
v. 31, 32)." *(Heavenly Arcana,* n. 8365)

Make music unto Jehovah, ye His merciful ones,
And confess for the remembrance of His holiness.
For His anger is sudden,
In His good pleasure is life.
In the evening weeping may tarry for the night,
But loud joy is in the morning.
And as for me, I said in my tranquility,
I shall never be moved. (Ps. 30:4-6)

To make music is to worship from spiritual truth (see Ps. 57:7);
Jehovah is the Lord as to Divine love (see Ps. 18:31, 28:1, 68:26,
82:1, 147:7); the merciful are those who are primarily in love to
the Lord (see Ps. 25:10, 26:3, 36:5, 89:14, 103:8). Confession is
worship from affection for the good of love (see Ps. 7:17, 35:18,
50:14, 89:24); the remembrance is presence or conjunction with
the Lord through love (see Ps. 8:4) which is from Divine truth
signified by His holiness (see Ps. 5:7, 65:4). Anger is punish-

ment due to evil (see Ps. 2:5, 78:49); good pleasure is is to be in happiness doing God's will (see Ps. 5:12, 40:8, 51:18, 69:13) in which there is eternal life. Night represents a state of obscurity as to truth, or falsity (see Ps. 3:8, 16:7, 32:4, 74:16, 91:6, 104:20, 136:9); weeping is grief of heart over deprivation of truth (see Ps. 6:6). Morning is the coming of the Lord, his kingdom, the good of love (see Ps. 46:5, 101:8, 110:3, 130:6, 143:7). To be in tranquility is to be in confidence from one's own self will – the word is related to Shiloh which signifies the Divine Human as to the celestial (see Ps. 78:60); to say signifies perception of the will (see Ps. 33:9). To believe that one shall not be moved is to have confidence in falsehood derived from one's own intelligence.

"And in Isaiah: *One calleth unto me out of Seir, Watchman, what of the night? Watchman, what of the night? The watchman said, The morning cometh, and also the night* (xxi. 11, 12). By watchman in the internal sense is meant one who observes the states of the church and its changes, thus every prophet; by night is meant the last state of the church, by morning its first state; by Seir, from which the watchman crieth, is signified the enlightening of the nations which are in darkness — that Seir has this meaning may be seen above (n. 4240); and that night is the last state of the church (n. 6000); the morning cometh, and also the night, signifies that though there is enlightening to those who are of the new church, yet there is night to those who are in the old. The like is signified by morning in David: *In the evening weeping may come to tarry for the night, but in the morning shall be singing* (Ps. xxx. 5); and in Isaiah: *At eventide behold terror; before the morning he is not* (xvii. 14)." *(Heavenly Arcana*, n. 10134.11)

Jehovah, in Your good pleasure You have made my mountain to stand strong,
You hid Your face, I was troubled.
To You, Jehovah, I called,
And toward Jehovah I sought grace.
What profit is there in my blood when I go down to the pit?

Shall the dust confess You? Shall it proclaim Your truth?
(Ps. 30:7-9)

The good pleasure is to be in happiness of doing God's will
(see Ps. 5:12, 40:8, 51:18, 69:13), one's mountain is one's will in
the good of love (see Ps. 18:7, 36:6, 46:2, 65:6, 68:15-16, 72:3, 97:8,
104:10, 114:4,6, 121:1, 133:3, 147:8, 148:9) and to stand strong is
to be firm from the power of good (see Ps. 21:13, 95:4, 96:6). For
the Lord to hide His face means to be left to the evils of one's own
self will (see Ps. 13:1, 22:24). To call to Jehovah is to pray from
affection for good; to receive grace is to receive spiritual good and
truth, and comfort and hope of mind in temptations (see Ps. 4:1)
and is sought by those in humiliation of thought (see Ps. 103:8).
Blood signifies truth falsified and profaned (see Ps. 5:6, 16:4,
105:29), and this leads to captivity from falsehood signified by
pit (see Ps. 28:1, 69:15, 88:4,6). Dust is the condemnation of hell
(see Ps. 22:29, 44:25, 72:9) in which there is no affection for the
good of love signified by confession (see Ps. 7:17, 35:18) nor is
there acknowledgment of truth.

Hear, Jehovah, and be gracious to me,
Jehovah, be a helper for me.
You have turned my wailing into dancing for me,
You have put off my sackcloth and girded me with joy (Ps. 30:10-11)

To receive grace is to receive comfort and hope of mind in
temptations (see Ps. 4:1) and comes from humiliation of thought
(see Ps. 103:8); to receive help is Divine aid against evil from
Divine mercy (see Ps. 10:14). Mourning is sadness due to falsity; dancing signifies the spiritual affection for the truth (see
Ps. 150:4):

"*With timbrels and with dances.* That this signifies celebration from joy and gladness is evident from the signification of
timbrel, as predicated of affection for spiritual good or of the
good of truth, and as signifying its enjoyment or joy... and from
the signification of dance, as predicated of affection for spiritual
truth and as signifying its pleasantness or gladness — of which
in what follows. In ancient times gladness of heart was attested

not only by musical instruments and songs, but also by dances. For joys of the heart or interior joys burst forth in the body into various acts, as into songs and also dances. And whereas in ancient times the gladnesses which excelled all others were spiritual gladnesses, that is, from affections of spiritual loves, which were those of good and truth, therefore also it was then allowed to adjoin dances to songs and musical harmonies, and so likewise in these ways to testify joy. This is why dances are mentioned in the Word, and thereby are signified gladnesses of affections for truth or faith, from good or charity — as in Jeremiah: *Again shalt thou deck thy timbrels, and shalt go forth into the dance of them who make merry. ...Their soul shall be as a watered garden; and they shall not sorrow any more at all. Then shall the virgin rejoice in the dance, and the young men and the old together* (xxxi. 4, 12, 13). Again: *The joy of our heart shall cease; our dance is turned into mourning* (Lam. v. 15). And in David: *Thou hast turned for me my mourning into dancing* (Ps. xxx. 11)." (*Heavenly Arcana*, n. 8339.1; see also *Heavenly Arcana*, n. 10416.2)

When sackcloth was put on the loins, it signified mourning on account of good that was destroyed:

"*And put sackcloth upon his loins.* That this signifies mourning for destroyed good, is evident from the signification of putting sackcloth upon the loins, as representative of mourning for destroyed good. For the loins signify marriage love, and hence all celestial and spiritual love... When king Hezekiah heard the blasphemies which Rabshakeh spoke against Jerusalem, *He rent his clothes, and covered himself with sackcloth* (Isa. xxxvii. 1; 2 Kings xix. 1). Because he spoke against Jehovah, the king, and Jerusalem, there was therefore mourning; that it was against truth, is signified by his rending his clothes (n. 4763); and that it was against good, by his covering himself with sackcloth. For where truth is treated of in the Word, good also is treated of, on account of the heavenly marriage, which is that of good and truth, and of truth and good, in every particular — as also in David: *Thou hast turned my mourning into dancing; Thou*

hast loosed my sackcloth, and girded me with joy (Ps. xxx. 11).
Dancing here is predicated of truths, and joy of goods, as also in
other passages in the Word; and so loosing sackcloth stands for
taking away mourning over destroyed good." (*Heavenly Arcana*,
n. 4779.1, 5)

If the sackcloth was put on the body for clothing instead of
the loins, it signified mourning on account of truth destroyed:

*"Thou hast turned for me my mourning into dancing, thou
hast loosed my sackcloth and hast girded me with joy (Ps. xxx.
11).*

In these passages, too, 'sackcloth' signifies mourning; and
'to gird sackcloth over the body instead of the vesture' signifies
mourning because of the destruction of the truth of the church;
and 'to gird sackcloth upon the loins and upon the flesh' signifies
mourning because of the destruction of the good of the church;
for 'the vesture' signifies the truth of the church, and 'loins and
flesh' signify the good of the church." (*Apocalypse Explained*,
n. 637.18)

"*Clothed in sackcloth*, signifies mourning meantime on
account of the non-reception of the truth. By being clothed in
sackcloth is signified mourning on account of the vastated truth
in the church; for garments signify truths (n. 166, 212, 328, 378,
379): and therefore, to be clothed in sackcloth, which is not a garment, signifies mourning that there is no truth; and where there
is no truth, there is no church. The children of Israel represented
mourning by various things, which were significative from correspondences; as by putting ashes upon the head, by rolling themselves in the dust, by sitting upon the earth in silence for a long
time, by shaving themselves, by wailing and howling, by rending their clothes, and also by putting on sackcloth; beside other
things: and each of them signified some evil of the church within
them, on account of which they were punished. And when they
were punished, they by such things represented repentance;
and on account of the representation of repentance, and that of
humiliation at the same time, they were heard. That mourning
on account of vastated truth in the church was represented by

putting on sackcloth, may be seen from these passages: *The lion hath come up from the thicket, he hath gone forth out of his place to lay waste the earth; for this gird ye on sackcloth, wail, howl* (Jer. iv. 7, 8). *Daughter of My people, gird thee with sackcloth, and roll thee in ashes, because the waster shall come suddenly upon you* (Jer. vi. 26). *Woe unto thee, Chorazin, and Bethsaida; for if the mighty works had been done in Tyre and Sidon which have been done in you, they would have repented in sackcloth and ashes* (Matt. xi. 21; Luke x. 13). *The king of Nineveh, after he heard the words of Jonah, laid aside his robe from him, and put on sackcloth, and sat in ashes and proclaimed a fast, and that man and beast should be covered with sackcloth* (Jonah iii. 5, 6. Beside other places, as Isa. iii. 24; xv. 2, 3; xxii. 12; xxxvii. 1, 2; l. 3; Jer. xlviii. 37, 38; xlix. 3; Lam. ii. 10; Ezek. vii. 17, 18; xxvii. 31; Dan. ix. 3; Joel i. 8, 13; Amos viii. 10; Job xvi. 15, 16; Ps. xxx. 11; xxxv. 13; lxix. 11; 2 Sam. iii. 31; 1 Kings xxi. 27; 2 Kings vi. 30; xix. 1, 2)." (*Apocalypse Revealed*, n. 492)

So that my glory may make music to You, and not be silent, O Jehovah my God, I will confess You forever. (Ps. 30:12)

Glory is Divine truth from the Lord (see Ps. 8:5, 19:1, 24:7-10, 29:1, 73:24, 96:3) and one's glory is the truth one has received from the Lord; to make music is to worship from spiritual truth (see Ps. 57:7); to be silent is to be in falsehood (see Ps. 4:4). The word for silence in the original Hebrew can also mean to be silenced in death in which case it represents praise for victory over death. Jehovah is the Lord as to Divine love (see Ps. 18:31, 28:1, 68:26, 82:1, 147:7); confession signifies worship from affection for the good of love (see Ps. 7:17, 35:18, 50:14, 89:24); forever is eternity in the celestial heaven of love (see Ps. 145:13).

Psalm 31

To the chief musician, a Psalm of David.

~

In You, Jehovah, I seek refuge, (1)
Let me never be ashamed.
In Your righteousness rescue me,
Incline Your ear to me; deliver me quickly. (2)
Be to me a rock of a stronghold,
For a house of a fortress to save me,
For You are my cliff and my fortress. (3)
And for Your name's sake lead me and guide me,
Pull me out of the net that they have hidden for me, (4)
For You are my stronghold.
Into Your hand I commit my spirit, (5)
You have ransomed me, Jehovah, God of truth.
I have hated those who take heed to vain vanities, (6)
But toward Jehovah I trust.
I will be glad and rejoice in Your mercy, (7)
Because You have seen my affliction,
You have known my soul in adversities.
And You have not surrendered me into the hand of the enemy, (8)
You have made my feet to stand in a broad place.
Be gracious to me, Jehovah, for I am in distress, (9)
My eye wastes away with provocation, my soul and my belly.
For my life is spent with sorrow, (10)
And my years with sighing.
My power stumbles in my iniquity,
And my bones waste away.
From all my adversaries I am a reproach, (11)

And a *calamity* to my fellow residents,
And a dread to my acquaintance.
They who saw me in the street fled from me,
I am forgotten as one dead from the heart, (12)
I am like a demolished vessel.
For I have heard the slander of many, (13)
Apprehension was round about.
While they took counsel together against me,
They schemed to take away my life.
But I trusted upon You, Jehovah, (14)
I said, You are my God.
My times are in Your hand, (15)
Deliver me from the hand of my enemies and from those who
pursue me.
Make Your face to shine upon Your servant, (16)
Save me in Your mercy.
Jehovah let me not be ashamed for I have called upon You, (17)
Let the wicked be ashamed, let them be silent in hell.
Let the lips of falsehood become dumb, (18)
Which speak arrogantly against the righteous with pride and
contempt.
How great is Your goodness which You have hidden for those who fear
You, (19)
You have wrought for those who seek refuge in You in front of the
sons of Man.
You shall hide them in the secret of Your presence from the league of
men, (20)
You shall keep them secretly in a pavilion from arguing tongues.
Blessed be Jehovah, (21)
For He has made His mercy wonderful in a defended city.
And as for me, I said in my haste, I am cut off from in front of Your
eyes: (22)
Surely You heard the voice of my supplications when I cried to You.
Love Jehovah, all ye His merciful ones: (23)
Jehovah preserves the faithful and plentifully repays the proud doer.
Persevere and He shall encourage your heart, (24)
All ye who hope for Jehovah.

Psalm
Commentary
31

Summary: Prayer of the Lord to the Father, that He may be protected from those who devise evil (v. 1-4). They want to slay him (v. 5) yet He trusts in the Father (v. 6-8). From this the Lord has grief of heart, and He was despised on the cross (v. 9-14). Prayer for deliverance from His enemies (v. 15-18). Through trust in the Father He is delivered from the enemies (v. 15-18). Praise of the Father for deliverance, thus let there be trust in the Lord (v. 19-24).

In You, Jehovah, I seek refuge,
Let me never be ashamed.
In Your righteousness rescue me,
Incline Your ear to me; deliver me speedily.
Be to me a rock of a stronghold,
For a house of a fortress to save me,
For You are my cliff and my fortress.
And for Your name's sake lead me and guide me,
Pull me out of the net that they have hidden for me, for You are
my stronghold. (Ps. 31:1-4)

    The Lord protects against falsity and evil: a refuge is protection from falsity and to not be ashamed is to not have shame from committing evil. To be rescued is to be led by truths out of falsity (see Ps. 91:14) towards what is good signified by righteousness (see Ps. 14:5, 36:6, 37:6,17, 72:2, 89:14, 92:12). For God to hear is Divine providence from mercy (see Ps. 17:6). A rock is Divine truth (see Ps. 18:46, 19:14, 28:1, 78:15) from the the power of good signified by stronghold (see Ps. 21:13, 29:1, 95:4, 96:6); a house of a fortress is good from spiritual truth as house is related to what is good (see Ps. 23:6, 65:4, 92:13, 105:21). Salvation is deliverance from evil by Divine mercy (see Ps. 14:7, 96:2). A cliff is external truth (see Ps. 18:2) and a fortress is spiritual truth defending against falsity. To be led is to be led towards good (see Ps. 5:8, 23:3, 27:11); to be guided is to be guided by truth. A net is external material desires (see Ps. 10:9).

Into Your hand I commit my spirit,
You have ransomed me, Jehovah, God of truth. (Ps. 31:5)

This was quoted by Jesus on the cross before he breathed his last (Luke 23:46) showing that the Psalms in the highest sense refer to the Lord during his temptations and combats with hell. God's hand is the power of truth (see Ps. 20:6, 44:3, 45:4, 80:15,17, 89:13,21, 110:1, 121:5) and the spirit here is one's spiritual life; to ransom means to liberate from falsity (see Ps. 49:15, 69:18, 71:23, 119:134, 130:7).

"*Into Thine hand I will commend my spirit; Thou hast ransomed me, O Jehovah, God of truth (Ps. xxxi. 5); 'to ransom' means to free from falsities and to reform by means of truths; and because this is signified by 'ransom' it is said, 'O Jehovah, God of truth.'*" (*Apocalypse Explained*, n. 328.15)

I have hated those who give heed to vain vanities,
But toward Jehovah I trust,
I will be glad and rejoice in Your mercy,
Because You have seen my affliction,
You have known my soul in adversities.
And have not surrendered me into the hand of the enemy,
You have made my feet to stand in a broad place. (Ps. 31:6-8)

To hate those who give heed to vain vanities is to reject the falsity of doctrine signified by vanity (see Ps. 4:2, 144:8). To trust is to have confidence of the will from the good of charity (see Ps. 33:21); to be glad is to be in affection for truth from thought and to rejoice in the Lord's mercy is to have joy from love (see Ps. 14:7). To be in affliction is to be lacking in knowledges of the truth (see Ps. 35:10, 37:14, 40:17); to be in adversities is to suffer from evils attacking good (see Ps. 3:1, 27:12). To not surrender into the hand of the enemy is to not submit to the power of falsity; for feet to stand is to live a new regenerate life (see Ps. 40:2); a broad place is to be increased in truth signified by breadth (see Ps. 4:1, 18:19, 104:25). The spiritual significance of standing upon the feet is described below:

"When I had prophesied about the spirit, the spirit entered into them, and they revived and stood upon their feet (Ezek. xxxvii. 10).

Here also 'to stand upon the feet' signifies a new life, such as the regenerate man has; for 'the dry bones' to which the house of Israel is likened signify the state of the church with them, namely, that it had no goods of love or truths of doctrine; and 'being clothed with sinews, flesh, and skin' signifies regeneration; and 'the spirit that entered in' signifies a new life through the influx and reception of Divine truth; therefore it is then said that 'they revived and stood upon their feet.' 'To stand upon the feet' has the same signification elsewhere in the same prophet:—

A voice speaking to me said, Son of man, stand upon thy feet that I may speak to thee; then the spirit entered into me when he spake unto me, and stood me upon my feet, and I heard him who spake to me (ii. 1, 2).

And again:—

I fell upon my face, but the spirit entered into me and raised me upon my feet (iii. 23, 24).

This was done because 'to stand upon the feet' signifies life itself when it is in its fullness; and life is in its fullness when the natural lives from the spiritual. For the ultimate of man's life is in his natural; this ultimate is like a base to man's interior and higher parts; for these close into the ultimate and subsist in it, consequently unless life is in the ultimate it is not full, and thus

not perfect. Moreover, all things interior or higher exist together
in the ultimate as in their simultaneous. For this reason such
as the ultimate is such are the interior or higher parts, for these
adapt themselves to the ultimate because it receives them. 'To
stand upon the feet' has a similar signification in *David:*—

> *Thou hast made my feet to stand in a broad place (Ps.* xxxi.
> 8).

'A broad place' signifies the truth of doctrine from the Word,
therefore 'to make my feet to stand in a broad place' signifies
to cause one to live according to Divine truths." (*Apocalypse
Explained,* n. 666.3-5)

"*In the length of it and in the breadth of it.* That this signifies the celestial and the spiritual, or what is the same, good
and truth [may be evident from the signification of length and
breadth]. That length signifies good, and breadth truth, may be
seen explained before (n. 650). The reason is, because the land
signifies the heavenly kingdom, or the church; of which no length
and breadth can be predicated, but those things which are applicable and correspondent, which are goods and truths. The celestial, or good, because it is primary, is compared to length; but
the spiritual, or truth, because it is secondary, is compared to
breadth.

"That breadth is truth, appears plainly enough in the prophetic Word. As in Habakkuk: *I raise up the Chaldeans, that
bitter and hasty nation; which walk through the breadths of the
land* (i. 6). The Chaldeans stand for those who are in falsity; to
walk through the breadths of the land, means to destroy truths;
for this is predicated of the Chaldeans. In David: *O Jehovah,
Thou hast not shut me up into the hand of the enemy; Thou hast
made my feet to stand in a broad place* (Ps. xxxi. 8). To stand in a
broad place means in truth. Again: *Out of straitness I called upon
Jah; Jah answered me in a broad place* (Ps. cxviii. 5). To answer
in a broad place means in the truth. In Hosea: *Jehovah will feed
them as a lamb, in a broad place* (iv. 16). To feed in a broad place
signifies to teach truth." (*Heavenly Arcana,* n. 1613.1-2)

"And behold, the land is broad in spaces before them. That this signifies extent, namely, of the truth of doctrine, is evident from the signification of land, as the church... and from the signification of broad in spaces, as extent as to truths, and thus as to what is of doctrine. In the Word, description according to measures does not signify measures in the internal sense, but qualities of state; for measures involve spaces, and in the other life there are not spaces, nor times, but states corresponding thereto... And as it is so, lengths, breadths, and heights which are of measured space, signify such things as belong to state... For this reason by a land broad in spaces is signified extent of truth which is of doctrine in the church.

"He who does not know that there is a spiritual meaning in the Word, other than what appears in the literal sense, cannot but wonder when told that by a land broad in spaces is signified extent of the truth which is of doctrine in the church. But that still it is so, may be evident from the places where breadth is mentioned in the Word — as in Isaiah: Assyria *shall go through Judah; he shall overflow and pass through; he shall reach even to the neck, and the stretchings out of his wings shall be the fullness of the breadth of thy land* (viii. 8). In David: O Jehovah, *Thou hast not shut me up into the hand of the enemy, Thou hast made my feet to stand in a broad place* (Ps. xxxi. 8). In the same: *Out of straitness I called upon Jah; Jah answered me in a broad place* (Ps. cxviii. 5). In Habakkuk: *I raise up the Chaldeans, that bitter and hasty nation, which walk through the breadths of the land* (i. 6) — where by breadths nothing else is signified than the truth of the church." (*Heavenly Arcana*, n. 4482.1-2)

Be gracious to me, Jehovah, for I am in distress,
My eye wastes away with provocation, my soul and my belly.
(Ps. 31:9)

To receive grace is to receive spiritual good and truth, and comfort and hope of mind in temptations (see Ps. 4:1) and is sought by those in humiliation of thought (see Ps. 103:8); distress is a state of temptation. Eye represents the spiritual understanding (see Ps. 11:4, 13:3, 31:9, 69:23) and the soul is one's spiritual life therefrom (see Ps. 22:10, 31:9, 71:23, 107:9); belly is internal reception of the truth (see Ps. 17:14, 31:9, 40:8, 127:3). To waste away with provocation is to be destroyed by falsity (see Ps. 10:14, 78:58).

"*Be gracious unto me, O Jehovah, for I am in distress; mine eye wasteth away with vexation, my soul and my belly* (Ps. xxxi. 9). 'Eye, soul, and belly,' here signify the understanding and exterior and interior thought of truth therefrom; thus the 'belly' signifies the interiors of the understanding, which are said 'to waste away with vexation' when they are destroyed by falsities." (*Apocalypse Explained*, n. 622.7)

"In *Jonah:*—

When my soul fainted upon me (ii. 7).

This treats of temptations; and that 'his soul fainted upon him' signifies that the truth fainted (or ceased) in the faith and understanding. In *David:*—

Mine eye wasteth away with vexation, and my belly (Ps. xxxi. 9).

In the same:—

My soul is bowed down to the dust, our belly cleaveth to the earth (Ps. xliv. 25).

This also describes the state of temptations. The 'eye' signifies the understanding, the 'soul' the belief in truth and the understanding of truth, and the 'belly' the belief in good and the understanding of good. This is the signification of 'belly' because the belly receives food, and 'food' and 'bread' signify good that nourishes, here the understanding and faith. The lack of these in temptation is signified by 'wasting away with vexation,' and 'bowing down to the dust,' and 'cleaving to the earth.'" (*Apocalypse Explained*, n. 750.14)

For my life is spent with sorrow,
And my years with sighing.
My power stumbles in my iniquity,
And my bones waste away. (Ps. 31:10)

One's life is one's spiritual life from love; sorrow is sadness due to evil and years in sighing is oppression from falsehood. For power to stumble from iniquity is for the power of truth (see Ps. 65:6) to falter due to evil against the good of truth (see Ps. 51:1-3); for bones to waste away is for one's external truth to be destroyed by falsehood (see Ps. 22:14,17, 34:20, 35:10).

From all my adversaries I am a reproach,
And a calamity to my fellow residents,
And a dread to my acquaintance.
They who saw me in the street fled from me. (Ps. 31:11)

Adversaries are evils which attack the good of love (see Ps. 3:1, 27:12); to be in calamity is to be in a weak state as to truth (see Ps. 18:18); a fellow resident are evils from falsity; a dread to an acquaintance is an opposing knowledge of falsehood. In a positive sense, a fellow resident (below translated as neighbor) is a similar good from truth:

"*Then shall he and his neighbor next unto his house take one.* That this signifies conjunction with the nearest good of truth, is evident from the signification of taking, namely, with his near neighbor one lamb together, as conjunction; and from the signification of neighbor next unto his house, as the nearest good of truth." (*Heavenly Arcana*, n. 7835)

They who saw me in the street fled from me,
I am forgotten as one dead from the heart,
I am like a demolished vessel.
For I have heard the slander of many,
Apprehension was round about.
While they took counsel together against me,
They schemed to take away my life. (Ps. 31:11-13)

Those in the street are those in external falsehoods. To be "forgotten as one dead from the heart" is to be rejected out of hatred for heart signifies love of the will (see Ps. 7:9, 22:10, 24:4, 51:10, 64:6, 66:18, 71:23, 78:8, 86:11); to be like a demolished vessel is for knowledges of good and truth to be destroyed (see Ps. 2:9) - demolish similar to perish signifies to spiritually die from falsehoods (see Ps. 88:11); to hear slander is for falsehoods to attack what is good. To take counsel is to plot falsity against the truth. To plan to take one's life in the literal sense means they plotted to take away the life of the Lord; in the spiritual sense it signifies the desire of hell to to take away the eternal life of heaven.

But I trusted upon You, O Jehovah,
I said, You are my God.
My times are in Your hand,
Deliver me from the hand of my enemies and from those who
pursue me.
Make Your face to shine upon Your servant,
Save me in Your mercy. (Ps. 31:14-16)

To trust is to have confidence of the will from the good of charity (see Ps. 33:21) and is thus mentioned with Jehovah who is the Lord as to Divine love (Ps. 18:31, 28:1, 68:26, 82:1, 147:7); God is the Lord as to Divine truth (see Ps. 18:31, 29:1, 68:17,24, 82:1, 95:3, 147:7); times concern man's state (see Ps. 69:13); hand is the power of truth (see Ps. 20:6, 44:3, 45:4, 80:15,17, 89:13,21, 110:1, 121:5). The hand of the enemies is the power of the falsehoods from hell (see Ps. 3:1, 27:12); those who pursue are the evils which attack what is good. The face of the Lord is Divine good (see Ps. 4:6, 13:1, 22:24, 27:8-9, 67:1); for the face to shine is to receive good from Divine mercy signified by face (see Ps. 13:1, 22:24, 27:8-9, 31:16, 67:1); a servant is one who lives by the truth (see Ps. 69:36, 78:70, 89:3,20). Salvation is deliverance from evil from Divine love (see Ps. 14:7, 96:2) which is signified by mercy (see Ps. 25:10, 26:3, 36:5, 89:14, 103:8).

"That 'the face,' in reference to Jehovah or the Lord, signifies the Divine love and the Divine good therefrom is evident from the following passages. In *David:*—

> *Make Thy faces to shine upon Thy servant; save me because of Thy mercy* (xxxi. 16).

'To make the faces to shine' signifies to enlighten in Divine truth from Divine love; this is signified by 'making the faces to shine,' because Divine truth, which proceeds from the Lord as a sun in the angelic heaven, gives all the light there, and also enlightens the minds of the angels and fills them with wisdom; consequently the Lord's face, in a proper sense, is the sun of the angelic heaven; for the Lord appears to the angels of the interior heavens as a sun, and this from His Divine love, for love in the heavens when presented before the eyes appears as fire, but the Divine love as a sun. From that sun both heat and light proceed, that heat is Divine good, and that light is Divine truth. From this it can be seen that 'Make Thy faces to shine upon Thy servant' signifies to enlighten with Divine truth from Divine good; therefore it is also added, 'save me because of Thy mercy;' mercy is of the Divine good. (But of the sun in the angelic heaven, and the heat and light from it, see in the work on *Heaven and Hell;* of The Sun there, n. 116-125; and of The Heat and Light from it, n. 126-140). In the same:—

> *Many say, Who will show us good? Jehovah, lift up the light of Thy faces upon us (Ps.* iv. 6).

In the same:—

> *They shall walk, O Jehovah, in the light of Thy faces (Ps.* lxxxix. 15).

In the same:—

> *Turn us back, O God, and cause Thy faces to shine, that we may be saved (Ps.* lxxx. 3, 7, 19).

And in the same:—

*God be merciful unto us and bless us, and cause His faces to
shine upon us (Ps. lxvii. 1).*

'The light of the faces' of Jehovah or of the Lord means Divine
truth from Divine love (as above) and intelligence and wisdom
therefrom, for both angels and men have all their intelligence
and wisdom from Divine truth, or the Divine light in the heavens, therefore 'make Thy faces to shine upon us,' 'lift up the light
of Thy faces upon us,' and 'cause Thy faces to shine,' in the above
passages signify to enlighten in Divine truth, and to bestow
intelligence and wisdom." (*Apocalypse Explained*, n. 412.2-3)

"Since the Lord in respect to Divine truth is called in the
Word 'a servant' from serving, so those who are in Divine truth
from the Lord and thereby serve others are there called 'servants,' as the prophets are in these passages. In *Jeremiah:—*

Jehovah sent unto you all His servants the prophets (xxv. 4).

In *Amos:—*

He hath revealed His secret unto His servants the prophets
(iii. 7).

In *Daniel:—*

*He hath set [His laws] before us by the hand of His servants
the prophets* (ix. 10).

So too:—

Moses is called The servant of Jehovah (Mal. iv. 4).

And also Isaiah, in his prophecy (*Isa.* xx. 3; l. 10).

For 'prophets' in the Word signify the doctrine of Divine
truth, thus Divine truth in respect to doctrine (see *A. C.,* n. 2534,
7269). So again, David calls himself 'a servant of Jehovah,' as in
the following passages:—

*I rejoice in Thy statutes; I do not forget Thy word. [Deal
well with Thy servant.] Thy servant doth meditate in Thy
statutes. Thou hast done good to Thy servant, O Jehovah,
according to Thy word. Deal with Thy servant according to*

Thy mercy, and teach me Thy statutes. I am Thy servant,
cause me to discern, that I may know Thy testimonies. Make
Thy faces to shine upon Thy servant, and teach Me Thy stat-
utes. I have gone astray like a lost sheep; seek Thy servant
(Ps. cxix. 16, 17, 23, 65, 124, 125, 135, 176).

In the same:—

Keep my soul, for I am holy; save Thy servant, for I trust
in Thee. Gladden the soul of Thy servant; for unto Thee, O
Lord, do I lift up My soul. Give strength unto Thy servant,
and save the son of Thy handmaid (Ps. lxxxvi. 2, 4, 16; and
elsewhere, as *Ps.* xxvii. 9; xxxi. 16; xxxv. 27; cxvi. 16; *Luke*
i. 69).

Since the Lord in respect to Divine truth is meant by 'David' in
the above cited passages, and thus 'David,' in like manner as
the prophets, means Divine truth, so 'servant' in these passages
also means in the spiritual sense, what is of service. One who is
ignorant of the spiritual sense of the Word might believe that
not only David but also others who are spoken of in the Word,
called themselves 'servants,' for the reason that all are servants
of God; but still wherever 'servants' are mentioned in the Word,
what is of service and effect is meant in the spiritual sense. For
this reason too:—

Nebuchadnezzar king of Babylon is called the servant of
Jehovah (Jer. xxv. 9; xliii. 10).

But in a particular sense, 'servant' and 'servants' in the Word
mean those who receive Divine truth and who teach it, since
Divine truth is what serves, and by means of it Divine good
produces effects. For this reason 'servants' and 'chosen' are
frequently mentioned together, 'servants' meaning those who
receive Divine truth and who teach, and 'chosen' those who
receive Divine good and who lead, as in *Isaiah:*—

I will bring forth a seed out of Jacob, and out of Judah an inheritor of My mountains; that My chosen may possess it, and My servants may dwell there (lxv. 9).

In the same:—

Thou, Israel, art My servant, and Jacob, whom I have chosen (xli. 8).

In the same:—

Hear, O Jacob, My servant; Israel, whom I have chosen. Fear not, O Jacob, My servant, and thou Jeshurun, whom I have chosen (xliv. 1, 2).

(That those are called 'chosen' who are in the life of charity, see A. C., n. 3755 near the end, n. 3900)." (*Apocalypse Explained*, n. 409.6)

Jehovah let me not be ashamed for I have called upon You,
Let the wicked be ashamed, let them be silent in hell.
Let the lips of falsehood become dumb,
Which speak arrogantly against the righteous with pride and contempt.
How great is Your goodness which You have hidden for those who fear You,
You have wrought for those who seek refuge in You in front of the sons of Man.
You shall hide them in the secret of Your presence from the league of men,
You shall keep them secretly in a pavilion from arguing tongues.
(Ps. 31:17-20)

To not be ashamed is to not have shame from falling into evil and falsity; the wicked are the evils of hell and for them to be silent is for their falsehoods to be silenced by truth (see Ps. 4:4). The "lips of falsehood" are false doctrines (see Ps. 12:4, 81:5) to become silenced by Divine truth; to speak arrogant things is to be in the falsehood of selfish pride against good, signified by righteous (see Ps. 14:5, 36:6, 37:6,17, 72:2, 89:14,

92:12). The goodness hidden for those who fear the Lord is the good of heaven hidden for those who live a life of love; to seek refuge is to be protected from falsehood by the Divine truth; the sons of Man (Hebrew *adam*) are spiritual truths (see Ps. 49:2, 57:4, 80:17, 89:47). Interior good and truth of heaven is kept secret from those in the evil of external falsehoods signified by "league of men" and from false persuasions signified by "arguing tongues" (see Ps. 35:28, 57:4, 140:11) in order to prevent them from being profaned. A pavilion, similar to Succoth, signifies the holy of truth (see Ps. 60:6).

"*Jehovah will create over every dwelling-place of mount Zion, and over her assemblies, a cloud by day, and a smoke and the shining of a flame of fire by night; for over all the glory there shall be a covering. And there shall be a tent* [succah] *for a shadow in the day-time, and for a refuge and covert from flood and from rain* (iv. 5, 6). A cloud is here also the literal sense of the Word, and the glory the internal sense, as also in Matthew (xxiv. 30; Mark xiii. 26; Luke xxi. 27). A tent here also stands for the holy of truth. Interior truths are said to be in hiding, for the reason that if they had been revealed, they would then have been profaned (see n. 3398, 3399, 4289); which is also set forth by these words in David: *Thou hidest them in the covert of Thy presence from the plottings of man; Thou keepest them secretly in a tent* [succah] *from the strife of tongues* (Ps. xxxi. 21)." (*Heavenly Arcana*, n. 4391.2)

"*Thou hidest them in the hiding place of Thy faces from the pride of man; Thou concealest them in a pavilion from the strife of tongues* (Ps. xxxi. 20).

'A hiding place of faces in which Jehovah hides them,' signifies the Divine good of the Divine love, for 'the face of Jehovah' signifies the good of love, and 'the hiding place' signifies inwardly in man; 'the pride of man' signifies the pride of self-intelligence; the 'pavilion in which He hides them' signifies Divine truth; and 'the strife of tongues' signifies the falsity of religion from which they reason against truths." (*Apocalypse Explained*, n. 455.10)

"Thou hidest them in the hiding place of Thy faces from the elations of man; Thou concealest them in Thy covert from the strife of tongues (Ps. xxxi. 20). 'To hide them in the hiding place of Thy faces' means in the Divine good that does not appear before others; and 'to conceal in Thy covert' means in the Divine truth; 'the elations of man' and 'the strife of tongues' mean the evils of falsity and the falsities of evil; for 'elations' are predicated of evils because they are of self-love, and 'man' signifies truth and falsity..." *(Apocalypse Explained,* n. 412.8)

Blessed be Jehovah,
For He has made His mercy wonderful in a defended city.
(Ps. 31:21)

To bless Jehovah is to acknowledge that all good and happiness comes from the Lord (see Ps. 3:8, 16:7, 21:6, 24:5, 28:6, 96:2); mercy is the Divine love (see Ps. 25:10, 26:3, 36:5, 89:14, 103:8); to make wonderful is to perform an act of Divine power which causes belief (see Ps. 71:7, 78:43, 105:5); a defended city are the doctrines of truth which defend against falsehoods (see Ps. 46:4, 48:8, 107:36, 122:3). The defended city also signifies heaven and the church which constantly defends against the falsities and evils of hell.

"...to bless the Lord is to sing to Him, to proclaim the good tidings of His salvation, to preach His wisdom and power, and thus to confess and acknowledge the Lord from the heart. They who do this cannot but be blessed by the Lord, that is, be gifted with those things which are of blessing, namely, with celestial, spiritual, natural, worldly, and corporeal good; these, when they follow each other in this order, are the good things in which is happiness.

"As to bless Jehovah, or the Lord, and to be blessed by Jehovah, or the Lord, was a common form of speech, it was therefore common also to say 'Blessed be Jehovah.' As in David: *Blessed be Jehovah, because He hath heard the voice of my supplications* (Ps. xxviii. 6). Again: *Blessed be Jehovah, for He hath made*

His mercy wonderful to me (Ps. xxxi. 21)." (*Heavenly Arcana*, n. 1422.2-3)

And as for me, I said in my haste, I am cut off from in front of Your eyes:
Surely You heard the voice of my supplications when I cried to You.
Love Jehovah, all ye His merciful ones:
Jehovah preserves the faithful and plentifully repays the proud doer.
Persevere and He shall encourage your heart,
All ye who hope for Jehovah. (Ps. 31:22-24)

To be "cut off in front of Your eyes" is be cut off from Divine truth or Divine foresight (see Ps. 17:6) as eyes signify spiritual understanding of the truth (see Ps. 11:4, 13:3, 31:9, 69:23); to hear signifies Divine providence against evil (see Ps. 17:6). Jehovah is the Lord as to Divine love (see Ps. 18:31, 28:1, 68:26, 82:1, 147:7) and the merciful ones are those who are in the good of love (see Ps. 25:10, 26:3, 36:5, 89:14, 103:8); the faithful are those who are in the truths of faith; one's recompense is eternal life in heaven according to how one lived their life (see Ps. 109:20). A "proud doer" here has the sense of one who does according to love. To persevere is to have power from truth; to be encouraged in heart is to be strengthened in the will to do good for heart signifies the will (see Ps. 7:9, 22:10, 24:4, 51:10, 64:6, 66:18, 71:23, 78:8, 86:11); hope is given to those who are in the good of faith (see Ps. 33:22).

Psalm 32

Of David, Maschil.

~

Happy is he whose transgression is forgiven, (1)
Whose sin is covered.
Happy is the Man to whom Jehovah reckons not iniquity, (2)
In whose spirit there is no deceit.
When I held my peace, (3)
My bones waxed old through my roaring all day.
For day and night Your hand was heavy upon me, (4)
It is turned *to my devastation* in the drought of summer. (Selah)
    I acknowledge my sin to You, (5)
    And I have not covered up my iniquity.
    I said, I will confess my transgressions unto Jehovah,
    And You forgave the iniquity of my sin. (Selah)
    Due to this shall every one who is merciful pray to You at a time of
    finding, (6)
    Surely in the overflowing of many waters they shall not touch him.
    You are a hiding place for me, (7)
    You shall preserve me from adversity,
    You shall compass me about with shouts of deliverance. (Selah)
        I will give prudence to you and direct you in the way which you
        shall go, (8)
        I will counsel you with My eye upon you.
        Be ye not as the horse, as the mule which have no
        understanding, (9)
        Whose *pleasure* must be held in with bit and bridle, lest they
        come near to you.

Much suffering shall be to the wicked, (10)
But he who trusts in Jehovah, mercy shall compass him about.
Rejoice in Jehovah and be glad, ye righteous, (11)
And shout for joy all ye who are upright in heart.

Psalm Commentary   32

Summary: One is happy who repents and turns away from evil (v. 1-2). The grievousness of temptations (v. 3-4). Confession of sins and deliverance from them (v. 5-7). From this is wisdom and enlightenment (v. 8-9). Let there be trust in the Lord (v. 10-11).

Happy is he whose transgression is forgiven,
Whose sin is covered.
Happy is the Man to whom Jehovah reckons not iniquity,
In whose spirit there is no deceit. (Ps. 32:1-2)

Happiness is the happiness of eternal life and from affections of love and charity (see Ps. 1:1). Transgression is evil done against the truth of faith, and sin is evil done against good of love (see Ps. 25:7, 32:1, 51:1-3). Iniquity is evil done against the good of faith (see Ps. 51:1-3) and deceit is to intentionally persuade others of falsehood against the truth (see Ps. 5:6). Sins, iniquities and transgressions are only forgiven and removed through repentance, which is done by acknowledgment of the sin and desisting from the evil.

"Mention is made of transgression and also of sin, because of the marriage of truth and good in everything of the Word; for transgression signifies evil against truth, which is less, and sin, evil against good, which is more grievous; hence it is that both are spoken of — as also in other passages: Jacob said to Laban, *What is my transgression? what is my sin? that thou hast pursued after me* (Gen. xxxi. 36). In Isaiah: *I will blot out as a thick*

427

cloud thy transgressions, and as a cloud thy sins (xliv. 22). In
Ezekiel: *In his transgression that he hath transgressed, and in
his sin that he hath sinned, in them shall he die* (xviii. 24). Again:
*In that your transgressions are discovered, so that in all your
doings your sins may appear* (xxi. 24). And in David: *Blessed
is he whose transgression is forgiven, whose sin is covered* (Ps.
xxxii. 1)." (*Heavenly Arcana*, n. 6563)

For the second verse angels explained to Swedenborg the
spiritual sense from the letters and syllables of the Hebrew
alone:

"[Angels] explained to me the meaning of the Word in Psalm
xxxii. 2, from the letters or syllables alone; showing that the sum
of their meaning was *that the Lord is merciful even to those who
do evil.*" (*Doctrine concerning Sacred Scripture*, n. 90)

When I held my peace,
My bones waxed old through my roaring all day. (Ps. 32:3)

To hold one's peace is to not acknowledge the truth (see
Ps. 28:1) by confessing one's sin (see v. 5). For bones to wax old
is for knowledges of truth to become dissipated due to the falsehood of sin (Ps. 22:14,17, 34:20, 35:10). Roaring is grief from a
desolation of truth:

"*And cried out with a great voice, as a lion roareth,* signifies
the testification of grievous distress on account of the desolation
of Divine truth in the church. This is evident from the signification of 'crying out with a great voice,' as being the testification of
grievous distress (of which presently); and from the signification
of 'as a lion roareth,' as being on account of the desolation of
Divine truth in the church; for a 'lion' signifies Divine truth in
its power (see above, n. 278), and 'to roar' signifies the result of
distress because of the desolation of truth... In *Isaiah:*—

*The anger of Jehovah is kindled against His people. He hath
lifted up an ensign to the nations from far, and hath hissed
to him from the end of the earth. His roaring is like that of a
lion, He roareth like young lions; He growleth and seizeth the
prey, he shall snatch and none shall deliver, and he growleth*

*against him like the growling of the sea; and if He shall look
unto the earth, behold darkness and distress, and the light
is darkened in the ruins thereof* (v. 25-30).

Here, too, 'the roaring like that of a lion, and like that of young
lions,' signifies grief and lamentation over the vastation of
Divine truth in the church by the falsities of evil. 'He seizeth
the prey and none shall deliver' signifies the deliverance and
salvation of those who are in truths from good. The vastation
itself is described by 'behold darkness, distress, and the light
is darkened in the ruins thereof;' 'darkness' meaning falsities;
'distress' evil; 'the darkening of the light' the disappearance of
Divine truth, and 'ruins' total overthrow. In *David:*—

> *The enemy hath destroyed all things in the sanctuary; the
> adversaries have roared in the midst of thy feast* (Ps. lxxiv.
> 3, 4).

'The enemy' signifies evil from hell; 'the sanctuary' the church,
and 'feast' worship. This makes clear what is signified by these
words in series. That roaring signifies grievous lamentation
from grief of heart can be seen from these passages. In *David:*—

> *When I kept silence my bones waxed old through my roaring
> all the day* (Ps. xxxii. 3).

In the same:—

> *I am weakened and crushed exceedingly; I have roared by
> reason of the roaring of my heart* (Ps. xxxviii. 3).

And in *Job:*—

> *My sighing cometh before bread, and my roarings are
> poured out like the waters* (iii. 24)." (*Apocalypse Explained*,
> n. 601.1, 16-17)

*For day and night Your hand was heavy upon me,
It is turned to my devastation in the drought of summer.* (Ps. 32:4)

Day and night signify states of enlightenment and obscurity as to truth (see Ps. 3:8, 16:7, 74:16, 91:6, 104:20, 136:9); for the hand to be heavy is to be oppressed in temptation due to the stubbornness of the will (see Ps. 4:2, 144:8) as things of weight signify one's state as to good or evil (see Ps. 38:4, 62:9, 69:1). The word for devastation is similar to the name of Shaddai, which signifies a state of temptation (see Ps. 68:14). The word can possibly be read as "field," which signifies the good of life conjoined with doctrine (see Ps. 8:7, 78:12, 96:12). Summer and winter refer to changing states of the will as they relate to heat. A "drought of summer" signifies a state of temptation as to the will.

"That day and night signify the state of the same, that is, the regenerate man, as to what is of the understanding, the alternations of which are as day and night, is evident from what has now been said. Summer and winter are predicated of what is of the will, from their cold and heat; for so it is with the will. But day and night are predicated of what is of the understanding, from their light and darkness; for so it is with the understanding." (*Heavenly Arcana*, n. 936)

I acknowledge my sin to You,
And I have not covered up my iniquity.
I said, I will confess my transgressions unto Jehovah,
And You forgave the iniquity of my sin. (Ps. 32:5)

Sin is evil against the good of love from a depraved will; iniquity is evil against the good of faith; and transgression is evil against the truth of faith (see Ps. 5:10, 25:7, 32:1, 51:1-3). To acknowledge is to acknowledge from the truth of thought; to confess is to acknowledge from the heart (see Ps. 7:17, 35:18, 89:24).

Due to this shall every one who is merciful pray to You at a time of finding,
Surely in the overflowing of many waters they shall not touch him. (Ps. 32:6)

Those who are merciful are in the good of love (see Ps. 25:10, 26:3, 36:5, 89:14, 103:8) who are those who find the Lord in prayer. As waters signify truths or falsehoods, a flood of great waters signifies temptations of falsehoods (see Ps. 18:4, 42:7, 69:1, 124:4). This is the spiritual meaning of the flood of Noah by which the antediluvians had perished, which Swedenborg had directly experienced:

"It has been granted me to learn by experience what a flood or deluge is in the spiritual sense. Such a flood is two-fold, one of lusts, and the other of falsities. The one of lusts belongs to the voluntary part, and is on the right side of the brain; but the one of falsities belongs to the intellectual part, in which is the left side of the brain. When a man who has lived in good is let back into his self-hood, thus into the sphere of his very life, there then appears a flood as it were. When he is in that flood, he is indignant, angry, thinks restlessly, desires impetuously. It is one way when the left side of the brain where there are falsities is flooded, and another when the right side where evils are is flooded. When however the man is kept in the sphere of life which he had received from the Lord by regeneration, he is then entirely out of such flood, and is as it were in a serene and sunny, cheerful and happy state, thus far from indignation, anger, unrest, passions, and the like. This is the morning or springtime of spirits; the other is their evening or autumn. It was given me to perceive that I was out of the flood, and this for quite a long time, while I saw that other spirits were in it. Afterward however I myself was immersed, and then I noticed the appearance of a flood. In such a flood are they who are in temptations. By it too I was instructed what the deluge signifies in the Word — that the last posterity of the most ancient people, who were of the Lord's celestial church, were completely flooded with evils and falsities, and so perished." (*Heavenly Arcana*, n. 5725; see also *Heavenly Arcana*, n. 739)

You are a hiding place for me,
You shall preserve me from adversity,

You shall compass me about with shouts of deliverance. (Ps. 32:7)

To be preserved from adversity is to be preserved from evil (see Ps. 3:1, 27:12), to be compassed with shouts of deliverance is to be protected from falsehood by truth as signified by deliverance (see Ps. 91:14).

I will give prudence to you and direct you in the way which you shall go,
I will counsel you with My eye upon you.
Be ye not as the horse, as the mule which have no understanding,
Whose pleasure must be held in with bit and bridle, lest they come near to you. (Ps. 32:8-9)

Prudence is wisdom from love, to direct is instruction in truth, and way is the truth itself (see Ps. 1:1, 18:42, 25:4,12, 37:23, 86:11). Counsel is guidance from Divine foresight signified by eye (see Ps. 17:6). A horse represents one's self derived intelligence (see Ps. 147:10); a mule represents one's own rational truth; pleasure is one's desire according to the love of self. The bit and bridle signifies the falsehoods which lead and direct one's understanding.

"*He shall be a wild-ass* [onager] *man.* That this signifies rational truth, which is thus described, is evident from the signification of a wild-ass, as rational truth. In the Word there is frequent mention of horses, horsemen, mules, and asses; and heretofore no one has known that they signify what is intellectual, rational, and of external knowledge. That they have such a signification will, by the Divine mercy of the Lord, be confirmed by many things in their proper places. Of the same class is the onager, for this is the mule of the wilderness, or wild-ass, and it signifies man's rational; not however the rational in its whole compass, but only rational truth." (*Heavenly Arcana*, n. 1949)

"In old times a judge rode upon a she-ass, and his sons upon young asses; for the reason that the judges represented the goods of the church, and their sons truths therefrom. But a king rode upon a she-mule, and his sons upon mules, by reason that kings and their sons represented the truths of the church (see n. 1672,

1728, 2015, 2069). That a judge rode upon a she-ass, is evident in the Book of Judges: *My heart is toward the lawgivers of Israel, that offered themselves willingly among the people; bless ye Jehovah ...ye who ride upon white she-asses, ye who sit upon carpets* (v. 9, 10). That the sons of the judges rode upon young asses: Jair the judge over Israel *had thirty sons, that rode on thirty young asses* (Judg. x. 3, 4; and in other places). Abdon the judge of Israel *had forty sons, and thirty sons' sons, that rode on seventy young asses* (Judg. xii. 14). That a king rode upon a she-mule: David *said unto them, Take with you the servants of your lord, and cause Solomon my son to ride upon the she-mule which is mine. ...And they caused Solomon to ride upon king David's she-mule, ...and Zadok the priest and Nathan the prophet anointed him king in Gihon* (1 Kings i. 33, 38, 44, 45). That the sons of a king rode upon he-mules: *All the sons of king David rose up, and rode each one upon his mule, and fled,* because of Absalom (2 Sam. xiii. 29).

"Hence it is manifest that to ride on a she-ass was the badge of a judge, and to ride on a she-mule, the badge of a king; and that to ride on a young ass was the badge of a judge's sons, and to ride on a mule was the badge of a king's sons; for the reason, as already said, that a she-ass represented and signified affection for natural good and truth, a she-mule the affection for rational truth, an ass or a young ass natural truth itself, and a mule and also the son of a she-ass rational truth." (*Heavenly Arcana*, n. 2781.6-7)

The truth by which the understanding is led is signified by a bridle:

"*And blood came out of the winepress, even unto the bridles of the horses,* signifies violence done to the Word by dreadful falsifications of truth, and the understanding so closed up thereby that man can scarce be taught any longer, and thus be led of the Lord by Divine truths. By the blood is signified violence done to the Word (n. 327), and the Divine truth of the Word falsified and profaned (n. 379): for by the blood out of the winepress is meant the grape juice and wine from the trodden clusters; and by grape

juice and wine similar things are signified (n. 316). By the bridles
of the horses are signified the truths of the Word, by which the
understanding is led; for a horse signifies the understanding of
the Word (n. 298): hence the truth by which the understanding is
led is signified by a bridle. *Even unto the bridles of the horses*, is
even into the mouth in which the bridle is inserted; and a horse
is watered and fed through the mouth; therefore it also signifies,
that such violence was done to the Word by dreadful falsifications, that man can scarce be taught any longer, and thus be led
of the Lord by Divine truths. That by which the understanding is
led is also signified by a bridle (Isa. xxx. 27, 28; xxxvii. 29): and
the Divine truth of the Word is signified by the blood of grapes
(Gen. xlix. 11; Deut. xxxii. 14); but here in the opposite sense."
(*Apocalypse Revealed*, n. 653)

Much suffering shall be to the wicked,
But he who trusts in Jehovah, mercy shall compass him about.
Rejoice in Jehovah and be glad, ye righteous,
And shout for joy all ye who are upright in heart. (Ps. 32:10-11)

Suffering is affliction from falsehoods (see Ps. 38:17); to trust
is to have confidence of the will from the good of charity (see
Ps. 33:21). Mercy is Divine love (see Ps. 25:10, 26:3, 36:5, 89:14,
103:8) from which one becomes protected from evils. To rejoice
is to have joy from love and to be glad is to be in affection for
truth (see Ps. 14:7). The righteous are those who do good (see
Ps. 14:5, 36:6, 37:6,17, 72:2, 89:14, 92:12); the upright in heart
are those who are in truth from good (see Ps. 9:8, 11:3, 25:21,
96:10, 143:10).

Psalm 33

Shout for joy in Jehovah, ye righteous, (1)
For praise is comely for the upright.
Confess unto Jehovah with harp, (2)
With a lute of ten strings make music to Him.
Sing to Him a new song, (3)
Play well with a trumpet blast.
   For the word of Jehovah is right, (4)
   And all His works are faithful.
   He loves righteousness and judgment, (5)
   The earth is full of the mercy of Jehovah.
   By the word of Jehovah were the heavens made, (6)
   And all the host of them by the breath of His mouth.
   He gathers the waters of the sea together as a heap, (7)
   He puts the depths in treasuries.
   Let all the earth fear Jehovah, (8)
   Let all the inhabitants of the world sojourn after Him.
   For He spake and it came into being, (9)
   He commanded and it stood fast.
      Jehovah nullifies the counsel of the nations, (10)
      He disallows the devices of the people.
      The counsel of Jehovah stands forever, (11)
      The devices of His heart to generation and generation.
      Happy is the nation whose God is Jehovah, (12)
      The people He has chosen for His own inheritance.
Jehovah looks from heaven, (13)
He sees all the sons of Man,
From the site of His habitation He gazes upon all the inhabitants
of the earth: (14)

Forming their hearts together, (15)
Understanding all their works.
No king is saved by the multitude of an army, (16)
A mighty one is not delivered by much power.
The horse is a false thing for victory, (17)
And by its abundant valour he shall not escape.
Behold, the eye of Jehovah is toward those who fear Him, (18)
Toward those who hope for His mercy,
To deliver their soul from death, (19)
And to keep them alive in famine.
Our soul waits for Jehovah, (20)
He is our help and our shield.
For our heart shall rejoice in Him, (21)
For we have trusted in His holy name.
Let Your mercy, Jehovah, be upon us, (22)
According as we hope in You.

Psalm Commentary

33

Summary: Praise of the Lord (v. 1-3) for the church is from Him through the Word (v. 4-9) which will continue even though evil will fight against it (v. 10-12). One is not saved through self intelligence, but through hope and trust in the Lord (v. 13-19). Acknowledgement of trust in the Lord and His mercy (v. 20-22).

Shout for joy in Jehovah, ye righteous,
For praise is comely for the upright.
Confess unto Jehovah with harp,
With a lute of ten strings make music to Him.
Sing to Him a new song,
Play well with a trumpet blast (Ps. 33:1-3)

The righteous are those who do good (see Ps. 14:5, 36:6, 37:6,17, 72:2, 89:14, 92:12) and the upright are those who are in truths from good (see Ps. 9:8, 11:3, 25:21, 96:10, 143:10). Joy is happiness from love of the will (see Ps. 14:7); praise is worship from affection for truth (see Ps. 7:17, 35:18). To confess Jehovah is to worship from affection for the good of love (see Ps. 7:17, 35:18, 50:14, 89:24); the harp is worship from spiritual truth (see Ps. 43:4, 49:4, 57:8, 71:22, 98:5, 147:7, 149:3); to make music with the lute is to worship from spiritual good (see Ps. 57:8, 71:22). To sing is to worship from spiritual good (see Ps. 57:7); a new song is glorification on account of the coming of the Lord (see Ps. 96:1); to play well with a trumpet blast is to worship from the good of love (see Ps. 47:5).

"*Sing aloud, ye righteous in Jehovah. Confess to Jehovah with the harp, sing psalms unto Him with the psaltery of ten strings. Sing unto Him a new song, play well with a loud noise* (Ps. xxxiii. 1-3).

As joy of heart is both from celestial love and from spiritual love, it is said, 'Sing aloud, ye righteous, in Jehovah, confess to Jehovah with the harp; sing psalms to Him with a psaltery of ten strings;' 'sing aloud, ye righteous,' is predicated of those who are in celestial love; 'Confess on the harp, and sing psalms with the psaltery,' of those who are in spiritual love. That those who are in celestial love are called 'righteous' see above (n. 204a), and that 'harp' and 'psaltery' are predicated of those who are in spiritual good (n. 323a, 323b); and as 'singing' means confession from the joy arising from these loves, it is said, 'Confess to Jehovah,' 'Sing unto Him a new song.' The exaltation of joy from its fullness is signified by 'play well with a loud noise.' In the same:—

> *I will praise the name of God with a song, and will magnify Him by confession* (Ps. lxix. 30).

In the same:—

> *When I shall have gone with them to the house of God, with the voice of jubilee and confession, the multitude keeping a festival* (Ps. xlii. 4).

In the same:—

> *Confess ye to Jehovah, call upon His name. Sing unto Him, sing psalms unto Him* (Ps. cv. 1, 2; cxlix. 1).

In the same:—

> *I will confess to Jehovah according to His righteousness, and I will sing psalms unto the name of Jehovah most high* (Ps. vii. 17).

In the same:—

> *My heart is prepared, O God; I will sing, and sing psalms. Awake thee, my glory; awake thee, psaltery and harp. I will*

*confess unto Thee, O Lord, among the nations; I will sing
psalms unto Thee among the peoples (Ps. lvii. 7-9).*

Because 'to sing a song' signifies confession from joy of heart, in
these passages two expressions are used, 'to confess and to sing,'
'confession and song,' 'voice of singing and voice of confession.'
(*Apocalypse Explained*, n. 326.9-10)

> "Confess unto Jehovah with the harp; sing psalms unto Him
> with the psaltery of ten strings. Sing unto Him a new song;
> play well with a loud noise. For the word of Jehovah is right;
> and His work is done in truth (Ps. xxxiii. 2-4).

As a 'harp' signifies confession from spiritual truths, it is said,
'confess unto Jehovah with the harp;' 'a psaltery of ten strings'
signifies the corresponding spiritual good; therefore it is said,
'sing psalms unto Him upon a psaltery of ten strings;' and for
the same reason also it is said, 'for the word of Jehovah is right,
and all His work is done in truth;' 'the word of Jehovah is right'
signifying the truth of good; 'His work is done in truth' signifying
the good of truth; the truth of good is the truth that proceeds
from good, and the good of truth is the good which is produced
by truth." (*Apocalypse Explained*, n. 323.3)

*For the word of Jehovah is right,
And all His works are faithful.
He loves righteousness and judgment,
The earth is full of the mercy of Jehovah.* (Ps. 33:4-5)

The "word of Jehovah" is Divine truth from Divine good, as
the word is Divine truth and Jehovah is the Lord as to Divine
good (see Ps. 18:31, 28:1, 68:26, 82:1, 147:7); right or upright also
signifies truth from good (see Ps. 9:8, 11:3, 25:21, 96:10, 143:10)
and refers to the Divine truth flowing into man as uprightness
as one lives by the truth. His works are the Divine works of good
that lead to the spiritual regeneration of man (see Ps. 107:24,
111:2,7); these are faithful or according to truth inasmuch one
follows the truth. Righteousness is good and judgment is truth
(see Ps. 36:6, 37:6, 72:2, 89:14, 92:12). The earth is the church

as to truth (see Ps. 9:8, 24:1, 60:2, 90:2, 96:13) and mercy is the Divine love (see Ps. 25:10, 26:3, 36:5, 89:14, 103:8); fullness is all truth and good of the church (see Ps. 24:1, 50:12, 89:11).

By the word of Jehovah were the heavens made,
And all the host of them by the breath of His mouth. (Ps. 33:6)

The word of Jehovah is the Divine truth from Divine good; and it is from the Divine truth from the Lord by which the spiritual heavens are created. The breath of His mouth is life from thence of which the angels are recipients (see Ps. 18:15, 51:11, 104:4, 143:10). The hosts are all the goods and truths of heaven and the church (see Ps. 103:21).

"That by the wind of Jehovah or His breath is signified the life which is of heaven, and which is of the man who is in heaven, that is, of a regenerate man, is evident in David: *By the Word of Jehovah were the heavens made; and all the host of them by the breath* [wind] *of His mouth* (Ps. xxxiii. 6)." (*Heavenly Arcana*, n. 8286.2)

"That Holy proceeding from the Lord, and flowing in through angels and spirits with man, whether manifestly or not, is the Holy Spirit with him; for it is Divine truth proceeding from the Lord that is called in the Word the holy (see n. 9680).

"For this reason it is that the Holy Spirit is called the Spirit of Truth, that it is said that *He will guide into all truth; for He shall not speak of Himself, but what things soever He shall have heard* from the Lord; and that *what He shall receive from Me* [the Lord] He shall declare (John xvi. 13, 14); and also that when the Lord departed from the disciples, *He breathed on them, and saith unto them, Receive ye the Holy Spirit* (John xx. 21, 22). Breathing signifies the life of faith (n. 9229, 9281); and hence breathing upon by the Lord signifies the faculty imparted of perceiving Divine truths, and thus of receiving that life. Wherefore also the name, spirit, is derived from blowing and from wind, because from breathing, and therefore spirit is sometimes called wind. That breathing, which is of the lungs, corresponds to the life of faith, and that the pulse, which is of the heart, corresponds to the life of love, may be seen above (n. 3883-3896, 9300, 9495).

"The same is signified by breathing into in the Book of Genesis: *And Jehovah breathed into man's nostrils the breath of lives* (ii. 7). Therefore the Lord is called, *The breath of our nostrils* (Lam. iv. 20). And because Divine truth consumes and vastates the evil, therefore it is said in David: *The foundations of the world were laid bare ...at the blast of the breath of Thy nostrils* [*nose*] (Ps. xviii. 15). And in Job: *By the breath of God they perish, and by the breath of His nostrils are they consumed* (iv. 9). And in David: *By the word of Jehovah were the heavens made; and all the host of them by the breath of His mouth* (Ps. xxxiii. 6). The Word of Jehovah is Divine truth, in like manner the breath or spirit of His mouth. That it means the Lord, is evident in John: *In the beginning was the Word, and the Word was with God, and God was the Word. ...All things were made by Him. ...And the Word became flesh, and dwelt among us* (i. 1, 3, 14)." (*Heavenly Arcana*, n. 9818.14-16)

"A word in a general sense signifies utterance of the mouth or speech; and since speech is thought of the mind uttered by vocal expressions, therefore a word signifies the thing which is thought, and hence everything which really exists and is anything is called in the original tongue a word. But in an eminent sense the Word is Divine truth, for the reason that everything which really exists and is anything, is from Divine truth. Therefore it is said in David: *By the word of Jehovah were the heavens made, and all the host of them by the breath of His mouth* (Ps. xxxiii. 6) — where the word of Jehovah is Divine truth proceeding from the Lord; the breath of the mouth of Jehovah is life thence; the heavens made by it and all the host of them are angels, so far as they are receptions of Divine truth. The heavens are angels because they constitute heaven; and since angels are receptions of Divine truth, therefore by angels in an abstract sense are signified Divine truths which are from the Lord (see n. 8192); and the host of heaven in the same sense are Divine truths (n. 3448, 7236, 7988)." (*Heavenly Arcana*, n. 9987.1)

"The Spirit of God is the Divine truth, and so too the light: the Divine truth is the Word; and therefore, when the Lord calls Himself the Word, He also calls Himself the Light (John i. 4, 8, 9). The same is also meant by these words in David: *By the Word of Jehovah were the heavens made, and all the host of them by the breath of His mouth* (Ps. xxxiii. 6). In fine, without the Divine truth of the Word, which in its essence is the Divine good of the Divine love and the Divine truth of the Divine wisdom of the Lord, a man cannot have life. Through the Word there is conjunction of the Lord with man, and of man with the Lord; and through that conjunction there is life. There must be something from the Lord, which can be received by man, by means of which there may be conjunction, and thence eternal life." (*Apocalypse Revealed*, n. 200.2; for other passages that show the "Spirit of God" is the Divine truth, see also *Apocalypse Explained*, n. 183.12)

"*Concerning the ineffable power of the Word.* Scarce any one at this day knows that there is any power in truths; for truth is supposed to be only a word spoken by some one in authority, which ought therefore to be done; consequently, to be like mere breath from the mouth, or sound in the ear; when yet truth and good are the first principles of all things in both worlds, the spiritual and the natural; and by means of them the universe was created, and by means of them the universe is preserved, and also by means of them man was made; wherefore those two are the all in all. That the universe was created by the Divine truth, is openly said in John: *In the beginning was the Word, and the Word was God ...all things that were made were made by it ... and the world was made by it* (i. 1, 3, 10). And in David, *By the Word of Jehovah were the heavens made* (Ps. xxxiii. 6). By the Word in both of these places is meant the Divine truth. Since the universe was created by this truth, therefore it is also conserved by it; for, as subsistence is perpetual existence, so conservation is perpetual creation. Man was made by the Divine truth because all things in man refer themselves to the understanding and the will; and the understanding is the receptacle of Divine truth, and the will of Divine good; consequently the human mind, which consists of those two principles, is no other than a form of Divine truth and Divine good, spiritually and naturally organized. The human brain is that form. And because the whole of man depends on his mind, all things in his body are dependencies, which are actuated by those two principles, and live from them." (*True Christian Religion*, n. 224)

Hosts signify all goods and truths of heaven, which is occasionally translated as "armies" in the following passages:

"That the goods and truths of heaven and the church are signified in the Word by armies, and in the opposite sense evils and falsities, may be evident from the passages where the sun, moon, and stars are called armies or hosts; and by the sun the good of love is signified, by the moon the truth of faith, and by the stars the knowledges of good and truth; and the contrary in the opposite sense (n. 51, 53, 332, 413). The former and the latter are called armies or hosts in these passages: *Praise Jehovah, all His hosts; praise Him, sun and moon; praise Him, all the stars* (Ps. cxlviii. 2, 3). *My hands have spread out the heavens, and I have commanded all their host* (Isa. xlv. 12). *By the Word of Jehovah were the heavens made, and all the host of them by the breath of His mouth* (Ps. xxxiii. 6). *The heavens and the earth were finished, and all the host of them* (Gen. ii. 1). *The horn of the he-goat grew even to the host of the heavens; and it cast down unto the earth from the host and from the stars; yea, it raised itself up even to the prince of the host: and the host was delivered to it on account of the continual sacrifice for transgression, because he cast down the truth to the earth: the holy one said, How long is the holy place and the host given to be trodden down?* (Dan. viii. 10-14). *Jehovah uttered His voice before His army* (Joel ii. 11). *Upon the roofs of the houses they have offered incense to all the host of the heavens* (Jer. xix. 13). *Lest thou shouldst bow thyself down and serve the sun, the moon, the stars, and all the host of the heavens* (Deut. iv. 19; xvii. 3; Jer. viii. 2): so too in Isa. xiii. 4; xxxiv. 4; xl. 26; Jer. xxxiii. 22; Apoc. xix. 14. Since the goods and truths of heaven and the church are signified by the hosts

or armies of the heavens, the Lord is therefore called Jehovah
Zebaoth, that is, Jehovah of armies or hosts; and on this account
the ministry of the Levites was called a military service (Num.
iv. 3, 23, 30, 39): and it is said in David, *Bless Jehovah, all His
hosts, His ministers that do His will* (Ps. ciii. 21)." (*Apocalypse
Revealed*, n. 447)

"'Armies' (or hosts) are frequently mentioned in the Word,
and the Lord is called 'Jehovah of Hosts or Zebaoth,' and 'armies'
there signify truths from good fighting against the falsities
from evil, and in the contrary sense falsities from evil fighting
against truths from good. Such is the signification of 'armies' in
the Word, because 'wars' in the Word, both in the histories and
prophecies, signify, in the internal sense spiritual wars, which
are waged against hell and against the diabolical crew there,
and such wars have relation to truths and goods opposing falsities and evils; this is why 'armies' signify all truths from good,
and in the contrary sense all falsities from evil. That 'armies'
signify all truths from good is evident from the sun, moon, stars,
and also the angels, being called 'the armies of Jehovah,' because
they signify all truths from good in the complex; also from the
sons of Israel being called 'armies,' because they signified the
truths and goods of the church. And as all truths and goods are
from the Lord, and the Lord alone fights for all in heaven and
for all in the church against the falsities and evils which are
from hell, so He is called 'Jehovah Zebaoth,' that is, 'Jehovah of
Hosts.' That the sun, the moon, and the stars, are called 'hosts'
is evident from the following passages. In *Moses:*—

*Thus the heavens and the earth were finished, and all the
host of them (Gen. ii. 1).*

In *David:*—

*By the word of Jehovah were the heavens made; and all
the host of them by the breath of His mouth (Ps. xxxiii. 6)."
(Apocalypse Explained*, n. 573.2-3; see also *Heavenly Arcana*,
n. 3448.5)

He gathers the waters of the sea together as a heap,
He puts the depths in treasuries. (Ps. 33:7)

The waters of the sea are general knowledges of truth (see Ps. 24:2, 69:34, 77:19, 89:25, 104:5-6,25), and also signifies the lowest heaven. The depths of the treasuries are lower knowledges from the senses, or the literal sense of the Word.

"*By the word of Jehovah were the heavens made; and all the hosts of them by the breath of His mouth. He gathereth the waters of the sea together as an heap; He giveth the deeps in treasuries* (*Ps.* xxxiii. 6, 7). 'The word of Jehovah by which the heavens were made,' and 'the breath of His mouth by which all the hosts of them were made,' signify Divine truth proceeding from the Lord 'the hosts of the heavens' are all things of love and faith 'the waters of the sea that He gathereth together as an heap' signify the knowledges of truth, and truths in general, which are together in the natural man; 'the deeps that He gives in treasuries' signify sensual knowledges (*scientifica sensualia*), which are the most general and ultimate things of the natural man, and in which at the same time are interior or higher truths, therefore they are called 'treasures.'" (*Apocalypse Explained*, n. 275.11)

"*I will dry up the sea of Babylon, and will make dry her spring: the sea shall come up upon Babylon; she shall be covered by the multitude of its billows* (Jer. li. 36, 42). By drying up the sea of Babylon, and making dry its spring, is signified to extinguish all the truth of that church from firsts to lasts. *After Jehovah shall they go, and the sons from the sea shall draw near with honor* (Hos. xi. 10). Sons from the sea are they who are in general or ultimate truths. *Jehovah, who buildeth His stairs in the heavens, and calleth the waters of the sea, and poureth them forth upon the face of the earth* (Am. ix. 6). *By the Word of Jehovah were the heavens made; He gathereth the waters of the sea together as a heap, He layeth up the deep in store-houses* (Ps. xxxiii. 6, 7). *By his rebuke I dry up the sea, I make the rivers a desert* (Isa. 1. 2: besides other places). Since by the sea Divine truths with those who are in the borders of heaven are signified, therefore by Tyre and Zidon, because they were by the sea, is signified the church as to the knowledges of good and truth: and therefore also by the islands of the sea those are signified who are in the more remote worship of the Lord (n. 34); and for that reason the sea in the Hebrew tongue is the west, that is, where the sun's light goes into its evening, or truth into obscurity." (*Apocalypse Revealed*, n. 238)

"As 'abysses' signify the hells, where and from which are falsities, so 'abysses' signify also the ultimates of heaven, where and from which are the knowledges of truth, which are the truths of the natural man. This is because the ultimates of heaven appear to be in waters, but such as are limpid and clear; for, as was said above, the atmosphere of the highest heaven is like an ethereal atmosphere, that of the middle heaven like an aerial atmosphere, and that of the lowest heaven like a watery atmosphere; this is like a watery atmosphere because the truths with those who are in it are truths of the natural man, and the atmosphere of the natural man is as it were watery. This is what gives rise to the appearances of rivers, lakes, and seas, in the spiritual world; consequently 'seas' signify also cognitions and knowledges (*cognitiones et scientifica*) in general, or in the whole complex (see above, n. 275, 342). 'Abysses' also have a like signification in the following passages. In *Moses:*—

> *Jehovah thy God bringeth thee to a good land, a land of rivers of waters, of fountains and abysses going forth from valley and mountain (Deut. viii. 7).*

(This may be seen explained above, n. 518a). In the same:—

> *God will bless Joseph with the blessings of heaven from above, with the blessings of the abyss that coucheth below (Gen. xlix. 25; Deut. xxxiii. 13).*

(This, too, is explained above, n. 448a). In *David:*—

> *By the word of Jehovah were the heavens made; and all the hosts of them by the breath of His mouth. He gathered the waters of the sea together as a heap; He giveth the abysses*

in storehouses (Ps. xxxiii. 6, 7)." (Apocalypse Explained,
n. 538.14-15)

"The church is according to the understanding of the Word,
because the church is according to the truths of faith and the
goods of charity, and these two are the universals, which are not
only spread through all the literal sense of the Word, but also
lie hidden within, like precious things in a treasury. The things
which are in its literal sense are apparent to every man, because
they present themselves directly to the eye; but the things which
lie hid in the spiritual sense are not apparent, except to those
who love truths because they are truths and do goods because
they are goods; to them the treasure is laid open, which the literal sense covers and guards; and these are they which essen-
tially make the church." (*Heavenly Arcana*, n. 244)

Let all the earth fear Jehovah,
Let all the inhabitants of the world sojourn after Him.
For He spake and it came into being,
He commanded and it stood fast. (Ps. 33:8-9)

The earth is the church as to truth and the world is the
church as to good (see Ps. 9:8, 24:1, 60:2, 90:2, 96:13); to fear is to
do according to God's will (see Ps. 2:11, 33:18, 128:1, 147:11) and
to sojourn is to be instructed (see Ps. 5:4). To speak or say (Heb.
amar) is the perception of the Divine will; to command is from
the Divine truth. Being is predicated of love; to exist or stand
fast is predicated of truth. The meaning of the word "saying"
(Heb. *amar*) depends on the context:

"Good is of love and its affections, consequently from it is perception; but truth is of faith, consequently this is of thought. The
former is signified in the historic parts of the Word by saying,
but the latter by speaking. But when saying is found alone, it
then sometimes signifies perceiving, and sometimes thinking;
because saying involves both." (*Heavenly Arcana*, n. 2619)

Jehovah nullifies the counsel of the nations,
He disallows the devices of the people.

The counsel of Jehovah stands forever,
The devices of His heart to generation and generation.
Happy is the nation whose God is Jehovah,
The people He has chosen for His own inheritance. (Ps. 33:10-12)

Counsel is falsehood derived from evil signified by nations (see Ps. 2:1, 18:43, 79:1, 80:8, 102:15, 106:5,27) which is constantly opposed by Divine good as signified by the name of Jehovah (see Ps. 18:31, 28:1, 68:26, 82:1, 147:7); the "devices of the people" are thoughts derived from falsity as signified by people (see Ps. 2:1, 3:8, 18:43, 65:7, 74:18, 102:15) which is opposed by Divine truth (see also *Apocalypse Explained*, n. 175.11, 331.11). The "counsel of Jehovah" is wisdom from Divine love and forever is eternity in the celestial heaven of love (see Ps. 145:13). The devices of His heart is Divine truth from Divine good; generation signifies eternity in the spiritual kingdom (see Ps. 14:5, 22:30, 145:13). Happiness is the happiness of eternal life (see Ps. 1:1) which is given to those who are in good signified by nation (see Ps. 2:1, 18:43, 79:1, 80:8, 102:15, 106:5,27). Inheritance refers to those who are in good from truth (see Ps. 69:35-36).

"Throughout their generations on the part of the sons of Israel. That this signifies eternity for the spiritual kingdom, is evident from the signification of generations, as what is eternal — of which in what follows; and from the signification of the sons of Israel, as the spiritual church (see n. 9340), and therefore the spiritual kingdom; for the spiritual kingdom of the Lord in the heavens is the spiritual heaven, and on earth it is the spiritual church. Generations mean what is eternal, because by them in the internal sense are meant the generations of faith and charity... and therefore the things which are of heaven and the church, which are eternal. By the sons of Israel, of whom the generations are predicated, is also signified the church (n. 9340). That by generations is signified what is eternal, is plain from the following passages in the Word — in Isaiah: *My justice shall be to eternity, and My salvation unto generations of generations. ... Awake as in the days of old, in the generations of eternities* (li. 8,

9). Again: *I will make thee an eternal excellency, a joy of genera-tion and generation* (lx. 15). Again: *The smoke thereof shall go up to eternity: from generation to generation it shall lie waste; none shall pass through it for ever and ever* (xxxiv. 10). In David: *The counsel of Jehovah shall stand to eternity, the thoughts of His heart to generation and generation* (Ps. xxxiii. 11)." (*Heavenly Arcana*, n. 9789)

Jehovah looks from heaven,
He sees all the sons of Man.
From the site of His habitation He gazes upon all the inhabitants of the earth:
Forming their hearts together,
Understanding all their works. (Ps. 33:13-15)

This concerns the Divine influx of Divine truth flowing from the Lord, first into heaven, then into sons of Man (Hebrew *adam*) who are those in spiritual truths (see Ps. 49:2, 57:4, 80:17, 89:47), then externally to those who are in truth signified by the earth (see Ps. 9:8, 24:1, 60:2, 90:2, 96:13). To form the heart is to regenerate the will as to love (see Ps. 7:9, 22:10, 24:4, 51:10, 64:6, 66:18, 71:23, 78:8, 86:11); to understand their works is to know the intentions of everyone's deeds.

No king is saved by the multitude of an army,
A mighty one is not delivered by much power.
The horse is a false thing for victory,
And by its abundant valour he shall not escape.
Behold, the eye of Jehovah is toward those who fear Him,
Toward those who hope for His mercy,
To deliver their soul from death,
And to keep them alive in famine. (Ps. 33:16-19)

A king is an internal falsehood from self-intelligence (see Ps. 2:2,10, 24:7-10, 72:11, 89:20,39, 95:3, 105:20,30, 110:5); a multitude of an army are knowledges of evil as the same word can be translated as "wealth" which signifies knowledge of good (see Ps. 49:6). Salvation is deliverance from evil which is from the mercy of the Lord alone (see Ps. 14:7, 96:2) and there is no salvation from one's self as the selfish ego is the origin of one's evil. A mighty one is one who is persuasive according to falsehood (see Ps. 21:13, 80:2) and power is the power of falsehood (see Ps. 65:6). A horse signifies one's understanding from self intelligence (see Ps. 147:10) and victory is overcoming the temptation of evil; abundant valour is power (see Ps. 18:32) to escape from evils. The eye of Jehovah is Divine foresight (see Ps. 17:6) which is upon those who live by the truth signified by fearing God (see Ps. 2:11, 33:18, 128:1, 147:11); those who hope in His mercy are those who have hope in the Lord's Divine love (see Ps. 25:10, 26:3, 36:5, 89:14, 103:8). To deliver the soul from death is to deliver one's spiritual life of the understanding signified by soul (see Ps. 22:10, 31:9, 71:23, 107:9) from falsity which leads to spiritual death (see Ps. 6:5, 9:13, 102:20, 106:28); to keep alive in famine is to be preserved from evil while lacking in knowledges of good (see Ps. 37:19, 105:16).

"*Behold, the eye of Jehovah is upon them who fear Him, to deliver their soul from death, and to keep them alive in famine* (*Ps.* xxxiii. 18, 19). 'Those who fear Jehovah' mean those who love to do His commandments; 'to deliver the soul from death' signifies from evils and falsities, and thus from damnation; and 'to keep them alive in famine' signifies to give spiritual life according to desire. A desire for the knowledges of truth and good is a spiritual affection of truth, which is given only to those who are in the good of life, that is, who do the Lord's commandments; and these, as has been said, are meant by 'those who fear Jehovah.'" (*Apocalypse Explained*, n. 386.18)

Our soul waits for Jehovah,
He is our help and our shield.
For our heart shall rejoice in Him,
For we have trusted in His holy name.
Let Your mercy, O Jehovah, be upon us,
According as we hope in You. (Ps. 33:20-22)

The soul is one's spiritual life of the understanding (see Ps. 22:10, 31:9, 71:23, 107:9). Help is Divine aid against evil (see Ps. 10:14) and a shield is truth which defends against falsity (see Ps. 144:2). The heart is one's will (see Ps. 7:9, 22:10, 24:4, 51:10, 64:6, 66:18, 71:23, 78:8, 86:11) which rejoices in happiness from love (see Ps. 14:7), for true happiness comes from love. To trust is to have confidence of the will (see Ps. 33:21) in the truth of doctrine signified by name (see Ps. 74:18, 96:2); the name can also refer to the Divine human (see Ps. 8:1). Holy is also predicated of the Divine truth (see Ps. 5:7, 65:4). Mercy is the Divine love (see Ps. 25:10, 26:3, 36:5, 89:14, 103:8) which is received according to one's reception of it in the hope of one's faith. Trust is of the will, and hope is of the understanding:

"*And he comforted them.* That this signifies hope, is evident from the signification of comforting, as allaying anxiety of mind with hope (see n. 3610).

"*And spake to their heart.* That this signifies confidence, is evident from the signification of speaking to the heart, as giving confidence, namely, that evil should not befall; for speaking is influx (see n. 2951, 5481, 5797), and heart is the will (n. 2930, 3888); thus speaking to the heart, is influx into the will, and thence confidence. From this is also plain that there is a marriage of truth which is of the understanding, and of good which is of the will, in all things of the Word; for comforting is spoken of the understanding, and speaking to the heart, of the will; therefore also his comforting them signifies hope, for this is of the understanding by truth, and his speaking to their heart signifies confidence, for this is of the will by good, inasmuch as genuine confidence cannot be given with others than those who are in the good of charity, nor genuine hope with others than those who are in the good of faith." (*Heavenly Arcana*, n. 6577-6578)

Psalm   34

Of David, when he changed his behaviour before Abimelech; who cast
him out, and he departed.

~

I will bless Jehovah at all times, (1) [*aleph*]
His praise shall continually be in my mouth.
In Jehovah my soul shall make her praise, (2) [*beth*]
The meek shall hear and rejoice.
Magnify Jehovah with me, (3) [*gimel*]
And let us exalt His name together.
I enquired after Jehovah and He answered me, (4) [*daleth*]
And He delivered me from all my fears.
They look to Him and are enlightened, (5) [*he*]
And their faces shall not be embarrassed.

    This afflicted one called and Jehovah heard, (6) [*zayin*]
    And saved him out of all his adversities,
    The angel of Jehovah encamps round about those who fear Him, (7)
    [*cheth*]
    And rescues them.
    Taste and see that Jehovah is good, (8) [*teth*]
    Happy is the mighty one who seeks refuge in Him.
    Fear Jehovah, ye His holy ones, (9) [*yod*]
    For there is no want to those who fear Him.
    The young lions shall lack and be hungry, (10) [*kaph*]
    But they who enquire after Jehovah shall not want any good.

        Come, ye sons, hearken to me, (11) [*lamed*]
        I will teach you the fear of Jehovah.
        Who is the man who delights in life, (12) [*mem*]
        Loving days to see good?

Guard your tongue from evil, (13) [*nun*]
And your lips from speaking deceit.
Depart from evil and do good, (14) [*samech*]
Seek peace and pursue it.
The eyes of Jehovah are toward the righteous, (15) [*ayin*]
And His ears are toward their cry.
The face of Jehovah is against those who do evil, (16) [*pe*]
To cut off the remembrance of them from the earth.
They cry and Jehovah hears, (17) [*tsade*]
And delivers them out of all their adversities.
Jehovah is near to those who are of a broken heart, (18) [*qoph*]
And He saves such as be of a contrite spirit.
Many are the evils of the righteous, (19) [*resh*]
But Jehovah delivers him out of them all.
He keeps all his bones, (20) [*shin*]
Not one of them is broken.
Evil shall put the wicked to death, (21) [*tav*]
And they who hate the righteous shall be guilty.
Jehovah ransoms the soul of His servants, (22) [*pe*]
And all who seek refuge in Him shall not be guilty.

Psalm Commentary 34

Summary: Song in praise of the Lord (v. 1-5) because He delivers those who trust in Him from all evil (v. 6-10). Do good and depart from evil (v. 11-14). The Lord protects the good from evil (v. 15-18). He saves the good, and the evil perish (v. 16-22).

I will bless Jehovah at all times,
His praise shall continually be in my mouth.
In Jehovah my soul shall make her praise,
The meek shall hear and rejoice.
Magnify Jehovah with me,
And let us exalt His name together. (Ps. 34:1-3)

To bless Jehovah means to acknowledge that all good and happiness originates from the Lord (see Ps. 3:8, 16:7, 21:6, 24:5, 28:6, 31:21); at all times signifies in every state (see Ps. 69:13); to praise is to worship from truth (see Ps. 7:17, 35:18). Praise is from the spiritual understanding signified by soul (see Ps. 22:10, 31:9, 71:23, 107:9); the meek are those humble at heart and thus hear from obedience (see Ps. 40:6) and rejoice from love (see Ps. 14:7). To magnify Jehovah is to worship by means of good as Jehovah is the Lord as to Divine love (see Ps. 18:31, 28:1, 68:26, 82:1, 147:7); to exalt His name is to worship be means of the Divine Human (see Ps. 8:1) or every truth of doctrine (see Ps. 74:18, 96:2).

I enquired after Jehovah and He answered me,
And He delivered me from all my fears.

455

They look to Him and are enlightened,
And their faces shall not be embarrassed. (Ps. 34:4-5)

To enquire and answer is to receive Divine influx from Divine truth (see Ps. 4:1); to be delivered from fears is to be delivered from the threats of evils. To be enlightened is to receive enlightenment from Divine truth; for the face not to be embarrassed is not have shame for doing evil against the good of faith. The word embarrassed is mentioned with the moon in Isa. 24:23, which signifies the good of faith (see Ps. 8:3, 72:5,7, 74:16, 89:37, 104:19, 136:9, 148:3).

This afflicted one called and Jehovah heard,
And saved him out of all his adversities.
The angel of Jehovah encamps round about,
Those who fear Him and rescues them. (Ps. 34:6-7)

To be afflicted is to be lacking in knowledges of the truth (see Ps. 35:10, 37:14, 40:17); to be in adversities is to suffer from evils attacking what is good (see Ps. 3:1, 27:12). Those who fear the Lord are those who do His will (see Ps. 2:11, 33:18, 128:1, 147:11) and from that are rescued from falsity (see Ps. 91:14). Those who are in good and truth are surrounded and protected by angels in the spiritual world:

"As regards temptations, they take place when man is in the process of regeneration; for no one can be regenerated, unless he also undergoes temptations, and they then arise from evil spirits who are about him. For man is then let into the state of evil in which he is, that is, in which is that itself which constitutes his proprium; and when he comes into this state, evil or infernal spirits encompass him, and when they perceive that he is interiorly protected by angels, the evil spirits excite the falsities which he has thought, and the evils which he has done, but the angels defend him from within. It is this combat which is perceived in man as temptation, but so obscurely that he scarce knows otherwise than that it is merely an anxiety; for man, especially if he believes nothing concerning influx, is in a state that is wholly obscure, and apperceives scarcely a thousandth part of the things about which evil spirits and angels are contending. And yet the battle is then being fought for the man and his eternal salvation, and it is fought from the man himself; for they fight from those things which are in man, and concerning them. That this is the case, has been given me to know with the utmost certainty. I have heard the combat, I have perceived the influx, I have seen the spirits and angels, and at the time and afterward have conversed with them on the subject." (*Heavenly Arcana*, n. 5036.2)

The "angel of Jehovah" is the Divine Human, which preexisted before Jehovah became incarnate in human form in Jesus Christ (see Ps. 57:5):

"That the redeeming Angel is the Lord as to the Divine Human, is evident from this, that by the Lord's assuming the Human and making it Divine, He redeemed man, that is, delivered him from hell; whence the Lord as to His Divine Human is called the Redeemer. That the Divine Human is called the Angel, is because the word angel means sent, and the Lord as to the Divine Human is said to be sent — as is plain from many passages in the Word of the Evangelists. And moreover the Divine Human before the Lord's coming into the world, was Jehovah Himself flowing in through heaven when He spake the Word; for Jehovah was above the heavens, but what passed from Him through the heavens, was then the Divine Human, inasmuch as by the influx of Jehovah into heaven, heaven was in the form of man, and the Divine Itself thence was the Divine man. This now is the Divine Human from eternity, and is what is called Sent, by which is meant proceeding, and is the same as Angel.

"But because Jehovah by this Divine Human of His could not flow in longer with men, since they had so far removed themselves from that Divine, therefore He assumed the Human and made this Divine, and thus by influx thereby into heaven He was able to reach even those of the human race who received the good of charity and the truth of faith from the Divine Human, which was thus made visible, and thereby deliver them from hell. Not otherwise could this have been effected; and this deliverance is called redemption, and the Divine Human Itself, which delivered or redeemed, is called the redeeming Angel.

"But it is to be known that the Lord as to the Divine Human, as well as, as to the Divine Itself, is above heaven; for He is the Sun which illumines heaven, and thus heaven is far beneath Him. The Divine Human which is in heaven, is the Divine truth which proceeds from Him, which is light from Him as from the sun. The Lord as to His essence is not Divine truth, for this is from Him as light from the sun, but He is Divine good Itself, one with Jehovah.

"The Lord's Divine Human is called Angel also in other places in the Word, as when He appeared to Moses in the bush, of which it is written in Exodus that, when Moses *came to the mountain of God, unto Horeb ...the Angel of Jehovah appeared unto him in a flame of fire out of the midst of a bush. ...Jehovah saw that Moses turned aside to see,* therefore *God called unto him out of the midst of the bush. ...Moreover He said, I am the God of thy father, the God of Abraham, the God of Isaac, and the God of. Jacob* (iii. 1, 2, 4, 6). It is the Lord's Divine Human which is here called the Angel of Jehovah, and it is plainly said that it was Jehovah Himself. That Jehovah was there in the Divine Human, may be evident from this, that the Divine Itself could not appear except by the Divine Human — according to the Lord's words in John: *No one hath seen God at any time, the only-begotten Son, Who is in the bosom of the Father, He hath declared Him* (i. 18); and in another place: *Ye have neither heard* the *voice* of the Father *at any time, nor seen His shape* (v. 37)." (*Heavenly Arcana*, n. 6280.1-4)

Taste and see that Jehovah is good,
Happy is the mighty one who seeks refuge in Him.
Fear Jehovah, ye His holy ones,
For there is no want to those who fear Him.
The young lions shall lack and be hungry,
But they who enquire after Jehovah shall not want any good.
(Ps. 34:8-10)

Jehovah is the Lord as to Divine love (see Ps. 18:31, 28:1, 68:26, 82:1, 147:7) and is thus said to be good. Taste is to learn

and perceive what is good, as eating signifies the appropriation of love (see Ps. 78:24, 128:2). The mighty are those who are
strong in the power of truth (see Ps. 21:13, 80:2) which comes to
those who seek refuge or have faith in the Lord. Happiness is
from eternal life (see Ps. 1:1). The holy ones who fear Jehovah
are those who live by the truth; those who fear who have no want
are those who are in the good of love (see Ps. 2:11, 33:18, 128:1,
147:11). The young lions are those who are lacking in interior
truths (see Ps. 91:13) and are thus hungry which is to be lacking
in good (see Ps. 34:10, 107:5,9, 146:7).

*"There is no want to them who fear Jehovah. The young lions
shall lack, and suffer hunger; but they who seek Jehovah shall
not want any good (Ps.* xxxiv. *9, 10).* Here, too, 'those who fear
Jehovah to whom there is no want,' signify those who love to
do the Lord's commandments; and 'they who seek Jehovah who
shall not want any good,' signify those who in consequence are
loved by the Lord, and receive truths and goods from Him. 'The
young lions that lack and suffer hunger,' signify those who have
knowledge and wisdom from themselves, 'to lack and suffer
hunger' meaning that they have neither truth nor good." (*Apocalypse Explained*, n. 386.19)

Come, ye sons, hearken to me,
I will teach you the fear of Jehovah.
Who is the man who delights in life,
And loves many days that he may see good?
Guard your tongue from evil,
And your lips from speaking deceit.
Depart from evil and do good,
Seek peace and pursue it. (Ps. 34:11-14)

For sons to hear signifies for those who are in truths (see
Ps. 17:14, 45:16, 127:3, 128:3,6) to come to obedience signified by
hearing (see Ps. 40:6). To be taught the fear of Jehovah is to be
led by truth to do God's will (see Ps. 2:11, 33:18, 128:1, 147:11).
In the original Hebrew life is in plural, which refers to eternal
life of the will and eternal life of the understanding; delight is

joy from love; to love many days is to be in affection for different states of truth (see Ps. 32:4, 74:16, 136:8) which leads to good. One's tongue signifies a false persuasion (see Ps. 35:28, 57:4, 140:11) which leads towards evil; lips is doctrine (see Ps. 12:4, 81:5) and deceit is to intentionally deceive. One must depart from evil before doing good; peace is a state of tranquility after having overcome the conflict of temptation (see Ps. 4:8, 29:11).

The eyes of Jehovah are toward the righteous,
And His ears are toward their cry.
The face of Jehovah is against those who do evil,
To cut off the remembrance of them from the earth. (Ps. 34:15-16)

The eyes of the Lord signify Divine foresight (see Ps. 17:6) and the righteous are those who do good (see Ps. 14:5, 36:6, 37:6,17, 72:2, 89:14, 92:12). Ears signify Divine providence (see Ps. 17:6). The face of Jehovah signifies Divine love or mercy (see Ps. 4:6, 13:1, 22:24, 27:8-9, 31:16, 67:1) which opposes evil; to be cut off is to become separated from heaven; remembrance is conjunction with the Lord (see Ps. 8:4); the earth is the church as to truth (see Ps. 9:8, 24:1, 60:2, 90:2, 96:13). In the spiritual world it is the evil who turn away their own face from the Lord (see Ps. 44:18):

"That the evil turn away their face from the Lord does not mean that they do it with the face of the body, but with the face of their spirit. Man can turn his face whatever way he pleases, since he is in a state of freedom to turn himself either towards heaven or towards hell, and moreover a man's face is taught to deceive for the sake of the appearance before the world; but when man becomes a spirit, which he does immediately after death, then he who had lived in evils turns the face altogether away from the Lord... This is what is meant by 'they have turned unto Me the back of the neck, and not the face,' and 'they have become turned backwards and not forwards.' And because such then come into the evil of punishment and hell, those who have turned themselves away suppose that this is from the Lord, and that He regards them with a stern countenance, and casts them down into hell, and punishes them just as an angry man would do, when yet the Lord regards no one in any other way than from love and mercy. It is from that appearance that these things are said in the Word... In *David:*—

> *It is burned with fire, it is cut down; they have perished at the rebuke of Thy faces (Ps. lxxx. 16).*

In the same:—

> *The faces of Jehovah are against them who do evil, to cut off the remembrance of them from the earth (Ps. xxxiv. 16)."* (*Apocalypse Explained*, n. 412.21; see also Ex. 20:35, 23:20-21; Num. 10:35; Rev. 20:11)

To be cut off signifies to be separated from heaven due to evil. The same word has the opposite sense meaning to make (or ratify) a covenant which signifies conjunction with the Lord through love (see Ps. 25:10, 89:3,28, 105:8, 111:9):

"*That soul shall be cut off from Israel.* That this signifies that he shall be separated from those who are of the spiritual church and that he shall be condemned, is evident from the signification of being cut off, as being separated and also condemned; and from the representation of the sons of Israel, as those who are of the spiritual church" (*Heavenly Arcana*, n. 7889)

They cry and Jehovah hears,
And delivers them out of all their adversities.
Jehovah is near to those who are of a broken heart,
And He saves such as be of a contrite spirit. (Ps. 34:17-18)

To cry is to have grief on account of falsehood (see Ps. 9:12); to be delivered from adversities is to be delivered from evils (see Ps. 3:1, 27:12). Those who have a broken heart are in grief of the will due to evil, signified by heart (see Ps. 7:9, 22:10, 24:4, 51:10, 64:6, 66:18, 71:23, 78:8, 86:11); those who have a contrite spirits are those who acknowledge the falsehoods of their own understanding. Contrite can also be translated as crushed, which is to be in a state of temptation where there is a lack of influx from heaven (see Ps. 44:19). To come near signifies the conjunction and presence of the Lord (see Ps. 65:4, 69:18):

"That coming near is conjunction and presence, is because in the other life the distances of one from another are altogether according to the differences and diversities of the interiors which are of thought and affection (n. 1273-1277, 1376-1381, 9104). Moreover withdrawing from the Lord and drawing near to Him are just according to the good of love and thence of faith from Him and to Him. For this reason the heavens are near to the Lord according to goods, and on the other hand the hells are remote from the Lord according to evils. Thus it is plain why it is that to be nigh and to draw near mean in the spiritual sense to be conjoined — as also in the following passages: *Jehovah is nigh unto all them who call upon Him, that call upon Him in truth* (Ps. cxlv. 18) — where being nigh stands for being present and being conjoined. Again: *Blessed is he whom Thou choosest, and causest to approach; he shall dwell in Thy courts* (Ps. lxv. 4) — where causing to approach stands for being conjoined. Again: *O Jehovah, draw nigh unto my soul ...deliver me* (Ps. lxix. 18). Again: *Jehovah is nigh unto them who are broken in heart* (Ps. xxxiv. 18)." (*Heavenly Arcana*, n. 9378.3)

Many are the evils of the righteous,
But Jehovah delivers him out of them all.
He keeps all his bones,
Not one of them is broken. (Ps. 34:19-20)

Those who remove evils come into doing good signified by righteousness (see Ps. 14:5, 36:6, 37:6,17, 72:2, 89:14, 92:12), for one can only do good only after having first removed any opposing evil. The Lord delivers from evils to those who repent. In the highest sense this refers to the purification of the evils in the Lord's external human form before it was made one with the Divine. Bones are external knowledges of the truth (see Ps. 22:14, 35:10); for them not to be broken is for them not to be destroyed by falsities. This was fulfilled in a literal sense when not one bone of Jesus was broken on the cross (see John 19:26); which spiritually signifies that the Jews were unable to destroy the Divine truth.

"*Neither shall ye break a bone thereof.* That this signifies that truth of knowledge also must be sound, is evident from the signification of bone, as the ultimate in which interior things terminate as on their base, that they may be supported and not part asunder. Such an ultimate in spiritual things is the truth of outward knowledge; for all spiritual truths and goods flow down according to order to lower forms, and terminate at length in those of outward knowledge, where they present themselves visibly to man. That not breaking it means that it must be sound, is plain. The knowledge is said to be sound when it admits into itself nothing but truths which agree with its good; for the outward knowledge is the general receptacle. Moreover outward knowledges are like the bones in a man: if these are not sound, or in their proper order, as when disjointed or distorted, the form of the body is changed thereby, and accordingly the actions. Truths of knowledge are doctrinal tenets." (*Heavenly Arcana*, n. 8005)

"To break the bones means to destroy the truths from the Divine which are the last in order, and on which interior truths and goods rest, and by which they are supported; for if these are destroyed, the interior which are built upon them fall also. Truths that are last in order are the truths of the literal sense of the Word, within which are the truths of the internal sense and upon which these latter rest as columns upon their bases. That bones mean truths maybe seen above (n. 3812, 6592, 8005). From these things it is plain what was represented and signified by what is written concerning the Lord, in John: *When they came to Jesus, and saw that He was dead, they brake not His legs. ... For this came to pass, that the Scripture might be fulfilled, A bone of Him shall not be broken* (xix. 33, 36.). The reason was that He was Divine truth itself both in the first and in the last of its order." (*Heavenly Arcana*, n. 9163.4)

Evil shall put the wicked to death,
And they who hate the righteous shall be guilty.
Jehovah ransoms the soul of His servants,

And all who seek refuge in Him shall not be guilty. (Ps. 34:21-22)

Evil leads to death which is spiritual death, or separation from heaven (see Ps. 6:5, 9:13, 33:19, 102:20, 106:28). The nature of evil is to hate what is good signified by the righteous (see Ps. 14:5, 36:6, 37:6,17, 72:2, 89:14, 92:12). To ransom is to deliver from falsity (see Ps. 25:22, 26:11, 31:5, 49:15, 69:18, 71:23, 119:134, 130:7); the soul is one's spiritual life of the understanding (see Ps. 22:10, 31:9, 71:23, 107:9); servants are those who live by the truth (see Ps. 31:16, 69:36, 78:70, 89:3,20). Those who seek refuge in the Lord are those in the good of love who are protected; guilt is the imputation of sin:

"That guilt is the blame or imputation of sin and of transgression against good and truth, may be evident from the passages of the Word where guilt is mentioned, and also described — as in Isaiah: *It pleased Jehovah to bruise Him, and He hath made Him weak: if thou shalt make His soul an offering for sin, He shall see His seed, He shall prolong His days, and the pleasure of Jehovah shall prosper in His hand* (liii. 10) — where the Lord is treated of; to make His soul an offering for sin means sin imputed to Him, thus blame by those who hated Him; not that in Himself He contracted anything of sin, that He should take it away. In Ezekiel: *Thou art become guilty through thy blood that thou hast shed, and art defiled in thine idols which thou hast made* (xxii. 4) — where shedding blood signifies offering violence to good (n. 374, 376, 1005), whence comes guilt. In David: *They that hate what is just shall have guilt, Jehovah redeemeth the soul of his servants; and none of them who trust in Him shall have guilt* (Ps. xxxiv. 21, 22). Thus guilt stands for all sin, which remains; its separation by good from the Lord is redemption, which was also represented by the expiation made by the priest, when they offered the sacrifice of guilt — as we read in Leviticus (vi. 1-26; vii. 1-10; xix. 20-22; Numb. v. 1-8)" (*Heavenly Arcana*, n. 3400)

Psalm 35

Of David.

~

Argue, Jehovah, with those who argue with me, (1)
Fight with those who fight with me.
Take hold of shield and scale armour, (2)
And arise in my help.
And draw out the spear, (3)
And close in against those who pursue me,
Say to my soul, I am your salvation.
Let them be ashamed and dishonoured who seek my soul, (4)
Let them be turned back and embarrassed who devise my evil.
Let them be as chaff before the wind, (5)
And let the angel of Jehovah push them away.
Let their way be dark and slippery, (6)
And let the angel of Jehovah pursue them.
For without cause have they hid for me a pit of their net, (7)
Without cause they have dug for my soul.
Let devastation which he knows not come upon him, (8)
And let his net that he has hid catch himself,
Into devastation let him fall.
And my soul shall be glad in Jehovah, (9)
It shall rejoice in His salvation.

All my bones shall say, Jehovah, who is like You, (10)
Delivering the afflicted from him who perseveres after him,
And the afflicted and the needy from him who robs him?
Witnesses of violence rose up, (11)
They asked me of what I knew not.
They repaid me evil instead of good, (12)
It was a bereavement to my soul.

And as for me, when they were sick, my clothing was sackcloth, (13)
I humbled my soul with fasting,
And my prayer returned upon my own bosom.
I walked as though *he were* a neighbour, as a brother to me, (14)
I was stooped down in black as one who mourns a mother.
But in my limping they rejoiced and gathered themselves
together, (15)
The lame gathered themselves together against me, and I knew not.
They rent and were not silent with profane scorners in *scorn*, (16)
They gnashed upon me with their teeth.
    Lord, how long will You look on? (17)
    Turn away my soul from their devastations,
    My only begotten from the young lions.
    I will confess You in the great assembly, (18)
    I will praise You with numerous people.
    Let not those who are falsely my enemies rejoice over me, (19)
    Who hate me without cause, who wink the eye.
    For they speak not peace, (20)
    And they devise deceitful words against those who are in repose
    in the land.
    And they widened their mouth against me, (21)
    They said, Aha, aha, our eye has seen it.
You have seen, Jehovah, hold not Your peace, (22)
Lord, be not far from me.
Stir up Yourself, and awake to my judgment, (23)
To my argument, my God and my Lord.
Judge me, Jehovah my God, according to Your righteousness, (24)
And let them not rejoice over me.
Let them not say in their heart, Ah, our soul: (25)
Let them not say, We have swallowed him up.
Let them be ashamed and embarrassed together who rejoice at my
evil: (26)
Let them be clothed with shame and dishonour who magnify them-
selves against me.
Let them shout for joy, and rejoice, who delight in my righteousness: (27)
And let them say continually, Let Jehovah be magnified,
Who has delight in the peace of His servant.
And my tongue shall meditate of Your righteousness, (28)
Your praise every day.

Psalm Commentary

35

Summary: The combats of the Lord against the hells, and their subjugation and overthrow (v. 1-9). They purpose putting Him to death for desiring their good, which causes Him grief (v. 10-16). Prayer that He may be preserved from them, whence He will have joy (v. 17-18) but they blaspheme Him (v. 19-21). From His Divine He will overcome them, hence the righteousness of the Lord will be praised in song (v. 22-28).

Argue, Jehovah, with those who argue with me:
Fight with those who fight with me. (Ps. 35:1)

To argue is to defend against falsity to be liberated from it; to fight is to fight against evils.

"*Jehovah ...shall thoroughly plead their cause, that He may give rest to the earth* (1. 34) — where pleading or disputing their cause stands for defending truths against falsities and liberating; the earth stands for the church, which has rest when it is in good and thereby in truths. Again: *O Lord, Thou hast pleaded the causes of my soul; Thou hast liberated my life* (Lam. iii. 58) — where pleading the causes of the soul stands for defending and liberating from falsities. In David: *Plead Thou my cause, and redeem me: quicken me according to Thy word* (Ps. cxix. 154) — where also pleading my cause means liberating from falsities. In Micah: *Contend Thou with the mountains, and let the hills hear Thy voice* (vi. 1) — where contending with the mountains stands for contending and defending against the self-exalted and also

467

against the evils of self-love. The hills which are to hear His voice are the humble and those who are in charity. In Isaiah: *I will not contend for ever, neither will I be always wroth* (lvii. 16) — where contending, or disputing, means contending against falsities." (*Heavenly Arcana*, n. 9024.3)

Take hold of shield and scale armour,
And arise in my help,
And draw out the spear, and close in against those who pursue me:
Say to my soul, I am your salvation. (Ps. 35:2-3)

A shield signifies truth which protects against falsehood (see Ps. 144:2) and scale armour is truth which protects against falsehoods which attack good (see Ps. 5:12); help is aid from Divine mercy against evil (see Ps. 10:14). A spear is protection in general. To say signifies perception of the will (see Ps. 33:9) and the soul is one's spiritual life of the understanding (see Ps. 22:10, 31:9, 71:23, 107:9); salvation is deliverance from evil by Divine mercy (see Ps. 14:7, 96:2). In the following passage scale armour is translated as "buckler," but Swedenborg notes that it was something that protected the entire body:

> "*Strive, O Jehovah, with them who strive with me, fight against them who fight against me, take hold of shield and buckler and rise up for mine help, draw out the spear, and stop the way against my pursuers; say unto my soul, I am thy salvation* (Ps. xxxv. 1-3).

Here 'to fight,' 'to take hold of shield and buckler,' and 'to draw out the spear,' does not mean to grasp these arms of war, since this is said of Jehovah, but it is so said because all arms of war signify such things as pertain to spiritual war. A 'shield,' because it protects the head, signifies protection against the falsities that destroy the understanding of truth; a 'buckler,' because it protects the breast, signifies protection against the falsities that destroy charity, which is the will of good; and a 'spear,' because it protects all parts of the body, signifies protection in general. Because such things are signified it is added, 'say unto my soul, I am thy salvation.'" (*Apocalypse Explained,* n. 734.7)

Let them be ashamed and dishonoured who seek my soul:
Let them be turned back and embarrassed who devise my evil.
(Ps. 35:4)

Those who seek after the soul are falsehoods which oppose the spiritual life of the understanding signified by soul (see Ps. 22:10, 31:9, 71:23, 107:9); those who devise evil concern evils of the will. To be ashamed is to have shame due to being destitute of good; to be dishonoured is to be destitute of truth; to be turned back is to turn back towards the love of self away from love of the Lord (see Ps. 34:16, 44:18); to be embarrassed is to have shame for doing evil against the good of faith (see Ps. 34:5). Shame and dishonour are mentioned together in the following passage, where the word for dishonour is translated as "confounded:"

> "*The wind shall feed all thy shepherds, and thy lovers shall go into captivity; then shalt thou be ashamed and confounded for all thy wickedness (Jer. xxii. 22).*

'Shepherds' in an abstract sense signify the goods of the church, and 'lovers' its truths; the 'wind' that shall feed the shepherds signifies the hollowness and emptiness of doctrine; the 'captivity' into which the lovers shall go signifies a *shutting* out from all truths and from the understanding of them; 'to be ashamed and confounded' signifies to be destitute of all good and truth; for thus, when they come among the angels, are they ashamed and confounded." (*Apocalypse Explained,* n. 811.13)

Let them be as chaff before the wind:
And let the angel of Jehovah push them away.
Let their way be dark and slippery:
And let the angel of Jehovah pursue them. (Ps. 35:5-6)

Chaff is external life in which there is no charity (see Ps. 1:4); wind is the influx of the Divine truth which judges the evil (see Ps. 18:15, 48:7, 78:26, 83:15); the angel of Jehovah is the Divine Human (see Ps. 34:7, 57:5) which opposes the evil to protect the good. A way represents truth but in the opposite sense falsity (see Ps. 1:1, 18:42, 25:4,12, 37:23, 86:11); to be dark is to be in the falsity of ignorance (see Ps. 18:28, 104:20); to be slippery is the falsity that leads to evil.

For without cause have they hid for me a pit of their net,
Without cause they have dug for my soul.
Let devastation which he knows not come upon him,
And let his net that he has hid catch himself:
Into devastation let him fall. (Ps. 35:7-8)

A net represents external material desires (see Ps. 10:9) from which one becomes captivated in falsehood signified by a pit (see Ps. 28:1, 69:15, 88:4,6). To dig a pit for the soul is to prepare internal falsehood which entrap the soul, which is one's life from the spiritual understanding (see Ps. 22:10, 31:9, 71:23, 107:9). Devastation is destruction from one's own evil; to fall into one's net is to be allured by material things; to fall is to pervert the truth (see Ps. 7:15).

And my soul shall be glad in Jehovah:
It shall rejoice in His salvation.
All my bones shall say, Jehovah, who is like You,
Delivering the afflicted from him who perseveres after him,
And the afflicted and the needy from him who robs him?
(Ps. 35:9-10)

The soul is one' spiritual life from the understanding (see Ps. 22:10, 31:9, 71:23, 107:9); to be glad is to have affection for truth (see Ps. 14:7); to rejoice is to have joy from love (see Ps. 14:7); salvation is deliverance from evil from Divine mercy (see Ps. 14:7, 96:2). Bones signify external knowledge of the truth (see Ps. 22:14,17, 34:20); to say who is like Jehovah is to acknowledge only one God (see Ps. 77:13, 88:6). The afflicted are those lacking in knowledges of the truth (see Ps. 37:14, 40:17) and the needy are those lacking in good (see Ps. 37:14, 40:17, 109:16, 113:7); the one who perseveres are those who have power from truth; the one who robs are those who seek to take away good (see Ps. 68:12, 76:5, 104:21). In the below passage the word afflicted is translated as needy, and needy as poor:

"*All my bones shall say, O Jehovah, who is like unto Thee, which deliverest the needy from him who is stronger than he, yea, the needy and the poor from them who spoil him?* (Ps. xxxv. 10.) Here bones are truths of knowledge (n. 8005); the needy are those who are in little truth, and the poor those who are in little of good and are infested by evils and falsities. From such infestations the needy are also called afflicted, in the original tongue, for to be afflicted means to be infested by falsities (n. 9196). Again, in like manner: *The wicked ...in the covert ...lieth in wait to catch the needy; he doth catch the needy, and draweth him into his net* (Ps. x. 9). In Isaiah: *Is not this the fast ...to break bread to the hungry? and to bring the needy that are cast out to thy house?* (lviii. 6, 7). Again: *Jehovah hath comforted His people, and will have mercy upon His needy ones* (xlix. 13). And in Zephaniah: *I will leave in the midst of thee a needy and feeble people, who hope in the name of Jehovah* (iii. 12). In these passages, the needy are those who are in ignorance of truth and desire to be instructed." (*Heavenly Arcana*, n. 9209.6)

"In the Word likewise the proprium, and indeed a proprium vivified by the Lord, is signified by bones — as in Isaiah: *Jehovah shall ...satisfy thy soul in dry places, and shall set free thy bones, and thou shalt be like a watered garden* (lviii. 11). Again: *And ye shall see, and your heart shall rejoice, and your bones shall flourish like the tender grass* (lxvi. 14). In David: *All my bones shall say, Jehovah, who is like unto Thee* (Ps. xxxv. 10). It is still more evident in Ezekiel, where it is said of bones that they should take on flesh, and breath should be put into them: *The hand of Jehovah was upon me ...in the midst of the valley, and it was full of bones. ...And He said unto me ...Prophesy over these bones, and say unto them, O ye dry bones, hear the Word of*

Jehovah. Thus saith the Lord Jehovih unto these bones, Behold I will cause breath to enter into you and ye shall live. And I will lay sinews upon you, and will bring up flesh upon you, and cover you with skin, and put breath in you, and ye shall live, and shall know that I am Jehovah (xxxvii. 1, 4-6). As seen from heaven man's proprium appears but as a bony, inanimate, and unsightly thing, and thus as in itself dead; but vivified by the Lord it appears as of flesh. For man's proprium is nothing but a dead thing; and yet it appears to him as something, indeed as everything. Whatsoever with him is living is of the Lord's life; and if this were withdrawn he would fall dead as a stone. For he is only an organ of life; and such as the organ is, such is the affection of the life. The Lord alone has proprium [or, what is truly His own]. From His proprium He redeemed man, and from His proprium He saves man. The Lord's proprium is Life; and from His proprium He vivifies man's proprium, which in itself is dead. The Lord's proprium is signified by His words in Luke: *A spirit hath not flesh and bones, as ye see Me have* (xxiv. 39). It is also signified by the command that not a bone of the paschal lamb should be broken (Exod. xii. 46)." (*Heavenly Arcana*, n. 149)

Witnesses of violence rose up:
They asked me of what I knew not.
They repaid me evil instead of good:
It was a bereavement to my soul. (Ps. 35:11-12)

"Witnesses of violence" are those in affirmation against the good of charity (see Ps. 27:12); to ask what one knew not is to falsify the truth for those in ignorance. To do evil for good is for evil to always desire to attack what is good; to bereave the soul is to remove truth from one's spiritual understanding (see Ps. 22:10, 31:9, 71:23, 107:9).

And as for me, when they were sick, my clothing was sackcloth:
I humbled my soul with fasting,
And my prayer returned upon my own bosom. (Ps. 35:13)

To be sick is to suffering from one's own evils (see Ps. 30:2). To be clothed in sackcloth means mourning on account of non-reception of the truth (see Ps. 30:11); to fast is to mourn over non-reception of good (see Ps. 34:10). Prayer is according to the good of one's life (see Ps. 4:1, 66:19, 72:15) and the bosom signifies one's own self (see Ps. 79:12). For the prayer to return signifies the wicked were non-receptive to good and did not receive the Lord.

"That the bosom is man's very self, thus his proprium, and hence appropriation and conjunction by love, is evident from the following passages: *Trust ye not in a friend, put ye not confidence in a guide; keep the doors of thy mouth from her who lieth in thy bosom* (Micah vii. 5) — where she who lieth in thy bosom, is one who is joined to another by love: hence also a wife is called the wife of the bosom of the husband (Deut. xxviii. 54; 2 Sam. xii. 8); and a husband is called the husband of the bosom of the wife (Deut. xxviii. 56); and this because the one is of the other. And in David: *My prayer shall return unto mine own bosom* (Ps. xxxv. 13) — meaning that it would return to himself. Again: *Remember, Lord, the reproach of Thy servants; how I do bear in my bosom all the great peoples* (Ps. lxxxix. 50) — meaning with himself, as his own. In Isaiah: *He feedeth His flock like a shepherd, He gathereth the lambs in His arms, and carrieth them in His bosom* (xl. 11) — where the sense is the same." (*Heavenly Arcana*, n. 6960.2)

I walked as thought he were a neighbour, as a brother to me:
I was stooped down in black as one who mourns a mother.
(Ps. 35:14)

A neighbor is one in a similar truth of faith (see Ps. 122:8) and a brother is one in the good of charity (see Ps. 22:22, 122:8, 133:1). To be cast down in black as one mourning a mother means sadness due to falsehood against the truth, as mother signifies truth conjoined to good (see Ps. 10:14, 27:10,13).

"Since in the churches before the Lord's coming, which were representative churches, mourning represented spiritual grief of mind on account of the absence of truth and good, for they mourned when oppressed by an enemy, on the death of a father or mother, and for like things, and oppression by an enemy signified oppression by evils from hell, and father and mother signified the church in respect to good and in respect to truth, because with them these things were represented by mourning, they at such times went in black. As in *David:*—

> *I say unto God my rock, why hast Thou forgotten me? Why shall I go in black because of the oppression of the enemy* (*Ps.* xlii. 9; xliii. 2).

In the same:—

> *I bowed myself in black as bewailing a mother* (*Ps.* xxxv. 14).

In the same:—

> *I was bent, I was bowed down exceedingly; I have gone in black all the day* (*Ps.* xxxviii. 6).

In *Malachi:*—

> *Ye have said, What profit is it that we walk in black before Jehovah?* (iii. 14).

In *Jeremiah:*—

> *For the breach of the daughter of my people I am broken down; I am made black* (viii. 21);

'daughter of the people' signifying the church. In *Jeremiah:*—

> *Judah hath mourned, and her gates have been made to languish, they are made black even to the earth; and the cry of Jerusalem hath gone up; for their nobles sent their little ones for water, they came to the pits and found no waters, their vessels return empty* (xiv. 2, 3).

That 'to be made black' signifies spiritual grief of mind because of the absence of truth in the church is evident from the particulars here in the internal sense; for 'Judah' signifies the church in respect to the affection of good; and 'Jerusalem' the church in respect to the doctrine of truth; 'gates' signify admission to the church. That there were no longer any truths is described by 'the nobles sent their little ones for water, they came to the pits and found no waters, their vessels return empty,' 'waters' signifying truths, and 'pits' the things that contain, which are the doctrinals from the Word and the Word itself, and in these truths are no longer seen. From this it can be seen that 'black (*nigrum*)' and 'black (*atrum*)' in the Word signify the absence of truth; and 'darkness,' 'clouds,' 'obscurity,' and many things from which blackness arises have a like signification. As in *Joel:*—

> *A day of darkness and of thick darkness, a day of cloud and of obscurity* (ii. 2)" (*Apocalypse Explained*, n. 372.6-7)

But in my limping they rejoiced and gathered themselves together, The lame gathered themselves together against me, and I knew not. (Ps. 35:15)

To be limping is to suffer from evils and the lame are those who are in evil, as legs signify one's power to do good (see Ps. 147:10). To rejoice is the joy of evil (see Ps. 14:7) against good; to gather against one who did not know is to attack those who are in ignorance of the truth.

"By the lame in the Word are also signified those who are in no good, and thence in no truth — as in Isaiah: *Then shall the prey of a great spoil be divided, the lame shall carry off the prey* (xxxiii. 23). In David: *When I am halting they are glad and gather themselves together; the lame whom I knew not gather themselves together against me* (Ps. xxxv. 15). And because such are signified by the lame, it was forbidden to sacrifice anything that was lame (Deut. xv. 21, 22; Mal. i. 8, 13); and forbidden that any one of the sons of Aaron who was lame should discharge the office of priest (Lev. xxi. 18). It is similar with the lame as with the blind, for the blind in a good sense signify those who are in ignorance of truth, and in an opposite sense those who are in falsities (n. 2383).

"In the original language the lame or halt is expressed by one word, and he who halteth by another, and by the lame in the proper sense are signified those who are in natural good into which spiritual truths cannot flow on account of natural appearances and the fallacies of the senses, and in an opposite sense those who are in no natural good, but in evil, which altogether obstructs the inflow of spiritual truth. But by him who halteth in the proper sense are signified those who are in natural good into which general truths are admitted, but not particular truths in detail, because of ignorance; and in an opposite sense those who are in evil and thus do not even admit general truths." (*Heavenly Arcana*, n. 4302.7-8)

They rent and were not silent with profane scorners in scorn,
They gnashed upon me with their teeth. (Ps. 35:15-16)

To tear or rend is to destroy what is good through falsity (see Ps. 7:2, 22:13); to not be silent is to be in falsehood (see Ps. 4:4); to gnash with the teeth is to argue against truth from falsehoods derived from external appearance (see Ps. 3:7, 57:4, 58:6):

"That teeth signify the ultimates of the life of man, which are called sensual, which when they are separated from the interiors of the mind are in mere falsities, and offer violence to truths, and destroy them, may be evident from the following passages: *My soul, I lie in the midst of lions, their teeth are spears and darts* (Ps. lvii. 4). *O God, break the teeth in their mouths, break out the great teeth of the young lions* (Ps. lviii. 6). *A strong nation hath come up upon My land, its teeth are the teeth of a lion, and it hath the great teeth of a lion* (Joel i. 6). *Jehovah, Thou breakest the teeth of the ungodly* (Ps. iii. 7). *A beast came up out of the sea, terrible, and dreadful, and strong exceedingly, which had great iron teeth; it devoured and crushed* (Dan. vii. 7). *Blessed be Jehovah, who hath not delivered us a prey to their teeth* (Ps. cxxiv. 6). Since sensual men do not see any truth in its light, but argue and wrangle about every thing as to whether it is so, and these altercations in the hells are heard out of them as gnashings of teeth, which in themselves are the collisions of falsity and truth, it is manifest what is signified by the gnashing of teeth (Matt. viii. 12; xiii. 42, 50; xxii. 13; xxiv. 51; xxv. 30; Luke xiii. 28): and in a measure what by gnashing with the teeth (Job xvi. 9; Ps.

xxxv. 16; xxxvii. 12; cxii. 10; Mic. iii. 5; Lam. ii. 16)." (*Apocalypse Revealed*, n. 435)

"Because the 'teeth' signify falsities in things most external, 'gnashing of teeth' signifies to fight with vehemence and anger from falsities against truths, in the following passages. In *Job:*—

He teareth me in his wrath, and hateth me; mine enemy gnasheth upon me with his teeth, he sharpeneth his eyes against me (xvi. 9).

In *David:*—

The halt whom I know not gather themselves together against me, they rend, nor are they silent. They gnash upon me with their teeth (Ps. xxxv. 15, 16).

In the same:—

The wicked plotteth against the just, and gnasheth upon him with his teeth (Ps. xxxvii. 12).

In the same:—

The wicked shall see and be provoked; he shall gnash with his teeth, and melt away (Ps. cxii. 10).

In *Micah:*—

Against the prophets that lead the people astray, that bite with their teeth (iii. 5).

In *Lamentations:*—

All thine enemies opened their mouth against thee, O daughter of Jerusalem, they hissed and gnashed the teeth (ii. 16).

In *Mark:*—

One said to Jesus, I have brought unto thee my son, who hath an evil spirit; and wheresoever it taketh him it teareth him; and he foameth and grindeth his teeth, and pineth away; and I spake to Thy disciples that they should cast it out, but they were not able. And Jesus said unto him, Thou

*dumb and deaf spirit, I command thee come put of him, and
enter no more into him* (ix. 17, 18, 25).

One who is ignorant of the spiritual sense of the Word might
suppose that they are said 'to gnash the teeth' merely because
they were angry and intent on evil, since men then press the
teeth together; but they are said 'to gnash the teeth' because the
endeavor to destroy and the act of destroying truths by means of
falsities are meant by it; this is said in the Word because 'teeth'
signify falsities in things most external, and 'gnashing' signifies
vehemence in fighting for them; this effort and act are also from
correspondence." (*Apocalypse Explained*, n. 556.16)

*Lord, how long will You look on?
Turn away my soul from their devastations,
My only begotten from the young lions.
I will confess You in the great assembly:
I will praise You with numerous people.* (Ps. 35:17-18)

The Lord (Hebrew *Adonai*) is Divine good in the Divine
Human (see Ps. 68:17,26, 105:21, 110:1, 114:7); the soul is the
spiritual life of the understanding (see Ps. 22:10, 31:9, 71:23)
and devastation is the destruction of truth. Young lions are interior falsehoods (see Ps. 91:13) which destroy what is good (see
Ps. 91:13), signified by only begotten. The only begotten also
refers to the only begotten Son, the incarnation of Jehovah in
human form, who was one with the Father as the body is with
its soul (see Ps. 22:20). Confession is from the love of good (see
Ps. 7:17, 89:24) and the great assembly are those in the internal
truths of the church (see Ps. 1:5, 68:26, 107:32); praise is worship
from affection for the truth (see Ps. 7:17) and "numerous people"
are also those who are in the external truths of the church (see
Ps. 2:1, 3:8, 18:43, 65:7, 74:18, 102:15):

"...confession has reference to the celestial of love, and is
distinguished from what relates to the spiritual of love; for it
is said confession and the voice of joy, confession and the voice
of them who make merry, I will confess unto Thee among the
nations, and I will sing praises unto Thee among the peoples

— confession and confessing being what is celestial, and the voice of joy, the voice of them who make merry and sing praises, being what is spiritual. It is also said, confess among the nations, and sing praises among the peoples, because nations signify those who are in good, and peoples those who are in truth (see n. 1416, 1849, 2928) — that is, those who are in celestial love, and those who are in spiritual love. In the Word, with the Prophets, two expressions for the most part occur, one having reference to the celestial or good, and the other to the spiritual or truth, in order that there may be a Divine marriage in every part of the Word, thus a marriage of good and truth... From this it is also manifest that confession involves the celestial of love, and that genuine confession, or that which is from the heart, can only be from good, the confession which is from truth being called the voice of joy, the voice of them who make merry, and that sing praises.

"So also in these passages — In David: *I will praise the name of God with a song, and will magnify Him with confession* (Ps. lxix. 30). Again: *I will confess to Thee with the psaltery, even Thy truth O my God; unto Thee will I sing with the harp, O Thou Holy One of Israel* (Ps. lxxi. 22). That singing with the harp and other stringed instruments signifies spiritual things, may be seen above (n. 418-420). Again: *Enter into His gates with confession, into His courts with praise; confess to Him, bless His name* (Ps. c. 4) — where confession and confessing proceed from the love of good, but praise and blessing from the love of truth. Again: *Respond unto Jehovah with confession; sing praises upon the harp unto our God* (Ps. cxlvii. 7). Again: *I will confess to Thee in the great congregation; I will praise thee among much people* (Ps. xxxv. 18). Again: *I will confess to Jehovah with my mouth, and in the midst of a multitude will I praise Him* (Ps. cix. 30). Again: *We Thy people and the flock of Thy pasture, will confess to Thee for ever: to generation and generation will we show forth Thy praise* (Ps. lxxix. 13). Again: *Let them confess to Jehovah His mercy, and His wonderful works to the sons of man. Let them*

sacrifice the sacrifices of confession, and declare His works with
singing (Ps. cvii. 21, 22)." (*Heavenly Arcana*, n. 3880.4-5)

Let not those who are falsely my enemies rejoice over me,
Who hate me without cause, who wink the eye.
For they speak not peace,
And they devise deceitful words against those who in repose in
the land.
And they widened their mouth against me,
They said, Aha, aha, our eye has seen it. (Ps. 35:19-21)

Enemies are external falsehoods which attack the truth (see
Ps. 3:1, 27:12); those who wink the eye are those in internal
falsehoods as the eye represents one's higher spiritual understanding (see Ps. 11:4, 13:3, 31:9, 69:23). To "speak not peace" is
to be opposed to the peaceful state of love (see Ps. 4:8, 29:11) and
to generate conflict; to devise deceitful words is to intentionally
deceive those who are in the truth, signified by land or earth
(see Ps. 9:8, 24:1, 60:2, 90:2, 96:13). To widen the mouth is to
multiply falsehoods, signified by width (see Ps. 4:1, 18:19, 31:8,
104:25), from the external understanding signified by mouth
(see Ps. 5:9, 37:30, 135:16); To say signifies perception of the
will (see Ps. 33:9); for the eye to see is for internal falsehoods to
attack the truth.

You have seen, Jehovah, hold not Your peace:
Lord, be not far from me.
Stir up Yourself, and awake to my judgment,
To my argument, my God and my Lord.
Judge me, Jehovah my God, according to Your righteousness,
And let them not rejoice over me. (Ps. 35:22-24)

To not hold peace is to is to speak the truth against falsehood
(see Ps. 28:1); the Lord (Hebrew *Adonai*) is Divine good in the
Divine Human (see Ps. 68:17,26, 105:21, 110:1, 114:7) to and to
be near is to be in a state of conjunction in good (see Ps. 34:18,
65:4, 69:18). Judgment is by Divine truth (see Ps. 36:6, 37:6,
72:2, 89:14, 92:12); argument is defense against falsehood and

to be liberated from it (see Ps. 35:1). Righteousness is to be in good from love (see Ps. 14:5, 36:6, 37:6,17, 72:2, 89:14, 92:12); to rejoice is the joy of evil to overcome good (see Ps. 14:7).

Let them not say in their heart, Ah, our soul:
Let them not say, We have swallowed him up.
Let them be ashamed and embarrassed together who rejoice at my evil:
Let them be clothed with shame and dishonour who magnify themselves against me.
Let them shout for joy, and rejoice, who delight in my righteousness:
And let them say continually, Let Jehovah be magnified,
Who has delight in the peace of His servant. (see Ps. 35:25-27)

To say signifies perception of the will (see Ps. 33:9) and is thus mentioned with heart which signifies the will (Ps. 7:9, 22:10, 24:4, 51:10, 64:6, 66:18, 71:23, 78:8, 86:11). To say "Ah, our soul" is for falsehood to overcome internal spiritual truth (see Ps. 22:10, 31:9, 71:23, 107:9); to swallow up is for falsehood to overcome external truth as signified by mouth (see Ps. 5:9, 37:30, 135:16). To be ashamed is to have shame due to committing evil against the good of love; to be embarrassed is to have shame for doing evil against the good of faith (see Ps. 34:5); to rejoice at evil is to have joy of doing evil against internal good (see Ps. 14:7); those who are clothed with shame and dishonour are those who do evil from the understanding against the good and truth of faith. The righteous are those who do good (see Ps. 14:5, 36:6, 37:6,17, 72:2, 89:14, 92:12) and rejoice from the joy of doing good (see Ps. 14:7); peace is a state of spiritual peace free from the conflict of temptation (see Ps. 4:8, 29:11); servants are those who live and do good by the truth (see Ps. 31:16, 69:36, 78:70, 89:3,20).

And my tongue shall meditate of Your righteousness,
Your praise every day. (Ps. 35:28)

Tongue signifies a principle of persuasion or confession of doctrine (see Ps. 57:4, 140:11); meditation is perception of good (see Ps. 19:14); righteousness is to do good (see Ps. 14:5, 36:6, 37:6,17, 72:2, 89:14, 92:12); praise is to worship from affection for the truth (see Ps. 7:17, 35:18); every day is in every state of enlightenment of the truth (see Ps. 32:4, 74:16, 136:8).

"That tongue, or language, in the internal sense signifies opinion, and so principles and persuasions, is because there is a correspondence of the tongue with the intellectual part of man, or with his thought, like that of an effect with its cause." (*Heavenly Arcana*, n. 1159)

"*And my tongue shall meditate of Thy righteousness and of Thy praise all the day* (Ps.xxxv. 28). Here, too, 'tongue' signifies confession from the doctrine of the church, for it is said 'to meditate of;' 'righteousness' is predicated of the good of the church, and 'praise' of its truth, as also elsewhere in the Word." (*Apocalypse Explained*, n. 455.15)

Psalm 36

To the chief musician. Of David the servant of Jehovah.

~

Transgression speaks to the wicked within *his* heart, (1)
There is no dread of God in front of his eyes.
For he flatters himself in his own eyes, (2)
Hating to find his iniquity.
The words of his mouth are iniquity and deceit, (3)
He has desisted from prudence and doing good.
He devises iniquity upon his bed, (4)
He stands upon a way that is not good, he does not reject evil.
Jehovah, Your mercy is in the heavens, (5)
And Your faithfulness reaches to the skies.
Your righteousness is like the mountains of God, (6)
Your judgments are a great deep:
You save man and beast, Jehovah.
How precious is Your mercy, God, (7)
And the sons of Man seek refuge in the shadow of Your wings.
They shall be satiated from the fatness of Your house, (8)
And You shall make them drink of the wadi stream of Your *Eden*.
For with You is the fountain of life: (9)
In Your light shall we see light.
Draw out Your mercy to those who know You, (10)
And Your righteousness to the upright in heart.
Let not the foot of pride come to me, (11)
And let not the hand of the wicked make me wander away.
There have the workers of iniquity fallen: (12)
They are pushed down, and shall not be able to rise.

Psalm Commentary

36

Summary: Hypocrites think only of evil, who are in the pride of self (v. 1-4). It should be acknowledged that all good and truth comes from the Lord (v. 5-9). Those who acknowledge the Lord possess all good and truth and will be protected from the evil, while the evil will perish (v. 10-12).

Transgression speaks to the wicked within his heart,
There is no dread of God in front of his eyes.
For he flatters himself in his own eyes,
Hating to find his iniquity.
The words of his mouth are iniquity and deceit,
He has desisted from prudence and doing good.
He devises iniquity upon his bed,
He stands upon a way that is not good, he does not reject evil.
(Ps. 36:1-4)

Transgression is evil against the truth of faith (see Ps. 5:10, 25:7, 32:1, 51:1-3) and the heart is one's will (see Ps. 7:9, 22:10, 24:4, 51:10, 64:6, 66:18, 78:8); eyes signifies understanding of the truth (see Ps. 11:4, 13:3, 31:9, 69:23) in which there is no acknowledgment of Divine truth, signified by God (see Ps. 18:31, 29:1, 68:17,24, 82:1, 95:3, 147:7). In place of God there is the falsity of the love of self, which increases towards iniquity, which is evil against the good of faith (see Ps. 51:1-3). The "words of his mouth" are false thoughts of the external understanding (see Ps. 5:9, 37:30, 135:16); iniquity is harm against the good of truth; and deceit is to intentionally deceive others (see Ps. 5:6). Prudence is wisdom from love and is thus mentioned with doing good. A bed is the lower natural (see Ps. 41:3) where there is a further derivation of iniquity, or evil against the good of faith. To "stand in a way that is not good" is to be in a falsehood signified by way (see Ps. 1:1, 18:42, 25:4,12, 37:23, 86:11) that does not lead to good by rejecting what is evil.

Jehovah, Your mercy is in the heavens,
And Your faithfulness reaches to the skies. (Ps. 36:5)

Mercy is the Divine love (see Ps. 25:10, 26:3, 89:14, 103:8) which is in the higher heavens; the lower heavens are in good from truth signified by faithfulness and are thus said to reside in the skies, which refer to the lower heavens (see Ps. 18:11).

"In David: *Thy mercy, O Jehovah, is in the heavens, thy truth even to the skies; Thy justice is like the mountains of God, Thy judgments are a great deep* (Ps. xxxvi. 5, 6). Here both mercy and justice are in like manner of love, and truth and judgments are of faith. In the same: *Truth shall spring out of the earth, and justice shall look down from heaven. Yea, Jehovah shall give good, and our land shall yield its increase* (Ps. lxxxv. 11, 12). Here truth, which is of faith, is used for judgment, and justice for love or mercy." (*Heavenly Arcana*, n. 2235.4)

"In many other passages also mention is made of judgment and justice, and by judgment is signified truth, and by justice good, as in Jeremiah: *Thus saith Jehovah, Execute ye judgment and justice; and deliver the spoiled out of the hand of the oppressor. ...Woe unto him who buildeth his house in what is not justice, and his chambers in what is not judgment. ...Did not thy father eat and drink, and do judgment and justice? then it was well with him* (xxii. 3, 13, 15) — where judgment stands for those things which are of truth, and justice for those things which are of good. In Ezekiel: *If the wicked turn from his sin, and do judgment and justice. ...All of his sins that he hath sinned shall not be remembered against him; he hath done judgment and justice; living he shall live. ...When the wicked turneth from his wickedness, and*

doeth judgment and justice, for these he shall live (xxxiii. 14, 16,
19); and in other places also (Isa. lvi. 1; ix. 7; xvi. 5; xxvi. 7, 9;
xxxiii. 5, 15; lviii. 2; Jer. ix. 24; xxiii. 5; xxxiii. 15; Hosea ii. 19, 20;
Amos v. 24; vi. 12; Ps. xxxvi. 5, 6; cxix. 164, 172). It is said judgment and justice because in the Word whenever truth is treated
of, good is also treated of, because of the heavenly marriage in
each thing therein, which is the marriage of good and truth...
Inasmuch as justice is of good, and judgment is of truth, it is also
said in other passages justice and truth (Zech. viii. 8; Ps. xv. 2;
xxxvi. 5, 6; lxxxv. 10, 11)." (*Heavenly Arcana*, n. 9263.9)

"That the Lord appears in the angelic heaven as a sun, and
that Divine truth proceeding from the Lord as a sun produces
all the light of heaven, thus all the intelligence and wisdom the
angels have, may be seen in the work on *Heaven and Hell*, n. 116-
125, and n. 126-140). It is said also that the 'air' was darkened,
meaning the light of truth, for the air gives light from the sun.
'Skies' (*aetheres*) have a similar signification in *David:*—

> *Thy mercy O Jehovah, is in the heavens; and Thy truth is
> even unto the skies* (Ps. xxxvi. 5; lvii. 10; cviii. 4).

'Mercy' signifies the Divine good of Divine love, and 'truth' Divine
truth; and as Divine truth is the light of heaven, as has just been
said, it is said, 'Thy truth is even unto the skies;' thus 'skies' in
the plural signify Divine light even to the highest heaven, where
it is in the highest degree. ("Skies" have a similar signification in
Ps. lxxvii. 17; *Ps.* lxxviii. 23, 24)." (*Apocalypse Explained*, n. 541)

Your righteousness is like the mountains of God,
Your judgments are a great deep (Ps. 36:6)

Righteousness is to be in good (see Ps. 14:5, 37:6,17, 72:2,
89:14, 92:12); mountains signify the good of love (Ps. 18:7, 36:6,
68:15-16, 72:3, 104:10, 114:4,6, 121:1, 133:3, 147:8, 148:9). Judgments are done by the Divine truth (see Ps. 36:6, 37:6, 72:2, 89:14,
92:12); the great deep are truths in general, similar in meaning
to the sea (see Ps. 24:2, 33:7, 69:34, 77:19, 89:25, 104:5-6,25).

"Jehovah, Thy righteousness is like the mountains of God; Thy judgments like a great deep (Ps. xxxvi. 6).

Because 'righteousness,' in the Word, is predicated of good, and 'judgment' of truth, it is said that 'the righteousness of Jehovah is like the mountains of God, and His judgments like a great deep;' 'the mountains of God' signifying the good of charity, and 'the deep' truths in general, which are called the truths of faith." *(Apocalypse Explained*, n. 405.20; see also *Apocalypse Explained*, n. 946.3)

You save man and beast, Jehovah. (Ps. 36:6)

Man and beast mentioned together signifies spiritual and natural affections; beasts can also signify lower natural desires (see Ps. 49:10, 73:22).

"By man and beast together is signified man as to spiritual and natural affection, in the following passages: Jer. vii. 20; xxi. 6; xxvii. 5; xxxi. 27; xxxii. 43; xxxiii. 10-12; xxxvi. 29; 1. 3; Ezek. xiv. 13, 17, 19; xxv. 13; xxxii. 13; xxxvi. 11; Zeph. i. 2, 3; Zech. ii. 7, 8; viii. 9, 10; Jonah iii. 7, 8; Ps. xxxvi. 6; Num. xviii. 15. By all the beasts which were sacrificed good affections were signified, and the same by the beasts which were eaten; and the contrary by the beasts which were not to be eaten (Lev. xx. 25, 26)." *(Apocalypse Revealed*, n. 567)

"Thy righteousness is like the mountains of God, Thy judgments are a great deep; O Jehovah, Thou preservest man and beast (Ps. xxxvi. 6). 'Man and beast' signify interior affection, which is spiritual, from which is intelligence, and exterior affection, which is natural, from which is knowledge (*scientia*) corresponding to intelligence." *(Apocalypse Explained*, n. 650.15; see also *Apocalypse Explained*, n. 1100.16-17)

"By man is signified interior good or evil because he is man from his internal man and its quality, but not from the external man; for the external man is not man without the internal; and that the external may be also man, it must be wholly subordinated to the internal, so as not to act from itself, but from the internal. By a beast is signified exterior good, and in the opposite sense exterior evil, because beasts have not an internal such as man has; the internal which they have is merged in the external, so that it is one with it, and together with it looks downward or toward the earth, without any elevation toward what is interior." (*Heavenly Arcana*, n. 7424)

"The interior good and also the interior evil which are signified by man, are what are of intention or end, for the intention or end is the inmost of man; but the exterior good and also the exterior evil which are signified by beast, are what are of the thought, and of the action thence when nothing opposes. That what is exterior is signified by beast, is because man as to his external or natural man is nothing else than a beast, for he enjoys like lusts and pleasures, and like appetites and senses. And what is interior is signified by man, because man is man as to the internal or spiritual man, enjoying there affections for good and truth, such as belong to angels in heaven, and because by that he rules his natural or animal man, which is a beast...

"Man and beast stand for interior and exterior good in the following passages: *I have made the earth, the man and the beast ...by My great power* (Jer. xxvii. 5). Again: *Behold the days come, saith Jehovah, that I will sow the house of Israel and the house of Judah with the seed of man, and with the seed of beast* (xxxi. 27). Again: The earth shall be a desolation, *without man or beast* (xxxii. 43). Again: *In the cities of Judah, and in the streets of Jerusalem, that are desolate, without man and without inhabitant and without beast* (xxxiii. 10; li. 62). In David: *Thy justice is like the mountains of God; Thy judgments are a great deep: O Jehovah, Thou preservest man and beast* (Ps. xxxvi. 6). Because such things were signified by man and beast, therefore the firstborn of the Egyptians died, both of men and beasts (Exod. xii. 29); and therefore the firstborn was sanctified, *both of man and beast* (Num. xviii. 15); and therefore also from a holy rite it was commanded by the king of Nineveh, *Let neither man nor beast ...taste anything ...but let them be covered with sackcloth* (Jonah iii. 7, 8)." (*Heavenly Arcana*, n. 7523.1,3)

How precious is Your mercy, God,
And the sons of Man seek refuge in the shadow of Your wings.
They shall be satiated from the fatness of Your house,
And You shall make them drink of the wadi stream of Your Eden.
(Ps. 36:7-8)

Mercy signifies Divine love; sons of Man (Hebrew *adam*) are
spiritual truths (see Ps. 49:2, 57:4, 80:17, 89:47); wings signify
spiritual truths which protect against falsehoods. (see Ps. 17:8,
18:10, 68:13, 91:4). Fat signifies celestial good (see Ps. 17:10,
23:5, 63:5, 65:11, 81:16, 92:14, 147:14) and a house is heaven
and the church in respect to good (see Ps. 23:6, 65:5, 105:21). To
drink is to be instructed in truth (see Ps. 78:15, 104:10, 110:7);
the stream of Eden is the spiritual truth of Divine love.

"*They shall be filled with the fatness of Thy house; and Thou*
makest them drink of the brook of Thy delights; for with Thee is
the fountain of life, in Thy light shall we see light (xxxvi. 8, 9).

'Fatness' signifies the good of love, and 'the brook of delights'
truth from that good; 'to make to drink' means to teach..." (*Apocalypse Explained*, n. 483.10)

"*And Jehovah God planted a garden in Eden, in the east,*
and there He put the man whom He had formed. By the garden
is signified intelligence, by Eden love, by the east the Lord. And
thus by a garden in Eden, in the east, is signified the intelligence
of the celestial man, which flows in through love from the Lord."
(*Heavenly Arcana*, n. 98)

"As to the signification of 'fat' — that it is the celestial itself,
which is of the Lord — the celestial is all that is of love. Faith
also is celestial when it is from love; charity is celestial; every
good of charity is celestial — all which were represented by the
fats of the sacrifices, and specially by the fat upon the liver or its
caul, the fat upon the kidneys, the fat that covers the intestines,
and upon the intestines. These were holy, and were offered up
on the altar (Exod. xxix. 13, 22; Lev. iii. 3, 4, 14; iv. 8, 9, 19, 26,
31, 35; viii. 16, 25). And they were therefore called 'the bread of
the offering by fire, for a rest unto Jehovah' (Lev. iii. 14, 16). And
on this account the Jewish people were forbidden to eat any fat

of beasts; and this was proclaimed 'a statute for ever throughout your generations' (Lev. iii. 17; vii. 23, 25). This was because that Church was such that they did not acknowledge internal, still less, celestial things.

"That fat signifies what is celestial, and the goods of charity, is evident in the prophets — as in Isaiah: *Wherefore do ye weigh silver for that which is not bread? and your labor for that which satisfieth not? Hearkening hearken unto Me, and eat ye that which is good, and let your soul delight itself in fatness* (lv. 2). In Jeremiah: *I will fill the soul of the priests with fatness, and My people shall be satisfied with My good* (xxxi. 14); where it is very evident that fatness is not meant, but celestial-spiritual good. In David: *They shall be filled with the fatness of Thy house, and Thou shalt make them drink of the river of Thy pleasures. For with Thee is the fountain of lives; in Thy light shall we see light* (Ps. xxxvi. 8, 9); where fatness and the fountain of life stand for the celestial, which is of love; the river of Thy pleasures and light, for the spiritual, which is of faith from love. In the same: *My soul shall be satisfied with marrow and fatness, and my mouth shall praise Thee with lips of songs* (Ps. lxiii. 5). Here likewise fat stands for the celestial, and 'lips of songs' for the spiritual. That it is the celestial is very evident, for the soul shall be satisfied. The first-fruits themselves, which were the first-born of the earth, were therefore called the fat (Num. xviii. 12)." (*Heavenly Arcana*, n. 353.2)

"'Fat things' signify what is good and thus satisfying, because the fat is the best part of flesh and because it resembles oil, which signifies the good of love. That 'fatness' signifies good and things pertaining to good, thus satisfactions and joys, can be seen from the following passages in the Word. In *Isaiah:*—

> *In hearkening hearken unto Me, and eat ye that which is good, that your soul may be delighted in fatness* (lv. 2),

'To eat that which is good' signifies to appropriate good to oneself; therefore 'to be delighted in fatness' signifies to be in a state of satisfaction and blessedness. In *Jeremiah:*—

*I will fill the soul of the priests with fatness, and My people
shall be satisfied with good* (xxxi. 14).

Here, too, 'fatness' signifies satisfaction and blessedness from
the good of love. In *David:*—

*With fat and fatness my soul shall be satisfied, and my
mouth will praise Thee with lips of songs* (Ps. lxiii. 5).

'To have the soul satisfied with fat and fatness' signifies to be
filled with the good of love and consequent joy; 'to praise with
lips of songs' signifies to worship by truths that gladden the
mind. In the same:—

*They shall be filled with the fatness of Thy house, and Thou
shalt make them drink of the river of Thy pleasures* (Ps.
xxxvi. 8).

The 'fatness' with which the house shall be filled signifies the
good of love and consequent satisfaction, 'house' being the things
of the mind; 'the river of pleasures' that he will make them to
drink of signifies intelligence and consequent happiness." (*Apocalypse Explained*, n. 1159.2)

*For with You is the fountain of life:
In Your light shall we see light.
Draw out Your mercy to those who know You,
And Your righteousness to the upright in heart.* (Ps. 36:9-10)

The fountain signifies truths from the Word and the Lord
(see Ps. 68:26, 87:7, 104:10, 114:8); the Lord is the source of all
life (see Ps. 27:13). Light is the Divine truth which enlightens
one's understanding (see Ps. 4:6, 11:4, 18:28, 43:3, 104:2, 139:12).
Mercy is Divine love (see Ps. 25:10, 26:3, 36:5, 89:14, 103:8);
righteousness is good derived from Divine love (see Ps. 14:5,
36:6, 37:6,17, 72:2, 89:14, 92:12); the upright are those who are
in truth from good (see Ps. 9:8, 11:3, 25:21, 96:10, 143:10).

"..."with Thee is the fountain of life" signifies that with the
Lord and from Him is Divine truth; because that is what is signified by 'the fountain of life' it is added, 'in Thy light shall we see

light,' for 'the light of the Lord' means Divine truth." (*Apocalypse Explained*, n. 483.10)

"'Life' signifies the Lord, and thence salvation and heaven, because all of life is from one only Fountain, and that only Fountain of life is the Lord, while angels and men are merely forms receiving life from Him. The Life itself that proceeds from the Lord and fills heaven and the world, is the life of His love, and in heaven this appears as light, and because this light is life it enlightens the minds of angels, and enables them to understand and be wise. From this it is that the Lord calls Himself not only 'the Life' but also 'the Light.' As in *John:*—

> *In the beginning was the Word, and the Word was with God, and God was the Word. In Him was life; and the life was the light of men. That was the true Light, which lighteth every man coming into the world* (i. 1, 4-12).

In the same:—

> *Jesus said, I am the Light of the world; he who followeth Me shall not walk in darkness, but shall have the light of life* (viii. 12).

In *David:*—

> *Jehovah, with Thee is the fountain of life, in Thy light shall we see light* (*Ps.* xxxvi. 9).

The light which is life from the Lord in heaven is there called Divine truth, because it shines in the minds of those who are there, and thence shines before their eyes. From this it is that in the Word 'light' signifies Divine truth, and intelligence and wisdom therefrom, and that the Lord Himself is called 'the Light.'" (*Apocalypse Explained*, n. 186.11)

"As He is life, and every man is a recipient of life from Him,. He also teaches that He gives life and makes alive, as in *John:*—

> *As the Father makes alive, the Son also makes alive* (v. 21).

In the same:—

> *I am the bread of God that cometh down out of heaven, and*
> *giveth life unto the world* (vi. 33).

In the same:—

> *Because I live ye shall live also* (xiv. 19).

Also in many passages, that He gives life to those who believe in Him. And for this reason God is called 'the fountain of life' (*Psalm* xxxvi. 9), and elsewhere, 'Creator,' 'Maker,' 'Former,' also 'Potter,' and we 'the clay, and the work of His hands.' As God is life, it follows that in Him we live, move, and have our being." (*Apocalypse Explained*, n. 1120.5)

> *Let not the foot of pride come to me,*
> *And let not the hand of the wicked make me wander away.*
> *There have the workers of iniquity fallen:*
> *They are pushed down, and shall not be able to rise.* (Ps. 36:11-12)

The foot signifies the external natural (see Ps. 8:6, 41:9, 49:5, 99:5, 105:18), which is in the pride of self love. The hand of the wicked is the falsity of evil as signified by hand (see Ps. 20:6, 44:3, 45:4, 80:15,17, 89:13,21, 110:1, 121:5); to wander is to not know truth and good (see Ps. 56:8). The "workers of iniquity" are those who do evil against the good of faith (see Ps. 51:1-3); to fall is to pervert the truth (see Ps. 7:15); to be pushed down is to be lowered towards hell so that they can no longer rise to attack the good.

Psalm   37

Of David.

~

Be not upset with evildoers, (1) [*aleph*]
Be not jealous against the workers of injustice.
For they shall quickly be cut down like the grass, (2)
And fade away as the greenery of tender herb.
Trust in Jehovah and do good, (3) [*beth*]
Reside in the land and shepherd faithfully.
And be content upon Jehovah, (4)
And He shall give you the requests of your heart.
Commit your way upon Jehovah, (5) [*gimel*]
And trust upon Him and He shall do it.
And He shall bring forth your righteousness as the light, (6)
And your judgment as the noonday.

~

Be silent for Jehovah, (7) [*daleth*]
And expectantly wait for Him.
Be not upset with him who prospers in his way,
With the man who executes schemes.
Cease from anger and forsake fury, (8) [*he*]
Be not upset, it is only toward evil.
For evildoers shall be cut off, (9)
But those who wait upon Jehovah, they shall possess the earth.
And yet a little while, and the wicked shall not be, (10) [*vav*]
And you shall consider his place, and it shall not be.
But the meek shall possess the earth, (11)
And shall be content in the abundance of peace.

The wicked scheme against the righteous, (12) [*zayin*]
And gnashes upon him with his teeth.
The Lord shall laugh at him, (13)
For He sees that his day is coming.
The wicked have drawn out the sword, (14) [*cheth*]
And have bent their bow,
To fell the afflicted and needy,
To butcher him who is upright in the way.
Their sword shall enter into their own heart, (15)
And their bows shall be broken.
    Better is a little that the righteous has, (16) [*teth*]
    Than the abundance of many wicked.
    For the arms of the wicked shall be broken, (17)
    But Jehovah supports the righteous.
    Jehovah knows the days of the perfect, (18) [*yod*]
    And their inheritance shall be forever.
    They shall not be ashamed in the time of evil, (19)
    And in the days of famine they shall be satisfied.
    For the wicked shall perish, (20) [*kaph*]
    And the enemies of Jehovah are like precious fattened lambs,
    They shall be consumed, as smoke they shall consume away.
        The wicked borrows and repays not, (21) [*lamed*]
        But the righteous is gracious and gives.
        For such as are blessed by Him shall possess the earth, (22)
        And they who are cursed by Him shall be cut off.
        The course of a mighty one is established by Jehovah, (23)
        [*mem*]
        And he is delighted in his way.
        Though he fall he shall not be cast down, (24)
        For Jehovah supports his hand.
I have been young, also old, (25) [*nun*]
And I have not seen the righteous forsaken,
Nor his seed begging for bread.
Every day he is gracious, and lends, (26)
And his seed is a blessing.
Depart from evil and do good, (27) [*samech*]
And reside forever.
For Jehovah loves judgment, (28)
And forsakes not His merciful ones.

They are kept forever, [*ayin*]
But the seed of the wicked shall be cut off.
The righteous shall possess the earth, (29)
And reside upon her for ever.
The mouth of the righteous meditates wisdom, (30) [*pe*]
And his tongue speaks judgment.
The law of his God is in his heart, (31)
His steps shall not falter.
The wicked watches the righteous, (32) [*tsade*]
And seeks to put him to death.
Jehovah will not forsake him in his hand, (33)
And not condemn him when he is judged.
Wait on Jehovah, (34) [*qoph*]
And keep His way,
And He shall exalt you to possess the earth:
When the wicked are cut off you shall see it.
I have seen the wicked as terrible, (35) [*resh*]
And exposing himself like a green native tree.
But he passed away, and, lo, he was not, (36)
And I sought him, but he was not found.
Take heed of the perfect and see the upright, (37) [*shin*]
For the latter end of that man is peace.
But the transgressors shall be destroyed together, (38)
The latter end of the wicked shall be cut off.
But the salvation of the righteous is from Jehovah, (39) [*tav*]
He is their stronghold in the time of adversity.
And Jehovah shall help them and rescue them, (40)
He shall rescue them from the wicked,
And save them for they seek refuge in Him.

Psalm Commentary 37

Summary: Although evil flourish for a short time, yet they perish and are cast down into hell while the righteous are established in heaven, so do not be angry due to the prosperity of the evil (v. 1-11). The falsity of evil always desires to attack the truth of the good (v. 12-15). The righteous should be content with what little they have, for their inheritance in heaven is eternal (v. 16-20). The wicked do evil and the righteous do good, and shall be judged accordingly (v. 21-24). The Lord shall provide for the righteous (v. 25-29). The righteous are guided by the truth (v. 30-34). The punishment of the evil and the reward of the righteous (v. 35-40).

Be not upset with evildoers,
Be not jealous against the workers of injustice.
For they shall soon be cut down like the grass,
And fade away as the greenery of tender herb. (Ps. 37:1-2)

Evildoers are those who do evil against the good of love; "workers of injustice" are those who do evil against the good of faith (see Ps. 7:3). Grass signifies external fallacies from evil in the natural; the green tender herb is knowledges of falsehoods in the natural as signified by green (see Ps. 92:14) and grass (see Ps. 23:1, 103:15, 104:14, 147:8). Grass has this meaning as it is the lowest thing towards the earth, and is also the food for animals which represents man's lower nature. Those who are evil become immersed into their lower natural, which leads to spiritual death.

"Inasmuch as creeping or moving things signify both pleasures of the body and pleasures of the senses, of which the green herb is predicated, the word in the original language is one which signifies both esculent and green — esculent in reference to pleasures of affections of the will, or celestial affections, and green in reference to pleasures of affections of the understanding, or spiritual affections.

"That the esculent herb and green herb signify what is vile, is evident in the Word — as in Isaiah: *For the waters of Nimrim shall be desolate;for the grass is dried up, the herbage is consumed, there is no green thing* (xv. 6). Again: *Their inhabitants were short of hand, they were dismayed, and put to shame; they became the herb of the field, and the green herbage, the grass on the house tops* (xxxvii. 27) — the green herbage standing for what is most vile. In Moses: *The land whither thou goest in to possess it, is not as the land of Egypt, front whence ye came out, where thou sowedst thy seed, and wateredst it with thy foot, as a garden of herbs* (Deut. xi. 10) — where a garden of herbs stands for what is vile. In David: *For the evil doers shall soon be cut down like the grass, and wither as the green herbage* (Ps. xxxvii. 2) — where the grass and the green herbage stand for what is most vile." (*Heavenly Arcana*, n. 996.2-3)

"*And all green grass was burnt up,* signifies that all true knowledge (*scientificum*) was destroyed by the cupidities of the same loves. This is evident from the signification of 'grass,' as being knowledge (*scientificum*) (of which presently); also from the signification of 'green,' as being truth and living from truth, because as green grass serves as food for animals, so true knowledge serves for spiritual nourishment for man; for whatever is produced in fields, in gardens, and in plains, and serves for nourishment either for man or beast, has a correspondence with such things as serve for the nourishment of the spirit and mind, and such nourishment is called spiritual nourishment... 'green grass' signifies true knowledge (*scientificum*), which is living, but 'grass burnt up' signifies false knowledge, which is dead. When truth and good, which come from heaven, find no receptacle in the cognitions and knowledges with man, but evils and falsities which are from hell are received, then knowledges (*scientifics*) are not living but dead, and correspond to grass withered and burnt up. It is similar with man himself, for a man is such a man as the cognitions and knowledges are alive in him; for from living knowledges (*scientiae*) he has intelligence, but from knowledges not living he has no intelligence; and if they are dead in consequence of the confirmation of falsities by them there is insanity and folly. Such a man, from correspondence, is compared in the Word to 'grass,' and is also called 'grass' in the following passages. In *Isaiah:*—

The inhabitants have become as the herb of the field, as the greenness of the tender herb, as the grass of the housetops and as a field scorched before it is grown up (xxxvii. 27; 2 *Kings* xix. 26). In *David:*—

> *The wicked are cut down in haste as the grass, and wither as the greenness of the herb (Ps.* xxxvii. 2)." (*Apocalypse Explained*, n. 507.1, 3-4; see also Ps. 103:15, 129:6)

Trust in Jehovah and do good,
Reside in the land and shepherd faithfully.
And be content upon Jehovah,
And He shall give you the requests of your heart.
Commit your way upon Jehovah,
And trust upon Him and He shall do it. (Ps. 37:3-5)

To trust is to have confidence of the will from the good of charity (see Ps. 33:21) and is thus mentioned with Jehovah who is the Lord as to Divine love (see Ps. 18:31, 28:1, 68:26, 82:1, 147:7); to reside in the land is to be in the church from truth (see Ps. 9:8, 24:1, 60:2, 90:2, 96:13); to shepherd faithfully is to lead in good and truth (see Ps. 23:1, 80:1) and to instruct (see Ps. 23:1, 78:71, 100:3). To be "content in Jehovah" is to be in the good of love; the requests of the heart are the desires of the will from love (see Ps. 7:9, 22:10, 24:4, 51:10, 64:6, 66:18, 78:8). To "commit one's way unto Jehovah" is to be in truth that leads towards love, as way signifies truth (see Ps. 1:1, 18:42, 25:4,12, 37:23, 86:11); "to trust in Him and He shall do" signifies that there is a reciprocal conjunction between man and God which is done through love; to trust is to have confidence of the will from the good of charity (see Ps. 33:21).

And He shall bring forth your righteousness as the light,
And your judgment as the noonday. (Ps. 37:6)

Righteousness is to do what is good (see Ps. 14:5, 36:6, 37:17, 72:2, 89:14, 92:12), and judgment is related to Divine truth (see Ps. 36:6, 72:2, 89:14, 92:12). Light signifies the Divine truth which comes from Divine love (see Ps. 4:6, 11:4, 18:28, 36:9); noonday signifies lower spiritual truth of the intellectual. Righteousness (or "justice" as below) is often paired with judgement in scripture to represent the union of Divine love with Divine truth:

"Since the Lord is the Divine good and the Divine truth, and the Divine truth is signified by judgment, and the Divine good by justice, therefore in many places, where the Lord is spoken of, justice and judgment are mentioned; as in the following: *Zion shall be redeemed with justice, and her restored one with judgment* (Isa. i. 27). *He shall sit upon the throne of David and upon his kingdom to establish it in judgment and justice* (Isa. ix. 7). *Jehovah shall be exalted, for He dwelleth on high, and hath filled the earth with judgment and justice* (Isa. xxxiii. 5). *Let him who glorieth glory in this, that Jehovah doeth judgment and justice in the earth* (Jer. ix. 24). *I will raise up unto David a just Branch, who shall reign King and execute judgment and justice in the earth* (Jer. xxiii. 5; xxxiii. 15). *I will betroth Me to thee in justice and in judgment* (Hos. ii. 19). *Judgment shall flow as water, and justice as a mighty stream* (Am. v. 24). *O Jehovah, Thy justice is like the mountains of God, and Thy judgments a great deep* (Ps. xxxvi. 6). *Jehovah shall bring forth thy justice as the light, and thy judgment as the noonday* (Ps. xxxvii. 6). *Jehovah will judge thy people with justice, and thy poor with judgment* (Ps. lxxii. 2). *Justice and judgment are the support of His throne* (Ps. lxxxix. 14). *When I shall have learned the judgment of Thy justice: seven times in a day do I praise Thee, because of the judgments of Thy justice* (Ps. cxix. 7, 164). And in other places, that men ought to do *justice and judgment*, as Isa. i. 21; v. 16; lvi. 1; lviii. 2; Jer. iv. 2; xxii. 3, 13, 15; Ezek. xviii. 5; xxxiii. 14, 16, 19; Am. vi. 12; Mic. vii. 9; Deut. xxxiii. 21; John xvi. 8, 10. In these passages justice has relation to the good of truth, and judgment to the truth of good. Since judgment relates to truth, and justice to good, therefore we read in some places of truth and justice; as Isa. xi. 5; Ps. lxxxv. 11: and in David, *The judgments of Jehovah are truth, they are just altogether; more to be desired than gold, sweeter than honey* (Ps. xix. 9, 10)." (*Apocalypse Revealed*, n. 668)

The word "noonday" refers to the lower light of spiritual truth which enlightens the natural:

"*For the men shall eat with me at noon.* That this signifies that they will be conjoined when with a medium, is evident from the signification of eating with, as communicated with, conjoined, and appropriated (n. 2187, 2343, 3168, 3513, 3596, 3832). And because they were with a spiritual medium, which is Benjamin (n. 5639), it is said, at noon; for noon signifies a state of light, thus a spiritual state which comes through a medium (n. 1458, 3708)." (*Heavenly Arcana*, n. 5643)

"That noon means a state of light is because the times of day, as morning, noon, and evening, correspond to different degrees of enlightenment in the other life, and the degrees of enlightenment there are those of intelligence and wisdom; for in the light of heaven is intelligence and wisdom. There are alternations of enlightenment there, like morning, noon, and evening on earth." (*Heavenly Arcana*, n. 5672)

The word "noonday" can also be translated as "window." The window of Noah's ark, and all windows in scripture, represents intellectual truth:

"That the window which was to be finished 'to a cubit from above' signifies the intellectual, any one may see from what has now been said; and also from this, that the intellectual can be compared only to a window from above, when the construction of the ark is being treated of, and by the ark is signified the man of the church. And so in other parts of the Word the intellectual of man is called a window — whether it be reason or mere reasoning — that is, his internal sight. Thus in Isaiah: *O thou afflicted, tossed with tempest and not comforted ...I will make thy suns (windows) of rubies, and thy gates of carbuncles, and all thy border of pleasant stones* (liv. 11, 12). Here suns are put for windows, from the light that is admitted, or transmitted. The suns or windows in this passage are intellectual truths, and indeed from charity, and therefore they are likened to a ruby; the gates are rational truths therefrom; and the border is outward knowledge from the senses. The Lord's church is there treated of." (*Heavenly Arcana*, n. 655)

Be silent for Jehovah,
And expectantly wait for Him.
Be not upset with him who prospers in his way,
With the man who executes schemes.
Cease from anger and forsake fury,
Be not upset, it is only toward evil.
For evildoers shall be cut off,
But those who wait upon Jehovah, they shall possess the earth.
And yet a little while, and the wicked shall not be,
And you shall consider his place, and it shall not be. (Ps. 37:7-10)

To be "silent for Jehovah" is to silence self-derived thoughts of falsehood (see Ps. 4:4); to "expectantly wait for Him" is to receive what is good. One who "prospers in his way" is one who follows falsehood, signified by way (see Ps. 1:1, 18:42, 25:4,12, 37:23, 86:11); the one who "executes plans" is one who does evil according to falsehood. Anger is from evil of the will and fury is from falsity of thought (see Ps. 2:5, 78:49), and as fury is of the mind it is mentioned with forsake which signifies the rejection of falsity (see Ps. 27:9). To be upset to do evil is to commit an external act from falsehood, but if anger of the will and fury of thought are

brought under restraint, so one can exercise restraint on one's
actions. To be cut off signifies to be separated from heaven and
condemned (see Ps. 34:16); to wait on Jehovah is to be in truth
ready to receive what is good (see Ps. 25:3) and to "possess the
earth" is to acquire the kingdom of heaven through good (see
Ps. 69:35-36). In the last judgment the wicked are deprived of
their place between heaven and hell and are cast down, and are
thus said not to exist in their place any longer.

But the meek shall possess the earth,
And shall be content in the abundance of peace. (Ps. 37:11)

The meek are those in the good of charity; to possess the earth
is to acquire the kingdom of heaven through good (see Ps. 69:35-
36). To be "content in the abundance of peace" is to have spiritual
peace after the removal of evil and falsity (see Ps. 4:8, 29:11).
This verse is quoted in the beatitudes in Matt. 5:5:
"In *Matthew:*—

Blessed are the meek, for they shall inherit the earth (v. 5).

'Inheriting the earth' signifies not possession of the earth, but
possession of heaven and blessedness there; the 'meek' mean
those who are in the good of charity." (*Apocalypse Explained,*
n. 304.44)

"*Blessed are the meek, for they shall inherit the earth* (Matt.
v. 5). *I am Jehovah that maketh all things, that spreadeth out*
the heavens alone, that stretcheth out the earth by Myself (Isa.
lxiv. 23, 24; Zech. xii. 1; Jer. x. 11-13; li. 15; Ps. cxxxvi. 6). *Let*
the earth open itself, let it bring forth salvation; thus said Jeho-
vah, that createth the heavens, that formeth the earth (Isa. xlv.
8, 12, 18, 19). *Behold, I create new heavens and a new earth*
(Isa. lxv. 17; lxvi. 22)... The reason why the church is signified
by the earth is because by earth or land the land of Canaan is
often meant, in which was the church: the heavenly Canaan
is nothing else: also because when the earth is mentioned,
the angels, who are spiritual, do not think of the earth, but
of the human race which is upon it, and their spiritual state;

and their spiritual state is the state of the church." (*Apocalypse Revealed*, n. 285)

The wicked scheme against the righteous,
And gnashes upon him with his teeth.
The Lord shall laugh at him,
For He sees that his day is coming. (Ps. 37:12-13)

The schemes of the wicked are evil intentions against good as signified by righteous (see Ps. 14:5, 36:6, 37:6,17, 72:2, 89:14, 92:12); to gnash the teeth means to fight against truths from external falsities (see Ps. 35:16). The Lord (Hebrew *Adonai*) is Divine good in the Divine Human (see Ps. 68:17,26, 105:21, 110:1, 114:7); laughter is internal affection for truth against falsity (see Ps. 2:4); the coming day is the day of judgment by the truth.

The wicked have drawn out the sword,
And have bent their bow,
To fell the afflicted and needy,
To butcher him who is upright in the way.
Their sword shall enter into their own heart,
And their bows shall be broken. (Ps. 37:14-15)

The sword represents falsity fighting against the truth (see Ps. 7:12, 22:16, 37:14, 45:3, 57:4, 78:62,64, 149:5); the bow is the doctrine of falsity (see Ps. 7:12-13, 11:2, 18:34, 46:9, 77:17-18, 78:9,57). The afflicted are those who are lacking in knowledges of the truth (see Ps. 35:10, 40:17) and the needy those lacking in knowledge of good (see Ps. 35:10, 40:17, 109:16, 113:7) and though lacking yet desire them; to cause them to fall is to pervert the truth with them (see Ps. 7:15). The upright are those who are in truth from good (see Ps. 9:8, 11:3, 25:21, 96:10, 143:10) and the way is the way of truth (see Ps. 1:1, 18:42, 25:4,12, 37:23, 86:11). For the sword to enter their own heart is for their falsity to destroy the good of the own will (see Ps. 7:9, 22:10, 24:4, 51:10, 64:6, 66:18, 78:8); for their bow to be broken is for their doctrine

of falsity (see Ps. 7:12-13, 11:2, 18:34, 46:9, 77:17-18, 78:9,57) to
be defeated by the truth.

> *"The wicked unsheathe the sword, and bend their bow, to
> cast down the miserable and needy. Their sword shall enter
> into their own heart, and their bows shall be broken (Ps.
> xxxvii. 14, 15).*

'Sword' signifies falsity fighting against truth, and 'bow' signifies
the doctrine of falsity; 'to cast down the miserable and the needy'
signifies to pervert those who are in ignorance of truth and good;
'their sword shall enter into their own heart' signifies that they
shall perish by their own falsity; and 'their bows shall be broken'
signifies that their doctrine of falsity shall be dispersed, which
also takes place after their departure from the world; then falsities destroy them, and so far as they have applied truths to
falsities their doctrine is dispersed." (*Apocalypse Explained*,
n. 357.13; see also *Apocalypse Explained*, n. 238.3)

Better is a little that the righteous has,
Than the abundance of many wicked.
For the arms of the wicked shall be broken,
But Jehovah supports the righteous. (Ps. 37:16-17)

The righteous are those who do good (see Ps. 14:5, 36:6, 37:17,
72:2, 89:14, 92:12), what little the righteous has refers to what
little knowledge of truth he or she may know. The word "better"
is predicated of good: although one's truth may be deemed insig-
nificant, if one lives according to the good of love one shall enter
heaven. Truth will then be multiplied as it can then be received
by those who were in the good of life. The "abundance of many
wicked" are the abundant fallacies and falsehoods that are
derived from evil which withdraws one from eternal life. The
spiritual treasures of heaven are those of good and truth:

"In spiritual life there are no other riches than the knowledges of good and truth, and no other possessions and inher-
itances than the felicities of life arising from goods and their
truths." (*Heavenly Arcana*, n. 5135.5)

To break the arm of the wicked is to destroy the power of evil by falsity as signified by arm (see Ps. 10:15, 77:15, 89:21, 136:12); Jehovah is the Lord as to Divine love (see Ps. 18:31, 28:1, 68:26, 82:1, 147:7) who is the origin of the good in the righteous. In the following quote the word for righteous is translated as "just":

"The just man is thus described in David: *Jehovah upholdeth the just. ...The just sheweth mercy, and giveth. ...The just ...all the day long sheweth mercy, and lendeth. ...The just shall inherit the land. ...The mouth of the just talketh of wisdom, and his tongue speaketh judgment. The law of his God is in his heart* (Ps. xxxvii. 17, 21, 26, 29-31). These things are the goods of charity, which are of the just. That these goods of charity are from the Lord, so that they are the Lord's with man, is known to the church. The just man is also described in other passages, as in Ezekiel (xviii. 5-9, 21; also xxxiii. 15-20)." (*Heavenly Arcana,* n. 9263.6)

Jehovah knows the days of the perfect,
And their inheritance shall be forever.
They shall not be ashamed in the time of evil,
And in the days of famine they shall be satisfied. (Ps. 37:18-19)

To be perfect is to be in good from truth (see Ps. 15:2) and days are their states of enlightenment (see Ps. 32:4, 74:16, 136:8); forever is eternity in the celestial heaven of love (see Ps. 145:13). To not be ashamed is to have no shame due to being destitute of good from evil (see Ps. 35:4); to be satisfied in the days of famine is to conquer temptations from evil when one is lacking in truth (see Ps. 37:19, 105:16).

"*Jehovah knoweth the days of the perfect, and He shall be their inheritance for ever. They shall not be ashamed in the time of evil; and in the days of famine they shall be satisfied* (Ps. xxxvii. 18, 19). 'The days of the perfect' signify the states of those who are in good and in truths therefrom, or those who are in charity and in faith therefrom. 'Jehovah shall be their inheritance for ever' signifies that they are His own and are in heaven; 'they shall not

be ashamed in the time of evil' signifies that they shall conquer
when they are tempted by evils; and 'in the days of famine they
shall be satisfied' signifies that they shall be upheld by truths
when they are tempted and infested by falsities, 'time of evil'
and 'days of famine' signifying the states of temptations, and
temptations are from evils and falsities." (*Apocalypse Explained*,
n. 386.22)

"Famine signifies the deprivation and the rejection of the
knowledges of truth and good, arising from evils of life. It also
signifies ignorance of the knowledges of truth and good arising from deficiency of them in the church; and it signifies also
a desire to know and understand them. I. That famine signifies the deprivation and rejection of the knowledges of truth
and good arising from evils of life, and the evils of life thence,
may be evident from the following passages: *By the sword and
by famine they shall be consumed, that their carcase may be for
food to the birds of the heavens and to the beasts of the earth*
(Jer. xvi. 4). *These two things shall come upon thee, devastation
and breaking in pieces, and famine and the sword* (Isa. li. 19).
*Behold, I will visit upon them; the young men shall die by the
sword, the sons and daughters shall die of famine*(Jer. xi. 22).
*Give his sons to famine, and pour out their blood by the power
of the sword; let the men be put to death* (Jer. xviii. 21). *I will
send against them the sword, famine, and pestilence, and I will
make them like wild figs that cannot be eaten for badness, and
I will pursue after them with the sword, famine, and pestilence*
(Jer. xxix. 17, 18). *I will send against them the sword, famine,
and the pestilence, until they are consumed from the earth* (Jer.
xxiv. 10). *I proclaim liberty for you to the sword, to famine, and
to the pestilence; and I will deliver you to the attack of all nations*
(Jer. xxxiv. 17). *Because ye have polluted My sanctuary, the third
part of thee shall die by the pestilence and shall be consumed
with famine, and the third part shall fall by the sword: when
I send the evil darts of famine against them, which shall be for
destruction* (Ezek. v. 11, 12, 16, 17). *The sword without, and the
pestilence and famine within* (Ezek. vii. 15). *On account of all the*

evil abominations, they shall fall by the sword, by famine, and by the pestilence (Ezek. vi. 11, 12). *My four evil judgments, the sword, the famine, and the evil beast, and the pestilence, will I send upon Jerusalem, to cut off from it man and beast* (Ezek. xiv. 13, 15, 21: besides other places, as Jer. xiv. 12, 13, 15, 16; xlii. 13, 14, 16-18, 22; xliv. 12,13, 27; Matt. xxiv. 7, 8; Mark xiii. 8; Luke xxi. 11). ...a sword is the destruction of spiritual life by falsities, famine is the destruction of spiritual life by evils, the beast of the earth is the destruction of spiritual life by the lusts of falsity and evil, and the pestilence and death are an utter wasting away, and thus condemnation. II. That famine signifies ignorance of the knowledges of truth and good arising from deficiency of them in the church, is evident also from various passages in the Word, as Isa. v. 13; viii. 19-22; Lam. ii. 19; v. 8-10; Amos. viii. 11-14; Job. v. 17, 20; and elsewhere. III. That famine or hunger signifies the desire of knowing and understanding the truths and goods of the church, is manifest from these, Isa. viii. 21; xxxii. 6; xlix. 10; lviii. 6, 7; 1 Sam. ii. 4, 5; Ps. xxxiii. 18, 19; xxxiv. 9, 10; xxxvii. 18, 19; cvii. 8, 9, 35-37; cxlvi. 7; Matt. v. 6; xxv. 35, 37, 44; Luke i. 53; John vi. 35: and elsewhere." (*Apocalypse Revealed*, n. 323)

For the wicked shall perish,
And the enemies of Jehovah are like precious fattened lambs,
They shall be consumed, as smoke they shall consume away.
(Ps. 37:20)

The wicked are those who are in falsehoods against the truth; to perish is to spiritually die from falsehoods (see Ps. 88:11); the enemies of Jehovah are the falsehoods (see Ps. 3:1, 27:12) which attack what is good, signified by Jehovah. To burn is to be punished by one's evil desires; smoke is the falsity of evil or the pride of one's own self intelligence (see Ps. 11:6, 18:8, 68:2, 144:5) which leads to spiritual destruction.

The wicked borrows and repays not,
But the righteous is gracious and gives. (Ps. 37:21)

The wicked are those who are in evil and to borrow is to be instructed; to not repay signifies to use one's knowledge for selfish gain. The righteous are in good (see Ps. 14:5, 36:6, 37:6,17, 72:2, 89:14, 92:12); to be gracious is to have affection from truth (see Ps. 103:8); to give is to do charity in act.

"In the Word where mention is made of borrowing and lending, being instructed and instructing from the affection of charity are signified — as in Matthew: *Give to every one that asketh thee, and from him who would borrow of thee turn not thou away* (chap, v. 42). That here by asking is not meant asking, is plain, for it is said, Give to every one that asketh; and so neither by borrowing is meant borrowing; for if one were to give to every one that asketh and also to every one that would borrow, he would be deprived of all his goods. But because the Lord spoke from the Divine, by asking and desiring to borrow, and by giving and receiving a loan, is meant the sharing of heavenly goods, which are knowledges of good and truth; for in regard to such sharing the case is this — the more an angel gives to another from the affection of charity, the more flows in with him out of heaven from the common stock, that is, from the Lord (n. 6478). Thus by giving to him who asketh, an angel is not deprived of, but enriched with goods. The case is the same with a man when he does good to another from the affection of charity. But it is charity to give to the good, and it is not charity to give to the evil what they ask and desire (n. 8120) — according to these words in David: *The wicked borroweth, and payeth not again: but the just sheweth mercy and giveth* (Ps. xxxvii. 21). And in Luke: *If ye lend to them of whom ye hope to receive, what thank have ye? …Rather love your enemies, and do good, and lend, hoping for nothing again; and your reward shall be great, and ye shall be the sons of the Most High* (vi. 34, 35).

"Here also by lending is meant doing good from the affection of charity, and thus sharing the goods of heaven, and also the goods of the world, but the latter for the sake of the former as an end. Affection of charity consists in sharing goods without having recompense as an end; but it is not affection of charity to impart goods for the sake of recompense as an end... Loving one's enemies and doing good to the evil is the affection of charity; but enemies are loved and good is done to them when they are instructed, and also when by suitable means they are corrected (n. 8121)." (*Heavenly Arcana*, n. 9174.3-4)

For such as are blessed by Him shall possess the earth,
And they who are cursed by Him shall be cut off.
The course of a mighty one is established by Jehovah,
And he is delighted in his way.
Though he fall he shall not be cast down,
For Jehovah supports his hand.
I have been young, also old,
And I have not seen the righteous forsaken,
Nor his seed begging for bread.
Every day he is gracious, and lends,
And his seed is a blessing. (Ps. 37:22-26)

The blessed are those who receive good and happiness from the Lord (see Ps. 3:8, 16:7, 21:6, 24:5, 28:6, 31:21, 96:2); to possess is to acquire from love (see Ps. 69:35-36) and the earth is the church (see Ps. 37:11, 46:2, 65:9, 104:5). The cursed are the evil who will be cut off from heaven (see Ps. 34:16). The course of a mighty one are those who live by the power of truth (see Ps. 21:13, 80:2); to be delighted in the way is to have affection for living by the truth signified by way (see Ps. 1:1, 18:42, 25:4, 86:11). To fall is to be deceived by a perversion of the truth (see Ps. 7:15), however though the righteous err at times they will not be cast down into hell. For Jehovah to support the hand is to recover from error from the power of truth as signified by hand (see Ps. 20:6, 44:3, 45:4, 80:15,17, 89:13,21, 110:1, 121:5). To be young is to be in a state of innocence lacking in truth (see Ps. 103:5) and to be old is to be wise from love. To be forsaken is lacking in truth (see Ps. 27:9) which those who are in good do not lack; seed signifies those in the faith of charity (see Ps. 18:50, 21:10, 22:23,30, 89:4, 106:27) who will never be lacking in love, signified by bread (see Ps. 23:2, 105:16). To be gracious is to have affection from truth (see Ps. 103:8); to lend is to exercise charity (see Ps. 37:21, 112:5); and from one's faith of charity one receives good and happiness from the Lord, signified by blessing (see Ps. 3:8, 16:7, 21:6, 24:5, 28:6, 31:21, 96:2).

Depart from evil and do good,
And reside forever.
For Jehovah loves judgment,
And forsakes not His merciful ones.
They are kept forever,
But the seed of the wicked shall be cut off.
The righteous shall possess the earth,
And reside upon her for ever. (Ps. 37:27-29)

Evil must first be removed before one can do good, thus "depart from evil" is mentioned before doing good. To reside forever is to live forever in the celestial heaven of love (see Ps. 145:13). Judgment is from Divine truth (see Ps. 36:6, 37:6, 72:2, 89:14, 92:12) and mercy is Divine love (see Ps. 25:10, 26:3, 36:5, 89:14, 103:8). To be kept forever is to be kept in good forever; the "seed of the wicked" are those in the falsity of evil who will be cut off from heaven (see Ps. 34:16). The righteous are those who do good (see Ps. 14:5, 36:6, 37:6,17, 72:2, 89:14, 92:12); to possess is to acquire from love (see Ps. 69:35-36) and the earth is the church (see Ps. 37:11, 46:2, 65:9, 104:5).

The mouth of the righteous meditates wisdom,
And his tongue speaks judgment. (Ps. 37:30)

The mouth is the external understanding (see Ps. 5:9, 135:16) derived from good signified by righteous (see Ps. 14:5, 36:6, 37:6,17, 72:2, 89:14, 92:12); to meditate is to have perception of good (see Ps. 19:14) and wisdom is truth from love. The tongue is one's opinion or principle of persuasion (see Ps. 35:28, 57:4, 140:11) and judgment signifies Divine truth (see Ps. 36:6, 37:6, 72:2, 89:14, 92:12).

"...in the Word that is said to be in the heart which is interior and proceeds from good, and that to be in the mouth which is exterior and proceeds from truth" (*Heavenly Arcana*, n. 3313) "the 'mouth' and the things belonging to the mouth signify the things of the understanding and of thought and speech therefrom, for these correspond to the mouth. For all the organs that are included in the one term *mouth,* as the larynx, the glottis, the throat, the tongue, the mouth, the lips, are organs that serve the understanding for utterance and for speech, and this is why the 'mouth' signifies the thought and reasoning therefrom. But as man's thought is interior and exterior, that is spiritual, natural, and sensual, so the 'mouth' signifies such thought as pertains to the man treated of... That the 'mouth' from correspondence, thus in the spiritual sense, signifies thought, but in the natural sense utterance, can be seen from the following passages. In *David:*—

> *The mouth of the righteous meditateth wisdom* (*Ps.* xxxvii. 30).

The 'mouth' here signifies thought from affection, for man from that meditates wisdom, but not from the mouth and its speech." (*Apocalypse Explained*, n. 580.1-2)

The law of his God is in his heart,
His steps shall not falter.
The wicked watches the righteous,
And seeks to put him to death.
Jehovah will not forsake him in his hand,
And not condemn him when he is judged. (Ps. 37:31-33)

The law of God are the internal things of the Word related to love (see Ps. 19:7) and is thus mentioned with the heart which concerns the love of one's will (see Ps. 7:9, 22:10, 24:4, 51:10, 64:6, 66:18, 78:8); steps are one's life according to the truth. The wicked who watch the righteous is falsehood which seeks to attack good; to put to death is to extinguish one's spiritual life (see Ps. 6:5, 9:13, 33:19, 102:20, 106:28). To forsake is to be deprived of truth against the falsity of evil (see Ps. 27:9); the hand here is the power of falsehood (see Ps. 89:42); to be condemned is to be condemned to hell due to evil.

Wait on Jehovah,

And keep His way,
And He shall exalt you to possess the earth:
When the wicked are cut off you shall see it.
I have seen the wicked as terrible,
And exposing himself like a green native tree.
But he passed away, and, lo, he was not:
And I sought him, but he was not found. (Ps. 37:34-36)

To wait on Jehovah is to have hope from the will; to keep His way is to follow the truth (see Ps. 1:1, 18:42, 25:4,12, 37:23, 86:11). To possess is to acquire from love (see Ps. 69:35-36) and the earth is the church (see Ps. 37:11, 46:2, 65:9, 104:5); for the evil to be cut off is to be separated from heaven and condemned (see Ps. 34:16). To be terrible is to do violence to the goods and truths of the church (see Ps. 54:3). To pass away and not be is to become separated from love; to not be found is to be separated from truth.

Take heed of the perfect and see the upright,
For the latter end of that man is peace.
But the transgressors shall be destroyed together,
The latter end of the wicked shall be cut off.
But the salvation of the righteous is from Jehovah,
He is their stronghold in the time of adversity.
And Jehovah shall help them and rescue them,
He shall rescue them from the wicked,
And save them for they seek refuge in Him. (Ps. 37:37-40)

To be perfect is to be in good from truth (see Ps. 15:2) and to be upright is to be in truth from good (see Ps. 9:8, 11:3, 25:21, 96:10, 143:10); peace is spiritual tranquility after the removal of evils and falsities where they no longer infest (see Ps. 4:8, 29:11). Transgression is evil against the truth of faith from a perverted understanding (see Ps. 5:10, 25:7, 32:1, 51:1-3); for the wicked to be cut off is to be cut off from heaven due to evil (see Ps. 34:16). Salvation is deliverance from evil from Divine love (see Ps. 14:7, 96:2); stronghold or strength is the power of good by truth (see Ps. 21:13, 29:1, 95:4, 96:6) and a time of adversity is a state of evil (see Ps. 3:1, 27:12). Help is aid from Divine mercy against evil (see Ps. 10:14) and to rescue is to lead away from falsity (see Ps. 91:14).

Psalm 38

A Psalm of David, for remembrance.

~

Jehovah, reprove me not in Your wrath, (1)
And chasten me not in Your fury.
For Your arrows stick fast in me, (2)
And Your hand presses upon me.
There is no wholeness in my flesh from before Your indignation, (3)
Nor peace in my bones from before my sin.
For my iniquities are passed over my head, (4)
As a heavy burden they are too heavy for me.
My bruises stink, (5)
They waste away from before my foolishness.
I am bent over; I am stooped down even exceedingly, (6)
Every day I go in black.
For my entrails are filled with loathing, (7)
And there is no wholeness in my flesh.
I am benumbed and exceedingly crushed, (8)
I have roared because of the groaning of my heart.
Lord, all my longing is in front of You, (9)
And my sighing is not hidden from You.
My heart quivers, my power forsakes me, (10)
And the light of my eyes, even they are no more with me.
   My loved ones and my neighbours stand aloof from my plague, (11)
   And my kin stand afar off.
   And they who seek after my life lay snares, (12)
   And they who enquired after my evil speak mischievous things,
   And meditate deceits every day.
   But I, as one deaf, heard not, (13)

And I was as one dumb who opens not his mouth.
And I was as a man who hears not, (14)
And in whose mouth are no reproofs.
For in You, Jehovah, I hope: (15)
You will answer, Lord my God.
For I said, Lest they should rejoice over me: (16)
When my foot slips, they become magnified against me.
For I am ready to limp, (17)
And my suffering is continually in front of me.
For I will tell my iniquity, (18)
I will be anxious about my sin.
But my enemies are lively, they are numerous, (19)
And they who hate me falsely are multiplied.
And they repay evil instead of good, (20)
They are my accusers though I pursue good.
Forsake me not, Jehovah: (21)
My God, be not far from me.
Hurry to my help, (22)
Lord of my salvation.

Psalm Commentary 38

Summary: The grievousness of the Lord's temptations is described (v. 1-10). Those who are of the church purpose to have Him put to death which he bore with tolerance (v. 11-14). Trust in the Father that the hells will not prevail (v. 15-20).

Jehovah, reprove me not in Your wrath,
Neither chasten me in Your fury. (Ps. 38:1)

Reproof is correction for falsehood (see Ps. 94:10), and chastisement correction for evil (see Ps. 2:10, 94:10). Anger is punishment due to evil and fury punishment from falsehood (see Ps. 2:5, 78:49). It is the mercy of the Lord to protect the good which causes Him to appear angry to those who are evil:

"That the zeal or mercy of the Lord when it protects the good appears as hostility, is manifest in Isaiah: *Jehovah shall go forth as a mighty man; He shall stir up zeal like a man of war: He shall cry, yea, He shall shout aloud. ...He shall prevail over His enemies* (xlii. 13). In Joel: *Jehovah shall be zealous for His land, and have pity on His people* (ii. 18)... In like manner the zeal of Jehovah is described as anger in other passages (Ps. xxxviii. 1: Ezek. xvi. 42; xxiii. 25; xxxviii. 19). From these examples it may be evident what is meant by the zeal of Jehovah, and what by a zealous God — namely, that in the genuine sense are meant love and mercy, but in a sense not genuine, such as is seen by those who are in evils and falsities, anger and vastation are signified." (*Heavenly Arcana*, n. 8875.6, 7)

517

For Your arrows stick fast in me,
And Your hand presses upon me.
There is no wholeness in my flesh from before Your indignation,
Nor peace in my bones from before my sin. (Ps. 38:2-3)

Arrows signify truths (see Ps. 18:14) which fight against falsehoods; hand is the power of truth (see Ps. 20:6, 44:3, 45:4, 80:15,17, 89:13,21, 110:1, 121:5) which fights against evil. To have no wholesomeness in one's flesh is to have no good in one's self will, signified by flesh (see Ps. 16:9, 63:1, 78:39); to have no peace in one's bones is to have conflicts from falsities (see Ps. 4:8, 29:11) in one's own knowledge, signified by bones (see Ps. 22:14,17, 34:20, 35:10). Indignation is punishment due to falsity against the truth of faith (see Ps. 78:49); sin is evil against the good of love (see Ps. 25:7, 32:1, 51:1-3).

For my iniquities are passed over my head,
As a heavy burden they are too heavy for me. (Ps. 38:4)

Iniquity is evil against the good of faith done from a perverted understanding (see Ps. 51:1-3); the head signifies interior spiritual things of good and truth (see Ps. 133:2) as feet signify the lowest natural things closer to the material world; thus for iniquities to go over the head is for one's spiritual understanding and wisdom to be closed due to a perverted understanding. A burden signifies the bondage of evil which is not removed due to falsity, as things of weight are related to good or evil (see Ps. 62:9, 69:1):

"Learn of Me, for I am meek and lowly of heart, and ye shall find rest to your souls; for My yoke is easy and My burden is light (Matt. xi. 29, 30). That the yoke of the Lord is easy and His burden light, is because as far as man resists the evils springing from the love of self and the world, he is led by the Lord and not by himself; and because the Lord then resists those evils in man and removes them." (*Heaven and Hell*, n. 359)

My bruises stink,
They waste away from before my foolishness. (Ps. 38:5)

Bruises signify profanation of the truth which injures the understanding of truth; a stench is aversion due to profaned truth; to waste away is for good to be thereby extinguished which is from foolishness or lack of understanding. In the following passages the word for bruise is translated as stripe:

"*Stripe for stripe.* That this signifies if anything of affection in the intellectual — be extinguished or injured — is evident from the signification of stripe, as the extinction or injury of affection in the intellectual, that is, of affection for truth. Stripe in the original tongue is expressed by a term which signifies blackness arising from a collection of blood or of gore, and blood in the internal sense is the truth of faith from the good of love, and in the opposite sense truth falsified and profaned... therefore stripe means truth injured or extinguished. This is also signified by the stripes or plagues in the Apocalypse (ix. 20; xi. 6; xv. 1, 6, 8; xvi. 21; xviii. 8); also in Jeremiah (xxx. 12, 14, 17; l. 13); in Zechariah (xiv. 12-15); in David (Ps. xxxviii. 5); and in Luke (x. 30-35) in the parable of him who fell among thieves, who inflicted stripes on him and left him half dead; and it is said that a Samaritan bound up his stripes or wounds, pouring on oil and wine, and set him on his own beast, and brought him to an inn." (*Heavenly Arcana*, n. 9057.1; see also *Heavenly Arcana*, n. 7524.1,4)

A stench due to bruising signifies aversion due to profaned truth:

"*And the river shall stink.* That this signifies aversion for it, is evident from the signification of stinking, as aversion (see n. 7161); and from the signification of river, here the river of Egypt turned into blood, as truth falsified. It is to be known that in the other life nothing is more abominable, and consequently nothing has a more grievous stench, than profaned truth; it is as the stench of a carcass, which is made when living flesh dies. For falsity has no smell, unless it be applied to truth, nor evil unless it be applied to good, the quality of each being made sensible not from itself, but from its opposite; hence it may be evident how great is the stench of profaned truth." (*Heavenly Arcana*, n. 7319)

"As odor is all that which is grateful to the Lord, so stench
is that which is ungrateful to the Lord, consequently stench is
aversion, and also abomination. Stench also actually corresponds
to the aversion and abomination which are of falsity and evil.
Because stench stands for that which is of aversion, in the Word
stench is used to express aversion — as in 1 Samuel: *Israel was
made to stink with the Philistines* (xiii. 4). Again: Achish says
of David, *He hath made himself utterly to stink with his people,
with Israel* (xxvii. 12). Again: *When the sons of Amman saw that
they were made to stink with David* (2 Sam. x. 6). Again: *Ahitho-
phel said unto Absalom ...all Israel shall hear that thou art
become a stench to thy father* (xvi. 21). In these passages stench
stands for aversion. And in Isaiah: The slain of the nations *shall
be cast out, and the stink of their carcases shall come up, and the
mountains shall be melted with blood* (xxxiv. 3) — where stink
stands for evil that is abominable. In like manner in Amos (iv.
10) and in David (Ps. xxxviii. 5, 6)." (*Heavenly Arcana*, n. 7161.2)

I am bent over; I am stooped down even exceedingly,
Every day I go in black.
For my entrails are filled with loathing,
And there is no wholeness in my flesh.
I am benumbed and exceedingly crushed,
I have roared because of the groaning of my heart. (Ps. 38:6-8)

To be bent over or stooped down is to be deprived of good
during temptation (see Ps. 31:9); to be black is to be in sadness
or mourning due to lack of truth (see Ps. 35:14). Entrails or
flanks are the sides between the last rib and the hip and are
closely related to the kidneys (see Lev. 3:4,10,15, 4:9, 7:4); the
same word is also translated as hope and foolishness indicating this signifies the understanding, as kidneys correspond to
truth which explores and judges (see Ps. 7:9). Flesh corresponds
to one's will which is here oppressed by evil (see Ps. 16:9, 63:1,
78:39); for there to be no wholeness is for one's spiritual life to be
affected by evils. To be benumbed and crushed is to be in a state
of temptation where there is a lack of influx of good and truth

from heaven (see Ps. 44:19); roaring of the heart signifies grief of the will due to lack of truth (see Ps. 32:3).

"That disease means evil, is because in the internal sense are signified such things as affect the spiritual life. The diseases which affect that life are evils, and are called desires and lusts. Faith and charity make spiritual life; this life sickens when falsity takes the place of the truth which is of faith, and evil takes the place of the good which is of charity; for these bring that life to death, which is called spiritual death and is damnation, as diseases bring the natural life to its death... Like things are signified by diseases in other passages — as in Moses: *Ye shall serve Jehovah your God, that He may bless thy bread, and thy waters; and I will take disease away from the midst of thee* (Exod. xxiii. 25). Again: *If ye shall reject My statutes, and if your soul abhor My judgments, so that ye will not do all My commandments, whilst ye make My covenant of none effect ...I will appoint terror over you, even consumption, and burning fever, that shall consume the eyes, and torment the soul* (Lev. xxvi. 15, 16) — signifying the decrease of truth and the increase of falsity; burning fever stands for the lust of evil. And in Isaiah: *Wherefore will ye revolt more and more? the whole head is sick, and the whole heart faint. From the sole of the foot even unto the head there is no soundness in it; but wound, and bruise, and fresh sore: they have not been closed, neither bound up, neither mollified with oil* (i. 5, 6) — where it is plain to every one that by sickness, wound, bruise, and sore are meant sins. In like manner in Ezekiel: *Woe unto the shepherds of Israel. ...The diseased sheep have ye not strengthened, neither have ye healed that which was sick, neither have ye bound up that which was broken* (xxxiv. 2, 4). And in David: *Mine iniquities are gone over my head. ...My wounds stink and are corrupt, because of my foolishness ...for my bowels are filled with burning; and there is no soundness in my flesh* (Ps. xxxviii. 4, 5, 7)." (*Heavenly Arcana*, n. 8364.2, 4)

Lord, all my longing is in front of You,
And my sighing is not hidden from You.

My heart quivers, my power forsakes me,
And the light of my eyes, even they are no more with me.
My loved ones and my neighbours stand aloof from my plague,
And those near to me stand afar off. (Ps. 38:9-11)

The Lord (Hebrew *Adonai*) is Divine good in the Divine
Human (see Ps. 68:17,26, 105:21, 110:1, 114:7); longing is the
desire of the will to be delivered from evil and sighing is the
desire of the thought to be delivered from falsehood. For the
heart to quiver signifies a change of state of the will; power is
the power of Divine truth (see Ps. 65:6) and to forsake is to be
deprived of truth (see Ps. 27:9). For there to be no more light
of one's eyes is to have no enlightenment of the understanding
(see Ps. 11:4, 13:3, 31:9, 69:23). Lovers are the goods of love and
neighbours are spiritual goods which withdraw during temptation (see Ps. 122:8). Plagues signify evils which destroy the soul
(see Ps. 78:50, 91:6); for those near to stand afar off is to not be
in a state of conjunction with external knowledges of the truth.
In the literal sense, it refers to the rejection of the Lord by those
who have knowledge of scripture.

"That plagues signify spiritual plagues, which affect men as
to their souls, and destroy them, which are evils and falsities,
may be evident from the following passages: *From the sole of the
foot even to the head there is, no soundness, a fresh plague not
closed, nor bound up, nor mollified* (Isa. i. 6). *Jehovah smiteth
the people in anger with an incurable plague* (Isa. xiv. 6). *O Jehovah, remove Thy plague from me, I am consumed by the blow
of Thine hand* (Ps. xxxix. 10). *Thy wound is incurable, with the
plague of an enemy have I smitten thee for the multitude of thine
iniquity, thy sins have become very many; but I will heal thee of
thy plagues* (Jer. xxx. 12, 14, 17). *If thou wilt not observe to do all
the words of the law, Jehovah will make thy plagues wonderful,
plagues great and lasting, and every plague which is not written in the book of this law, even until thou art destroyed* (Deut.
xxviii. 58, 59, 61). *There shall no evil befall thee, and neither
shall any plague come nigh thy dwelling* (Ps. xci. 10). *Edom shall*

be a desolation, every one that passeth by shall hiss at all her plagues (Jer. xlix. 17). *It shall be a desolation, every one that passeth by Babylon shall be astonished, and shall hiss at all her plagues* (Jer. l. 13). *In one day shall plagues come upon Babylon* (Apoc. xviii. 8). *The two witnesses shall smite the earth with every plague* (Apoc. xi. 6). By the plagues of Egypt, which were in part similar to those described in the following chapter, nothing else was signified but evils and falsities; which plagues you may see enumerated above (n. 503): they are also called *plagues* (Exod. ix. 14; xi. 1). From this it is manifest, that by plagues nothing else is signified but spiritual plagues, which affect men as to their souls, and destroy them; as also Isa. xxx. 26; Zech. xiv. 12, 15; Ps. xxxviii. 5, 11; Apoc. ix. 20; xvi. 21; Exod. xii. 13; xxx. 12; Num. xi. 33; Luke vii. 21; and elsewhere." (*Apocalypse Revealed*, n. 657)

And they who seek after my life lay snares,
And they who enquired after my evil speak mischievous things,
And meditate deceits every day.
But I, as one deaf, heard not,
And I was as a dumb man who opens not his mouth.
And I was as a man who hears not,
And in whose mouth are no reproofs. (Ps. 38:12-14)

One's life is one's spiritual life; snares signify the allurement and deception of evil (see Ps. 18:5, 38:12); to speak mischievous things is falsity attacking good and to utter deceits is to deceive by distorting the truth (see Ps. 5:6). To be deaf and not hear is to have no perception of good to oppose evil; to be dumb and not open one's mouth is the inability to oppose falsehood. One's mouth is the external understanding (see Ps. 5:9, 37:30, 135:16) and reproof is to correct falsehoods (see Ps. 94:10).

"That a snare therefore signifies the destruction of spiritual life and perdition, is plain from the following passages... In Luke: *Lest ...that day come on you suddenly: for as a snare shall it come upon all them who dwell on the face of the whole earth* (xxi. 34, 35) — where the subject is the last time of the church

when there is no faith because no charity, since the loves of self
and of the world will then reign, and from these loves comes
perdition, which is the snare. In Jeremiah: *Among My people
are found wicked men: they watch, as fowlers stretch nets; they
set a trap, they catch men* (v. 26). In David: *They that seek after
my soul stretch snares; and they who seek my hurt speak mischievous things, and imagine deceits all the day long* (Ps. xxxviii.
12). Again: *Keep me from the hands of the gin which they have
laid for me, and from the snares of the workers of iniquity. Let the
wicked fall into their own nets, whilst that I pass over* (Ps. cxli. 9,
10)." (*Heavenly Arcana*, n. 9348.9)

For in You, Jehovah, I hope:
You will answer, Lord my God.
For I said, Lest they should rejoice over me:
When my foot slips, they become magnified against me.
For I am ready to limp,
And my suffering is continually in front of me. (Ps. 38:15-17)

Jehovah is the Divine itself or Divine love (see Ps. 18:31, 28:1,
68:26, 82:1, 147:7); the Lord (Hebrew *Adonai*) is Divine good in
the Divine Human (see Ps. 68:17,26, 105:21, 110:1, 114:7) and
God is the Lord as to Divine truth (see Ps. 18:31, 29:1, 68:17,24,
82:1, 95:3, 147:7). This thus refers to the Divine Trinity of the
Divine itself, the Divine Human and the Divine proceeding.
To hope is to have faith in the Lord; to answer is Divine influx
giving perception and help (see Ps. 4:1). For evil to rejoice is for
evils to overcome love (see Ps. 14:7); for the foot to slip is to be
overcome by one's lower natural (see Ps. 8:6, 41:9, 49:5, 99:5,
105:18); to be magnified is for falsehood to become exalted over
truth. To be ready to limp is to acknowledge one is not in good,
signified by being lame (see Ps. 35:15); suffering (or sorrows) is
grief of mind due to temptations of falsehood. The same word
appears in Ex. 3:7:

"*For I have known their sorrows.* That this signifies foresight,
how much they would be immersed in falsities, is evident from
the signification of knowing, when said of the Lord, as foresight

— knowing is foresight because the Lord knows everything from eternity; and from the signification of sorrows, as immersion in falsities; for they who are in good, when they are immersed in falsities, come into anguish and anxieties, and are tormented; for they love truths and abhor falsities, and think continually about salvation, and about their unhappiness if falsities should prevail with them. But they who are not in good, care not whether they be in falsities or in truths, for they do not think at all about salvation, nor about unhappiness, because they do not believe such things." (*Heavenly Arcana*, n. 6853)

For I will tell my iniquity,
I will be anxious about my sin.
But my enemies are lively, they are numerous:
And they who hate me falsely are multiplied.
And they repay evil instead of good,
They are my accusers though I pursue good.
Forsake me not, Jehovah:
My God, be not far from me.
Hurry to my help,
Lord of my salvation. (Ps. 38:18-22)

Iniquity is evil done against the good of faith (see Ps. 51:1-3); sin is is evil done against the good of love (see Ps. 5:10, 25:7, 32:1, 51:1-3). Enemies are falsehoods which attack the truth (see Ps. 3:1, 27:12); they who hate are evils which attack what is good. There are two kinds of evil spirits: devils who are primarily in evil against good, and satans who are in falsehoods against the truth (see *Heavenly Arcana*, n. 9993.6). The devils are those who repay evil for good; the accusers (Hebrew *satan*) are satans that falsely accuse (see Ps. 71:13, 109:4); to pursue good is to be in truth from good. For Jehovah to forsake is for Divine love to appear absent; to be far from God is for Divine truth to appear distant. Help is aid from Divine mercy (see Ps. 10:14); the Lord (Hebrew *Adonai*) is Divine good in the Divine Human (see Ps. 68:17,26, 105:21, 110:1, 114:7); salvation is deliverance from evil by Divine good (see Ps. 14:7, 96:2).

Psalm 39

To the chief Musician, to Jeduthun, a Psalm of David.

~

I said, I will keep my ways, (1)
From sinning with my tongue,
I will keep a muzzle for my mouth,
While *wickedness* is in front of me.
I was dumb with silence, (2)
I was still from good.
And my pain was befoul.
My heart was hot within me, (3)
While I was meditating the fire burned,
I spoke with my tongue:
Jehovah, make me to know my end, (4)
And the measure of my days what it is,
That I may know how fleeting I am.
Behold, You have given my days as a handbreadth, (5)
And my age is as nothing in front of You,
Surely every Man standing is altogether vanity. (Selah)

~

Surely every man walks in an image, (6)
Surely he heaps up vain things of abundance,
And knows not who shall gather them.
And now what do I wait for, Lord? (7)
My hope is in You.
Deliver me from all my transgressions, (8)
Make me not the reproach of the foolish.
I was dumb, I opened not my mouth, (9)
For You did it.

Remove Your stroke away from me, (10)
From the blow of Your hand I am consumed.
With reproofs You chastise man due to iniquity, (11)
And You make his desire to melt like a moth,
Surely every Man is vanity. (Selah)
    Hear my prayer, Jehovah, and give ear to my cry, (12)
    Hold not Your peace at my tears.
    For I am a stranger with You,
    A resident alien as all my fathers were.
    Look away from me and I will smile, (13)
    Before I go and be no more.

Psalm Commentary 39

Summary: The Lord's tolerance in the state of temptations, and His desire for the end of temptations (v. 1-5, 6-11). Prayer to the Father that He be not forsaken (v. 12-13).

I said, I will keep my ways,
From sinning with my tongue,
I will keep a muzzle for my mouth,
While wickedness is in front of me.
I was dumb with silence,
I was still from good.
And my pain was befoul,
My heart was hot within me.
While I was meditating the fire burned,
I spoke with my tongue: (Ps. 39:1-3)

To take heed to one's ways is to guard against falsehood signified by way (see Ps. 1:1, 18:42, 25:4,12, 37:23, 86:11). To sin is to do evil against the good of love (see Ps. 25:7, 32:1, 51:1-3); a tongue signifies a false persuasion (see Ps. 35:28, 57:4, 140:11). To keep a muzzle to the mouth is to guard against falsehood of the external understanding (see Ps. 5:9, 37:30, 135:16); wickedness is falsehood from evil. To be dumb with silence is to be lacking in truth; to be still from good is to be lacking in good (see Ps. 28:1). For pain to be befoul is to have pain from falsehood corrupting truth – befoul is used for a falsehood that falsifies other truths if not discovered and removed (see Gen. 34:30, Josh.

6:18, 7:25). For one's heart to be hot is to have discomfort of the will due to evil. To meditate is to have internal perception of good (see Ps. 19:14) and fire burning is related to the desire of the will; to speak with the tongue is teach truth from one's confession of doctrine.

Jehovah, make me to know my end,
And the measure of my days what it is,
That I may know how fleeting I am.
Behold, You have given my days as a handbreadth,
And my age is as nothing in front of You,
Surely every Man standing is altogether vanity. (Ps. 39:4-5)

To measure is to know one's spiritual quality as to good and truth (see Ps. 31:8, 39:4, 40:5); days are one's states as to truth (see Ps. 32:4, 74:16, 136:8); to be fleeting is to acknowledge that one has no good from one's self. A Man (Hebrew *adam*) is one who is in self love (see Ps. 36:6); vanity is falsity of doctrine (see Ps. 4:2, 144:8).

> *"Make known to me, Jehovah, my end, and the measure of my days what it is, that I may know how transitory I am; behold Thou hast given my days as handbreadths, and my time is as nothing before Thee* (xxxix. 4, 5).

It appears as if by these words times of life only are meant, the limit of which he wishes to know, and that these times pass away quickly; but in the spiritual sense times are not meant, but states of life instead; so 'Make known to me, Jehovah, my end, the measure of my days what it is,' signifies that he might know the state of his life and its quality, thus what kind of life he would continue in. 'Behold Thou hast given my days as handbreadths' signifies that it is of very little consequence what the state of one's life is; 'and my time is as nothing before Thee' signifies that the state of one's life is of no value; for 'time and day' signify states of life in respect to truth and good, and thence in respect to intelligence and wisdom; so it is here meant that all these, so far as they are from oneself, are of no value. That there is such a meaning in these words cannot be seen by those who think only naturally, because natural thought cannot be separated from the idea of time. But spiritual thought, like that of angels, has nothing in common with time or space or with person." (*Apocalypse Explained*, n. 629.15-16)

Surely every man walks in an image
Surely he heaps up vain things of abundance,
And knows not who shall gather them.
And now what do I wait for, Lord?
My hope is in You. (Ps. 39:6-7)

An image signifies man's reception of truth from the Lord. Walking signifies how one lives according to the truth (see Ps. 1:1, 56:13, 81:13); image here is one's own false understanding from the self; to heap up vain things of abundance is to gather and arrange false knowledges. To wait on the Lord is to be receptive to good from the Lord; to hope upon Him is to be receptive of Divine truth from the Lord. The Lord (Hebrew *Adonai*) is Divine good in the Divine Human (see Ps. 68:17,26, 105:21, 110:1, 114:7); in the highest sense to wait upon Him is to await His coming.

"And God created man in His own image; in the image of God created He him. The word image is twice used here, because faith, which is of the understanding, is called His own image; and love, which is of the will — and which in the spiritual man comes after, but in the celestial man precedes — is called the image of God." (*Heavenly Arcana*, n. 53)

"And they gathered them together in heaps and heaps. That this signifies that those false reasonings were arranged in groups in the natural, is evident from the signification of being gathered together in heaps and heaps, as being arranged in groups. Being gathered together in heaps has this signification because all things in the mind of man are arranged into series, and as it were into groups; and into series within series, or into groups within groups (see n. 5339, 5530, 5881)." (*Heavenly Arcana*, n. 7408)

Deliver me from all my transgressions:

Make me not the reproach of the foolish.
I was dumb, I opened not my mouth,
For You did it. (Ps. 39:8-9)

Transgressions are evils against the truths of faith (see Ps. 5:10, 25:7, 32:1, 51:1-3); to be a reproach of the foolish is to be in aversion due to falsehood (Ps. 94:10). To be dumb is lacking in internal truth; to not open one's mouth is to be lacking in external truth (see Ps. 5:9, 37:30, 135:16).

Remove Your stroke away from me:
From the blow of Your hand I am consumed.
With reproofs You chastise man due to iniquity,
You make his desire to melt like a moth:
Surely every Man is vanity. (Ps. 39:10-11)

A stroke or plague signifies evil which destroys internal good (see Ps. 38:11); a blow or wound is destruction of external good (see Ps. 64:7); hand signifies the power of truth (see Ps. 20:6, 44:3, 45:4, 80:15,17, 89:13,21, 110:1, 121:5). Reproofs are corrections for falsehood (see Ps. 94:10) and to chastise is to correct evils (see Ps. 2:10, 94:10); iniquity is evil done from the understanding against the good of faith (see Ps. 51:1-3). For desire to melt like a moth is for one's lust for evil to become dissipated; Man (Hebrew *adam*) is one's self love (see Ps. 36:6) and vanity is falsity of doctrine (see Ps. 4:2, 144:8).

Hear my prayer, Jehovah, and give ear to my cry,
Hold not Your peace at my tears.
For I am a stranger with You,
A resident alien as all my fathers were.
Look away from me that I may smile,
Before I go and be no more. (Ps. 39:12-13)

Prayer is worship from spiritual good (see Ps. 4:1, 66:19, 72:15); to hold not peace is is to put an end to falsehood (see Ps. 28:1); tears signify grief of mind due to deprivation of truth (see Ps. 6:6). A stranger is one who is not instructed in the truths of the church and yet desires it (see Ps. 146:9); a resident alien is one who lacks spiritual good and is in mere natural good and is thus mentioned with fathers which is related to what is good (see Ps. 27:10, 45:16). To smile is to have affection for truth (Ps. 2:4); before one goes and is no more is to be separated from heaven due to lack of good. In the following passage the word resident alien is translated as sojourner, but resident alien is more accurate as it comes from a word meaning "to dwell" which is predicated of good:

"*A sojourner and a hired servant shall not eat thereof.* That this signifies that they who from mere natural disposition do good and those who do it for the sake of gain are to be with them, is evident from the signification of sojourner, as those who do good from mere natural disposition — of which below; from the signification of hired servant, as those who do good for the sake of gain — of which also below; and from the signification of not eating thereof, as not to be with them — of which just above (n. 8001). That a sojourner means those who do good from mere natural disposition, is because sojourners were those who came from other peoples, and became inhabitants, and dwelt with the Israelites and Jews in one house; and to dwell together signifies to be together in good. But because, as was said, they were from peoples out of the church, the good which is signified is not the good of the church, but is a good not of the church. This good is called natural good, because it is possessed hereditarily by birth, and also by some in consequence of ill health and infirmity. This good is meant by the good which they do who are signified by sojourners.

"This good differs altogether from the good of the church, for by the good of the church conscience is formed in man, which is the plane into which angels flow and by which there is fellowship with them; whereas by natural good no plane for the angels can be formed. They who are in this good do good in the dark from blind instinct, not in the light of truth by virtue of influx from heaven. Wherefore in the other life they are led away, like chaff by the wind, by every one as well evil as good, and more by an evil one who knows how to adjoin to reasonings something of affection and persuasion; nor then can they be led by angels, for the angels operate through the truths and goods of faith, and flow into the plane which has been formed inwardly in man from the truths and goods of faith. From these things it is plain that those who do good from mere natural disposition cannot be consociated with angels...

"That sojourners are those who stay not in their own land nor in their own house, but in a strange land, is evident in Moses: *The land shall not be sold in perpetuity; for the land is Mine: for ye are strangers and sojourners with Me* (Lev. xxv. 23); and in David: *Hear my prayer, O Jehovah ...hold not Thy peace at my tears: for I am a stranger with Thee, a sojourner, as all my fathers were* (Ps. xxxix. 12); and in the Book of Genesis: *Abraham ...spake unto the sons of Heth, saying, I am a stranger and a sojourner with you: give me a possession of a sepulchre* (xxiii. 3, 4). By a stranger, just as by a sojourner, is signified a comer and inhabitant from another land, but by a stranger are signified those who were instructed in the truths of the church and who received those truths, and by sojourners those who were not willing to be instructed in the truths of the church, because they were not willing to receive them." (*Heavenly Arcana*, n. 8002.1-3)

Psalm 40

To the chief musician, a Psalm of David.

~

Waiting, I waited for Jehovah, (1)
And He inclined to me and heard my cry.
And He brought me up out of the pit of *devastation*, (2)
Out of the miry clay.
And He raised my feet upon a cliff,
He established my steps.
And He gave a new song in my mouth, praise to our God: (3)
Many shall see, and fear, and shall trust in Jehovah.
Happy is the mighty one who makes Jehovah his confidence, (4)
And faces not towards those of Rahab and those who fall away to a
lie.

~

Many, Jehovah my God, are Your wondrous works which You have
done, (5)
And Your devised things toward us, none can be set in order to You,
I will proclaim and speak, they are more than can be numbered.
You did not delight *in* sacrifice and offering, (6)
My ears You have bored for me,
You have not asked for burnt offering and sin offering.
Then I said, Behold, I come, (7)
In the scroll of the book it is written of me.
I delight to do Your good pleasure, my God, (8)
And Your law is in the midst of my bowels.
 I have brought tidings of righteousness in the great assembly, (9)
 Behold, I have not restrained my lips, Jehovah, You know.

I have not covered Your righteousness in the midst of my
heart, (10)
I have spoken of Your faithfulness and Your salvation,
I have not hidden Your mercy and Your truth from the great
assembly.
You, Jehovah, restrain not Your compassion from me, (11)
Let Your mercy and Your truth continually preserve me.
For evils have surrounded me until they were innumerable, (12)
My iniquities have overtaken me and I am not able to see.
They are more than the hairs of my head,
And my heart forsakes me.

    Be pleased, Jehovah, to deliver me, (13)
    Jehovah hurry to help me.
    Let them be ashamed and embarrassed together who seek after
    my soul to obliterate it, (14)
    Let them be turned backward and dishonoured who are
    delighted in my evil,
    Let them be desolate as a consequence of their shame who say to
    me, Aha, aha. (15)
    Let all those who seek You be joyful and rejoice in You, (16)
    Let such as love Your salvation say continually, Jehovah be
    magnified.
    But I am afflicted and needy, (17)
    The Lord will reckon me.
    You are my help and my deliverer,
    My God, delay not.

Psalm Commentary 40

Summary: Thanksgiving and celebration of the Father, that He has helped Him (v. 1-4). He came into the world, as is written in the Word, that He might do the will of the Father (v. 5-8). He also preached the gospel of the kingdom of God, and taught (v. 9-10). Trust from His Divine against those who purpose to put Him to death (v. 11-12). Prayer for deliverance from evil (v. 13-18).

Waiting, I waited for Jehovah,
And He inclined to me and heard my cry.
And He brought me up out of the pit of devastation,
Out of the miry clay.
And He raised my feet upon a cliff,
He established my steps. (Ps. 40:1-2)

To wait for Jehovah is to have faith to receive Divine love; for Him to hear one's cry is to receive Divine truth after grief on account of falsehood signified by cry (see Ps. 9:12). The pit is the falsity of hell (see Ps. 28:1, 69:15, 88:4,6); devastation is the deprivation of truths; clay is evil from falsity signified by mire (see Ps. 18:42, 69:14) into which one sinks as one withdraws from heaven towards the lower natural. Cliff is truth from good (see Ps. 137:9, 141:6); for one's feet to be raised is to be elevated from lower falsehoods of the external natural, signified by the feet (see Ps. 8:6, 41:9, 49:5, 99:5, 105:18) towards external truths signified by cliff (see Ps. 18:2).

537

Devastation or desolation signifies the deprivation of truth among the evil (see Ps. 46:8). In undergoing temptation the righteous also undergo a state of deprivation of truth which differs in nature from the state of the evil:

"With those who are regenerated, that is, who the Lord foresees will suffer themselves to be regenerated, those truths are greatly multiplied, for they are in the affection for knowing truths; but when they come nearer to the very act of regeneration, they are deprived as it were of those truths, for they are drawn inward, and then the man appears in desolation; nevertheless those truths are successively let back into the natural, and are there conjoined with good, during man's regeneration. But with those who are not regenerated, that is, who the Lord foresees will not suffer themselves to be regenerated, truths are indeed usually multiplied, for they are in the affection for knowing such things for the sake of reputation, honor, and gain; yet when they advance in years and submit those truths to their own sight, then either they do not believe them, or they deny them, or they turn them into falsities; thus with them truths are not withdrawn inward, but are cast forth, although they still remain in the memory for the sake of ends in the world, though without life. This state also is called in the Word desolation or vastation, but differs from the former state in the desolation of the former being apparent, while the desolation of this state is absolute; for in the former state man is not deprived of truths, while in this state he is entirely deprived of them…

"Again: *Then shall they not thirst; He shall lead them in waste places: He shall cause the waters to flow out of the rock for them; He cleaveth the rock also, so that the waters flow out* (xlviii. 21) — speaking of the state after desolation. Again: *Jehovah will comfort Zion: He will comfort all her waste places; and He will make her wilderness like Eden, and her desert like the garden of Jehovah; joy and gladness shall be found therein, thanksgiving, and the voice of a song* (li. 3) — where the subject is the same; for, as said above, desolation is for the end that man may be regenerated, that is, that after evils and falsities are separated, truths may be conjoined to goods, and goods to truths. The regenerate man as to good is what is compared to Eden, and as to truths to the garden of Jehovah. In David: *Jehovah brought me up out of the pit of devastation, out of the miry clay, and set my feet upon a rock* (Ps. xl. 2).

"The vastation and desolation of the man of the church, or of the church in man, was represented by the captivity of the Jewish people in Babylon, and the raising up of the church by the return from that captivity — as described in Jeremiah throughout, especially chapter xxxii. 37 to the end; for desolation is captivity, man then being kept as it were bound, wherefore too by those who are bound, in prison, and in the pit, are signified those who are in desolation..." (*Heavenly Arcana*, n. 5376.2, 7-8)

Clay signifies evil from which is falsity:

"*In clay, and in bricks.* That this signifies on account of the evils which they contrived, and the falsities which they devised, is evident from the signification of clay, as good, and in the opposite sense evil — of which in what follows; and from the signification of bricks, as the falsities which they devise (see n. 1296) — as to the evils and falsities which the infernals contrive and devise, see above (n. 6666). That clay is evil from which is falsity, is plain from these passages in the Word — in Isaiah: *The wicked are like the troubled sea, when it cannot rest, and its waters cast up mire and clay* (lvii. 20) — mire being falsity from which is evil, and clay evil from which is falsity.

"In Jeremiah: *Thy feet are sunk in the clay, they are turned away back* (xxxviii. 22). The feet sunk in the clay, are the natural sunk in evil. In Nahum: *Draw thee water for the siege, strengthen thy fortresses: go into the mire, and tread the clay, repair the brick-kiln. There shall the fire devour thee, and the sword shall cut thee off* (iii. 14, 15) — where treading the clay stands for thinking from evil what is false. In Habakkuk: *He shall say, Woe to him who increaseth that which is not his! how long? and that ladeth himself with clay! Shall they not rise up suddenly that shall bite thee?* (ii. 6, 7) — to lade himself with clay standing for evil.

"In David: *Jehovah ...brought me up also out of a pit of dev-astation, out of the miry clay, and He set my feet upon a rock* (Ps. xl. 2). Again: *I sink in deep clay where there is no standing, I am come into deep waters, and the floods overwhelm me. ...Deliver me out of the clay, that I sink not ...and out of the deep waters ...and let not the deep swallow me up* (Ps. lxix. 2, 14, 15) — clay standing for evil from which is falsity. In Isaiah: *He shall come upon the rulers as upon clay, and as the potter treadeth the mire* (xli. 25)." (*Heavenly Arcana*, n. 6669.1-3)

And He gave a new song in my mouth, praise to our God:
Many shall see, and shall fear, and shall trust in Jehovah.
Happy is the mighty one who makes Jehovah his confidence,
And faces not towards those of Rahab and those who fall away to
a lie. (Ps. 40:3-4)

A new song is glorification on account of the coming of the Lord (see Ps. 96:1); the mouth is the external understanding (see Ps. 5:9, 37:30, 135:16) and praise is worship from affection for truth (see Ps. 7:17, 35:18). To see is to understand the truth, to fear is to live by the truth (see Ps. 2:11, 33:18, 128:1, 147:11), and to trust is to have confidence of the will from the good of charity (see Ps. 33:21). Happiness is the happiness of eternal life (see Ps. 1:1); a mighty one is one who receives power from Divine truth (see Ps. 21:13, 80:2).

The name Rahab and its variants are often translated as proud, and is first mentioned in reference to the harlot Rahab (see Josh. 2:1-3). It is also used as an epithet for a sea monster (Job 26:12) and for Egypt (see Isa. 30:7). The sea signifies external knowledge in general (see Ps. 24:2, 33:7, 69:34, 77:19, 89:25, 104:5-6,25) as does Egypt (see Ps. 78:9, 80:8). It spiritually signifies those who pervert and profane the truth through persuasion, which is mentioned in scripture as whoredom; to fall away to a lie is to follow falsity in regards to one's life (see Ps. 4:2, 144:8). To "face not" is to not let falsehood influence one's will to do good, signified by face (see Ps. 4:6, 13:1, 22:24, 27:8-9, 31:16, 67:1).

Many, Jehovah my God, are Your wondrous works which You
have done,
And Your devised things toward us cannot be set in order to You,
I will proclaim and speak:
They are more than can be numbered. (Ps. 40:5)

Wondrous works are acts of Divine power which cause belief (see Ps. 71:7, 78:43, 105:5); devised things are plans from Divine foresight which are hidden. To proclaim and speak is to announce the Divine truth; to be numbered is to know the quality of a thing (see Ps. 147:4), thus it signifies the things of Divine power are not only infinite but also beyond human comprehension. In the highest sense this refers to the incarnation of Jehovah in human form. The Divine truth was fully present in Jesus, and was not given in measure as with other men as indicated by John 3:34:

> "*He whom the Father hath sent speaketh the words of God,*
> *for not by measure hath God given the spirit unto Him* (iii. 34).
>
> The 'spirit' that God giveth signifies Divine truth, and intelligence and wisdom therefrom; 'not by measure' signifies above every measure and quality of men, therefore infinitely, for the infinity that belongs to the Lord is without measure or quality, for measure and quality are properties of the finite, since measure and quality determine what is finite and set limits to it, but what is without limit is infinite. From this it follows that 'measure' also here signifies quality, since 'not by measure' signifies not predicating what a thing is, or its quality." (*Apocalypse Explained*, n. 629.15)

You did not delight in sacrifice and offering,
My ears You have bored for me,
You have not asked for burnt offering and sin offering. (Ps. 40:6)

Ears or hearing signify obedience; the boring of the ears refers to the external ritual of boring the ear of a servant by an awl to a door (Ex. 21:6). Sacrifice signifies external worship representing the truths of faith (see Ps. 40:6, 50:8); an offering is external worship in general (see Ps. 20:3); burnt offering is worship from the good of love (see Ps. 20:3, 50:8, 66:15); a sin offering represents a state of conjunction as to love.

"That by ear is signified obedience, and in the internal sense faith therefrom, is still more plainly manifest from the ritual respecting a servant who was not willing to depart from service — of whom it is thus written in Moses: *If a man-servant or maid-servant shall not be willing to depart from service, his master shall bring him unto God, and shall bring him to the door, or unto the door-post, and his master shall bore his ear through with an awl, and he shall serve him for ever* (Exod. xxi. 5, 6; Deut. xv. 17). Boring the ear through with an awl at the door-post signifies serving or obeying perpetually; in the spiritual sense it signifies not willing to understand truth, but willing truth from obedience, which is relatively not freedom.

"Because the obedience of faith is understood by ears in the internal sense, and obeying by hearing, it is evident what is signified by these words of the Lord, which He so often uttered: *He who hath an ear to hear, let him hear* (Matt. xiii. 9, 43; Mark iv. 9, 23; vii. 16; Luke viii. 8; xiv. 35; Apoc. ii. 7, 11, 29; iii. 13, 22)." (*Heavenly Arcana*, n. 3869.11-12)

The rituals of animal sacrifices were but external rituals that represented repentance and a life according to God's will. The blood was separated from the animal and the flesh was burned, which signified the separation of that which is holy from lower natural desires through repentance. The external rituals of the Jews were abolished when God became incarnate to be the ultimate sacrifice, where He conquered the hells by resisting sin and temptation in His human body, until the human form was made Divine. Thus animal sacrifices were representative of the Lord Himself:

"...burnt offerings and sacrifices were nothing else than representatives of internal worship; and that when they were separated from internal worship, they became idolatrous. This any one of sound reason may see. For what is an altar but something of stone, and what is burnt offering and sacrifice but the slaying of a beast? If there be Divine worship, it must represent something heavenly which they know and acknowledge, and from which they worship Him Whom they represent.

"That these were representatives of the Lord no one can be ignorant, unless he is unwilling to understand anything about the Lord. It is by internal things, namely, charity and faith therefrom, that He Who is represented is to be seen and acknowledged and believed — as is clearly evident in the prophets, for example, in Jeremiah: *Thus saith Jehovah of hosts, the God of Israel: Add your burnt offerings unto your sacrifices, and eat ye flesh. For I spake not unto your fathers, and I commanded them not in the day that I brought them out of the land of Egypt, concerning burnt offerings and sacrifices: but this thing I commanded them, saying, Hearken unto My voice, and I will be your God* (vii. 21-23). To hearken to or obey the voice is to obey the law, which all relates to the one command, to love God above all things and the neighbor as one's self, for in this is the law and the prophets (Matt. xxii. 35-40; vii. 12). In David: *O Jehovah ...sacrifice and offering Thou hast not desired ...burnt offering and sin offering hast Thou not required ...I have desired to do Thy will, O my God; yea, Thy law is within my heart* (Ps. xl. 7, 9).

"In Samuel, who said to Saul — *Hath Jehovah as great pleasure in burnt offerings and sacrifices as in hearkening to the voice of Jehovah? Behold, to hearken is better than sacrifice, and to obey than the fat of rams* (1 Sam. xv. 22). What is meant by hearkening to the voice may be seen in Micah: *Shall I come before Jehovah with burnt offerings, with calves of a year old? Will Jehovah be pleased with thousands of rams, with ten thousands of rivers of oil? ...He hath showed thee, O man, what is good; and what doth Jehovah require of thee, but to do judgment, and to love mercy, and to walk humbly with thy God?* (vi. 6-8.) This is what is signified by burnt offerings and sacrifices of clean beasts and birds. So in Amos: *Though you offer Me burnt offerings and your meat offerings, I will not accept them: neither will I regard the peace offerings of your fat beasts. ...But let judgment flow like waters, and justice like a mighty river* (v. 22, 24). Judgment is truth, and justice is good, both from charity, and these are the burnt offerings and sacrifices of the internal man. In Hosea: *For I desire mercy and not sacrifice, and the knowledge of God more than burnt offerings* (vi. 6)." (*Heavenly Arcana*, n. 922.1-3)

The reason for animal sacrifices was also on account of idolatry:

"The command came on this account, that the worship of sacrifices had, with them as with the nations, been turned into idolatry; and from this worship they could not be withdrawn, because they regarded it as the chief holy thing. For what has once been implanted from infancy, as holy, especially if by fathers, and so enrooted, this, unless it be against order itself, the Lord by no means breaks, but bends. This is the reason that it was directed that they should be instituted in the way described in the books of Moses.

"That sacrifices were by no means acceptable to Jehovah, and thus were only permitted and tolerated for the reason which has been stated, is plainly manifest in the Prophets, as we read in Jeremiah: *Thus saith Jehovah Zebaoth, God of Israel, Add your burnt-offerings unto your sacrifices, and eat ye flesh. I spake not unto your fathers, and I commanded them not in the day that I brought them out of the land of Egypt, concerning burnt-offering and sacrifice; but this thing I commanded them, saying, Hearken unto My voice, and I will be your God* (vii. 21-23). In David: *O Jehovah, sacrifice and offering Thou hast not desired …burnt-offering and sin-offering hast Thou not required. I have desired to do thy will, O my God* (Ps. xl. 6, 8). In the same: *Thou delightest not in sacrifice, that I should give it; burnt-offering Thou dost not accept. The sacrifices of God are a broken spirit* (Ps. li. 16, 17). In the same: *I will take no bullock out of thy house nor he-goats out of thy folds. …Offer unto God the sacrifice of confession* (Ps. l. 9, 13, 14; cvii. 21, 22; cxvi. 17; Deut. xxiii. 19)." (*Heavenly Arcana*, n. 2180.6)

Then I said, Behold, I come,
In the scroll of the book it is written of me.

I delight to do Your good pleasure, my God,
And Your law is in the midst of my bowels. (Ps. 40:7-8)

The coming of the Lord is foretold throughout scripture, and all of Divine truth testifies concerning the Lord. To delight to do the Lord's good pleasure is to be in happiness doing God's will (see Ps. 5:12, 51:18, 69:13). The law is the internal things of the Word (Ps. 19:7) and bowels signifies love to the Lord and the neighbour which is the essence of the entire law (see Ps. 22:14).

"In *Isaiah:*—

Wilt thou call this a fast, and the day of Jehovah's good pleasure? Is it not to break thy bread to the hungry; and when thou seest the naked that thou cover him? (lviii. 6, 7).

That 'Jehovah's good pleasure,' in reference to men, signifies to live according to His commandments, which is to love God and the neighbor (as was said above) is evident; for it is said that 'His good pleasure is to break the bread to the hungry, and to cover the naked;' 'to break bread to the hungry' signifies from love to do good to the neighbor who desires good; and 'to cover the naked' signifies to instruct in truths him who desires to be instructed. In *David:*—

I delight in doing Thy good pleasure (that is, Thy will) *O my God; and Thy law is in my bowels* (Ps. xl. 8).

In the same:—

Teach me to do Thy good pleasure; Thy good spirit shall lead me into the land of uprightness (Ps. cxliii. 10).

In the same:—

Bless ye Jehovah, all His hosts; ye ministers of His that do His good pleasure (Ps. ciii. 21).

To 'do the good pleasure of Jehovah God' signifies to live according to His commandments; this is His good pleasure or His will, because from Divine love He wills that all should be saved, and by it they are saved. Moreover, in the Hebrew expression 'good pleasure' also means *will*; for whatever is done according to the will is well pleasing, and the Divine love wills nothing else than that love from itself may be with angels and men, and His love is with them when they love to live according to His commandments. That this is to love the Lord He teaches in *John* xiv. 15, 21, 23, 24; xv. 10, 14; xxi. 15-17)." (*Apocalypse Explained*, n. 295.11-12)

I have brought tidings of righteousness in the great assembly,
Behold, I have not restrained my lips, Jehovah, You know.
I have not covered Your righteousness in the midst of my heart,
I have spoken of Your faithfulness and Your salvation,
I have not hidden Your mercy and Your truth from the great
assembly. (Ps. 40:9-10)

To bring tidings is to announce the coming of the Lord, to evangelize, and declare the gospel (see Ps. 96:2). Righteousness is to do what is good (see Ps. 14:5, 36:6, 37:6,17, 72:2, 89:14, 92:12) and the great assembly are those in the internal truths of the church (see Ps. 1:5, 68:26, 107:32). Lips signify the doctrine of truth (see Ps. 12:4, 81:5). The heart is the will to do good (see Ps. 7:9, 22:10, 24:4, 51:10, 64:6, 66:18, 78:8); faithfulness is the Divine truth and salvation is deliverance from evil by Divine mercy (see Ps. 14:7, 96:2). Mercy and truth are the two aspects of the Divine; mercy is the Divine love which is conjoined with Divine truth (see Ps. 25:10, 26:3, 36:5, 89:14, 103:8).

You, Jehovah, restrain not Your compassion from me,
Let Your mercy and Your truth continually preserve me. (Ps. 40:11)

Jehovah is the Lord as to Divine love (see Ps. 18:31, 28:1, 68:26, 82:1, 147:7). The Hebrew word for compassion can also be translated as womb, which signifies innocence which is the origin of love and truth:

"*That, behold, twins were in her womb.* That this signifies both things of the church, is evident from the signification of twins, as both good and truth (n. 3299); and from the signification of the womb, as where good and truth lie conceived, and so where that is which is of the church. The womb in the genuine sense signifies the inmost of marriage love in which is innocence, because the womb corresponds to that love in the Greatest Man; and as marriage love has its origin from the love for good and truth which is of the heavenly marriage, and as this marriage is heaven itself, or the Lord's kingdom, and as the Lord's kingdom on earth is the church, therefore the church also is signified by the womb; for the church is where the marriage of good and truth is. For this reason it is, that opening the womb means the doctrines of churches therefrom (n. 3856), and also the ability of receiving the truths and goods of the church (n. 3967); and that coming forth from the womb means being reborn or regenerated (see n. 4904), that is, being made a church; for whoever is reborn or regenerated, is made a church." (*Heavenly Arcana*, n. 4918)

"*And of the womb.* That this signifies their conjunction, namely, the conjunction of good and truth, is evident from the signification of womb, as the inmost of marriage love; and because marriage love exists from the heavenly marriage, which is the conjunction of good and truth, therefore by the womb this conjunction is signified." (*Heavenly Arcana*, n. 6433)

For evils have surrounded me until they were innumerable,
My iniquities have overtaken me and I am not able to see.
They are more than the hairs of my head,
And my heart forsakes me. (Ps. 40:12)

In the highest sense this describes the temptations of the hells against the Lord while He was incarnate in human form. The evils are the evils of hell which attack the good of love; iniquity is evil done against the good and faith (see Ps. 51:1-3); to not see is to not have spiritual understanding of truth due to falsity (see Ps. 11:4, 13:3, 31:9, 69:23). Hairs signify external falsities (see also Ps. 69:4, Matt. 10:30) and the head represents interior truths (see Ps. 133:2); the heart is one's love of the will (see Ps. 7:9, 22:10, 24:4, 51:10, 64:6, 66:18, 78:8).

Let it be acceptable, Jehovah, to deliver me,
Jehovah hurry to help me.

*Let them be ashamed and embarrassed together who seek after
my soul to obliterate it,*
*Let them be turned backward and dishonoured who are delighted
in my evil.*
*Let them be desolate as a consequence of their shame who say to
me, Aha, aha.*
Let all those who seek You be joyful and rejoice in You,
*Let such as love Your salvation say continually, Jehovah be mag-
nified.* (Ps. 40:13-16)

A deliverer is one who leads away from falsity (see Ps. 91:14);
help is aid from Divine mercy (see Ps. 10:14). Those who seek
after the soul to obliterate it are the falsehoods of hell that wish
to destroy one's spiritual understanding (see Ps. 22:10, 31:9,
71:23, 107:9); those who are delighted in evil are the evils of hell
that wish to destroy what is good. For them to be ashamed is to
have shame due to committing evil; to be embarrassed is to have
shame for doing evil against the good of faith (see Ps. 34:5). To
be turned back is to turn back towards the love of self away from
love of the Lord (see Ps. 34:16, 44:18); to be dishonoured is to be
destitute of truth (see Ps. 35:4); to be desolate is to be deprived
of truth (see Ps. 40:2). To seek is to search for the truth; to rejoice
is to have joy from love (see Ps. 14:7). Those who love the Lord's
salvation are those who are in the good of love, as salvation is
from Divine love (see Ps. 14:7, 96:2).

But I am afflicted and needy,
The Lord will think upon me.
You are my help and my deliverer,
My God, delay not. (Ps. 40:17)

To be afflicted is to be lacking in knowledges of the truth (see
Ps. 35:10, 37:14); to be needy is lacking in knowledge of good
(see Ps. 35:10, 37:14, 109:16, 113:7); the Lord (Hebrew *Adonai*)
is Divine good in the Divine Human (see Ps. 68:17,26, 105:21,
110:1, 114:7). Help is aid from Divine mercy (see Ps. 10:14) and
a deliverer is one who leads away from falsity (see Ps. 91:14); to

not delay is hope for the end of temptation. The word afflicted is translated as needy in the below passage:

"That by the poor and needy are meant in the internal sense those outside the church who are in ignorance of truth, because they have not the Word, and yet desire to be instructed, and by means of that which they know are still in some little good, and those also within the church who from various causes are ignorant of truth, but yet from some good with them desire it, is evident from passages where the poor and needy are mentioned in the Word — as in David: *I am needy and poor: make haste unto me, O God: my help and my deliverer, O Jehovah* (Ps. lxx. 5). These words were spoken by David, who was not poor and needy, from which it is plain that spiritual poverty and need is to be understood. In like manner in another passage: *I am needy and poor; O Lord, think upon me, my help and my deliverer* (Ps. xl. 17). Again: *God shall judge His people in justice, and His needy in judgment. The mountains shall bring peace to the people, and the hills injustice. He shall judge the needy of the people. He shall save the sons of the poor, and shall break in pieces the oppressor* (Ps. lxxii. 2-4). The needy in this passage are those who are in spiritual need and thus in hunger, that is, in the desire to be willing to be instructed in truths." (*Heavenly Arcana*, n. 9209.5; see also *Apocalypse Revealed*, n. 209)

Psalm 41

To the chief Musician, a Psalm of David.

~

Happy is he who has prudence toward the poor, (1)
In the day of evil Jehovah will rescue him.
Jehovah will keep him and make him live, (2)
He shall be happy in the earth,
And You will not give him to the will of his enemies.
Jehovah will sustain him upon the couch of illness, (3)
You will overturn all his bed in his sickness.
I said, Jehovah be gracious to me, (4)
Heal my soul for I have sinned against You.
My enemies speak evil of me: (5)
"When shall he die, and his name perish?"
   And if he come to see me he speaks vanity, (6)
   His heart gathers iniquity to itself,
   He goes outside, he speaks of it.
   All who hate me whisper together against me, (7)
   Against me they devise evil towards me.
   A word of Belial is poured into him: (8)
   "And now that he lies he shall rise up no more."
   Even my man of peace in whom I trusted, (9)
   Who ate of my bread,
   He has lifted up his heel against me.
But You Jehovah, be gracious to me, (10)
And raise me up that I may repay them.
By this I know that you are delighted in me, (11)
For my enemy does not shout in triumph over me.
And as for me, You uphold me in my integrity, (12)

And set me before You forever.
Blessed be Jehovah God of Israel, (13)
From everlasting to everlasting,
Amen and Amen.

Psalm Commentary 41

Summary: the happiness of those who are righteous, who are in charity and love towards others (v. 1-2). The hells among themselves devise evils against the Lord who sought His death and destruction (v. 3-5). The opposition of the falsified church against the Lord (v. 6-9). The defeat of the hells and the resurrection of the Lord, by whom the righteous are sustained (v. 10-13).

Happy is he who has prudence toward the poor:
In the day of evil Jehovah will rescue him.
Jehovah will keep him and make him live,
He shall be happy in the earth,
And You will not give him to the will of his enemies. (Ps. 41:1-2)

Happiness is the happiness of eternal life (see Ps. 1:1) which is to be of use and serve those who are in need; to have prudence is to have wisdom from love; the poor are those who are lacking in truth (see Ps. 109:16, 113:7); to be rescued in the day of evil is to be delivered from temptation of evil. To be kept alive is to have eternal life in heaven; to be happy in the earth is to be happy in church as to truth (see Ps. 9:8, 24:1, 60:2, 90:2, 96:13). The "will" can be literally translated as soul, and refers to the desire of one's understanding (see Ps. 22:10, 31:9, 71:23, 107:9). The will of enemies thus refers to the false intents derived from falsehoods which attack the truth signified by enemies (see Ps. 3:1, 27:12). The spiritual meaning of poor is indicated by the following commentary on Exodus 23:3:

553

"And a poor man thou shalt not overrate in his strife. That this signifies that the falsities in which they are who are in ignorance of truth, are not to be favored, is evident from the signification of a poor man, as they who are in few truths and are also in falsities from ignorance." (*Heavenly Arcana,* n. 9253)

Jehovah will sustain him upon the couch of illness,
You will overturn all his bed in his sickness. (Ps. 41:3)

A couch of illness is to be in incorrect doctrine regarding good, and a bed of sickness is false doctrine (see Ps. 4:4). To overturn the bed is to convert or turn one away from the falsity of doctrine. Verse 1 concerns the righteous in the good of love, verse 2 concerns the spiritual who are in good from truth, and this verse concerns those who are in external obedience. To be remote from from good and truth is to be in the lower natural:

"That a bed is the natural, is because the natural is beneath the rational and serves it as a bed; for the rational lies down as it were upon the natural, and because the natural is thus spread out underneath, it is therefore called a bed — as also in Amos: *As the shepherd rescueth out of the mouth of the lion two legs, or a piece of an ear; so shall the children of Israel be rescued that dwell in Samaria in the corner of a bed, and on the end of a couch* (iii. 12). 'In the corner of a bed' means in the lowest of the natural; and 'on the end of a couch' means in the sensual. For by the people Israel, who had Samaria for a metropolis, was represented the Lord's spiritual kingdom. Of this it is said, as of the father Israel here, that it is upon the head of the bed, for spiritual good, which is represented by the father Israel, is the head of the bed. But when they turn themselves thence to those things which are of the lowest natural and which are of the sensual, it is then said that they are in the corner of the bed and on the end of the couch.

"Again in the same prophet: *They that lie upon beds of ivory, and stretch themselves upon their couches ...but they are not grieved for the breach of Joseph* (vi. 4, 6). Beds of ivory stand for the pleasures of the lowest natural, which are the pleasures of the proud; not to be grieved for the breach of Joseph, is to have no concern about the dissipation of good from the internal. So in David: *Surely I will not come into the tent of my house, nor go up upon the couch of my bed* (Ps. cxxxii. 3). The tent of my house stands for the holy of love (n. 414, 1102, 2145, 2152, 3312, 4128, 4391, 4599); to go up upon the couch of the bed means upon the natural to the truth which is from the good of love." (*Heavenly Arcana*, n. 6188.2-3)

I said, Jehovah be gracious to me,
Heal my soul for I have sinned against You.
My enemies speak evil of me:
"When shall he die, and his name perish?"
And if he come to see me he speaks vanity,
His heart gathers iniquity to itself,
He goes outside, he speaks of it. (Ps. 41:4-6)

To receive grace is to receive spiritual good and truth, and comfort and hope of mind in temptations (see Ps. 4:1) and is sought by those in humiliation of thought (see Ps. 103:8). To heal is to preserve from evil (see Ps. 30:2, 38:4-7) and sin is evil against the good of love (see Ps. 25:7, 32:1, 51:1-3). Enemies are falsehoods which attack the truth (see Ps. 3:1, 27:12); death is spiritual death as to the will and to perish is spiritual death from falsity (see Ps. 88:11). To speak vanity is to teach the falsity of doctrine (see Ps. 4:2, 144:8); iniquity is evil done against the good of faith (see Ps. 51:1-3); to speak of it outside is to teach external falsehoods from the false doctrine.

All who hate me whisper together against me,
Against me they devise evil towards me.
A word of Belial is poured into him:
"And now that he lies he shall rise up no more."
Even my man of peace in whom I trusted,
Who ate of my bread,
He has lifted up his heel against me. (Ps. 41:7-9)

Those who whisper are the evil who secretly plot falsehood; to devise evil is to plot evil. A thing of Belial is a falsehoods that perverts the truth; for one to lie down and not rise up is to be spiritually dead. A man of peace is one who appears in similar truth; the one who eats of one's bread is one who appears in a similar good signified by bread (see Ps. 23:2, 105:16). This was literally fulfilled by Judas who betrayed Jesus after having shared bread with Him at the Last Supper, which spiritually signifies the rejection of Jesus by majority of the Jews at the time. To lift up the heel is to elevate falsehood from the literal sense of the Word or the external natural (see Ps. 8:6, 41:9, 49:5, 99:5, 105:18), and also concerns those who distort the literal sense of the Word:

"He who did eat of My bread hath lifted up his heel against Me (Ps. xli. 9). This is said of the Jews, who had Divine truths because they had the Word, as can be seen in *John* (xiii. 18), where these words are applied to the Jews; therefore 'to eat the Lord's bread' signifies the appropriation of Divine truth, but here a communication of it, for the Jews could not appropriate it. 'Bread' signifies the Word, from which is spiritual nutrition. 'To lift up the heel against Him' signifies to pervert the sense of the letter of the Word even to denial of the Lord, and the falsification of every truth. For the Divine truth is presented in image as a man; this is why heaven in its whole complex is called the Greatest Man, and corresponds to all things of man; for heaven is formed according to the Divine truth proceeding from the Lord; and as the Word is the Divine truth, this, too, before the Lord is in image like a Divine Man; for this reason its ultimate sense, which is the mere sense of the letter, corresponds to the heel. The perversion of the Word, or of the Divine truth, by applying the sense of the letter to falsities, such as were the traditions of the Jews, is signified by 'lifting up the heel against the Lord.'" (*Apocalypse Explained*, n. 617.17)

But You Jehovah, be gracious to me,
And raise me up that I may repay them.

By this I know that you are delighted in me,
For my enemy does not triumph over me. (Ps. 41:10-11)

To receive grace is to receive spiritual good and truth, and comfort and hope of mind in temptations (see Ps. 4:1) and is sought by those in humiliation of thought (see Ps. 103:8); to be raised is to be elevated from falsehoods into interior truths (see Ps. 27:5) after which the evil spirits withdraw. To be delighted is to have conjunction with the Lord through love; an enemy is a falsehood that attacks the truth (see Ps. 3:1, 27:12).

And as for me, You uphold me in my integrity,
And set me before You forever.
Blessed be Jehovah God of Israel,
From everlasting to everlasting,
Amen and Amen. (Ps. 41:12-13)

Integrity is to be in truth from good (see Ps. 25:21); to be stationed before the Lord is to be in good from love; forever is eternity in the celestial heaven (see Ps. 145:13). To bless Jehovah is to acknowledge that all good and happiness comes from the Lord alone (see Ps. 3:8, 16:7, 21:6, 24:5, 28:6, 31:21, 96:2); everlasting is eternity in the celestial heaven of love (see Ps. 145:13). Amen signifies confirmation of the truth, and is also used here to mark the end of the first book of the Psalms.

END OF VOLUME I